AVERSION, AVOIDANCE, AND ANXIETY

Perspectives on Aversively
Motivated Behavior

AVERSION, AVOIDANCE, AND ANXIETY

Perspectives on Aversively
Motivated Behavior

Edited by
Trevor Archer
Lars-Gören Nilsson
University of Umeå

LAWRENCE ERLBAUM ASSOCIATES, PUBLISHERS
1989   Hillsdale, New Jersey   Hove and London

Lawrence Erlbaum Associates, Inc., Publishers
365 Broadway
Hillsdale, New Jersey 07642

Library of Congress Cataloging-in-Publication Data

Aversion avoidance, and anxiety : perspective on aversively motivated
behavior / edited by Trevor Archer, Lars-Göran Nilsson.
   p.   cm.
   Includes bibliograpies and indexes.
   ISBN 0-8058-0132-4
   1. Aversive stimuli—Congresses. 2. Avoidance (Psychology)—
Congresses. 3. Conditioned response—Congresses. 4. Motivation
(Psychology)—Congresses. 5. Motivation (Psychology)—Physiological
aspects—Congresses. 6. Anxiety—Congresses. I. Archer, Trevor.
II. Nilsson, Lars-Göran, 1944–
BF319.5.A8A89   1988
153.8'5—dc19   88-24487
                                          CIP

Printed in the United States of America
10 9 8 7 6 5 4 3 2 1

Contents

IV NEUROBIOLOGICAL PERSPECTIVES ON AVERSIVELY MOTIVATED BEHAVIOR

V COGNITIVE PERSPECTIVES

VII METHODOLOGICAL AND CONCEPTUAL PERSPECTIVES ON AVERSIVE CONDITIONING

15. How One Might Find Evidence for Conditoning in Adult Humans   381
Robert A. Boakes

16. The Yoked Control Design   403
Russell M. Church

VIII SUMMARY AND INTEGRATION

Preface

The conference "Perspectives on Aversively motivated behavior" was held at the University of Umeå, Sweden, June 17-20, 1987. The prime objective of the conference was to review the scientific status of the field of aversive learning from historical, affective, clinical, neurobiological, cognitive, neuroethological and conceptual perspectives. In our previous (1984) conference prominent scientists were assembled to discuss and develop common grounds for conceptualizations in the learning and memory of human and sub-human species. We have taken pains to conform to that same endeavour, i.e. to pursue the comparative analysis between human and animal behavior, both in the Umeå conference (of 1987) and in the present volume.

Without wishing to deny the importance of individual cases of pathology and other approaches to the development of maladies originating from unpleasant experiences, the selection of the various perspectives was overridingly empirical although whereever possible other orientations have been allowed to infiltrate. Thus, some fleeting reference will be made to areas such as psychosomatics, neuroimmunomodulation, stress-induced analgesia, ethological approaches to aggression, animal models in depression and anxiety and psychopharmacology. It will be noted throughout that one recurring premise has arisen from what John Garcia would call a "Darwinian Perspective" through which all organisms are confronted by the same basic challenges to survival. By this token, it seems only true to observe that the very conceptualizations of aversive learning and the methodologically paradigmatic issues that contribute to such learning are still evolving. Therefore, our current theoretical appreciations must of necessity be humble in comparison with the vastness of the behavior of those various organisms we are attempting to catalogue, analyse and eventually understand.

By a perfect accident, we were informed at this time that John Garcia would be retiring from his formal academic endeavours to his own "eagle's nest" in the Cascades. How appropriate then to reveal that the original construction of the conference and the volume (both conceived nearly a decade ago) was centred upon the work of this man. Our dedication of this book is to John Garcia. Thank you, John.

The conference was made possible by financial support from the University of Umeå, the City of Umeå, Stiftelsen Seth M. Kempes Minne, Västerbottens Läns Landsting, Nordisk Ministerråd, The Swedish Council for Research in the Humanities and the Social Sciences, The Swedish Medical Research Council and several companies including AB Ferrosan, AB Leo, ASTRA Läkemedel AB, Linjeflyg, Searle Research and Development, Semper AB, and Sandoz Ltd. The support from these institutions and companies is gratefully acknowledged.

We are indebted to the following persons for invaluable help in organizing the conference: Björn Andersson, Agneta Herlitz, Arto Hiltunen, Stig Lindqvist, Annacari Lundquist, Timo Mäntylä, Ulrich Olofsson, Karl Sandberg, Mona Wiklund, Jan-Åke Åkerlund, but above all Margareta Json Lindberg. Publication of this volume would have been impossible without the impeccable services of Margareta Json Lindberg and Helena Lundberg.

Trevor Archer
Lars-Göran Nilsson

LIST OF CONTRIBUTORS

Trevor Archer, Department of Psychology, University of Umeå, S-901 87 Umeå, Sweden.

Richard J. Beninger, Department of Psychology, Queen's University, Kingston, Ontario K7L 3N6, Canada.

Federico Bermúdez-Rattoni, Departemento de Neuroscienceis, Centro de Investigacion en Fisiologia Celular, Universidad Nacional Autonoma, Apartado Postal 70-600, 04510 Mexico, D.F.

Giorgio Bignami, Instituto Superiore Di Sanita, Viale Regina Elena, 229, I-00161 Roma, Italy.

Robert A. Boakes, Laborotory of Experimental Psychology, University of Sussex, Falmer, Brighton, BN1 9QG, England.

Larry Cahill, Center for the Neurobiology of Learning and Memory, University of California, Irvine, CA 92717, USA.

Sven-Åke Christianson, Department of Psychology, University of Umeå, S-901 87 Umeå, Sweden.

Russell M. Church, Department of Psychology, Brown University, Providence, R.I. 02912, USA.

Ulf Dimberg, Department of Applied Psychology, University of Uppsala, Box 1225, S-751 42 Uppsala, Sweden.

Francisco Esteves, Department of Applied Psychology, University of Uppsala, Box 1225, S-751 42 Uppsala, Sweden.

Michael W. Eysenck, Department of Psychology, Royal Holloway and Bedford New College, University of London, Egham Hill, Egham, Surrey TW20 0EX, England.

John Garcia, 1950 A, Chilberg Road, MT Vernon, WA 98273, USA.

Tommy Gärling, Department of Psychology, University of Umeå, S-901 87 Umeå, Sweden.

Kenneth Hugdahl, Department of Somatic Psychology, University of Bergen, Årstadsveien 21, N-5000 Bergen, Norway.

Ines B. Introini-Collison, Center for the Neurobiology of Learning and Memory, University of California, Irvine, CA 92717, USA.

Torbjörn Järbe, Department of Psychology, University of Uppsala, Box 227, S-751 04 Uppsala, Sweden.

Elizabeth F. Loftus, Department of Psychology, University of Washington, Seattle, Washington 98195, USA.

Ingvar Lundberg, Department of Psychology, University of Umeå, S-901 87 Umeå, Sweden.

James L. McGaugh, Center for the Neurobiology of Learning and Memory, University of California, Irvine, CA 92717, USA.

Susan Mineka, Northwestern University, College of Arts and Sciences, Department of Psychology, Evanston, Illinois 60201, USA.

Alan H. Naghara, Center for the Neurobiology of Learning and Memory, University of California, Irvine, CA 92717, USA.

Lars-Göran Nilsson, Department of Psychology, University of Umeå, S-901 87 Umeå, Sweden.

Arne Öhman, Department of Applied Psychology, University of Uppsala, Box 1225, S-751 42 Uppsala, Sweden.

J. Bruce Overmier, Center for Research in Human Learning, 205, Elliot Hall, 75, East River Road, Minneapolis, Minnesota 55455, USA.

Roberto A. Prado-Alcalá, Departemento de Neuroscienceis, Centro de Investigacion en Fisiologia Celular, Universidad Nacional Autonoma, Apartado Postal 70-600, 04510 Mexico, D.F.

Terje Sagvolden, Institute of Neurophysiology, Karl Johans Gate 47, N-0162 Oslo 1, Norway.

Marco Antonio Sánches, Departemento de Neuroscienceis, Centro de Investigacion en Fisiologia Celular, Universidad Nacional Autonoma, Apartado Postal 70-600, 04510 Mexico, D.F.

Per-Olow Sjödén, Department of Applied Psychology, University of Uppsala, Box 1225, S-751 42 Uppsala, Sweden.

Richard F. Thompson, Department of Psychology, University of Southern California, Seeley, G. Mudd Building, Los Angeles, California, 90098-1061, USA.

Andrew J. Tomarken, Department of Psychology, University of Wisconsin, 1202 West Johnson Street, Madison, WI 53706, USA.

INTRODUCTION

1 Historical Perspectives on the Study of Aversively Motivated Behavior: History and New Look

J. Bruce Overmier and Trevor Archer
University of Minnesota and University of Umeå

PROLEGOMENON

The purpose of this chapter is two-fold: first, to provide a historical background to the current studies of aversively motivated behaviors, and secondly, to introduce the six perspectives on aversively motivated behaviors that make up the balance of this volume. The contrast between these two sections is, in itself, rather a point of interest. Despite the historical importance of the study of aversively based behaviors in stimulating theoretical developments and these in generating empirical research, many of the historically important lines of research are seen only in vestigial form in the contemporary perspectives presented in the present volume. This occurs in part because a substantial portion of the historically important research was devoted to various challenges to strict S-R theories. These challenges emphasized analyses of avoidance. Nowadays, the S-R theories have at last been abandoned in favor of approaches to learning that emphasize cognitions rather than responses, and outcomes rather than strict performance (Blanchard & Blanchard, 1969; Dickinson & Shanks, 1985; Staddon & Simmelhag, 1971; Wagner, 1978).

Secondly, concurrent with the emergence of the cognitive perspective has been a reawakening of the long dormant interest in the Pavlovian or classical conditioning paradigm as a tool for exploring the cognitive processes in both humans and animals (Davey, 1983, 1987; Estes, 1973). Thirdly, some of the most challenging contemporary research on and analyses of the nature of what is learned has arisen from the relatively

3

recent rediscovery by Garcia and his associates of learning of food *specific* aversions, concerning the ecology of toxic plants and animals (Poulton, 1887) and hence did not play a part in the early history of aversively based learning as studied by psychologists in the first two-thirds of this century. Garcia's research emphasized the powerful biological constraints on associations and influenced not only animal research but stimulated anew human research in classical defense conditioning.

Given this curious partial disjunction between history and the contemporary scene, the current "perspectives" will require their own introduction. Nonetheless, some better appreciation of how far we have come may be gained by review first of some aspects of the early study of aversively motivated behavior as it transpired.

HISTORICAL BACKGROUND

1. Introduction

The basic empirical fact that sensory experiences of pleasures and pains direct behavioral acts surely has been known to mankind from the earliest times and has been recognized in statements of hedonistic principles. These first appeared formally in the philosophy of Epicurus (ca. 300 BC) and were reiterated later by Spinoza and l'Mettrie. This philosophy became a cornerstone of contemporary psychology through Thorndike's "Law of Effect" and Freud's "Id".

The two halves of the Law of Effect--"satisfiers" and "annoyers"--were, at least initially, considered to be of equal importance (Thorndike, 1931). Yet, in the domain of the psychology of learning, *very* much more attention and research has been directed towards an understanding of "appetitively" based reward learning than "aversively" based conditioning, escape, punishment, and avoidance learning. Indeed, Mackintosh's encyclopedic *Psychology of Animal Learning* (1974) devotes only 20 percent of its pages to aversively based learning! The same is true of other surveys of the learning literature (e.g. Bitterman, LoLordo, Overmier & Rashotte, 1979; Catania, 1979).

This is especially surprising because aversively based control of behavior is a prominent feature of training for both our children (Walters & Grusec, 1977) and our pets (Tortera, 1985), and probably ourselves! Moreover, aversive procedures result in some of the most striking and dramatic instances of behavior of animals including extraordinary persistence (Brown, 1969; Solomon, Kamin, & Wynne, 1953) and, by way of contrast, striking failures to respond (Overmier & Seligman, 1967) and even sudden death in response to threat (Richter, 1957).

In humans, equally striking phenomena are found to result from aversive procedures, ranging from the successful treatment in a matter of minutes through response contingent shock punishment of an otherwise therapy resistant self-injurious behavior (Whaley & Tough, 1970), to the elicitation from an unemotional autistic child of his first *positive* affective response by means of shock avoidance training (Garmezy & Rutter, 1983; Lovass, Schaeffer & Simmons, 1965), and further to, by way of contrast, the despair and "giving up" occasionally witnessed (Engel, 1967; Schein, 1956). Aversively based behaviors have proved a continuing challenge for theoretical development in (a) classical conditioning -- especially with respect to selectivity of associations between potential cues and hedonic events (Foree & LoLordo, 1973; Garcia & Koelling, 1966; Kamin, 1968; Öhman, Fredrikson, Hugdahl & Rimino, 1976), (b) punishment and the cause of the response suppression (Church, 1963; Goodall & Mackintosh, 1981; Solomon, 1964), (c) escape and how it reduces the "severity" of the experienced aversive events (Mowrer & Viek, 1948), and (d) avoidance learning and the mechanisms of response selection and reinforcement (Bolles, 1970; Konorski, 1967; McAllister, McAllister & Douglas, 1971; Mowrer, 1948).

In the paragraphs that follow, we shall comment upon the various paradigms that have been used to study aversively motivated behaviors, some key concepts, animal models of human "dysfunction", and experiments which set the stage for the perspectives presented in this volume.

2. Paradigms

One focus of the present and succeeding chapters is the changes in behavior that are observed when aversive stimuli are presented or withdrawn contingent upon some prior event or response -- the particular arrangement specifying the paradigm. There are several paradigms to be distinguished because their consequences are different. We shall turn to these anon.

First, we must direct our attention to one element of these paradigms, the putative aversive stimuli. Electric shock is the most extensively used aversive stimulus, typically applied to the feet of freely moving rats, in punishment paradigms, to condition suppress of appetitively reinforced bar-pressing (e.g. Annau & Kamin, 1961; Estes & Skinner, 1941). The technical definition of an aversive or noxious stimulus has long proved problematic. One might wish for a definition in terms of physical properties. But, this seems not possible in a broad general sense because of differences across individuals and species; there is disagreement in all but extreme cases as to whether a particular sight, sound, or other stimulation is "aversive" (e.g., the sight of a decapitated head, Hebb, 1946), and occasionally disagreement even in extreme cases (e.g., masochism, Brown, 1965). Failing this, operational definitions have been proffered including as one example Thorndike's Law of Effect. Thorndike's definition was criticized on the basis of its circularity (Meehl, 1950) but with the suggestion that the concept of "trans-situationality" of effects would break the chain of circularity. Unfortunately, trans-situationality of effects, while common, is sufficiently unreliable that we cannot use it to define aversive stimuli with unique behavioral properties.

This difficulty of definition is ubiquitously commented upon critically (Solomon, 1964; Church, 1963). But should this be so? Perhaps not, because exactly the same set of problems besets the definition of "rewards" and Thorndike's "satisfiers," yet the study of appetitively motivated behaviors has proceeded uninterruptedly. The tack has been to define the stimuli as appetitive rewards on a situational basis as a result of the observed effects of the contingency upon behavior. And so it must be for aversively motivated behavior. In both cases we are guided by our own hedonistic intuitions in the selection of the stimulus events to use, but the determination is largely empirical. Thus, the paradigms and their outcomes become the focus.

With respect to the paradigms, we may usefully distinguish the paradigms shown in Figure 1.1. These include (a) stimulus dependent presentation of aversive events, (b) stimulus dependent omission of aversive events, (c) response dependent presentation, (d) response dependent omission, (e) response dependent continuation, (f) response dependent termination, and, finally, (g) stimulus *and* response *independent* presentations of aversive events. In common parlance, the first two paradigms are "a" excitatory classical or Pavlovian defense conditioning and "b" inhibitory Pavlovian or "safety" conditioning. Paradigm "c" is punishment training, while "d" is instrumental avoidance training. The fifth, "e", has no common designation although Church (1963) has called it the "preservation" paradigm, but we prefer "cessation". Paradigm "f" we recognize as escape training. Finally, paradigm "g" is a complete zero contingency procedure used in whole or in part in "learned helplessness" and "learned irrelevance" experiments (e.g., Mackintosh, 1973; Overmier & Seligman, 1967) and is a concatenation of uncontrollability and unpredictability over repeated presentations (Seligman, 1968).

Each of these paradigms has been employed in research sufficiently that we have strong general expectations about their outcomes when the contingent event is aversive -- although these outcomes are not always obtained. For example, contrary to intuitions, punishment for correct responses can under some circumstances lead to improved appetitive choice response learning (Muenzinger, 1934; see Overmier, 1979, for discussion of other instances). This listing does not exhaust all the procedural distinctions one might draw (viz., Bitterman, 1962; Solomon & Brush, 1956), but it does set forth the major, distinctive operational paradigms through which we study aversively motivated behaviors.

The distinctions among these paradigms, perhaps obvious to us today, were not always recognized nor appreciated. Consider for example, excitatory Pavlovian conditioning and instrumental avoidance. The latter appears to have emerged out of efforts in Bekhterev's laboratory to translate Pavlov's paradigm of "psychic" (salivary) responses based on appetitive USs into one using motor responses and defensive USs. In the translation, the situation was altered such that the US was received only if the CR did not occur (Razran, 1956). A similar translation error occurred in the United States (e.g., Hamel, 1919) as researchers emmulated the work described by Bekhterev (1913); this instantiation of the *avoidance* paradigm was unintentional and unrecognized (Watson,

Selected Paradigms

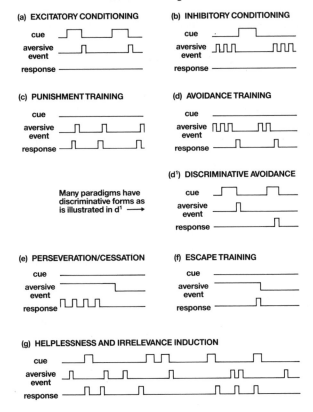

FIG. 1.1. Aversively-multivated learning procedures; cues, aversive events and some response consequences.

1916). Later, after the operational difference was recognized, its functional importance was vigorously contested (e.g., Hunter, 1935, vs. Schlosberg, 1934). Even after the functional importance was recognized -- at least for some classes of motor responses (Warner, 1932, vs. Logan 1951 but see Moore & Gormezano, 1961), the theoretical significance was still controversial (Schlosberg, 1937) and denied by some (Hull, 1943); the existence of these operational differences appears a central issue (Konorski & Miller, 1937; Skinner, 1935, 1937). Nevertheless, the conundrum for traditional theories was becoming clear: the reinforcing event for defensive classical conditioning, escape training, and avoidance learning could not be the same (Gibson, 1952; Mowrer, 1940; Mowrer & Lamoreaux, 1942; Mowrer & Solomon, 1954; Osgood, 1950).

Even later, as new forms of avoidance technology were being developed (Sidman, 1953), mistaken identification of an avoidance paradigm for one of escape led May (1948) and influential others (Kimble,

1961) to misunderstand the nature of avoidance and the origin of the initial avoidance responses, which they attributed to escapes from an aversive CS. "Replication" of the May experiment controlling for the previously unrecognized imbedded avoidance contingency made clear the mis-attribution (Ehrman & Overmier, 1976).

Similarly, the classic experiment of Watson and Rayner (1920) with Little Albert involves a paradigmatic confusion. The experiment is virtually everywhere described as one of Pavlovian or classical conditioning of "fear" in which the sight of a white rat (CS) was paired with a loud noise (US). But in point of fact, the actual procedure was one of punishment with the loud noise being sounded only when Little Albert approached and or reached out to touch the rat! This confusion and its persistence is surprising given the centrality of this demonstration to the development of learning based models of neurotic behavior and behavior therapies.

We should not, however, feel too superior to these earlier failures to adequately characterize a given paradigm. There may be paradigms that we have yet to recognize clearly. For example, the defensive classical conditioning paradigm, in which the cue is labeled CS and the defensive event to US, has been used by many to characterize conditioned taste aversion learning. But it has been argued that we cannot apply this to conditioned taste aversions because the cue here (consumption of some palatable substance) is really a US and the defensive event is feedback from gastric distress (Garcia, Lasiter, Bermudez-Rattoni & Deemo, 1985; Solomon, 1977; Spiker, 1977). Thus, it may well be that the paradigms described above do not yet accurately characterize all those procedures we use.

3. Emergent Concepts

The early controversies, of course, stimulated continuing research (see Mowrer, 1960, chapter 1, for one summary) which in turn led to new theoretical analyses and invocation of new constructs and conceptualizations. Some have stood the test of time and served us well; others have not. But all have proved useful -- and sometimes quite powerful -- heuristics for research leading to further advances.

Two Response Processes. It was the early studies contrasting the classical conditioning and instrumental avoidance paradigms using a variety of skeletal-motor and autonomic responses that led to efforts to distinguish the two learning processes in "two-process" theories. Given the origin of the impetus, it is not surprising that the effort focused upon response "types". Some of the proposed type distinctions are shown in Table 1.1.

These proposed distinctions have never really proved satisfactory because researchers were quite adept at finding and demonstrating " exceptions" -- such as instrumental training of the heart rate response (DiCara & Miller, 1968), although the mechanisms underlying response control in these exceptions has been challenged (Black, 1974) and,

TABLE 1.1
Some distinctions between Response types.

Hypothesized response system characteristics

Theorist (S)		Classical	Instrumental
Konorski	1948	little sensory feedback	rich sensory feedback
Schlosberg	1937	diffuse emotional	precise adaptive
Skinner	1935	elicited	emitted
Mowrer	1947	autonomic	skeletal motor
Kimble	1962	involuntary	voluntary
Turner & Solomon	1962	high reflexivity, short latency	low reflexivity

sometimes, the demonstrations themselves have proved unreliable (Dworkin & Miller, 1986; Miller, 1972). Alternatively, challenges sometimes focused upon cases in which the "same" response was established under both classical and instrumental procedures (e.g., Logan, 1951; Wahlston & Cole, 1972). This led to important new questions about response similarity (e.g., Cotton, 1953; Logan, 1956) and new technologies for measuring responses. Are two instances of a particular molar response (e.g., leg flexions or eyeblinks) to be considered instances of the same class of response when there are systematic detectable differences in response topography (see Spence & Ross, 1959; on voluntary vs. conditioned responses)? Different theorists gave different answers. Another problem is that there is little direct evidence of response-produced feedback in instrumental learning. Turner and Solomon (1962) noted that college students failed to avoid shock delivered to a toe if toe-flexion be the required response but did learn rapidly to pull a lever. These theoretical dilemma were never fully resolved, and the issue of response topography continues to be of concern, especially in human psychophysiology.

One reason that this theoretical issue was not resolved, of course, is because it arises primarily from an S-R or response learning view. If by contrast, one believes that what is learned is some cognitive expectancy (Dickinson, 1980) or event representation (Rescorla, 1980) or proposition (Furedy & Riley, 1987), then the issue of the response is believed to be moot -- a matter of organism convenience. Actually, the issue of response performance is a continuing problem that cognitive psychologists must face, but often -- even typically -- do not, leading Furedy and Riley (1987) to complain that the "cognitive imperalism" of today is still subject to Guthrie's jibe made half a century ago that cognitivists leave the rat buried in thought at the choice point.

Mediation. More central to two-process theories was the idea put forward by Mowrer (1938, 1940), trying to account for neurotic behaviors, that classical conditioning established a mediating motivational state that was the basis for both the initiation of the avoidant behavior and its reinforcement. Mowrer called the mediating state "anxiety" and later "fear", which, in the then popular S-R language, was characterized as the fractional anticipatory detachable component of the pain reaction to a noxious stimulus. At this point two issues appear to have become confused: (a) mediation by fear and (b) encoding or representation of fear.

These two issues roughly correspond to fear as an intervening variable and fear as a hypothetical construct, respectively (MacCorquodale & Meehl, 1948). The first is central to any two-process theory; the second is not. Yet it is this second which often garnered much of the attention of researchers. They tried to establish through concurrent measurement and correlational techniques that fear *was* increases in heart rate -- or some other autonomic response (e.g., Black, 1959). Alternatively, the autonomic function was impaired with the expectation that fear motivated avoidance would now be blocked; and while avoidance was disrupted to some extent, it was rarely blocked (Wenzel, 1968; Wynne & Solomon, 1955). Eventually, autonomic responses were relegated to the status of correlated but imperfect indicies of the mediational state.

Conceptually similar efforts were made to localize fear in particular brain structures -- typically some limbic structure (e.g., Kriekhaus, 1967) -- with a similar pattern of disappointing results so far. This latter line of CNS research has not been abandoned and continues in two forms, one focusing on anatomical structures and one focusing on neurochemical systems (see chapters in this volume by Thompson, by Beninger, and by McGaugh). Unless one is prepared to be a dualist, there can be no question that the state of fear has some physiological basis somewhere, as psychopharmacology confirms. In this search, however, behavioral analysis plays a central role for it provides the "target" which the physiological functions must map onto to validate the identification of the physiological substrate.

If there were ever any doubt about the early unsatisfactory conception of fear as the "detachable component of pain", recent work by Gray (1977, 1982) has put it to rest. Gray reports a double dissociation between antianxiety drugs, which act on responses to *signals* for noxious events but not on responses to the events themselves, and opiates and analgesics, which act on responses to noxious events but not on responses to signals for noxious events. This is *not*, however, to say that fear and anxiety do not mediate responses, merely that the conceptualization of fear as a component of the pain response is inadequate. They are different systems as the recent analysis by Bolles and Fanselow (1980) confirms. The failure of escape training to reliably enhance avoidance learning reflects this same separation (Bolles, 1969; Zielinski & Soltysik, 1964).

The viability of "fear" as a mediator lies not in the ability to measure it directly (although that would certainly be appropriate) but rather in the successful use of it as an intervening variable -- as a predictive bridge between operations and consequent behavior. To test mediational theories in which fear is only an intervening variable, a new class of experiment was called for, one in which the mediational process and the response process were independently manipulated. This class of experiment is referred to as "transfer of control" experiments. A classic example is Solomon and Turner's (1962) demonstration that discriminative defensive classical conditioning of dogs while immobilized by curare endowed the CS+ with the power to later control immediately and completely an instrumental avoidance response previously established to another stimulus. Other exemplars of this class are demonstrations of (a) fear as an acquired drive (Miller, 1948), (b) the power of classical conditioned CSs of several types to modulate instrumental responding (Overmier & Lawry, 1979; Rescorla & Solomon, 1967; Trapold & Overmier, 1972; provide analytic reviews), as well as (c) response switching among available responses (Overmier & Brackbill, 1977). The concept of classically conditioned fear as a mediator of responses continues to play a central role in several hypotheses of neurotic behaviors (see Mineka, 1979, 1985a, for especially perceptive reviews). Unfortunately, many of these latter theoretical efforts have not generally maintained contact with contemporary developments in conditioning theory or research.

Reinforcement. The preceding paragraphs focused on fear as mediating response occurence. Another function, response reinforcement through fear reduction, has also been an issue of interest. This hypothesized basis for learning of avoidance responses is in contrast to the alternative views of the avoidance response as being either a classically conditioned CR, a "short-latency" escape response, or as reinforced by shock frequency reduction. The first two alternative views faltered on the problem of the dissimilarity between the avoidance response and the CR or the escape response (Bolles, 1969; Gibson, 1952; Fonberg, 1958; Keehn, 1959; Mowrer & Lamoreaux, 1946). The third alternative has had difficulty with the fact that *overall* shock frequency reduction is not necessary to maintain avoidance (Gardner & Lewis, 1976), although Mackintosh (1983) considers this a pseudo-difficulty.

Advantages of the fear reduction concept of reinforcement are found in its ability not only to resolve Mowrer's paradox of how the non-occurence of an event (the noxious stimulus) can act as a reinforcer but also to account for selected performance issues. For example, this function of fear accounts for the fact that one-way avoidance is learned faster than two-way avoidance and that this difference increases with intensity of the noxious stimulus (McAllister & McAllister, 1967; Theios, Lynch & Lowe, 1966). It does so by noting that fear reduction will be greater if a response carries an animal into, or allows access to, a place where the noxious stimulus has never occurred before than if the response produces little environmental change. Similarly, it rationalizes, without reference to species-specific defense reactions, why learning of a bar press as an avoidance response is typically poor (D'Amato & Shiff, 1964) but can be made excellent by allowing the bar press to open an exit door (Crawford & Masterson, 1978; Masterson & Crawford, 1982; Miller, 1948).

Above, we have given the impression of widespread support for the two-process fear-mediational theory of avoidance and punishment -- of a theory standing firm against the onslaughts of challengers. It has done well, but it is no longer clearly *THE* primary theory that it once was.

This is because it metamorphized out of a strict S-R, behavioristic tradition; it has cognitive overtones but is still burdened with S-R baggage. Newer theories have abandoned rather completely S-R related accounts in favor of ones involving memories, representations, expectancies, and/or other cognitive constructs (Bolles, 1972; Dickinson, 1980; Seligman & Johnson, 1973). So far, these cognitive accounts of aversively motivated learning have led to few new exprimental results inconsistent with the former theory, but they are just beginning to be tested seriously.

Dissociation of Fear and Avoidance. One speculation on fear both as a mediator and a source of reinforcement was proposed to account for what has been described as the special resistance of avoidance -- and by implication, phobic responses -- to extinction (Solomon, Kamin & Wynne, 1953). Solomon and Wynne (1954) suggested (a) that the degree of extinction of fear response was proportional to the level to which fear rose before responding, but (b) that the magnitude of the elicited fear reaction did not directly determine the vigor of the instrumental avoidance response. Indeed they argued, only a little fear was needed because organisms need not wait until maximally afraid before responding *and* that the vigor of the avoidance response was a function of the *instrumental* response strength derived from previous fear reduction reinforcement. The avoidance response, it was argued, terminated the fear state before it was maximally aroused and hence "conserved" the anxiety or fear so as to continue to mediate responses for a long time.

This speculation seemed to be able to account not only for the persistence of avoidance behavior in experimental studies but also for the persistence of fear motivated neurotic behaviors in clinical populations. However, this "explanatory" power came with real costs. This speculation created fundamental problems for the testing of any fear mediational model of avoidance behavior. The problem it creates is that it implies a dissociation between the fear state and possible indices of the fear.

The dissociation of fear and avoidance implied by Solomon and Wynne's analysis was demonstrated empirically by Kamin, Brimer and Black (1963). They showed that as avoidance training proceeded to a high level, the classically conditioned fear of the CS appeared to diminish. Mineka and Gino (1980) have confirmed this using improved designs (see also Mineka, Cook & Miller, 1984). Additionally, Coover, Ursin, and Levine (1973) obtained a similar result using corticosterone levels as their index of the level of chronic fear. Whatever it is that controls avoidance performance levels, it is not directly correlated with fear as indexed by CER or ACTH. This at least partial independence or desynchrony among measures of fear and fear mediated behaviors is potentially a serious problem for any type of mediational theory of avoidance -- or of neurotic behaviors. The problem is possibly a less serious one for theories that argue fear is a cognitive process only indirectly and loosely related to any particular response system such as motor, psychophysiological, or verbal. One such view is Lang's (1964, 1968) three factor conceptualization of fear which is currently of substantial interest to behavior therapists (e.g., Rachman, 1978).

The issue of dissociation also appears in another form in the human classical conditioning literature: Can conditioning occur in the absence of awareness of the subject about the contingencies? Human defensive conditioning and its dependence upon awareness has long been controversial (cf., Dawson & Schell, 1985). The early view was that it was not (Lacey & Smith, 1954); indeed, many human eyeblink conditioning experiments explicitly included "masking" conditions to prevent such awareness so that "true" classical conditioning (as opposed to avoidance) could proceed (Hartman & Ross, 1961). Conditioning without awareness was claimed at its most dramatic form in the perceptual defense based "subception" phenomenon of Lazarus and McCleary (1951) in which apparently discriminative autonomic CRs occurred in response to threatening words that could not be recognized (see also Reiss, 1980). Ericksen (1956) suggested this was at least in part a measurement problem in which the autonomic response had more variation available to it than the verbal response (see also Overmier, 1970). Today, little is heard of such perceptual defense -- although this "preprocessing" concept is still with us in the guise of pre-attentive stimulus selection and orienting (Öhman, 1979).

The general view today seems to be that higher cognitive processes play a role in human conditioning and that awareness is a necessary mediator of the conditioning process (Dawson & Schell, 1987; but see also the chapter by Boakes, this volume). Evidence for the role of these higher mental processes include the observation that instructions can modulate conditioning and extinction -- harking back to Mowrer's point years ago. But this view that awareness is necessary for conditioning is seen as posing some serious problems for the view that phobias are defensive classically conditioned responses because phobic patients are often unable to identify any historical associative basis (Marks, 1969; but see Hugdahl, 1980). Perhaps a little familiarity with contemporary animal learning research would obviate this concern. For example, Holland (1981) demonstrated that if an animal had two separate experiences, first a CS paired with a novel taste and later that CS paired with the induction of nausea, then the animal showed an aversion to the *taste* even though the taste was never paired with the nausea! Could this solve the mystery of the missing associative history in some phobics? If so, the classical conditioning literature abound with such examples of higher-order conditioning in aversively motivated paradigms (cf. Rizley & Rescorla, 1972). In any case, it does illustrate the point that many currently used learning concepts of neurotic disorders may not be based upon the most contemporary research (see Davey, 1983; Mineka, 1985a; and Siddle & Remington, 1987 for counter examples).

Inhibition of Fear. One account of the desynchrony or dissociation between CS elicited fear and the persistence of avoidance rests on the assertion that the avoidance response is maintained by response contingent occurence of conditioned inhibitors of fear. This notion is clearly related to Mowrer's original view that the response is reinforced by fear reduction; after all, an inhibitor of fear is presumed to produce fear reduction. The idea differs in asserting that these inhibitors become reinforcing themselves (see Boakes & Halliday, 1972).

Aside from constituting the introduction of a whole new construct -- albeit one of long standing (Pavlov, 1927), the concept of conditioned inhibition has some clear merits. In fact, it has been demonstrated that when such conditioned inhibitors are contingent upon responses, they influence learning (Morris, 1975), rate of responding (Weisman & Litner, 1969), and choice behavior (Rescorla, 1969). But the full conceptualization here is more: it derives from Konorski's (1967) theory of reciprocal relations between appetitive and aversive motivational systems. This theory sees an excitor for one motivational system as an inhibitor for the other, the CER experiments of Estes and Skinner (1941) being one instance. Reciprocally, an inhibitor for one motivational system would be an *excitor* for the other. Direct confirmations of this aspect are limited (Dickinson & Dearing, 1979, may be one example). This theory is consistent with the persistence of avoidance responses seen even when fear weakens because it views the response contingent inhibitory stimuli as sustaining the avoidance behavior. Reduction in the inhibitory properties of response contingent stimuli does reduce their capacity to sustain avoidant behavior (Cicala & Owen, 1976).

One important feature of this theory is that it makes central the concept of inhibition. Thus, we must be concerned with the basis for conditioning of inhibition. Inhibition, some hypothesize, is conditioned by virtue of a CS being paired with a condition opposite the excitatory state induced by the noxious event (e.g., Denny, 1971). The clearest statement of this process is given by the opponent-process theory (Solomon & Corbit, 1974). In one sense, it is a theory of habituation to the CS; this occurs by virtue of interaction of a primary, event-induced hedonic process with a "homeostatic" counterprocess of opposite hedonic quality, which although initially sluggish recruits through repitition and persists after the primary event is gone. Important is the assertion that CSs paired with either net hedonic state will become conditioned elicitors of that state: in particular, because the anti-excitatory state persists after the end of the frequently experienced noxious events, backward CSs should become conditioned elicitors of this state. Several deductions follow from this theory of inhibitory classical conditioning. For example, a novel noxious event should readily support excitatory conditioning to a forward CS, but it should not support inhibitory conditioning to a backward CS. In contrast, an habituated noxious event should not support excitatory conditioning to a forward CS, but it should readily support inhibitory conditioning to a backward CS. Such predictions have been confirmed (Overmier, Payne, Brackbill, Linder, and Lawry, 1979).

To the extent that conditioned inhibitors based upon aversive events are "reinforcers", this theory provides a potential account of the observed desynchrony between fear measures and well learned avoidance behaviors based on having experienced the US many times. We suppose, also, that to the extent an aversive stimulus is habituated and the post-event hedonic state has become opposite, this theory gives an account of self-punitive and masochistic behaviors.

Punishment and Fear as Discriminative Stimuli. The hedonic properties of aversive events have been emphasized so far. But of course, they have stimulus properties as well. At low intensities, it is these stimulus properties that predominate (Church, 1963; Solomon, 1964). One presumes that anticipations or expectancies of them have stimulus properties as well. Indeed, some experiments have been designed to elucidate exactly these stimulus properties of expectancies of distinctive aversive events (Desiderato & Newman, 1971; Overmier, Bull & Trapold, 1971).

The notion that aversive events and expectancies of them have stimulus or cue properties produces some special phenomena. For example, the occurence of response contingent punishers can enhance appetitive responding in the absence of further rewards. This occurs if the organism had previously learned a discrimination between two schedules of reward (VI vs. EXT) for which the presence of response independent noxious events was the discriminative stimulus for the richer schedule (Azrin & Holz, 1961). Similarly, if animals have learned to perform a response to get food but have also received partial punishment concurrently, later presentations of a classically conditioned fear CS will *enhance* response vigor, not suppress it as would normally be expected in such a CER paradigm (Rosellini & Terris, 1976).

It is likely that it is these discriminative properties that are responsible for the *facilitation* of behaviors, previously learned under aversive motivations, when punishment is introduced -- the so-called "vicious circle" behavior (Brown, 1969; Gwinn, 1949). Such phenomena are not restricted to animals, but have been reported for human patients for whom stuttering was (presumed to have been) learned under aversive motivation and for whom punishment was introduced (Bloodstein, 1958; but see Siegel, 1970).

Other instances of facilitative interactions may be found in the cross-tolerance between partial punishment and frustration induced by partial reward (Brown & Wagner, 1964; Linden, 1974). Partial reinforcement experience results in later resistance to punishment; similarly, partial punishment experience results in later resistance to frustration. Thus, it appears that fear and frustration states have elements in common. In related work, Fonberg (1956) has shown that, if a dog is first trained in an avoidance response and then later trained in an *appetitive* discrimination, as the discrimination is made more difficult (frustrating?) the *avoidance* response begins to spontaneously reoccur -- like a neurotic tic! All these effects are presumed to be based upon the similarity of the stimulus properties of the induced aversive states and these stimuli's role in controlling behavior.

Another less obvious way in which aversive stimuli or motivations may act as "discriminative stimuli" is in prompting recall. We treat this later in the section on memory below.

Memory. One might presume that after having learned that a stimulus signals danger, and one response leads to pain or another response leads to relief or safety, it would be advantageous for the organism to remember these events precisely and well. It seems, in fact, that animals often do remember aversively motivated responses effectively (Gleitman & Holmes, 1967; Thomas, 1979), but how precise is the memory is another issue.

Eysenck (1968) has argued that at least under some circumstances fears may "incubate" over time and, hence, yield recall of levels of distress that never occurred. This idea has been subject to experimental tests (e.g., Bindra & Cameron, 1953) but with less than dramatic results (Bersh, 1980).

Do fears incubate or are they forgotten? It seems that, in part, the answer depends upon how the question is asked experimentally. Memories of the conditions under which the aversive event occurred seem to generalize more broadly with the passage of time; one result of this is that if the test for remembered fear happens to be in a context that differs from that in which the aversive event was experienced, two outcomes are possible depending upon the promptness of test. Early tests in the new context will show little remembered fear (because of the context change), but later tests will show considerable remembered fear (because of the generalization; Riccio, Richardson, Ebrer, 1984). Thus, the late test in the changed context might lead one to infer incubation; on the other hand late tests given in the original context could lead to an inference of no change! (Further discussions on the role of context events are provided in the next section on context).

When one tests for retention of fear to a CS+ using summation tests wherein the CS+ is superimposed on a baseline of behavior established using exactly the same noxious event, then retention is remarkably insensitive to the passage of time. However, when the testing is on a baseline established using a different noxious event, retention *appears* to improve over time (the CS+ increases the baseline further; Hendersen, Patterson & Jackson, 1980)! We say "appears" because Hendersen (1985) has shown that this increase occurs because of *forgetting* of exactly what one was afraid of and, hence, generalizing across USs more broadly with the passage of time. Moreover, the animal can be 'tricked' into misremembering the source of the original fear by presenting false "reminders" to the animal, and the degree of one's ability to trick the animal increases with time. This seems closely related to Loftus's "red-herring" phenomenon (this volume).

In addition to the above, it may be that information about motivational state is part of how memories are stored. That is, motivational context or state dependency may be one of the retrieval cues for learned responses in animals and man. Motivational state may act as an analogue to drugs as in state-dependent learning (Overton, 1984). The work of Bower (1981) and Ellis (1985) on mood and human memory is consistent with this view. Conceptually similar experiments in animals not only confirm that motivational state plays a role in modulating recall, but also give insight into the mechanism (McGaugh, this volume, Riccio & Concannon, 1981). In essence, it seems that motivational states have their own endogenous neurohumoral "drug" state, and that recall is dependent upon reinstatement of that neurohumoral state (Izquierdo, 1984; Stewart, Krebs & Kaczander, 1971).

The implications of this for human recall are obvious: If you wish a client to recall an event, recall will be improved if the client is put into a motivational state similar to that during the original learning.

Additionally, it also implies that if one wants to change (therapeutically) a patient's memory of an event, this too will be facilitated by getting the subjects into the original motivational state. Indeed, this may be one of the keys to the successes of "flooding" or "implosive" therapies (Stampfl & Levis, 1967). Confirmation of this last principle can be found in a clever set of experiments by Robbins and Meyer (1970). After they first trained rats in form discrimination #1 as an escape and then trained form discrimination #2 as an appetitive task, they found that ECS administered after a new escape trial functionally "erased" form discrimination #1 -- not the last learned task! But if the ECS were administered after a new appetitive trial, it "erased" form discrimination #2. The motivation reinstated by the final trial determined which memory was susceptible to modulation.

One further speculation that follows from this line of analysis is that the ruminative thinking about earlier fears and frustrations that accompanies anxious-depressive states may be a direct manifestation of this neurohumoral modulation of recall (Overmier & Hellhammer, in press).

Context. Although early described by Pavlov as a "synthetic environmental reflex" (1927) the influence of contextual (or background) events has received more consistent and explicit notice within the last decade (e.g. Balsam, 1984; Balsam & Schwartz, 1981; Domjan & Burkhard, 1982; Honig & Staddon, 1977; Jenkins, Barnes & Barrera, 1981). Context determines the way in which a given stimuli is initially learned and a shift of context could mean that subjects are required to utilise a stimulus-context configuration, as retrieval cues, different from that of the initial learning phase.

In aversively motivated conditioning procedures, context learning appears to be rapid, both for the formation of CS-context associations (Anderson, Wolf & Sullivan, 1969; Rudy, Rosenberg & Sandell, 1977) and US-context associations (Baker, Mercier, Gabel & Baker, 1981; Odling-Smee, 1975b). Balsam (1985) has reviewed techniques by which contextual influence can be studied with aversive conditioning procedures: (a) *Context-Shift* tests by which initial training (conditioning) occurs within one context and later performance can be assessed in either the same or in a different context (e.g. Archer, Sjödén, Nilsson & Carter, 1979; Archer & Sjödén, 1980, 1981; Bouton & King, 1983; Rescorla, Durlach & Grau, 1985; Sjödén & Archer, 1981). (b) *Retardation* tests use essentially a latent inhibition technique (Lubow, 1965; Lubow & Moore, 1959) by pretraining or preexposure to the contextual cues followed by CS conditioning in that or in a different context. There are two main variations: the CS is absent during the pretraining phase and introduced during the second phase or present during the initial phase and context is varied during the second phase. The rationale is that prior context conditioning will disrupt subsequent learning acquisition. (c) *Preference* tests measure contextual learning by applying a choice between contexts that have undergone different training histories or procedures (e.g. Fanselow, 1980; Odling-Smee, 1975a; Randich, 1981; Randich, Jacobs, LoLordo & Sutterer, 1978; Randich & Ross, 1984). (d) *Summation* tests evaluate context conditioning effects upon ongoing operant behaviors. For example, Patterson and Overmier (1981) inferred context conditioning from the effects of nonreinforced presentation of contextual cues on response rate in a CER procedure.

Other demonstrations of the summation tests are present (Bouton & Bolles, 1979; Bouton & King, 1983; Dweck & Wagner, 1970). Some of these tests are aimed at measuring conditioning to a CS embedded with the CS-context configuration, others the associative strength accruing to the context independent of the presence or absence of the CS; both tactics provide instances of phenomena relevant to current learning theories.

Several experiments have indicated that the latent inhibition phenomenon (e.g. Lubow, 1973) may be context specific, i.e. if a stimulus (the CS) is repeatedly presented in one context this CS will be conditioned slowly when paired with a US in that context, but if the CS-US pairings occur in a different context conditioning will occur relatively rapidly (Anderson, O'Farrell, Formica & Coponigri, 1969; Balaz, Capra, Hartl & Miller, 1981, 1982; Bouton & Bolles, 1979; Channell & Hall, 1981; Dexter & Merrill, 1969; Lubow, Rifkin & Alek, 1976). As noted by Mackintosh (1985), few context experiments of this type control for the possibility that the physical characteristics of the CS may be altered as a result of contextual changes, as in the case of context-specific extinction effects (Lovibond, Preston & Mackintosh, 1984). Context-specific latent inhibition demonstrations may hold consequences for our notions on the role of fear in aversively conditioned behavior. The 'weaker' fear of the different context (during preexposure) groups indicated that these animals learn that the CS could occur without the US in the preexposure context; there was no explicit contingency by which to expect an association between the CS, context and US events. Thus, this class of experiments may offer further evidence of the utility of the fear mediation concept as an intervening variable.

Contextual cues have been shown to be responsible for the reinstatement of fear responses after they have been extinguished (Bouton, 1984; Bouton & Bolles, 1985; Hoffman, 1965; Quinsey & Ayres, 1969; Rescorla & Cunningham, 1977; Rescorla & Heth, 1975). The following general procedure is used: First, CS-US (shock) pairings are made and then the CR (suppression of responding, for example) is extinguished. Later, the US is presented a few times independently of the CS. After this, the CS is presented and is found to suppress responding once again, i.e. it appears that the CS has regained some of its ability to evoke conditioned fear. Bouton and King (1983) make clear the role of background context on this fear reinstatement in conditioned suppression. Other evidence that contextual cues can affect fear conditioning both measurably and manipulatively are provided by Odling-Smee (1975a, b, 1978), and Jacobs and Nadel (1985) suggest this may be the key to neurotic and phobic learning.

The purpose of this section is to maintain the awareness of the importance of background context in the control of aversively motivated behaviors. Awareness of context implies that the experimenter considers the momentary reactions of the subject, that is to say CS and shock events, within the larger, global context of the subject's overall history of experience of these events (Bouton & Bolles, 1985); this consideration may be of fundamental importance for aversive conditioning.

Generality of Laws. The traditions in the psychology of learning have been to search for general principles derived from simple, controlled situations, which may or may not be considered arbitrary! Prototypic examples are the text book "laws" such as the matching law according to which the relative response frequencies match the relative reinforcement frequencies and the contiguity law according to which the strength of association is related to the degree of contiguity. According to the latter, the optimal CS-US interval in classical conditioning is 0.5 seconds; every introductory text book says so! The finding that when a novel taste occurs followed by induced gastric distress, aversion learning can occur despite intervals of *hours* between the two events has itself upset many psychologists (for relevant discussions, see Bolles, 1985a, b). So much so that they proposed new principles (Garcia, Rusiniak & Brett, 1977) or abandoned all hope and denied the possibility of general laws of learning (Seligman, 1970). Similar difficulties in accounting for task specificity (see Bignami, this volume), led Bolles (1970) to propose that avoidance learning followed special new principles that reflected species specific defense reactions (SSDRs).

Defense systems were presumably evolved to give animals significant evolutionary advantages (Hollis, 1982). Moreover, defense systems are not a singularity but involve several discrete subsystems with their own associated psychological states. These subsystems likely include intraspecific social defense, toxiphobia gut defense, and predator-skin defense (Garcia, this volume; Öhman, 1986). The last appears to be further subdivided into pain (local) and fear (distal) defense systems (Bolles & Fanselow, 1980). Arousal states for each of these systems -- emotions? -- may, in addition to being response-action modulators, also be a signal system to self, conspecifics, and predators (Darwin, 1872). As such, perceptions of these emotional signals (e.g., grimacing face) may be highly specialized by evolution, as is apparently the case for language (Lenneberg, 1969). Hence, we may well see selective association between events within a given system and the elicited emotional consequences.

These problems have received considerable attention (e.g., Domjan 1983), including accounts of why human phobias appear to occur to a restricted range of stimuli (Mineka, 1985a; Seligman, 1971; Öhman, et al, 1976). But in what sense do they constitute cases against the generality of laws of learning? Let us consider the case of the CS-US long-delay effect in taste aversion learning. What principle is violated here?

The basic principle most commonly asserted to be challenged is that of contiguity and the 0.5 second optimum. And, 0.5 seconds is close together. But 0.3 seconds is closer, while 0.1 is closer still. Yet, learning of the eyeblink response does not improve with these increasing degrees of contiguity. That there is an optimal CS-US interval that is non-zero is already a challenge to the principle of contiguity that has long existed. Moreover, 0.5 seconds is the optimum for eyeblink conditioning in humans but not for other stimulus-response sets in humans or animals, and this too has been long known. The optimum for gross motor movements in pigs seems to be nearer to 10 seconds, (Noble & Adams, 1963), and Pavlov (1927) rarely used less than 30 seconds. In all cases, there is an optimum CS-US value; the principle is the same for all, only the parameter value of the optimum varies. True, we do not know the reasons for the variation yet, but there are likely a number of different contributing factors (including operational ones such as measurement technique), but no principle is violated. One possible contributing factor may be a sensory preconditioning effect mediated by contextual cues that 'bridge' the CS-US delay interval (for discussion, see Archer & Sjödèn, 1982). Moreover, taste aversion learning shows most all of the other known phenomena of classical conditioning (see Krane & Wagner, 1975; Logue, 1979; Spiker, 1977, for reviews).

With respect to stimulus differences in associability, these too may be overdrawn because many of the procedures used failed to control for potentially important differences in nonassociative factors. Indeed, Linwick, Patterson, and Overmier (1981) have illustrated exactly this problem that occurs whenever bidirectionally sensitive baselines are not used, and they usually are not. This is not to claim that all stimuli become associated with any reinforcer with equal facility. No one ever assumed equal salience of stimuli. Moreover, a number of stimulus properties and their similarity between the CS and the US modulate rate of both nonassociative and associative factors (Rescorla, 1985; Testa, 1974; Wickens & Wickens, 1942). Until these are well articulated, we should be wary of arguing against any generality of principles of learning.

We do not wish to foreclose the possibility that there *are* several types or classes of learning, each with its own sets of laws. Our conceptualizations of what is learned and the nature of the elements that enter into this learning are still maturing. Under such conditions, one would be foolhardy to claim that our current theoretical appreciation is as sophisticated as the organisms the behavior of which we wish to account for.

Nonetheless, all organisms are faced with the same basic challenges to survival. Given the physical constraints on the world, we should not be surprised that the optimally effective solutions are limited in number and that evolution of each species would access many of these. On the other hand, physiology does vary across species and is related to the ecological niche occupied. So identity, too, might be quite surprising, although the dimensionality of the variability may be quite limited. When one compares the similarity of learning phenomena identified across species as divergent as the honeybee and the teleost fish and the rat, one is struck much more by the parallels than the divergences (Bitterman, 1975, 1987).

With respect to aversively motivated behaviors, Gray (1982) reports that hundreds of anti-anxiety drugs have been tested over a wide range of species (goldfish to human) using a variety of signals and response tasks, and there are only rare occasions when there is need to qualify the description of the observed effect. This, he suggests means that fear (or anxiety), its behavioral expression, and its neural bases are phylogenetic primitives. What we learn in animal experiments can guide us in understanding the human condition.

II. CURRENT PERSPECTIVES

"Perspectives on Aversively Motivated Behavior" includes contributions from six different conceptual orientations. All are empirical, experimental. This selection is not to dinigrate other orientations nor the importance of individual cases of pathology. Applications are of concern. Within each of the orientations, we shall seek to link the particular orientation to the problems of maladaptive behaviors and cognitions that are of concern to us all. Indeed, the view is that a solid scientific understanding of the mechanisms of psychological function will give us the greatest leverage on disordered and maladaptive human behavior. The six orientations include:

1. Perspectives on determinants of hedonic value
2. Clinical Perspectives
3. Cognitive perspectives
4. Neurobiological perspectives
5. Neuro-ethological perspectives
6. Methodological and conceptual perspectives

Each deserves brief introductory comment.

Perspectives on the determinants of hedonic value grows out of the research on taste aversion learning. Experiment in taste averison learning assumed a major significance in the field, globally influencing our conceptions of the nature of learning and the learning organism. This research has not toppled the ediface of general process theories of learning but it surely shook the foundations for awhile, and we may yet find that it has reoriented the structure. John Garcia initiated this dislodgement by showing a special "double dissociation" between the associabilities of particular stimuli and particular consequences. Tastes were shown to be more readily associated with induced gastric distress than with tactual pain, while noises and lights were shown to be more readily associated with tactual pain than gastric distress. This finding was not readily accepted and challenged on many grounds, but it proved to be a highly robust phenomenon of great generality. Some saw this as a death knell for general process views of learning, sometimes even claiming that our traditional research practices were incapable of producing general laws of learning -- ignoring that it was just such a research practice using arbitrary events that produced this special but generalizable finding.

Revusky (1971, 1977; but see also Revusky & Garcia, 1970) began the "salvage" operation by inquiring into the factors that permitted selective associations, especially over long delays, in the case of taste aversions and proposed an answer out of traditional general process learning theory -- concurrent and retroactive interference, an operational issue. As will be discussed by Sjödén & Archer, both the differential associability of events and the bridging of long-delays may, at least in part, be consequences of particular experimental procedures. Is this special discovery going to disappear into procedural "trivia"? Likely not, but it is time to assess the future impact or the perspectives of taste-aversion learning.

Clinical Perspectives focus on selective associations and biases in the conditioning of emotions and how these aversive motivations serve as warning signals that function to increase classes of behaviors that are adaptively correct -- but sometimes become maladaptive. The clinical perspective promises to provide us with a deep analysis of various processes underlying human fear and anxiety, phobias, and memory for emotional episodes. A deeper understanding of cognitive function and dysfunction as they relate to behavioral dysfunction is sought. Kenneth Hugdahl, Arne Öhman and Susan Mineka present different experimental approaches to conditioning and anxiety. We shall learn about the "preparedness principle" in hemispheric lateralization of emotions, "preattentive" selective processes in emotional learning, and the roles of cognitive biases in the origins and maintenance of fear and anxiety disorders.

Cognitive Perspectives are included for two main reasons. First, the general function of cognitive processes in aversively motivated behavior are as of the same fundamental importance as in any other behaviors, and their study in aversively motivated subjects may yield new insight into the degree to which cognitive functioning can modify emotions and responding. Secondly, it may well also be that motivations and emotions reciprocally modify perceptions and other cognitive processes including memory. Do anxiety eliciting stimuli result in a state of narrowed cognitive field or heightened attentiveness, thoughtfulness, or problem solving. Micheal Eysenck deals with the issue of causality in anxious subjects versus other persons. Christianson and Nilsson explore how unpleasant, traumatic events can lead to problems of remembering, while Elizabeth Loftus demonstrates how such traumatic effects may -- purposefully or inadvertantly -- result in altered memory or deficits that in turn lead to difficulties in assessing the reliability of eyewitness accounts.

Neurobiological perspectives on the study of fear and anxiety have changed dramatically in the last ten years. The work used to focus discovering and mapping the brain structures that participated in the production of various forms of avoidance behaviors. The work typically lesioned or stimulated structures such as mammillary bodies or septum and the consequences for various avoidance learning procedures assessed. The emergence of compounds with relative pharmacological selectivity and the discovery of multitudes of neuroreceptors and active peptides have shifted the focus of much or the research. There is still an important search on for localized engrams by Richard Thompson, but here he presents some very exciting evidence regarding the essential cerebellar circuitry mediating Kamin's blocking effect (1968). Additionally, however, there is a search for hormonal and neurotransmitter specific substrates. The biological substrate has eluded us so far, but we are getting closer. Jim McGaugh utilizes the retention of aversively motivated tasks to demonstrate the involvement of neurotransmitters and hormones in the amygdala. Rick Beninger is exploring the role of dopamine in mediating incentive in various avoidance tasks with special response initiation constraints.

Neuroethological perspectives are viewed with much expectation and a little trepidation. The importance of ethological considerations will have already been raised in the context of taste-aversion learning. But other perspectives are necessary. Giorgio Bignami has taken on the task of analysis of response systems and their interaction with task demands. He studies these in multiple species using a systematic set of task variations within the avoidance paradigm. Pharmacological interventions they yield additional insights into the ethological, physiological, and behavioral interdependencies. Stephen Suomi discussed hereditary patterns of aversively motivated behaviors in Rhesus monkey and related these to concommitant physiological and pharmicological changes. He also made an interesting case for a *contructively valid* separation model of a depressed state.

Methodological and Conceptual perspectives bring to the fore issues fundamental to any analysis of aversively motivated behavior -- or any behavioral system for that matter. Russ Church directly addresses the necessity as well as the usefulness of studying psychological processes using aversively motivated behavior, and he supports this with clear exemplars. To illustrate the conceptual issue he describes the problem of the yoked control group (see also Church & Getty, 1972). Terje Sagvolden takes a methodological orientation and demonstrates the special values of parametric research strategies in uncovering psychological processes. Finally, Bob Boakes suggests that particular foci of concerns in human psychophysiology research have led to experimental methods and designs that are less than optimal for the study of some key psychological questions. In particular Boakes discusses the role of "awareness" in causal relationships. These are likely to be generalizable arguments of interest to researchers from all perspectives.

It will be noted from the choice of topics and the particular individual orientations incorporated that there is a desire to pursue the comparative analysis between human and animal behavior. It is intended that this comparative theme will be a recurring one permeating all the perspectives. The contributions in the six major sections should will give us some important new insight into aversively motivated behaviors in man and animals and the mechanism that underlie them. The reader will notice that there are important emerging topics in the field that are not covered including psychosomatics, neuroimmunomodulation, stress induced analgesia, ethological approaches to aggression (the aggressor-victim problem) and even continuing developments in the psychopharmacology of avoidance, aversion and anxiety. It is not that we do not think these important, quite the contrary. But we believe that the perspectives herein included can do more to shape progress in those areas than the reverse. Perhaps in the future, we can provide a fully integrated overview as research and understanding progresses.

We hope that the Umeå conference (held in June, 1987) will prove simply the first to be held on perspectives in aversively motivated behaviors. Expression of such a hope may strike some as odd. But we believe (as does Revusky, 1987) that very real obstacles to future research in these areas present themselves. These arise from the recent promulgations of government regulations on the conduct of research with humans and animals. Some of these literally remove certain important research problems from the domain of answerable questions, or promise to do so (for an intense, lucid and candid discussion of the ethics of animal experimentation the paper by Revusky, ibid, is essential reading).

For human research in the United States, one must now clearly and explicity assure volunteer participants in experiments that they can withdraw at any time without penalty. This means that the future of research on models of depression such as "learned helplessness" cannot be effective pursued as we shall explain. Geer, Davidson and Gatchel (1970) have shown that merely giving subjects information that they can control a situation in some way -- even if they do not exercise that control -- prevents the development of learned helplessness related effects in humans. Gardner (1978) has provided a direct demonstration that asking for such this "informed consent" blocks obtaining the phenomenon. So in general, we should not expect many future studies from the United States to provide new experimental, empirical data on important facets of this important model of human dysfunction. Nor should we expect many future animal experiments in this area either because they typically use uncontrollable electric shocks (but see Seiden, Dahms & Shaughnessy, 1985; Seiden & O'Donnell, 1985; for details of the Differential-reinforcement-of-low-rate schedule (DRL-72) drug screen for antidepressant compounds). Such procedures are to be highly restricted -- if not banned -- according to new regulations promulgated in many countries. *BUT*, the quests are neither removed nor discarded just placed further away, and we are required simply to exercise more inventiveness to attain them.

These new regulations on animal experiments follow closely a classificatory scheme for "stressful" experiments that puts the use of uncontrollable aversive events in the most restricted category. This scheme follows closely one proposed by Orleans (1986) which seems to have more intuition as its basis that scientific facts. Experiments on learned helplessness, endogenous stress-induced opioid analgesia, and indeed most behavioral and physiological studies using classical defensive conditioning (USs are by definition uncontrollable) will be restricted. Additionally, any attempts to develop an animal model of a "psychotic" disorder will be restricted. Whether "psychotic-like behavior", the phrase used, includes also neurotic behaviors or even models of Alzheimer's disease in uncertain as yet. But there is little reason for optimism.

The key to hope here is that volumes such as the present one will show the positive contributions to our understanding of both normal and abnormal functioning that studies in aversively motivated behaviors have provided. That is the challenge.

ACKNOWLEDGEMENTS

Preparation of this manuscript was supported in part by grants from the National Institute of Child Health and Human Development and by the Norwegian Marshall Found to J. Bruce Overmier. The authors thank Susan Mineka and Robert Murison for their comments on an earlier draft.

REFERENCES

Anderson, D. C., Wolf, D., & Sullivan, P. (1969). Preconditioning to the CS: Variation in place of testing. *Psychonomic Science, 14,* 233-235.

Anderson, D. C., O'Farrell, T., Farmica, R., & Coponigri, V. (1969). Preconditioning CS exposure: Variation in place of conditioning and of presentation. *Psychonomic Science, 15,* 54-55.

Annau, Z., & Kamin, L. J. (1961). The conditioned emotional response as a function of intensity of the US. *Journal of Comparative and Physiological Psychology, 54,* 428-432.

Archer, T., & Sjödèn, P. O. (1980). Context-dependent taste-aversion learning with a familiar conditioning context. *Physiological Psychology, 8,* 40-46.

Archer, T., & Sjödèn, P. O. (1981). Environment-dependent taste-aversion extinction: A question of stimulus novelty at conditioning. *Physiological Psychology, 9,* 102-108.

Archer, T., & Sjödèn, P. O. (1982). Higher-order conditioning and sensory preconditioning of a taste aversion with an exteroceptive CS_1. *Quarterly Journal of Experimental Psychology, 34B,* 1-17.

Archer, T., Sjödèn, P. O., Nilsson, L. G., & Carter, N. (1979). The role of exteroceptive background context in taste-aversion conditioning and extinction. *Animal Learning and Behavior, 7,* 17-22.

Azrin, N. H., & Holz, W. C. (1961). Punishment during fixed interval reinforcement. *Journal of the Experimental Analysis of Behavior, 4,* 343-347.

Baker, A. G., Mercier, P., Gabel, J., & Baker, P. A. (1981). Contextual conditioning and the US preexposure effect in conditioned fear. *Journal of Experimental Psychology: Animal Behavior Processes, 7,* 109-128.

Balaz, M. A., Capra, S., Hartl, P., & Miller, R. R. (1981). Contextual potentiation of acquired behavior after devaluing direct context - US associations. *Learning and Motivation, 12,* 383-397.

Balaz, M. A., Capra, S., Kasprow, W. J., & Miller, R. R. (1982). Latent inhibition of the conditioning context. Further evidence of contextual potentiation of retrieval in the absence of appreciable context-US associations. *Animal Learning and Behavior, 10,* 242-248.

Balsam, P. D. (1984). Bringing the background to the foreground: The role of contextual cues in autoshaping. In M. Commons, R. Herrnstein & A. R. Wagner (Eds.), *Quantitative analyses of behavior: Volume 3: Acquisiton.* Cambridge, Mass.: Balinger.

Balsam, P. D. (1985). The functions of context in learning and performance. In P. D. Balsam & A. Tomie (Eds.), *Context and Learning,* pp. 1-21. Hillsdale, New Jersey: Lawrence Erlbaum Associates.

Balsam, P. D., & Schwartz, A. L. (1981). Rapid contextual conditioning in autoshaping. *Journal of Experimental Psychology: Animal Behavior Processes, 1,* 382-393.

Bekhterev, V. M. (1913). *La Psychologie Objective.* Paris.

Bersh, P. J. (1980). Eysenck's theory of incubation: a critical analysis. *Behaviour Research & Therapy, 18,* 11-17.

Bindra, D., & Cameron, L. (1953). Changes in experimentally produced anxiety with the passage of time: Incubation effect. *Journal of Experimental Psychology, 45,* 197-203.

Bitterman, M. E. (1962). Techniques for the study of learning in animals: Analysis and classification. *Psychological Bulletin, 59,* 81-93.

Bitterman, M. E. (1975). The comparative analysis of learning. *Science, 188,* 699-709.

Bitterman, M. E. (1987). Vertebrate-invertebrate comparisons. In H. J. Jerison and I. L. Jerison (Eds.), *Intelligence and Evolutionary Biology.* Springer.

Bitterman, M. E., LoLordo, V. M., Overmier, J. B., & Rashotte, M. E. (1979). *Animal Learning: Survey and Analysis.* NY: Plenum.

Black, A. H. (1959). Heart rate changes during avoidance learning in dogs. *Canadian Journal of Psychology, 13,* 229-242.

Black, A. H. (1974). Operant autonomic conditioning: The analysis of response mechanisms. In P. A. Obrist, A. H. Black, J. Brenner, L. V. DiCara (Eds.), *Cardiovascular Psychophysiology,* pp. 229-250. Aldine Publ.

Blanchard, R. J., & Blanchard, D. C. (1969). Crouching as an index of fear. Journal of *Comparative and Physiological Psychology, 67,* 370-375.

Bloodstein, O. (1958). Stuttering as an anticipatory struggle reaction. In J. Eisenson (Ed.), *Stuttering: A Symposium,* pp. 1-69. New York: Harper.

Boakes, R. A., & Halliday, S. (1972). *Inhibition and Learning.* London: Academic Press.

Bolles, R. C. (1969). Avoidance and escape learning: simultaneous acquisition of different response. *Journal of Comparative and Physiological Psychology, 68,* 355-358.

Bolles, R. C. (1970). Species-specific defense reactions and avoidance learning. *Psychological Review, 77,* 32-48.

Bolles, R. C. (1972). Reinforcement expectancy, and learning. *Psychological Review, 79,* 394-409.

Bolles, R. C., & Fanselow, M. S. (1980). A Perceptual-defense-recuperative model of fear and pain. *Behavioral and Brain Sciences, 3*, 291-300.

Bouton, M. E. (1984). Differential control by context in the inflation and reinstatement paradigms. *Journal of Experimental Psychology: Animal Behavior Processes, 10*, 56-74.

Bouton, M. E., & Bolles, R. C. (1979). Contextual control of the extinction of conditioned fear. *Learning and Motivation, 10*, 445-466.

Bouton, M. E., & Bolles, R. C. (1985). Contexts, Event-memories, and extinction. In P. D. Balsam & A. Tomie (Eds.), *Context and Learning*, pp. 133-166. Hillsdale, New Jersey: Lawrence Erlbaum Associates.

Bouton, M. E., & King, D. A. (1983). Contextual control of the extinction of conditioned fear: Tests for the associative value of the context. *Journal of Experimental Psychology: Animal Behavior Processes, 9*, 248-265.

Bower, G. H. (1981). Mood and memory. *American Psychologist, 36*, 129-148.

Bower, G., Monteiro, K. P., & Gilligan. S. G. (1979). Emotional mood as a context for learning and recall. *Journal of Verbal Learning and Verbal Behavior, 17*, 573-585.

Brown, J. S. (1965). A behavioral analysis of masochism. *Journal of Experimental Research in Personality, 1*, 65-70.

Brown, J. S. (1969). Factors affecting self-punitive locomotor behavior. In B. A. Campbell & R.-M. Church (Eds.), *Punishment and Aversive Behavior*, pp. 467-514. N.Y.: Appleton Century Crofts.

Brown, J. S., & Wagner, A. R. (1964). Resistance to punishment and extinction following training with shock or nonreinforcement. *Journal of Experimental Psychology, 68*, 503-507.

Catania, C. C. (1979). *Learning*. Englewood Cliffs, N. J.: Prentice Hall.

Cicala, G. A., & Owen, J. W. (1976). Warning signal termination and a feedback signal may not serve the same function. *Learning and Motivation, 7*, 356-367.

Channell, S., & Hall, G. (1981). Facilitation and retardation of descrimination learning after exposure to the stimuli. *Journal of Experimental Psychology: Animal Behavior Processes, 7*, 437-446.

Church. R. M. (1963). The varied effects of punishment on behavior. *Psychological Reviews, 70*, 369-402.

Church, R. M., & Getty. D. G. (1972). Some concequences of the reaction to an aversive extent. *Psychological Bulletin, 78*, 21-27.

Coover. G. D., Ursin, H., & Levine, S. (1973). Plasma-corticosterone levels during active avoidance learning in rats. *Journal of Comparative and Physiological Psychology, 82*, 170-174.

Cotton, J. W. (1953). Running time as a function of amount of food deprivation. *Journal of Experimental Psychology, 46*, 188-198.

Crawford, M., & Masterson. F. (1978). Components of the flight response can reinforce barpress avoidance. *Journal of Experimental Psychology: Animal Behavior Process, 4*, 144-151.

D'Amato, M. R., & Schiff, D. (1964). Long-term discrimination avoidance performance in the rat. *Journal of Comparative and Physiological Psychology, 57,* 123-126.

Darwin, C. P. (1872). *The Expression of Emotions in Man and Animals.* London: John Murray.

Davey, G. (1983). An associative view of human classical conditioning. In S. Davey (Ed.), *Animal Model of Human Behavior.* Chichester: John Wiley & Sons.

Davey, G. (Ed.). (1987). *Cognitive processes and pavlovian conditioning in humans.* Chicester: Wiley.

Dawson, M. E., & Schell, A. M. (1985). Information processing and human autonomic classical conditioning. In P. K. Ackles, J. R. Jennings and M. G. H. Coles (Eds.), *Advances in Psychophysiology, Vol. 1,* pp. 89-165. Greenwich, CT.: JAI Press.

Dawson, M. E., & Schell, A. M. (1987). Human autonomic and skeletal classical conditioning: The role of conscious cognitive factors. In G. Davey (Ed.), *Cognitive Processes and Pavlovian Conditioning in Humans,* pp. 27-55. Chichester: John Wiley & Sons.

Denny, R. M. (1971). Relaxation theory and experiments. In F. R. Brush (Ed.), *Aversive Conditioning and Learning,* pp. 235-295. N.Y.: Academic Press.

Desiderato, O., & Newman, A. (1971). Conditioned suppression produced in rats by tones paired with escapable or inescapable shock. *Journal of Comparative and Psychological Psychology, 11,* 427-431.

Dexter, W. R., Merrill, H. K. (1969). Role of contextual discrimination in fear conditioning. *Journal of Comparative and Physiological Psychology, 69,* 677-681.

DiCara, L. V., & Miller, N. E. (1968). Long term retention of instrumentally learned heart-rate changes in the curarized rat. *Communication in Behavioral Biology, Part A, 2,* 19-23.

Dickinson, A. (1980). *Contemporary Animal Learning Theory.* Cambridge: Cambridge University Press.

Dickinson, A., & Dearing, M. F. (1979). Appetitive-aversive interactions and inhibitory processes. In A. Dickinson & R. A. Boakes (Eds.), *Mechanisms of Learning and Motivation,* pp. 203-232. Hillsdale: N.J: Erlbaum.

Dickinson, A., & Shanks, D. (1985). Animal conditioning and human causality judgement. In L.-G. Nilsson & T. Archer (Eds.), *Perspectives on learning and memory,* pp. 167-191. Hillsdale, N. J.: Lawrence Erlbaum Associates.

Domjan, M. (1983). Biological constraints on instrumental and classical conditioning: Implications for general process theory. *Advances in the Study of Behavior, 17,* 215-277.

Domjan, M., & Burkhard, B. (1982). *The principles of learning and behavior.* Monterey, Calif.: Brooks/Cole.

Dweck, C. S., & Wagner, A. R. (1970). Situational cues and correlation between CS and US as determinants of the conditioned emotional response. *Psychonomic Science, 18,* 145-147.

Dworkin, B. R., & Miller, N. E. (1986). Failure to replicate visceral learning in the acute curarized rat preparation. *Behavioral*

Neuroscience, 100, 299-277.

Ehrman, R. N., & Overmier, J. B. (1976). Dissimilarity of the mechanisms for the vocation of escape and avoidance responding. *Animal Learning and Behavior, 4,* 347-351.

Ellis, H. C. (1985). Mood and schematic organization in memory. Paper presented at 26th Meeting of the Psychonomic Society, Boston, MA. (Abstr. #179).

Engel, M. L. (1967). A psychological setting of somatic disease: the "giving up - given up" complex. *Proceedings of the Royal Society of Medicine, 60,* 553-555.

Ericksen, C. W. (1956). Subception: fact or artifact. *Psychological Review, 63,* 74-80.

Estes, W. K., & Skinner, B. F. (1941). Some quantitative properties of anxiety. *Journal of Experimental Psychology, 29,* 390-400.

Estes, W. K. (1973). Memory and conditioning. In F. J. McGuigan & D. B. Lumsden (Eds.), *Contemporary approaches to conditioning and learning,* pp. 265-286. Washington, D. C.: Winston.

Eysenck, H. J. (1968). A theory of the incubation of anxiety / fear responses. *Behaviour Research and Therapy, 6,* 309-321.

Fanselow, M. S. (1980). Extinction of contextual fear an preference for signaled shock. *Bulletin of the Psychonomic Society, 16,* 458-460.

Fonberg, E. (1956). On the manifestation of conditioned defensive reactions in stress. *Bulletin of the Society of Science & Letter of Lodz. III, 1,* 1.

Fonberg, E. (1958). Transfer of instrumental avoidance reactions in dogs. *Bulletin of Academy Polish Sciences, 6,* 353-356.

Foree, D. D., & LoLordo, V. M. (1973). Attention in the pigeon: the differential effects of food-getting vs shock-avoidance procedures. *Journal of Comparative and Physiological Psychology, 85,* 551-558.

Furedy, J., & Riley, A. (1987). In G. Davey (Ed.), *Cognitive Processes and Pavlovian Conditioning in Humans,* pp. 27-55. Chichester: John Wiley & Sons.

Garcia, J., Lasiter, P. S., Bermudez-Rattoni, F., & Deemo, D. A. (1985). A general theory of aversion learning. In N. Bravman & P. Bronstein (Eds.), *Experimental Assessment and Clinical Applications of Conditioned Taste Aversions,* pp. 3-41. (Annals of the New York Academy of Sciences).

Garcia, J., & Koelling, R. A. (1966). Relation of cue to consequence in avoidance learning. *Psychonomic Science, 4,* 123-124.

Garcia, J., Rusiniak, K. W., & Brett, L. P. (1977). Conditioning food-illness aversions in wild animals: In H. Davies & H. M-B. Hurwitz (Eds.), *Operant-Pavlovian Operations,* pp. 273-316. Hillsdale: N. J.: Lawrence Erlbaum Associates.

Gardner, G. T. (1978). Effects of federal humen subjects regulations on data obtained in environmental stressor research. *Journal of Personality and Social Psychology, 36,* 628-634.

Gardner, E. T., & Lewis, P. (1976). Negative reinforcement with shock-frequency increase. *Journal of Experimental Analysis of*

Behavior, 25, 3-14.

Garmezy, N., & Rutter, M. (Eds.) (1983). *Stress, Coping, and Development in Children.* N. Y.: McGraw Hill.

Geer, J., Davidson, G. C., & Gatchel, R. I. (1970). Reduction of stress in humans through non-verdical perceived control of aversive stimuluation. *Journal of Personality and Social Psychology, 16,* 731-738.

Gibson, E. (1952). The role of shock in reinforcement. *Journal of Comparative Physiological Psychology, 45,* 18-30.

Gleitman, H., & Holmes, P. A. (1967). Retention of incompletely learned CER in rats. *Psychonomic Science, 7,* 19-20.

Goodall, G., & Mackintosh, N. J. (1981). Analysis of the Pavlovian properties of signals for punishment. *Quarterly Journal of Exerimental Psychology, 39B,* 1-22.

Gray, J. A. (1977). Drug effects on fear and frustration. In L. L. Iversen, S. D. Iversen & S. M. Snyder (Eds.), *Handbook of Psychopharmacology, Vol. 8,* pp. 433-530. New York: Plenum.

Gray, J. A. (1982). *The Neuropsychology of Anxiety.* Oxford University Press.

Gwinn, G. T. (1949). The effects of puishment on acts motivated by fear. *Journal of Experimental Psychology, 39,* 260-269.

Hamel, I. A. (1919). A study and analysis of the conditioned reflex. *Psychological Monographs, 27,* Whole No. 118.

Hartman, T. F., & Ross, L. E. (1961). An alternative criterion for the elimination of "voluntary" responses in eyelid conditioning. *Journal of Experimental Psychology, 61,* 334-338.

Hebb, D. O. (1946). On the nature of fear. *Psychological Review, 53,* 259-276.

Hendersen, R. W. (1985). Fearful memories: The motivational significance of forgetting. In J. R. Brush & J. B. Overmier (Eds.), *Affect, Conditioning, and Cognition: Essays on the Determinants of Behavior,* pp. 43-53. Hillsdale, N. J.: Lawrence Erlbaum Associates.

Hendersen, R. W. Patterson, J., & Jackson, R. L. (1980). Acquisition and retention of control of instrumental behavior by a cue signaling airblast: How specific are conditioned anticipations? *Learning & Motivation, 11,* 407-426.

Hoffman, H. S. (1965). The stimulus generalization of conditioned suppression. In D. I. Mostofsky (Ed.), *Stimulus generalization,* pp. 175-229. Stanford, Calif.: Stanford University Press.

Holland, P. C. (1981). Acquisition of representation-mediated conditioned food aversions. *Learning & Motivation, 12,* 1-18.

Hollis, K. L. (1982). Pavlovian conditioning of signal-centered action patterns and autonomic behavior: A biological analysis of function. *Advances in the Study of Behavior, 12,* 1-65.

Honig, W. K., & Staddon, J. E. R. (1977). *Handbook of operant behavior.* Engelwood Cliffs, N. J.: Prentic-Hall.

Hugdahl, K. (1980). Is biology relevant for phobic fears? *Scandinavian Journal of Behavior Therapy, 9,* 115-132.

Hull, C. L. (1943). *Principles of Behavior.* New York: Appleton-Century-Crofts.

Hunter, W. S. (1935). Conditioning and extinction in the rat. *British Journal of Psychology, 26 (II)*, 135-148.

Izquierdo, J. (1984). Endogenous state-dependency: Memory depends on the relation between the neuro and hormonal states present after training at the time of testing. In G. Lynch, J. McGaugh, & N. Weinberg (Eds.), *Neurobiology of Learning & Memory*, pp. 65-77. N.Y.: Guilford.

Jacobs, W. J., & Nadel, L. (1985). Stress-induced recovery of fears and phobias. *Psychological Review, 92*, 512-532.

Jenkins, H. M., Barnes, R. A., & Barrera, F. J. (1981). Why autoshaping depends on trial spacing. In C. M. Locurto, H. S. Terrace & J. Gibbon (Eds.), *Autoshaping and Conditioning Theory*, pp. 255-284. N. Y.: Academic Press.

Kamin, L. J. (1968). Attention-like processes in classical conditioning. In M. R. Jones (Ed.), *Miami Symposium on the Prediction of Behavior: Aversive Stimulation*, pp. 9-33. Miami: University of Miami Press.

Kamin, L. J., Brimer, C. J., & Black, A. H. (1963). Conditioned suppression as a monitor of fear of the CS in the course of avoidance training. *Journal of Comparative and Physiological Psychology, 56*, 497-501.

Keehn, J. D. (1959). On the non-classical nature of avoidance behavior. *American Journal of Psychology, 72*, 243-247.

Kimble, G. (1961). *Hilgard and Marguis' Conditioning and Learning.* (2nd Ed.). New York: Appleton-Century Crofts.

Konorski, J (1967). *The Integrative Activity of the Brain.* Chicago: University of Chicago Press.

Konorski, J., & Miller, S. (1939). On two types of conditioned reflex. *Journal of Psychology, 16*, 155-170.

Krane, R. V., & Wagner, A. R. (1975). Taste aversion learning with a delayed shock US: Implications for the "generality of the laws of learning". *Journal of Comparative and Physiological Psychology, 88*, 882-889.

Kriekhaus, E. E. (1967). The mammillary bodies: Their function and anatomical connections. *Acta Biological Experimentalis, 27*, 319-337.

Lacey, J. I., & Smith, R. L. (1954). Conditioning and generalization of unconscious anxiety. *Science, 120*, 1045-1052.

Lang, P. J. (1964). Experimental studies of desensitizaton psychotherapy. In J. Wolpe, A. Salter & L. J. Reyna (Eds.), *The Conditioning Therapies*, pp. 38-53. New York: Holt, Rinehart & Winston.

Lang, P. J. (1968). Fear reduction and fear behavior: Problems in treating a construct. In J. M. Shlein (Ed.), *Research in Psychotherapy, Vol. III*, pp. 90-103. Washington, D. C.: American Psychological Association.

Lazarus, R. S., & McCleary, R. A. (1951). Autonomic discrimination without awareness: a study of subception. *Psychological Review*, *58*, 113-122.

Lenneberg, E. (1969). *Biological Foundations of Language*. New York: Wiley.

Linden, D. R. (1974). Transfer of approach responding between punishment, frustrative non-reward, and the combination of punishment and non-reward. *Learning and Motivation*, *5*, 498-510.

Linwick, D., Patterson, J., & Overmier, J. B. (1981). On inferring selective associations: Methodological issues. *Animal Learning & Behavior*, *9*, 508-512.

Logan, F. A. (1951). A comparison of avoidance and non-avoidance eyelid conditioning. *Journal of Experimental Psychology*, *42*, 390-393.

Logan, F. A. (1956). A micromolar approach to behavior theory. *Psychological Review*, *63*, 63-73.

Logue, A. (1979). Taste aversion and the generality of the laws of learning. *Psychological Bulletin*, *86*, 276-296.

Lovass, O. I., Schaeffer, B., Simmons, J. Q. (1965). Experimental studies in childhood schizophrenia: Building social behavior in autistic children by the use of electric shock. *Journal of Experimental Research in Personality*, *1*, 99-109.

Lovibond, P. F., Preston, G. C., & Mackintosh, N. J. (1984). Context specificity of conditioning, extinction and latent inhibition. *Journal of Experimental Psychology: Animal Behavior Processes*, *10*, 360-375.

Lubow, R. E. (1965). Latent inhibition: Effects of frequency of nonreinforced preexposure of the CS. *Journal of Comparative and Physiological Psychology*, *60*, 454-457.

Lubow, R.E. (1973). Latent inhibition. *Psychological Bulletin*, *79*, 398-407.

Lubow, R. E., & Moore, A. V. (1959). Latent inhibition: The effect of nonreinforced preexposure of the CS. *Journal of Comparative and Physiological Psychology*, *52*, 415-419.

Lubow, R. E., Rifkin, B., & Alek, M. (1976). The contextual effect: The relationship between stimulus pre-exposure and environmental pre-exposure determines subsequent learning. *Journal of Experimental Psychology: Animal Behavior Processes*, *2*, 38-47.

MacCorquodale, K., & Meehl, P. E. (1948). On a distinction between hypothetical constructs and intervening variables. *Psychological Review*, *55*, 95-107.

Mackintosh, N.J. (1974). *The Psychology of Animal Learning*. N.Y.: Academic Press.

Mackintosh, N. J. (1973). Stimulus selection: learning to ignore stimuli that predict no change in reinforcement. In R. A. Hinde & J. S. Hinde (Eds.), *Constraints on Learning*, pp. 75-96. London: Academic Press.

Mackintosh, N. J. (1983). *Conditioning and associative learning*. Oxford: Oxford University Press.

Mackintosh, N. J. (1985). Contextual specificity or State dependency of human and animal learning. In L. G. Nilsson & T. Archer (Eds.), *Perspectives on learning and memory*, pp. 223-242. Hillsdale, New Jersey: Lawrence Erlbaum Associates.

Marks, I. (1969). *Fears and Phobias*. N.Y.: Academic Press.

Masterson, F. A., & Crawford, M. (1982). The defense motivation system: A theory of avoidance behavior. *Behavioral and Brain Sciences, 4*, 661-675.

May, M. A. (1948). Experimentally acquired drives. *Journal of Experimental Psychology, 38*, 66-77.

McAllister, W. R., & McAllister, D. E. (1967). Drive and reward in aversive learning. *American Journal of Psychology, 80*, 377-383.

McAllister, W. R., McAllister, D. E., & Douglas, W. K. (1971). The inverse relationship between shock intensity and shuttlebox avoidance learning in rats: A reinforcement explanation. *Journal of Comparative and Physiological Psychology, 74*, 426-433.

Meehl, P. E. (1950). On the circularity of the law of effect. *Psychological Bulletin, 47*, 52-75.

Miller, N. E. (1948). Studies of fear as an acquirable drive. *Journal of Experimental Psychology, 38*, 99-101.

Miller, N. E. (1972). Interactions between learned and physical factors in mental illness. *Seminars in Psychiatry, 4*, 239-253.

Mineka, S. (1979). The role of fear in theories of avoidance learning, flooding, and extinction. *Psychological Bulletin, 86*, 985-1010.

Mineka, S. (1985). Animal models of anxiety-based disorders: Their usefulness and limitations. In A. H. Tuma & J. D. Maser (Eds.), *Anxiety and the Anxiety Disorders*, pp. 199-259. Hillsdale, N. J.: Lawrence Erlbaum Associates. (a)

Mineka, S. (1985). The frightful complexity of the origins of fears. In F. R. Brush & J. B. Overmier (Eds.), *Affect, Conditioning, and Cognition: Assays on the Determination of Behavior*, pp. 55-73. Hillsdale, N. J.: Lawrence Erlbaum Associates. (b)

Mineka, S., Cook, M., & Miller, S. (1984). Fear conditioned with escapable and inescapable shock: the effects of a feedback stimulus. *Journal of Experimental Psychology: Animal Behavior Processes, 10*, 307-323.

Mineka, S., & Gino, A. (1980). Dissociation between conditioned emotional response and extended avoidance performance. *Learning and Motivation, 11*, 416-502.

Moore, J. W., & Gormezano, I. (1961). Yoked comparisons of instrumental and classical eyelid conditioning. *Journal of Experimental Psychology, 62*, 552-559.

Morris, R. G. M. (1975). Preconditioning of reinforcing properties to an exteroceptive feedback stimulus. *Learning and Motivation, 6*, 289-298.

Mowrer, O. H. (1938). Preparatory set (expectancy) - a determinant in motivation and learning. *Psychological Review, 45*, 62-91.

Mowrer, O. H. (1940). Anxiety reduction and learning. *Journal of Experimental Psychology, 27*, 497-516.

Mowrer, O. H. (1948). On the dual nature of learning. *Harvard Educational Review, 12,* 102-148.

Mowrer, O. H. (1960). *Learning Theory and Behavior.* N. Y.: John Wiley & Sons.

Mowrer, O. O., & Lamoreaux, R. R. (1942). Fear as an intervening variable in avoidance conditioning. *Journal of Comparative Psychology, 39,* 29-50.

Mowrer, O. H., & Solomon, L. N. (1954). Contiguity vs drive-reduction in conditioned fear: The proximity and abrtuptness of drive reduction. *American Journal of Psychology, 67,* 15-25.

Mowrer, O. H., & Viek, P. (1948). An experimental analogue of fear from a sev of helplessness. *Journal of Abnormal and Social Psychology, 83,* 193-200.

Muenziner, K. F. (1934). Motivation in learning: I. Electric shock for correct response in a visual discrimination habit. *Journal of Comparative Psychology, 17,* 167-277.

Noble, M., & Adams, C. K. (1963). Conditioning in pigs as a function of the interval between CS and US. *Journal of Comparative and Physiological Psychology, 56,* 215-219.

Odling-Smee, F. J. (1975). The role of background stimuli during Pavlovian conditioning. *Quarterly Journal of Experimental Psychology, 27,* 201-209. (a)

Odling-Smee, F. J. (1975). Background stimuli and the interstimulus interval during Pavlovian conditioning. *Quarterly Journal of Experimental Psychology, 27,* 201-209. (b)

Odling-Smee, F. J. (1978). The overshadowing of background stimuli by an informative stimulus in aversive Pavlovian conditioning. *Animal Learning and Behavior, 6,* 43-51.

Orleans, F. B. (1986). Classification System for Degree of Animal Harm. *Scandinavian Journal of Laboratory Animal Science, 13,* 93-97.

Öhman, A. (1979). The orienting response, attention, and learning. In H. D. Kimmel, E. H. von Olst, & J. F. Orlebeke (Eds.), *The Orienting Reflex in Humans,* pp. 443-471. Hillsdale, N. J.: Lawrence Erlbaum Associates.

Öhman, A. (1986). Face the beast and fear the face: Animal and social fears as prototypes for an evolutionary analysis of emotion. *Psychophysiology, 23,* 123-145.

Öhman, A., Fredrikson, M., Hugdahl, K., & Rimino, P. A. (1976). The premise of equipotentiality in human classical conditioning. *Journal of Experimental Psychology: General, 105,* 313-337.

Osgood, C. E. 1950). Can Tolman's theory of learning handle avoidance training? *Psychological Review, 57,* 133-137.

Overmier, J. B. (1970). A note on subception. *Psychological Reports, 27,* 519-524.

Overmier, J. B. (1979). Punishment. In M. E. Bitterman, V. M. LoLordo, J. B. Overmier & M. E. Rashotte (Eds.), *Animal Learning: Survey and Analysis,* pp. 279-311. N.Y.: Plenum Press.

Overmier, J. B., & Brackbill, R. M. (1977). On the independence of stimulus evocation of fear and fear evocation of responses. *Behavior Research Therapy, 15,* 51-56.

Overmier, J. B., Bull, J. A., & Trapold, M. A. (1971). Discriminative cue properties of different fears and their role in response selection. *Journal of Comparative and Physiological Psychology, 76,* 478-482.

Overmier, J. B., & Hellhammer, D. (in press). The learned helplessness psychological model for human depression. In P. Simon, P. Soubrie, & D. Widlocher (Eds.), *Animal Models of Psychiatric Disorders.* Basel, Switzerland, Karger.

Overmier, J. B., & Lawry, J. A. (1979). Pavlovian conditioning and the mediation of behavior. *The Psychology of Learning and Motivation, 13,* 1-55.

Overmier, J. B., Payne, R. J., Brackbill, R. M., Linder, B., & Lawry, J. A. (1979). On the mechanism of post-asymptotic decrement phenomenon. *Acta Neurobiologic Experimentalis, 39,* 603-620.

Overmier, J. B., & Seligman, M. E. P. (1967). The effects of inescapable shocks upon subsequent escape and avoidance learning. *Journal of Comparative and Physiological Psychology, 63,* 28-33.

Overton, D. A. (1984). State dependent learning and drug discrimination. In L. L. Iversen, S. D. Iversen, & S. H. Snyder (Eds.), *Handbook of Psychopharmacology, Vol. 18,* pp. 59-128. N. Y.: Plenum Press.

Patterson, J., & Overmier, J. B. (1981). A transfer of control test for contextual associations. *Animal Learning and Behavior, 9,* 316-321.

Pavlov, I. P. (1927). *Conditioner reflexes.* Oxford: Oxford University Press.

Poulton, E. B. (1887). The experimental proof of the protective value of color and marking in insects in reference to their vertebrate enemies. *Proceedings Zoological Society of London,* pp. 191-274.

Quinsey, V. L., & Ayres, J. J. B. (1969). Shock-induced facilitation of a portially extinguished CER. *Psychonomic Science, 14,* 213-214.

Rachman, S. (1978). *Fear and Courage.* San Francisco: Freeman Press.

Randich, A. (1981). The US preexposure phenomenon in the conditioned suppression paradigm: A role for conditioned situational stimuli. *Learning and Motivation, 12,* 321-341.

Randich, A., Jacobs, W. J., LoLordo, V. M., & Stutterer, J. R. (1978). Conditioned suppression of DRL responding: Effect of UCS intensity, Schedule parameter and schedule context. *Quarterly Journal of Experimental Psychology, 30,* 141-150.

Randich, A., & Ross, R. T. (1984). Mechanisms of blocking by contextual stimuli. *Learning and Motivation, 15,* 106-117.

Razran, G. (1956). On avoidance learning before the familiar american studies: Avoidant and non-avoidant conditioning and partial reinforcement in Russian laboratories. *American Journal of Psychology, 69,* 127-129.

Reiss, G. (1980). Pavlovian conditioning and human fear: an expectancy model. *Behavior and Therapy, 11,* 380-396.

Rescorla, R. A. (1969). Establishment of a positive reinforcer through contrast with shock. *Journal of Comparative and Physiological Psychology, 67,* 260-263.

Rescorla, R. A. (1980). *Pavlovian Second-order Conditioning: Studies in Associative Learning.* Hillsdale, N. J.: Lawrence Erlbaum Associates.

Rescorla, R. A. (1985). Pavlovian conditioning analogues to gestalt perceptual principles. In J. R. Brush & J. B. Overmier (Eds.), *Affect, Conditioning, and Cognition: Essays on the Determinants of Behavior,* pp. 113-129. Hillsdale, N. J.: Lawrence Erlbaum Associates.

Rescorla, R. A., & Cunningham, C. L. (1977). The erasure of reinstated fear. *Animal Learning and Behavior, 5,* 386-394.

Rescorla, R. A., & Heth, C. D. (1975). Reinstatement of fear to an extinguished conditioned stimulus. *Journal of Experimental Psychology: Animal Behavior Processes, 1,* 88-96.

Rescorla, R. A., & Solomon, R. L. (1967). Two-process learning theory: Relationship between Pavlovain conditioning and instrumental learning. *Psychological Review, 74,* 151-182.

Rescorla, R. A., Durlach, P. J., & Grau, J. W. (1985). Contextual learning in Pavlovian conditioning. In P. D. Balsam & A. Tomie (Eds.), *Context and Learning,* pp. 23-56. Hillsdale, New Jersey: Lawrence Erlbaum Associates.

Revusky, S. H. (1971). The role of interference in association over a delay. In W. K. Honig & P. H. R. James (Eds.), *Animal Memory,* pp. 155-213. New York: Academic Press.

Revusky, S. (1977). Learning as a general process with an emphasis on data from feeding experiments. In N. W. Milgram, L. Krames & T. M. Alloway (Eds.), *Food aversion learning,* pp. 1-51. New York, Plenum Press.

Revusky, S. (1987). About the Canadian council on animal care. *The Newfoundland Psychologist, 9,* 33-44.

Revusky, S., & Garcia, J. (1970). Learned associations over long delays. In G. H. Bower & J. T. Spence (Eds.), *The psychology of learning and motivation: Advances in research and theory (Vol IV),* pp. 1-84. New York: Academic Press.

Riccio, D. C., & Concannon, J. T. (1981). ACTH and the reminder phenomenon. In J. L. Martinez, Jr., R. A. Jensen, R. B. Messing, H. Rigter & J. L. McGaugh (Eds.), *Endogenous Peptides and Learning and Memory,* pp. 117-142. N.Y.: Academic Press.

Riccio, D. C., Richardson, R., & Ebrer, D. L. (1984). Memory retrieval deficits based upon altered contextual cues: A paradox. *Psychological Bulletin, 96,* 152-165.

Richter, C. (1957). On the phenomenon of sudden death in animals and man. *Psychosomatic Medicine, 19,* 191-198.

Rizley, R. C., & Rescorla, R. A. (1972). Associations in second-order condtioning and sensory precondtioning. *Journal of Comparative and Physiological Psychology, 81,* 1-11.

Robbins, M. J., & Meyer, D. R. (1970). Motivational control of retrograde amnesia. *Journal of Experimental Psychology, 84,* 220-225.

Rosellini, R. A., & Terris, W. (1976). Fear as a discriminative stimulus for an appetitive instrumental response. *Learning and Motivation, 7,* 327-339.

Rudy, J. W., Rosenberg, L., & Sandell, J. H. (1977). Disruption of a taste familiarity effect by novel exteroceptive stimulation. *Journal of Experimental Psychology: Animal Behavior Processes, 3,* 26-36.

Schein, E. H. (1956). The Chinese indoctrination program for prisoners of war. *Psychiatry, 19,* 149-172.

Schlosberg, H. (1934). Conditioned responses in the white rat. *Journal of Genetic Psychology, 45,* 303-335.

Schlosberg, H. (1937). The relationship between success and the laws of learning. *Psychological Review, 44,* 379-394.

Seiden, L. S., Dahms, J. L., & Shaughnessy, R. A. (1985). Behavioral screen for antidepressants. The effects of drugs and electro-convulsive shock on performance under a differential-reinforcement-of-low-rate schedule. *Psychopharamcology, 86,* 55-60.

Seiden, L. S., & O'Donnell, J. M. (1985). Effects of antidepressant drugs on DRL behavior. In L. S. Seiden & R. L. Balster (Eds.), *Behavioral Pharmacology: The current status,* pp. 323-338. New York: Alan R. Liss Inc.

Seligman, M. E. P. (1968). Chronic fear produced by unpredictable electric shock. *Journal of Comparative and Physiological Psychology, 66,* 402-411.

Seligman, M. E. P. (1970). On the generality of the laws of learning. *Psychological Review, 77,* 408-418.

Seligman, M. E. P. (1971). Phobias and preparedness. *Behavior Therapy, 2,* 307-320.

Seligman, M. E. P., & Johnson, J. C. (1973). A cognitive theory of avoidance learning. In F. J. McGuigan & D. B. Lumsden (Ed.), *Contemporary Approaches to Conditioning and Learning,* pp. 69-110. Washington, D. C.: U. H. Winston.

Siddle, D. A. T., & Remington, B. (1987). Latent inhibition and human Pavlovian conditioning: Research & Relevance. In G. Davey (Ed.), *Cognitive Processes and Pavlovian Conditioning in Humans,* pp. 115-146. Chicester: John Wiley & Sons.

Sidman, M. (1953). Avoidance conditioning with brief shock and no exteroceptive warning signal. *Science, 188,* 157-158.

Siegel, G. (1970). Punishment, stuttering, and disfluency. *Journal of Speech and Hearning Research, 13* 677-714.

Sjödèn, P. O., & Archer, T. (1981). Associative and nonassociative effects of exteroceptive context in taste-aversion conditioning with rats. *Behavioral and Neural Biology, 33,* 74-92.

Skinner, B. F. (1935). Two types of conditioned reflex and a pseudo-type. *Journal of General Psychology, 12,* 66-77.

Skinner, B. F. (1937). Two types of conditioned reflex: A reply to Konorski and Miller. *Journal of General Psychology, 16,* 272-279.

Solomon, R. L. (1964). Punishment. *American Psychologist, 19,* 239-252.

Solomon, R. L. (1977). An opponent-process theory of motivation: V. Affective dynamics of eating. In L. Barker, M. Best & M. Domjan (Eds.), *Learning Mechanisms in food selection,* pp. 255-269. Waco: Baylor Univ. pr.

Solomon, R. L., & Brush, E. S. (1956). Experimentally derived condeptions of anxiety. *Nebraska Symposium on Motivation, 4,* 212-305.

Solomon, R. L., & Corbit, J. (1974). An opponent-process theory of motivation: I. The temporal dynamics of affect. *Psychological Review, 81,* 119-145.

Solomon, R. L., Kamin, L. J., & Wynne, L. C. (1953). Traumatic avoidance learning: The outcomes of several extinction procedures with drugs. *Journal of Abnormal and Social Psychology, 48,* 291-302.

Solomon, R. L., & Turner, L. H. (1962). Discriminative classical conditioning in dogs paralyzed by curare can later control discriminative avoidance responding in the normal state. *Psychological Review, 69,* 202-219.

Solomon, R. L., & Wynne, L. C. (1954). Traumatic avoidance learning: The principles of anxiety conservation and partial irreversibility. *Psychological Review, 61,* 353-385.

Spence, K. W., & Ross, L. E. (1959). A methodological study of the form and latency of eyelid response in conditioning. *Journal of Experimental Psychology, 58,* 376-381.

Spiker, V. A. (1977). Taste aversion: A procedural analysis and an alternative paradigmatic classification. *Psychological Record, 27,* 753-769.

Staddon, J. E. R., & Simmelhag, V. L. (1971). The "Superstition experiment": A reexamination of its implications for the principles of adaptive behavior. *Psychological Review, 78,* 3-43.

Stampfl, T. G., & Levis, D. J. (1967). The essentials of implosive therapy. *Journal of Abnormal Psychology, 72,* 496-503.

Stewart, J., Krebs, J., & Kaczander, E. (1971). State dependent learning produced with steroids. *Nature, 216,* 1233-1234.

Testa, T. (1974). Causal relationship and the acquisition of avoidance responses. *Psychological Review, 81,* 491-505.

Theios, J., Lynch, A. D., & Lowe, W. G. (1966). Differential effects of shock intensity on one-way and shuttle avoidance conditioning. *Journal of Experimental psychology, 72,* 294-299.

Thomas, D. (1979). Retention of conditioned inhibition in a bar-press suppression paradigm. *Learning and Motivation, 10,* 161-177.

Thorndike, E. L. (1931). *Human learning.* New York: Century.

Tortera, D. (1985). *Understanding Electronic Dog Training.* Tucson, Ariz.: TriTronics.

Trapold, M. A., & Overmier, J. B. (1972). The second learning process in instrumental learning. In A. H. Black & W. F. Prokasy (Ed.), *Classical Conditioning II: Current Research and Theory.*

pp. 427-452. N. Y.: Appleton-Century-Crofts.

Turner, L. H., & Solomon, R. L. (1962). Human traumatic avoidance learning: theory and experiments on the operant-respondent distinction and failure to learn. *Psychological Monographs, 76* (Whole No. 559).

Wagner, A. R. (1978). Expectancies and the priming of STM. In S. Hulse, H. Fowler, & W. K. Honig (Eds.), *Cognitive processes in animal behavior*, pp. 238-251. Hillsdale, N. J.: Lawrence Erlbaum Associates.

Wahlston, D-L., & Cole, M. (1972). Classical and avoidance training of leg flexion in the dog. In A. H. Black & W. F. Prokasy (Eds.), *Classical Conditioning II: Current Theory & Research*, pp. 379-407. N.Y.: Appleton Century Crofts.

Walters, G. C., & Grusec, J. (1977). *Punishment*. San Francisco: Freeman & Co.

Warner, L. H. (1932). The association span of the white rat. *Journal of Genetic Psychology, 41*, 57-90.

Watson, J. B. (1916). The place of the conditioned reflex in psychology. *Psychological Review, 23*, 89-116.

Watson, J. B., & Rayner, R. (1920). Conditioned emotional reactions. *Journal of Experimental Psychology, 3*, 1-14.

Weisman, R. G., & Litner, J. S. (1969). Positive conditioned reinforcement of sidman avoidance behavior in rats. *Journal of Comparative and Physiological Psychology, 68*, 597-603.

Wenzel, B. M. (1968). Beharioral studies of immunosympathectomized mice. *Journal of Comparative and Physiological Psychology, 66*, 354-362.

Whaley, D. L., & Tough, J. (1970). Treatment of a self-injuring mongoloid with shock-induced suppression and avoidance. In R. Ulrich, T. Stachnik & J. Mabry (Eds.). *Control of Human Behavior II: from Cure to Prevention*, pp. 154-155. Glenview: Scott, Foresman, Co.

Wickens, D. D., & Wickens, C. D. (1942). Some factors related to pseudoconditioning. *Journal of Experimental Psychology, 31*, 518-526.

Wynne, L. C., & Solomon, R. L. (1955). Traumatic avoidance learning: Acquisition and extinction in dogs deprived of normal autonomic function. *Genetic Psychology Monograph, 52*, 241-284.

Zielinski, K., & Soltysik, S. (1964). The effect of pretraining on the acquisition and extinction of avoidance reflex. *Acta Biological Experimentalis, 24*, 73-87.

Perspectives on the Determinants of Hedonic Value (Taste-Aversion Learning)

Trevor Archer
University of Umeå

Although the basic finding that taste stimuli are well associated with illness inducing events was noted and documented well over 30 years ago (see Garcia, Kimeldorf & Hunt, 1956), it is the finding of a differential associability of taste and visual-auditory conditioned stimuli (CSs) with illness and shock unconditioned stimuli (USs), commonly know as the "Garcia effect", that proved to be of some considerable consequence for prevailing notions of conditioning and learning theory. Thus, it was proposed by Seligman (1970) that "rats are prepared, by virtue of their evolutionary history, to associate tastes with malaise.... Further, rats are contraprepared to associate exteroceptive events with nausea" (p. 409).

This 'preparedness' principle seemed reasonable in view of suggestions by Revusky and Garcia (1970) that rats "tend to ignore external events" (p. 22) and that "time-space contextual information... is dispensed with as unnecessary" (p. 828) (Garcia, Hankins & Rusiniak, 1974); and as will become more evident from the treatises of Clinical Perspectives (pp. 139-144) and Neuroethological Perspectives (pp. 335-342) the consideration of preparedness factors may well be essential to any comprehensive understanding of aversively motivated behavior. With regard to the issue of preparedness in taste-aversion there seems to be a general consensus that most taste-averison learning phenomena can be accounted for by contemporary accounts of conditioning without special reference to preparedness (Charlton & Ferraro, 1982; Dickinson & Mackintosh, 1978; Logue, 1979; Revusky, 1977).

In view of the massive scientific endeavour that has been applied to the investigation of illness induced aversion learning it is probably timely to take some steps towards assessing the full significance of this behavior for an understanding of (a) the processes involved in taste-aversion learning, and (b) the broader aspect of aversively motivated behavior in general. The chapters by John Garcia, Per-Olow Sjödén and Trevor Archer, and Frederico Bermudez-Rattoni all give insights into the processes involved in taste-aversion learning whether this be with regard to the relative status of the taste and poison events as the functional CSs and USs, or the relative role of the taste and contextual elements in the conditioning process, or as to the neuroanatomical and neurochemical substrate of the phenomenon. The assessment of the contribution of taste-aversion learning to a broader understanding of aversively motivated behavior is much more difficult to derive. It is clear that our *awareness* of the specialized adaptations and stimulus-response complexity over animal species and behavioral situations has benefited but it may also be that the theoretical significance the taste-aversion endeavour for general avoidance learning is waning. Indeed, it is probably no great exaggeration to suggest that with the asymptote of taste-aversion publications having been reached that the bulk of this endeavour is oriented to neuroscientific applications and investigations of a decidedly pharmacological and toxicological nature. Perhaps a new awakening with procedures to stimulate wider controversal issues should be sought after.

In the present volume, the chapter presented by Frederico Bermudez-Rattoni (pp. 121-138) offers an exciting search for the neuropharmacological basis of aversion learning, although developments along this theme may well produce a unique double dissociation, but, more importantly, Bermudez-Rattoni indicates that the brain transplant procedures may be applied to taste-aversion systems in the central nervous system. Bermudez-Rattoni, Fernandez, Sanchez, Aguilar-Roblero and Druker-Colin (1987) demonstrated that gustatory neocortex or amygdaloid lesions disrupted taste aversions but that the aversions could be reinstated by transplantations of homologous brain tissue from 17-day-old fetuses into the lesioned area.

It may be that the broader aspects of aversively motivated behavior can be approached through a consideration of two basic processes which regulate the animals behavior in the particular situation (i.e. the feeding situation) where taste-aversion learning takes place. These processes, which govern the behavior of individual animals and particular species as a whole are: variation and adaptation. Variation may occur in any of three following ways: (a) in the type of behavior produced by an organism within its particular ecological niche. i.e. the variation in behavior in a situation, prior to reinforcement, which reflects such factors as past experience, motivation, and stimulus factors such as novelty or intensity, referred to by Staddon and Simmelhag (1971) as the "principles of behavioral variation," (b) in the type of behavior produced by a particular animal of a particular species in a given situation, (c) in the type of environmental context which confronts an organism at any particular moment in time, and (d) in the type of reception given to stimuli and their relations (e.g. CSs and USs) by any given individual in a particular species. Variation is assumed to be a basic property of all behavior and all environments and allowes for the operation of *selection*. Two basic examples of apdaptation may be considered: (a) those processes which account for the survival of a particular species within its particular ecological niche, and in spite of the changes that may occur in the environment in which that species exists.

Here, adaptation works via selective pressures leading to the development of particular characteristics in a specics that allow maximum efficiency in coping with the environment, (b) those processes which account for the survival of an organism as a result of the consequences of a particular behavior. Adaptation in this respect works via the selective pressures exerted by the 'validity' of a particular type of behavior. Thus, in general, behaviors followed by aversive consequences are suppressed while behaviors leading to rewarding consequences are increased. Taste-aversion conditioning exerts selective pressures upon the organism such that the consumption of a particular novel taste that has illness consequences will be avoided subsequently. The former type of adaptation process corresponds roughly to what has been termed to be due to the "contingencies of reinforcement" (Skinner, 1969), and the second to what has been termed due to the "contingencies of survival" (Skinner, 1969). However, a word of caution, the adaptive consequences of behavior are neither obvious nor straightforward, e.g. some responses elicited by an aversive stimulus can prove impervious to the avoidance contingency (Turner & Solomon, 1962) whereas it may also be that the behavioral changes are independent of the avoidance contingency (Gormezano, 1965; Woodard & Bitterman, 1973). Thus, this account, a tentative formulation, may help to derive validity and utility through viewing taste-aversion learning from the broader aspects of aversively motivated behavior.

REFERENCES

Bermudez-Rattoni, F., Fernandez, J., Sanchez, M. A., Aguilar-Roblero, R., & Drucker-Colin, R. (1987). Fetal brain transplants induce recuperation of taste aversion learning. *Brain Research, 416,* 147-152.

Charlton, S. G., & Ferraro, D. P. (1982). Effects of deprivation on the differential conditionability of behavior in golden hamsters. *Experimental Animal Behavior, 1,* 18-29.

Dickinson, A., & Mackintosh, N. J. (1978). Classical conditioning in animals. *Annual Review of Psychology, 29,* 587-612.

Garcia, J., Hankins, W. G., & Rusiniak, K. W. (1974). Behavioral regulation of the miliew interne in man and rat. *Science, 185,*

823-831.

Garcia, J., Kimeldorf, D. J., & Hunt, E. L. (1956). Conditioned responses to manipulative procedures resulting from exposure to gamma radiation. *Radiation Research, 5,* 79-87.

Gormezano, I. (1965). Yoked comparisons of classical and instrumental conditioning of the eyelid response; and an addendum on "voluntary responders". In W. F. Prokasy (Ed.), *Classical Conditioning: A symposium,* pp. 48-70. New York: Appleton-Century-Crofts.

Logue, A. W. (1979). Taste aversion and the generality of the laws of learning. *Psychological Bulletin, 86,* 226-296.

Revusky, S. (1977). Learning as a general process with an emphasis on data from feeding experiments. In N. W. Milgram, L. Krames & T. M. Alloway (Eds.), *Food aversion learning,* pp. 3-51. New York: Plenum Press.

Revusky, S., & Garcia, J. (1970). Learned associations over long delays. In G. H. Bower (Ed.), *The Psychology of learning and motivation: Advances in research and theory (vol. 4).* pp. 1-84. New York: Academic Press.

Seligman, M. E. P. (1970). On the generality of the laws of learning. *Psychological Review, 77,* 400-418.

Skinner, B. F. (1969). *Contingencies of reinforcement.* New York: Appleton-Century-Crofts.

Staddon, J. E. R. (1983). *Adaptive Behavior and Learning.* Cambridge, England: Cambridge University Press.

Staddon, J. E. R., & Simmelhag, V. L. (1971). The "superstition" experiment: A reexamination of its implications for the principles of adaptive behavior. *Psychological Review, 78,* 3-43.

Turner, L. H., & Solomon, R. L. (1962). Human traumatic avoidance learning: theory and experiments on the operant-respondent distinction and failure to learn. *Psychological Monographs, 76,* (40, Whole No. 559).

Woodard, W. T., & Bitterman, M. E. (1973). Pavlovian analysis of avoidance conditioning in the goldfish (Carassius auratus). *Journal of Comparative and Physiological Psychology, 82,* 123-129.

2 Food for Tolman: Cognition and Cathexis in Concert

John Garcia
University of California at Los Angeles

ABSTRACT

Tolman distinguished two kinds of learning: Field expectancies or cognitions are acquired in Pavlov's CS-US and Thorndike's R-US paradigms, wherein animals "map" the spatiotemporal context of the stimulus field and subsequently modify their behavior. Cathexis is a Darwinian process exemplified by flavor aversions, wherein the affective value of a goal object (US) is modified according to homeostatic feedback (FB). The latter process is characterized by one-trial learning over long temporal spans often occuring in the absence on any observable reaction to the prolonged paired stimulation. Flavor paired with a nauseous agent results in an aversion even at doses too low to induce nausea. In feeding, taste plays the pivotal US role ending the cognitive CS-US coping sequence and initiating the affective US-FB adjustment. In addition, taste potentiates weak distal CSs for feeding. Implications of the CS-US-FB schema for theories of CS-US associative similarity, CS-CS facilitation of long-delay learning and CS-CS competitive blocking are discussed. Examples of the duality of cognitive-affective processing are drawn from evolution and comparative neuroanatomy as well as from experiments and observations of animal and human behavior. Tolman's legacy is fondly recalled.

INTRODUCTION

Edward C. Tolman (1949) presented an address as the Chairman of the Division of General Psychology of the American Psychological Association in Boston on September 7, 1948, entitled "There is more than one kind of learning". He began with the following comment:

I wish to suggest that our familiar theoretical disputes about learning may *perhaps* (I emphasize "perhaps") be resolved, if we can agree that there are really a number of different kinds of learning. For then it may turn out that the theory and laws appropriate to one kind may well be different from those appropriate to other kinds. Each of the theories of learning now current may, in short, still have validity for some one or more varieties of learning if not for all. But to assume that this will settle our squabble is, I know, being overly optimistic (p. 144).

Not wishing to surpass my Sainted Professor, I will confine my discussion to two kinds of learning which Tolman called "Field Expectancies" and "Cathexes". I suggest that classical conditioning results in a cognitive field expectancy while flavor aversion conditioning results in a negative cathexis and that parametric laws and associative processes of these two kinds of learning are indeed different as Tolman hypothesized. But, with the same hopes and trepidations, I suggest that if we adopt a simple and consistent notation system, classical conditioning theory on the one hand and conditioned taste aversion theory on the other hand, can be unified into a single explanation of feeding behavior. The scheme flows naturally from the pragmatic study of many data sources, mostly collected since Tolman made his distinction 38 years ago. Still, those wedded to a strict hypothetico-deductive format may deem it "post-hoc". But the utility of the scheme can be tested anew. It is part of what Bolles (1985), my fellow Tolmanic, calls an "emerging functionalism" in the explanation of learning and behavior.

The trouble with flavor aversions

Taste aversions do not fit comfortably within the present framework of classical or instrumental conditioning: These aversions selectively seek flavors to the exclusion of other stimuli. Interstimulus intervals are a thousandfold too long. But these are only minor difficulties because selective associations and long interstimulus intervals are ubiquitous in the animal learning literature as we and others have argued (Garcia & Ervin, 1968; Garcia & Levine, 1976; Logue, 1979). Some intractable biological constraints on conditioning theorists still remain (Garcia, McGowan & Green, 1972).

Consider for a moment the ordinary Pavlovian demonstration of defensive conditioning pairing a tone as the conditioned stimulus (CS) and an electrocutaneous shock as the unconditioned stimulus (US). The CS must be intense enough to elicit an orienting response (OR) and the shock must be intense enough to elicit unconditioned escape reactions (UR). The onset of stimulation seems to be the most important feature of both CS and US for rapid associative learning though the duration of stimuli can affect the formation of the conditioned response (CR) pattern. After a number of trials in which the onsets of the paired stimuli are separated by about 0.5 s, the subject on hearing the tone will exhibit a defensive CR as if it "expects" the shock US.

We confront the real problems when considering an ordinary conditioned flavor aversion (CFA) demonstration using the same classical notation. The flavor of saccharin water (CS) is paired with ionizing radiation (US). In this case, the duration of the paired stimuli as well as the interval from CS onset to US onset can be extended for hours yet the CFA is acquired in one trial (Garcia & Kimeldorf, 1957; Garcia, Hankins, & Rusiniak, 1974). Furthermore, the total amount of energy emitted during the US exposure is its most important parameter (Garcia, Kimeldorf, & Hunt, 1961; Buchwald, Garcia, Feder, & Bach-y-Rita, 1964). If the radiation US intensity is reduced and duration is prolonged, no UR is obvious. There is no apparent discomfort during and immediately after radiation. Animals given the flavor CS will drink readily enough during US exposure but later they will display the CFA when the CS is presented alone in an extinction test (Garcia et al., 1972).

Classical CS-US notation simply cannot encompass CFA. To reiterate this crucial point, there are more examples, old and new. If rats are given a thiamine-deficient diet or a low-grade chronic toxin they will develop a CFA for a familiar diet over days and weeks (Harris, Clay, Hargreaves & Ward, 1933; Richter, 1943). If a distinctive diet is presented for 10 days while a tumor known to produce "anorexia" is growing then a genuine CFA develops and becomes stronger with the continued use of the diet and growth of the tumor (Bernstein, 1985; Bernstein, 1978). In all such cases, it is difficult to point to the onset of the CS or US or FB; the CFA, in other words the CR, is the only sign of conditioning. It is as if in Pavlov's paradigm, we reduced both the tone CS and the infused vinegar US to such a low degree that neither an OR or a UR was discernable, then after we left them both on for a week or two, salivation gradually appeared and steadily became more copious.

Paradoxical effects are also observed when a toxic solution serves as the US. In the absence of a flavor CS, rats cannot effectively reduce their poison intake to "escape" the US malaise in repeated trials. But given a flavor CS in conjunction with the US they will avoid the CS after a single trial (Rusiniak, Hankins, & Garcia, 1976). Once the flavor CS has been presented, a delayed toxic US is effective even if it is presented while the rat is anesthetized (Roll & Smith, 1972) or deeply tranquilized and unresponsive to pinches and probes (Forthman Quick, 1984) or when its electrocortical activity is depressed (Buresova & Bures, 1973; Davis & Bures, 1972). In other words, learning can occur without behavioral signs of US or UR or when the subject is in a drugged sleep state during delivery of the putative US. To speak of a psychological US or UR in such cases is to invoke gratuitous unconscious events giving CFA the hollow status of a hypothetical construct. But CFA is an empirically established form of associative learning dependent upon the conditional pairing of a taste and any member of a specific class of physiochemical agents and events.

CFAs have been discussed *ad nauseum*, which is entirely appropriate for nauseous agents promote taste aversions: Any physiological, emotional, or perceptual event or any physiochemical agent causing nausea will establish a taste aversion even at doses insufficient to produce overt signs of nausea. Not just any poison or toxin will do, the event or agent must affect the emetic system of the midbrain and brainstem. Drugs and toxins attacking the nervous system or metabolic processes such as nembutal and cyanide will not cause aversions as we discussed recently (Garcia, Lasiter, Bermudez-Rattoni, & Deems, 1985). Allergies, bloating and lower intestinal discomfort may cause a judicious subject to avoid specific foods but it will not cause a CFA (Pelchat, Grill, Rozin, & Jacobs, 1983). CFA is an active dislike for the flavor of the food which can spread to the place where the food was eaten under special conditions; olfactory and visual cues associated with the feeding place will elicit signs of disgust in animals (Garcia & Rusiniak, 1980). Hearing or thinking about CFA elicits reports of nausea and facial expressions of loathing in humans.

The empirical evidence can be found in three recent volumes: Barker, Best and Domjan (1977) organized a conference on "learning mechanisms in food selection" and edited a volume providing data analysis, theoretical discussions and an extensive bibliography. Bravemen and Bronstein (1985) continued this synthetic process with a similar conference and volume "Experimental assessments and clinical applications of conditioned food aversions". Burish, Levy and Meyerowitz (1985) conducted a conference on medical implications of "Cancer, nutrition and eating behavior" and edited the volume mainly concerned with aversions induced in human patients by medical treatments.

Cognitive vs affective processing of stimuli

The clash of CFA and classic paradigms has gone on for decades but a reconciliation based on biological adaptation is possible (Rozin, 1977). I suggest that some of the confusion can *perhaps* (I emphasize "perhaps" also) be cleared up if we divide the poisoned food (or drink) into two components using US to denote the stimulation of food in the mouth and FB to denote the visceral feedback from food in the gut. This expansion depicted in Fig. 2.1a and 2.1b allows us to deal more comfortably with CFA phenomena.

I assume these elements and associations to be different types of events mediated by different sensory and brain systems. Obviously the sensory systems cannot be neatly divided into CS, US and FB channels. For example, over a wide range of just noticeable increments, auditory stimulation acts as a neutral CS. The subject will simply habituate if the noise is not followed by a US. If auditory stimulation is raised to an intense level it can be used as a US to condition avoidance responses. In order to avoid such ambiguities, I will invoke that conceptual cliche "paradigm" referring to a specific experimental arrangement which yields verifiable facts. Auditory stimulation can be a CS in one training paradigm and a US in another training paradigm. This is not a satisfactory solution by any means, for it leaves us mired down in a mass of training procedures, but it is the best we can do at this state of the game we play.

CLASSICAL FEEDING PARADIGMS

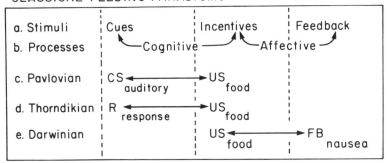

FIG. 2.1. This expanded notion for food conditioning involves: (a) three stimulus categories and (b) two associate processes to unify classical conditioning (CS-US) and conditioned flavor aversions (CFA). For simplicity, Pavlovian and Thorndikian paradigms are considered varients differing only in CS and R respectively. In both forms a map of the CS-US in its spatiotemporal context is acquired when the subject is awake and intersimulus interval (ISI) is brief. Darwin proposed a form of a CFA as an outcome of natural selection. In US-FB processing, a simple hedonic shift (CFA) is acquired in one trial even when the ISI is prolonged and conscious appreciation of the associated FB is held constant by Pavlovians and Thorndikians. FB is the principle independent variable for Darwinians and its reflexive connections to the US accounts for the selective nature of the hedonic shift.

In general, the molar behavioral categories and processes atop Fig. 2.1 are taken from Tolman (1949). Cues are the distal stimuli (CS) guiding the subject towards goals and away from danger during the coping phase of a behavioral sequence. Incentives are the pleasant proximal stimuli (US) resulting from contact with a desired "goal-object" or the unpleasant stimuli arising from contact with a "disturbance-object". Feedback (FB) stems from the internal homeostatic regulatory system following the consummatory bout which usually ends a behavioral sequence, as when food consumption brings satiation or nausea.

CSs and USs are associated by a cognitive processing system resulting in *behavior modification* as the subject utilizes environmental information to form field expectancies or "cognitions" evidenced by its movements towards goals and away from disturbances. Subsequently the animal acts as if it has acquired a memorial "cognitive map" of the CS-US field by anticipating stimuli and taking appropriate detours and shortcuts resulting in new pathways. Examples of maplike memories can be found in rats (Olton, 1977) chimpanzees (Menzel, 1978) and birds (Shettleworth, 1983).

USs and FBs are integrated by an affective processing system resulting in *incentive modification*, thus the subject acquires "cathexes". According to Tolman (1949) cathexes are "...the acquisition by the organism of positive dispositions *for* certain *types* of food, drink, sex-object, etc. or of negative dispositions *against* certain *types* of disturbance-object". CFA research demonstrates that a strong negative cathexis for a food-object can be acquired in a single trial. Rejection of the formerly positive food is attended by negative affective signs (Garcia, Forthman Quick, & White, 1984; Grill & Norgren, 1978).

CFAs are curiously isolated from field expectancies lending support to the notion that two kinds of learning may be involved. For example, rats given saccharin water in a T-maze learned to turn towards the sweet fluid in preference to unflavored water on the other side. Later in another place, saccharin was paired with nausea. When the rats returned to the maze they persisted in running to the side of the sweet water. But they would not drink backing away in disgust. Apparently the rats did not "know" they had acquired a CFA for saccharin (Garcia, Kovner, & Green, 1970). Similar results were obtained in lever-boxes. Rats were trained to press a lever for a reinforcing flavor in one place and then presented with the flavor followed by toxin in another place. When they were returned to the lever box under extinction conditions they continued to press at the lever for a fluid which was now aversive (Holman, 1975). As we shall discuss below under "Taste-potentiation: some practical and theoretical implications", other investigators using other procedures found some depression in instrumental responding after the reinforcering flavor is made aversive by CFA treatment. However, in its totality that evidence supports the point we make here, namely, poisoning the flavor has little effect upon instrumental responding for the flavor under extinction conditions compared to its huge effect on consuming the flavor.

Apologies and acknowledgments

It was a big mistake (mine, I'm afraid) to designate taste as a CS and nausea as a US because taste was Pavlov's original US and there are compelling reasons for keeping it so. Nausea is not a proper US or UR; it is an FB whose function is to decrease the incentive value of the taste US. I ask everyone to make this simple correction in their mental computers: Where I have written taste CS and nausea US in the past, please plug in US and FB, respectively.

I am indebted to Revusky and Solomon for lighting my path. Revusky (1971) presents a tripartite theory of concurrent interference, which yields several forms of blocking similar to the compound conditioning phenomena I discuss below. His analysis of concurrent interference makes sense out of other long delay paradigms as we shall see below. But Revusky makes no assumption that his elements are different kinds of events and specifies that one element must precede another element by definition. This is exactly how I made my big mistake. On the other hand, Solomon (1977) emphatically points out that food is a US, not a CS. He argues that biological prepotency and survival value are the hallmarks of a US. Furthermore, he points out that most (I say all) USs, whether pleasant or unpleasant, arouse lingering affective reactions.

Recently Domjan (1985) raised this question: Why is the aversion weakened as the interstimulus interval between US and FB is increased? Decay of the taste memory is not a very good answer because humans can recall the taste. Interference by other tastes is a possibility but the diminution occurs in the absence of tastes during the interval. Solomon and Corbit (1974) offer us an attractive alternative, the opponent-process theory of motivation: Essentially any positive FB is terminated by an open-loop negative FB in the opposite hedonic direction. The converse is also true. Green and Garcia (1971) provide an example of how this works in CFA. Apomorphine injections induce a brief bout of nausea followed by receuperative relief. A taste presented before nausea becomes aversive while a second taste presented before recuperation becomes preferred illustrating the opponent processes. Therefore when a single taste US is followed by a toxic FB, the aversion diminishes as time passes because the opponent (recuperative) process gradually counter-conditions the taste aversion set up by the illness process. (Jim McGaugh, my favorite expert on memory traces, argues that the opponent-process must operate on the flavor, not the nausea, in order to produce the ISI delay gradient.)

Solomon (1977) notes that US-US conditioning may also involve long ISIs. He describes how a monkey, shown a fear-evoking toy snake in its feeding place many hours after eating a particular food, may thereafter avoid that food even in the home cage. In the main, I concur. However, I would emphasize this paradigmatic distinction: (1) If fear elicited by the snake US makes the monkey sick to its stomach, then that nauseous FB may establish a true taste aversion which is manifested in any context where *that food* is encountered. (2) Alternatively, if some CS attribute of the feeding situation is inducing a cognitive expectancy of the fearful snake US, then that expectancy may interfere with the monkey's consumption of *any* food in that particular CS context. The US-FB notation makes this distinction explicit.

Finally, studying Rescorla's (1967) article entitled "Pavlovian Conditioning and Its Proper Control Procedures" started me thinking about classical conditioning and taste aversions in abstract procedural terms. To my surprise, that cognitive exercise led to the CS-US-FB schema. And it was fun. As Tolman (1959) advised us:

> Since all the sciences, and especially psychology, are still immersed in such tremendous realms of the uncertain and the unknown, the best that any individual scientist, especially any psychologist, can do seems to be to follow his own gleam and his own bent, however inadequate they may be. In fact, I suppose that actually this is what we all do. In the end the only sure criterion is to have fun. And I have had fun.

Three classic paradigms of food conditioning

Pavlov's original food conditioning paradigm is an excellent example of cognitive processing resulting in a field expectancy (Fig. 2.1c). The dog is thoroughly adapted to the experimental situation so that no distractions disturb its singular task of associating the distal auditory CS with the peripheral taste US. The dog orients to the CS and the US is delivered into its mouth. After acquisition the CS elicits salivation as if the dog "expects" the taste to follow. The dog's behavior indicates that it has mapped the CS and US in the spatiotemporal context of the apparatus and the experimental procedures.

Thorndike's instrumental food conditioning paradigm is a similar example of cognitive processing of cues and incentives (Fig. 2.1d). Consider the situation where a cat is confined to a puzzle box and the cat's pulling response trips the latch, releasing the cat to eat food outside. The latch response (R) serves the same function for Thorndike's cat as the auditory CS served for Pavlov's dog. Admittedly there are some differences between the two situations, the dog has a clear sensory CS and a food US gratuitously presented without work requirement, while the cat has to retrieve the memory of R and labor at the latch in order to eat. There are, however, persuasive parametric similarities which indicate that the underlying associative processes may be rather similar (Garcia & Holder, 1985).

The conditioned food aversion paradigm, historically associated with Charles Darwin and A.R. Wallace, is an excellent example of the affective processing of a US incentive and a homeostatic FB (Fig. 2.1e). The taste US is followed by nausea FB some time later reversing the palatability of the taste US for the next trial. Originally Darwin posed the problem of tender caterpillars flaunting their colorful patterns on bare twigs exposed to insectivorous birds and other predators searching for food. Clearly, such behavior seems maladaptive. Wallace suggested a hypothetical answer; these colorful caterpillars are either disgusting or poisonous and their vivid color patterns serves to turn away potential predators. In 1887, Poulton summarized twenty years of research supporting Wallace's hypothesis and establishing a biological research area concerned with the ecology of toxic plants and animals. This research validated a theory of associative conditioning which predates the Pavlovian and Thorndikian theories by several decades (Garcia & Hankins, 1977; Garcia y Robertson & Garcia, 1988).

For the sake of clarity and historical reference, the three paradigms are presented as distinct dual entities but obviously, all three components (cues, incentives and feedback) are involved in each paradigm. Consumption of food by Pavlov's dog and Thorndike's cat provides a positive homeostatic FB maintaining the palability of the food so that when it is presented again the hungry animal will eat avidly. Thorndike and Pavlov were both adaptive theorists concerned with homeostatic functions. The Darwinian researchers were enormously interested in adaptive value of distal cues for poisonous species and their nontoxic mimics. These theorists were well aware that both cognitive and affective processes act in concert in their respective paradigms.

Selective cue-consequence learning

There are many examples of selective CFA learning but for the moment I will concentrate on a single experiment which caused some theoretical discussion (Garcia, McGowan, Ervin and Koelling, 1968). We employed two food cues, the size or the taste of the food pellet, juxtoposed against two forms of punishment, shock to the feet or illness induced by X-ray exposure, in four independent groups of rats. Animals presented with the size cue visible at a distance learned the discrimination when punished with foot-shock but not when punished with illness. Conversely animals given a taste cue dependent upon oral contact acquired an aversion when punished by illness but not when punished with foot shock. In other words, strong associations were formed between the distal (size) CS and the proximal (skin-shock) US as indicated in Fig. 2.2a. Strong aversions were formed to the taste US followed by nausea FB as indicated in Fig. 2.2b. In the present scheme of things the strong associations are Pavlovian and Darwinian conditioning respectively.

SELECTIVE AND POTENTIATED LEARNING

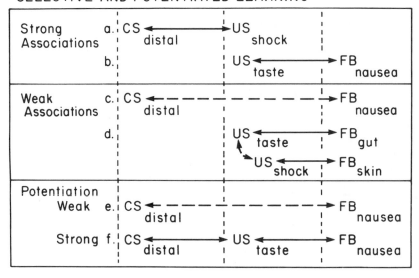

FIG. 2.2. This is a continuation of Fig. 2.1. Garcia's paradigm of selective cue-consequence learning is accounted for by dual processing: (a) A strong cognitive association is acquired by classically pairing a distal CS with a foot-shock US. (b) A strong hedonic shift is acquired by pairing a proximal flavor US with a nausea FB. (c) A weak CS-FB hedonic shift occurs in the absence of a US. (d) A weak association is acquired when two USs from antagonistic systems are paired. Potentiation: a weak CS-FB affective adjustment (c) is potentiated by (d) the addition of the appropriate US. Note that if the distal stimulus and the proximal taste are considered to be compound CS then potentiation contradicts the principle of blocking or overshadowing where weak CS components are blocked by stronger CS components.

The non-existent or weak associations are of two varieties. The failure of the CS-FB association is due to the absence of a US (Fig. 2.2c). We will elaborate on the capacity of the taste US to strengthen the CS-FB association in our discussion of potentiation below. The failure of the taste-shock association results from challenging two relatively isolated defense (US-US) systems (Fig. 2.2d). We have discussed the evolutionary significance of this dichotomy previously (Garcia y Robertson & Garcia, 1985). Essentially auditory and visual CSs and the electrocutaneous US impinge upon a skin-defense system evolved under the natural selective pressures of predation. Taste and emetic toxins impinge upon a gut-defense system evolved under the pressure of plants and animals which employ toxins to fend off foragers and predators. These two systems are mutually inhibitory and it is difficult for animals to make connections across systems in a few trials. I will offer more evidence for this dichotomous learning in the final sections of my discussion.

Selective CFA learning is a robust phenomenon which has been replicated under a wide variety of experimental arrangements (Domjan, 1983). Selective associations have been demonstrated in neonate rats (Gemberling & Domjan, 1982) and it has been reported that flavor and toxin can be associated by fetal rats (Smotherman, 1982). Selective effects can be obtained by drug injections: The motor paralytic agent, gallamine, produces a stronger place avoidance than taste aversion like pain. In contrast the nauseous agent, lithium chloride, produces a stronger taste aversion than place aversion (Lett, 1985a). Amphetamine produces both a taste aversion and a place preference presumably by simultaneously disrupting gut defense mechanisms and facilitating skin defense mechanisms (Reicher & Holman, 1977).

Any reasonable person, on observing the many different receptor systems possessed by animals, is forced to conclude that selective associations must be omnipresent in this world. Each receptor system is structurally and functionally unique. For example, the auditory system locates sounds from all quarters so it is ideally suited to warn the animal of impending attacks on the sensitive skin completely enveloping its body. The visual system provides a richer detail of information but it is focused on one segment of the environment at any given moment therefore it is better suited to select escape routes or food objects (Garcia & Ervin, 1968). Accordingly, Shettleworth (1972) found that baby chicks use an auditory CS more effectively when shocked to the feet but a visual signal when shocked to the beak for drinking. Similar selective effects are reported when conditioning adult pigeons. These birds utilize the visual component of a compound signal for feeding but the auditory component for defending against shock (Lolordo & Furrow, 1976). There is also stimulus selectivity depending on the species as anyone whoever cornered a wild animal can testify; birds flutter against the brightest window while rats scurry to the darkest shadow. Thus Allison, Larson and Jensen (1967) found frightened rats chose the black compartment in preference to the white one regardless of where they were shocked. However to cast taste-nausea affinity as simply another case of CS-US selectivity is to belittle a profound learning phenomenon. The crucial point, as I said above, is that the visceral FB is impossible to define in traditional US-UR terms.

Taste-Potentiation of distal CSs: 12 empirical points

The hypothesis linking taste and nausea by neural convergence of the paired afferents to a specialized gut-defense mechanism in the brain raises an immediate question: "How does the subject learn to avoid poison at a distance especially when the poison was delayed and experienced only once? Wild-bred coyotes, wolves and hawks can do this in one trial (Garcia & Brett, 1977). The answer is: "Distal cues are associated with delayed nausea by the mediation of taste or the expectancy of taste. When the animal is thus focused on ingestion, distal stimuli become feeding cues as if a "sensory and-gate" channelled them into the gut-defense system (Garcia, et al., 1984; Garcia et al., 1985). This process called "synergistic taste-potentiation of distal cues" is supported by a voluminous literature; I will only summarize and enumerate the salient points here.

(1) Distal cues (color, odor, noise, etc.) are weak CSs for delayed nauseous FB in the absence of a taste US (see Fig. 2.2e). For example, odor is a weak signal for poison in the absence of taste for rats (Garcia & Koelling, 1967; Rusiniak, 1976, Rusiniak, Hankins, Garcia, & Brett, 1979). A visual cue used alone is a weak signal for hungry hawks (Brett, Hankins, & Garcia, 1976).

(2) Interpolation of taste between the distal CS and the delayed FB potentiates the distal CS so that it becomes a powerful ingestive deterrent (see Fig. 2.2f). For example, when saccharin is added to almond-scented water, the weak odor becomes a strong aversive stimulus for rats (Rusiniak et al., 1979).

(3) Addition of a potentiating taste can block aversion to a familiar taste. After repeated trials without a distinctive taste cue, hawks rejected both black (poisoned) and white (safe) mice presumably because both mice taste alike. However, when a distinctive taste was added to the black mice and paired with poison in a single trial, other hawks rejected black mice on sight at a distance exhibiting disgust signs. But they accepted the taste of white mice avidly indicating that the added taste had blocked conditioning to the mouse taste (Brett et al., 1976).

(4) Taste-potentiation is a phenomenon of great generality. It has been demonstrated in thirsty pigeons using colored water (Clarke, Westbrook, & Irwin, 1979) and in hungry rats using colored capsules of food (Galef & Osborne, 1978). Potentiation has been studied in a series of avian species (Martin & Lett, 1985) and a similar phenomenon has been observed in human patients undergoing nauseous chemotherapy for cancer (see Garcia y Robertson & Garcia, 1985).

(5) Taste-potentiation is much stronger than second-order conditioning when the same taste and odor are tested in both paradigms. In the latter paradigm, taste becomes aversive when followed by nausea in first-order conditioning. Then odor is paired with the aversive taste in the second

order. Tests of odor indicate that second-order conditioning is completely ineffective or very weak (Best, Batson, Meachum, Brown, & Ringer, 1985; Rusiniak et al., 1979). This cumbersome second-order process may seldom if ever operate in natural foraging situations however reliable it may appear in strictly controlled laboratory situations.

(6) Taste-potentiation is much stronger than sensory preconditioning when the same taste and odor are tested in both paradigms. In the latter paradigm odor and taste are paired in the first phase. Then taste is paired with nausea in the second phase. Finally tests of odor reveal that sensory preconditioning is ineffective or weak (Lett, 1985b; Palmerino, 1979; Palmerino, Rusiniak, & Garcia, 1980).

(7) Taste-potentiation and CTA have different neural substrates. A small precise lesion in the gustatory neocortex will disrupt CTA sparing taste-potentiation (Kiefer, Rusiniak, & Garcia, 1982). Another small precise lesion in the same general region will disrupt both functions (Lasiter, Deems & Garcia, 1985). Anesthesia applied to the limbic system will disrupt odor-nausea association but spare odor-shock and taste-nausea associations (Bermúdez-Rattoni, 1985; Bermudez-Rattoni, Rusiniak, & Garcia, 1983).

(8) Taste-potentiation can be manifested in the absence of a CTA. Even a taste too weak to garner any aversive conditioning when paired with nausea can serve to potentiate an odor aversion. This paradoxical effect can be achieved by using a very weak saccharin solution in intact rats (Rusiniak et al., 1979) or by blunting their taste sensitivity with neocortical lesions (Kiefer et al., 1982).

(9) In an odor-taste-nausea conditioning sequence, the odor-taste interval must be a matter of minutes or perhaps seconds. But the taste-nausea interval can be extended to a half hour or more. The empirical evidence was gathered in a wind tunner apparatus delivering puffs of scented air to the rat drinking saccharin water (Coburn, Garcia, Rusiniak, & Kiefer, 1984; Holder & Garcia, 1987).

(10) Enriched experience with odor and taste facilitates the utilization of odor but not taste in rats. Unlike wild-bred species, laboratory rats reared in barren cages do not utilize distal cues effectively to avoid poisoned baits (Garcia, Rusiniak, & Brett, 1977). However, given "enriched" experience with only one odor and one taste in their drinking water for about a month, laboratory rats demonstrate much stronger odor aversion when a second odor and taste are paired with nausea. But they do not display a stronger taste aversion which appears maximal in both groups. Furthermore, enriched rats demonstrate direct odor-toxin aversions over 30 min intervals while impoverished rats do not (Rusiniak, Garcia, Palmerino & Cabral, 1983).

(11) When used in contiguity with taste the most unlikely cues can be potentiated when followed by poison. A noise activated by the rats feeding responses and emanating from the food cup is an ineffective CS for a toxic FB. However, when that noise is combined with taste in acquisition it will suppress feeding when tested alone in extinction. But if the noise emanates from a nearby locus, it will not be potentiated by taste (Ellins, Cramer, & Whitmore, 1985; Ellins & Von Kluge, 1987). Garcia and

Koelling (1966) used a compound signal composed of a bright-noisy flash and a sweet taste activated by the licking of thirsty rats at the water spout. They failed to obtain taste potentiation of the bright-noisy flash presumably because the distal flash was not contiguous with the sweet water.

(12) Perhaps any cue which induces a taste expectancy in the subject can serve in the role of the taste US. Holland (1981) first presented rats with a tone CS followed with a distinctive food US, then he paired the tone CS with lithium FB and subsequently the rats displayed a decrement in consumption of the distinctive food. Thus he obtained an aversion when the expectancy of a distinctive food is followed by nausea. The effect seems small compared to the aversion obtained when genuine food is followed by illness, nevertheless the effect is reliable. Holland (1983) also obtained potentiation of a distal odor by substituting a signal associated with a distinctive food for the taste of the actual food US. Potentiation does not appear as strong as when an actual flavor US is used but replication has demonstrated reliability of the phenomenon (Holland, 1983).

Taste-potentiation: Devaluated reinforcers and taste artifacts

Now I will discuss those studies which reported depressed instrumental responding for a flavor under extinction conditions after the flavor is made aversive by CFA treatment. For example, rats trained to go down a runway for a tasty reinforcer slowed down after that taste was paired with poison as if they "knew" the reinforcer was "bad" (Chen and Amsel, 1980). The paradigm has been called "Instrumental responding for a devaluated reinforcer" (Bob Boakes, my favorite historian, informs me that the label "Instrumental responding for a devaluated reinforcer" originates from Dickinson. See Dickinson, A. (1985) Actions and Habits in Weiskrantz, L. (Ed.), *Animal Intelligence*, Oxford, Clarendon Press. which clearly implies the dual feeding process of a CS-US coping and US-FB hedonic shift. Colwill and Rescorla (1985a: 1985b) report on a series of interesting and complex experiment in which instrumental responding is depressed after the reinforcing flavor has been "devaluated" by pairing it with poison. They also provide a review of the conflicting studies.

A detailed analysis of all these studies is beyond my purpose and interest, but I will discuss how potentiation and other well-known variables effect instrumental responding in rats working for devaluated flavor. Then I will concentrate upon the agreements which outweigh the differences among researchers. I am indebted to Eric Holman (personal communication, April 6, 1987) who discussed many of the procedures and variables with me in a most collegial manner but of course he should not be held responsible for anything I write. First let me dispense with the matter of salt hunger. In a sensory-preconditioning paradigm rats put into a sudden need for salt will return to the instrumental habits that yielded salt in the past (Fudin, 1978; Krieckhaus and Wolfe, 1968). Holman believes salt need is more like hunger than toxiphobia; hungry rats will seek food where they found it before. I agree.

In simple conditioning the powerful associative affinity of taste for nausea is supreme but relative. It was known early on that other cues would also become aversive paricularly when higher toxic doses and repeated acquisition trials are imposed. Odor stands next in the hierarchy of associative affinity (Garcia and Koelling, 1967. Palmerino et al, 1980, Taukulis and St. George, 1982). Next come other cues impinging upon the mouth such as moisture of the food (Garcia, Hankins, Robinson & Vogt, 1972) temperature of the fluid and distinctive features of the spout (Nachman, Rauschenberger & Ashe, 1977; Archer, Sjöden, and Nilsson, 1985; Archer, Sjöden, Nilsson, & Carter, 1980).

The use of any oral stimulation, other than taste, raises a classic question known as the "doctrine of specific energies of nerves". As a thumb in the eye or a blow to the back of the skull can cause the victim to see lights and stars, so tactual and other stimuli applied to the tongue or the buccal cavity can fire gustatory receptors causing the subject to perceive taste. Alternatively they may fire other receptors whose fibers may or may not converge centrally with taste fibers. Aversions for tongue-tactual cues, rather than aversions for visual cues stemming from spouts and jars, have been reported by Nachman, Rauschenberger and Ashe (1977) who assume that only trigeminal stimulation is involved. Archer, Sjöden and Nilsson (1985) describe tactual spout differences as "contextual cues" as opposed to "taste cues", but they offer no evidence that oral-tactual stimuli are not taste-related, in any case they can scarcely be called "contextual". Furthermore, use of plastic tubes and bottles in conditioning apparatus can impart a flavour to the water which rats can detect.

It is generally agreed that a compartment with distinctive visual, auditory and paw-tactual features will become aversive when paired with illness, but the aversion is relatively weak compared to taste and odor aversions (Archer, Sjöden, Nilsson & Carter, 1980; Best, Best & Henggeler, 1977; Garcia, Kimeldorf & Hunt, 1961; Garcia & Koelling, 1967). Therefore, when instrumental training and testing is carried out in the same compartment where the reinforcing flavor is devalued by CFA treatment is repeated trials, then it is likely that some cue emanating from the compartment may depress instrumental responding.

This problem is exacerbated by taste potentiation (see empirical points; 2,3,8,11,12, above). Garcia, Kovner and Green (1970) and Holman (1975) tested the animal in one place and established the CFA in another; they did not observe a depression in instrumental responding. Others who observed a depression in strumental responding tested the animals and established the CFA in the same place (e.g. Colwill & Rescola, 1985a; 1985b) Significantly, Wilson, Sherman and Holman (1981) found depressed instrumental conditioning for a devaluated flavor in extinction testing, if and only if, the lever press was followed by the noisy operation of the feeder. Therefore any spatial or temporal cue which by design or accident induces an expectancy of the target flavor and/or nausea or any cue which is contiguous with taste and followed with poison can depress instrumental responding during extinction. But in spite of these procedural differences Colwill and Rescola (1985b) agree with us when they conclude "In each of the experiments we found persistent (instrumental) behavior in animals that were unwilling to consume any (devaluated) reinforcers".

The fact that the taste-potentiation mechanism is more sensitive than the taste-aversion mechanism means that in practical search for a suspected taste in food or water, the test for a potentiated odor is more sensitive than a direct test for the taste aversion itself (point 8). Furthermore, mixing the odorant in the water is a risky procedure since it may add an unspecified taste to the water which can potentiate the odor in "odor only" groups. Some investigators using this mixing procedure reported potentiation (e.g., Durlach & Rescorla, 1980; Rusiniak et al., 1979; Holland, 1981, 1983). However, others using the mixing procedure reported strong odor aversions and blocking of taste by odor (Bouton & Whiting, 1982; Mikulka, Pitts, & Philput, 1982; Rosellini, DeCola, & Lashley, 1981). I suspect that the odor aversions were potentiated by an unspecified taste of the odorant mixed in the water which also served to block aversive conditioning to the target taste (see point 3; also Coburn et al., 1984).

Conversely, mixing a taste in the water may provide an unspecified odor component. This is a special problem when a compound flavor is followed by footshock because odor is more effective than taste for shock avoidance (Hankins, Garcia, & Rusiniak, 1973; Hankins, Rusiniak, & Garcia, 1976). In shock experiments, rats can detect the odor component of 1.0 gm/liter saccharin solution (Hankins et al., 1976). That is the same concentration that we used in the original cue-consequence experiment. Fortunately odor was not effective in that experiment probably because saccharin spillage below the grid provided masking odor on both shock and nonshock trials (we now use this technique to mask the odor, when required). Unspecified odor components can cause problems, for example Krane and Wagner (1975) assume that they are dealing with taste only when they pair a 7.0 gm/liter saccharin solution with shock. They obtained rapid learning indicating the presence of an effective but unspecified saccharin odor.

Paradoxically, when flavor is paired with shock the rat tends to drink more of the shocked flavor (Dietz & Capretta, 1966; Garcia, Ervin, & Koelling, 1966; Lasiter & Braun, 1981). This fact should not escape the notice of clinicians who attempt to reduce drinking of alcoholic beverages with contingent shock treatment. Usually this increased drinking of the shocked fluid is described as a "nonassociative" effect however, even when the rat displays a taste-shock association in one place it will drink more of the fluid in another time and place (see Fig. 2.5). Because of the vastly different functional properties of odor and taste, many flavor studies are difficult to interpret and may have to be repeated analyzing the separate contributions of odor and taste components.

Taste potentiation: Some theoretical implications

Association by contiguity in time and space are both crucial in potentiation as indicated by points 9 and 11 respectively. Any experience which enables the animals to separate the target cue from the potentiating taste is apt to disrupt potentiation. For example, when Ellins and Von Kluge (in press) gave their animals prior experience with an entirely different sound emanating from the same speaker which later projected the target sound, taste-potentiation of noise was completely disrupted probably because the rats had learned that the source of noise was not really in the food. Cognitive mapping of cues in the food is critical for potentiation by food taste.

Rats are also sensitive to contiguity of odor and taste sources. Given prior experience with both stimuli emanating from a single locus, odor and taste in the water, subsequent tests of potentiation of odor by taste are strengthened (see point 10, Rusiniak, et al, 1983). But given prior experience with the two stimuli emanating from two adjacent loci, odor on a disc around the spout and taste in the water, subsequent potentiation is weakened (Palmerino, 1979; Palmermino, et al. 1980). Once the odor is aversive it is a different matter; changing the odor from the disc to the water or vice versa has no effect of the aversion (Rusinak, et al. 1982). During repeated extinction trials the odor remains aversive even when the taste aversion is extinguished (Palmerino, 1979). During extinction, we have observed rats scratching out the offensive filter from the odor disc, disposing of it through the mesh floor and then drinking from the spout. When odor is made fearful by pairing it with shock, it is still another story; the subtle change of odor from disc to water or vice versa completely disrupts fear conditioning (Rusiniak, et al, 1982). These differences have evolutionary significance. When protecting its gut from nausea, the rat simply avoids the odor emanating from the tainted water no matter where it is subsequently found. When protecting its skin from painful attacks, exactly where the fearful odor is coming from is critical to guide the rat's avoidance responses.

Potentiation presents a problem for those who argue that selective associations may be due to CS-US similarity (Testa, 1974; Testa & Ternes, 1977). A buzzer is said to be similar to vibratory foot-shock but not to nausea. A lingering taste in the mouth is said to be similar to a lingering illness in the gut. From one perspective, Testa's hypothesis resembles our own similarity hypothesis (Garcia & Ervin, 1968; Garcia & Koelling, 1966). To a certain degree, the structure of an organism is topologically isomorphic with its hereditary environmental niche. Auditory receptors and cutaneous receptors evolved from common sources to form the external defense system. Oral receptors and visceral receptors rose out of the primordial gut to form the internal defense system. But Testa does not defend similarity on evolutionary or neurological grounds, he argues on the empirical basis of the spatiotemporal correlative similarity of the paired stimuli used in conditioning. However, odor is a weak CS for delayed nausea implying its dissimilarity to illness, yet after a single taste-potentiation trial the same odor followed by the same illness becomes strongly aversive implying similarity. Furthermore, the similarity hypothesis does not seem applicable to a replication of the cue-consequence effect in which the size of the food pellet replaced the buzzer. Pellet size can scarcely be said to be more similar to shock than to illness (Garcia, McGowan, Ervin, & Koelling, 1968).

Domjan (1985) discusses the similarity hypothesis citing some supporting evidence for Testa's notion. Sullivan (1979) reported that if exploratory handling of small objects is followed 35 min later by a series of shocks correlated with the amount and pattern of the handling, then future handling of the small objects is suppressed. But Domjan points out that in the typical CTA experiment, the bout of illness by injection is independent of the amount and pattern of consummatory licking at the flavored water. Historically, association by similarity has been viewed as a weak law and rightly so; it may be sufficient for learning on occasion but it is not necessary for CTA.

Varieties of blocking paradigms

In overshadowing and blocking paradigms, a strong signal and a weak signal are combined into a compound CS and paired with a US. Conditioning accrues to the stronger one as if the two components compete during acquisition and the weaker one is blocked out. Viewed abstractly, taste-potentiation of odor seems to belong to the same paradigmatic class since a compound stimulus made up of weak odor and strong taste precedes a toxic stimulus, but paradoxically in this case, the weaker odor component is potentiated by the stronger taste component. Another paradox occurs when the same compound is followed by immediate shock rather than delayed illness. In this case odor is more effective than taste, but now the weak taste component blocks the strong odor component (Rusiniak, Palmerino, Rice, Forthman, & Garcia, 1982). Both paradoxes vanish when we abandon the Rescorla (1982) notion that odor and taste are similar elements within a compound CS and instead view odor as a CS and taste as a US.

Fig. 2.3 presents overshadowing or blocking and potentiation phenomena in terms of the CS-US-FB schema. Blocking occurs whenever there is competition between similar stimulus events in association. In the 2CSs-US competition paradigm (Fig. 2.3a) two CS components (eg., auditory and visual) compete for association with a single US (e.g., foot-shock). One component is given a competitive advantage in any number of ways, the stronger one can be more salient or more predictive of the US, the weaker one can be made redundant. In this case the weaker component can be totally or partially blocked depending on the degree of competitive edge possessed by the stronger component. The results can be understood in terms of the information value of both components, that is, in communication or cognitive terminology (Egger & Miller, 1963; Kamin, 1969; Rescorla, 1969).

In the 2USs-FB competition paradigm shown in Fig. 2.3b, two flavor USs compete for association with a single nauseous FB in the gut. For example, Revusky and Bedarf (1967) paired two successive flavors, one familiar and one novel, with a single toxic dose: the novel flavor acquired much greater aversive strength regardless of whether it was first or second

BLOCKING PARADIGMS

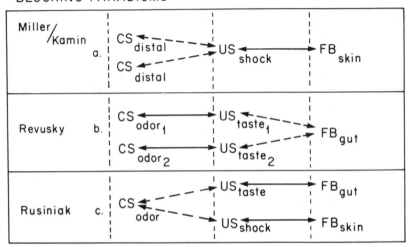

FIG. 2.3. This is a continuation of Fig. 2.2. The contradiction between blocking-overshadowing and potentiation is accounted for by dual processing: (a) Miller-Kamin; two distal CSs compete for association with a single US. (b) Revusky; two taste USs compete for a single gut FB. (c) Rusiniak; two US's from antagonistic systems compete for a single odor CS. In each case the more salient member of the competing pair is favored.

in temporal order. In similar competitions, the more salient flavor US wins out (Cannon, Best, Batson, Brown, Rubenstein, & Carrell, 1985; Kalat & Rozin, 1971). In Fig. 2.3b, the critical feature appears to be the two taste USs (each attended by its potentiated odor CS) competing for association with one FB. It may be well to repeat this paradigm under arrangements in which the contribution of odor is eliminated or assessed independently of taste.

The CS-2USs competition paradigm illustrated in Fig. 2.3c is a mirror image of the 2CS-US competition paradigm; two USs (each bound to its FB) compete for association with a single CS. Rusiniak et al. (1982) used an overshadowing paradigm. When used alone odor is a powerful CS for foot-shock, but as the saliency of taste is increased, odor loses associative strength with the shock US and gains associative strength with the taste US. When the same flavor series is followed by poison, odor gains aversive strength through potentiation as the saliency of taste is increased (see Figs. 2.2e, 2.2f). Rusiniak achieved his effects by varying the locus and the strength of taste, whether the same effects can be achieved by varying the novelty, reliability and the temporal parameters of the competing USs remains to be tested.

Long-delay tactics in cognitive paradigms

Traditional methodology enhances the principle of contiguity and imparts a mystical urgency to reinforcement by imposing brief ISIs within the trial and a long ISI between the trials. But decades ago, it was demonstrated that the long ISI could be imposed within the trial and that reinforcement was not a magic property of an undefined class of stimuli. The various delay paradigms can be organized into three categories according to where the delay is imposed on an animal coping with an instrumental task (Garcia & Levine, 1976). In the traditional paradigms where the long-delay occurs between trials (Fig. 2.4a), the probability of a correct response (R) increases from one trial to the next when a deprived animal is coping with an experimental situation (S) in order to obtain a goal (US). Obviously the animal must remember the S-R-US association from one trial to the next over lapses of hours or even days. Thorndike (1913) believed that the reinforcing US "stamped in" the S-R bond enabling it to endure over the long period. But Premack (1965) demonstrated that R and US activities are interchangeable. For example, under the usual paradigmatic arrangement, thirsty rats run in order to drink, but under another arrangement, restless rats drink in order to run. These data demonstrated that there is no essential difference between R and US activities, both are dependent upon state of the organism.

OTHER LONG-DELAY PARADIGMS

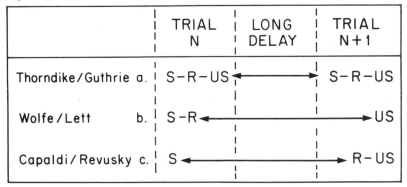

FIG. 2.4. Long-delayed learning is ubiquitous: Thorndike-Guthrie; Elements within trials are separated by brief ISIs but trials are separated by prolonged ISIs. Thorndike believed the US reinforced the within-trial associations enabling them to endure between trials. Guthrie believed removing the subject from the trial situation protected the within-trial associations from between-trial interference. Wolfe-Lett; Long delays can be imposed in within-trial associations with the aid of a marking stimulus applied immediately after R. The same effect can be obtained classically with an intervening stimulus between CS and US. Capaldi-Revusky; In delayed alternation, a stimulus or response (S) from yesterday's trial serves as a memorial cue for today's trial (R-US). Adapted from Garcia and Levine (1976).

Guthrie (1940) thought the unique function of the reinforcing US was to remove the animal from S after it emitted R. For example, when a hungry animal hits the trigger releasing it from a problem box to find food outside the animal escapes both confinement and hunger. The animal's interim behavior is associated with the free-feeding situation and thus does not interfere with behavior associated with the problem box. When the cat is returned to S it merely retrieves R, the last act of the previous trial. Revusky's (1971) concurrent interference theory elaborates on this notion and applies it to long-delay paradigms.

Wolfe (1934) provided some experimental evidence for learning with long delays between R and the US (Fig. 2.4b). After a correct R in a T-maze the rat was removed to a distinctive box and the food US was presented after a delay. After an error the rat was placed in another box without food. Rats learned the discrimination. More recently Lett (1975) provided some definitive evidence in a similar paradigm. Immediately after R the rat was removed to the box for the delay period and then fed in the stem of the T-maze. Animals learned with delays of one hour between R and US. Garcia and Levine (1976) suggested the essential function of the US is to "flag" R making it easy to retrieve on the next trial. Lieberman, McIntosh and Thomas (1979) demonstrated that rats will learn if they are simply handled after R and then wait in the maze for food. If handling is delayed for 30 s after R the animals fail to learn. Auditory and visual signals work as well as handling. These authors said that immediate stimulation "marks" the relevant R. Finally, there is evidence that monkeys and rats will display one-trial long-delay conditioned preference in a variation of this paradigm (D'Amato & Buckiewitz, 1980; Safarjan & D'Amato, 1981).

The delayed alternation paradigm is evidence for learning with long delays between S and R (Fig. 2.4c). Given a choice between two alternatives, the animal must reject the one visited on the last trial, thus the memory of R on the previous trial is the cue for the alternative R on the present trial (e.g., Petrinovich & Bolles, 1954). More recently Capaldi (1967) provided the US in a runway on alternate days and rats learned to adjust their running speeds appropriately. Revusky (1974) used black and white runways; on any given day, food was contingent upon the color of the runway on the day before; these rats also adjusted their running speeds appropriately even though a full day was interpolated between S and R.

Semantic variation and conceptual confusion

Two classical paradigms which resemble the Wolfe-Lett instrumental version (Fig. 2.4b) have made a recent appearance in the literature and as a result we now have at least five labels for essentially one function: flag, marker, bridge, catalyst and intervening stimulus (IS). Naturally I prefer the first term because it is mine and has a cognitive ring to it, but in keeping with Tolman's ecumenical spirit I will use the last term because it has a neutral procedural connotation. Two studies are variants of the "autoshaping" paradigm (Kaplan & Hearst, 1982; Rescorla, 1982). If a key or target is lighted (CS) just before grain (US) is delivered, hungry pigeons will peck at the key-light demonstrating an expectation of food much as Pavlov's dog did when salivating at the bell (Brown & Jenkins, 1968). In the current versions, there is a temporal gap between the CS and the US and the effect of inserting an IS into the gap is tested. An IS completely filling the gap appears to be most effective, be it visual or auditory. If the IS does not completely fill the gap then the IS is more effective if it is presented adjacent to the CS rather than later in the gap, an effect similar to that reported by Lieberman et al. (1979) in the instrumental version of the paradigm.

The other study makes use of the "conditioned suppression" or "conditioned emotional response" paradigm (Pearce, Nicholas, Dickinson, 1981). If a signal (CS) is followed by an electrocutaneous shock (US) while a rat is working at a lever for food, the animal will cease working in order to defend its skin against shock (Estes & Skinner, 1941). The insertion of an IS into a 30s gap between the CS and the US resulted in superior conditioned suppression to the CS. Unfortunately Pearce et al. (1981) refer to their effect as "potentiation" and draw a parallel between their effect and taste-potentiation. In a similar fashion. Rescorla (1982) discussing his "catalytic" effect recalls taste-potentiation and refers to "within-compound associations".

I say "unfortunately" because now we have one term and a single explanation for two completely different phenomena. When an IS is inserted into the CS-US interval. it serves as an aid to cognitive processing of the CS-US association. Presumably any two signals can be used either as the CS or the IS and their roles can be interchanged in the interest of experimental symmetry. But taste-potentiation is asymmetrical, e.g., taste potentiates odor but odor does nothing for taste, more like a CS-US interaction than a CS-IS relationship.

When all is said about long delays in learning, one glaring temporal discrepancy remains. If we consider the interval between the CS and whatever S follows it, be it an IS or a US, we find a brief gap which is best measured in seconds. The same is true for the interval between an instrumental R and the S which follows it. be it a marking S or a reinforcing S. On the other hand. if we consider the interval between a taste US and a nauseous FB we find a prolonged interval *without supporting intervention* which can best be measured in hours (Garcia & Holder, 1985). Finally, when a response towards a distinctive arm in a T-maze and a drink of saccharin are both followed by delayed nausea affording a direct comparison, delayed reinforcement has a substantially greater negative impact upon acquisition of the instrumental response than upon acquisition of the saccharin aversion (D'Amato & Safarjan, 1981).

Smell and taste of poison by the rat pup

Taste is the most powerful arbiter of what is fit to eat. smell comes next (Garcia & Koelling, 1967; Palmerino et al., 1980; Taukulis & St.George,

1982). The natural relationship between olfaction and gustation owes much to the peripheral placement of the external nares just above the mouth. This contiguous external arrangement, so advantageous in foraging and feeding, is common to most terrestrial vertebrates. Internally, olfactory receptors located primarily in the respiratory system send fibers to limbic and paleocortical regions of the brain; while gustatory receptors located in the alimentray system send fibers to the nucleus solitarius in the brainstem which receives visceral fibers also. Thus the anatomical arrangement also indicates odor plays a plastic CS role while taste plays a reflexive US role in feeding.

Olfaction presents a puzzle in the developing rat. The rat pup has a functional olfactory system at birth and uses odors in its search for the nourishing nipple of its mother. It is soon able to associate odor with nausea (Rudy & Cheatle, 1977) and uses its experience with odor to choose its food (Bronstein & Crockett, 1976). Since there is evidence indicating the taste buds are not functional in the first week of life (Bradley & Minstretta, 1971) it is likely that the odor component of flavor is an effective CS for fetal rats (Smotherman, 1982) and neonate rats (Gemberling & Domjan, 1982). Neonate rats apparently are able to connect odor with shock to the belly before they connect odor with shock to the hips (Haroutunian & Campbell, 1979). Shock to the belly may stimulate the end organs of the vagus. These data indicate that the critical job for the neonate is feeding and the pup's skin protection, like temperature regulation, is left largely to the mother for the first week of life. On the other hand, although the adult rat is described as a macrosmatic animal and it is constantly sniffing, it makes poor use of odor cues to modulate its food preferences. It can make effective use of odor to defend against shock (Hankins et al., 1976) but it prefers taste and taste-potentiated odor cues to defend against poison (Hankins et al., 1973; Palmerino et al., 1980; Rusiniak et al., 1979). It is almost as if the pup and the adult are two different species of rat.

A recent report supports the idea that rat pups may utilize odors more effectively than adults to modulate feeding (Molina, Serwatka, Spear, & Spear, 1985). The odor of alcohol arising from beneath the mesh floor is paired with either nausea or recuperation from nausea induced by apomorphine. When given a two bottle preference test the pups exhibit appropriate hedonic shifts depressing or increasing consumption respectively, but the adult rats do not. When given a spatial test both young and old rats avoid the place with nauseous odor and, if anything, the adult rats are superior to the pups in associate the odor with place but unlike the pups they do not utilize the odor for ingestive purposes.

When the flavor of a solution is paired with the nausea and recuperation from apomorphine adult rats are able to modulate their preferences appropriately in either direction (Green & Garcia, 1971). Furthermore, hungry adult rats can also modulate their preference for arbitrary flavors paired with entubed doses of alcohol. Given too high a dose they will exhibit an aversion, but they will display a preference for lower doses presumably because alcohol has the caloric value to satisfy their hunger (Sherman, Hickis, Rice, Rusiniak, & Garcia, 1983). In contrast, thirsty rats will develop an aversion for the same dose preferred by the hungry rats indicating that in the absence of the compensatory caloric need, the nauseous property of the low alcohol dose is unmasked (Deems, Oetting, Sherman, & Garcia, 1986). But in all these cases, the adult rat has taste (as well as odor) on which to base its hedonic adjustment, so there is no conflict with Molina et al. (1985) where odor alone is paired with nausea.

There may be a critical period for consolidation of olfactory function in the developing mammal. The rat pup lives in a rich odorous environment with its mother and its littermates. In contrast, the adult rat is confined to a barren individual laboratory cage after it is weaned. When rats are given "enriched" experience with odor and taste after weaning, their adult capacity to utilize odor in response to delayed nausea is vastly improved (see potentiation point 10 above). It appears that uniform tasting tap water with its constant weak odor may impose a sensory deprivation upon the animal specifically disrupting the capacity to use odor to modulate ingestive behavior. This conclusion is supported by comparisons of wild-bred species with laboratory-bred species (Garcia et al., 1977). Wild-bred canines quickly incorporate odor and other cues to avoid poison prey at a distance. So do wild-bred hawks. But laboratory-bred rats and ferrets persist in tracking and attacking prey which they reject in disgust as food. Humans reared in richly flavored environments like wild-bred species, can easily acquire an aversion for familiar foods (Bernstein & Sigmundi, 1980). Novelty may be more critical for laboratory rats and other creatures reared in barren environments.

Phylogenetic evidence for skin-gut duality

The skin-gut dichotomy is the natural result of the selective pressure of the food chain in which all organisms including plants are involved. In order to survive and reproduce, all organisms evolved coping mechanisms for obtaining nutrients and protective mechanisms to keep from becoming nutrients (Garcia y Robertson & Garcia, 1985). Learning within each of these systems has been extensively studied in both invertebrate and vertebrate species (Garcia et al., 1984). The interest of psychologists has traditionally centered on out closest relatives, the mammalian and avian species, but a study of anatomical structure of our more distant relatives is very revealing. The dichotomy is clear in Herrick's (1948) description of anatomical structure and function of the two systems in the salamander. Essentially, auditory and cutaneous receptors send inputs to the somatosensory neuropil which sends its outputs to the skeletal motor system. Taste and visceral receptors send inputs to the viscereosensory neuropil which sends its outputs to the smooth musculature of the viscera. Appropriately, the olfactory and visual afferents send inputs to both neuropils (Garcia, et al., 1985).

An odor CS gated into the gut-defense system and associated with a taste US and emetic FB, will thereafter produce gaping and retching.

When channelled into the skin-defense system and associated with electrocutaneous shock the same odor CS will thereafter elicit pawing defense reactions (Garcia et al., 1984). The FB in the skin defense system appears to be endogenous analgesia. Rats exposed to shock will exhibit an opioid analgiesic response which is reversed by the opioid antagonist, naltrexone. The timid rat will show the same reaction when a cat is present or when a frightened conspecific is present (Fanselow, 1985; Fanselow & Boakes, 1982; Lester & Fanselow, 1985).

There is a striking parallel between endogenous analgesia FB and nauseous FB. First, both FBs operate to "devaluate" their respected USs by hedonic shifting, albeit in opposing directions, nauseous FB makes the taste US less tolerable while analgesic FB renders pain more tolerable. Second, neither function is impaired when the animals are rendered unconscious; for example, delayed lithium injections (FB) delivered to rats under pentobarbital anesthesia induce CTA for substances tasted (US) earlier (Bermúdez-Rattoni, Forthman Quick, Sanchez, Perez, & Garcia, in press). Likewise, pentobarbital has no effect upon endogenous analgesia (FB) induced by continuous foot-shock (US) (Terman, Shavit, Lewis, Canon & Liebeskind, 1984). In both cases, motives are modified in absence of any memory of the affective US-FB associations, a feature often discussed in historic theories of unconscious motivation (Garcia & Holder, 1984).

The feeding sequence is divided into a CS-US vs US-FB dichotomy with the mouth as the transition zone. The dual function is obvious in the anatomical structure of an even more distant relative, the bullhead catfish (Finger & Morita, 1985). The taste receptors in the anterior part of the tongue and the lips send afferent pulses via the facial nerve to a lobe in the medulla whose efferents flow to spinal motor control serving CS-US instrumental behavior. The afferents from taste buds at the back of the mouth and palate course via the vagal nerve to a nearby lobe whose efferents flow to muscular swallowing mechanisms serving US-FB consummation. If the facial lobes are bilaterally lesioned, the fish cannot find food in its watery environment but will swallow food placed in its mouth. If the vagal lobes are lesioned, the fish can locate and seize the food but will not swallow it. As the food accumulates in its mouth the fish simply releases it.

The same ambivalent behavior observed in snakes attacking toxic frogs has been described to me by George T. Barthalmus and David K. Woodworth (personal communication, February 4, 1986). When the African clawed frog is seized by the hognose snake in an experimental arena, the snake stops all ingestive jaw movements within 30 s. Holding on to the frog, the snake slows all movements as the frog struggles releasing a viscous creamy mucus. After a half hour or more, the snake increases its ingestive jaw movements and its general locomotor activity: The frog escapes but the snake does not pursue; instead it acts as if it has just eaten exhibiting the exaggerated tongue flicking and the yawning jaw actions used to re-align its mandibles after swallowing a bulky prey.

Analysis of the frog's mucosa reveals a number of peptides which are involved in digestion and satiety in vertebrates. When the frog is injected with epinephrine it will secrete copious amounts of mucosa and snakes attacking the excited slimy amphibian will promptly release it. But when the excited frog is washed clean of mucus, the snake will immediately swallow it. The authors offer this intriguing hypothesis: The frog's mucous may produce satiety in the reptile with low doses and toxicosis with higher doses. That may be the way chemical protection gradually evolves; those organisms which can quickly induce satiety in foragers stand a better chance of having their kind survive. Perhaps it is no accident that many phytochemicals such as caffeine, nicotine and digitalis cause a loss of appetite in vertebrates including humans, thus providing an excellent protection against continued munching by foragers.

While these two systems are obscured by the complex elaboration of the medulla during evolution, two homologous subsystems can be discerned in mammals (Hamilton & Norgren, 1984). The facial nerves innervating the anterior taste buds in the mouth project to the rostral part of the nucleus solitarius while the glossopharyngeal nerves innervating the posterior taste buds on the palate and pharynx terminate in the caudal part of the same nucleus. Sweet is the natural signal for nutrition and bitter is the natural signal for poison (Garcia & Hankins, 1975). Significantly, sweet receptors predominate in the front of the mouth and thus are intimately associated with the reinforcing US terminating the coping phase of feeding. Bitter receptors predominate in the back of the mouth and thus are intimately associated with ingestion FB and the affective phase of feeding.

Experimental evidence for skin-gut duality

The same duality of function was observed in the behavior of thirsty rats using a shuttlebox with a water bottle at each end and a shock grid as the floor (Garcia & Hankins, 1977). One bottle contained a strong saccharin solution (7.0 gm/liter) and the other contained water. Half the animals were rendered anosmic with zinc sulphate treatment of the nasal mucosa. Preference for saccharin was measured in a two-bottle test before and after saccharin-shock training. Ten trials a day were conducted for nine days with immediate shock contingent upon licking saccharin on five trials unsystematically interspersed with five water shock-free trials. The shock was just intense enough to interrupt drinking without causing complete cessation of drinking in the apparatus. Total fluid intake was measured each day and displayed as a saccharin preference score in Fig. 2.5.

With repeated trials both groups learned to associate saccharin with shock. The intact rats had a definite advantage because they could stretch their necks and sniff the spout and turn away without licking. Note also that the intact rats show about a 42% preference for saccharin flavor in the first encounter with the novel fluid while anosmic animals exhibit about a 72% preference. This indicates that neophobic reactions to foods may be primarily due to olfaction with its extensive afferents to the limbic system. However the anosmic rats also acquired the taste-shock association with repeated trials. When tested in the home cages, both

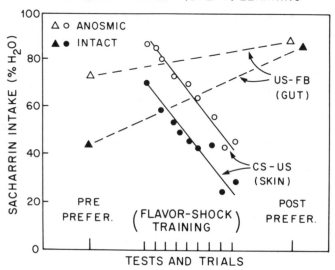

FIG. 2.5. Learning in opposing directions to the same flavor in the antagonistic skin and gut systems: Flavor is used as a CS for foot-shock in a two-way avoidance alley for thirsty rats. The rats learn to use flavor as a CS to defend against the foot-shock US in context of the shock apparatus (flavor-shock training). But when tested in their home cages after shock training, the rats exhibit an increased preference (post-prefer) for the flavor US which reduced thirst (FB) while they were learning to run away from it. Cognitive and effective conditioning proceeds simultaneously in opposing directions (adapted from Garcia & Hanskins, 1977).

groups demonstrated an increased preference for the same saccharin solution they were turning away from in the shuttlebox (Garcia & Hankins, 1977).

Brett (1977) demonstrated the same effect using the conditioned suppression method. She trained a number of groups employing various paired and unpaired stimuli but the anosmic rats tested with bitter water are the most interesting in this context. A naturally aversive quinine solution was paired with shock at the midpoint of a one min drinking trial for five trials unsystematically interspersed with five safe water trials each day for ten days; taste was the only cue for shock. As training progressed, bitter water consumption decreased prior to shock but increased during the post-shock period until it reached water baseline levels. The thirsty rats learned to use the bitter taste to defend their skin from external shock and simultaneously acquired an increased preference for the bitter water slaking their internal need. CS-US cognitive learning and US-FB affective conditioning progressed concurrently in opposing directions with surprisingly little interference.

Similar splits in function are also evident in a completely different experimental context, namely the transfer of conditioned inhibition in mammals (Finch, 1985). In classical inhibitory training, a negative correlation between the CS and US is established, then the inhibitory CS is tested in other situations (Rescorla, 1969, 1974). When acid serves as the aversive US in one phase and food serves as the appetitive US in another phase, conditioned inhibition transfers from acid to food (Pavlov, 1927). This is as expected, since both USs impinge upon the internal (gut) system eliciting adaptive salivary responses: One thin and watery to dilute the acid, the other thick and slimy to lubricate the food bolus for swallowing.

Rescorla and Holland (1977) also found transfer within the feeding (gut) system using two CSs (auditory and visual) which evoked two different conditioned responses supporting the notion that the components of the bright-noisy CS are comparable but distinctive cues (see Fig. 2.2a). In contrast, they found no transfer of inhibition between US food training and US shock training. They deemed food and shock to be "antagonistic" USs supporting the hypothesis that the internal (gut) system and external (skin) system operate somewhat independently (see Fig. 2.2d). Rescorla and Holland, as well as Konorski (1967), concluded that conditioned inhibitory training was specific to the US, as opposed to the CS. However, Nieto (1984) and Nieto and Boakes (1983) reported transfer of inhibition between training phases involving "two different aversive USs". Significantly, they used shock and a loud horn as the aversive stimuli. In our scheme of things, noise and shock are not antagonistic, they are compatible stimuli impinging upon the skin defense system evoking adaptive "startle" responses and defensive motor movements.

Cognitive-affective duality in human reactions

The cognitive-affective dichotomy is evident in human experimental studies. Zajonc (1980) reviews a vast literature extending over the last century and culminating in the modern investigations of cognitive processing. He entitles his study: "Feeling and thinking: Preferences need no inferences" and concludes that affect and cognition are controlled by separate and partially independent psychobiological systems. Zajonc offers some suggestions concerning the different neural substrates for affect and cognition in the mammalian brain but it is his synthesis of the behavioral data which is most illuminating. Contrary to common sense, affective reactions often occur without prior perceptual and cognitive processing.

The primacy of affect over cognition is not accepted by Lazarus (1982, 1984) who defends the primacy of cognition over affect. The issue has become quite complex and my brief discussion is unlikely to resolve anything. Essentially Lazarus is impressed with findings indicating that emotions always appear to have some traces of cognitive appraisal in human judgements. He agrees that affective reactions (e.g., galvanic skin response) can occur without accurate identification of the target stimuli but he says, that errors more often than not, bear a semantic (i.e., cognitive) relation to correct response. Zajonc (1980, 1984) is impressed by evidence indicating that human subjects can make reliable affective judgements (like-dislike ratings) in total absence of any recognition memory (new-old judgements). I am impressed with the fact that in humans the connection between cognition and affect is a two-way street: Affects are often followed by cognitive rationalizations and cognitive suggestions can be used to induce or block nauseous FB (Burish, Redd, & Carey, 1985; Redd, Burish, & Andrykowski, 1985). This implies that the two systems are reciprocally inhibitory to some degree but that each can affect the other and often act in concert.

Independent systems and the primacy of affect over cognition in some situations raises the following question: "How do you know you don't like 'it' when you do not know what 'it' is?" Taste aversions also display the same logical failure. John Locke points to a honey aversion without memory raising the question, "How can you dislike the taste of honey when you cannot remember that it made you ill?" (Garcia, 1981). But cognitions, memories and awareness of the US-FB association are not necessary, simple disgust will best protect the gut. Cognitive appreciation of peripheral or shadowy stimuli is not necessary, a simple fear or phobia will protect the skin nicely. Nature is not constrained by semantic logic, it follows the functional logic of evolution: First evolve an affective system dependent upon *what* is good or bad for survival; later evolve a cognitive system to identify what *that* is!

In the main, I have dealt with cathexes (US-FB) for food. When hungry, warm spicy food brings repletion and becomes more palatable; its savory glow tinges our thoughts and the society of our mother's kitchen. But Tolman (1949) offers us a general proposition for which other homeostatic examples can be found (Cabanac, 1979; Garcia & Holder, 1985). If the homeostatic core is cold, a warm US applied to our skin is pleasant, because that warmth is useful in regulating our internal temperature. When courtship is new, the odors emanating from our mate seem odd and novel, but after the consummation of desire, the odors become erotic. Thus, we become addicted to our ethnic cuisine, attached to our old sweaters and bonded to our lovers.

Temperature regulation offers the most favorable opportunity to test the CS-US-FB scheme anew. A cue or signal from a warm place may serve as the CS. Skin temperature sensitivity may operate as a US, and internal core temperature may provide the FB. When the core temperature is low, the FB adjusts the hedonic tone of the skin so that a warm sweater is a pleasant US, as the core temperature rises the warm US becomes unpleasant and the sweater comes off. After the sweater repeatedly protects us from the cold, it becomes a positive US eliciting vasomotor FB reactions preparing us for cold weather, thus an old sweater is preferred to a new sweater not evoking the appropriate FB. One can ask questions comparable to those asked in conditioned taste aversions. What is the relative effectiveness of the distal CSs (e.g., sights, sounds, odors) for temperature reinforcement? Can a distal CS emanating from a warm place be directly associated with FB from a cool core when skin US temperature is held constant (see Fig. 2.3a)? Will the CS be potentiated by a warm US drawing positive FB from the cool core (see Fig. 2.3b)?

Tolman's historic legacy

Tolman's (1949) address to the Division of General Psychology may not have been his most significant contribution but it reveals the complexity of his sometimes bewildering intellect, the depth of his concern for his chosen field and the warmth of his completely captivating personality. His scope is catholic and his appeal is ecumenical. He attributes his motives to social needs rather than mystical ferver. Free of condescension, he generously cites both his theoretical friends and his reputed rivals calling for the unification of psychology.

To the gestalt theorists, he credits the perceptually organized nature of his field expectancies as follows:

> It is, of course, the facts of latent learning plus the facts of taking short-cuts and roundabouts, when forced or permitted, which have driven me and others to the notion that when a rat, or a human being, is practiced in a particular set of activities in a particular environment, an essential part of what he acquires is an expectancy, a sign-Gestalt, a cognitive structure, a cognitive map (to use some of the terms which have been suggested) relative to that environment.

Tolman agreed with Clark Hull, usually considered his main theoretical rival, as far as positive cathexes were concerned saying:

> It would seem that animals or human beings acquire positive cathexes for new foods, drinks, sex-objects, etc., by trying out the corresponding consummatory responses upon such objects and finding that they work--that, in short, the consummatory reactions to these new objects do reduce the corresponding drives. Hence, here I believe, with Hull, in the efficacy of reinforcement or need reduction.

Tolman went on to discuss how the hypothetical cathexis might be tested. He required a dog with esophogeal and stomach fistulas so that the taste of food could be separated from its nutritional value in order to test whether a dog's hunger could be "cathected" to the food "re-introduced" into its stomach and "de-cathected" to the food which is not. CTA research has now supplied the crucial data for positive and negative cathexes with simpler procedures.

In his discussion of "motor patterns" he refers to Guthrie's "interference hypothesis" of one-trial learning.

Any response (i.e., any movement) which goes off will, according to Guthrie, get conditioned on a single trial to whatever stimuli were then present. Therefore a movement which removes the individual from out the range of those stimuli tends to be the one which remains conditioned to them because no other movements have a chance to occur and to displace it. A motor pattern thus gets learned without reinforcement.

But alas, Tolman was a man of his time; he accepts Guthrie and Horton's (1946) explanation of cats learning a stereotyped motor pattern by "getting out of their hit-the-barber-pole type of problem-box" in order to get food outside. But so did the rest of us until Moore and Stuttard (1979) showed us that the cats were simply greeting the experimenters in the hereditary flank and head-rubbing ritual of feline species.

Tolman was aware that species differences were important pointing out the necessity for fact-finding concerning; (1) the perceptual sensitivity of the species obviously important in building up field expectancies, (2) their ability to connect and associate different parts of the field, (3) their abilities to form inferences and expectancies beyond the specific parts of the field in which they were exercised. Unfortunately he did not do much with either comparative behavior or brain mechanisms. Though the psychology department at Berkeley was housed in the Life Sciences building at that time, Tolman and most of his colleauges were interested in human problems. Animals were merely convenient "stand-ins" for humans in the experimental laboratory: So do I study rats to better understand my fellows. Tolman's concern for humanity is most clear when he pokes fun at himself. He rarely made fun of others. Sometimes I wish I could be so generous.

Why do I want to complicate things; why do I not want one simple set of laws for all learning? I do not know. But I suppose it must be due to some funny erroneous equivalence belief on my part to the effect that being sweeping and comprehensive, though vague, is equivalent to more love from others than being narrow and precise. No doubt, any good clinician would be able to trace this back to some sort of nasty traumatic experience in my early childhood. Let, then, the clinician unravel this sort of causal relationship in me or in others and I will attempt to show him its analogue in rats, or at least in chimpanzees or perhaps dogs.

ACKNOWLEDGEMENT

This research was supported by the following grants: USPHS NIH NS11618 and HDO5958. Send requests for reprints to Dr. John Garcia, Neuropsychiatric Institute, Rm. 58-228, University of California at Los Angeles, Department of Psychology, Franz Hall, Los Angeles, CA 90024.

REFERENCES

Allison, J., Larson, D., & Jensen, D. (1967). Acquired fear, brightness preference and one-way shuttlebox performance. *Psychonomic Science, 8,* 267-270.

Archer, T., Sjöden, P. O., & Nilsson, L.-G. (1985). Contextual control of taste-aversion conditioning and extinction. In P. D. Balsam & A. Tomie (Eds.), *Context and learning,* pp. 225-271. Hillsdale, NJ: Lawrence Erlbaum.

Archer, T., Sjöden, P. O., Nilsson, L.-G., & Carter, N. (1980). Exteroceptive context in taste-aversion conditioning and extinction: Odour, cage, and bottle stimuli. *Quarterly Journal of Experimental Psychology, 32,* 197-214.

Barker, L. M., Best, M. R., & Domjan, M. (Eds.). (1977). *Learning mechanisms in food selection.* Waco, TX: Baylor University Press.

Bermudez-Rattoni, F. (1985). *Flavor-illness aversions: Potentiation of odor by taste is regulated by the limbic system.* Unpublished doctoral dissertation, University of California, Los Angeles.

Bermudez-Rattoni, F., Forthman Quick, D. L., Sanchez, M. A., Perez, J. L., & Garcia, J. (in press). Odor and taste aversions conditioned in anesthetized rats. *Behavioral Neuroscience.*

Bermudez-Rattoni, F., Rusiniak, K. W., & Garcia, J. (1983). Flavor-illness aversions: Potentiation of odor by taste is disrupted by application of novocaine into amygdala. *Behavioral and Neural Biology, 37,* 61-75.

Bernstein, I. L. (1978). Learned taste aversions in children receiving chemotheraphy. *Science, 24,* 185-208.

Bernstein, I. L. (1985). Learned food aversions in the progression of cancer and its treatment. *Annals of the New York Academy of Sciences, 443,* 365-380.

Bernstein, I. L., & Sigmundi, R. A. (1980). Tumor anorexia: A learned food aversion? *Science, 209,* 416-418.

Best, M. R., Batson, J. D., Meachum, C. L., Brown, E. R., & Ringer, M. (1985). Characteristics of taste-mediated environmental potentiation in rats. *Learning and Motivation, 16,* 190-209.

Best, P. J., Best, M. R., & Henggeler, S. (1977). The contribution of environmental non-ingestive cues in conditioning with aversive internal consequences. In L. M. Barker, M. R. Best & M. Domjan (Eds.), *Learning mechanisms in food selection,* pp. 371-393. Waco, TX: Baylor University Press.

Bolles, R. C. (1985). Associative processes in the formation of conditioned food aversions: An emerging functionalism. *Annals of the New York Academy of Sciences, 443,* 1-7.

Bouton, M. E., & Whiting, M. R. (1982). Simultaneous odor-taste ande-taste compounds in poison-avoidance learning. *Learning and Motivation, 13,* 472-494.

Bradley, R. M., & Minstretta, C. M. (1971). The morphological and functional development of fetal gustatory receptors. In N. Emmlin & Y. Zotterman (Eds.), *Oral physiology,* pp. 239-253. NY:

Pergamon.

Braveman, N., & Bronstein, P. (Eds.). (1985). *Experimental assessments and clinical applications of conditioned taste aversions*, Vol. 443. NY: New York Academy of Sciences.

Brett, L. P. (1977). *Experimental extensions of the cue-consequence aversive conditioning paradigm*. Unpublished doctoral dissertation, University of California at Los Angeles.

Brett, L. P., Hankins, W. G., & Garcia, J. (1976). Prey-lithium aversions. III. Buteo hawks. *Behavioral Biology, 17*, 87-98.

Bronstein, P., & Crockett, D. (1976). Exposure to the odor of food determines the eating preference of rat pups. *Behavioral Biology, 18*, 387-392.

Brown, P. L., & Jenkins, H. M. (1968). Autoshaping of the pigenon's key-peck. *Journal of the Experimental Analysis of Behavior, 2*, 1-8.

Buchwald, N. A., Garcia, J., Feder, B. H., & Bach-y-Rita, G. (1964). Ionizing radiation as a perceptual and aversive stimulus. II. Electrophysiological studies. In T. J. Haley & R. S. Ryder (Eds.), *The second international symposium on the responses of the nervous system to ionizing radiation*, pp. 688-699. Boston, MA: Little, Brown Publishing Co.

Buresova, O., & Bures, J. (1973). Cortical and subcortical components of the conditioned saccharin aversion. *Physiology and Behavior, 11*, 435-439.

Burish, T. G., Levy, S. M., & Meyerowitz, B. E. (Eds.) (1985). *Cancer, nutrition and eating behavior: A biobehavioral perspective.* Hillsdale, NJ: Lawrence Erlbaum.

Burish, T. G., Redd, W. H., & Carey, M. P. (1985). In T. G. Burish, S. M. Levy & B. E. Meyerowitz (Eds.), *Cancer, nutrition and eating behavior: A biobehavioral perspective*, pp. 205-224. Hillsdale, NJ: Lawrence Erlbaum.

Cabanac, M. (1979). Sensory pleasure. *Quarterly Review of Biology, 54*, 1-29.

Cannon, D. S., Best, M. R., Batson, J. D., Brown, E. R., Rubenstein,rell, L. E. (1985). Interfering with taste aversion learning in rats: The role of associative interference. *Appetite, 6*(1), 1-19.

Capaldi, E. (1967). A sequential hypothesis of instrumental learning. In K. Spence & J. Spence (Eds.), *The psychology of learning and motivation: Advances in Research and theory*, Vol. 1, pp. 67-156. NY: Academic Press.

Chen, J. S., & Amsel, A. (1980). Recall (versus recognition) of taste and immunization against aversive taste anticipations based on illness. *Science, 209*, 851-853.

Clarke, J. C., Westbrook, R. F., & Irwing, J. (1979). Potentiation instead of overshadowing in the pigeon. *Behavioral and Neural Biology, 25*, 18-29.

Coburn, K. L., Garcia, J., Kiefer, S. W., & Rusiniak, K. W. (1984). Taste potentiation of poisoned odor by temporal contiguity. *Behavioral Neuroscience, 98*(5), 813-819.

Colwill, R. M., & Rescorla, R. A. (1985a). Postconditioning devaluation of a reinforcer affects instrumental responding. *Journal of Experimental Psychology: Animal Behavior Processes, 11,* 120-132.

Colwill, R. M., & Rescorla, R. A. (1985b). Instrumental responding remains sensitive to reinforcer devaluation after extensive training. *Journal of Experimental Psychology: Animal Behavior Processes, 11,* 520-536.

D'Amato, M. R., & Safarjan, W. R. (1981). Differential effects of delay of reinforcement on acquisition of affective and instrumental responses. *Animal Learning and Behavior, 9*(2), 209-215.

D'Amato, M. R., & Buckiewicz, J. (1980). Long-delay, one-trial conditioned preference and retention in monkeys (Cebus apella). *Animal Learning and Behavior, 8*(3), 359-362.

Davis, J. L., & Bures, J. (1972). Disruption of saccharin-aversion learning in rats by cortical spreading depression in the CS-US interval. *Journal of Comparative and Physiological Psychology, 80,* 398-402.

Deems, D. A., Oetting, R. L., Sherman, J. E., & Garcia, J. (1986). Hungry, but not thirsty, rats prefer flavors paired with ethanol. *Physiology and Behavior, 36,* 141-144.

Dietz, M. N., & Capretta, P. J. (1966). Modification of sugar and sugar-saccharin preferences in rats as a function of electric shock to the mouth. *Proceedings of the American Psychological Association* (New York), September, 161-162.

Domjan, M. (1983). Biological constraints on instrumental and classical conditioning: Implications for a general process theory. In G. H. Bower (Ed.), *The psychology of learning and motivation,* Vol. 17, pp. 215-277. New York: Academic Press.

Domjan, M. (1985). Cue-consequence specificity and long-delay learning revisited. *Annals of the New York Academy of Sciences, 443,* 54-66.

Durlach, P. J., & Rescorla, R. A. (1980). Potentiation rather than overshadowing in flavor-aversion learning: An analysis in terms of within-compound associations. *Journal of Experimental Psychology: Animal Behavior Processes, 6,* 175-187.

Egger, M. D., & Miller, N. E. (1963). When is a reward reinforcing? An experimental study of the information hypothesis. *Journal of Comparative and Physiological Psychology, 56,* 132-137.

Ellins, S. R., Cramer, R. E., & Whitmore, C. (1985). Taste potentiation of auditory aversions in rats: A case for spatial contiguity. *Journal of Comparative Psychology, 99.* 108-111.

Ellins, S. R., & Von Kluge, S. (1987). Extinction, spontaneous recovery, and preexposure effects of taste-potentiated lithium chloride induced auditory food aversions in rats. *Behavioral Neuroscience, 101,* 164-169.

Fanselow, M. S. (1985). Odors released by stressed rats produce opioid analgesia in unstressed rats. *Behavioral Neuroscience, 99,* 589-592.

Fanselow, M. S., & Boakes, M. P. (1982). Conditioned fear-induced opiate analgesia on the formalin test: Evidence for two aversive motivational systems. *Learning and Motivation, 13,* 200-221.

Estes, W. K., & Skinner, B. F. (1941). Some quantitative properties of anxiety. *Journal of Experimental Psychology, 29,* 390-400.

Finch, B. (1985). *Effects of excitatory contexts on conditioned inhibition in taste aversion.* Unpublished doctoral prospectus, University of California at Los Angeles.

Finger, T. E., & Morita, Y. (1985). Two gustatory system: Facial and vagal gustatory nuclei have different brainstem connections. *Science, 227,* 776-778.

Forthman Quick, D. (1984). *Reduction of crop damage by Olive Baboons (Papio anubis): The feasibility of conditioned taste aversion.* Unpublished doctoral dissertation, University of California at Los Angeles.

Fudim, O. K. (1978). Sensory preconditioning of flavors with a formalin-produced sodium need. *Journal of Experimental Psychology: Animal Behavior Processes, 4,* 276-285.

Galef, B. G., & Osborne, B. (1978). Novel taste facilitation of the association of visual cues with toxicosis in rats. *Journal of Comparative and Physiological Psychology, 92,* 907-916.

Garcia, J. (1981). Tilting at the paper mills of academe. *American Psychologist, 36,* 149-158.

Garcia, J., & Brett, L. P. (1977). Conditioned responses to food odor and taste in rats and wild predators. In M. Kare (Ed.), *The chemical senses and nutrition,* pp. 227-289. NY: Academic Press.

Garcia, J., & Ervin, F. R. (1968). Gustatory-visceral and telereceptor-cutaneous conditioning. Adaptation in the internal and external milieus. *Communications in Behavioral Biology, Part A, 1,* 389-415.

Garcia, J., Ervin, F. R., & Koelling, R. A. (1966). Learning with prolonged delay of reinforcement. *Psychonomic Science, 5,* 121-122.

Garcia, J., Forthman Quick, D., & White, B. (1984). Conditioned disgust and fear from mollusk to monkey. In D. L. Alkon & J. Farley (Eds.), *Primary neural substrates of learning and behavioral change,* pp. 47-61. Cambridge, MA: Cambridge University Press.

Garcia, J., & Garcia y Robertson, R. (1985). The evolution of learning mechanisms. *American Psychological Association, Master Lecture Series,* Vol. 4, pp. 191-243. Washington, D.C.: American Psychological Association.

Garcia, J., & Hankins, W. G. (1975). The evolution of bitter and the acquisition of toxiphobia. In D. Denton & J. Coghlan (Eds.), *Olfaction and taste,* Vol. 5, pp. 39-41. New York: Academic Press.

Garcia, J., & Hankins, W. G. (1977). On the origin of food aversion paradigms. In L. Baker, M. Domjan & M. Best (Eds.), *Learning mechanisms in food selection,* pp. 3-19. Waco, TX: Baylor University Press.

Garcia, J., Hankins, W. G., & Rusiniak, K. W. (1974). Behavioral regulation of the milieu interne in man and rat. *Science, 185,* 824-831.

Garcia, J., Hankins, W. G., Robinson, J. H., & Vogt, J. L. (1972).

Baitshyness: Tests of CS-US mediation. *Physiology and Behavior, 3,* 807-810.

Garcia, J., & Holder, M. D. (1985). Time, space and value. *Human Neurobiology, 4,* 81-89.

Garcia, J., & Kimeldorf, D. J. (1957). Temporal relationships within the conditioning of a saccharin aversion through radiation exposure. *Journal of Comparative Physiology and Psychology, 50,* 180-183.

Garcia, J., Kimeldorf, D. J., & Hunt. E. L. (1956). Spatial avoidance behavior in the rat as a result of exposure to ionizing radiation. *British Journal of Radiation Research, 5,* 79-87.

Garcia, J., Kimeldorf, D. J., & Hunt, E. L. (1961). The use of ionizing radiation as a motivating stimulus. *Psychological Review, 68,* 383-395.

Garcia, J., & Koelling, R. A. (1966). The relation of cue to consequence in avoidance learning. *Psychonomic Science, 5,* 123-124.

Garcia, J., & Koelling, R. A. (1967). A comparison of aversions induced by x-rays, drugs, and toxins. *Radiation Research Supplement, 7,* 439-450.

Garcia, J., Kovner, R., & Green, K. F. (1970). Cue properties vs. palatability of flavors in avoidance learning. *Psychonomic Science, 20,* 313-314.

Garcia, J., Lasiter, P. S., Bermudez-Rattoni, F., & Deems, D. A. (1985). A general theory of aversion learning. *Annals of the New York Academy of Sciences, 443,* 8-21.

Garcia, J., & Levine, M. S. (1976). Learning paradigms and the structure of the organism. In M. Rosenzweig & E. Bennet (Eds.), *Neural mechanisms of learning and memory,* pp. 421-442. New York: Academic Press.

Garcia, J., McGowan, B. K., & Green, K. F. (1972). Biological constraints on conditioning. In A. Black & W. Prokasy (Eds.), *Classical conditioning,* pp.3-27. Hamilton, Ontario: McMaster University.

Garcia, J., McGowan, B. K., Ervin, F. R., & Koelling, R. A. (1968).Their relative effectiveness as a function of the reinforcer. *Science, 160,* 794-795.

Garcia, J., & Rusiniak, K. W. (1977). Visceral feedback and the taste signal. *NATO conference series* (III-human factors) *Biofeedback and behavior,* Vol 2, pp. 59-71. New York: Plenum Press.

Garcia, J., & Rusiniak, K. W. (1980). What the nose learns from the mouth. In D. Muller-Schwarze & R. N. Silverstein (Eds.), *Chemical signals.* New York: Plenum.

Garcia, J., Rusiniak, K. W., & Brett, L. P. (1977). Conditioning food-illness aversions in wild animals: Caveant canonici. In H. Davis & H. Hurowitz (Eds.), *Operant Pavlovian interactions,* pp 273-316. Hillsdale: NJ: Lawrence Erlbaum.

Garcia, J., Rusiniak, K. W., Kiefer, S. W., & Bermúdez-Rattoni, F. (1982). The neural integration of feeding and drinking habits. In C. D. Woody (Ed.), *Conditioning: Representation of involved neural functions,* pp. 567-579. New York: Plenum.

Garcia y Robertson, R., & Garcia, J. (1985). X-Rays and learned taste aversions: Historical and psychological ramifications. In T. G. Burish, S. M. Levy & B. E. Meyerowitz (Eds.), *Cancer, nutrition and eating behavior: A biobehavioral perspective*, pp. 11-41. Hillsdale, NJ: Lawrence Erlbaum.

Garcia y Robertson, R., & Garcia, J. (1988). Darwin was a learning theorist. In R. C. Bolles & M. D. Beecher (Eds.), *Evolution and learning*, pp. 17-38. Hillsdale, NJ: Lawrence Erlbaum.

Gemberling, G. A., & Domjan, M. (1982). Selective associations in one-day-old rats: Taste-toxicosis and texture-shock avoidance learning. *Journal of Comparative and Physiological Psychology, 96*, 105-113.

Green, K. F., & Garcia, J. (1971). Recuperation from illness: Flavor enhancement in rats. *Science, 173*, 749-751.

Grill, H. J., & Norgren, R. (1978). The taste reactivity test. I. Mimetic responses to gustatory stimuli in neurologically normal rats. *Brain Research, 143*, 263-279.

Guthrie, E. R. (1940). Association and the law of effect. *Psychological Review, 47*, 127-128.

Guthrie, E. R., & Horton, G. P. (1946). *Cats in a puzzle box.* New York: Rinehart.

Hamilton, R. B., & Norgren, R. (1984). Central projections of gustatory nerves in the rat. *Journal of Comparative Neurology, 222*, 560-577.

Hankins, W. G., Garcia, J., & Rusiniak, K. W. (1973). Dissociation of odor and taste in baitshyness. *Behavioral Biology, 8*, 407-419.

Hankins, W. G., Rusiniak, K. W., & Garcia, J. (1976). Dissociation of odor and taste in shock-avoidance learning. *Behavioral Biology, 18*, 345-358.

Harris, L. J., Clay, J., Hargreaves, F. J., & Ward, A. (1933). Appetite and choice of diet. The ability of the vitamin B deficient rat to discriminate between diets containing and lacking the vitamin. *Proceedings of the Royal Society of London, 63*, 161-190.

Haroutunian, V., & Campbell, B. A. (1979). Emergence of interoceptiveive control of behavior in rats. *Science, 205*, 927-929.

Herrick, C. J. (1948). *The brain of the tiger salamander.* Chicago, IL: University of Chicago Press.

Holder, M. D., & Garcia, J. (1978). Role of temporal order and odor intensity in taste-potentiated odor aversions. *Behavioral Neuroscience.*

Holland, P. C. (1981). Acquisition of representation-mediated conditioned food aversions. *Learning and Motivation, 12*, 1-18.

Holland, P. C. (1983). Representation-mediated overshadowing and potentiation of conditioned aversions. *Journal of Experimental Psychology: Animal Behavior Processes, 9*(1), 1-13.

Holman, E. W. (1975). Some conditions for the dissociation of consummatory and instrumental behavior in rats. *Learning and Motivation, 6*, 358-366.

Kalat, J. W., & Rozin, P. (1971). Role of interference in taste-aversion learning. *Journal of Comparative and Physiological Psychology, 77*, 53-58.

Kamin, L. J. (1969). Predictability, surprise, attention and conditioning. In B. Campbell & R. M. Church (Eds.), *Punishment and aversive behavior*, pp. 279-296. NY: Appleton-Century-Crofts.

Kaplan, P. S., & Hearst, E. (1982). Bridging temporal gaps between CS US in autoshaping: Insertion of other stimuli before during, and after CS: *Journal of Experimental Psychology, 8*(2), 187-203.

Kiefer, S. W., Rusiniak K. W., & Garcia, J. (1982). Flavor-illness aversions: Gustatory neocortex ablations disrupt taste but not taste-potentiated odor cues. *Journal of Comparative and Physiological Psychology, 96*(4), 540-548.

Konorski, J. (1967). *Integrative activity of the brain* Chicago, IL: University of Chicago Press.

Krane, R. V., & Wagner, A. R. (1975). Taste aversion learning with a delayed shock US: Implications of the "generality of the laws of learning." *Journal of Comparative and Physiological Psychology, 88*, 882-889.

Krieckhaus, E. E., & Wolf, G. (1968). Acquisition of sodium by rats: Interaction of innate mechanism and latent learning. *Journal of Comparative and Physiological Psychology, 65*(2). 197-201.

Lasiter, P. S., & Braun, J. J. (1981). Shock facilitation of taste aversion learning. *Behaivoral and Neural Biology, 32*, 277-281.

Lazarus, R. S. (1982). Thoughts on the relations between emotion and cognition. *American Psychologist, 37*(9), 1019-1024.

Lazarus, R. S. (1984). On the primacy of cognition. *American Psychologist, 39*(2), 124-129.

Lester, L. S., & Fanselow. M. S. (1985). Exposure to a cat produces opioid analgesia in rats. *Behavior Neuroscience, 99*, 756-759.

Lett, B. T. (1975). Long delay learning in the T-maze. *Learning and Motivation, 6*, 80-90.

Lett, B. T. (1985a) The painlike effect of gallamine and naloxone differs from sickness induced by lithium chloride. *Behavioral Neuroscience, 99*(1), 145-150.

Lett, B. T. (1985b). Taste potentiation in poison avoidance learning. In M. L. Commons, R. J. Herrnstein & A. R. Wagner (Eds.), *Quantitative analyses of behavior: Vol. 3, acquisition*, pp. 273-293. Cambridge: Ballinger.

Lieberman, D. A., McIntosh, D. C., & Thomas, G. V. (1979). Learningard is delayed: A marking hypothesis. *Journal of Experimental Psychology, 5*(3), 224-242.

Louge, A. W. (1979). Taste aversion and the generality of the laws of learning. *Psychological Bulletin, 86*, 276-296.

Lolordo, V. M., & Furrow, D. R. (1976). Control by the auditory element or the visual element of a compound discriminative stimulus: Effects of feedback. *Journal of the Experimental Analysis of Behavior, 25*, 251-256.

Martin, G. M., & Lett, B. T. (1985). Formation of associations of colored and flavored food with induced sickness in five avian species. *Behavioral and Neural Biology, 43*. 223-237.

Menzel, E. W. (1978). Cognitive mapping in chimpanzees. In S. H.

Hulse, W. K. Honig & H. Fowler (Eds.), *Cognitive processes in animal behavior*, pp. 375-421. Hillsdale, New Jersey: Erlbaum.

Mikulka, P. J., Pitts, E., & Philput, C. (1982). Overshadowing not potentiation in taste aversion conditioning. *Bulletin of the Psychonomic Society, 20*, 101-104.

Molina, J. C., Serwatka, J., Spear, L. P., & Spear, N. E. (1985). Differential ethanol olfactory experiences affect ethanol ingestion in preweanlings but not in older rats. *Behavioral and Neural Biology, 44*, 90-100.

Moore, B. R., & Stuttard, S. (1979). Dr. Guthrie and Felis domesticus or: Tripping over the cat. *Science, 205*, 1031-1033.

Nachman, M. (1970). Learned taste and temperature aversions due to lithium chloride sickness after temporal delays. *Journal of Comparative and Physiological Psychology. 73*, 22-30.

Nachman, M., Rauschenberger, J., & Ashe, J. (1977). Studies of learned aversions using non-gustatory stimuli. In L. M. Barker, M. R. Best & M. Domjan (Eds.), *Learning mechanisms in food selection*, pp. 395-417. Waco, TX: Baylor University Press.

Nieto, J. (1984). Transfer of conditioned inhibition across different aversive reinforcers in the rat. *Learning and Motivation, 15*, 37-57.

Nieto, J., & Boakes, R. A. (1983). The effects of horn devaluation on the transfer of conditioned inhibition between horn and shock. *Revista Mexicana de Analisis de la Conducta, 9*, 145-162.

Olton. D. S. (1977). Spatial memory. *Scientific American, 236*, 82-98.

Palmerino, C. C. (1979). *Associative interactions of odor and taste in illness-induced aversions*. Unpublished doctoral dissertation, University of California, Los Angeles.

Palmerino, C. C., Rusiniak, K. W., & Garcia, J. (1980). Flavor-illness aversions: The peculiar roles of odor and taste in memory for poison. *Science, 208*, 753-755.

Pavlov, I. P. (1927). *Conditioned reflexes*. Oxford: Oxford University Press.

Pearce, J. M., Nicholas, D. J., & Dickinson, A. (1981). The potentiation effect during serial conditioning. *Quarterly Journal of Experimental Psychology, 33*B, 159-179.

Pelchat, M. L., Grill, H. J., Rozin, R., & Jacobs. J. (1983). Quality of acquired responses to tastes by *Rattus Norvegicus* depends on type of associated discomfort. *Journal of Comparative Psychology, 97*, 140-153.

Petrinovich, L., & Bolles, R. (1954). Deprivation states and behavioral attributes. *Journal of Comparative and Physiological Psychology, 47*, 450-453.

Premack, D. (1965). Reinforcement theory. In D. Levine (Ed.), *Nebraska symposium in motivation*, pp. 123-180. Lincoln, NE: University of Nebraska Press.

Poulton, E. B. (1887). The experimental proof of the protective value of color and marking in insects in reference to their vertebrate enemies. *Proceedings of the Zoological Society of London*, pp. 191-274.

Redd, W. H., Burish, T. G., & Andrykowski, M. A. (1985).

Aversiveing and cancer chemotherapy. In T. G. Burish, S. M. Levy & B. E. Meyerowitz (Eds.), *Cancer, nutrition and eating behavior: A biobehavioral perspective*, pp. 117-132. Hillsdale, NJ: Lawrence Erlbaum.

Reicher, M. A., & Holman, E. W. (1977). Location preference and flavor aversion reinforced by amphetamine in rats. *Animal Learning and Behavior, 5*, 343-346.

Rescorla, R. A. (1967). Pavlovian conditioning and its proper control procedures. *Psychological Review, 74*, 71-80.

Rescorla, R. A. (1969). Pavlovian conditioned inhibition. *Psychological Bulletin, 72*, 77-94.

Rescorla, R. A. (1973). Information variables in Pavlovian conditioning. In G. H. Bower (Ed.), *The psychology of learning and motivation*, Vol. 6, pp. 1-46. New York: Academic Press.

Rescorla, R. A. (1974). A model of Pavlovian conditioning. In V. S. Rusinov (Ed.), *Mechanisms of formation and inhibition of conditional reflex*, pp. 25-39. Moscow: Academy of Sciences of the U.S.S.R.

Rescorla, R. A. (1982). Effect of a stimulus intervening between CS and US in autoshaping. *Journal of Experimental Psychology, 8(2)*, 131-141.

Rescorla, R. A., & Holland, P. C. (1977). Associations in Pavlovian conditioned inhibition. *Learning and Motivation, 8*, 429-447.

Revusky, S. H. (1971). The role of interference in association over a delay. In W. Honig & H. James (Eds.), *Animal memory*, pp. 155-213. New York: Academic Press.

Revusky, S. H. (1977). The concurrent interference approach to delay learning. In L. M. Baker, M. R. Best & M. Domjan, M. (Eds.), *Learning mechanisms in food selection*, pp. 319-363. Waco, Texas: Baylor University Press.

Revusky, S. H., & Bedarf, E. W. (1967). Association of illness with the prior consumption of novel foods. *Science, 155*, 219-220.

Richter, C. P. (1943). Total self-regulatory functions in animals and human beings. *Harvey Lecture Series, 38*, 63-103.

Roll, D. L., & Smith, J. C. (1972). Conditioned taste aversion in anesthetized rats. In M. E. P. Seligman & J. L. Hager (Eds.), *Biological boundaries of learning*, pp. 98-102. New York: Appleton-Century-Crofts.

Rosellini, R. A., DeCola, J. P., & Lashley, R. L. (1981). Overshadowing and potentiation of odor by taste: The role of stimulus saliency. Paper presented at the meeting of the Psychonomic Society, Philadelphia.

Rozin, P. (1977). The significance of learning mechanisms in food selection: Some biology, psychology, sociology of science. In L. Barker, M. Domjan & M. Best (Eds.), *Learning mechanisms in food selection*, pp. 557-583. Waco, TX: Baylor University Press.

Rozin, P., & Zellner, D. (1985). The role of Pavlovian conditioning in the acquisition of food likes and dislikes. *Annals of the New York Academy of Sciences, 443*, 189-202.

Rudy, J. W., & Cheatle, M. D. (1977). Odor-aversion learning in neonatal rats. *Science, 198,* 845-846.

Rusiniak, K. W. (1976). *Roles of olfaction and taste in appetitive and consummatory behavior during illness aversion conditioning.* Unpublished doctoral dissertation, University of California at Los Angeles.

Rusiniak, K. W., Garcia, J., Palmerino, C. C., & Cabral, R. J. (1983). Developmental flavor experience affects utilization of odor, not taste in toxiphobic conditioning. *Behavioral and Neural Biology, 39,* 160-180.

Rusiniak, K. W., Hankins, W. G., & Garcia, J. (1976). Baitshyness: Avoidance of the taste without escape from the illness. *Journal of Comparative Physiology and Psychology, 90,* 460-467.

Rusiniak, K. W., Hankins, W. G., Garcia, J., & Brett, L. P. (1979). Flavor-illness aversions: Potentiation of odor by taste in rats. *Behavioral and Neural Biology, 25,* 1-17.

Rusiniak, K. W., Palmerino, C. C., Rice, A. G., Forthman, D. L., & Garcia, J. (1982). Flavor-illness aversions: Potentiation of odor by taste with toxin but not shock in rats. *Journal of Comparative and Physiological Psychology, 96,* 527-539.

Safarjan, W. R., & D'Amato, M. R. (1981). One-trial, long-delay, conditioned preference in rats. *The Psychological Record, 31,* 413-426.

Sherman, J. E., Hickis, C. F., Rice, A. G., Rusiniak, K. W., & Garcia, J. (1983). Preferences and aversions for stimuli paired with ethanol in hungry rats. *Animal Learning and Behavior, 11(11),* 101-106.

Shettleworth, S. J. (1972). Conditioning of domestic chicks to visual and auditory stimuli: Control of drinking by visual stimuli and control of conditioned fear by sound. In M. E. P. Seligman & J. L. Hager (Eds.), *Biological boundaries of learning,* pp. 228-236. NY: Appleton-Century-Crofts.

Shettleworth, S. J. (1983). Memory in food-hoarding birds. *Scientific American, 248,* 201-210.

Smotherman, W. P. (1982). Odor aversion learning by the rat fetus. *Physiology and Behavior, 29,* 769-771.

Solomon, R. L. (1977). An opponent-process theory of motivation, V. Affective dynamics of eating. In L. M. Barker, M. R. Best & M. Domjan (Eds.), *Learning mechanisms in food selection,* pp. 255-269. Waco, TX: Baylor University Press.

Solomon, R. L., & Corbit, J. D. (1974). An opponent-process theory of motivation. *Psychological Review, 81,* 119-145.

Sullivan, L. G. (1979). Long-delay learning with exteroceptive cue and exteroceptive reinforcement in rats. *Australian Journal of Psychology, 31(1),* 21-32.

Taukulis, H., & St. George, S. (1982). Overshadowing of emotional *Learning and Behavior, 10,* 288-292.

Testa, T. J. (1974). Causal relationships and the acquisition of avoidance responses. *Psychological Review, 81(6),* 491-505.

Testa, T. J., & Ternes, J. W. (1977). Specificity of conditioning mechanisms in the modification of food preferences. In L. M. Baker, M. Domjan & M. R. Best (Eds.), *Learning mechanisms in food selection*, pp. 229-253. Waco, TX: Baylor University Press.

Thorndike, E. (1913). *The psychology of learning* (Educational Psychology II). NY: Teachers College.

Tolman, E. C. (1949). There is more than one kind of learning. *Psychological Review, 56,* 144-155.

Tolman, E. C. (1959). Principles of purposive behaviorism. In S. Koch, *Psychology: A study of a science,* Vol. 2, pp. 92-157. NY: McGraw Hill.

Wilson, C. J., Sherman, J. E., & Holman, E. W. (1981). Aversion to reinforcer differentially affects conditioned reinforcement and instrumental responding. *Journal of Experimental Psychology: Animal Behavior Processes, 7,* 165-174.

Wolfe, J. B. (1934). The effect of delayed reward upon learning in the white rat. *Journal of Comparative Psychology, 17,* 1-21.

Zajonc, R. B. (1980). Feeling and thinking: Preferences need no inferences. *American Psychologist, 35*(2), 151-175.

Zajonc, R. B. (1984). On the primacy of affect. *American Psychologist, 39*(2), 117-123.

3 Taste-Aversion Conditioning: The Role of Contextual Stimuli

Per-Olow Sjödén and Trevor Archer
Uppsala University and Umeå University, Sweden

In a series of studies, we have documented the influence of contextual stimuli on the conditioning and extinction of taste-aversions in rats. Our general conclusion is that a contextual compound stimulus consisting of bottles, compartments and an odor element exerts strong control over postconditioning intake of the aversive substance (saccharin). The relative salience of the contextual elements has been demonstrated to be in the order of bottles > compartments > odor, and tongue-tactile bottle stimuli are likely to be the most salient. In a recent comment, Holder (1988) has raised several objections to our conclusions. His main point is that our methodology harbors a serious artifact in that the manipulations of bottle cues have been confounded by the possible influence of a "plastic" taste, emanating from the drinking bottles. In recent experiments we have shown (1) that bottle cues control both the postconditioning intake of saccharin and extinction of the saccharin aversion, and (2) that inhibitory learning of drinking spout characteristics is possible, in spite of the fact that "plastic" taste cues were controlled for. We also have data from a number of studies in which aversions to spout characteristics were produced although all the animals drank water from plastic or glass bottles. Thus, the empirical findings demonstrate that although Holder's criticism may indeed prove to be valid if lacks substance.

In a series of previously unpublished studies, we exposed different groups of animals to a stimulus compound composed of novel bottles and compartments during 1, 2, or 3 saccharin-aversion conditioning trials. The intake of saccharin was then measured in the same or a different context. For the groups tested in a different context (bottles and compartments), the number of conditioning trials did not affect aversion strength. However, for those tested in the conditioning context, a strong and reliable trials effect was evident. The suggested interpretation of these findings is that what rats learn about the aversiveness of the saccharin stimulus is achieved in one trial. On later trials, learning seems to concern the aversiveness of contextual cues only. Furthermore, the aversion to saccharin in the different-context groups was extinguished in one trial, whereas the same-context groups showed a depressed intake during 3-8 test trials, depending upon the number of conditioning trials. Similar results were obtained when bottle cues only were manipulated.

In another series of studies, we used the research paradigm to investigate the influence of neurochemical manipulations on selective attentional processes. The results of several studies demonstrated that forebrain noradrenaline manipulations, using the DSP4- and 6-hydroxydopamine dorsal bundle lesion DNAB, attenuated or antagonised completely the context-dependent latent inhibition effect and the context-mediated sensory preconditioning effect.

Contextual stimuli are most commonly defined as exteroceptive stimuli within an experimental environment that are not purposely correlated with CS and US presentations. In learning experiments, contextual stimuli are often more familiar to the organism than are CSs and USs. Also, contextual stimuli have a more static character, whereas CSs and USs are of a more phasic nature. Examples are lights that illuminate the environment, background noise, odors, and the walls and floor of the test box. When taste substances are employed as CSs, properties of the fluid source (e. g. the fluid container) also need to be considered. In most early studies of associative learning, these kinds of stimuli were usually not varied systematically with CS and US presentations. Neither were analytical experiments performed to ascertain their possible role in the conditioning process. This practice was presumably a consequence of the then prevalent assumption that they acquire no associative strength when conditioning processes take place within the context which they constitute. In spite of its relatively recent nature, the field of taste-aversion learning was dominated by a similar assumption for some time, due mostly to the results of some early studies.

Lately however, considerable efforts have been directed at mapping the contextual influences on various learning phenomena. In a recent overview of the field, Balsam and Tomie (1985) compiled fourteen contributions from various areas of learning such as Pavlovian conditioning, autoshaping, taste-aversion learning, operant responding and drug-state-dependent learning. The topic of contextual influences was to a certain extent considered in some earlier works (e. g. Dickinson, 1980; Estes, 1975), but was not given the prominent role that it has been recently designated. The theoretical importance of an analysis of contextual conditioning phenomena has been amply documented (Estes, 1973, 1975; Rescorla & Wagner, 1972; Wagner, 1976; Wagner & Rescorla, 1972).

Contextual Stimuli in Taste-Aversion Learning: Early Notions

In a now classical taste-aversion learning experiment, Garcia and Koelling (1966) presented rats with a compound CS composed of taste, auditory, and visual elements, which was paired with either an electric shock or an illness-type US. During subsequent testing, rats that had the compound paired with illness avoided only the taste element, whereas rats that had the compound paired with shock avoided only the auditory-visual element. One of several implications of this result was that of a differential associability of interoceptive (taste) and exteroceptive (auditory, visual) stimuli with illness-type USs. Thus, in rats, associations between exteroceptive stimuli and nausea were considered difficult, if not impossible to establish, at least in comparison to taste-nausea associations (Garcia, Kimeldorf, & Hunt, 1961; Green, Holmstrom, & Wollman, 1974). In several other studies, where exteroceptive stimuli were paired with illness, subsequent water intake in the presence of these stimuli was suppressed very little (Domjan & Wilson, 1972; Garcia & Koelling, 1967; Garcia, McGowan, Ervin, & Koelling, 1968).

There are also a large number of subsequent studies in which rats were presented with a taste-auditory-visual compound paired with illness, and which demonstrate that aversions are learned to the taste element but not to the auditory-visual elements (Best, Best, & Mickley, 1973; Garcia, Kovner, & Green, 1970; Hargrave & Bolles, 1971; Larsen & Hyde, 1977; Slotnik, Brown, & Gelhard, 1977; Wilcoxon, Dragoin, & Kral, 1971; Woods, Makous, & Hutton, 1969). On the basis of these findings from experiments in which exteroceptive stimuli were paired with illness either singly or in compound with taste, it was concluded that contextual elements in general were of little or no relevance in the taste-aversion learning paradigm. Thus, it was proposed by Revusky and Garcia (1970) that rats "tend to ignore external events (p. 22)" and that, according to Garcia, Hankins, and Rusiniak (1974) "...time-space contextual information...is dispensed with as unnecessary (p. 828)" in taste-aversion learning. The independence of taste-aversion learning from contextual stimuli was thought to be one characteristic setting this form of learning apart from more traditional types of associative conditioning, and a neoevolutionary theoretical framework was proposed to handle this observation (Seligman, 1970). It was suggested that "Rats are prepared, by virtue of their evolutionary history, to associate tastes with malaise...Further, rats are contraprepared to associate exteroceptive events with nausea (p.409)".

In this tradition, Garcia and coworkers have developed a neuroethological theory of taste-aversion learning based on knowledge concerning the natural habitats of species and neural pathways involved in interoceptive and exteroceptive stimulation (Garcia, Lasiter, Bermudez-Rattoni, & Deems, 1985). In the 1985-version of the theory, the role of contextual stimulus elements is not discussed. However, a plausible interpretation of Figure 2 in Garcia and coworkers (1985) seems to be that exteroceptive contextual events are not available for associations with toxic USs. In a more recent version (Garcia, this volume) it is at least acknowledged that noise stimuli may come to control aversion strength by way of potentiation. Thus, the finding of an unequal associability of taste and visual-auditory CSs with illness and shock USs (the "Garcia effect") seems amply documented. In the preceding studies, the exteroceptive stimuli were mostly presented in compound with taste, and no efforts were made to study the influence of more static features of the environment. This procedural choice was dictated by the main interest of this research: to investigate the relative roles of interoceptive and exteroceptive stimulus events in aversively motivated behavior in general. However, the conclusions from this research regarding the role of contextual stimuli in taste-aversion learning were too far ranging in view of the procedures employed. We maintain that the role of static as well as phasic contextual stimuli in taste-aversion learning needs to be examined with other procedures and experimental designs.

Contextual effects in taste-aversion learning: Procedures

We define the central problem in the area of contextual influences on taste-aversion learning as follows: Does the presence or absence of contextual stimuli (e. g. during conditioning) influence whether and to what extent the animal "attributes" the cause of an illness experience to a preceding taste stimulus (as tested e. g. during extinction)? The central concern in the study of contextual stimulus control is thus the effect of one stimulus on the control of behavior exercised by other stimuli (e. g. nominal CSs) (Thomas, 1985).

A straightforward way of investigating the influence of contextual stimuli in taste-aversion learning was suggested by Estes' (1973) model of memory and conditioning, i. e. testing of postconditioning aversion strength in the presence and absence of the conditioning background context. We chose to vary some aspects of contextual stimuli in a systematic fashion during the phases of acquisition and extinction of taste aversions. Our initial experiments studied the role of stimuli pertaining to: (1) the bottle in which the taste CS is presented; (2) the animal housing environment in which the taste CS is consumed; and (3) an odor component. In some of the experiments, we employed a conditioning context consisting of these several components and then studied the extinction of the taste aversion in situations where none, one or more of the conditioning stimulus elements were present. In some experiments, we retested the animals in the conditioning context after their taste aversion was extinguished in contexts characterized by a varying number of conditioning stimulus components.

The basic design used in these experiments is as follows: Rats were first trained to drink a daily water ration during a 30-min period per day. On the taste-aversion conditioning trials, a .2% saccharin solution was substituted for water and an intraperitoneal .15M lithium chloride (LiCl) solution (10 ml/kg bodyweight) was administered within 15-20 min of the end of saccharin drinking. Manipulations of contextual stimuli consisting of an animal compartment and an odor element were achieved by presenting this stimulus compound either on a 24-hr basis beginning at the first saccharin-conditioning trial, or only during the 30-min saccharin-drinking periods. Contextual bottle stimuli were always presented only in conjunction with the saccharin presentations.

After conditioning, saccharin aversions were extinguished in the presence of either the entire contextual stimulus compound or some, one or none of its elements. Daily 30-min saccharin-drinking periods constituted extinction trials. A context-dependent conditioning effect is said to occur if, during extinction, the saccharin intake of animals drinking in the presence of the same context as during conditioning is less than that of animals not drinking in the presence of contextual conditioning cues. Postextinction saccharin preference tests (one bottle of saccharin vs. one bottle of water) were performed in the presence of the entire conditioning context, and/or the extinction context of each specific group. A context-dependent extinction effect is defined as a lower saccharin preference in groups not exposed to conditioning contextual cues during extinction as compared to those that had drunk saccharin in the conditioning context during the extinction phase.

Contextual effects in taste-aversion learning: A demonstration

In our first demonstration of contextual effects (Archer, Sjödén, Nilsson, & Carter 1979b), four groups of rats (n = 6) were given two 30-min presentations of a saccharin solution followed either by a LiCl injection (3 groups), or by a sodium chloride (NaCl) solution (1 group). All animals were placed in an unfamiliar context during a 6-day drinking training period prior to conditioning. The unfamiliar context consisted of a darkened, opaque plastic box, in which a thin layer of menthol-smelling ointment was smeared on one inner wall to give a distinct odor stimulus. In these "contextual" compartments, water was presented in "noisy" bottles with metal nozzles that had a 6-mm hole at the tip and contained two small metal balls, which created considerable noise when the animals licked the nozzles. Beginning at the first conditioning trial, the animals were returned to "normal" compartments, consisting of individual Perspex cages with metal grid covers, no explicit odor stimulus, and fluids presented in "silent" standard glass bottles with metal nozzles having a 2-mm hole at the tip. They remained in these cages on a 24-hr basis during conditioning. Thus, cage and odor stimuli were present on a 24-hr basis, whereas the bottles (also considered to be a contextual aspect for taste presentations) were present only during saccharin drinking. The animals had previously experienced the cages during a 2-week period of acclimatization to laboratory conditions.

All animals were given saccharin + LiCl (or saccharin + NaCl) pairings in relatively unfamiliar contexts. Group labels refer to: (1) the number of conditioning trials (viz., 2), and (2) whether they were placed in the same (S) or a different (D) context during saccharin-aversion extinction as during conditioning. In addition, W indicates that water was presented instead of saccharin during the extinction phase, and C (control) alludes to the fact that this group was given NaCl instead of LiCl at conditioning.

The results are illustrated in Figure 3.1. The data from the extinction phase (E1-E5) indicate that the background stimuli of the conditioning phase exerted considerable control over the amount of fluid drunk during extinction (Fig. 3.1, left-hand panel). Thus, only Group 2S showed a strong and consistent saccharin aversion in comparison to Groups 2DW (water) and 2DC (saccharin), whereas Group 2D (saccharin) evidenced an aversion only on E1. A context-specific saccharin aversion is clearly indicated. After the extinction phase, three preference tests were performed, the two first in the conditioning context of all groups ("normal" cages, no odor, "silent" bottles) and the third in the context prevailing during the extinction phase ("contextual" compartments, mentholated odor, "noisy" bottles). The preference test data (Fig 3.1, right-hand panel) illustrate that extinction of the saccharin aversion in a context different from that of the conditioning trials (Group 2D) did not result in a decrease of the aversion in the conditioning context (T1 and T2). However, reinstatement of the extinction context for Group 2D on T3 yielded no evidence of a saccharin aversion. These observations warrant the conclusion that a context-specific extinction effect was demonstrated.

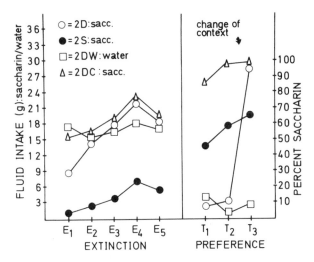

FIG. 3.1. Fluid intake during extinction phase (left) and percentage saccharin preference on preference tests (right) for Groups 2D, 2S, 2DW, and 2DC. Fluids presented during extinction are indicated in the left-hand panel. (Copyright 1979 Psychonomic Society, Inc. Reprinted by permission of the publisher from T. Archer, P. O. Sjödén, L. G. Nilsson, & N. Carter, Role of exteroceptive background context in taste-aversion conditioning and extinction, Animal Learning and Behavior, 1979, 7, 17-22.)

In a second experiment of the same study (Archer et al., 1979b), we switched the background stimuli across conditioning and extinction phases, so that conditioning took place in "contextual" compartments, and extinction in "normal" cages. Also, the effects of one versus two trials were investigated. The results were essentially the same and the context-dependent conditioning effect was smaller after one than after two conditioning trials.

On the basis of these results, we concluded that the background context of the conditioning trial exerts a major control over the amount of saccharin consumed on subsequent one-bottle tests. In fact, evidence of a saccharin aversion was obtained on a number of extinction tests only when the background contexts of the conditioning and extinction trials were identical. Moreover, the background context present during the extinction phase largely determined the degree of aversion on subsequent preference tests. Thus, the importance of contextual stimuli was clearly illustrated, whereas the specific stimulus components exerting contextual control and the precise nature of this control could not be decided from the results of the first study (Archer et al., 1979b).

Further studies of contextual effects

The background stimuli used in our first studies consisted of a compound of visual, auditory, tactual, and olfactory elements. In two studies (Archer, Sjödén, & Carter, 1979a; Archer, Sjödén, Nilsson, & Carter, 1980), we attempted to reach a specification of the relative importance of odor, bottle, and compartment stimuli for the contextual control of learned taste aversions. The purpose of the first experiment (Archer et al., 1980) was to compare the degree of control over subsequent saccharin aversion exerted by an odor stimulus (menthol) and by compartment+bottle elements present on a saccharin-aversion conditioning trial. Thus, saccharin-LiCl pairings were given either in the presence of a novel odor or a novel compartment+drinking bottle. The main results were that the odor stimulus of the conditioning trial did not control saccharin intake during extinction. In contrast, the compartment+bottle contextual compound did so to a considerable extent. Thus, a strong and reliable context-dependent conditioning effect was evident for the compartment+bottle compound but not for the odor element. Furthermore, the compound was found to yield a significant context-dependent extinction effect as opposed to the odor stimulus.

To pinpoint more precisely which aspect of the compartment+bottle compound that controls postconditoning saccharin intake, we varied each of these elements separately in a further experiment (Archer et al., 1980). The presence of the conditioning compartment+bottle compound during extinction resulted in a lesser saccharin intake than when these stimuli were absent. These results also suggest that the presence of the bottle element alone resulted in a suppression of saccharin intake at least on the first extinction trial, whereas there was no suppression due to the compartment alone. The same pattern of results was replicated during the postextinction preference tests, but the control exerted by the bottle cue was considerably stronger than on extinction tests.

The bottle stimulus employed in the present studies provides the animals with contextual elements pertaining to several sensory modalities. Apart from differences of tongue-tactile stimulation arising from the use of nozzles of different sizes, and steel balls in the case of "noisy" bottles, a difference of auditory stimulation is created by the clicking noise produced when drinking from the "noisy" bottles. In a further study (Archer et al., 1979a), we investigated the possible effect of the clicking sound on postconditioning saccharin intake. We found no evidence of an effect of the auditory element neither during extinction nor during postconditioning preference tests. Bottle stimuli were again demonstrated to exert strong control. Thus, tongue-tactile stimuli remain as the likely basis for the contextual bottle control over learned taste aversions.

From these data, it seems that stimuli arising from the animal compartment are ignored in this situation. However, in further studies we have demonstrated (1) a strong context-dependent extinction effect but no conditioning effect of compartmental stimuli, provided that familiar bottles were used (Archer & Sjödén, 1981), and (2) significant context-dependent effects of compartmental stimuli (Archer, Sjödén, & Nilsson, 1985, Fig. 9.5), provided that two-bottle tests are used to measure saccharin intake. Thus, exteroceptive control over taste-aversion strength can be demonstrated provided a suitable methodology is chosen.

Contextual effects: Conclusions from previous studies

On the basis of the results from the studies presented above we propose the following main conclusions: A contextual compound stimulus consisting of bottles, compartments and an odor element was demonstrated to exert strong control over postconditioning saccharin intake. Context-dependent conditioning as well as extinction effects were observed. This indicates that rats learn about contextual stimuli both during acquisition and extinction of taste aversions. The relative salience of the contextual elements was demonstrated to be in the order of bottles > compartments > odor, and tongue-tactile stimuli are likely to be the most salient.

A number of further studies of contextual control of learned saccharin aversions in rats have produced data compatible with the following additional conclusions: (1) Rats seem to learn more readily about those contextual events that are present during CS-periods (drinking) than about those presented during US-periods (Archer, Sjödén, & Nilsson, 1984). However, evidence for context-US associations were also obtained (Archer & Sjödén, 1982; Archer et al., 1984); (2) Novel contextual stimuli appear to gain significantly more associative strength at saccharin-aversion conditioning trials than do familiar contextual stimuli. This relationship is quantitative rather than qualitative (Archer & Sjödén, 1980, 1981; Sjödén, & Archer, 1981); (3) The contextual effects demonstrated are of an associative nature rather than the result of nonassociative influences (e.g. resulting from varying degrees of novelty of the extinction context) (Sjödén, & Archer, 1981); (4) Taste stimuli can be shown to potentiate the conditioning of an aversion to bottle stimuli in the taste-aversion learning paradigm (Sjödén & Archer, 1983); (5) Contextual elements can be used to support second-order conditioning as well as sensory preconditioning of a taste aversion, further illustrating that context-US associations can be formed (Archer & Sjödén, 1982).

A possible challenge: Methodological confounding

In a recent comment, specifically adressing four of our studies (Archer et al., 1980; Archer et al., 1979a, b; Sjödén & Archer, 1983), Holder (1988) has raised several objections to our conclusions. The objections were based upon perceived problems with our experimental methodology. Since Holder's criticism is, if uncontested, potentially serious for the status of most of our research, we find it essential to deal with it here.

Among the four studies discussed by Holder (1988), there is one to which he seems to take particular exception (Sjödén & Archer, 1983). In that study, we reported six experiments investigating the roles of taste and bottle stimuli in taste-aversion learning in rats. Specifically, we found that a taste stimulus (saccharin) was more salient than stimuli from the drinking bottle when paired singly with illness (LiCl). When a novel compound stimulus consisting of saccharin and bottle elements was paired with illness, the bottle element acquired greater aversive strength than the taste. Finally, in an overshadowing/potentiation paradigm, we found that the taste stimulus potentiated conditioning to the bottle stimulus. Thus, animals that had experienced the taste + bottle compound paired with illness evidenced a stronger aversion to the bottle than did animals for which the bottle alone had been paired with illness.

At the heart of Holder's criticism is the suggestion that our methodology harbors a serious artifact. Since the "noisy" bottles that we have used throughout our studies were always made of plastic, and the "silent" ones were made of glass, Holder (1988) suggests that the saccharin may have tasted differently when taken from plastic as opposed to glass containers. Thus, a taste difference, rather than a difference of tongue-tactile stimulation may have formed the basis for the rats' discriminative behavior.

Meeting the challenge: Experiment 1

The most effective argument against Holder's proposal of an artifact should, of course, be based on empirical data. Such a demonstration should show that rats can form an aversion to saccharin which is specific to the drinking spout used, irrespective of the material of which the fluid container is made.

We have performed two experiments to specifically address this question (Sjödén & Archer, 1988). Both experiments employed our standard methodology with the following exceptions. Two types of fluid containers were used: one made of glass and one made of plastic. Both types could be fitted with "noisy" or "silent" spouts. The "noisy" spouts had a 6-mm wide opening at the tip and contained two stainless steel balls with a diameter of 6.3 mm. The "silent" spouts were standard stainless steel spouts with a 2-mm opening at the tip.

   Method. Four groups of animals were employed (n = 8). Groups GS and GD (G = glass) drank saccharin from glass bottles at conditioning, whereas Groups PS and PD (P = plastic) drank from plastic bottles. All bottles were fitted with "noisy" spouts. During the subsequent extinction period, Groups GS and PS (S = same) continued their saccharin intake from the same ("noisy") spouts as during conditioning, whereas the "noisy" spouts were replaced by "silent" spouts for Groups GD and PD (D = different). Five extinction tests were employed. During postextinction preference tests, all animals were given two bottles, one with saccharin and one with water for 8 hours. Groups GS and GD were given glass bottles, and Groups PS and PD plastic bottles. All bottles were fitted with "noisy" spouts, i. e. the same kind as was used at conditioning. The percent preference for saccharin in relation to total fluid intake was computed.

   Split-plot analyses of variance were run separately for the conditioning and extinction phases. Nonparametric statistics were used for the preference test data.

   Results. The results are presented in Figure 3.2. During conditioning, there was a significant effect of Groups [F (3,28) = 5.5, p <.01], but the Tukey HSD-test indicated no pairwise between-group differences. Thus, there were no differences between the S and D groups drinking from glass or from plastic bottles.

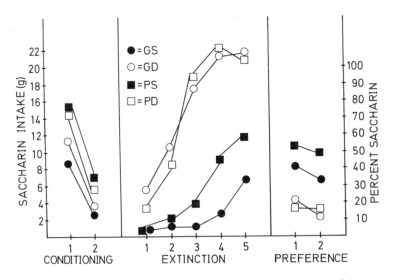

FIG. 3.2. Saccharin intake during conditioning, extinction and preference tests for Groups GS, GD, PS, and PD of Experiment 1. (Copyright 1988 Psychonomic Society, Inc. Reprinted by permission of the publisher from P. O. Sjödén & T. Archer, Exteroceptive cues in taste-aversion learning, no artifact: Reply to Holder, Animal Learning and Behavior, 1988.)

The extinction data indicate that the presence (S groups) or absence (D groups) of the drinking spout employed during conditioning heavily influenced saccharin intake. There was a Groups by Trials interaction [F (12,112) = 6.6, p <.01]. HSD-tests revealed significant GS < GD differences on extinction trials 2-5, and PS < PD differences on trials 3-5. Thus, the change of drinking spout affected saccharin intake from glass as well as from plastic bottles.

The analysis of preference test data was complicated by several strongly skewed distributions for what reason the Mann-Whitney U-test was used. U-values varied between 12 and 15 for all within-trial GS > GD and PS > PD comparisons (p <.05). This indicates that the animals experiencing a drinking spout during extinction, which was different from that at conditioning, retained their aversion to a higher degree than those having the conditioning spout during extinction as well. Thus, spout-specific conditioning as well as extinction effects were demonstrated in spite of the fact that a possible "plastic taste" was controlled for. Thus, we feel we can safely reject Holder's (1988) suggestion that the results of our previous studies are due to an artifact of our experimental methodology.

Defeating the challenge: Experiment 2

In previous studies, we have demonstrated that contextual stimuli are salient enough in taste-aversion learning to support second-order as well as sensory preconditioning (Archer, Cotic, & Järbe, 1986; Archer & Sjödén, 1982). Instead of replicating these studies with the "plastic taste" controlled for, we decided to explore whether or not another well-documented phenomenon could be shown for contextual bottle stimuli with proper controls executed.

It has been repeatedly shown that the preconditioning presentation of a potential CS retards subsequent conditioning and facilitates extinction of that CS (Mackintosh, 1974). This phenomenon has been termed latent inhibition, and it has been shown also after taste preexposure in taste-aversion learning (Nachman, 1970; Revusky & Bedarf, 1967; Wittlin & Brookshire, 1968). Our aim was to show that preexposure to a specific drinking spout retards the establishment of an aversion to saccharin drunk from that type of spout, although "plastic taste" was controlled for.

Method. Thirty-six male Sprague-Dawley rats were randomly assigned to four groups. Before conditioning, four daily trials of preexposure to saccharin for 30 min/day were given to all animals in their home cages. Group GP (P = preexposure) was offered saccharin in glass bottles (G = glass) fitted with "noisy" spouts, Group GN (N = no preexposure) was given glass bottles with "silent" spouts, Group PP was given plastic bottles with "noisy" spouts (P = plastic), and Group PN received plastic bottles with "silent" spouts. Two conditioning trials were administered on which all groups drank saccharin from "noisy" spouts, G-groups from glass bottles and P-groups from plastic bottles. All groups were then given three postconditioning test trials with the same saccharin/bottle/spout combination as during conditioning.

Results. There were no significant differences between the groups during the preexposure phase or on the first conditioning trial (prior to LiCl injections). Saccharin intake from the second conditioning trial and from the test trials is illustrated in Figure 3.3. If spout characteristics are as salient as we maintain, the preexposure of Groups GP and PP to these cues should serve to reduce aversion strength in comparison to Groups GN and PN. U-tests revealed GP > GN differences of saccharin intake on the second conditioning trial and the first two test trials (U-values between 14 and 18), and PP > PN on the first two test trials (U-values = 11 and 21). Thus, overall, the results verified our prediction based on inhibitory learning to the spout characteristics. Again, there is no possibility that the animals used "plastic" taste cues.

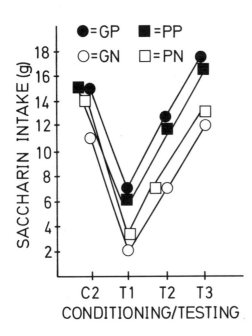

FIG. 3.3. Saccharin intake on the second conditioning trial and three tests trials by Groups GP, GN, PP, and PN of Experiment 2. (Copyright 1988 Psychonomic Society, Inc. Reprinted by permission of the publisher from P. O. Sjödén & T. Archer, Exteroceptive cues in taste-aversion learning, no artifact: Reply to Holder, Animal Learning and Behavior, 1988.)

Holder's contention that rats can discriminate, using taste, water in plastic tubes from water in glass bottles, is not at all unreasonable, but quite mistaken here. Thus we consider it most unlikely as an explanation of the strong effects we have found in many studies. In the first place, in most of our experiments, rats must discriminate not between water in different containers but between saccharin solutions. The saccharin taste may mask any "plastic taste". Secondly, Holder cites a study by Garcia, McGowan and Green (1972) to support his contention of an aversion to an equipment-based stimulus. In that study, rats given radiation as a US were found to have developed an aversion to water stored in plastic bottles. The authors' conclusion (Garcia et al., 1972) that "the rats could discriminate the water in plastic bottles... on the basis of taste (p. 6)", is based on a highly suspect piece of empirical evidence. In fact, the report states that the procedure used was "informal tests by Robert A. Koelling, conducted by hand in the animal room (p. 6)". A less reliable methodology is hard to conceive.

In conclusion, we maintain that tongue-tactile stimulation from drinking is sufficiently salient to serve as the basis for spout-specific taste aversion learning in rats. The data from Experiment 2 extend our previous findings by showing reliable inhibitory learning to drinking spout characteristics in spite of the fact that the animals could not use taste cues from the fluid containers. Thus, Holder's position was demonstrated to be untenable.

Taste-aversion learning: a true one-trial phenomenon?

Our very first demonstration of contextual effects (Archer et al., 1979b) included an experiment in which we compared the effects of one vs. two conditioning trials. Using a contextual compound stimulus consisting of bottles, compartments and an odor, we gave two groups of rats (n = 6) two saccharin-aversion conditioning trials (Groups 2D and 2S), while two groups received one trial (1D and 1S). The results from postconditioning extinction and preference testing are illustrated in Figure 3.4. A context-specific conditioning effect is evidenced by the 2S < 2D and the 1S < 1D differences for extinction trials 1-4 and 2, respectively.

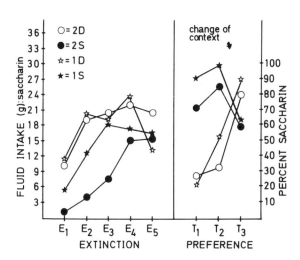

FIG. 3.4. Fluid intake during extinction phase (left) and percentage saccharin preference on preference tests (right) for Groups 2D, 2S, 1D, and 1S. (Copyright 1979 Psychonomic Society, Inc. Reprinted by permission of the publisher from T. Archer, P. O. Sjödén, L. G. Nilsson, & N. Carter, Role of exteroceptive background context in taste-aversion conditioning and extinction, Animal Learning and Behavior, 1979, 7, 17-22.)

With respect to the differential effect of one vs. two conditioning trials, pairwise comparisons indicated that Group 2S drank less saccharin than Group 1S on extinction trials 2 and 3. No differential effects of the number of trials were observed in the D groups. This pattern of results seems to indicate that what is learned about the aversiveness of taste is accomplished in one trial, and is not further increased after two trials, since 2D = 1D throughout. When differential effects of one vs. several trials are observed under normal (i. e. no change of context) conditions, these may be due to the animals learning more about the background context with the higher number of trials since 2S < 1S for extinction trials 2 and 3. In our 1979 (b) article, we ended the comments on this point by saying "Clearly, this pattern of effects needs to be replicated before too much weight is given to it (p. 20)".

We have now performed a series of experiments in order to explore this finding with a larger number of trials and to extend our results.

One, two and three trials: Experiment 3

Method. Six groups of male Sprague-Dawley rats (n = 6) were given 1, 2 or 3 saccharin-aversion conditioning trials in a novel context consisting of "contextual" compartments and "noisy" bottles. Animals were placed in "contextual" compartments or normal cages on a 24-hr basis during the different phases of the study. Saccharin was presented in plastic bottles with "noisy" nozzles (see Archer et al., 1979b). During a one-week preconditioning acclimatization period, animals were housed in normal Perspex cages and were served water in normal "silent" glass bottles. These conditions were also maintained on days when conditioning trials were not given. Conditioning trials were given every other day according to a staggered pattern so that the conditioning trial of the 1-trial groups coincided with the last trial of the 3-trial groups. After conditioning, nine daily saccharin-drinking extinction tests were performed either in the same context as during conditioning (Groups 1S, 2S, and 3S; S = same), or in normal cages with saccharin presented in "silent" bottles (Groups 1D, 2D, and 3D; D = different). All drinking trials up to this point lasted 30 min. Four postextinction preference tests (8 hours), comparing saccharin and water intake from different bottles were performed, the 1st and the 3rd under the same contextual conditions as during conditioning (i. e. two "noisy" bottles in "contextual" compartments), and the 2nd and 4th in normal cages with two "silent" bottles.

Results. The data from the conditioning phase indicated stable and similar degrees of conditioning in all groups on all trials, resulting in a progressively stronger aversion with an increasing number of trials. There were no differences between S and D groups.

Our hypotheses for the extinction phase, based on previous results, was that there would be an increasing degree of suppression of saccharin-drinking in 1 vs. 2 vs. 3 trial groups in the S-condition, but not in the D-condition and that the suppressed intake in the D-groups would be evident only on the first trial. The findings from the extinction phase are illustrated in Figure 3.5. Analysis of variance showed significant main effects and two-factor interactions for all major variables (Trials = 1, 2, 3; Conditions = Same, Different; and Days = 1-9). In addition, there was a Trials by Conditions by Days interaction [F (16, 240) = 2.99, p <.05]. Tukey HSD-tests (p <.05) showed no significant differences between the D-groups on any of the days. However, Group 3S drank less than Group 1S on Days 2-6 and less than Group 2S on Days 3-6. Group 2S drank less than Group 1S on Days 2-5. This pattern of results parallell our previous findings (Archer et al., 1979b) with respect to 1 vs. 2 trials and extend them to 3 trials.

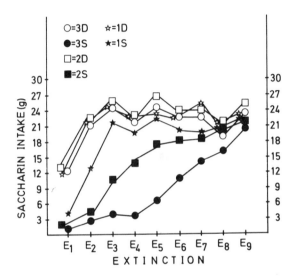

FIG. 3.5. Saccharin intake during extinction of Groups 3D, 3S, 2D, 2S, 1D, and 1S of Experiment 3. Contextual stimuli consisted of compartments and bottles.

Several aspects of these findings deserve comments. Firstly, it is astonishing that we find no more aversion to saccharin as a result of an increasing number of conditioning trials in the D-groups. In addition, the degree of aversion shown by the D-groups is very weak. Secondly, the S-groups show considerable aversions to saccharin, which are in proportion to the number of conditioning trials, and which show the expected strong resistance to extinction. Thus, it seems that when differential effects of the number of conditioning trials are seen under normal (no change of context) experimental conditions, the major portion of associative strength may pertain to the contextual stimuli.

Figure 3.6 illustrates the data from the preference tests. There were no significant effects due to the number of conditioning trials. However, main effects of Conditions and Tests and their interaction [F (3, 90) = 45.0, p <.01] were significant. This was due to the fact that the mean saccharin preference in the S condition was signficantly stronger than in the D condition on Tests 1 and 3, when preference was assessed in the extinction context of the S groups. No differences were detected on Tests 2 and 4. The number of trials at conditioning seems to affect postextinction preference tests data very little. Instead, the presence or absence of the conditioning context during extinction is of great importance.

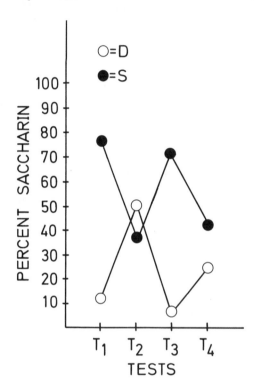

FIG. 3.6. Percentage saccharin preference on preference tests for animals from the D (different context during extinction) and S (same context) conditions of Experiment 3. T_1 and T_3 were performed in the extinction context of the S-animals, and T_2 and T_4 were performed in the context prevailing during extinction for the D-animals. Contextual stimuli consisted of compartments and bottles.

It is tempting to conclude that taste-aversion learning is indeed a one-trial learning phenomenon in a sense that is not usually intended: all that is learned about taste is accomplished in one trial, and nothing more is learned with repeated trials. Instead, additional conditioning seems to concern contextual stimuli only. It may be that multiple-trial groups have a better chance to learn about exteroceptive stimuli than do one-trial groups in taste-aversion learning experiments. The intake of saccharin was rather low on conditioning trials 2 and 3 (means were around 6 and 2 g of saccharin respectively). Thus, the animals in the 2- and 3-trial groups spent very little time drinking and therefore had a chance to learn about other aspects of their environment, in contrast to the 1-trial groups. However, this line of reasoning disregards the fact that the most salient contextual stimulus has been found to be the bottle cue, and more is probably learned about it the more time the animals spend drinking. Execution of the drinking response may therefore be of importance.

Trial-one-learning about taste and the importance of the drinking response: Experiment 4

The results of Experiment 3 are clearcut: Groups tested during extinction with bottles and compartments different from that of conditioning show no differential effects of 1-3 conditioning trials. In order to investigate the hypothesis that taste aversion learning is accomplished in only one trial, and to elucidate the contribution of the drinking response we performed an additional study.

Method. Forty-eight animals were assigned to 8 groups (n = 6). Groups 3D, 3S, 1D, and 1S were identical to those of Experiment 3. Groups 3DW (W = water) and 3SW were treated identically to Groups 3D and 3S with the exception that they drank water instead of saccharin on the last two conditioning trials. They were included in order to test the hypothesis that only one trial is needed to learn about the taste stimulus, and that a similar degree of suppression of saccharin intake can be achieved by (1) 3 saccharin + LiCl trials and (2) 1 saccharin + LiCl trial plus 2 water + LiCl trials in the same context. If the hypothesis is correct, Groups 3DW and 3SW should show aversions similar to those of Groups 3D and 3S, respectively.

An additional pair of groups, 3D$ and 3S$, was included. They first received a regular saccharin + LiCl trial. However, during the last two conditioning trials no drinking fluid was presented. The animals were placed in the compartments and left there for 30 min. after which LiCl injections were administered. Water was given daily to these groups in "silent" bottles in the home cages 6 hours after conditioning. These groups were used to assess the extent of learning about contextual stimuli on conditioning trials 2 and 3 in the absence of performance of the drinking response, or, to put it differently, when there is no chance to learn a water aversion.

In the present study, the staggered pattern of conditioning trials was reversed in comparison to Experiment 3 so that the first (for 1-trial groups: the only) conditioning trial was given on the same day to all groups.

Results. During conditioning, reliable saccharin aversions were obtained in Groups 3D and 3S, whereas no depression of fluid intake on the day after the conditioning trial was evident in Groups 3D$, 3S$, 1D and 1S. Groups 3DW and 3SW showed an increasing depression of fluid intake between trials 2 and 3, on which they drank water in the conditioning context. One day of 30-min. water drinking was interpolated between conditioning and extinction. There were no between-group differences of fluid intake on that day.

The extinction phase data are shown in Figure 3.7 (data from Groups 3D$ and 3 S$ are shown in a separate table to increase clarity). The results from Groups 3D, 3S, 1D and 1S replicated those from the identical groups in Experiment 3. Thus, the 3-trial group showed a significantly greater suppression of saccharin intake than the 1-trial group in the S-condition whereas there was no difference between 3 and 1 trials in the D-condition. Main effects of Conditions (Same, Different), Trials (1 and

3) and Days (1-9) and their two-factor interactions were signficant. Also, the three-factor interaction (Conditions by Trials by Days) was significant [F (24, 320) = 2.53, p < .01]. This was mainly due to the fact that Group 3S drank less saccharin than Group 3D on Days 1-8, and less than Group 3SW on Days 3-7 (HSD-tests, p < .05). Thus, the expectation that Groups 3S and 3SW would show identical results was fulfilled only for the first two extinction trials. However, Groups 3D and 3DW showed virtually identical results. This shows that when extinction is performed in a context different from that of conditioning, two additional saccharin-LiCl pairings (Group 3D) add nothing beyond what is learned on the first trial. This finding is in line with our hypothesis. However, the strong suppression of intake of Group 3S (as compared to Group 3SW) during trials 3-7 seems to involve more than is learned about taste on the first conditioning trial. One possibility is that the presence of the taste stimulus on the latter two conditioning trials may potentiate learning to the contextual elements (cf. Sjödén & Archer, 1983).

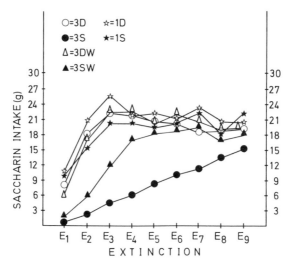

FIG. 3.7. Saccharin intake during extinction of Groups 3D, 3S, 3DW, 3SW, 1D, and 1S of Experiment 4. Compartments and bottles were used as contextual stimuli.

Group 3 SW drank less saccharin than Group 3DW on Days 2-4. This indicates that the two additional trials of water drinking+contextual stimuli+LiCl resulted in an increased aversive strength of some contextual stimulus elements, evident only when testing is performed in the conditioning context. Thus, learning about contextual elements takes place on LiCl-trials following a taste-aversion trial involving the identical elements even when no saccharin is presented.

The mean saccharin intake of Groups 3S$ and 3D$ over extinction trials is shown in Table 3.1. There were no significant differences between the groups on any of the days of testing. This indicates that the drinking response (or water ingestion, but not a water aversion) is essential for learning about contextual elements in taste-aversion learning experiments. This conclusion is further underlined when the intake of Group 3S$ is compared to that of Group 3SW: Group 3SW showed a significantly lower saccharin intake than Group 3S$ on Days 1-4 and 7-8. Thus, the two additional water + LiCl trials experienced by Group 3SW contributed to a depression of saccharin intake beyond that shown by Group 3S$. The latter finding can be accounted for either in terms of the importance of the drinking response or a water aversion.

TABLE 3.1

Mean saccharin intake of Groups 3S$ and 3D$ during extinction trials 1-9

	1	2	3	4	5	6	7	8	9
3S$	14.5	20.0	22.0	22.0	22.0	21.8	24.5	22.3	21.5
3D$	11.5	19.7	22.3	22.3	19.2	21.3	23.7	20.8	19.8

Overall, the patterns of data in Figure 3.7 and Table 3.1 indicate that only Groups 3S and 3SW show any appreciable saccharin aversion. The remaining groups, irrespective of whether they were given 3 saccharin + LiCl trials (3D), or 1 saccharin + LiCl trial plus 2 water + LiCl trials (3DW), or 1 saccharin + LiCl trial plus 2 "placements" in the conditioning context (3S$) or 1 saccharin + LiCl trial only (1D) showed an aversion on the first extinction test day only. It should be noted that the concept of neophobic responses cannot explain the data. The relative familiarity with saccharin in the different groups do not form a pattern parallell to the data. The saccharin intake of these groups did not differ appreciably from each other.

Our conclusions from Experiment 4 are the following: (1) The data at least partly support our contention that taste-aversion learning is largely accomplished on the first trial, and that learning about contextual elements proceeds also on later trials. If additional associative strength is contributed by taste on later trials, this may be in terms of potentiation of learning about exteroceptive stimuli. (2) Performance of the drinking response appears essential for learning about the contextual stimuli used in the present experimental setup. An alternative interpretation in terms if a water aversion cannot be ruled out in the 3SW < 3S$ comparisons.

Replication with bottle cues only: Experiment 5

All multiple-trials experiments sofar were performed with a contextual stimulus compound consisting of compartments and bottles. The bulk of our data from other studies indicates the bottle stimulus to play a major role in contextual control of taste aversions. We therefore decided to replicate Experiment 3 but with bottle cues as the only manipulated contextual element. Thus, groups were identical to those of Experiment 3. "Noisy" bottles were used for conditioning and "silent" bottles served as the "different" context during extinction and preference testing.

Results. The conditioning phase data indicated reliable conditioning in all groups in proportion to the number of trials given. There were no differences between the S and D groups.

The data from extinction are presented in Figure 3.8. There were significant main effects of Trials, Conditions and Days and their two-factor interactions. Also, the Trials by Conditions by Days interaction was significant [F (16, 240) = 17.0, p < .01]. HSD-tests were used to investigate pairwise between-group differences (p < .05).

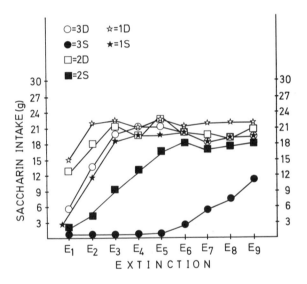

FIG. 3.8. Saccharin intake during extinction of Groups 3D, 3S, 2D, 2S, 1D, and 1S of Experiment 5. Contextual stimuli consisted of bottles.

Overall, the results form a pattern parallel to that of Experiment 3. In the S-condition, aversions were strong and proportional to the number of conditioning trials. Thus, Group 3S drank less saccharin than Groups 2S and 1S on Days 2-9. Group 2S drank less than 1S on Days 2-4. In the D-condition, Group 3D drank less saccharin than Groups 2D and 1D on Days 1and 2. Also, Group 2D showed a stronger aversion than 1D on Day 2. Aversions were extinguished in the D-condition by Day 3. The finding of a differential effect of the number of conditioning trials in the D-condition differs from the results of Experiment 3, when compartments + bottles were used as contextual elements.

This pattern of data illustrate that bottle stimuli are salient contextual elements and that, apparently, more is learned about taste with 3 than with

1 and 2 taste-aversion conditioning trials. Still, it is remarkable that the aversions shown by Groups 3D and 1S are virtually identical. In fact, the aversion in Group 1S is stronger than that in Group 3D on Days 1 and 2.

The results from the preference-test phase are illustrated in Figure 3.9. Tests 1 and 3 were performed in the extinction context of the S-groups ("noisy" bottles), and Test 2 was performed with saccharin and water in normal "silent" bottles. All main effects and two-factor interactions were signficant in addition to the Trials by Conditions by Tests interaction [F (4, 60) = 14.2, P <.01]. The S-groups showed weaker aversions than Groups 3D and 2D on Tests 2 and 3. Also, 1D showed a weaker aversion than 3D and 2D on Test 1 and on Test 3 there was a progressively weaker aversion in the D-groups the smaller the number of conditioning trials. Thus, the expected context-dependent extinction effect was demonstrated along with a suggestion of a trials effect.

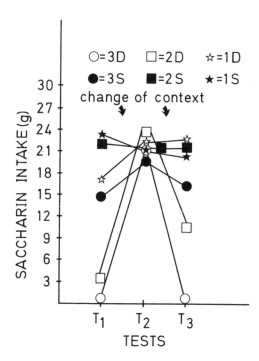

FIG. 3.9. Percentage saccharin preference of Groups 3D, 3S, 2D, 2S, 1D, and 1S of Experiment 5. T_1 and T_3 were performed in the extinction context of the S-animals, and T_2 was performed in the context prevailing during extinction for the D-animals. Contextual stimuli consisted of bottles.

One-trial learning about taste: Conclusions

The results of the multiple-trials experiments warrant the following conclusions: (1) When the same exteroceptive context (either compartments+bottles or bottles alone) is employed at conditioning and extinction there is a strong and reliable effect of the number of conditioning trials in taste-aversion learning. However, when the context is changed from conditioning to extinction, either there is no evidence of a trials effect (with compartments + bottles) or a weak effect (with bottles alone). Partial support was obtained for the hypothesis that most of what is learned about taste is accomplished on the first trial, and that learning concerns exteroceptive stimuli on the succeeding trials. This implies qualitative differences between positions on a quantitative learning variable: the number of acquisition trials. (2) Performance of the drinking response appears essential for learning about contextual (probably bottle) stimuli in this situation.

The notion that taste-aversions can be established within only one trial is an often repeated "truth" (e. g. Logue, 1979; Revusky & Garcia, 1970; Seligman, 1970; Testa & Ternes, 1977). It is, by some authors, considered to be a characteristic particular to this form of learning (and maybe a few others). However, there seems to exist very little systematic research comparing the effects of single and multiple conditioning trials. The 1977-bibliography complied by Riley and Clarke lists 188 references under the topical heading of "CS-US association: Repeated trials". However, very few of these studies include the effects of the number of trials as a major research question. In most investigations, the trials variable is only included in passing.

Garcia, Ervin & Koelling (1966) found a progressively greater aversion to saccharin from 1 to 4 saccharin-US pairings. Brackbill and Brookshire (1971) administered 1, 2, 4, 8, or 16 saccharin-US trials to different groups of rats and demonstrated a marked aversion after two trials, which represented the asymptote reached in that study.

In theoretical discussions of taste-aversion learning (e. g. Garcia et al., 1985; Revusky, 1977; Revusky & Garcia, 1970), the rapidity of acquisition is seldom singled out as a problem. Instead, the discussion usually focuses on the selectivity of associations, long-delay learning and some other characteristics. Apparently, the relation between the number of conditioning trials and the strength of taste aversions is considered unproblematic, maybe because there exists a large number of demonstrations of 1-trial learning (see e. g. Gustavson, 1977 for a cross-species review). No theoreticians seems to have even attempted to say anything interesting about it. If the present results can be replicated, the issue of one vs. multiple trials effects in taste-aversion learning may be revived.

Taste-context associations and forebrain noradrenaline

The role of forebrain noradrenaline (NA) in various learning tasks has been studied extensively utilising different techniques to lesion noradrenergic pathways and with various measures of behavioral performance (Anzelark, Crow, & Greenway, 1973; Crow & Wendlandt, 1976; Mason & Iversen, 1985; Sessions, Kant, & Koob, 1976). The role of NA in associative learning has been both implied and denied by a vast number of experimental studies (see Robbins, Everitt, Cole, Archer, & Mohammed, 1985). Recent evidence, however, derived from classical conditioning procedures such as latent inhibition and sensory preconditioning indicates that forebrain NA may well be implicated in associative learning processes.

Latent inhibition refers to the fact that nonreinforced preexposure to the CS prior to CS-US pairings retards conditioning of that CS (Lubow, 1965; Lubow & Moore, 1959). In taste-aversion learning, taste (CS) preexposure in the absence of poisoning leads to an attenuation of the aversion to that taste after conditioning (e. g. Domjan, 1972). In the area of contextual influences, we have previously investigated latent inhibition of conditioning of "noisy" bottle cues (Experiment 2 above). In the NA-studies to be reported below, groups of rats received preexposure to either saccharin plus "noisy" bottle, saccharin alone (in familiar "silent" bottles), "noisy" bottle alone (with tap water), or neither of these stimuli. Saccharin was then presented in "noisy" bottles for all groups on taste-aversion conditioning trials based on LiCl injections. At testing, saccharin was presented in "noisy" bottles.

Sensory preconditioning has two criteria: initial nonreinforced paired presentation of two CSs (CS1 and CS2), and later pairing of CS1 with a US. Testing for sensory preconditioning is done with CS2 (Rizley & Rescorla, 1972). In taste-aversion learning, a convenient and reliable method for investigating sensory preconditioning consists of presentations of saccharin (CS2) in "noisy" bottles (CS1) during the first phase. In the second phase, drinking water from the "noisy" bottles (CS1) is paired with LiCl (US). Sensory preconditioning of an aversion to saccharin (CS2) is then tested for with the fluid in "silent" bottles (Archer & Sj d, 1982).

Noradrenergic involvement in latent inhibition and sensory preconditioning in taste-aversion conditioning was studied by inflicting depletions of forebrain NA using two techniques: systemic administration of N-2-chloroethyl-N-ethyl-2-bromobenzylamine hydrochloride (DSP4) and by microinjections of 6-hydroxydopamine (6-OHDA) in the dorsal noradrenergic bundle (DNAB). A single i. p. injection of DSP4 (50 mg/kg) causes a sustained and long-lasting reduction of endogenous NA, neuronal accumulation of NA and dopamine-§-hydroxylase activity in rat brain regions (cf. Jonsson, Hallman, Ponzio, & Ross, 1981; Ross, 1976). Controls were injected with saline (5 ml/kg bodyweight). Lesions of the DNAB were inflicted by intracerebral injection of 6-OHDA, as described by Everitt, Robbins, Gaskin and Fray (1983). 6-OHDA was injected manually over 12 min through a microcannula, connected by polyethene tubing to a 5-μl Hamilton syringe. Sham-operated rats were treated identically but received infusions of the vehicle (.9 % saline containing .02% ascorbic acid) only. Following both DSP4 or DNAB lesions, rats were given a two-week recovery period before preexposure and preconditioning trials.

Latent inhibition - DSP4 experiment (Experiment 6)

The experimental chronology is presented in Table 3.2. On Day 1 (first preexposure), DSP4-N + S and CONT-N + S (CONT = vehicle-injected

TABLE 3.2

Experimental treatments and chronology for latent inhibition (Exp. 6-7) and sensory preconditioning (Exp. 8-9) experiments

GROUPS	Acclimatization and deprivation schedule	Pre-exposure (Phase I)	Conditioning (Phase II)	Testing (Phase III)
EXPERIMENT 6				
DSP4-N+S	Water/silent	Sacc/noisy	Sacc/noisy+LiCl	Sacc/noisy
CONT-N+S	Water/silent	Sacc/noisy	Sacc/noisy+LiCl	Sacc/noisy
DSP4-S	Water/silent	Sacc/silent	Sacc/noisy+LiCl	Sacc/noisy
CONT-S	Water/silent	Sacc/silent	Sacc/noisy+LiCl	Sacc/noisy
DSP4-N	Water/silent	Water/noisy	Sacc/noisy+LiCl	Sacc/noisy
CONT-N	Water/silent	Water/noisy	Sacc/noisy+LiCl	Sacc/noisy
DSP4-0	Water/silent	Water/silent	Sacc/noisy+LiCl	Sacc/noisy
CONT-0	Water/silent	Water/silent	Sacc/noisy+LiCl	Sacc/noisy
EXPERIMENT 7				
DNAB-N+S	Water/silent	Sacc/noisy	Sacc/noisy+LiCl	Sacc/noisy
SHAM-N+S	Water/silent	Sacc/noisy	Sacc/noisy+LiCl	Sacc/noisy
DNAB-S	Water/silent	Sacc/silent	Sacc/noisy+LiCl	Sacc/noisy
SHAM-S	Water/silent	Sacc/silent	Sacc/noisy+LiCl	Sacc/noisy
		(CS1-CS2)	(CS1-US)	(CS2 test)
EXPERIMENT 8				
DSP4-PP	Water/silent	Sacc/noisy	Water/noisy+LiCl	Sacc/silent
CONT-PP	Water/silent	Sacc/noisy	Water/noisy+LiCl	Sacc/silent
DSP4-UP	Water/silent	Sacc/silent[1]	Water/noisy+LiCl	Sacc/silent
CONT-UP	Water/silent	Sacc/silent[1]	Water/noisy+LiCl	Sacc/silent
EXPERIMENT 9				
DNAB-PP	Water/silent	Sacc/noisy	Water/noisy+LiCl	Sacc/silent
SHAM-PP	Water/silent	Sacc/noisy	Water/noisy+LiCl	Sacc/silent
DNAB-UP	Water/silent	Sacc/silent[1]	Water/noisy+LiCl	Sacc/silent
SHAM-UP	Water/silent	Sacc/silent[1]	Water/silent+LiCl	Sacc/silent

Note: Sacc = saccharin, noisy = "noisy" bottle, silent = "silent" bottle, LiCl = lithium chloride injection.

[1] Water presented in "noisy" bottles 24 hrs prior to sacc/noisy presentation

control) groups were offered a novel saccharin solution (S) in novel "noisy" (N) bottles, DSP4-S and CONT-S groups were offered novel saccharin in familiar "silent" bottles, DSP4-N and CONT-N groups were given water in novel "noisy" bottles, and DSP4-0 and CONT-0 groups (0 = no novel cues at preexposure) received water in "silent" bottles. All fluid presentations lasted 30 min. On Days 2, 4, 6, 7, 9, 11, 13, 14, 16, 18, 20, 21, 23, 25, 27, 28, and 30 the standard 30-min water presentation in "silent" bottles was maintained. On Days 3, 5, 8, 10, and 12 an identical procedure to that of Day 1 was instituted. These constituted preexposure trials 2-6. On Day 15, all groups were offered saccharin in the "noisy" bottles for 30 min and were injected with LiCl shortly thereafter. This constituted the first conditioning trial. The 2nd and 3rd conditoning trials were performed on Days 17 and 19. Three saccharin intake tests were carried out on Days 22, 24, and 26 (T1 - T3). On Day 29, an 8-hour saccharin preference test was performed (1000 - 1800 hrs).

The results from Tests 1-3 and the preference test (Fig. 3.10) indicated the following pairwise between-group differences (HSD-tests, p < .05), performed when analysis of variance indicated signficant main effects or interactions. Test 1: CONT-N+S drank more saccharin than the CONT-S group. Test 2: CONT-N+S > CONT-S, and DSP4-N+S > DSP4-S > DSP4-0 and Test 3: CONT-N+S > CONT-S, and DSP4-N+S > DSP4-S > DSP4-N > DSP4-0, and DSP4-S > CONT-S. Test 4: CONT-N+S showed a higher saccharin preference than CONT-S and DSP4-S > CONT-S but did not differ from the DSP4-N+S group. The conclusion from these results is that the presence of the "noisy" bottle cue controlled whether or not a latent inhibition effect of saccharin exposure was obtained or not; NA depletion as a result of DSP4 treatment abolished this effect.

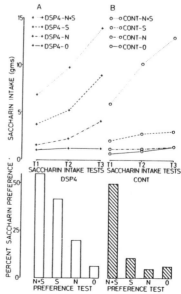

FIG. 3.10. Mean saccharin intake in noisy bottles by DSP4-treated (A) and control (B) rats during the saccharin intake tests (top). Percentage saccharin preference (bottom) during the preference test was measured in the noisy bottles. (Behavioral and Neural Biology. Archer, Mohammed, & Järbe, 1983.)

Latent inhibition - DNAB experiment (Experiment 7)

An identical procedure to that of the latent inhibition - DSP4 experiment (Exp. 6) was maintained with the exception that two groups, DNAB-N+S and SHAM-N+S received preexposure to saccharin in "noisy" bottles during 6 preexposure trials, and two groups, DNAB-S and SHAM-S received preexposure to saccharin in "silent" bottles alone (see Table 2). All four groups received saccharin in "noisy" bottles followed by LiCl on three conditioning trials. Three saccharin intake tests (T1-T3) from "noisy" bottles were followed by an 8-hr saccharin preference test. The results (Fig. 3.11) were comparable to those of Experiment 6. HSD tests showed that the SHAM-N+S group consumed more saccharin than the SHAM-S group on the test trials. In addition, the DNAB-S group consumed more saccharin than the SHAM-S group. This effect was obtained for all four test trials. The presence or absence of the "noisy" bottles during the preexposure phase controlled postconditioning saccharin aversion strength for the SHAM rats but not for the DNAB rats. Thus, although latent inhibition per se does not appear to be affected by NA loss, there seems to be strong evidence to indicate that NA may modulate the contextual control of latent inhibition in taste-aversion learning.

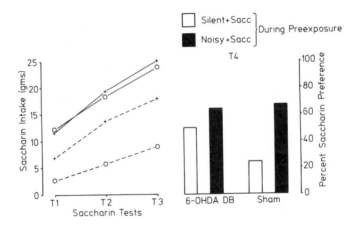

FIG. 3.11. Effect of dorsal bundle lesion (DB) on latent inhibition. Left panel shows mean saccharin intake from the noisy bottles during Tests 1 - 3. Right panel shows the percent saccharin preference during Test 4. Symbols: DNAB-N+S= +——+, SHAM-N+S=0——0, DNAB-S= +----+, SHAM-S=0----0. (6-OHDA DB=DNAB). (Behavioural Brain Research, Mohammed, Callenholm, Järbe, Swedberg, Danysz, Robbins, & Archer, 1986.)

Sensory preconditioning - DSP4 experiment (Experiment 8)

Rats were randomly assigned to DSP4, CONT, DNAB or SHAM conditions and an experimental design comparable to that of the latent inhibition - DNAB experiment (Exp. 7) was employed, with the exception that there were two groups within each of the four NA-conditions. Group designations refer to manipulations during Phases 1 and 2 (see Table 3.2). P equals paired presentations of stimuli and U equals unpaired presentations of stimuli manipulated during that phase. The procedure consisted of three phases.

Phase I: Sensory preconditioning of CS1-CS2 associations.

On Day 0, groups in the PP condition were offered saccharin in "silent" bottles, whereas UP groups were offered water in "noisy" bottles. On Day 1 (1st preconditioning trial, P1), the PP groups were offered a saccharin solution (CS2) in "noisy" bottles (CS1) for 30 min, whereas the UP groups were offered saccharin in "silent" bottles (see Table 2). On Days 2 and 4, a procedure identical to that of Day 0 was employed, whereas on Days 3 and 5 (P2 and P3), the Day-1 procedure was maintained. On Days 6 and 7, water was presented for 30 min in "silent" bottles.

Phase II: Conditioning of aversion to CS1

On Day 8 (1st conditioning trial, C1), all groups were offered water in "noisy" bottles (CS1) for 30 min and were then given a 10 ml/kg i. p. injection of .15M LiCl (US) shortly thereafter. On Days 9, 11, 13, 14, 16, 18, 20, 21, 23, 25, 27, 28, 30, 32, 34, 35, 37, and 39 water was presented in "silent" bottles for 30 min. On days 10, 12, 15, 17, 19, 22, 24, 26, 29, 31, and 33 (C2-C12), a procedure identical to that of Day 8 was carried out.

Phase III: Testing for sensory preconditioning.

On Days 36 (Test 1) and 38 (Test 2), all groups were offered one "silent" bottle containing saccharin and one containing water during an 8-hr saccharin (CS2) preference test (0800 -1600 hrs). The positions of the saccharin and water bottles was reversed between days. The percent preference for saccharin in relation to total fluid intake was computed.

Clear evidence of sensory preconditioning of a saccharin aversion, mediated by the first-order aversion to water in the "noisy" bottles was obtained in the CONTR condition (saline treated animals) (Fig. 3.12). However, no sensory preconditioning was seen among the DSP4 groups. Thus, analysis of variance indicated a significant effect of Groups, and HSD-tests revealed that the CONT-PP groups showed significantly more saccharin aversion than the DSP4-PP and CONT-UP groups. The DSP4-PP group showed a significantly stronger saccharin aversion than the DSP4-UP group. These results warrant the conclusion that NA depletion as a result of DSP4 treatment attenuated sensory preconditioning of a taste aversion, since the CONT-PP group showed a stronger aversion than the DSP4-PP group.

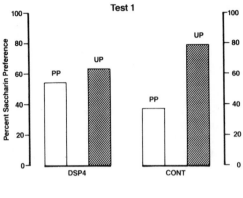

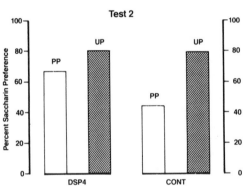

FIG. **3.12.** Percent saccharin preference by DSP4-treated and the saline-treated control rats during Tests 1 and 2 (testing for aversions to CS_2 only). All the rats received one silent bottle with saccharin (CS_2 and one silent bottle with water in the 8-h saccharin preference tests. (Behavioural Brain Research, Archer, Mohammed, Danysz, Järbe, & Jonsson, 1986.)

Sensory preconditioning - DNAB experiment (Experiment 9).

The design and procedures were identical to those used in the sensory preconditioning - DSP4 experiment (Exp. 8) (see Table 3.2). A similar result was obtained (Figure 3.13). The SHAM-operated rats demonstrated sensory preconditioning and this effect was abolished in the DNAB animals.

HSD-tests of the significant Groups effect in the analysis of variance, revealed that the SHAM-PP group showed significantly more saccharin aversion than the DNAB-PP and SHAM-UP groups. The aversion of the DNAB-PP group did not differ from that of the DNAB-UP group. In the SHAM condition, the PP group which received paired presentations of both CS1-CS2 and CS1-US showed a stronger CS2 aversion than the SHAM-UP group, which received unpaired CS1-CS2 presentations. Corresponding between-groups differences were not seen in the DNAB condition.

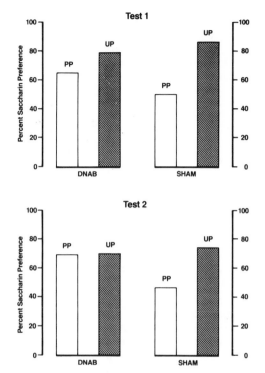

FIG. 3.13. Percent saccharin preference by DNAB and the sham-operated control rats during Tests 1 and 2 (testing for aversions to CS_2 only). (Behavioural Brain Research, Archer, Mohammed, Danysz, Järbe, & Jonsson, 1986).

Taste-context associations and forebrain noradrenaline: Conclusions

The results presented above indicate that sensory preconditioning of a saccharin aversion can be established with a first-order stimulus, consisting of the presentation of tap water in "noisy" bottles (CS1). Sensory preconditioning is evidenced in all of the experiments by the occurrence of a significantly greater saccharin (CS2) aversion in the PP groups than in the UP groups. We have previously argued that the UP control group is probably most critical for any demonstration of sensory preconditioning (Archer & Sjödén, 1982), although the PU control (CS1-CS2 paired , CS1-US unpaired) is often used. Archer, Cotic and Jrbe (1986) utilized both the UP and PU controls as well as a NP condition (N = no CS1-CS2 presentation. CS1-CS2 paired), but obtained a considerable attenuation of sensory preconditioning in the NA depleted (DSP4) condition. It should be noted that NA depletion did not affect first-order conditioning to the "noisy" bottles, which would have compromised demonstration of the sensory preconditioning effect. The disruption of the CS1-CS2 association indicates the possibly associative nature of the deficit induced by lesioning of forebrain NA pathways.

ACKNOWLEDGEMENTS

Research for this chapter was supported by grants 54/79, 897/80, 422/81, and 424/82 from the Swedish Council for Research in the Humanities and Social Sciences, and by grants from Astra Läkemedel AB, Södertälje, Sweden.

REFERENCES

Anzelark, G. M., Crow, T. J., & Greenway, A. P. (1973). Impaired learning and decreased cortical norepinephrine after bilateral locus coeruleus lesions. *Science, 181*, 682-684.

Archer, T., Cotic, T., & Järbe, T. U. C. (1986). Noradrenaline and sensory preconditioning in the rat. *Behavioral Neuroscience, 100*, 704-711.

Archer, T., Mohammed, A. K., Danysz, W., Järbe, T. U. C., & Jonsson, G. (1986). Attenuation of sensory preconditioning by noradrenaline depletion in the rat. *Behavioural Brain Research, 20*, 47-56.

Archer, T., & Sjödén, P. O. (1980). Context-dependent taste-aversion learning with a familiar conditioning context. *Physiological Psychology, 8*, 40-46.

Archer, T., & Sjödén, P. O. (1981). Environment-dependent taste-aversion extinction: A question of stimulus novelty at conditioning. *Physiological Psychology, 9*, 102-108.

Archer, T., & Sjödén, P. O. (1982). Higher-order conditioning and sensory preconditioning of a taste aversion with an exteroceptive CS1. *Quarterly Journal of Experimental Psychology, 34B*, 1-17.

Archer, T., Sjödén, P. O., & Carter, N. (1979). Control of taste-aversion extinction by exteroceptive cues. *Behavioral and Neural Biology, 25*, 217-226. (a)

Archer, T., Sjödén, P. O., & Nilsson, L. G. (1984). The importance of contextual elements in taste-aversion learning. *Scandinavian Journal of Psychology, 25*, 251-257.

Archer, T., Sjödén, P. O., & Nilsson, L. G. (1985). Contextual control of taste-aversion conditioning and extinction. In P. D. Balsam & A. Tomie (Eds.), *Context and learning*. pp. 225-271. Hillsdale, N. J.: Lawrence Erlbaum Associates.

Archer, T., Sjödén, P. O., Nilsson, L. G., & Carter, N. (1979). Role of exteroceptive background context in taste-aversion conditioning and extinction. *Animal Learning and Behavior, 7*, 17-22. (b)

Archer, T., Sjödén, P. O., Nilsson, L. G., & Carter, N. (1980). Exteroceptive context in taste-aversion conditioning and extinction: Odour, cage and bottle stimuli. *Quarterly Journal of Experimental Psychology, 32*, 197-214.

Balsam, P. D., & Tomie, A. (Eds.). (1985). *Context and learning.*

Psychology, 85, 250-257.
Brackbill, R. M., & Brookshire. K. H. (1971). Conditioned taste aversions as a function of the number of CS-US pairs. *Psychonomic Science, 22,* 25-26.
Crow, T. J., & Wendlandt. S. (1976). Impaired acquisition of a passive avoidance response after lesions in the locus coeruleus by 6-OH-dopamine. *Nature, 259,* 42-44.
Dickinson, A. (1980). *Contemporary animal learning theory.* Cambridge: Cambridge University Press.
Domjan, M. (1972). CS pre-exposure in taste-aversion learning. *Learning and Motivation, 3,* 389-402.
Domjan, M., & Wilson. N. E. (1972). Specificity of cue to consequence in aversion learning in the rat. *Psychonomic Science, 26,* 143-145.
Estes, W. K. (1973). Memory and conditioning. In F. J. McGuigan & D. B. Lumsden (Eds.), *Contemporary approaches to conditioning and learning,* pp. 265-286. Washington, D. C.: Winston.
Estes, W. K. (1975). *Handbook of learning and cognitive processes. (Vol. 2): Conditioning and behavior theory.* Hillsdale, N. J.: Lawrence Erlbaum Associates.
Everitt, B. J., Robbins, T. W., Gaskin. M., & Fray. P. J. (1983). The effects of lesions to ascending noradrenergic neurone on discrimination learning and performance in the rat. *Neuroscience, 10,* 397-410.
Garcia. J., Ervin. F. R., & Koelling, R. A. (1966). Learning with prolonged delay of reinforcement. *Psychonomic Science, 5,* 121-122.
Garcia, J., Hankins, W. G., & Rusiniak. K. W. (1974). Behavioral regulation of the milieu interne in man and rat. *Science, 185,* 823-831.
Garcia, J., Kimeldorf, D. J., & Hunt. E. L. (1961). The use of ionizing radiation as a motivating stimulus. *Psychological Review, 68,* 383-395.
Garcia, J., & Koelling, R. A. (1966). Relation of cue to consequence in avoidance learning. *Psychonomic Science, 4,* 123-124.
Garcia, J., & Koelling. R. A. (1967). A comparison of aversions induced by X-ray toxins, and drugs in the rat. *Radiation Research Supplement, 7,* 439-450.
Garcia, J., Kovner. R., & Green, K. F. (1970). Cue properties vs. palatability of flavors in avoidance learning. *Psychonomic Science, 20,* 313-314.
Garcia, J., Lasiter, P. S., Bermudez-Rattoni, F., & Deems. D. A. (1985). A general theory of aversion learning. In N. S. Braveman & P. Bronstein (Eds.), *Experimental assessments and clinical applications of conditioned food aversions. Annals of the New York Academy of Sciences, 443,* 8-21.
Garcia, J., McGowan. B. K., Ervin, F. R., & Koelling, R. A. (1968). Cues: their relative effectiveness as a function of the reinforcer. *Science, 160,* 794-795.
Garcia, J., McGowan. B. K., & Green. K. F. (1972). Biological

constraints on conditioning. In M. E. P. Seligman & J. L. Hager (Eds.), *Biological boundaries of learning*, pp. 21-43. New York: Appleton-Century-Crofts.

Green, K. F., Holmstrom, L. S., & Wollman, M. A. (1974). Relation of cue to consequence in rats: Effect of recuperation from illness. *Behavioral Biology, 10*, 491-503.

Gustavson, C. R. (1977). Comparative and field aspects of learned food aversions. In L. M. Barker, M. R. Best & M. Domjan (Eds.), *Learning mechanisms in food selection*, pp. 23-43. Baylor, Texas: Baylor University Press.

Hargrave, G. E., & Bolles, R. C. (1971). Rat's aversion to flavors following induced illness. *Psychonomic Science, 23*, 91-92.

Holder, M. D. (1988). Possible role of confounded taste stimuli in conditioned taste aversions. *Animal Learning and Behavior*.

Jonsson, G., Hallman, H., Ponzio, F., & Ross, S. B. (1981). DSP4(N-2-chloroethyl-N-ethyl-2-bromobenzylamine)-a useful noradrenaline denervation tool for central and peripheral noradrenaline neurons. *European Journal of Pharmacology, 72*, 173-188.

Larsen, J. D., & Hyde, T. S. (1977). A comparison of learned aversions to gustatory and exteroceptive cues in the rat. *Animal Learning and Behavior, 5*, 17-20.

Logue, A. W. (1979). Taste aversion and the generality of the laws of learning. *Psychological Bulletin, 86*, 276-296.

Lubow, R. E. (1965). Latent inhibition: Effects of frequency of nonreinforced preexposure of the CS. *Journal of Comparative and Physiological Psychology, 60*, 454-457.

Lubow, R. E., & Moore, A. V. (1959). Latent inhibition: The effect of nonreinforced preexposure of the CS. *Journal of Comparative and Physiological Psychology, 52*, 415-419.

Mackintosh, N. J. (1974). *The psychology of animal learning*. London: Academic Press.

Mason, S. T., & Iversen, S. D. (1975). Learning in the absence of forebrain noradrenaline. *Nature, 258*, 422-424.

Nachman, M. (1970). Learned taste and temperature aversions due to lithium chloride sickness after temporal delays. *Journal of Comparative and Physiological Psychology, 73*, 31-37.

Rescorla, R. A., & Wagner, A. R. (1972). A theory of Pavlovian conditioning. Variations in the effectiveness of reinforcement and nonreinforcement. In A. H. Black & W. F. Prokasy (Eds.), *Classical conditioning II: Current research and theory*, pp. 64-99. New York: Appleton-Century-Crofts.

Revusky, S. (1977). Learning as a general process with an emphasis on data from feeding experiments. In N. W. Milgram, L. Krames, & T. M. Alloway (Eds.&), *Food aversion learning*, pp. 3-51. New York: Plenum Press.

Revusky, S. H., & Bedarf, E. W. (1967). Association of illness with ingestion of novel foods. *Science, 155*, 219-220.

Revusky, S., & Garcia, J. (1970). Learned associations over long delays. In G. H. Bower & J. T. Spence (Eds.), *The psychology of learning and motivation: Advances in research and theory*, Vol. IV, pp. 1-84. New York: Academic Press.

Riley, A. L., & Clarke, C. M. (1977). Conditioned taste aversions: A bibliography. In L. M. Barker, M. R. Best, & M. Domjan (Eds.), *Learning mechanisms in food selection*. Baylor, Texas: Baylor University Press.

Rizley, R. C., & Rescorla, R. A. (1972). Associations in second-order conditioning and sensory preconditioning. *Journal of Comparative and Physiological Psychology*, *81*, 1-11.

Robbins, T. W., Everitt, B. J., Cole, B. J., Archer, T., & Mohammed, A. K. (1985). Functional hypotheses of the coeruleocortical noradrenergic projection: A review of recent experimentation and theory. *Physiological Psychology*, *13*, 127-150.

Ross, S. B. (1976). Long-term effects of N(2-chloroethyl)-N-ethyl-2-bromobenzylamine hydrochloride on noradrenergic neurons in the rat brain and heart. *British Journal of Pharmacology*, *58*, 521-527.

Seligman, M. E. P. (1970). On the generality of the laws of learning. *Psychological Review*, *77*, 400-418.

Sessions, G. R., Kant, G. J., & Koob, G. F. (1976). Locus coerulens lesions and learning in the rat. *Physiology and Behavior*, *17*, 852-859.

Sjödén, P. O., & Archer, T. (1981). Associative and nonassociative effects of exteroceptive context in taste-aversion conditioning with rats. *Behavioral and Neural Biology*, *33*, 74-92.

Sjödén, P. O., & Archer, T. (1983). Potentiation of a bottle aversion by taste in compound conditioning with rats. *Experimental Animal Behaviour*, *2*, 1-18.

Sjödén, P. O., & Archer, T. (1988). Exteroceptive cues in taste-aversion learning, no artifact: Reply to Holder. *Animal Learning and Behavior*.

Slotnik, B. M., Brown, D. L., & Gelhard,. R. (1977). Contrasting effects of location and taste-cues in illness-induced aversion. *Physiology and Behavior*, *18*, 333-335.

Testa, T. J., & Ternes, J. W. (1977). Specificity of conditioning mechanisms in the modification of food preferences. In L. M. Barker, M. R. Best, & M. Domjan (Eds.), *Learning mechanisms in food selection*, pp. 229-253. Baylor, Texas: Baylor University Press.

Thomas, D. R. (1985). Contextual stimulus control of operant responding in pigeons. In P. D. Balsam & A. Tomie (Eds.), *Context and learning*, pp 295-321. Hillsdale, N. J.: Lawrence Erlbaum Associates.

Wagner, A. R. (1976). Priming in STM: An information-processing mechanism for self-generated or retrieval-generated depression in performance. In T. J. Tighe & R. N. Leaton (Eds.), *Habituation: Perspectives from child development, animal behavior, and neurophysiology*, pp. 95-128. Hillsdale, N. J.: Lawrence Erlbaum Associates.

Wagner, A. R., & Rescorla, R. A. (1972). Inhibition in Pavlovian conditioning. Application of a theory. In M. S. Halliday & R. A. Boakes (Eds.), *Inhibition and learning*, pp. 301-336. London: Academic Press.

Wilcoxon, H. C., Dragoin, W. B., & Kral, P. A. (1972). Illness-induced aversions in rats and quail: Relative salience of visual and gustatory cues. *Science, 171*, 826-828.

Wittlin, W. A., & Brookshire, K. H. (1968). Apomorphine-induced conditioned aversion to a novel food. *Psychonomic Science, 12*, 217-218.

Woods, S. C., Makous, W., & Hutton. R. A. (1969). Temporal parameters of conditioned hypoglycemia. *Journal of Comparative and Physiological Psychology, 69*, 301-307.

Learning of External and Visceral Cue Consequences May Be Subserved by Different Neuroanatomical Substrates

4

Federico Bermúdez-Rattoni, Marco Antonio Sánchez and Roberto A. Prado-Alcalá
Universidad Nacional Autónoma de México

For animals, feeding behavior is the most important processes involved in the uptake of energy. In order to survive the animal must select nutrients and avoid toxins (Darwin, 1859/1985; Garcia, Rusiniak, Kiefer & Bermúdez-Rattoni, 1982). The ability for animals to recognize through odor and taste toxic components of plants, have produced influences in the evolution of both herbivorous and plants (Chapman & Blaney, 1979). A wide variety of animals to *associate* flavor with toxic effects apparently as a result of the coevolution of protective mechanisms on the host species and corresponding discrimination habits in feeding species (Garcia, Rusiniak & Brett, 1977). The same mechanism works to increase consumption as well. Many nutrients taste sweet and most feeders naturally prefer sweets. Many plants have taken advantage of this by evolving the dispersal mechanism of enclosing their indigestible seed in the sweet fruit; the feeder consumes the sweet fruits, absorbs the nutrient, but passes the seed far from the plant that bore it.

The selection of food resources and defense from depredation, that go along with the feeding chain, eventually produced adaptative pressures to the organisms (Rhoades, 1979; Sih, Crowley, Mc Peek, Petronka & Strohmeir, 1985). These pressures produce modifications of body structure and physiology, instinctive behavior and learning mechanisms that made it possible for organisms to become adapted to their environment (Garcia & Garcia Y. Robertson, 1985).

In this evolutionary regard, Garcia and coworkers have proposed *functional* dual mechanisms whereby animals cope with their defending their gut against toxins and their skin against predators (see Bolles, 1985; Garcia, Lasiter, Bermúdez-Rattoni & Deems, 1985). The existence of this dual learning mechanism is supported by work from different laboratories. Thus, taste is readily associated with illness producing the conditioned flavor aversions (CFA) after a single flavor-illness experience. Unlike most other demonstrations of classical conditioning, the delay between the taste and the illness can be an hour or more in the formation of a strong CFA. In contrast an audio-visual signal was a poor CS for illness conditioning, acquiring little or no aversive properties following a single toxic US. If footshock is used, the converse is true, the audio-visual signal was readily associated with the footshock US whereas taste was a poor CS in shock avoidance conditioning (Garcia et al., 1982; 1985). This difference in conditioning has been termed cue-consequences specificity (Garcia & Koelling, 1966; see Domjan, 1985).

In regard to the internal gut defense system, parametric research has shown that the temporal gradient for odor is steep; that is, odor must be followed immediately by poison to produce strong odor aversion learning. The temporal gradient for taste, on the other hand, is shallow; strong taste aversions may be conditioned even when poison administration is delayed several hours. When odor and taste are combined to produce a compound "flavor" CS, the conditionability of the odor component changes markedly, switching from the steep gradient characteristic of odor alone to the shallow gradient characteristic of taste alone. This effect was termed *potentiation* to reflect the fact that a previously weak odor cue became a strong associative cue simply by presenting it in conjunction with a taste (Rusiniak, Hankins, Garcia, & Brett, 1979; Rusiniak, Palmerino, Rice, Forthman & Garcia, 1982). This potentiation of odor by taste is a robust phenomenon, and it depends critically on close temporal contiguity between the odor and taste components in acquisition (Coburn, Garcia, Kiefer & Rusiniak, 1984). Moreover, the aversion to flavors can be acquired even if the animal's cortical electroactivity is depressed by chemicals or if the animal is rendered flaccid and unresponsible by drugs (Bermúdez-Rattoni, Forthman-Quick, Sánchez, Pérez & Garcia, submitted; Roll & Smith, 1972; Buresova & Bures, 1973). All this indicates that the visceral system operates below the level of awareness (Bermúdez-Rattoni et al., submitted; Garcia, et al., 1985).

The potentiation of food-related cues is not limited to odor stimuli on rats. It has been shown in birds that the concomitant presentation of taste and color cues, when followed by illness, results in color aversions much stronger than if the color is conditioned alone (Brett, Hankins & Garcia, 1976; Clark, Westbrook & Irwin, 1979). Recently, however, there has been some speculation that all external stimuli can be potentiated by taste in animals (Holder, Bermúdez-Rattoni & Garcia, in press). Ellins, Cramer & Whitmore (1985) showed that a noise contingent on consumption could be associated with illness. However, Holder et al (1987) were not always able to find noise potentiated by taste aversions, when similar procedures used for potentiated odor aversion were employed, despite the fact that the noise used was an effective external cue for footshock. Close spatiotemporal contiguity of the noise source and the flavored food is vital for noise potentiation (Ellins & von Kluge, in press). The complex polysynaptic routes of auditory and visceral pathways towards their ultimate convergence may account for the increased difficulty in developing noise-illness integration. In contrast, taste-illness is subserved by immediate convergence of gustatory and visceral pathways to the solitary nucleus. Additionally, it has been postuated that taste stimulation facilitates the integration of external stimuli with feeding responses by means of a sensory "and-gate" mechanism.

THE NEURAL INTEGRATION OF ODOR AND TASTE AVERSIONS

We have been engaged in neurophysiological and neuropharmacological experiments in order to explore the neural mechanisms involved in the potentiation of odor by taste during toxiphobia conditioning. By means of a switching mechanism odor may be gated into the memory stores associated with the external defense system against peripheral insults such as a shock US. On the other hand, the same may be gated into the visceral (feeding) system where it can be potentiated by taste (Garcia et al., 1982; 1985). Assuming the anatomical existence of this neural "and-gate" switching odor into the feeding system, we have examined several regions of the central nervous system where odor-taste interactions might possibly occur.

One region hypothesized to be crucial for taste potentiation of odor stimuli was the gustatory neocortex. Stimulation of the pyriform cortex produces antidromic responses in the olfactory bulb (Allen, 1923) indicating that there are indeed, projections from the olfactory bulb to the pyriform cortex. From the pyriform cortex, there are also axonal projections directly to the agranular insular cortex and to the terminal projections field in the orbital frontal neocortex (OFN) of the rat (Haberly & Price, 1978). Laiter and coworkers, based in studies using retrograde transport of horseradish peroxidase suggest that the primary gustatory neocortical projection field receives axonal projections from the pontine taste area (PTA) (Lasiter, Glanzman & Mensah, 1982). Ablations of this region disrupt taste-illness conditioning (Braun, Lasiter & Kiefer, 1982; Hankins, Garcia & Rusiniak, 1974). There is a close topographical relationship of the OFN and gustatory neocortext (Braun et al., 1982), as well as an abundant projection between the OFN and gustatory neocortex (GN) (Lasiter & Glanzman, 1982). This suggests that olfactory and gustatory information may converge, at least in part, to the GN and that this convergence contributes to the compound sensations described by humans as "flavors".

To determine the role of the cortex in potentiation, intact rats and rats lacking the dorsal region of the gustatory neocortex were given either a taste, an odor, or an odor-taste compound followed by intragastric administration of LiCl (Kiefer, Rusiniak & Garcia, 1982). On the first exposure to the stimuli, rats lacking gustatory neocortex failed to display normal neophobia for the odor-taste compound. After two acquisition trials, the test trials with the odor and taste components revealed relatively specific effects of the lesions. Taste conditioning was severely disrupted. In contrast, the ablation did not appreciably affect taste potentiation of the odor aversion despite the fact that the operated rats trained with the odor-taste compound (OT) did not form any aversion to the taste; these rats displayed potentiated odor aversions relative to the odor-alone group. Apparently, integrity of the dorsal gustatory neocortex is necessary for the acquisition of a taste aversion but not for taste potentiation of an odor aversion. Lasiter, Deems & Garcia (1985) verified this finding and reported that lesions in the ventral insular region disrupted both taste aversions and potentiated odor aversions.

THE INVOLVEMENT OF THE LIMBIC SYSTEM IN THE INTEGRATION OF ODOR POTENTIATED TASTE AVERSIONS

The amygdala is another likely site for the integration of odor with taste and toxicosis, as it receives both gustatory and olfactory afferents (Norgren, 1974; White, 1965). Neurons responding to both gustatory and visceral stimuli are found in the pontine taste area of the parabrachial complex (second gustatory relay); these neurons project also to the limbic system. Olfactory input reaches the amygdala from the accessory olfactory bulbar formation and olfactory cortex, thus the amygdala appears to receive all three modalities necessary for the mediation of taste-potentiated odor-illness conditioning. Accordingly, permanent lesions of the amygdala disrupt conditioned flavor aversions induced by a variety of unconditioned stimuli, such as amphetamine, lithium chloride, and x-rays (Grupp, Linseman & Coppel, 1976; McGowan, Hankins & Garcia, 1972; Elkins, 1980). Temporary amygdaloid lesions produced by disruptive electrical stimulation also impair apomorphine-induced flavor aversions (Kesner, Berman, Burton & Hankins, 1975). Furthermore, Buresova, Aleksanyan and Bures (1979) have shown that conditioned aversive flavors inhibit unit activity in the amygdala, as well as in the ventromedial hypothalamus and gustatory neocortex of the rat.

a) Acute Interference with Amygdala Function

We propose that the amygdala and other portions of the limbic system may perform the gating of odor by taste and that the local applications of selected drugs directly to relevant areas of the limbic system may be a reasonable research strategy. To test this proposition, we have been conducting a series of studies to examine the role of the amygdala in potentiation (Bermúdez-Rattoni, Chávez, Coburn & Garcia, 1983; Bermúdez-Rattoni, Grijalva, Kiefer & Garcia, 1986). In such experiments, rats are implanted with bilateral cannulae aimed at the amygdala. To produce "reversible" amygdala lesions, infusions of procaine are made. Such infusions suppress normal electrophysiological activity for about 2 hours. In an initial experiment, four groups of rats were given a single exposure to an odor-taste (OT) compound. One group was a normal control, a second group was given procaine just prior to presentation of the compound OT, a third group was given procaine following OT exposure, and a fourth group received the procaine just before LiCl application. The administration of LiCl was given to all rats 30 minutes after exposure to the odor and taste. Following OT-illness, all groups displayed approximately equivalent taste aversions, reducing saccharin consumption. However, the group given procaine prior to the OT exposure (Pre-CS), displayed attentuated odor aversions. These data suggest that disruption of odor potentiation might have been produced by amygdaloid dysfunction just prior to the CS experience (Bermúdez-Rattoni, Rusiniak & Garcia, 1983).

The deficits in odor potentiation found with procaine-treated rats could be related to disruptions of the integration of odor and taste information. It is also possible that pre-CS infusion of procaine in the amygdala disrupts simple odor detection or odor-illness associations. To test if odor perception was affected by procaine treatment, three groups of rats (normal, procaine pre-CS, and handled control) were given a single exposure to almond odor while drinking familiar tap water. After a one-minute exposure the rats were given a footshock (1 mA, 1 sec). The results from the subsequent odor test indicated that all three groups showed significant suppression of consumption in the presence of the odor. These data indicate that procaine-treated rats were not anosmic, since they could develop normal associations between an odor and footshock, in fact the treated rats exhibited superior odor-shock performance.

A third experiment tested whether amygdala dysfunction produced by procaine infusion would disrupt direct odor-illness conditioning induced by immediate toxic injections. Control rats (both saline infused and handled) and rats given procaine prior to odor exposure, were conditioned with a single odor-illness trial using immediate administration of the poison so that direct odor-illness learning could be obtained. The results of the subsequent odor test indicated that pretreatment with procaine disrupted conditioning. These results suggest that the disruptions in potentiation of odor aversions described above can be attributed to a deficit in the formation of odor-illness associations, and that the amygdala dysfunctions may not have been related to odor-taste integration but rather to odor-illness associative learning. The effect was specific to toxiphobia conditioning because odor-shock learning was not affected by procaine treatment (Bermúdez et al., 1983).

b) Chronic Interference with Amygdala Function

In another series of experiments we have produced permanent lesions to find out which of the specific nuclei of the amygdaloid complex is more involved in the gating of odor by taste in toxiphobic conditioning. In a first experiment we made relative large lesions since our procaine research indicated that large areas of the amygdala might be involved (McGowan et al., 1972; Grupp et al., 1976).

Therefore, rats were given extensive electrolytic lesions in the amygdala including lateral, dorsolateral, basal and medial nuclei of amygdala and one group received sham lesions. These groups of rats were divided into 3 subgroups: with odor, taste or the OT compound as CS's and all of them received LiCl 30 minutes later; the procedure was the same as described above. The results showed that the lesioned animals did not acquire either odor, taste or OT aversions as compared with those with the sham lesions. We concluded that the integrity of the amygdala is essential for odor and taste aversion learning. However, if the novocaine produces disruption only for odor but not for taste when applied to the amygdala it is possible that some of the nuclei are discretely involved rather than the whole amygdala (Bermúdez-Rattoni et al., 1986).

Therefore, in our second experiment we used smaller lesions directed at specific nuclei. The role of separate nuclei of the amygdalar complex was tested in the conditioning of aversions to the flavor compound and its odor-taste components. Rats were given small electrolytic lesions in the basal amygdala including the lateral and basolateral, medial nuclei, central amygdalar nucleus, or sham operations. Following postoperative recovery, each group received conditioning to an OT compound followed by delayed illness. Almond odor and saccharin were the CS's while the US was LiCL (i.p.). After conditioning, the tests with odor or taste alone showed that all groups presented strong taste and odor aversions, except the group which had sustained lateral amygdaloid lesions, which displayed a significant disruption of odor aversion learning (Bermúdez-Rattoni et al., 1986).

c) Cholinergic Activity of the Amygdala and Dorsal Hippocampus

From these results, it seems that the neural integration of odor and taste during the conditioned flavor aversions may be mediated by neurochemical changes, since permanent lesions of the amygdala disrupt both odor and taste, but reversible alterations disrupt only the integration of odor aversions (Bermúdez-Rattoni et al., 1983). Therefore a series of experiments were made in order to find which of the neurotransmitters of the amygdala might be involved in the potentiation effect. Elsewhere, it has been shown that the amygdaloid complex and dorsal hippocampus are involved in memory functions and that the basomedial and basolateral nuclei of the amygdala seem to be the most important areas in these functions (McGaugh & Gold, 1977; Grossman, Grossman & Walsh, 1975). The basolateral nucleus of the amygdala has a high content of acetylcholine (ACh) (Woolf & Butcher, 1982), and it has been postulated that the cholinergic activity in the amygdala and hippocampus are highly involved in retention of learned tasks (Todd & Kesner, 1978). Thus, it is likely that amygdalar cholinergic activity is involved in potentiation, i.e., the gating of odor into the visceral system.

Rats implanted with bilateral cannulae in the amygdala received physostigmine, scopolamine or saline infused over 3 min; almond odor and saccharin were the CS's and LiCl was the US. During acquisition the drugs were given 30 min before the presentation of odor and taste and were followed by delayed lithium illness. Then the animals were tested with odor or taste alone in separate tests days with water days in between. Results of the manipulations showed that when given prior to acquisition, physostigmine significantly decreased the odor aversion, while scopolamine produced a non-significant increase. Meanwhile taste aversions remained unaffected (Bermúdez-Rattoni et al., 1983). We concluded, therefore, that the cholinergic activity of the amygdala is involved in the potentiation effect.

Another limbic structure which has been given a role in memory processes for a long time is the hippocampus (O'Keefe & Nadel, 1978; Olton, Becker, Handelman, 1979; Thompson, 1983), which also has a high content of acetylcholine (Kuhar, 1975). Therefore we conducted experiments to determine if the hippocampal cholinergic activity has some involvement in the potentiation effect. The procedure was the same as in the studies described above. The results showed again that the physostigmine significantly reduced the odor aversions, but did not have any effect on taste aversions. On the contrary, the scopolamine significantly enhanced the odor aversions, but not the taste averisons (Bermúdez-Rattoni, Coburn, Fernández, Chávez & Garcia, 1987).

INVOLVEMENT OF THE NEOSTRIATUM IN MEMORY OF EXTERNAL CUE CONSEQUENCES

It has been postulated that the neostriatum, or cuadate-putamen (CP) is critically involved in memory processes when external cue-consequences are used. This is supported by the results of a great variety of experiments. It has been shown that acute or chronic interference with striatal functioning produced by electrolytic and mechanical lesions, or by local injections of anesthetics, potassium chloride or neurotoxins produce marked impairments in the consolidation and retrieval of instrumentally-learned associations (for reviews see Oberg & Divac, 1979 and Prado-Alcalá, 1985).

Further experimentation provides clues about possible neurochemical events within the CP, that may take place in the establishment of learning. For example, cholinergic blockade of the CP, induced shortly after training of passive avoidance, produces a state of retrograde amnesia (Giordano & Prado-Alcalá, 1986; Haycock, Deadwyler, Sideroff & McGaugh, 1973; Prado-Alcalá, Fernández-Samblancat & Solodkin-Herrera, 1985); this amnesic state is time-dependent since as the interval between training and intrastriatal injection of anticholinergic drugs is increased, the amnesic state is less evident or not evident at all

(Prado-Alcalá, Signoret-Edward & Figueroa, 1981). Interestingly, application of anticholinergic drugs to other brain structures (hippocampus and neocortex) only produce a mild impairment, or no impairment at all in passive avoidance responding (Haycock et al., 1973; Prado-Alcalá, Signoret-Edward, Figueroa, Giordano & Barrientos, 1984). Amnesia is also readily produced when atropine and scopolamine are injected into the CP of animals that have been trained in other instrumental tasks such as active avoidance (Neill & Grossman, 1970; Prado-Alcalá, 1985). Other lines of evidence converge to indicate that striatal cholinergic activity is involved in the learning of external cue-consequences. When the neurotoxin AF64A (a drug that produces a specific lesion of ACh-containing neurons) is injected into the CP, the treated animals are unable to show signs of learning of passive avoidance (Sandberg, Sanberg, Hanin, Fisher & Coyle, 1984).

If cholinergic blockade of the neostriatum is causally related to the amnesic states described above, then it would be expected that stimulation of acetylcholine receptors of that structure would produce an enhancement in retention and performance of instrumental tasks. Indeed, such is the case. There is a significant improvement in passive avoidance (Fernández, Solodkin & Prado-Alcalá, 1977) and active avoidance (Prado-Alcalá, Cepeda, Verduzco, Jiménez & Vargas-Ortega, 1984) after intrastriatal injections of choline, the ACh precursor. These series of experiments also lead to the prediction that training of an instrumental task should induce changes in ACh activity. Barker, Glick, Green & Khandelwal (1982) showed that shortly after training of passive avoidance there is a significant increase of ACh content in the striatum but not in other areas of the barin. Similarly, we have recently found a reliable increase in the formation of muscarinic receptors in the CP after training of that aversively-motivated task (unpublished observations).

Cholinergic activity of the striatum is mediated by intrinsic interneurons (Butcher & Butcher, 1974; McGeer, McGeer, Grewaal & Sing, 1975). They are functionally connected to afferent dopamine (DA) and, to efferent and to intrinsic GABA-containing neurons (Lehman & Langer, 1983). Hence, it should be expected that these neurons also contribute to the establishment of memory, since changes in their neurochemical activity bring about changes in the activity of ACh interneurons. Furthermore, important modifications in memory should be produced when an imbalance in the activity of the nigro-neostriatal system is produced by altering the activity of any of its components (ACh, DA or GABA neurons).

As predicted, intrastriatal injections of DA (Kim & Routtenberg, 1976a), bicuculine and picrotoxin (Chávez-Martinez & Prado-Alcalá, 1986) or GABAergic blockade of the substantia nigra (SN) (Kim & Routtenberg, 1976b) produce retrograde amnesia. Similar effects can be seen when the CP or the SN are electrically stimulated (Wyers & Deadwyler, 1971; Stabuli & Huston, 1978).

By far, the majority of studies germane to the involvement of the neostriatum or of any other brain structure in memory processes, have only looked upon the effects of manipulations of that structure on the performance of relatively undertrained behaviors. As described above, the general picture that emerges from those studies is that normal activity of the CP is necessary for the consolidation of memory of instrumental tasks. During the last few years we have been systematically studying the involvement of different neural structures in overtrained learned behaviors. When animals are trained to press a positively-rewarded lever and are then injected into the CP with anticholinergic drugs or potassium chloride, they become amnesic. However, when the animals are overtrained (i.e., when the number of training sessions is increased severalfold) those treatments fail to produce memory impairments (Prado-Alcalá & Cobos-Zapiaín, 1977, 1979; Prado-Alcalá, Kaufmann & Moscona, 1980). Equivalent effects are obtained in the case of passive avoidance, where atropine (Giordano & Prado-Alcalá, 1986) and procaine (Pérez-Ruiz & Prado-Alcalá, 1986) are tested.

It thus seems that the CP is involved in the consolidation of relatively untrained behaviors, but not in the performance of overtrained responses. We have proposed that in overtraining memory functions are transferred from the CP to other neurochemical systems (Prado-Alcalá & Cobos Zapián, 1977). Along these lines, Miller (1981) has recently advanced the hypothesis that in overtaining the engrams for operant learning are switched from the striatum to the neocortex.

IS THE NEOSTRIATUM INVOLVED IN THE ACQUISITION OF TASTE AVERSION LEARNING?

From the present results, it is clear that the CP is involved in the acquisition of external cue-consequences learning. However, there are only a few experiments that attempted to demonstrate that the CP is directly involved in the acquisition of conditioned flavor aversions. Lasiter, Deems & Glanzman (1985) reported that the integrity of the projections from the ventroposterior medial nuclei of the thalamus to the anterior insular gustatory neocortex are necessary for the development of normal taste aversion learning. Lesions in the ventrolateral neostriatum produced disruption of CFA learning, therefore it was suggested that the destruction of striatum should disrupt CFA by eliminating normal path information between thalamus and the gustatory neocortex (Lasiter et al., 1985).

Recently a series of experiments were conducted in our laboratories to assess to what extent is the CP involved in the acquisition of both taste and odor aversions using similar procedures to those mentioned above for the limbic system experiments. In one experiment we gave procaine to three different cannulated groups. The cannulae were aimed at the dorsal or ventral neostriatum, or at the amygdala. The microinjections were made during the acquisition of an odor-taste compound followed by LiCl. The preliminary results of these experiments are shown in Figure 4.1, where the mean suppression of fluid consumption (calculated as a percentage of a water baseline) is shown for extinction. Odor or taste alone were tested on different days. The group which received the procaine in the amygdala showed a taste aversion similar to the controls, but a disrupted odor aversion (near 100% of baseline). These results replicated the effects of disrupted odor aversion when the procaine was injected into the amygdala (Bermúdez-Rattoni et al., 1983). In contrast, we failed to find any disruptive effects when the procaine was applied to the dorsal or ventral neostriatum.

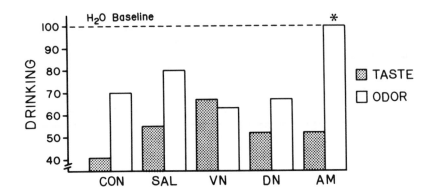

FIG. 4.1. Mean percent consumption by normal rats (CON) and rats that received saline (SAL), procaine into the ventral neostriatum (VN), dorsal neostriatum (DN) or into amygdala (AM). The procaine infusions only had effects in the amygdala group, where it disrupted odor aversions but not taste aversions. Note that both neostriatum groups develop normal odor and taste aversions (*p < 0.05; U-Mann-Whitney relative to controls).

However, in this first experiment the aversions were not very reliable and therefore we decided to replicate this experiment with a different experimental approach. In the second experiment we made large electrolytic lesions intended to produce damage to the ventral or dorsal neostriatum or amygdaloid complex. As reported above, all of these lesions have effects in different tasks and programs (see Bermúdez-Rattoni et al., 1986; Prado-Alcalá, 1985). The procedure was similar to that described above except that we used two acquisition trials in order to insure strong aversion responses (Kiefer et al., 1982). Figure 4.2 shows the results of this experiment when odor or taste were tested on different days. As expected, the control groups showed a strong water intake suppression in the presence of odor or saccharin in the water. The amygdala lesion group showed, as expected, disrupted odor and taste aversions. In marked contrast, both the dorsal and ventral neostriatum lesioned groups showed a strong taste and odor aversion. These results indicate that acute or chronic functional interferences in the neostriatum have an insignificant effect upon acquisition of flavor conditioning

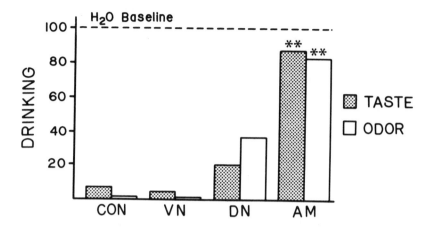

FIG. 4.2. Mean percent consumption by normal rats (CON) and rats with electrolitic lesions into the ventral neostiatum (VN), dorsal neostriatum (DN) and amygdala (AM) during test days. Note that lesions of amygdala significantly disrupted odor and taste aversions (**$p < 0.001$; U-Mann-Whitney, relative to controls).

learning. Of course, more research with different approaches is needed to elucidate the role of the CP in the acquisition of flavor aversions. As pointed out by Lasiter et al., (1985) the destruction of the ventral lateral CP produces the disruption of CTA by affecting of the normal pathways between thalamus and gustatory neocortex. In summary, it seems that the CP does not participate directly as a memory store for learning of internal cue-consequences.

DISCUSSION

In the presence of taste, odor information appears to be selectively gated out of an external defense system and into the internal defense system. These findings prompted a great deal of research to find the neural mechanisms involved in the gating of odor by taste to the internal system. The anatomical localization of neurons performing gating and potentiating functions has been found in studies employing lesions of the gustatory neocortex (Kiefer et al., 1982; Lasiter et al., 1985). The magnitude of the disruption of taste and odor functions depends on the location of the lesion. As mentioned, lesions in the dorsal somatic region of the anterior insular gustatory neocortex disrupted taste aversions but spared taste potentiation of odor (Kiefer et al., 1982; Lasiter et al., 1985).

From the results presented here and elsewhere (Bermúdez-Rattoni et al., 1986; 1987) it is conceivable that the mechanism by which the odor is indexed into the visceral system is, at least in part, regulated by the limbic system. This idea is supported by the results described above (Bermúdez-Rattoni et al., 1983; 1986; 1987; Garcia et al., 1982; 1985). Thus, amygdala anesthesia produced greater disruption in potentiated odor aversions than in taste aversions. These deficits found with procaine-treated rats may be related to disruption of the integration of odor and taste information since amygdaloid anesthesia did not disrupt simple odor-shock or odor-illness associations.

Animals which sustained large amygdalar lesions were unable to acquire either odor, taste, and odor-taste aversions. These data derived from our large lesions along with data from other lesion studies, demonstrate that extensive damage to the amygdala can have devastating effects upon acquisition of both external and visceral cue consequences avoidance tasks (McGowan et al., 1972; Gurpp et al., 1976; Elkins, 1980; Bermúdez-Rattoni et al., 1986). However, small lesions of the lateral nuclei of amygdala or manipulations of cholinergic activity of the dorsal hippocampus produced disruption in the odor aversions but spared taste aversions (Bermúdez-Rattoni et al., 1986; 1987). These results support the idea that the limbic system is regulating the indexing of odor into the internal visceral cue consequences system.

The neostriatum does not seem to be actively involved in the potentiated odor by taste and odor aversions learning. As mentioned, its involvement is reduced to being a through-station for the fiber pathway between thalamus and gustatory neocortex (Lasiter et al., 1985). However, there is a clear functional involvement of the striatum in the acquisition and maintenance of tasks mediated by external cue consequences (Prado-Alcalá et al., 1985).

In summary, the functional classification of cue-consequence learning in terms of visceral and external systems may be correlated with different but defined structures of the central nervous system. Thus, it seems that the striatum as well as some parts of the limbic system, such as the amygdala, are involved in the learning processes maintained by external cue consequences. Moreover, the limbic system, particularly the basolateral amygdala nuclei, the dorsal hippocampus and the insular neocortex are involved in the odor indexing into the visceral cue-consequences system. And finally, the dorsal somatic region of gustatory neocortex is importantly involved in the acquisition of the taste component in the flavor aversion conditioning.

ACKNOWLEDGEMENTS

This research was supported by the following grant: CONACyT PCSABNA-022045 to FB-R, and by Fundacion Miguel Aleman, A. C. We thank L. Salcedo, M. Escobar, B. Corte and S. Alvarez for technical assistance and/or advice given during this study.

REFERENCES

Allen, W. F. (1923). Origin and distribution of the tractus solitarious in the guinea pig. *Journal of Comparative Neurology, 35,* *171-204.*

Barker, L. A., Glick, S. D., Green, J. P., & Khandelwal, J. (1982). Acetylcholine metabolism in the rat hippocampus and striatum following one-trial passive training. *Neuropharmacology, 21,* 183-185.

Bermúdez-Rattoni, F., Grijalva, C. V., Kiefer, S. W., & Garcia, J. (1986). Flavor-illness aversions: the role of the amygdala in the acquisition of taste-potentiated odor aversion. *Physiology and Behavior, 38,* 503-508.

Bermúdez-Rattoni, F., Chávez, A. F., Coburn, K., & Garcia, J. (1983). The role of the amygdala cholinergic activity in taste potentiated odor aversion learning. *Society for Neuroscience Abstracts,* *9,* 827.

Bermúdez-Rattoni, F., Coburn, K. L., Fernández, J., Chávez, A. F., & Garcia, J. (1987). Potentiation of odor by taste and odor aversion in rats are regulated by cholinergic activity of dorsal hippocampus. *Pharmacology, Biochemistry and Behavior, 26,* 553-559.

Bermúdez-Rattoni, F., Rusiniak, K. W., & Garcia, J. (1983). Flavor-illness aversions: potentiation of odor by taste is disrupted by application of novocaine into amygdala. *Behavioral Biology, 37,* 61-75.

Bermúdez-Rattoni, F., Forthman Quick, D. L., Sánchez, M. A., Pérez, J., & Garcia, J. (submitted). Odor and taste aversions conditioned in anasthetized rats.

Bolles, R. (1985). Introduction: Associative processes in the formation of conditioned food aversions - An emerging functionalism? In: Braveman, N.S. & Bronstein, P. (Eds.), Experimental Assessment and Clinical Applications of Conditioned Food Aversions. *Annals of New York Academy of Science, 443,* 1-7.

Braun, J. J., Lasiter, P. S., Kiefer, S. W. (1982). The gustatory neocortex of the rat. *Physiological Psychology, 10,* 13-45.

Brett, L. P., Hankins, W. G., & Garcia, J. (1976). Prey-lithium aversions. III. Butea Hawks. *Behavioral Biology, 17,* 87-98.

Buresova, O., & Bures, J. (1973). Cortical and subcortical components of the conditioned saccharin aversion. *Physiology and Behavior, 11,* 435-439.

Buresova, O., Aleksanyan, Z. A., & Bures, J. (1979). Electrophysiological analysis of retrieval of conditioned taste aversions in rats: Unit activity changes in critical brain regions. *Physiology Bohemoslov, 28,* 525-539.

Butcher, S. G., & Butcher, L. L. (1974). Origin and modulation of acetylcholine activity in the neostriatum. *Brain Research, 71,* 167-171.

Chapman, R. F., & Blaney, W. M. (1979). How animal perceive secondary compounds. In G. A. Rosenthal & D. H. Jenzen

(Eds.), *Herbivores their interaction with secondary plant metabolities*, pp. 161-198. Academic Press, New York.

Chávez-Martínez, M. E., & Prado-Alcalá, R. A. (1986). Amnesia retrógrada producida por la aplicación de picrotoxina en el cuerpo estriado. X Congreso Nacional de Farmacología, Taxco, México.

Clarke, J. C., Westbrook, R. F., & Irwin, J. (1979). Potentiation instead of overshadowing in the pigeon. *Behavioral and Neural Biology, 25,* 18-29.

Coburn, K. L., Garcia, J., Kiefer, S. W., & Rusiniak, K. W. (1984). Taste potentiation of poisoned odor by temporal contiguity. *Behavioral Neuroscience, 98,* 813-819.

Darwin, C. (1859/1985). El origien de las especies. Original title: On the origin of species by means of natural selection, or the preservation of favoured races in the struggle for life. Sarpe. México. Vol. 10.

Domjan, M. (1985). Long-delay learning revisited. *Annals of New York Academy of Science, 443,* 54-66.

Elkins, R. L. (1980). Attenuation of x-ray induced taste aversion by the olfactory bulb or amygdaloid lesion. *Physiology and Behavior, 24,* 515-521.

Ellins, S. R., Cramer, R. E., & Whitmore, C. (1985). Taste potentiation of auditory aversion in rat: A case for spatial contiguity. *Journal of Comparative Psychology, 99,* 102-111.

Ellins, S. R., & von Kluge, S. Extinction, spontaneous recovery and preexposure effects of taste-potentiated lithium chloride induced auditory food aversions in rats. *Behavioral and Neural Biology,* (in press).

Fernández, S. M., Solodkin, M. H., & Prado-Alcalá, R. A. (1977). Blockade and activation of caudate cholinergic activity. *Society for Neurosciences Abstracts, 3,* 232.

Garcia, J., Lasiter, P. S., Bermúdez-Rattoni, F. & Deems, D. A. (1985). A general theory of aversions learning. In: Experimental assessments and clinical applications of conditioned food aversions. N.S. Braveman & P. Bronstein (Eds.), *Annals of the New York Academy of Sciences, 443,* 8-21.

Garcia, J., & Koelling, R. (1966). Relation of cue to consequence inavoidance learning. *Psychonomic Science, 4,* 123-124.

Garcia, J., & Garcia Y. Robertson. (1984). The evolution of learning mechanisms. Master lectures. American Psychological Association. USA. pp. 191-243.

Garcia, J., Rusiniak, K. W., & Brett, L. P. (1977). Conditioning food-illness aversions in wild animal: caveant canonici. In H. David & H. M. B. Hurwitz (Eds.), *Operant pavlovian interactions,* pp. 273-316. Hillsdale, N.J.: Lawrence Erlbaum Associates.

Garcia, J., Rusiniak, K. W., Kiefer, S. W., & Bermúdez-Rattoni, F. (1982). The neural integration of feeding and drinking habits. In C. D. Woody (Ed.), *Conditioning: representation of involved neural functions,* pp. 567-579. New York: Plenum Press.

Giordano, M., & Prado-Alcalá, R. A. (1986). Retrograde amnesia induced by post-trial injection of atropine into the caudate-putamen.

protective effect of the negative reinforcer. *Pharmacology Biochemistry and Behavior, 24*, 905-909.

Grossman, S. P., Grossman, L., & Walsh, L. (1975). Organization of the rat amygdala with respect to avoidance behavior. *Journal of Comparative Physiological Psychology, 88*, 829-850.

Grupp, L. P., Linseman, M. A., & Coppel, H. (1976). Effects of amygdala lesions of taste aversion produced by amphetamine and LiCl. *Pharmacology, Biochemistry and Behavior, 4*, 541-546.

Haberly, L. B., & Price, J. L. (1978). Association and commisural fiber systems of the areas. *Journal of Comparative Neurology, 178*, 711-740.

Hankins, W. G., Garcia, J., & Rusiniak, K. W. (1974). Cortical lesions: Flavor-illness and noise-shock conditioning. *Behavioral Biology, 10*, 173-181.

Haycock, J. W., Deadwyler, S. A., Sideroff, S. I., & McGaugh, J. L. (1973). Retrograde amnesia and cholinergic systems in the caudate-putamen complex and dorsal hippocampus of the rat. *Experimental Neurology, 41*, 201-213.

Holder, M. D., Bermúdez-Rattoni, F., & Garcia, J. (1987). Taste potentiated noise-illness association. *Behavioral Neuroscience* (in press).

Kesner, R. P., Berman, R. F., Bourton, B., & Hankins, W. G. (1975).of electrical stimulation of amygdala upon neophobia on taste aversion. *Behavioral Biology, 13*, 349-358.

Kiefer, S. W., Rusiniak, K. W., & Garcia, J. (1982). Flavor-illness aversions: Potentiation of odor by taste in rats with gustatory neocortical ablation. *Journal of Comparative Physiological Psychology, 96*, 540-548.

Kim, H. J., & Routtemberg, A. (1976a). Retention deficits following post-trial dopamine injection in rat neostriatum. *Society for Neurosciences Abstracts, 21*, 631.

Kim, H. J., & Routtemberg, A. (1976b). Retention disruption following post-trial picrotoxin injection into the substantia nigra. *Brain Research, 113*, 620-625.

Kuhar, M. J. (1975). Cholinergic neurons: septal-hippocampal relationships. In R. L. Isaacson & K. H. Pribram (Eds.), *The Hippocampus*, pp. 269-283. New York: Plenum Press.

Lasiter, P. S., Glanzman, D. L., & Mensah, P. A. (1982). Direct connectivity between pontine taste areas and gustatory neocortex in rat. *Brain Research, 234*, 111-121.

Lasiter, P. S., & Glanzman, D. L. (1982). Cortical substrates of taste aversion learning: Dorsal prepiriform (insular) lesions disrupt taste aversion learning. *Journal of Comparative and Physiological Psychology, 96*, 376-392.

Lasiter, P. S., Deems, D. A., & Garcia, J. (1985). Involvement of the anterior insular gustatory neocortex in taste-potentiated odor aversion learning. *Physiology, Psychology and Behavior, 34*, 71-77.

Lasiter, P. S., Deems, D., & Glanzman, D. L. (1985). Thalamocortical relations in taste aversion learning: I. Involvement of gustatory thalamocortical projections in taste aversion learning. *Behavioral Neuroscience, 99(3)*, 454-476.

Lehmann, J., & Langer, Z. (1983). The striatal cholinergic interneuron: synaptic target of dopaminergic terminals? *Neuroscience, 10*, 1105-1120.

McGaugh, J. L., & Gold, P. E. (1977). Modulation of memory by electrical stimulation of the brain. In M. R. Rosenzweig & E. Bennet (Eds.), *Neural Mechanisms of Learning and Memory*, pp. 549-560. Massachusetts: MIT Press.

McGeer, E. G., McGeer, P. L., Grewaal, D. S., & Sing, V. K. (1975). Striatal cholinergic interneurones and their relation to dopaminergic nerve endings. *Journal of Pharmacology, Paris, 6*, 143-152.

McGowan, B., Hankins, W. G., & Garcia, J. (1972). Limbic lesions and control of the internal and external environment. *Behavioral Biology, 7*, 841-852.

Miller, M. (1981). *Meaning and Purpose in the Intact Brain.* Oxford University Press.

Neill, D. B., & Grossman, P. S. (1970). Behavioral effects of lesions or cholinergic blockade of dorsal and ventral caudate of rats. *Journal of Comparative and Physiological Psychology, 71*, 311-317.

Norgren, R. (1974). Gustatory afferents to ventral forebrain. *Brain Research, 81*, 285.

Oberg, R. G. E., & Divac, I. (1979). "Cognitive" functions of the Neostriatum. In I. Divac & R. G. E. Oberg (Eds.), *The Neostriatum*, pp. 291-313. Oxford: Pergamon Press.

O'Keefe, J., & Nadel, L. (1978). *The hippocampus as a cognitive map.* New York: Oxford University Press.

Olton, D. D., Becker, J. T., & Handelman, G. E. (1979). Hippocampus space and memory. *Behavioral Brain Science, 2*, 313-365.

Pérez-Ruiz, C., & Prado-Alcalá, R. A. (1986). Differential effects of Lidocaine injections into the striatum on short- and long-term retention of passive avoidance in overtrained rats. Presented at the 16th Annual Meeting Society for Neuroscience, Washington, E.U.A.

Prado-Alcalá, R. A. (1985). Is cholinergic activity of the caudate nucleus involved in memory? *Life Science, 37*, 2135-2142.

Prado-Alcalá, R. A., Bermúdez-Rattoni, F., Velázquez-Martínez, D., & Bacha, M. G. (1978). Cholinergic blockade of the caudate nucleus and spatial alternation performance in rats: overtraining-induced protection against behavioral deficits. *Life Science, 23*, 889-896.

Prado-Alcalá, R. A., & Cepeda, G., Verduzco, L., Jiménez, A., & Vargas-Ortega, E. (1984). Effects of cholinergic stimulation of the caudate nucleus on active avoidance. *Neuroscience Letters, 51*, 31-36.

Prado-Alcalá, R. A., & Cobos-Zapiaín, G. G. (1977). Learning deficits induced by cholinergic blockade of the caudate nucleus as a function of experience. *Brain Research, 138*, 190-196.

Prado-Alcalá, R. A., & Cobos-Zapiaín, G. G. (1979). Interference with caudate nucleus activity by potassium chloride. Evidence for a "moving" engram. *Brain Research, 172,* 577-583.

Prado-Alcalá, R. A., Fernández-Samblancat, M., & Solodkin-Herrera, M. (1985). Injections of atropine into the caudate nucleus impair the acquisition and the maintenance of passive avoidance. *Pharmacology, Biochemistry and Behavior, 22,* 243-247.

Prado-Alcalá, R. A., Kaufmann, P., & Moscona, R. (1980). Scopolamine and KCl injections into the caudate-putamen. Overtraining-induced protection against deficits of learning. *Pharmacology, Biochemistry and Behavior, 12,* 249-253.

Prado-Alcalá, R. A., Signoret-Edward, L., & Figueroa, M. (1981). Time-dependent retention deficits induced by post-training injections of atropine into the caudate nucleus. *Pharmacology, Biochemistry and Behavior, 15,* 633-636.

Prado-Alcalá, R. A., Signoret-Edward, L., Figueroa, M., Giordano, M., & Barrientos, M. A. (1984). Post-trial injection of atropine into the caudate nucleus interferes with long-term, but not with short-term retention of passive avoidance. *Behavioral and Neural Biology, 42,* 81-84.

Rhoades, D. F. (1979). Evolution of plant chemical defense against herbivores. In G.A. Rosenthal & D. H. Jensen (Eds.), *Herbivores: Their Interaction with Secondary Plant Metabolites,* pp. 4-54. New York: Academic Press, Inc.

Roll, D. L., & Smith, J. C. (1972). Conditioned taste aversion in anesthetized rats. In M. E. P. Seligmon & J. L. Hager (Eds.), *Biological boundaries of learning,* pp. 98-102. New York: Appleton-Century-Crofts.

Rusiniak, K. W., Hankins, W. G., Garcia, J., & Brett, L. P. (1979). Flavor-illness aversions: Potentiation of odor by taste in rats. *Behavioral and Neural Biology, 25,* 1-17.

Rusiniak, K. W., Palmerino, C. C., Rice. A. G., Forthman, D. L., & Garcia, J. (1982). Flavor-illness aversions: Potentiation of odor by taste with toxin but not shock in rats. *Journal of Comparative and Physiological Psychology, 96,* 527-539.

Sandberg, K., Sanberg, P. R., Hanin, I., Fisher, A., & Coyle, T. (1984). Cholinergic lesion of striatum impairs acquisition and retention of a passive avoidance response. *Behavioral Neuroscience, 98,* 162-165.

Sih, A., Crowley, P., McPeek, M., Petronka, J., & Strohmeir, K. (1985). Predation, competition and prey communities: A review of field experiments. *Annual Review of Ecology and Systematics, 16,* 269-311.

Stabuli, U., & Huston, J. P. (1978). Effects of post-trial reinforcing vs subreinforcing stimulation of the substantia nigra on passive avoidance learning. *Brain Research Bulletin, 3,* 519-524.

Todd, J. W., & Kesner, R. P. (1978). Effects of posttraining injections of cholinergic agonist and antagonist into the amygdala on retention of passive avoidance in rats. *Journal of Comparative and Physiological Psychology, 2,* 958-968.

Thompson, R. (1983). Brain systems and long-term memory. *Behavioral and Neural Biology, 37*, 1-45.

White, L. (1965). Olfactory bulb projections of the rat. *Anatomical Record, 152*, 465.

Woolf, N. J., & Butcher, L. L. (1982). Cholinergic projections to the basolateral amygdala: A combined Evans Blue and acetylcholinesterase analysis. *Brain Research Bulletin, 8*, 751-763.

Wyers, E. J., & Deadwyler, S. A. (1971). Duration and nature of retrograde amnesia produced by stimulation of caudate nucleus. *Physiology and Behavior, 6*, 97-103.

Clinical Perspectives on Aversively Motivated Behavior

Trevor Archer and Lars-Göran Nilsson
University of Umeå

It may be appropriate to initiate the clinical perspectives on aversively motivated behavior with a consideration of the case of 'little Albert' and the white rat (Watson & Rayner, 1920), which remains an interesting example of the possible involvement of classical conditioning in the development of an emotional disorder. Eleven-month-old Albert showed no initial fear of the rat and even indicated some attempt to play with it. Each attempt to reach the rat was accompanied by a crashing sound resulting from a steel bar being banged behind Albert's head, frightening the child. Five instances of this experience led to agitated or disturbed reactions by Albert at the presence of the white rat in the absence of the crashing bar. The phobia of the white rat appears a clear instance of Pavlovian conditioning whereby the fear (fright, agitation and withdrawl of reaching response) associated with each crash (US) came to be evoked by the white rat (CS) which was subsequently a source of disturbance (CR) to the boy (see also Overmier & Archer, this volume). The anecdotal aspect of the little Albert story ought not to blind us to the advantages to be obtained from considerations of the involvement of conditioning principles in the complex and difficult etiology of depressive illness and anxiety states.

Discussions of clinical perspectives on aversively motivated behavior may in principle take many different forms. For example, one may choose to interpret 'clinical perspective' as a clinical application of basic research on aversively motivated behavior. From this point of view an obvious and straightforward clinical perspective would seem to be to apply the taste aversion paradigm and results into a clinical setting. Cytostatic treatment of cancer patients would seem to qualify as such a clinical setting especially so since many of these patients develop aversion towards certain sorts of food (Olafsdottir, Sjödén, & Westling, 1986), but see also the volume edited by Burish, Levy and Meyerowitz (1985). Thus, Garcia y Robertson & Garcia (1985) have observed a taste aversion and taste-potentiation phenomenon in human patients undergoing nauseous chemotherapy for cancer (see Redd, Burish & Andrykowski, 1985 also). Another clinical perspective of some considerable significance remains the issue of the usage of electroconvulsive shock (ECS) or therapy (ECT) in many cases of mental illness. The ECS/ECT issue also offers a unique instance where memory and learning deficits in humans and animals can be fruitfully compared (cf. Rönnberg & Ohlsson, 1985).

Rather than interpreting the term "Clinical Perspective" as a topic for application of basic research, the authors of the three chapters to be presented in this section have taken the term to mean an area of its own of basic research on aversively motivated behavior. More explicitly, all three chapters deal with various aspects of fear and anxiety. Whereas the experimental paradigms used differ somewhat between these three approaches there are striking similarities with respect to theory and these similarities are interesting such that they should be pointed out and elaborated upon.

In each of the three chapters (Hugdahl, Chapter 5; Öhman, Dimberg & Esevetes, Chapter 6; and Mineka & Tomarken, Chapter 7) there is a background in traditional conditioning theory and in each case there is a modification of this traditional framework in terms of cognitive psychology. In all three chapters there is an explicit urge to broaden the conceptual machinery of conditioning theory to be able to account for fine grain analyses of the data obtained. We will discuss this development of conditioning theory in more general terms in Chapter 18.

With regard to each single contribution in this section a few major points should be pointed out. First, with respect to the chapter by Hugdahl (Chapter 5) it should be noted that the approach taken to relate brain asymmetry and lateralization to conditioning is an interesting speculation that may have far-reaching consequences for interpreting results from conditioning experiments and, more importantly, this approach may serve as a basis to come to grips with contradictory results previously reported in the literature. The chapter by Öhman et al. (Chapter 6) discusses a problem of general importance in studies of aversively motivated behavior in human subjects, namely the role of automatic and controlled processes. Öhman et al. presents an interesting and clever backward masking technique for desynchrony among verbal, motor, and physiological processes. As it seems there are still some challenging problems to solve before this technique can be the break through it promises to be. If one is to account for the selective associations that Öhman et al. discuss one must reasonably first identify the mechanisms and their modulators. This is an important and challenging enterprise not only for studies of aversively motivated behavior in particular but also for the psychology of learning in general.

In Chapter 7, Mineka and Tomarken take on the important task to update conditioning theories of neurotic processes. As pointed out by Overmier and Archer in the introductory chapter such an updating has been desperately needed in the psychological literature for some time now. Overmier and Archer also discuss through several examples of how such models of neuroses could benefit from greater familarity with contemporary conditioning research. For example, the discrepancies between current measures of fear and fear-mediated behaviors poses problems for mediational type theories of avoidance or neurotic behavior that may, at least, partially be alleviated through use of the hypothetical construct that fear is a cognitive process only loosely related to motor, psychophysiological or verbal response systems (e.g. Lang, 1964, 1968). One interesting illustration of this type of conceptualization of fear appears to be provide by the different behaviors observed from infant monkeys in the presence or absence of the surrogate mothers, i.e. exploration and manipulation on the one hand and freezing and terror on the other (cf. Harlow, McGaugh & Thompson, 1971; but see also Davey & Arulamnala, 1982; Davey & McKenna, 1983).

The invocation of some concepts in Mineka and Tomarken's updating of conditioning theories of neurotic processes might be a source of some concern unless the concepts are more fully and independently assessed and verified. The integration of concepts from, for example, animal learning and human memory research is something we have endorsed in previous writings (Nilsson & Archer, 1985), but in that context we also pointed out the risks involved in such enterprises. Overmier and Archer (this volume) alert the reader to that danger again. An example of a seemingly problematic concept that Mineka and Tomarken want to introduce in research on aversively motivated behavior is the concept of schema. This concept is widely used in the cognitive literature, but it would seem to require some more specification in order for it to be properly used in research on aversively motivated behavior.

ECT is most commonly used in the treatment of endogenous depression and has been shown to be reliably efficacious (Fink, 1974) even in comparison with tricyclic antidepressants (Davidson, McLeod, Law-Yone & Linnoila, 1978), atypical antidepressants (Kiloh, Child, & Latner, 1960), or monoamine oxidase inhibitors (Shepard, 1965). As stated by Fink (1979) the impairment of memory functions by ECT is the most known, most studied and most pervasive consequence of the treatment. Wide aspects of the retrograde and anterograde amnesic conditions have been examined using numerous types of tests with variations of modality, content (verbal or figural), test method, etc., (e.g. Cronholm & Ottosson, 1961; Dornbush & Williams, 1974; Harper & Wiens, 1975; Squire, 1977), although it is known that ECT does improve the memory and performance of depressed patients (Sand-Strömgren, 1977). Amnesic effects in animals are extremely robust and have been reviewed (Kesner & Conner, 1974). The enormous wealth of evidence on memory loss following ECS in animals and humans provides a unique instance where the types of amnesic effect can be compared over numerous procedures in order to link processes in the memory and learning capacities of humans and animals; but examples of such direct comparisons appear to be sparse. The most common approach towards linking the human and animal memory data from ECS studies pertains to the derivations of neurochemical theories of ECT action that may or may not be related to memory (Essman, 1973; Kety, 1974). From a clinical perspective, the relations of ECT and depresive illness makes deep inroads essentials to considerations of aversively motivated behavior; and, the memory dimension poses essential grounds for the development of both multidisciplinary and interspecies pursuit of mechanism and therapy.

It should also be pointed out in this context that animal models seem to be appropriate for testing the 'preparedness hypothesis' (Seligman, 1970). However, such models would seem to be lacking in generality if one wants to take on the task of studying human behavior like phobias. Thus, evidence of any 'primitive' conditioning in human conditioning studies appears to be singularly lacking (e.g. Brewer, 1974; Dawson, Schell & Tweddle-Banis, 1986; Wilson, 1968; but see also Boakes, this volume; Dawson & Schell, 1987) except in human subjects at very early ages (2 years or less) when language abilities are clearly limited (Bentall, lowe & Beasty, 1985; Lowe, 1979). Boakes (this volume) proposes that the 'primitive' conditioning may prevail in human experiments until a particular threshold is reached and 'awareness' triggered together with decision processes that affect later responding. These considerations are necessary since it may be that the principles we derive are too powerfully based on the animal conditioning data and other analyses are required. Such studies would seem to require human rather than animal subjects, if the goal is to arrive at some general principles of utility to a broad clinical perspective.

REFERENCES

Bentall, R. P., Lowe, C. F., & Beasty, A. (1985). The role of verbal behavior in human learning: II. Developmental differences. *Journal of the Experimental Analyses of Behavior, 43,* 165-181.

Brewer, W. F. (1974). There is no convincing evidence for operant and classical conditioning in human beings. In W. B. Weimer & D. J. Palermo (Eds.), *Cognition and the symbolic processes,* pp. 1-42. Hillsdale, N. J.: Lawrence Erlbaum Associates.

Cronholm, B., & Ottoson, J. O. (1961). Memory functions in endogenous depression before and after electroconvulsive therapy. *Archives of General Psychiatry, 5,* 193-199.

Davey, G. C., & Arulamnalam, T. (1982). Second-order 'fear' conditioning in humans: Persistence of CR 2 following extinction of CR 1. *Behavioral Research Therapy, 20,* 391-396.

Davey, G. C., & McKenna, I. (1983). The effects of postconditioning revaluation of CS and UCS following Pavlovian second-order electrodermal conditioning in humans. *Quarterly Journal of Experimental Psychology, 35*, 125-133.

Davidson, J., McLeod, M., Law-Yone, B., & Linnoila, M. (1978). Comparison of electroconvulsive theropy and combined phenelzine-amitnyptyline in refractory depression. *Archives of General Psychiatry, 35*, 639-644.

Dawson, M. E., & Schell, A. M. (1987). Human autonomic and skeletal conditioning: The role of consious cognitive factors. In G. C. L. Davey (Ed.), *Cognitive processes and pavlovian conditioning in humans*, pp. 27-56. Chicester: Johan Wiley.

Dawson, M. E., Schell, A. M., & Tweddle-Banis, H. T. (1986). Greater resistence to extinction of electrodermal responses conditioned to potentially phobic CS_s: A noncognitive process? *Psychophysiology, 23*, 552-561.

Dornbush, R. L., & Williams, M. (1974). Memory and ECT. In M. Fink, S. Kety, J. McGaugh & T. Williams (Eds.), *Psychobiology of Convulsive therapy*, pp. 199-205. Washington D. C.,: V. H. Winston & Sons.

Essman, W. B. (1973). *Neurochemistry of cerebral electroshock.* New York: Spectrum Publications.

Fink, M. (1974). Clinical progress in convulsive therapy. In M. Fink, S. Kety, J. McGaugh & T. Williams (eds.), *Psychobiology of convulsive therapy*. pp. 271-278. Washington D. C.,: V. H. Winston & Sons,

Fink, M. (1979). *Convulsive therapy: Theory and practice.* New York: Raven Press.

Garcia y Robertson, R., & Garcia, J. (1985). X-Rays and learned taste-aversions: Historiacal and psychological ramifications. In T. G. Burish, S. M. Levy & B. E. Meyerowitz (Eds.), *Cancer, nutrition and eating behavior: A biobehavioral perspective*, pp. 11-41. Hillsdale, N. J.: Lawrence Erlbaum Associates.

Harlow, H. F., McGaugh, J. L., & Thompson, R. F. (1971). *Psychology.* San Francisco: Albion.

Harper, R. G., & Wiens, A. N. (1975). Electroconvulsive therapy and memory. *Journal of Nervous and Mental Disorders, 161*, 245-254.

Kesner, R. P., & Conner, H. S. (1974). Effects of electrical stimulation of rat limbic system and midbrain reticular formation upon short- and long-term memory. *Physiology and Behavior, 12*, 5-12.

Kety, S. S. (1974). Biochemical and neurochemical effects of electroconvulsive shock. In M. Fink, S. Kety, J. McGaugh & T. Williams (Eds.), *Psychobiology of Convulsive Therapy*, pp. 285-294. Washington, D. C.: V. H. Winston & Sons.

Kiloh, L. G., Child, J. P., & Latner, G. (1960). A controlled trial of iproniazid in the treatment of endagenous depression. *Journal of Mental Science, 106*, 1139-1144.

Lang, P. J. (1964). Experimental studies of desensitization psychotherapy. In J. Wolpe, A. Salter & L. J. Reyna (Eds.), *The Conditioning Therapies*, pp. 38-53. New York: Holt, Rhinehart &

Winston.

Lang, P. J. (1968). Fear reduction and fear behavior: Problems in treating a construct. In J. M. Shlein (Ed.), *Research in Psychotherapy, Vol. III*, pp. 90-103. Washington DC: American Psychological Association.

Lowe, C. F. (1979). Determinants of human operant behavior. In M. D. Zeiler & P. Harzem (Eds.), *Advances in the analyses of behavior, 1*, pp. 159-192. New York: Wiley.

Nilsson, L.-G., & Archer, T. (1985). Basic theoretical concepts. In L.-G. Nilsson and T. Archer (Eds.), *Perspectives on learning and memory*, pp. 15-18. Hillsdale, New Jersey: Lawrence Erlbaum Associates.

Olafsdottir, M., Sjödén, P.-O., & Westling, B. (1986). Prevalence and prediction of chemotherapy-related anxiety, nausea and vomiting in cancer patients. *Behaviour Research Therapy, 24*, 59-66.

Redd, W. H., Burish, T. G., & Andry-Kowski, M. A. (1985). Aversive conditioning and concer chemotherapy. In T. G. Burish, S. M. Lavy & B. E. Meyerowitz (Eds.), *Cancer, nutrition and eating behavior: A biobehavioral perspective*. pp. 117-132. Hillsdale: N. J.: Lawrence Erlbaum Associates.

Rönnberg, J., & Ohlsson, K. (1985). The challenge of integrating animal learning and human memory research. In L.-G. Nilsson and T. Archer (Eds.), *Perspectives on learning and memory*, pp. 293-324. Hillsdale, New Jersey: Lawrence Erlbaum Associates.

Sand-Strömgren, L. S. (1977). The influence of depression on memory. *Acta Psychiatrica Scandinavia, 56*, 109-128.

Seligman, M. E. P. (1970). On the generality of the laws of learning. *Psychological Reviews, 77*, 406-418.

Shepard, M. (1965). Clinical trial of the treatment of depressive illness. *British Medical Journal, 1*, 881-886.

Squire, L. R. (1977). ECT and memory loss. *American Journal of Psychiatry, 134*, 997-1001.

Watson, J. B., & Rayner, R. (1920). Conditioned emotional reactions. *Journal of Experimental Psychology 3*, 1-14.

Wilson, G. D. (1968). Reversal of differential GSR conditioning by instructions. *Journal of Experimental Psychology, 76*, 491-493.

5 Human Pavlovian Aversive Conditioning: Effects of Brain Asymmetry and Stimulus Lateralization

Kenneth Hugdahl
University of Bergen

INTRODUCTION

In the present chapter I will argue that recent data on human Pavlovian conditioning may be interpreted in terms of brain asymmetry and lateralization (see also Hugdahl, 1987 a, b; for other reviews). The concepts of asymmetry and lateralization denote the fact that the two cerebral hemispheres are functionally different for the processing of sensory information, and in particular for linguistic and visuo-spatial materials (Kimura, 1961; Sperry, 1974; Wada & Rasmussen, 1960). While the left hemisphere is dominant, or specialized, for the processing of verbal stimuli, the right is dominant, or specialized, for the processing of visuo-spatial and emotionally relevant stimuli (Bradshaw & Nettleton, 1981).

I will start out my review by describing in detail an experiment recently performed in our laboratory (Hugdahl & Brobeck, 1986), using what we have called "the dichotic extinction paradigm". Before that I would however like to present a brief theoretical account of lateralization of conditioning.

There are several theoretical arguments, although perhaps speculative, for a lateralized perspective on human Pavlovian conditioning. As I have argued elsewhere (e.g. Hugdahl, 1987 a, b) it is surprising that so less attention has been paid to the issue of asymmetry of conditioning considering the overlap in conceptual and theoretical concepts used to describe both the asymmetry and conditioning phenomena. I will here only list a few of these arguments, and the interested reader is referred to Hugdahl (1987 a, b; see also Hugdahl & Brobeck, 1986; Hugdahl, Kvale,

145

Nordby & Overmier, 1987) for further information. First of all, from the conceptualization of human Pavlovian conditioning in information-processing terms, stressing "attention", "information", and "expectancy" (e.g. Öhman, 1983; Maltzman, 1979; Dawson, Schell, Beers, & Kelly, 1982) it is a short step to infer that conditioning to language-related CSs should differ in strength depending on whether the stimulus is initially fed to the left or to the right hemisphere. Furthermore, if conditioning involve higher-order extraction of information of the CS-UCS contingency (cf. Rescorla, 1980), then the left hemisphere should be at an advantage relative the right if the CS has a semantic processing load, and the right hemisphere should be at an advantage relative the left if the CS has a non-verbal processing load. A possible example of the latter would be conditioning to fear-relevant CSs like pictures of snakes and spiders (Öhman, 1979; Hare & Blevings, 1975). From our knowledge of functional brain asymmetry it could be predicted that conditioning should be more easily acquired and/or more resistent to extinction when fear-relevant CSs are initially processed in the right hemisphere (cf. Schwartz, Davidson & Maer, 1975 for the relation of the right hemisphere to emotionally relevant stimuli).

Finally, it could be argued that the theory of prepared learning and the concept of preparedness (Seligman, 1970; Seligman & Hager, 1972) is possible to integrate into a lateralized perspective on conditioning and learning. Seligman (1970) suggested that the general laws of learning may not be valid for all kinds of stimuli and responses. Instead he suggested that organisms had evolved a biologically determined "preparedness" to more easily associate certain stimuli with certain reinforcers. The prototype of the "prepared paradigm" was the taste-aversion phenomenon (Garcia & Koelling, 1966) where rats easily developed an avoidance response to saccharin-flavored water if previously paired with injections of lithium chloride (which makes the animal sick), but not when paired with external shocks. Prepared learning made the way for the introduction of stimulus-significance as a critical factor in conditioning. I would, however, like to argue that stimulus-significance is not only related to biological evolution through "prepared" contingencies, but that the significance of a verbal CS as compared to a visuo-spatial CS is a biologically relevant to the organism as is the "prepared" attribute of the stimulus.

The dichotic extinction paradigm

From these introductory remarks, I will now turn to a review of empirical data from our laboratory (Hugdahl & Brobeck, 1986) followed by a more thorough discussion of the issues involved.

A general outline of the "dichotic extinction paradigm" is presented in Figure 5.1.

The dichotic listening technique is a frequently used method for the study of hemispheric asymmetry and brain lateralization (e.g. Kimura, 1961; see also Hugdahl, in press, for reviews of dichotic listening

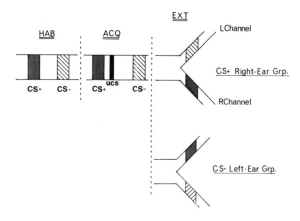

FIG. 5.1. Schematic description of the basic procedure in the "dichotic extinction paradigm". R = Right; L = Left; Hab = Habituation phase; Acq = Acquisition phase; Ext = Extinction phase. Note that the CSs are presented binaurally and separated during the habituation and acquisition phases, but dichotically and simultaneously during the extinction phase. See text for further explanations.

research).   However,   the   technique   is   seldom   used   in   classical conditioning studies (see von Wright, Andersson & Stenman, 1975; Dawson & Schell, 1982 for exceptions).

Forty-two right-handed men participated in the experiment, which was divided into three phases; a habituation, an acquisition, and a dichotic extinction phase.   During the habituation phase, all forty-two subjects were presented with the two consonant-vowel (CV) syllables "Ba" and "Pa".   Each syllable was 320 msec in duration, and the intertrial interval was varied between 25-40 sec.   On each trial, the subjects heard either "Ba" or "Pa", and there were four randomized presentations of each. The sounds were presented binaurally on each trial, i.e. the subject heard the same sound in both ears on each trial.   Skin conductance responses (SCRs) were recorded as dependent measures.

During the next, acquisition phase, 28 of the 42 subjects had one of the two CV-syllables always followed by a 106 db white noise, while the other CV was not followed by noise.   Which of the two CVs that was followed by noise was counterbalanced across subjects.   Thus, one of the CVs was turned into a CS +, with the other as a control (CS-), using a differential conditioning design (Prokasy & Kumpfer, 1973).   There were 10 CS +/UCS presentations, and 10 CS- presentations.   The remaining 14 subjects acted as a control group for the 28 conditioned subjects.   They had no UCS-presentations during the acquisition phase, but only CS presentations.   The 28 conditioned subjects were all treated alike, 10 CS +/UCS presentations and 10 CS- presentations.   All stimuli were delivered binaurally and separated in time.

During the extinction phase of the experiment, all 42 subjects had *both* the CS+ and the CS- presented at the same time in a dichotic mode. This meant that "Pa" and "Ba" was heard at the same time on each trial, one from the right ear and one from the left ear.

The decision of which of the two CSs (the CS+ and CS-) that should be presented in the right ear (contralateral to the left hemisphere), and which should be presented in the left ear (contralateral to the right hemisphere) was the only experimental manipulation performed on the 28 conditioned subjects).

By simply reversing the headphones so that half of the conditioned subjects had the CS+ in the right ear, and the CS- in the left ear, while the other half had the CS+ in the left ear, and the CS- in the right ear, two different groups of 14 subjects each were created. Thus, during the dichotic extinction phase, the 42 subjects were divided into; 14 previously conditioned subjects with the CS+ in the right ear and the CS- in the left ear; 14 previously conditioned subjects with the CS+ in the left ear, and the CS- in the right ear; and 14 control subjects with no conditioning experience, but also with dichotic presentations of the CS+ and CS-. (Since these subjects never had been presented with the UCS during acquisition, the terms CS+ and CS- simply means "Pa" and "Ba" without any conditioned difference between the sounds).

The control group was predicted to cease responding almost on the first extinction trial since they had never been conditioned. The important aspect of the experiment is however the predictions for the two conditioned groups. Remember that all of these subjects had been treated exactly alike during the habituation and acquisition phases of the experiment, and that the only difference between the groups during the extinction phase was the reverse of the headphones. Thus, the physical stimuli were the same for all subjects. From a learning theory point of view, the two conditioned groups should not differ in extinction performance. This is a prediction that can be made from any learning theory, whether cognitively (Rescorla & Wagner, 1972) or biologically based (Seligman, 1970; Eysenck, 1979).

Thus, from a learning theory perspective it should not matter in which ear the CS+ was presented during the extinction phase. However, from a brain lateralization perspective it should matter. It could be predicted that the group with the CS+ in the right ear should reveal delayed extinction performance compared to the group with the CS+ in the left ear. The reasons for this prediction are as follows:

One of the basic assumtions behind the dichotic listening technique is that the crossed auditory pathways are both more preponderant and more efficient than the uncrossed ones (Kimura, 1967). The empirical foundation for this assumption is derived from both recordings of brain potentials (Rosenzweig, 1951) and regional cerebral blood flow (Maxmilian, 1982). The result is then that information projected to the contralateral or opposite hemisphere should be better processed than information projected to the ipsilateral or same hemisphere. Since a clear majority of right-handers have been found to have language lateralized to the left hemisphere (Wada & Rasmussen, 1960; Rasmussen & Milner, 1977) better recall should then occur to the right ear input compared to

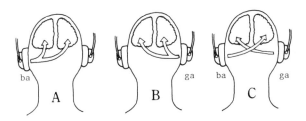

FIG. 5.2. Schematic description of the principles behind the dichotic listening technique. Contralateral projections are more preponderant than the ipsilateral ones. Figures 5.2A and 5.2B illustrate the monaural presentation of a single syllable to the left and the right ear, respectively. In the rightmost Figure (2C), the effect of a dichotic presentation of two syllables is shown. Stimulus transmission from the ear to the ipsilateral hemisphere is suppressed relative to the contralateral transmission. Typically, the right ear input is more accurately recalled than the left ear input in right-handed individuals. (From Hughdahl, 1987b. Reprinted with permission from the publisher John Wiley & Sons.)

the left ear input when the stimulus is verbal in nature. The basic outline of the dichotic listening technique is shown in Figure 5.2.

In general, this has also usually been found (see Bryden, 1982; Springer, 1986 for reviews), and the Right Ear Advantage (REA) for verbal material is perhaps one of the more robust empirical phenomenon in experimental psychology, indicating a left hemisphere specialization for the processing of language related stimuli.

Taking these assumptions together, it could then be hypothesized that since the contralateral pathways are more efficient than the ipsilateral ones, and since the left hemisphere is specialized for language processing in right-handers, then a verbal CS+ dichotically presented to the *right* ear should be more efficiently processed than a CS+ dichotically presented to the *left* ear. The skin conductance (SCR) results for the habituation and acquisition phases of the Hugdahl and Brobeck (1986) study are seen in Figure 5.3.

As can be seen in Figure 5.3, there is an overall decrease in response amplitudes for all subjects from the first trial. This is interpreted in terms of habituation of the electrodermal orienting response (OR) (Sokolov, 1963; Öhman, 1971). During the acquisition phase, there is a dramatic increase in response amplitudes from the second trial to the CS+ as compared to the CS- in all subjects. This is interpreted in terms of conditioned acquisition (Prokasy & Kumpfer, 1973). Note that the labellings "CS+ Left Ear" and "CS+ Right Ear" groups *do not* imply that the subjects were treated differentially during the habituation and acquisition phases. The labels mean those subjects that *later* during the dichotic extinction phase received the CS+ in the right and left ears,

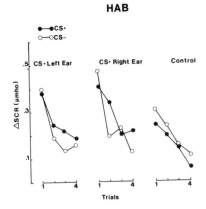

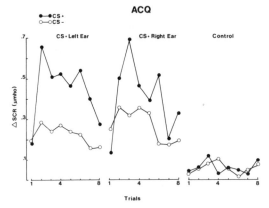

FIG. 5.3. The dichotic extinction paradigm. Mean skin conductance responses (SCRs) in μS as function of trials during the habituation (Hab) and acquisition (Acq) phases of the experiment. (From Hughdahl & Brobeck, 1986. Reprinted with permission from Psychophysiology.)

respectively. Thus, the splitting up of the subjects into the CS+ Right and CS+ Left ear groups already from the start of the experiment was made as a control for the possibility that any differences existed between the groups also during the habituation and accquistition phases. However, as can be seen in Figure 5.3, there were no significant differences between the "groups" during habituation and acquisition.

During the extinction phase, there was a large difference between the groups in response amplitudes across the entire extinction period. These data are shown in Figure 5.4.

Note that the abscissa is plotted in blocks of four trials, thus the entire extinction period involved 32 trials.

It should be noted that the only experimental difference between the two groups during the extinction phase was that the headphones were reversed for half of the subjects.

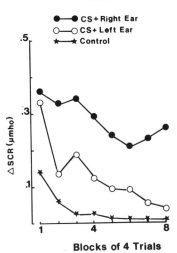

FIG. 5.4. The dichotic extinction paradigm. Mean skin conductance responses (SCRs) in μS as a function of trials during the dichotic extinction phase for the three groups in the experiment. (From Hugdahl & Brobeck, 1986. Reprinted with permission from the journal Psychophysiology.)

An interesting aspect of the data is the initial similar increase in responding in both groups on Trialblock 1. This effect is probably caused by the reinstatement of the orienting response on the first dichotic trial as an effect of the change in presentation mode of the CS stimuli (cf. Grings, 1960). Interestingly however, the groups differ in responding from Trialblock two and onwards, with the CS+ right ear group revealing superior performance.

The findings by Hugdahl and Brobeck (1986) were essentially similar to the findings by Hugdahl, Qundos and Vaittinen (1982a). Thus the dichotic extinction effect for the CS+ Right Ear group has been observed in two different experiments. The results from the extinction phase of the Hugdahl et al. (1982a) study are seen in Figure 5.5.

Hugdahl et al. (1982a) also included two groups that received two pianochords as the CS+ and CS-, with the assumption that since a Left Ear Advantage (LEA) sometimes is reported for musical stimuli, indicating a right hemisphere specialization for the processing of music (Kimura, 1967; Goodglass & Calderon, 1977) stronger resistance towards extinction should be observed in the *CS+ Left ear group* compared to the *CS+ Right ear group*. The results showed, however, no significant differences between the two groups.

There may be several reasons why no differences were observed to the musical stimuli. Some studies have revealed that whereas musically trained subjects reveal a REA, nonmusicians reveal a LEA (Bever & Chiarello, 1974; Gordon, 1970; Schweiger & Maltzman, 1985). Since this factor was not controlled for in the Hugdahl et al. (1982a) study, spontaneous mixing of musicians and nonmusicians in the sample could have contributed to the absence of a difference between the groups.

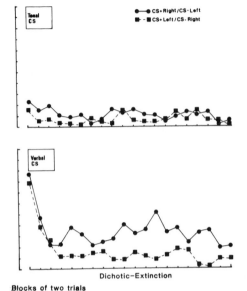

FIG. 5.5. The dichotic extinction paradigm. Mean skin conductance responses (SCRs) in μS as a function of trials for the two groups (CS+ Right ear and CS+ Left ear, respectively). (From Hugdahl, Qundus & Vaittinen, 1982a. Reprinted with permission from the Pavlovian Journal of Biological Science).

Before the results from the dichotic extinction paradigm are discussed in a broader theoretical framework, one further experiment related to the paradigm and two extensions will be presented.

Dichotic extinction and attentional control

An important criticism of the interpretation that the reviewed experiments have revealed a relationship between conditioning on the one hand, and brain asymmetry and lateralization on the other hand, is the lack of control for attentional biases.

It has recently been suggested by some students of the dichotic technique that the REA-effect in general may be caused by a bias to selectively attend to the right side in space (Bryden, 1982; Bryden, Munhall & Allard, 1983; Hugdahl & Andersson, 1986; Geffen & Wale, 1979). It is further argued that right-handed subjects should more easily be biased to attend to the right ear input (Bryden, 1982). Thus, directed attention is obviously a possible confounding factor that could explain reported REA effects in the literature.

The same kind of criticism could also be applied to the present findings of lateralized conditioning. If it is easier for a right-handed subject to attend to the right ear in a dichotic presentation, then the observed difference between the CS+ Right ear and CS+ Left ear groups could have been caused by perceptual or attentional bias.

Thus, the increased responding observed in the CS+ Right ear group could be due to a perceptual or attentional gating mechanism preventing the processing of the CS-. Similarly, the smaller response amplitudes observed in the CS+ Left ear group could be the effect of the same gating mechanism, but favoring the processing of CS-. As a consequence, the CS+ Right ear group should reveal larger response amplitudes than the CS+ Left ear group.

One way to test this would be to split each of the two groups during extinction into two subgroups, with one subgroup explicitly instructed to attend only to the right ear input, and the other subgroup explicitly instructed to attend only to the left ear input.

Such an experiment should also reveal something of the empirical basis of the previous results, whether they are basically perceptual or associative in nature. It is hard, if not impossible, to rule out the possibility that the previous findings are perceptual and therefore reveal nothing about conditioning and brain asymmetry. However, this may not be so damaging to the arguments put forward in this chapter, since the distinction between perceptual and "true" associative processes in itself is difficult to encompass when dealing with human conditioning. I will return to this in a later section when discussing orienting and conditioning.

Now, if the CS+ Right ear group-effect observed in the Hugdahl and Brobeck (1986) and Hugdahl et al. (1982a) studies was due to a right ear *attentional* bias, then there should be a difference between a CS+ Right ear subgroup which is instructed to attend to the right ear, and a CS+ Right ear group which is instructed to attend to the left ear. In a similar vein, it could be predicted that a CS+ Left ear/Attend right subgroup should be below a CS+ Left ear/Attend left subgroup. The reason for this latter prediction is that attending to the right ear while the CS+ is presented in the left ear would indicate "functional dissociation" between the effect of the CS and the effect of the instruction.

However, if attentional instructions have no differential effect on response amplitudes in the four subgroups, but that the two CS+ Right ear subgroups still are superior to the two CS+ Left subgroups, then an interpretation in terms of lateralization of conditioning will be strengthened. The results of this experiment are shown in Figure 5.6 (only the extinction phase is shown).

As can be seen in Figure 5.6 there were overall greater response amplitudes in the CS+ Right ear subgroups compared to the CS+ Left ear subgroups, with no apparent effect of the attentional instruction. Thus, the basic difference between the CS+ Right and CS+ Left ear grouping was replicated. Furthermore, the effect is obviously not caused by attentional bias.

The dichotic acquisition and dichotic blocking paradigms

Two extensions of the basic paradigm are "the dichotic acquisition", and "dichotic blocking paradigm", respectively. Starting out with the dichotic

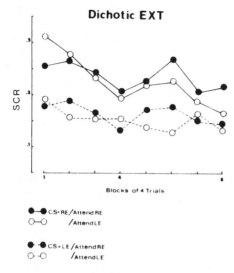

FIG. 5.6. The dichotic extinction paradigm-attention control. Mean skin conductancer responses (SCRs) in μS as a function of trials for the four groups. CS + RE = CS+ Right ear group; CS + LE = CS+ Left ear group.

acquisition paradigm, the major difference to the dichotic extinction paradigm is that the dichotic mode of the CS presentations occurs during the acquisition phase instead of during the extinction phase. The logic behind the dichotic acquisition paradigm is as follows: If two different verbal stimuli ("Ba" and "Pa") are simultaneously presented, one in each ear, in contiguity with the UCS, then the right ear CS should be more easily associated with the UCS than the left ear CS. Conversely, it could be argued that if emotionally relevant CSs are used, then the left ear CS should be more easily associated with the UCS, considering recent evidence showing a right hemisphere specialization for the processing of emotionally relevant information (Gainotti, 1972). These predictions could be tested by first presenting the two CSs dichotically during the acquisition phase, and then to present them separated and binaurally, during the extinction phase. If verbal stimuli are used, then the CS presented in the right ear during acquisition should reveal larger responses during the extinction phase, compared to the CS presented in the left ear. In the only experiment so far performed in our laboratory on the dichotic acquisition paradigm, we have not been able to demonstrate any asymmetry effects. It therefore seems that asymmetry of conditioning is more of an extinction than of an acquisition effect.

The dichotic blocking paradigm is similar to the dichotic acquisition paradigm in the sense that the dichotic CS presentations occur during the acquisition phase. However, in the dichotic blocking paradigm, one of the CSs (called the CSl) is previously associated with the UCS (cf. Kamin, 1969). Half of the subjects receive the CSl in the right ear during dichotic acquisition, with the other CS (called the CS2), simultaneously presented in the left ear. The other half of the subjects have the headphones reversed. During extinction, both CSs are used, and it is predicted that the group with the CSl in the right ear during the dichotic acquisition phase will reveal responses during extinction, because of the blocking effect. This was also obtained in a study with CV-syllables paired with a 106 db white noise UCS (see Hugdahl, 1987b for further details).

The dichotic blocking paradigm is theoretically appealing since conditioned blocking seldom has been studied in humans. One of the reasons for this has been problems in finding good blocking stimuli, i.e. different CSs within the same sensory modality that could be simultaneously presented to the subject with exact control over stimulus parameters. The series of dichotic conditioning paradigms presented so far seem however interesting and promising in this respect. The argument could perhaps be pushed one step further if the analysis of human associative conditioning is made in terms of higher-order information-processing (Dawson, Schell, Beers & Kelly, 1982), stressing the role of the CS in providing information about the UCS (Rescorla, 1972). It could then easily be argued that the cerebral hemispheres are differentially capable of extracting the information in the CS depending on the nature of the stimulus, and/or the nature of the processing requirements inherent in the conditioning task (see Hugdahl, 1987b). With such a cognitive view of conditioning in mind, the dichotic paradigms, and perhaps especially the dichotic blocking paradigm, would be well fitted for the study of conditioning and asymmetry. In the next section I will show how a visual analogue to the auditory dichotic paradigms was used in our laboratory to study asymmetry of conditioning to lateralized visual CS presentations.

The dichoptic acquisition paradigm

The visual experiment (Hugdahl, Kvale, Nordby & Overmier, 1987) employed a modified compound CS paradigm (cf. Rescorla, 1972) in which the different cues in the compound were initially fed only to the left or right hemisphere. During the acquisition phase, a compound of four different CS elements (two verbal and two non-verbal) were simultaneously presented to the subject followed by an 105 db aversive white noise-UCS. The four CS elements were two different color-words each written in two other different conflicting colors (the word "BLÅ" (blue) written in red, and the word "GUL" (yellow) written in green. The elements in the compound CS were tachistoscopically presented during acquisition with the help of the visual half-field (VHF) technique (see McKeever, 1986; Young, 1982 for reviews of the VHF-technique). Thus, during the acquisition phase, one color-word written in a conflicting color was presented in the right half-field (i.e. with initial left hemisphere input), with another color-word written in another conflicting color simultaneously presented in the left half-field (i.e. with intial right hemisphere input). The UCS-noise was delivered binaurally contingent on each compound CS presentation during the acquisition phase of the experiment. Thus, all CS elements in the compound was presented exactly at the same time in both the habituation and acquisition phases. Further, during the acquisition phase, the CS compound was paired synchronously with the UCS.

During the extinction phase, *each element* of the compound CS was presented separately. This was done by presenting each of the four elements in a bilateral display (see Figure 5.7).

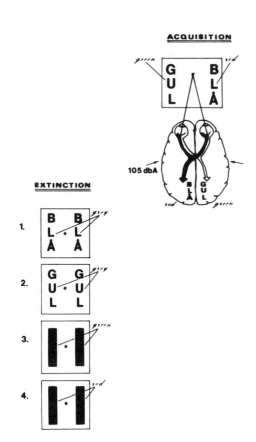

FIG. 5.7. A description of the basic outline of the "dichoptic acquisition paradigm". In the example in the Figure, two Norwegian color-words "GUL" and "BLÅ" (yellow and blue), written in two conflicting colors (green and red) are simultaneously presented in the left and right visual half-fields, respectively, as a compound CS during the acquisition phase. The stimuli are presented against a black background. Note the initial cortical occipital representation of each cue due to the crossing over of the visual pathways. A 105 db noise was used as the UCS, and presented contingent upon the display of the compound CS during acquisition.

During the extinction phase, each of the four CS cues (BLÅ, GUL, green and red) are presented separately, as shown in the Figure (Panels 1-4) are presented as green and red color-bars against a black background. Note the omission of the habituation phase in the Figure. (From Hugdahl, Kvale, Nordby & Overmier, 1987. Reprinted with permission from the journal Psychophysiology.)

The paradigm is thus called a "dichoptic acquisition paradigm" as a visual analogue to the dichotic paradigms previously described (Hugdahl et al., 1982a; Hugdahl & Brobeck, 1986). In order to control for non-associative factors, a control group was run post-hoc with exactly the same CS set-up as the conditioned subjects during acquisition and extinction, but with the exception that no UCSs were presented during the acquisition phase.

Following the outline of the dichoptic acquisition paradigm the following predictions were made:

It was predicted that the word element of the compound CS presented to the *left* hemisphere during acquisition would show greater conditioned responding during the extinction phase than the word element presented to the *right* hemisphere. The hypotheses are for same stimuli across half-field. Another set of hypotheses involve different stimuli in the same half-field: Left hemisphere will condition better to words than colors and vice versa.

Following the same logic, it was predicted that the color, i.e. the non-verbal element of the compound CS, presented to the *right* hemisphere during acquisition would show greater conditioned responding than the color element presented to the *left* hemisphere. This prediction was based on the finding of Pennal (1977) of a right hemisphere superiority for the perception of color-spots presented in the left visual half-field.

As for the auditory experiments, the visual study employed phasic bilateral skin conductance responses (SCRs) to evaluate conditioning. Subjects were right-handed males, and the CS presentations were made from slide projectors with high-speed shutters mounted in front of the lens to achieve brief tachistoscopic stimulus presentations (< 200 msec). The results are seen in Figure 5.8 (habituation and acquisition) and Figure 5.9 (extinction).

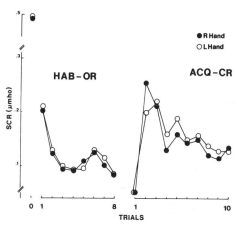

FIG. 5.8. The dichoptic acquisition paradigm. Mean skin conductance responses (SCRs) in μS as a function of trials during orienting and habituation (left panel), and during the acquisition phase (right panel). OR = Orienting response; CR = Conditioned response. R = Right; L = Left. (From Hugdahl, Kvale, Nordby & Overmier, 1987. Reprinted with permission from the journal Psychophysiology.)

As can be seen in Figures 5.8 and 5.9, the initial habituation was followed by a marked increase in response amplitudes to the compound CS display during acquisition. Note that the data are plotted separately for the left and right hand SCR recordings.

Furthermore, as can be seen in Figure 5.9, conditioning to the CS color-word previously presented in the right half-field during acquisition resulted in larger SCRs during extinction, than the color-word previously presented in the left half-field. In contrast, the CS color cue previously presented in the left half-field during acquisition resulted in larger SCRs during the first extinction trial, than the CS color cue presented in the right half-field. It is thus obvious from Figure 5.9 that differential skin conductance responding was demonstrated to the word relative to the color element depending on which hemisphere the compound CS was initially presented to *during acquisition*. The effect was furthermore most prominent during the first extinction trial where hemisphere asymmetry effects were demonstrated for both the word and the color elements. The

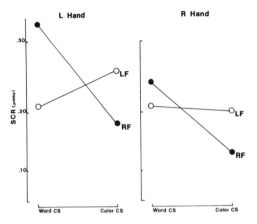

FIG. 5.9. The dichoptic acquisition paradigm. Mean skin conductance response magnitudes (SCRs) in μS to the first extinction trial separately for the left and right hands. LF = Left field presentation during acquisition. RF = Right field presentation during acquisition. (From Hugdahl, Kvale, Nordby & Overmier, 1987. Reprinted with permission from the journal Psychophysiology.)

asymmetry effect for the non-verbal color element however dissipated across trials. It is thus evident from the results that the right hemisphere asymmetry of conditioning to a non-verbal color CS is a more transient phenomenon than the left hemisphere asymmetry of conditioning to a word CS. This is also in agreement with other studies of hemispheric asymmetry that have revealed lateralization of the processing of word stimuli to be a more robust phenomenon than lateralization of the processing of non-verbal stimuli like color-patches, or color-bars (e.g. Hugdahl & Franzon, 1985; Franzon & Hugdahl, 1986; Davidoff, 1976).

An interesting aspect of the "dichoptic acquisition paradigm" is that the observed differences to the left- and right hemisphere CSs during extinction cannot have been caused by different instructions or cognitive sets, or by differences in CS cue onset-time, since all subjects had identical instructions and all four CS cues were presented at exactly the same time on each trial during the acquisition phase. This is important when arguing for a lateralized associative effect because it rules out the possibility that different instructional sets and time differences between hemisphere stimulations could have caused the observed differences in responding.

Summarizing both the data for the auditory and the visual paradigms, it is evident that the results favor an interpretation in terms of a hemisphere asymmetry influence on human Pavlovian conditioning, and especially when verbally relevant CSs are used. The effect seems however to require lateralized CS presentations in order to show up. Although these data seem interesting and promising, it should be kept in mind that they are preliminary and subject to criticism. One hitherto not discussed aspect of the results is whether the effect is a perceptual/attentional or an associative one. Although, as previously shown, an attentional explanation seems less likely as the basis for the results, the perceptual hypothesis have not yet been properly investigated. This should be done before any firm conclusions are reached. I have further argued that it has not been exclusively demonstrated that associative learning is lateralized in one hemisphere, but rather that it occurs with differential facility as a function of the nature of the CS and/or of the nature of the processing requirements in the conditioning task.

In the next section I will turn to a discussion of possible theoretical integrations of a lateralized perspective on human Pavlovian conditioning. For a more thorough discussion see Hugdahl (1987).

Asymmetry and conditioning: A theoretical framework

Compared to studies of perceptual asymmetries (see Bradshaw & Nettleton, 1981; Benson & Zaidel, 1985), studies of asymmetry of learning, and especially conditioning are rare in the literature. Looking at human conditioning, the possible role played by hemispheric asymmetry is perhaps most possible when skin conductance (SCR), or electrodermal conditioning is considered. There are several arguments for such a position. In the first place, the cortical hemispheres, and especially the frontal and temporal lobes, have been related to the control of electrodermal activity (Kimble, Bagshaw & Pribram, 1965; Wang, 1964; Wilcott & Bradley, 1970). Furthermore, when comparing response amplitudes from the left and right hand recordings to hemisphere specific stimuli, significant differences have been obtained indicating a mechanism of contralateral inhibition in the electrodermal system (Lacroix & Comper, 1979; Boyd & Maltzman, 1983; Myslobodsky & Rattok, 1977). These findings should however be interpreted cautiously since other studies (e.g. Gross & Stern, 1980; Hugdahl, Wahlgren & Wass, 1982b) have failed to report a difference between the hands to about the same kinds of stimuli. Another area of research possibly connecting associative functions and SCR conditioning to hemispheric asymmetry is recent research showing asymmetry of the orienting response (OR) and of subsequent habituation to repeated auditive and visual stimulation. Gruzelier (1973) found more spontaneous SCRs in the left compared to the right hand in a standard habituation paradigm in institutionalized schizophrenics.

This has later been elaborated upon in a more recent work (Gruzelier, 1984) where it has been argued that different schizoprenic syndromes may be related to either left or right hemisphere overactivation. Similarly, Hugdahl et al. (1982b, 1983) found a significant delay in habituation rate when visual stimuli were repeatedly presented to the right hemisphere. I will now argue that these apparent non-related studies actually may tell us something about asymmetry and SCR conditioning. My arguments rest on the assumption that the orienting response and its habituation play a crucial role in the process of human conditioning. This is perhaps best expressed by Öhman (1983) who argues that instead of being a nuisance factor in the process of conditioning, the OR "provides an important link for the understanding of Pavlovian conditioning, and perhaps learning in general" (p. 317). Öhman's argument is that the OR is related to learning in such a way that it habituates only as the subject learns something about the CS-UCS contingency, which in turn is a necessary prerequisite for the emergence of a conditioned response (CR).

The first author to relate the concepts of OR and conditioning to brain asymmetry was probably Maltzman (1979). Maltzman (1979) based his arguments on the distinction between involuntary (stimulus-elicited) and voluntary (significance-elicited) ORs. Maltzman (1979) argued that the involuntary OR, i.e. the response to a novel stimulus presented for the first time, is regulated primarily by the Pavlovian "first signal system", whereas voluntary ORs, elicited by verbal instructions related to stimulus significance, should be regulated by the Pavlovian "second signal system". From this I will argue that information processed in the first signal system should be regulated by the right hemisphere, whereas information processed in the second signal system should be regulated by the left hemisphere. These suggestions fit with the data reported by Hugdahl et al. (1982b) where it was found that stimulus-elicited ORs to visual flash-stimuli were slower to habituate when they were projected to the right hemisphere compared to when they were projected to the left hemisphere.

The argument that asymmetry of orienting behavior is related to asymmetry of conditioning and learning is further supported by animal data, and especially by the studies by Rogers and her colleagues (e.g. Howard, Rogers & Boura, 1980; Rogers & Anson, 1979; see also Rogers, 1980; 1986). Rogers employs a technique where pharmacological agents are used to selectively inhibit ribosomal protein synthesis in the left and right forebrain of chickens. Injections into the left hemisphere showed impairment of both auditory habituation and visual discrimination learning. In a similar way, Andrew and Rainey (1982) reported hemispheric differences in responding to presentations of novel emotional stimuli in chicken.

Rogers (e.g. 1980), and Andrew and Rainey (1982) have further used a technique where the left or right eye is covered during the learning task. As stated by Zaidel (1985) when citing Hamilton (1987), their data lead to the "attractive if speculative hypothesis that a bird searches for food with its right eye, while it watches for predators with its left" (pp. 49-50).

Effects of hemispheric asymmetry on learning in animals is also reported by Stokes and McIntyre (1985) in a state-dependent learning paradigm. Stokes and McIntyre (1985) produced state-depending through eliciting kindled seizures in the left or right hippocampus in a split-brain operated rat. When the animal was later tested in an avoidance paradigm it was shown that those animals that were kindled in the left side of the brain showed better evidence of conditioning in one experimental condition and impaired conditioning in a second condition. Asymmetry of learning in the animal may finally be inferred from recent studies by Archer and his colleagues (e.g. Archer, Mohammed & Järbe, 1983). Archer (1982) used a noradrenaline-neurotoxin (DSP4) which selectively destroys noradrenergic neurons. By injecting DSP4 into experimental animals, Archer (1982) has been able to demonstrate the importance of noradrenaline in avoidance conditioning. This finding may be crucial for an understanding of asymmetry of learning since several authors (e.g. Oke, Keller, Mefford & Adams, 1978) have reported higher concentrations of noradrenaline in the right somatosensory input area of the thalamus. Since this area has ample cortical connections to the parietal lobe (Jutai, 1984), an area critical for attention and orienting, then asymmetry of catecholamine concentrations in the brain may thus be linked to asymmetry of learning and conditioning. This line of arguments may be taken one step further if also the findings of asymmetrical distributions of dopamine reported by Glick, Ross and Hough (1982) are taken into consideration.

The findings by Glick et al. (1982) are especially intriguing in the present context since Mintz and Myslobodsky (1983) have suggested that it is the dopaminergic circuitry of the right hemisphere that may be responsible for bilateral control of electrodermal orienting and habituation. Mintz and Myslobodsky (1983) studied the electrodermal orienting response to simple visual stimuli in Parkinsonian patients with either a left or a right-sided extrapyramidal lesion syndrome. Among their many findings, it was observed that absence of an electrodermal OR was correlated with a right hemisphere dysfunction, and that the dysfunction was caused by a dopamine deficit. Asymmetry of the nigrostriatal dopamine system was also reported by Jerussi and Taylor (1982) with higher dopamine metabolities in the contralateral striatum to the dominant direction of rotation in haloperidol (a dopamine-antagonist) treated animals. It is thus possible that the motor laterality imbalance found in schizophrenics (e.g. Gur, 1977) with a pronounced left-sidedness on most tests for asymmetry, is a reminiscence of an unequal distribution of dopamine in the two halves of the brain.

Whether asymmetry of the distribution of neurotransmitters in both the animal and human brain is actually related to conditioning, including CSs that presumably differentially activates the hemispheres, is at present an open question. However, considering the intimate relationship between the orienting response and attention on the one hand, and Pavlovian conditioning on the other hand (Öhman, 1983; Maltzman, 1979) every demonstration of asymmetry of brain functions related to orienting and attention (Mintz & Myslobodsky, 1983; Jutai, 1984; Gruzelier, 1984; Gruzelier, Brow, Perry, Rhonder & Thomas, 1984) is of relevance for a lateralized perspective on Pavlovian conditioning. The issue of asymmetry of neurotransmitters in the brain and their importance for learning could perhaps be tested by developing adequate animal models where either unilateral depletions of transmitters are performed, or the effects of unequal distributions of transmitters between the two halves of the brain otherwise are manipulated while the animals are undergoing a conditioning experience. The DSP4-technique developed by Archer (e.g. 1982) seems a promising method in this respect.

Awareness of conditioning

Returning to the human level, the question of awareness of conditioning has been a lively debated area of research (see Psychophysiology, 1973, vol. 10 devoting a special issue to the role of awareness).

In a frequently cited paper, Corteen and Wood (1972) demonstrated that the conditioning of electrodermal responses to auditory presentations of city names could be elicited without the subject being aware of the stimulus. In a first phase of the Corteen and Wood (1972) experiment, subjects received an electric shock as the UCS contingent upon the presentation of the verbal CS (the city name). During this phase, subject's attention was directed towards the words they heard in the earphones. In a second phase, the conditioned words were presented in the left ear while prose-passages were presented in the other ear in a dichotic shadowing task. The subjects were instructed to attend only to the prose-passages in the right ear, ignoring the left ear input. The results showed that the previously shocked city names elicited more responses than control words when presented in the non-attended ear during the dichotic phase of the experiment. Corteen and Wood (1972) interpreted their findings as that CR was elicited although the subject was not aware of the CS. This finding was later replicated by von Wright, Andersson and Stenman (1975), by Dawson and Schell (1982), and by Martin, Stambrook, Tartaryn, and Biehl (1984). However, Wardlaw and Kroll (1976) failed to replicate the original Corteen and Wood (1972) experiment. Instead they claimed that Corteen and Wood's results might have been an artifact. What is perhaps more important is the quite remarkable fact that the methodological discrepancy between the Corteen and Wood (1972) study and the replication by Wardlaw and Kroll (1976) not have been noticed in the literature, and the possibility that these differences interacted with brain asymmetry to yield the difference in outcomes (see however Martin et al., 1984).

Thus, as also pointed out by Martin et al. (1984), Corteen and Wood (1972) presented the critical CSs in the left ear on all trials for all subjects, with the prosa-passages in the right ear, whereas Wardlaw and Kroll (1976) counterbalanced CS presentations between the ears. From what has been previously argued, paying attention to a verbal stimulus presented under dichotic competition should be more effective in the right ear, whereas conditioning to a shock-reinforced CS having an emotional aspect should be more effective in the left ear. Thus, by counterbalancing the presentation of the CSs and the prosa-passages between the ears, it is not surprising that Wardlaw and Kroll (1976) failed to find evidence of unaware conditioning. That brain asymmetry may play a role in unaware conditioning in humans was actually first suggested by Dawson and Schell (1982) who found that when the unattended words (CSs) were presented in the right ear there were indications of a different mode of responding related to attentional shifts, than when the same CSs were presented in the left ear. This was commented upon in a note by Öhman (1983) who stated that: "While this finding may indicate a different relationship between verbal awareness and orienting depending on what hemisphere is activated more data are certainly needed before firmer statements can be made" (p. 357). I agree with Öhman (1983) that more data are necessary and that adequately designed experiments hopefully can further elucidate the role played by the cerebral hemispheres in both unaware and aware human conditioning.

REFERENCES

Andrew, R.J., & Rainey, C. (1982). Right-left asymmetry of response to visual stimuli in the domestic chick. In D.J. Ingle, M. A. Goodale, & R.J.W. Mansfield (Eds.). *Analysis of visual behavior*, pp. 197-209. Cambridge, Mass., MIT Press.

Archer, T. (1982). DSP4, a new noradrenaline neurotoxin, and the stimulus conditions affecting acquisition of two-way active avoidance. *Journal of Comparative and Physiological Psychology, 96*, 476-490.

Archer, T., Mohammed, A. K., & Järbe, T. U. C. (1983). Latent inhibition following systemic DSP4: Effects due to presence and absence of contextual cues in taste-aversion learning. *Behavioral and Neural Biology, 38*, 287-306.

Benson, D. F., & Zaidel, E. (Eds.). (1985). *The dual brain*. New York: Guilford Press.

Bever, T. G., & Chiarello, R. J. (1974). Cerebral dominance in musicians and nonmusicians. *Science, 185*, 537-539.

Boyd, G. M., & Maltzman, I. (1983). Skin conductance response and muscle activity during adutitory, visual and memory tasks (Abstract). *Psychophysiology, 19*, 308.

Bradshaw, J. L., & Nettleton, N. C. (1981). The nature of hemispheric specialization in man. *The Behavioral and Brain Sciences, 4*, 51-91.

Bryden, M. P. (1982). *Laterality: functional asymmetry in the intact brain*. New York: Academic Press.

Bryden, M. P., Munhall, K., & Allard, F. (1983). Attentional biases and the right-ear effect in dichotic listening. *Brain and Language, 18*, 236-248.

Corteen, R. S., & Wood, B. (1972). Autonomic response to shock-associated words in an unattended channel. *Journal of Experimental Psychology, 94*, 308-313.

Davidoff, J. (1976). Hemispheric sensitivity differences in the perception of color. *Quarterly Journal of Experimental Psychology, 28*, 387-394.

Dawson, M. E., & Schell, A. M. (1982). Electrodermal responses to attended and nonattended significant stimuli during dichotic listening. *Journal of Experimental Psychology: Human Perception and Performance, 8*, 82-86.

Dawson, M. E., Schell, A. M., Beers, J. R., & Kelly, A. (1982). Allocation of processing capacity during human autonomic classical conditioning. *Journal of Experimental Psychology: General, 111*, 273-295.

Eysenck, H. J. (1979). The conditioning model of neurosis. *The Behavioral and Brain Sciences, 2*, 155-199.

Franzon, M., & Hugdahl, K. (1986). Visual half-field presentations of incongruent color words: Effects of gender and handedness. *Cortex, 22*, 433-445.

Gainotti, G. (1972). Emotional behavior and hemispheric side of the lesion. *Cortex, 8*, 41-55.

Garcia, J., & Koelling, R. A. (1966). Relation of cue to consequence in avoidance learning. *Psychonomic Science, 4*, 123-124.

Geffen, G., & Wale, J. (1979). Development of selective listening and hemispheric asymmetry. *Developmental Psychology, 15*, 138-146.

Glick, S. D., Ross, D. A., & Hough, L. B. (1982). Lateral asymmetry of neurotransmitters in human brain. *Brain Research, 234*, 53-63.

Gordon, H. W. (1970). Hemispheric asymmetries in perception of musical chords. *Cortex, 6*, 387-398.

Goodglass, H., & Calderon, M. (1977). Parallel processing of verbal and musical stimuli in right and left hemispheres. *Neuropsychologia, 15*, 397-407.

Grings, W. W. (1960). Preparatory set variables related to classical conditioning of autonomic responses. *Psychological Review, 67*, 243-252.

Gross, J. S., & Stern, J. A. (1980). An investigation of bilateral asymmetries in electrodermal activity. *Pavlovian Journal of Biological Science, 15*, 74-81.

Gruzelier, J. H. (1973). Bilateral asymmetry of skin conductance orienting activity and levels in schizophrenia. *Biological Psychology, 1*, 21-41.

Gruzelier, J. H. (1984). Hemispheric imbalances in schizophrenia. *International Journal of Psychophysiology, 1*, 227-240.

Gruzelier, J. H., Brow, T., Perry, A., Rhonder, J., & Thomas, M. (1984). Hypnotic susceptibility: A lateral predisposition and altered cerebral asymmetry under hypnosis. *International Journal of Psychophysiology, 2*, 131-139.

Gur, R. C. (1977). Motoric laterality imbalance in schizophrenia. *Archives of General Psychiatry, 34*, 33-37.

Hamilton, C. R. (1987). Hemispheric specialization in monkeys. In C. B. Trevarthen (Ed.). *Brain circuits and functions of the mind.* Cambridge, UK: Cambridge University Press.

Hare, R. D., & Blevings, G. (1975). Conditioned orienting and defensive responses. *Psychphysiology, 12*, 289-297.

Howard, K. J., Rogers, L. J., & Boura, A. L. A. (1980). Functional lateralization of the chicken forebrain revealed by use of intracranial glutamate. *Brain Research, 188*, 369-382.

Hugdahl, K. (1987a). Lateralization of associative processes: Human conditioning studies. In D. Ottosson (Ed.). *Duality and unity of the brain,* pp. 223-235. Hampshire, UK: Macmillan press.

Hugdahl, K. (1987b). Pavlovian conditioning and hemispheric asymmetry: A perspective. In G. Davey (Ed.). *Cognitive processes and Pavlovian conditioning in humans,* pp. 147-182. Chichester: John Wiley & Sons.

Hugdahl, K. (Ed.) (in press). *Handbook of dichotic listening.* Chichester, UK: John Wiley & Sons.

Hugdahl, K., Kvale, G., Nordby, H., & Overmier, B. J. (1987). Hemispheric asymmetry and human classical conditioning to verbal and non-verbal visual CSs. *Psychophysiology, 24*, 557-565.

Hugdahl, K., & Andersson, L. (1986). The "forced-attention paradigm" in dichotic listening to CV-syllables: A comparison between adults and children. *Cortex, 22,* 417-432.

Hugdahl, K., & Brobeck, C. G. (1986). Hemispheric asymmetry and human electrodermal conditioning: The dichotic extinction paradigm. *Psychophysiology, 23,* 491-499.

Hugdahl, K., Broman, J. E., & Franzon, M. (1983). Effects of stimulus content and brain lateralization on the habituation of the electrodermal orienting reaction (OR). *Biological Psychology, 17,* 153-168.

Hugdahl, K., & Franzon, M. (1985). Visual half-field presentations of incongruent color-words reveal mirror reversal of language lateralization in dextral and sinistral subjects. *Cortex, 21,* 359-374.

Hugdahl, K., Qundos, O., & Vaittinen, J. (1982,a). Effects of hemispheric asymmetry on electrodermal conditioning in a dichotic listening paradigm. *Pavlovian Journal of Biological Science, 17,* 120-129.

Hugdahl, K., Wahlgren, C., & Wass, T. (1982b). Habituation of the electrodermal orienting reaction is dependent on the cerebral hemisphere initially stimulated. *Biological Psychology, 15,* 49-62.

Jerussi, T. P., & Taylor, C. A. (1982). Bilateral asymmetry in stritial dopamine metabolism: Implications for pharmacotherapy of schizophrenia. *Brain Research, 246,* 71-75.

Jutai, J. W. (1984). Cerebral asymmetry and the psychophysiology of attention. *International Journal of Psychophysiology, 1,* 219-225.

Kamin, L. (1969). Predictability, surprise, attention, and conditioning. In B. A. Campbell, and R. M. Church (Eds.). *Punishment and aversive behavior,* pp. 279-296. New York: Appelton.

Kimble, D. P., Bagshaw, M. H., Pribram, K. H. (1965). The GSR of monkeys during orienting and habituation after selective ablations of the cingulate and frontal cortex. *Neuropsychologia, 3,* 121-128.

Kimura, D. (1961). Cerebral dominance and the perception of verbal stimuli. *Canadian Journal of Psychology, 15,* 166-171.

Kimura, D. (1967). Functional asymmetry of the brain in dichotic listening. *Cortex, 3,* 163-178.

Lacroix, J. M., & Comper, P. (1979). Lateralization in the electrodermal system as a function of cognitive/hemispheric manipulations. *Psychophysiology, 16,* 116-129.

Maltzman, I. (1979). Orienting reflexes and classical conditioning in humans. In H. D. Kimmel, E. H. van Olst and J. F. Orlebke (Eds.). *The orienting reflex,* pp. 323-353. Hillsdale, N.J.: Erlbaum Associates.

Martin, D. G., Stambrook, M., Tataryn, D. J., & Biehl, H. (1984). Conditioning in the unattended left ear. *International Journal of Neuroscience, 23,* 95-102.

Maxmilian, V. A. (1982). Cortical blood flow asymmetry during monaural verbal stimulation. *Brain and Language, 15,* 1-11.

McKeever, W. (1986). Tachistoscopic methods in neuropsychology. In J. Hannay (Ed.). *Experimental techniques in human neuropsychology,* pp. 161-211. New York: Oxford University Press.

Mintz, M., & Myslobodsky, M. S. (1983). Two types of hemisphere imbalance in hemi-Parkinsonianism coded by brain electrical activity and electrodermal activity. In M. S. Myslobodsky (Ed.). *Hemisyndromes: Psychobiology, Neurology, Psychiatry*, pp. 213-238. New York: Academic Press.

Moscovitch, M. (1979). Information processing and the cerebral hemispheres. In M. S. Gazzaniga (Ed.). *Handbook of neurobiology*, vol. 2, pp. 379-446. New York: Plenum Press.

Myslobodsky, M. S., & Rattok, J. (1977). Bilateral activity in waking man. *Acta Psychologica, 41*, 273-282.

Öhman, A. (1971). Differentiation of conditioned and orienting response components in eletrodermal conditioning. *Psychophysiology, 8*, 7-22.

Öhman, A. (1979). Fear relevance, autonomic conditioning, and phobias: A laboratory model. In P. O. Sjödén, S. Bates, & W. S. Dockens (Eds.). *Trends in behavior therapy*, pp. 107-133. New York: Academic Press.

Öhman, A. (1983). The orienting response during Pavlovian conditioning. In D. Siddle (Ed.). *Orienting and habituation: Perspectives in human research*, pp. 315-370. Chichester, Sussex, UK, John Wiley & Sons.

Oke, A., Keller, R., Mefford, I., & Adams, R. N. (1977). Lateralization of norepinephrine in human thalamus. *Science, 200*, 1411-1413.

Pennal, B. (1977). Human cerebral asymmetry in color discrimination. *Neuropsychologia, 15*, 563-568.

Prokasy, W. F., & Kumpfer, K. L. (1973). Classical conditioning. In W. F. Prokasy and D. C. Raskin (Eds.), *Electrodermal activity in psychological research*. New York: Academic Press.

Rasmussen, T., & Milner, B. (1977). The role of early left-brain injury in determining lateralization of cerebral speech functions. *Annals of the New York Academy of Sciences, 299*, 355-369.

Rescorla, R. A. (1972). Information variables in Pavlovian conditioning. In G. H. Bower (Ed.), *Learning and motivation*, Vol. VI, pp. 1-44. New York: Academic Press.

Rescorla, R. A. (1980). *Pavlovian second-order conditioning*. New York: Academic Press.

Rescorla, R. A., & Wagner, A. R. (1972). A theory of Pavlovian conditioning: Variations in the effectiveness of reinforcement and nonreinforcement. In A. Black and W. F. Prokasy (Eds.). *Classical conditioning II: Current theory and research*, pp. 64-99. New York: Appelton.

Rogers, L. J. (1980). Lateralization in the avian brain. *Bird Behaviors, 2*, 1-12.

Rogers, L. J. (1986). Lateralization of learning in chicks. In Rosenblatt, J. S., Beer, C., Busnel, M-C., & Slater, P.J.B: (Eds.), *Advances in the study of behavior*, Vol. 16, pp. 147-190. New York: Academic Press.

Rogers, L. J., & Anson, J. M. (1979). Lateralization of function in the chicken fore-brain. *Pharmacology, Biochemistry and Behavior, 10,* 679-689.

Rosenzweig, M. R. (1951). Representation of the two ears at the auditory cortext. *American Journal of Physiology, 167,* 147-158.

Schwartz, G. E., Davidson, R. J., & Maer, F. (1975). Right hemisphere lateralization for emotion in the human brain: Interaction with cognition. *Science, 190,* 266-268.

Schweiger, A., & Maltzman, I. (1985). Behavioral and electrodermal measures of lateralization for music perception in musicians and nonmusicians. *Biological Psychology, 20,* 129-145.

Seligman, M. E. P. (1970). On the generality of the laws of learning. *Psychological Review, 77,* 400-418.

Seligman, M. E. P., & Hager, J. L. (Eds.) (1972). *Biological boundaries of learning.* New York: Appelton.

Sokolov, E. N. (1963). *Perception and the conditioned reflex.* London: Pergamon Press.

Sperry, R. W. (1974). Lateral specialization in the surgically separated hemispheres. In F. O. Schmitt and F. G. Worden (Eds.), *The Neurosciences: Third study program,* pp. 5-19. Cambridge, Ma.: MIT Press.

Springer, S.P. (1986). Dichotic listening. In J. Hannay (Ed.), *Experimental techniques in human neuropsychology.* New York: Oxford University Press.

Stokes, K. A., & McIntyre, D. C. (1985). Lateralized state-dependent learning produced by hippocampal kindles convulsions: Effects of split-brain. *Physiology and Behavior, 34,* 217-224.

Wada, J. A., & Rasmussen, T. (1960). Interacarotid injection of sodium amytal for the lateralization of cerebral speech dominance. *Journal of Neurosurgery, 17,* 266-282.

Wang, G. H. (1964). Neural control of sweating. Madison, Wi.: University of Wisconsin Press.

Wardlaw, K. A., & Kroll, N. E. (1976). Autonomic responses to shock-associated words in a nonattended message: A failure to replicate. *Journal of Experimental Psychology: Human Perception and Performance, 2,* 357-360.

Wilcott, R. C., & Bradley, H. H. (1970). Low frequency electrical stimulation of the cat's auterior cortex and inhibition of skin potential responses. *Journal of Comparative and Physiological Psychology, 72,* 350-355.

von Wright, J. M., Andersson, K., & Stenman, U. (1975). Generalization of conditioned GSRs in dichotic listening. In P. M. Rabbit and S. Dornic (Eds.), *Attention and performance,* Vol. V, pp. 194-204. New York: Academic Press.

Young, A. W. (1982). Methodological, theoretical issues. In J. G. Beaumont (Ed.), *Divided visual field studies of cerebral organization.* London: Academic Press.

Zaidel, E. (1985). Introduction. In D. F. Benson and E. Zaidel (Eds.), *The dual brain.* New York: Guilford Press.

6 Preattentive Activation of Aversive Emotions

Arne Öhman, Ulf Dimberg, and Francisco Esteves
University of Uppsala

Aversive emotions are rooted in the defense systems of organisms. Fear provides the prototypical example. Animals display behavior that we understand as fearful in various contexts where, broadly speaking, their well-being, safety, or survival are threatened. The behavior in question may include escape, freezing (immobility), or attack (e.g. Archer, 1979), and, perhaps, seeking the proximity of conspecifics for shelter and protection (e.g. Bowlby, 1969; Klein, 1981). By utilizing Pavlovian contingencies, animals may be able to execute these defense responses more efficiently, thus gaining critical advantages in relation to, for example, a predator (see Hollis, 1982). From a biological perspective, therefore, fear, both unlearned and learned, has important adaptive functions, helping animals to survive and breed in their ecological niches.

Despite its utility in these apparently concrete situations, the fear concept is elusive because it cannot be reduced to any simple set of indicators that invariably provide pointers to its identification. As indicated by Archer (1979), "fear responding involves a flexible repertoire of available responses, many of which are shared with other motivational control systems" (p. 65). Framed in a somewhat different language derived from studies of fearful humans, fear is displayed in partly independent response systems comprising verbal reports, overt motor behavior, and physiological responses (Lang, 1968). This implies that fear has the conceptual status of a hypothetical construct with connotative meanings that cannot be exhaustively reduced to simple operations (Kozak & Miller, 1982; Öhman, in press).

The aim of the present chapter is to present a view of fear that seeks to unite biological, cognitive and clinical perspectives. Starting from considerations of the biological functions of fear, its role in cognition is examined in an effort to elucidate some of the mechanisms that intervene between a fear stimulus and a fear response. Throughout this analysis, examples are taken from a prominent form of human distress, namely social fear and anxiety.

VARIETIES OF FEAR

According to everyday experience, fear seems to be part of ideosyncratic contexts, and to take such diverse forms as to defy simple classification. Torgerson (1979) asked subjects to rate their fear of many types of situations, and subjected the ratings to factor analysis. In this way, he isolated five clusters of feared situations: separation fears, social fears, animal fears, mutilation fears, and nature fears. Similar, albeit not identical, factors have been identified in many investigations (see Öhman, Dimberg, & Öst, 1985, for a review).

Taking a broad biological point of departure, Öhman, et al. (1985) examined fear from the perspective of a general classification of behavior proposed by the eminent evolutionary biologist, Ernst Mayr (1974). He suggested that behavior is either communicative or noncommunicative in terms of the type of response it elicits from the surrounding world. Communicative behavior prompts active responses from the environment, that is to say, it is directed towards other living creatures.

Noncommunicative behavior, on the other hand, does not elicit such active responses but is directed toward the physical surroundings. The category of communicative behavior, finally, can be subdivided into inter- and intraspecific communicative behavior. The former refers to behavior directed towards members of other species such as the relationships between predators and preys, or between parasites and hosts. Mayr (1974) went on to argue that the role of genetic programs in the guidance of behavior may differ between these behavior systems, being larger in communicative than in noncommunicative behaviors.

At least three of the fear categories isolated by Togerson (1979) fall neatly into this simple tripartite classification. Nature fears would be cases of noncommunicative behavior, social fears would be cases of intraspecific communicative behavior, and animal fears would be cases of interspecific communicative behavior. This classification also dovetails nicely with Marks' (1969) grouping of clinical fears into social phobias, animal phobias, and miscellaneous specific phobias. The classification is illustrated in Figure 6.1.

Because these behavior systems have different evolutionary origins and thus different adaptive functions, it would be expected that the characteristics of fear and fear behavior exhibited within the systems would be different. Öhman et al. (1985) provided a detailed analysis of two of these systems, inter- and intraspecific communicative fears, and demonstrated that important differences between social and animal phobias may be explained from the assumption that their origins rest in different behavior systems. An important conclusion of this analysis is that there is nothing like generalized fear. That is to say, findings from one context,

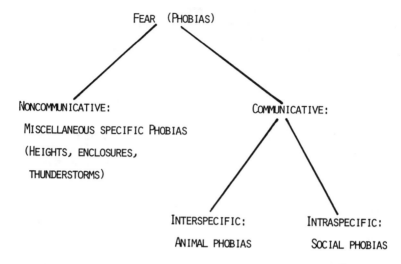

FIG. 6.1. Mayr's (1974) classification of behavior as applied to fears and phobias (see Marks, 1969). This classification system is further discussed in Öhman et al. (1985).

e.g. a social one, may not legitimately be generalized to a different context such as nature. Because the research to be reported in this chapter used social stimuli such as angry faces, caution is called for when generalizing the data to nonsocial contexts.

A THEORETICAL ANALYSIS

Functional-Biological Considerations

The most obvious adaptive function of fear, alluded to above, is to motivate the organism to escape and avoid potentially harmful circumstances. However, fear, like many other emotions, is not restricted to subserve adaptive functions only at the output stage of environment-organism interactions.

The signaling function of fear. As pointed out by Hamburg, Hamburg, and Barchas (1975), "distressing experiences may be quite useful although unpleasant. They have a *signal function* which warns the organism and other individuals significant to him that something is wrong, attention must be paid, learning capacities utilized, resources mobilized to correct the situation" (p. 239, italics added).

Fear is, indeed, communicative in several different senses. First, its outward expression communicates to the threatener, whether a predator or a rival conspecific, that escape (or other defense maneouvres) is imminent. Second, as suggested in the quotation, the same expressive aspects of fear communicate to conspecifics that circumstances potentially harmful to all of them, such as a predator, have been identified by one member of the group. Finally, fear is intrapsychically communicative in the sense that it prompts the organism to focus its attention on the threat. In this latter sense, emotions like fear have functional properties similar to those of the orienting response (OR) (see Öhman, in press). From considerations of these complex functional properties of fear responses, it follows that their nature and expression must reflect a series of evolutionary compromises, which may help to explain their lack of cohesion and the low correlations between various components.

It is, of course, vital for the organism that it is able to locate and respond appropriately to threats in its environment. Thus, it must be endowed with a sensory apparatus which can recognize the relevant stimuli, and which is, more or less conditionally, connected to the efferent mechanisms that mediate the emotional response. These sensory-perceptual mechanisms must have been tuned by evolutionary circumstances to respond promptly whenever threatening stimuli are encountered, whereever they are placed in the potential perceptual field. Furthermore, once activated, they must have preferential access to output mechanisms mediating overt defensive behavior. Thus, the sequence of internal and external events that constitutes fear includes a powerful interrupt function, so that priority is given to the fear response, regardless of the organism's current activity. Stated in somewhat different terms, this account implies that the organism is able to keep track of potentially threatening events occurring in any of a very large number of perceptual channels, which all converge on the defensive behavior we associate with fear.

Conscious control. In lower animals, fear-related behavior is more or less under complete automatic control. Thus, although the neural programs that control it clearly are derived from open genetic programs that need specific environmental input to become operational (see Mayr, 1974; Öhman & Dimberg, 1984), the mechanisms involved may be assumed to be relatively simple. In humans, however, the situation is much more complex. In our species, the automatic level of functioning has been superseded by, and subordinated under, another much more advanced and complex functional level, whether we call it consciousness, controlled processing or focal attention.

The evolution and function of consciousness, of course, are highly controversial issues (see e.g. Mandler, 1975). Let it suffice for our purpose to indicate that a main function of conscious control may be to integrate all the actions controlled from the automatic level into one coherent stream of behavior. To fulfill this function, the conscious level is needed to translate between various sensory modalities, to generalize patterns of information processing and action between different contexts, and to select one particular course of action by inhibiting alternative ones (Posner, 1978). In fact, this latter function is facilitated by the central characteristic of consciousness, its selectivity or limited capacity (James, 1890), which prevents other activated systems to gain access to consciousness once priority is given to one particular system (Shallice, 1972).

From this brief sketch, it is clear that consciousness can intervene and interrupt automatically controlled action sequences either to inhibit them completely in favor of some alternative action or merely to provide time for further information processing before an action is taken. Thus, similar to fear and other emotions, consciousness has an important interrupt function to allow establishment of new priorities in hierarchies of action alternatives. However, whereas the interrupt signal occasioned through fear activation operates automatically from the outside, the conscious interrupt has a deliberate internal origin, reflecting controlled operation on memory information in relation to the actual external situation.

Interaction between conscious and automatic processes. The two types of interrupt functions may be assumed to interact. Humans, like other animals, are equipped with mechanisms to respond to fear stimuli of phylogenetic or ontogentic origin, regardless of where in the total perceptual field they occur. Thus, the sensory-perceptual systems are tuned to automatically detect such stimuli independently of where the limited capacity of conscious attention is focused. Once a fear-evoking stimulus is detected, ongoing behavior is interrupted and an emotional response is set into motion. However, the interrupt also automatically calls on conscious processing resources which allow futher analysis of the situation and maybe a consicous interrupt of the emotional response. Thus, an interrupt through fear arousal from the periphery may be followed by a second interrupt from the conscious level in order to give time for further analysis of the situation, or in order to replace the skeletal components of the automatically evoked emotional response with a more deliberately controlled action. In humans, therefore, locating an emotional stimulus may have several more or less simultaneous consequences: consciousness is aroused, part of the emotional response is activated, and attention is bracketed on to the eliciting stimulus. These events may in concert set the stage for the phenomenal unity of each emotional experience, which integrates the stimulus, the affective tone and awareness of the emotional response into an undivisible whole.

As in Zajonc's (1980) influential thesis that preferences need no inferences, the present analysis suggests that affect preceeds and does not need inferences. Rather, it is an immediate and automatic consequence of an unconscious, preattentive analysis of the stimulus. But affect activates conscious activity and inferences in the next step of cognitive analysis. By activating consciousness, the whole repertoire of voluntary action can be brought to bear on the emotional situation, which provides for a flexibility of response which most often, but not invariably, is adaptively advantageous, and which is hard to match in the behavior of members of other species.

However, behind this apparent complexity, part of the archaic emotional response is still running its course much as it does in our fellow animals that are untouched by cultural evolution. Thus, inhibitory influences from the conscious level are unlikely to completely block the emotional response but mostly may be assumed to affect its skeletal components which mediate the overt behavior, thus providing the basis for an important instance of between system convergence (e.g. Hodgson & Rachman, 1974). The autonomic responses, which are part of the metabolic housekeeping preparing the organism for taxing defense responses like flight or fight, are likely to become activated even though their motor outlet may be blocked. Similarly, reflexive muscle movements such as in facial expressions are likely to be only partially masked by higher inhibitory influences. Thus, in spite of efforts to "keep a straight face" or "keep a stiff upper lip" there may be an "emotional leakage", which may provide important cues to the attentive observer. The physiological activation is collateral to the activation of consciousness and it may provide input to the conscious system which is critical for emotional experience (see Mandler, 1984).

An information processing translation

For those inclined to be more persuaded by information processing jargon than the biologically inspired common sense language above, the analysis can be specified and related to concepts and topics in contemporary cognitive psychology.

Automatic and controlled information processing. Briefly summarized, the present analysis entails that organisms are able to simultaneously and effectively monitor a large number of perceptual channels to locate potentially threatening events in their surroundings. Should such events be encountered by humans, emotions are activated and control is relinquished from this automatic perceptual level to a consciously controlled level which further analyses the situation before action is taken.

A similar distinction between automatic and controlled information processing is commonplace in modern cognitive psychology (e.g. Hasher & Zacks, 1979; Öhman, 1979b; Posner, 1978; Shiffrin & Schneider, 1977; see particularly Schneider, Dumais & Shiffrin, 1984 for an up-to-date and comprehensive review of this distinction). Automatic processing can occur in parallel across many sensory channels without interference. It is involuntary in the sense that it runs its course independently of intentions once started. It does not interfere with focal attention (i.e., consciousness), nor is it susceptible to easy interference from attended activites. In other words, it does not draw on cognitive resources associated with effort. Finally it typically takes place outside of awareness. Thus, it is clear that automatic processes as delineated by cognitive psychologists have exactly the attributes that were given to the automatic perceptual processes in the analysis presented above.

Controlled processing, on the other hand, is governed by intentions. It is strictly resource-limited in the sense that interference is marked between tasks that have to be performed at a controlled processing level. Because the system can only perfform one task at a time, controlled processing works sequentially and it requires cognitive effort. Finally, it is performed at a high level of awareness, i.e., controlled processing is typically conscious.

In the present context, it is important to note that the automatic processes have a monitoring capacity for sensory events that vastly exceeds that of the controlled processes. Thus, the automatic monitoring processes can keep track of a large number of sensory channels only one of which typically can be selected for controlled analysis. According to the present analysis this arrangement is adaptively exploited by links between the automatic identification of some significant event and the mobilization of controlled processing resources. This mobilization is associated with priming of the efferent parts of the emotional response, and thus with the initiation of emotion. At the controlled or conscious level, the emotional impact of the event is further evaluated in relation to past experience through controlled memory search (primary appraisal) and in relation to available action alternatives (secondary appraisal) (see Öhman, in press). The conceptual framework developed so far is illustrated in Figure 6.2.

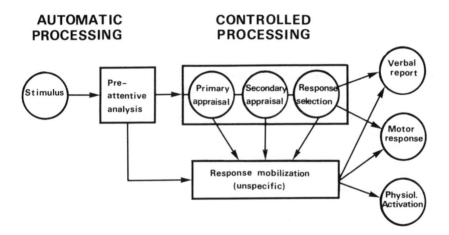

FIG. 6.2. Summary of the theoretical argument. Automatic processing mechanisms are able to locate emotionally significant stimuli in a preattentive analysis which initiates controlled processing of the stimulus and primes response mobilization systems. Controlled processing may include further evaluation of the stimulus against memory information (Primary appraisal) and in relation to action alternatives (Secondary appraisal). As a result of these appraisals, an action is selected (Response selection). At the output stage this sequence of operations is manifested in the three response systems (see Öhman, in press, for further discussions).

The boundary between "conscious" and "unconscious". As pointed out by Dixon (1981), the type of functional analysis of emotions outlined above, implies that emotions have unconscious or preattentive origins. Under the proper circumstances, therefore, it should be possible to elicit emotions without the individual being aware of the basis for the emotion. Such a claim, of course, is related to some of the most controversial issues in experimental psychology, such as subliminal preception and perceptual defense (Eriksen, 1960; see Bowers, 1984, and Dixon, 1981, for reviews).

However, these issues have been put in a new perspective by the theoretical developments in modern cognitive psychology, which, at least tacitly, provide abundant room for nonconscious psychological mechanisms (Erdelyi, 1974; Shevrin & Dickman, 1980). These potentialities have been further developed at the empirical level by research demonstrating nonconscious priming in lexical decision tasks (Balota, 1983; Fowler, Wolford, Slade, & Tassinary, 1981; Marcel, 1983b; McCauley, Parmelee, Sperber, & Carr, 1980). This research indicates that subjects encode and use the meaning of words, even if they are presented under backward masking conditions that prevent their conscious perception. Although still controversial (see Hollender, 1986), these demonstrations provide a conceptual basis for the claim that the emotional meaning of stimuli can be evaluated at the preattentive level before the conscious level is called.

An important issue in this context concerns the specification of the boundary between the conscious and the unconscious level. The controversy about perceptual defense during the fifties resulted in acceptance of perceptual discrimination as the conservative criterion (Eriksen, 1960). According to this criterion, subjects are conscious of stimuli as long as they are able to discriminate them at above chance accuracy in a forced choice task. However, as pointed out by Bowers (1984), verbal discrimination as the criterion restricts perception to the conscious level by definition, and thus precludes an empirical approach to the issue. Furthermore, this criterion does not capture the common sense meaning of "conscious" which is heavily dependent on phenomenological quality. To use Bowers example, an optometrist using above chance discrimination between D and H on his eye chart as the criterion for not recommending glasses to his clients, would soon be out of business. Clearly, "to see" in the ecological sense is fundamentally different from "being able to discriminate above chance" (e.g. Lundh, 1979). In other words, a distinction between "perceiving" and "noticing" is called for (Bowers, 1984), where the former refers to discrimination and the latter to being aware of the stimulus. Much as in the theoretical analysis presented above, this distinction suggests that stimuli may be perceived and reacted to at an automatic level, but that attention must be focused on them before they can reach consciousness.

Discussing the boundary between conscious and unconscious processes, or between noticing and perceiving, implies that there is some type of a threshold which marks the demarcation line between the two states or processes. For example, a stimulus may be too weak to enter the conscious state, or it may be masked from availability to conscious processing. At the conceptual level, the term threshold is difficult, because, strictly speaking, there is no absolute threshold but only a distribution of values around a central tendency. Conventionally, the threshold is statistically located at the median of this distribution. Using this concept, it is clear that a subject, by definition, should discover a target on 50% of the trials even if it is followed by a mask with an interval located exactly on the threshold for conscious report. If the target is an emotional stimulus, this may be sufficient to produce emotional effects even though no such effects are obtained on the other 50% of the trials. In other words, effects that on the surface may appear to be unconsciously mediated, may still be observed because on some proportion of the trials the subjects' sensitivity is more or less accidently enhanced. As a result, the stimulus is consciously perceived on these trials even if the particular target-mask interval (or stimulus-onset asynchrony, SOA) on the average does not allow recognition (see Massaro, 1975). Given these circumstances, at the conceptual level a firm dichotomy between conscious and unconscious states may be difficult to maintain.

Rather, we may be dealing with "early" and "late" effects in a more or less continuous information processing chain. If pressed, it can be conceded that for the present analysis, the important thing is that the emotional effects we are discussing are "early" rather than "unconscious", and that they precede later more consciously controlled operations such as, say, active rehearsal. Only if qualitatively different effects can be demonstrated between masking intervals supposed to be "unconscious" and "conscious" may it be legitimate to use these terms (see Cheesman & Merikle, 1986).

Cheesman and Merikle (1986) have developed this issue further by suggesting operational definitions of objective and subjective thresholds. The former refers to chance level performance in a detection task, and the latter to a level of discriminative responding at which subjects report chance level performance. Cheesman and Merikle (1986) went on to demonstrate the usefulness of this criterion by showing that stimuli presented below subjective threshold affected performance in a *Stroop task* (i.e., a task were the subject is required to react to the color instead of the meaning of words), but that the strategy effects observed for above threshold presentations were not evident at this level. Thus, they argued that different principles held for unconsciously and consciously governed performance, which substantiates the usefulness of the distinction. Furthermore, they argued that studies failing to report unconscious priming in lexical decision tasks (Cheesman & Merikle, 1984; Purcell, Stewart, & Stanovich, 1983) used an objective threshold criterion, whereas those reporting such effects more or less inadvertently used subjective threshold criteria (Fowler et al., 1981; Marcel, 1983b; McCauley et al., 1980).

Marcel's theory. Marcel (1983a) has developed a theoretical framework which stresses the distinction between, and independence of, conscious and nonconscious information processing mechanisms. According to this theory, automatic unconscious perceptual mechanisms segregate sensory information into any categories the organism is capable of appreciating, whether by nature or by individual experience. This categorization provides input to further information processing mechanisms in "bottom-up" types of analyses, providing material for perceptual hypotheses. One such hypothesis is selected to become consciously represented in a "top-down" act of recovery where the hypothesis is matched against sensory codes. It is this recovery process which is assumed to be disrupted by backward pattern masking, thus preventing the sensory information to reach awareness.

Theories of this type leave quite elaboratedly analysed meanings lingering around in the information processing system without gaining access to consciousness. It is but a small step to assume that this meaning has important unconscious effects. For example, Marcel (1983a) posits that the results of the initial perceptual analysis may provide support for postural adjustments or orientation in space. According to the present analysis a further unconscious effect may be the initiation of emotional responses, and particularly their physiological underpinnings.

AN EMPIRICAL ANALYSIS

Methodological considerations.

To corroborate the theoretical analysis presented above, it is necessary to demonstrate that stimuli presented under conditions preventing access to consciousness nevertheless are sufficient to elicit physiological responses associated with emotions. Such a demonstration, however, is fraught with methodological difficulties. To begin with, in normal circumstances the automatic preattentive mechanisms are inseparably interwoven with the controlled processing mechanisms. Thus, the first undertaking is to be able to experimentally dissociate these two levels from each other. This can be achieved by help of Marcel's (1983a) assertion that backward pattern masking blocks the recovery process by which sensory information is entered into awareness. However, the decision to use backward masking is only a first step. Next, it must be determined which type of mask and which masking intervals should be used. But to take these methodological decisions is secondary to the solution of another basic problem, namely which stimuli should be chosen to elicit emotions. This, in turn, is one of the basic problems in the experimental psychology of emotion.

Notwithstanding these constrains, part of the origin of the present research involve studies of Pavlovian conditioning to "fear-relevant" stimuli, such as pictures of snakes or angry faces (see Öhman, 1979a; 1986; 1987; Öhman & Dimberg, 1984; and Öhman et al., 1985, for reviews). These studies have demonstrated persistent conditioning of human autonomic responses to such stimuli after they have been coupled with an electric shock unconditioned stimulus (e.g., Öhman & Dimberg, 1978; Öhman, Fredrikson, Hugdahl & Rimmö, 1976; Cook, Hodes & Lang, 1986; Dawson, Schell & Banis, 1986). In important respects, this type of conditioned response provide "mini models" of human phobic fears (e.g., Öhman, 1979a).

Picture of faces are particularly relevant in the present context, because they are so suitable for masking studies. Whereas angry faces provide exceptionally good fear conditioning, happy faces are, if anything, inhibitory when coupled with an aversive US (Dimberg, 1986). One face may easily serve as a mask for another face. For example, after conditioning to an angry face, expected to result in good response acquisition, this facial conditioned stimulus could be presented masked by another face with a neutral expression in a test phase. In a control condition, a happy face, expected to give poor conditioning, could be similarly masked by the neutral face during testing. If larger autonomic responses, such as skin conductance responses, were observed under masking in the former than in the latter condition, support would have been otained for the basic prediction of the theory.

With the choice of target and masking stimuli made, the next crucial methodological problem, that of threshold determination, must be addressed. In the present research, two methods for threshold determination were used. One was phenomenological in scope and instructed subjects to report on what they saw, giving them ample opportunity to find out whether they saw anything or not. The other procedure was a conventional forced choice method with one group of subjects required to report whether they saw one or two stimuli, and another group required to report whether the first stimulus was an angry or a happy face. The particular SOA finally chosen was outside the range of confident identifications in the first procedure, and did not result in above chance performance in the second procedure.

Selection of masking interval

In the first type of threshold determination study, subjects were exposed to pairs of brief presentations of the Ekman and Friesen pictures of faces. The second face, serving as mask, always had a neutral emotional expression and a duration of 30 ms. The first face, the target, could be happy, angry or neutral, and its duration coincided with the SOA, that is, the interval between the onsets of the two stimuli. Both the target and the mask pictures could be male or female. The method of limits was used, starting at a SOA of 10 ms and then incrementing in steps of 10 ms. Each stimulus presentation was cued by a tone starting 1-4 sec before the stimulus pair. The subjects were carefully instructed that there were always two stimuli presented together, but that sometimes the interval betweeen them was too short to allow discovery of both. Their task was described so as to identify some characteristic of the first face, such as its sex, emotional expression or identity. They were instructed to report (a) when they discovered that something preceded the mask, (b) when they suspected or felt able to guess the particular attribute they were instructed to look for, and (c) when they felt sure about the attribute. In the particular experiment to be reported here, one group of subjects had the task of identifying the emotional expression, another group identified the sex of the target face, and the third group was first given training to identify four stimulus persons, and were then instructed to identify them in the target position.

The results are shown in Table 6.1 It is clear from this table that the thresholds for "seeing something", "believing" and "being sure" are similar regardless of whether the subjects judge emotional expression, sex or identity, with a nonsignificant tendency for somewhat shorter time for expression. However, happy faces were reliably more easy to identify than were angry and neutral faces, particularly when the judgement category was emotional expression. Two subjects of thirty were able to guess correct emotional expression twice each at a SOA of 30 ms. This is about 3% of all judgments made in the experiment. There were no "sure" identifications at this interval.

TABLE 6.1

Mean stimulus onset asynchrony (in ms) between target and mask at which subjects reported that they saw something more than the mask ("something"), believed (and correctly guessed) that they were able to identify the attribute ("believes") of the target, and were confidently sure that they did ("sure"). Three different groups of subjects judged emotional expression (angry, happy or neutral), sex, or identity (four different persons) of the target.

| | Response category | | |
Attribute	"Something"	"Believes"	"Sure"
Emotion	42	100	126
Sex	53	109	144
Person	47	113	142

In the forced-choice experiment, the method of constant stimuli was used with one group of subjects required to indicate whether the emotional expression of the first stimulus in each pair was anger or happiness. Another group of subjects indicated whether they saw one or two stimuli. The stimulus series involved seven pairs with the SOA varied between 30 and 330 ms and a control condition involving only the mask. As can be seen in Figure 6.3, the reports of two stimuli rose from about 5% in the control condition to about 12% with a 30 ms SOA and asymptoted at 95% at about a SOA of 100 ms. The correct identifications was slightly, but nonsignificantly, above a control level at the 30 ms SOA, and then rose steadily with SOA to assymptote at about 90% correct performance.

These two studies indicate that a SOA of 30 ms provides effective backward masking of the emotional expression of a briefly presented face for all subjects examined. Because it was deemed advantageous to have one and the same value for all subjects, the value may have been further below the threshold for some subjects than for others.

Preattentive elicitation of conditioned responses

The theoretical analysis presented above basically suggests that the emotional effects of stimuli should be possible to demonstrate even if the

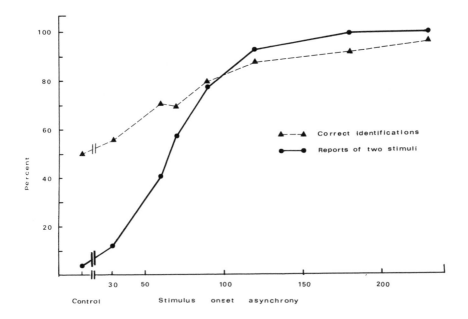

FIG. 6.3. Results of the forced choice discrimination experiment, where one group of subjects was required to guess whether the stimuli preceding the neutral face masking stimulus were angry or happy (correct identifications). Another group of subjects was required to merely report whether they saw one or two stimuli (reports of two stimuli). Data are plotted against the interval between target and mask (stimulus onset asynchrony).

subject is unable to consciously report on the event. This question can now be addressed by help of facial stimuli and the masking intervals determined above.

In the first experiment, we examined two groups of 20 subjects each, both of which were exposed to pictures of angry and happy faces taken from the Ekman and Friesen set, while skin conductance responses (SCRs) were measured. In an introductory phase of the study, both groups were given opportunities to habituate to two 60 ms duration presentations of each of the angry and happy faces, as well as to two 30 ms presentations of each of these two faces masked by a 30 ms neutral face with a SOA of 30 ms. In the following acquisition phase, one group of subjects was conditioned to angry and the other to happy faces by presentation of a brief electric shock to the fingers following the face stimuli. The shock had an intensity subjectively defined as "uncomfortable but not painful". The pictures were shown for 60 ms and the interval between the conditioned and unconditioned stimulus (CS and US, respectively) was 500 ms. For the group having the angry face reinforced by shock (CS+), a 60 ms presentation of the happy face served as nonreinforced control stimulus (CS-), with the contingency reversed for the group conditioned to happy faces. Interspersed between 12 reinforced CS+ and 12 nonreinforced CS- were 3 nonreinforced CS+ test trials, which allowed assessment of the conditioning effects. In addition, there were 12 randomly interspersed test trials involving 6 trials with the angry face masked by a neutral face and 6 trials where the happy face was masked by another neutral face. As in the masked habituation trials, each picture had a 30 ms duration and the SOA was also 30 ms.

Figure 6.4 shows data from the habituation phase and from the CS+ test trials and the closest CS- trials. It is evident that reliable response acquisition took place in both groups, because responding to the CS+ clearly exceeded that to the CS-. In support of the hypothesis of preattentive emotional responding, Figure 6.5 show that at least part of the differential responding to CS+ and CS- survived backward masking. This effect was statistically reliable on early trials for the group conditioned to angry faces. For the group conditioned to happy faces, there were virtually no evidence of differential responding under conditions of backward masking.

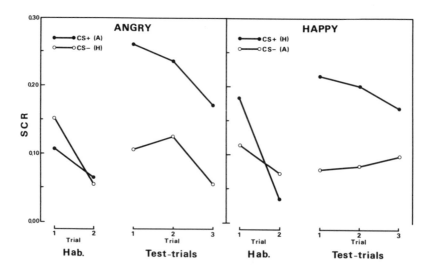

FIG. 6.4. Mean skin conductance responses (SCRs) (range-corrected) to 60 ms presentations of angry (A) and happy (H) faces during habituation (Hab.) and on nonreinforced testtrials during an acquisition series where the pictures were either paired (CS+) or unpaired (CS-) with an electric shock unconditioned stimulus. The conditioning procedure resulted in highly reliable conditioning in both subjects conditioned to angry and to happy faces.

These data appear to demonstrate that responses conditioned a visual stimulus can be elicited very early in the information processing chain,

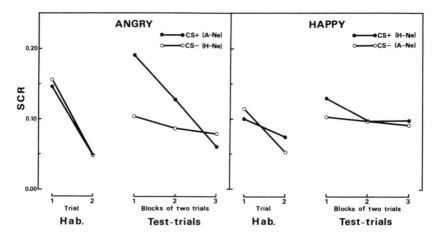

FIG. 6.5. Mean skin conductance responses (SCRs) (range-corrected) to 30 ms presentations of angry (A) or happy (H) faces which were masked by a 30 ms presentation of a neutral (Ne) face. Data are presented for a habituation (Hab.) series and for masked test trials during an acquisition series where the angry and happy faces were presented unmasked and paired (CS+) or unpaired (CS-) with an electric shock unconditioned stimuli. Differential responding (cf. Fig. 6.3) was retained only for on early trials for groups conditioned to angry faces.

even if its access to awareness is blocked through backward masking. This effect, furthermore, appears to be specific to biologically fear relevant stimuli like angry faces (see Öhman & Dimberg, 1984, Öhman et al., 1985, and McNally, 1987, for discussions of biological fear relevance and conditioning). Even though an equal amount of conditioning was evident in the group conditioned to happy faces during unmasked test trials (Fig. 6.4), this differential response did not survive backward masking.

The data presented in Figures 6.4 and 6.5 are partly inconsistent with data reported by Ross, Ferreira and Ross (1974). These investigators examined differential eye-blink conditioning to the letters T and H with an air-puff to the cornea as US. After one training session they selected good conditioners for a second session where they presented the CS unmasked or pattern masked with backward masking intervals of 40 or 120 ms for different groups of subjects. Contrary to our results with angry faces, the short masking interval wiped out differential responding completely. Thus, the data reported by Ross et al. (1974) are more similar to our results for the Happy condition, where masking blocked differential responding. Clearly, Ts and Hs are emotional neutral stimuli, and therefore the Ross et al. study underscores the conclusion that our results may be attributed to the use of fear-relevant stimuli.

However, the effects we observed with angry CSs were not strong and they disappeared over trials. This loss of the effect over test trials may be partly due to inhibitory conditioning to the mask stimulus, because upon closer scrutiny the conditions were inadvertently arranged for inhibition to occur. If a preattentive analysis is sufficient for conditioning, we had a situation where a consistently reinforced stimulus (an angry face) was never reinforced when occurring in a compound with another cue, the masking stimulus. This is a standard situation for generating inhibition to the cue occurring in the place of the masking stimulus in the present experiment. Thus, the falling trend over trials for the angry CS + may perhaps be attributed to this factor. To avoid this possible source of confounding, a second experiment was performed, whereby the masked test trials were now presented in extinction, without any interspersed reinforced trials.

This experiment used only a group conditioned to angry faces (CS+) with happy faces as control stimuli (CS-). In this type of paradigm, previous research has shown that responses conditioned to happy faces extinguish quite instantaneously when the US is witheld (Dimberg, 1986; Öhman & Dimberg, 1978). The subjects were conditioned to an angry face presented for 200 ms, which was followed by the shock US after an onset-to-onset CS-US interval of 500 ms. There were 2 habituation, 12 conditioning, and 16 extinction trials. The masking trials involved a 30 ms presentation of the angry face immediately followed by a 30 ms neutral face as masking stimulus. The results confirmed the previous findings. During the masked extinction trials, responding was reliably higher to the masked CS + than to the masked CS-. It appears, therefore, that the basic hypothesis was confirmed: emotional stimuli are capable of evoking physiological responses after a very quick stimulus analysis and even if the stimuli are blocked from entering consciousness.

Attentional resources and elicitation of emotional responses

As was pointed out above, the distinction between preattentive and controlled processing, or unconscious and conscious effects, would be easier to make if one could demonstrate that different principles held for the two levels. The most straightforward way to accomplish this purpose is to demonstrate that there are independent variables that operate at one level but not at the other. Controlled processing is assumed to be capacity-dependent whereas the preattentive processing is not. This implies that attentional demands should affect controlled processing but not preattentive processing. To examine this hypothesis, we arranged backward masking conditions to exclude or allow controlled processing. That is to say, we compared the previous condition where the SOA was 30 ms with another condition where it was 180 ms. The latter interval should, according to the threshold studies reported above, allow quite confident identification of the stimulus. The SOA conditions were orthogonally crossed with two levels of attention demands to the masking stimulus. In the low attention condition the subjects did not receive any particular instructions concerning the mask. In the high attention condition, however, they were instructed to count the number of females they saw in the mask position. In the first part of the experiment, the subjects were conditioned to angry faces with happy faces as control stimuli without any masks, exactly as in the previous two experiments. In the second part of the experiment, the CS+ and the CS- were presented masked by different neutral faces that were male or female, with the attention instructions described above. The specific hypothesis was that attention should have an effect only with the long SOA, which allowed central processing.

The results from the extinction test phase are given in Figure 6.6. Skin conductance responses were overall larger to the masked CS+ than to the masked CS- for all the four groups studied in the experiment, as attested by the main effect of stimulus. However, as is obvious in the figure, this effect appeared clearer in the low than in the high attention condition, and although the interaction between stimulus and attention failed to reach significance. reliable differential responding by t-tests was observed only in the low attention groups, both with the short and the long SOA. Thus, contrary to the hypothesis, the attention manipulation appeared to dilute the stimulus effect in both the short and the long SOA

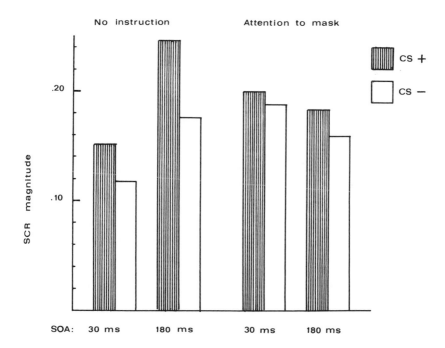

FIG. 6.6. Mean skin conductance responses (microsiemens) during masked extinction trials with different stimulus onset asynchronies (SOA) for subjects conditioned to an angry face (CS+) with a happy face as nonpaired control stimulus (CS-). Half the subjects attended to the mask by looking for a specific face (Attention to mask) whereas the other half had no instructions with regard to the mask (No instructions). Note that responses were larger for CS+ than for CS- particularly for the groups not attending to the mask.

condition. This implies that attention to the mask draws capacity away from eliciting the response conditioned to the CS+, which argues against the presumed capacity independence of preattentive processing.

If the failure to achieve differential responding in the high attention condition is accepted as real, it has important theoretical consequences. This is because an effect of attention to the mask on preattentive evocation of skin conductance responses precludes fulfilment of the criteria for strong automaticity for this phenomenon. Such criteria demand that the effect of the masking stimulus should be the same regardless of whether the stimulus is attended or not (Kahneman & Treisman, 1984). Thus, these data suggest that preattentive recognition of emotionally charged targets is not independent of the direction of attention. Rather such identification could be partially automatic and thus assisted, for example, by attention directed to relevant stimulus attributes. However, given that the data are somewhat ambiguous since we failed to demonstrate a reliable interaction between attention to mask and differential responding to CS+ and CS-, definite conclusions have to await further experimental work. Still, it is worth emphasizing that we replicated the basic phenomenon of preattentive elicitation of autonomic responses in the low attention condition with a 30 ms SOA.

Conditioning to masked stimuli

The discussion so far has been restricted to the elicitation of already acquired responses under conditions of backward masking. This is what is implied in the basic prediction of the theoretical framework. However, it is of general theoretical interest to determine whether acquisition of new responses could occur during backward masking. According to conventional learning theory notions, acquisition of CRs requires that the subjects is aware of the stimulus contingency (Dawson & Schell, 1975; Öhman, 1979b; 1983) or that the stimulus contingency is actively rehearsed (Shiffrin, 1976; Wagner, 1976; 1981). From such perspectives, one would expect that new associations between stimuli or between stimuli and responses can be established only through central processing.

In a pilot study to explore this issue, 20 subjects were exposed to a standard differential conditioning paradigm where a picture of an angry face was followed by an electric shock at a 500 ms interval, whereas a happy face was followed by nothing. Both types of visual stimuli were terminated after 30 ms exposure by a 30 ms presentation of a neutral face masking stimulus. Thus, the subjects were unable to see the angry and happy faces during this acquisition phase of the experiment. However, in the final extinction phase, both the angry and the happy faces were presented for 60 ms, without any masking stimulus. Much to our surprise, the subjects responded to a reliably larger extent to the angry than to the happy face during this extinction phase, suggesting that they had actually learned something about the masked stimuli during acquisition.

The results from the pilot study were followed up in an experiment which included various control groups. One group of 20 subjects received the same procedure as the one used in the pilot experiment. A second group had the contingency reversed during acquisition so that shock followed masked happy rather than masked angry faces. Finally, a third group was given only the two different neutral faces during acquisition, without any preceeding target stimuli. During extinction all three groups were given 60 ms presentations of angry and happy faces. Similar to the pilot data, the group conditioned to masked angry faces showed larger responses to the CS+ than to the CS- during extinction, but the differences did not reach statistical significance. In the two other groups, no differences emerged between the CS+s and the CS-s. Thus, the previously obtained preattentive conditioning effect did not survive replication.

A criticism that can be directed at these two experiments is that they were designed to prove the null hypothesis. Thus, there were no theoretical grounds for expecting response acquisition in any of the groups. Indeed, one could question whether it is at all possible to obtain conditioning effects in this type of paradigm, even with SOAs that would allow confident identification of the CSs. For example, it could be argued that the neutral mask stimulus would overshadow the targets, even with much longer SOAs. According to a quite extensive literature, most of the associative strength of compound stimuli tend to accumulate in the most salient component, which then "overshadows" the less salient components (e.g. Mackintosh, 1974). In the present context, the angry and happy CSs in effect were so weak that they did not even enter conscious perception, whereas the neutral masks were much more clearly perceived. Thus, the third experiment in the series compared a Preattentive Conditioning Group given similar treatment to the "angry" conditioning groups in the two previous experiments with two control groups. The Conditioning Control Group was given angry and happy faces masked by two different neutral faces during acquisition but with a SOA of 330 ms, which allowed clear identification of the angry and happy target stimuli. The interval between the CS (i.e., the angry face) and the US was 500 ms. The Sensitization Control Group, finally, was identical with the one in the second experiment, that is, neither angry nor happy faces were presented during acquisition. During the extinction test all the groups were given 200 ms presentations of the angry and happy faces used during acquisition.

The results are shown in Table 6.2, which presents the response probabilities to the CS+ and the CS- during extinction. As can be seen in the table, there was quite clear evidence of differential responding in the group given the long SOA. However, once again there was also some evidence of differential responding with the short SOA, although it reached significance only with an one-sided t-test. The Sensitization control group, finally, showed no evidence of differential responding. These results gave a group by stimulus interaction terms that approached, but did not quite reach, the 5% level of significance. Thus, although the data suggest that evidence of response acquisition may be obtained even with masked CS, they are not very strong. However, to the extent that they are accepted, they clearly contradict established theoretical notions suggesting that controlled processing is a prerequisite for learning (e.g. Dawson & Schell, 1985; Öhman, 1979b; Wagner, 1976). Given the pivotal nature of this notion in the psychology of learning, its falsification would have far-reaching consequences. Our data so far hardly justify seeking a theoretical alternative, but should our results be replicated and extended, such a search must be initiated.

TABLE 6.2

Probability of skin conductance responses during 16 unmasked extinction trials following backwardly masked conditioning trials with SOAs of 30 ms (Preattentive Conditioning) or 330 ms (Conditioning Control), or without any target stimuli (Sensitization). The CS+ was the previously masked angry face and the CS- the previously masked happy face.

| Stimulus | Experimental Groups | | |
	Preattentive Conditioning	Conditioning Control	Sensitization Control
CS+	.22	.28	.24
CS-	.18	.21	.25
$t(57)$	1.93*	2.77**	<1

* $p < .05$
**$p < .01$

SUMMARY AND CLINICAL IMPLICATIONS

The present chapter has outlined a theoretical perspective on aversive emotions which stresses early information processing mechanisms in their elicitation. According to this analysis, aversive emotions such as fear are set in motion after an essentially automatic stimulus analysis which is able to efficiently monitor multiple information channels for potentially threatening stimuli. When such stimuli are located, both autonomic and skeletal response systems are activated as part of a "call" for more advanced controlled information processing resources in the further analysis of the stimulus. This basic theoretical reasoning was summarized in Figure 6.2.

In the second part of the chapter, a series of experiments was described which provides support for the basic contention of the theory. That is to say, it was demonstrated that autonomic responses can be elicited from emotional stimuli blocked from consciousness through backward masking. One of the experiments provided some doubts as to whether the effects observed are truly automatic in the sense that they are completely independent of attention. Finally, some experimental data were reported which suggested that responses can actually be conditioned to masked stimuli.

The present analysis suggests that humans have a perceptual apparatus that is equiped to pick out potentially threatening information from the outside world in order to cope successfully with the threat. It is but a small step to suggest that this apparatus is differentially sensitive to threat in different individuals. A person with a more sensitive apparatus would be more likely to react to threat more often and thus be more likely to experience fear and anxiety. In other words, a perceptual bias to discover threat in the surroundings would be one factor promoting fear and anxiety episodes. This possibility has been nicely corroborated in a series of studies by Mathews, MacLeod, Eysenck and coworkers (see Eysenck, this volume). They have demonstrated that anxiety patients are particularly distracted by threat contents of words in a Stroop paradigm, and furthermore, that this sensitivty is linked to whether their anxiety concerns social or physical events (Mathews and MacLeod, 1985). Anxiety patients' attention seems to be dragged towards threat stimuli, which distinguish them sharply from normal controls, who tend to direct attention away from mild threats (MacLeod, Mathews, & Tata, 1986). Finally, and perhaps most importantly for the present analysis, this type of bias appears to operate already at a preattentive, unconscious level (Mathews & MacLeod, 1986). This series of studies, therefore, strongly suggests that the type of early emotional mechanism discussed in the present chapter operates with a biased setting in anxiety patients, which underscores the potential clinical utility of the approach (see further Mineka and Tomarken, this volume, for discussions of such issues).

The convergence of evidence from clinical and experimental studies on the importance of preattentive mechanism in the generating of fear is both reassuring and promising. But the research on these issues has only begun, and certainly it is much too early to speak of any breakthroughs. The findings must be confirmed and the theoretical formulations must be critically scrutinized. However, if they survive these tests, an important step forward in our understanding of the generation of fear and other aversive emotions may be marked.

ACKNOWLEDGEMENT

The research reported in this chapter was supported by grants from the Swedish Council for Research in Humanities and Social Sciences. Address correspondence to: Arne Öhman, Department of Clinical Psychology, University of Uppsala, P.O. Box 1225, S-751 42 Uppsala, Sweden.

REFERENCES

Archer, J. (1979). Behavioural aspects of fear. In W. Sluckin (Ed.), *Fear in animals and man*, pp. 56-85. New York: Van Nostrand Reinhold Company.

Balota, D. A. (1983). Automatic semantic activation and episodic memory encoding. *Journal of Verbal Learning and Verbal Behavior*, 22, 88-104.

Bowers, K. S. (1984). On being unconsciously influenced and informed. In K. S. Bowers & D. Meichenbaum (Eds.), *The unconsious reconsidered*, pp. 227-272. New York: John Wiley & Sons.

Bowlby, J. (1969). *Attachment and loss: Vol. 1. Attachment.* London: Hogarth Press.

Cheesman, J., & Merikle, P. M. (1984) Priming with and without awareness. *Perception and Psychophysics, 36*, 387-395.

Cheesman, J., & Merikle, P. M. (1986). Distinguishing conscious from unconscious perceptual processes. *Canadian Journal of Psychology, 40*, 343-367.

Cook, E. W., Hodes, R. L., & Lang, P. J. (1986). Preparedness and phobia: Effects of stimulus content on human visceral conditioning. *Journal of Abnormal Psychology, 95*, 195-207.

Dawson, M. E., & Schell, A. M. (1985). Information processing and human autonomic classical conditioning. In P. K. Ackles, J. R. Jennings, & M. G. H. Coles (Eds.), *Advances in psychophysiology*, Vol. 1, pp. 89-165. Greenwich, CT: JAI Press.

Dawson, M. E., Schell, A. M., & Banis, H. T. (1986). Greater resistance to extinction of electrodermal responses conditioned to potentially phobic CSs: A noncognitive process? *Psychophysiology, 23*, 552-561.

Dimberg, U. (1986). Facial expression as excitatory and inhibitory stimuli for conditioned autonomic responses. *Biological Psychology, 22*, 37-57.

Dixon, N. F. (1981). *Preconscious processing.* Chichester: John Wiley & Sons.

Erdelyi, M. H. (1974). A new look at The New Look: Perceptual defense and vigilance. *Psychological Review, 81*, 1-25.

Eriksen, C. W. (1960). Discrimination and learning without awareness. *Psychological Review, 67*, 279-300.

Fowler, C. A., Wolford, G., Slade, R., & Tassinary, L. (1981). Lexical access with and without awareness. *Journal of Experimental Psychology: General, 110*, 341-362.

Hamburg, D. A., Hamburg, B. A., & Barchas, J. D. (1975). Anger and depression in perspective of behavioral biology. In L. Levi (Ed.), *Emotions: Their parameters and measurement*, pp. 235-278. New York: Raven Press.

Hasher, L., & Zacks, R. T. (1979). Automatic and effortful processes in memory. *Journal of Experimental Psychology: General, 108*, 356-388.

Hodgson, R., & Rachman, S. (1974). II. Desynchrony in measures of fear. *Behavioural Research and Therapy, 12,* 319-326.

Holender, D. (1986). Semantic activation without conscious identification in dichotic listening, parafoveal vision, and visual masking: A survey and appraisal. *Behavioural and Brain Sciences, 9,* 1-66.

Hollis, K. L. (1982). Pavlovian conditioning of signal-centered action patterns and autonomic behavior: A biological analysis of function. In J. S. Rosenblatt, R. A. Hinde, C. Beer, & M.-C. Busness (Eds.), *Advances in the study of behavior,* Vol. 12, pp. 1-64. New York: Academic Press.

James, W. (1890). *The principles of psychology.* New York: Henry Holt & Co.

Kahneman, D., & Treisman, A. (1984). Changing views of attention and automaticity. In R. Parasuraman & D. R. Davies (Eds.), *Varieties of Attention,* pp. 29-61. Orlando, FL: Academic Press.

Klein, D. F. (1981). Anxiety reconceptualized. In D. F. Klein & J. Rabkin (Eds.), *Anxiety: New research and changing concepts,* pp. 235-263. New York: Raven Press.

Kozak, M. J., & Miller, G. A. (1982). Hypothetical constructs vs. intervening variables: A re-appraisal of the three-system model of anxiety assessment. *Behavior Assessment, 4,* 347-358.

Lang, P. J. (1968). Fear reduction and fear behavior: Problems in treating a construct. In J. M. Shlien (Ed.), *Research in Psychotherapy,* Vol. III, pp. 90-102. Washington, D. C.: American Psychological Association.

Lundh, L.-G. (1979). Introspection, consciousness, and human information processing. *Scandinavian Journal of Psychology, 20,* 223-238.

McCauley, C., Parmelee, C. M., Sperber, C. D., & Carr, T. H. (1980). Early extraction of meaning from pictures and its relation to conscious identification. *Journal of Experimental Psychology: Human Perception and Performance, 6,* 265-276.

Mackintosh, N. J. (1974) *The psychology of animal learning.* New York: Academic Press.

MacLeod, C., Mathews, A., & Tata, P. (1986). Attentional bias in emotional disorders. *Journal of Abnormal Psychology, 95,* 15-20.

Mandler, G. (1975). *Mind and emotion.* New York: John Wiley & Sons.

Mandler, G. (1984). *Mind and body: The psychology of emotion and stress.* New York: W. W. Norton & Company.

Marcel, A. J. (1983a). Conscious and unconscious perception: An approach to the relations between phenomenal experience and perceptual processes. *Cognitive Psychology, 15,* 238-300.

Marcel, A. J. (1983b). Conscious and unconscious perception: Experiments on visual masking and word recognition. *Cognitive Psychology, 15,* 197-237.

Marks, I. M. (1969). *Fears and phobias.* London: Heineman Medical Books.

Massaro, D. W. (1975). *Experimental psychology and information processing.* Chicago: Rand McNally College Publishing Company.

Mathews, A., & MacLeod, C. (1985). Selective processing of threat cues in anxiety states. *Behavioural Research and Therapy, 23,* 563-569.

Mathews, A., & MacLeod, C. (1986). Discrimination of threat cues without awareness in anxiety states. *Journal of Abnormal Psychology, 95,* 131-138.

Mayr, E. (1974). Behavior programs and evolutionary strategies. *American Scientist, 62,* 650-659.

McNally, R. J. (1987). Preparedness and phobias: A review. *Psychological Bulletin, 101,* 283-303.

Öhman, A. (1979a). Fear relevance, autonomic conditioning, and phobias: A laboratory model. In P.-O. Sjödén, S. Bates, & W. S. Dockens III (Eds.), *Trends in behavior therapy,* pp. 107-134. New York: Academic Press.

Öhman, A. (1979b). The orienting response, attention, and learning: An informationprocessing perspective. In H. D. Kimmel, E. H. van Olst & J. F. Orleboke (Eds.), *The orienting reflex in humans,* pp. 443-471. Hillsdale, N. J.: Erlbaum.

Öhman, A. (1983). The orienting response during Pavlovian conditioning. In D. A. T. Siddle (Ed.), *Orienting and habituation: Perspectives in human research,* pp. 315-369. Chichester: Wiley.

Öhman, A. (1986). Face the beast and fear the face: Animal and social fears as prototypes for evolutionary analyses of emotion. *Psychophysiology, 23,* 123-145.

Öhman, A. (1987). Evolution, learning and phobias: An interactional analysis. In D. Magnusson & A. Öhman (Eds.), *Psychopathology: An interactional perspective,* pp. 143-158. New York: Academic Press

Öhman, A. (in press). The psychophysiology of emotion: An evolutionary-cognitive perspective: In P. K. Ackles, J. R. Jennings, & M. G. H. Coles (Eds.), *Advances in psychophysiology* (Vol. 2). Greenwich, CT: JAI Press.

Öhman, A., & Dimberg, U. (1978). Facial expressions as conditioned stimuli for electrodermal responses: A case of "preparedness"? *Journal of Personality and Social Psychology, 36,* 1251-1258.

Öhman, A., & Dimberg, U. (1984). An evolutionary perspective on human social behavior. In W. M. Waid (Ed.), *Sociophysiology,* pp. 47-86. New York: Springer-Verlag.

Öhman, A., Dimberg, U., & Öst, L.-G. (1985). Animal and social phobias: Biological constraints on learned fear responses. In S. Reiss & R. R. Bootzin (Eds.), *Theoretical issues in behavior therapy,* pp. 123-178. New York: Academic Press.

Öhman, A., Fredrikson, M., Hugdahl, K., & Rimmö, P.-A. (1976). The premise of equipotentiality in human classical conditioning: Conditioned electrodermal responses to potentially phobic stimuli. *Journal of Experimental Psychology: General, 105,* 313-337.

Posner, M. I. (1978). *Chronometric explorations of mind.* Hillsdale,

N.J.: Lawrence Erlbaum Associates.

Purcell, D. G., Stewart, A. L., & Stanovich, K. E. (1983). Another look at semantic priming without awareness. *Perception and Pasychophysics, 34,* 65-71.

Ross, L. E., Ferreira, M. C., & Ross, S. M. (1974). Backward masking of conditioned stimuli: Effects on differential and single-cue classical conditioning performance. *Journal of Experimental Psychology, 103,* 603-613.

Schneider, W., Dumais, S. T., & Shiffrin, R. M. (1984). Automatic and control processing and attention. In R. Parasuraman & D. R. Davies (Eds.), *Varieties of attention,* pp. 1-28. Orlando, FL: Academic Press.

Shallice, T. (1972). Dual functions of consciousness. *Psychological Review, 79,* 383-393.

Shiffrin, R. M. (1976). Capacity limitations in information processing, attention, and memory. In W. K. Estes (Ed.), *Handbook of learning and cognitive processes: Vol. 4. Attention and memory,* pp. 177-236. Hillsdale, N. J.: Lawrence Erlbaum Associates.

Shiffrin, R. M., & Schneider, W. (1977). Controlled and automatic human information processing: II. Perceptual learning, automatic attending, and a general theory. *Psychological Review, 84,* 127-190.

Shevrin, H., & Dickman, S. (1980). The psychological unconscious: A necessary assumption for all psychological theory. *American Psychologist, 35,* 421-434.

Torgersen, S. (1979). The nature and origin of common phobic fears. *British Journal of Psychiatry, 134,* 343-351.

Wagner, A. R. (1976). Priming in STM: An information-processing mechanism for self-generated and retrieval-generated depression in performance. In T. J. Tighe & R. N. Leaton (Eds.), *Habituation: Perspectives from child development, animal behavior, and neurophysiology,* pp. 95-128. Hillsdale, N. J.: Lawrence Erlbaum Associates.

Wagner, A. R. (1981). SOP: A model of automatic memory processing in animal behavior. In N. E. Spear & R. R. Miller (Eds.), *Information processing in animals: Memory mechanisms,* pp. 5-48. Hillsdale, N. J.: Lawrence Erlbaum associates.

Zajonc, R. B. (1980). Feeling and thinking. Preferences need no inferences. *American Psychologist, 35,* 151-175.

7

The Role of Cognitive Biases in the Origins and Maintenance of Fear and Anxiety Disorders

Susan Mineka and Andrew J. Tomarken
University of Texas at Austin[*] and University of Wisconsin-Madison

The two dominant approaches to understanding the origins and maintenance of acquired fear and anxiety both date back to the early part of the 20th century. Freud, and other theorists of the psychoanalytic tradition, have viewed anxiety as a signal of, and reaction to, real or imagined dangers often associated with infantile wishes. Pavlov and Watson, by contrast, viewed acquired fear and anxiety as originating out of instances of classical conditioning in which neutral cues had been paired with noxious or traumatic events. Elaborations of the behaviorist theory were made in the 1940's and 1950's when other theorists, (e.g., Dollard & Miller, 1950; Mowrer, 1947; Solomon & Wynne, 1954) developed avoidance conditioning models of fear and anxiety to help explain the notorious persistence of many fear/anxiety responses (see Eysenck & Rachman, 1965).

Sources of dissatisfaction with the psychoanalytic view are well-known within mainstream experimental psychology. Perhaps the most important criticism is the failure to operationalize constructs so that they could be subjected to empirical tests. Dissatisfaction with conditioning and avoidance models of fear and anxiety disorders has also become widespread in the past 10-15 years as researchers have tried (and often failed) to document similarities between classically conditioned fear or avoidance responses occurring in the laboratory, and fear and anxiety disorders appearing in clinical populations. One major source of dissatisfaction has stemmed from the observation that in many instances people with clinically significant fear and anxiety have no known traumatic conditioning history. This has led to speculation that in many instances

---

[*]Now at Northwestern University, Evanston, Illinois 60201

vicarious or observational conditioning may be involved in the origins of fear and anxiety rather than direct traumatic conditioning. A second source of dissatisfaction has been that such models have been vastly oversimplistic in viewing these disorders as originating out of simple instances of classical conditioning or avoidance learning occurring more or less in a vacuum. In doing so they have ignored the influence that a host of experiential variables that may occur prior to, during, or after a traumatic experience may have on how much fear or anxiety is experienced at the time, or how much is conditioned to stimuli present at the time, or how much is maintained in the future.

A third source of dissatisfaction with these traditional models has stemmed from the increasing recognition of, and evidence for, the important role that cognitive biases play in the origins and maintenance of fear and anxiety disorders. Some of these biases can be conceptualized in the terms of more contemporary S-S conditioning theories such as those of Rescorla and Mackintosh, and in terms of current conditioning research on selective associations (e.g., Domjan, 1983; LoLordo, 1979). However, other sources of cognitive bias do not translate as easily into contemporary conditioning theory, and seem to require a framework that incorporates the concepts and paradigms of current information processing research.

In this chapter we will review the highlights of recent research that addresses each of these three major sources of dissatisfaction with traditional conditioning models. In doing so we will attempt to come up with a richer, more complete framework for understanding the origins and maintenance of fear and anxiety disorders. It is our contention that conditioning models *do* have a considerable amount to offer in explaining the origins and maintenance of anxiety. However, this will happen only if they acknowledge the role of vicarious as well as direct conditioning, and only if they acknowledge a complex set of interacting experiential variables as they impact on the results of any direct or vicarious conditioning experience. Finally, we will also argue that by themselves conditioning models may not be adequate to provide a complete understanding of all the factors involved in the etiology and maintenance of fear and anxiety; a complete framwork must also incorporate concepts from current information processing research.

The Role of Vicarious Conditioning in the Origins of Fear

The observation that many people with intense fears or anxiety disorders have no known traumatic conditioning history has led to speculation that vicarious or observational conditioning may play an important role in the origins of these disorders (e.g., Marks, 1969; Rachman, 1978). In support of this hypothesis, we have developed a primate model for the acquisition of phobic fears through observation in a series of experiments completed in the last few years at the Wisconsin Harlow Primate Laboratory (see Mineka, in press; Mineka & Cook, in press, for reviews). Building on earlier observations that wild-reared, but not lab-reared, monkeys exhibit an intense fear of snakes, a paradigm was developed in which lab-reared monkeys served as observers who watched a wild-reared monkey model (live or on videotape) exhibit his/her fear of snakes. A discriminative observational conditioning procedure was developed in which the observers watched the model exhibiting a fear of live and toy snakes on some trials, and exhibiting no fear of neutral objects on other trials. About 3/4 of the observers acquired an intense and persistent fear of snakes, with the major determinant of the intensity of the observers's acquired fear being the intensity of the model's fear performance exhibited during the observational conditioning sessions [r(42) = .69] (Mineka & Cook, submitted). This fear was at asymptotic intensity after only two sessions of observational conditioning involving a total of only 8 minutes of exposure to the wild-reared model reacting fearfully to snakes. The observationally acquired fear also showed no signs of diminution at three month follow-up (Cook et al., 1985: Mineka et al., 1984; Cook & Mineka, in preparation). These results strongly support the view that intense phobic-like fears can indeed be acquired through observation alone in a very short period of time.

Experiential Variables Affecting Fear Acquisition and Maintenance

Much contemporary research also addresses the second source of dissatisfaction with traditional conditioning models that tended to view these disorders as arising out of simple instances of conditioning or avoidance learning occurring more or less in a vacuum. Such overly simplistic models were unable to explain large individual differences in the responses of people undergoing traumatic or observational conditioning experiences. Some might develop a mild fear that extinguished fairly easily, while others might develop an intense phobic fear that was highly persistent, and yet others might develop no fear at all. Such individual differences become understandable if one recognizes the multitude of experiential variables occurring *prior to, during, and following* a traumatic or observational conditioning experience that can interact and affect the level of fear that is experienced, conditioned and maintained over time. A few examples of each of these kinds of variables will be briefly reviewed to illustrate this point (see Mineka, 1985a and b, for more detailed reviews).

Regarding experiential variables occurring *prior* to a traumatic or observational experience and how they affect the level of fear that is experienced or conditioned, at least two important examples from our research stand out. Mineka, Gunnar, and Champoux (1986) showed how early experience with control and mastery over appetitive events can reduce the level of fear that is experienced in novel and frightening situations. They reared 4 peer groups of 4 infant monkeys each in one of two kinds of environments. The two groups of master monkeys were reared in cages in which they had access to manipulanda, the operation of which would result in the delivery of food, water and treats. The two groups of yoked monkeys lived in identical cages except that their manipulanda were inoperative; whenever a member of the Master group successfully operated its manipulandum, a reinforcement was delivered to the Yoked group as well. Between 7 and 10 months of age both Master and Yoked groups were tested in several different fear-provoking situations. The results indicated that relative to Yoked monkeys, Master monkeys habituated more rapidly to a fear provoking toy monster, showed more eagerness to enter a novel somewhat frightening playroom situation, and showed far more exploratory behavior once in the playroom.

Prior exposure to the object that will later be involved in an observational conditioning experience provides a second example of an experiential variable occurring prior to a conditioning experience that can reduce the level of fear that is learned. For example, Mineka and Cook (1986) found that prior exposure to a nonfearful model behaving nonfearfully with snakes immunized against the effects of subsequent exposure to a fearful model behaving fearfully with snakes. That is, if one first learns that an object is "safe", then one is much less likely to subsequently learn a fear of that object. This may help to account for why most investigators have not found as high correlations between parent's and their children's fears as might be expected given the potency of observational conditioning suggested by our monkey experiments. If a child has had prior exposure to a nonfearful parent or peer behaving nonfearfully with some object, this may immunize against the effects of observing a phobic parent behaving fearfully with that object.

The controllability of the UCS is one variable occurring *during* a conditioning experience that affects the amount of fear that is conditioned. Although Pavlovian conditioning has usually been studied in the traditional paradigm where the subject has no control over the CS or the US, in many everyday situations where Pavlovian conditioning occurs the subject does have some control over the US--such as when it will terminate. And for some years it has been known that less fear is conditioned to a neutral stimulus paired with controllable (escapable) as opposed to uncontrollable (inescapable) shock (e.g. Desiderato & Newman, 1971; Mineka, Cook & Miller, 1984; Mowrer & Viek, 1948).

Among variables that can occur *following* a conditioning experience that affect the level of fear maintained over time is subsequent exposure to a more intense US than involved in the original conditioning. Rescorla (1974) first conditioned a weak fear CR by pairing a CS with a mild US. When these rats were subsequently exposed to a few noncontingent intense USs, their fear CR was inflated in the direction that would have been expected had the more intense US been involved in the conditioning in the first place. Bouton (1984) also showed that such inflation effects are independent of the context in which the inflation experience occurs. Hendersen (1985) further showed that the longer the time interval between the original conditioning and the inflation experience (1 versus 60 days), the greater the inflation effect. In sum, research on inflation suggests that the organism has a memorial representation of the US following conditioning, and that when this representation is altered through subsequent experiences with a more intense US, the fear CR changes accordingly. Hendersen's work further suggests that the malleability of that fear memory increases with time.

In summary, many of the problems of earlier conditioning models of fear and anxiety are circumvented if one adopts more contemporary S-S conditioning theories in which US representations can be altered. In addition, it is important to recognize the significance of a wide range of variables occuring prior to, during, and following direct or observational conditioning experiences and their effect on the level of fear that is experienced, conditioned and maintained into the future. Acknowledging such complexity allows us to appreciate the wide array of individual differences in how much fear is acquired and maintained in people undergoing the same traumatic or observational conditioning experiences.

COGNITIVE BIASES IN FEAR AND ANXIETY

The third source of dissatisfaction with traditional conditioning models stems from increasing recognition of the role that cognitive biases play in the origins and maintenance of fear and anxiety. A wide variety of phenomena could potentially be termed cognitive biases. In the present context, we use the term to denote selective or non-veridical processing of fear-or threat-relevant information that serves to promote the development, maintenance, or exacerbation of fear or anxiety. Such processing may be learned or unlearned, conscious or unconscious, and may occur at any stage of cognition (e.g. attention, memory, or judgment and decision-making).

Given this definition, there appear to be at least three general types of cognitive bias associated with fear and anxiety. One is a bias to associate certain fear-relevant or prepared cues with aversive outcomes, either when they are contingently or when they are randomly related. A second is a tendency toward selective processing of threat/danger cues. A third bias is a tendency to overgeneralize fear, especially with the passage of time. Research pertinent to each of these three types of cognitive bias will be discussed in turn.

Selective associations in fear conditioning

Since the classic demonstration of Garcia and Koelling (1966) showing selective associations of tastes with gastrointestinal illness, and of audiovisual cues with exteroceptive footshock. much attention in the conditioning literature has been devoted to issues of selective associations. One prominent theory to describe such effects as they pertain to the origins of phobic fears is Seligman's (1971) preparedness theory, elaborated on later by Öhman and his colleagues (e.g., 1978, 1985, 1986, this volume). These theories purport to explain the commonly observed nonrandom distribution of fears and phobias. That is, many more people have fears of snakes, spiders, water, heights, etc., than of bicycles, electric stoves, electric outlets. etc.. even though the latter objects may have equally or more often been associated with trauma. To account for the nonrandom distribution of fears, this theory proposes that in the struggle for existence there was a selective advantage for human and nonhuman primates who rapidly acquired fears of certain objects or situations that may have posed a threat to our early ancestors.

Öhman and his colleagues have conducted an impressive series of experiments using human subjects, the results of which are generally consistent with this view (see McNally, 1987; Öhman, this volume, for reviews). Briefly, they have found superior electrodermal conditioning, primarily indexed through heightened resistance to extinction, when slides of prepared or fear-relevant CSs such as snakes and spiders are paired with a mild electric shock US; this superiority is relative to conditioning found when slides of unprepared or fear-irrelevant CSs such as flowers and mushrooms are used in the same paradigm. This elegant series of experiments provides the best evidence for selective associations in human aversive conditioning. The question might be raised, however, whether such conditioned associations are evidence of biases that are specifically "cognitive" in nature. Indeed, according to Seligman's original formulation, preparedness effects are "non-cognitive" in the sense of being resistant to instructions or other forms of information (e.g., about the non-aversiveness of feared stimuli). In support of this notion, several studies by Öhman and his colleagues have found enhanced resistance to extinction to fear-relevant stimuli despite instructions indicating that shocks will no longer be presented (e.g. Hugdahl, 1978; Hugdahl & Öhman, 1977). However, several studies have failed to replicate these effects (see McNally, 1987, for a review).

More importantly, from a theoretical perspective, a line of reasoning that denotes as "non-cognitive" instances of resistance to instructions overly restricts the range of processes that can be termed "cognitive". By focussing solely on verbalizable expectancies and other conscious cognitive processes, this perspective ignores unconscious or pre-conscious processes occurring outside the scope of awareness. In fact, as will be described below (see Selective Processing of Threat Cues section), recent research by Öhman and his associates allows for such a reconceptualization of prepared selective associations in terms of these latter processes. This reconceptualization suggests that conditioned associations involving fear-relevant CSs differ from other conditioned associations more in the *types* of cognitive processes that mediate effects than in the presence or absence of "cognition" per se.

A second issue raised by preparedness experiments with human subjects is whether such effects are truly rooted in phylogenetic factors. As several commentators have noted (e.g., Delprato, 1980), the contribution of ontogenetic factors cannot be ruled out, since subjects, though often preselected for absence of snake or spider fear, all have prior associations to snakes, spiders, mushrooms, flowers, etc. One way to circumvent this problem inherent in the human prepared conditioning literature is to use lab-reared primate subjects that have no prior experiences with the fear-relevant or the fear-irrelevant stimuli. Two recent experiments using an observational conditioning paradigm similar to that described above have done exactly that. Because prior research had demonstrated the importance of the precise level of fear exhibited by models in determining how much fear the observer acquires (Cook et al., 1985; Mineka et al., 1984; Mineka & Cook, submitted), it was necessary to equate the amount of fear the model exhibited to the fear-relevant stimuli (toy snakes) and to the fear-irrelevant stimuli (brightly colored artificial flowers). An earlier experiment (Cook & Mineka, in preparation) had shown that observers acquire as much fear simply through watching a videotape of fearful models behaving fearfully with snakes as through watching a live model. This finding indicated that it would be feasible to do an experiment in which naive monkeys would watch edited videotapes on which the model looked as if he/she was reacting fearfully to either toy snakes, or to brightly colored artificial flowers, although in reality the model had been reacting to a live snake in the original unedited videotape.

For the first experiment (Cook & Mineka, in preparation) two different kinds of videotapes were made. The SN+FL- group watched a videotape on which they saw a model monkey reacting fearfully to toy snakes on some trials and nonfearfully to brightly colored artificial flowers on other trials. (Toy snakes rather than real snakes were used to control for possible effects of differences in animateness or movement between snakes and flowers). The FL+SN- group watched a videotape on which they saw a model monkey reacting fearfully to flowers on some trials and nonfearfully to toy snakes on other trials. It is important to note that the actual fear performance that both groups saw on SN+, and FL+, trials, respectively, was identical. This was accomplished by editing out the image of the real snake from the original videotape and editing in images of toy snakes and flowers for the two groups, respectively. The results of this experiment indicated that most subjects in the SN+FL-group did indeed acquire a fear of toy (and real) snakes, but not of flowers. Most subjects in the FL+SN- group, by contrast, did not acquire a fear of either flowers or snakes. Figure 7.1 illustrates these results for one of the measures of acquired fear (fear or disturbance behaviors).

A second experiment (Cook & Mineka, in preparation) examined whether monkeys could acquire a fear of the flowers when a simpler, nondiscriminative conditioning procedure was used, i.e., one in which they saw model monkeys reacting fearfully to flowers, but in which snakes were never presented. Accordingly, one group of monkeys (FL+) watched a videotape on which they saw a model reacting fearfully to flowers, and a second group (SN+) watched the same fear performance when models were reacting fearfully to toy snakes. Consistent with the results of the first experiment, most subjects in the SN+ group acquired a fear of snakes, but most subjects in the FL+ group did not acquire a fear of flowers.

Although the results of these two experiments provide some of the best evidence yet available that monkeys (and probably humans) have a phylogenetically based predisposition to acquire fears of certain kinds of fear-relevant objects more easily than fears of other fear-irrelevant objects, these results are not in and of themselves definitive on this point. In

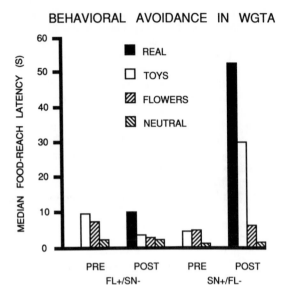

FIG. 7.1. Mean number of fear/disturbance behaviors exhibited by SN+FL- and FL+SN- groups during pretest and posttest (following observational conditioning) in the presence of real and toy snakes, artificial flowers, and neutral stimuli. (From Cook & Mineka, in preparation).

research on selective associations it is important to demonstrate that the stimulus (in this case flowers) which has not shown evidence of conditioning, can indeed be learned about in some other context such as an appetitive one. That is, one might expect flowers to be not easily associated with fear, but to be more easily be associated with, say, food. We are currently in the process of examining this issue. We have developed a complex discriminative appetitive operant paradigm, in which monkeys must solve two PAN (positive-ambiguous-negative) discrimination problems. For one problem they must discriminate between two different snake stimuli, and for the other they must discriminate between two different flower stimuli. The procedure is sufficiently complex that to date only four monkeys have learned the discriminations. However, these four monkeys have learned at a comparable rate about flowers and about toy snakes. Thus it does indeed seem that they can learn about flowers in an appetitive paradigm, suggesting that flowers are not simply an inadequate stimulus.

Fear-relevant selective associations and covariation bias.

In recent years, we have also conducted several studies assessing fear-relevant selective associations in human populations (Tomarken, Mineka, & Cook, in preparation). A major theme guiding this line of research is that such selective associations need not be restricted to the domain of classical conditioning. In our view, prepared conditioning may be one manifestation of a more generalized schema-induced *covariation bias*.

Broadly defined, the term 'schema' refers to an organized representation of knowledge that guides the processing of current situational information (e.g., Alloy & Tabachnik, 1984; Neisser, 1967). Such representations often prove beneficial to the individual, by promoting the perception of, memory for, and appraisal of, meaningful information. However, as a large body of contemporary research has shown, schematic processing often, though not always (e.g., Hastie, 1980), results in distorted processing of information in a direction consistent with prior expectancies (e.g., Brewer & Nakamura, 1984; Higgins & Bargh, 1987; Nisbett & Ross, 1980).

While such biases can be manifest in a variety of contexts, studies in which subjects have been required to estimate the degree of contingency between events have provided perhaps the greatest mass of findings illustrating this phenomenon. These investigations have shown that individuals with strong expectancies for covariations between two classes of events often strikingly overestimate the veridical contingency between them (Alloy & Tabachnik, 1984; Crocker, 1981).

Most important from the perspective of our research are the evident parallels between schema-induced covariation bias and selective associations between fear-relevant conditioned stimuli and aversive unconditioned stimuli. Perhaps, then, similar mechanisms underly the two sets of phenomena. Consistent with this latter assertion is the evidence that: the conditioned responses of animals in classical and instrumental paradigms are often sensitive to the same factors that affect humans' contingency judgments (e.g., Alloy & Tabachnik, 1984; Dickinson & Shanks, 1985); and, the detection of contingency itself underlies the development of conditioned responding (e.g., Mackintosh, 1983).

In our experiments, we have also assessed whether individual differences in fear moderate susceptibility to biased perception of the contingency between fear-relevant stimuli and aversive outcomes. This result would be consistent with the evidence from covariation and other paradigms that emotions often induce selective processing of information in a manner that may serve to reinforce or maintain affective states (e.g., Isen, 1984; Leventhal & Tomarken, 1986). Particularly relevant in the present context are Alloy and Abramson's intriguing series of experiments demonstrating marked differences between depressives and nondepressives in the perception of the contingency between instrumental responses and behavioral outcomes (e.g., Alloy & Abramson, 1979, 1982). However, no previous studies have assessed the effects of fear, or anxiety, on the perception of contingencies involving fear-relevant stimuli. In our experiments, we hypothesized that individuals high in fear of phobic-relevant stimuli would be particularly likely to overestimate the covariation between these stimuli and aversive outcomes.

To assess covariation bias in high and low fear subjects, we have used an illusory correlation paradigm. First developed by Chapman and

Chapman (1967, 1969) in their classic studies on biases in clinical judgment, this paradigm involves exposure to categories of stimuli that, across trials, are veridically uncorrelated. In our experiments, categories of stimuli were fear-relevant and fear-irrelevant slides randomly paired with aversive and non-aversive outcomes.

In the initial experiment, subjects were females selected from the top and bottom quartiles of the distribution of responses to standardized snake and spider fear questionnaires (High and Low Fear groups). They were exposed to 72 trials, on each of which a slide (8 sec. duration) was followed by an outcome. Slides came from one fear-relevant category, either snakes or spiders, and from two fear-irrelevant categories, mushrooms and flowers. These latter two categories were chosen because they have been used frequently as fear-irrelevant stimuli in studies assessing autonomic conditioning to prepared and non-prepared CSs. Following each slide, subjects experienced either a mildly aversive shock, a non-aversive tone (both 2 sec. in duration), or nothing at all.

Before the series of trials subjects were informed that their task was to decide if there was any relationship between any of the slide categories and any of the three possible outcomes. In reality, there was no correlation between any type of slide and any of the three outcomes. Specifically, the conditional probabilities of any outcome given the prior occurrence of any category of slide were all equivalent at .33. Subjects' perceptions of the relationships between slide types and outcomes were assessed immediately after the series of trials. Several formats were used to assess perceptions of contingency. We report here the results of a question format in which subjects make conditional probability estimates indicating their perceptions of the probability of experiencing each of the three outcomes given the prior occurrence of each of the three types of slides.

Figure 7.2 shows selected mean conditional probability estimates of the High and Low fear groups in Experiment 1. For the sake of brevity, in all figures and in subsequent text, the pooled snake/shock and spider/shock estimates are denoted simply as 'snake/shock'. As revealed by Figure 7.2, High Fear subjects demonstrated a dramatic bias to associate fear-relevant slides with aversive outcomes. Indeed, the results of analyses indicated that High Fear subjects' snake/shock estimates were significantly greater than all other relevant comparison estimates. Low fear subjects showed an attenuated bias. Although their snake/shock estimates were significantly greater than their snake/nothing and flower/shock estimates, the former failed to differ significantly from snake/tone and mushroom/shock probability estimates. Furthermore, a between-group comparison revealed that High Fear subjects had a significantly greater bias to associate snakes with shock than did Low Fear subjects.

A second experiment was designed to replicate the previous findings and to assess those features of an aversive outcome that are linked to fear-relevant stimuli in the development of illusory correlations. Concerning the latter issue, it is likely that shock was the most salient, as well as most aversive, of the three outcomes in the first experiment. Given the evidence that illusory correlations can be generated merely by

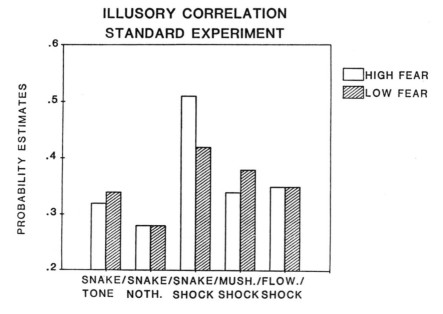

FIG. 7.2. Selected mean probability estimates for High and Low Fear subjects in first illusory correlation experiment. (From Tomarken, Mineka & Cook, in preparation).

co-occurrences of distinctive stimuli (e.g., Hamilton, Dugan, & Trolier, 1985; Hamilton & Gifford, 1976), the results of Experiment 1 leave unclear precisely what properties of the shock accounted for covariation bias.

To address this issue, the tone outcome used in the previous experiment was replaced by a more attention-getting but non-aversive combination of a ringing chime and flashing colored lights. The chime was identical to that used in public settings (e.g., airports) to alert people to subsequent important events (e.g., announcements). All other aspects of the procedure were identical to that of the first experiment. Ratings completed at the end of the series of trials indicated that although subjects found shock more aversive than the chime-light outcome, they rated the two outcomes equally salient or attention-getting. However, as indicated by Table 7.1, High Fear subjects still demonstrated a robust bias to associate fear-relevant stimuli with shock.

Their snake/shock probability estimates were significantly greater than all relevant comparison estimates, including the Low Fear group's snake-shock estimate. This finding suggests that it is the specifically aversive qualities of shock that are responsible for its association with fear-relevant stimuli. The Low Fear group showed some mild trends toward covariation bias, but there were no significant differences among their estimates.

TABLE 7.1
Illusory Correlation Experiment
Assessing Effects of Salience:
Conditional Probability Estimates

	Snake/ Nothing	Snake/Flashing Light-Chime	Snake/ Shock	Flower/ Shock	Mushroom/ Shock
Hi Fear Ss (N=13)	28.58%	28.04%	55.98%	35.73%	32.77%
Lo Fear Ss (N=12)	32.03%	31.37%	41.41%	32.96%	43.84%

In the first two experiments, there were only slight hints of a bias among Low Fear subjects to associate fear-relevant stimuli with aversive outcomes. As a result, the third experiment assessed the effects of two factors that, on the basis of previous findings, appeared likely to increase the magnitude and consistency of effects among Low Fear subjects. Concerning the first of these factors, previous studies have shown that increases in the sheer frequency of schema-congruent occurrences can lead to greater bias in contingency estimates (e.g., Alloy & Abramson, 1979). Therefore, we increased the number of snake-shock pairings for half the subjects. These groups received shock outcomes 50% of the time rather than 33% of the time. It should be emphasized that shock still occurred with equivalent probability after each of the three slide categories. In other words, slides and outcomes remained uncorrelated. The second factor introduced was based on the evidence that individuals frequently show enhanced recall for schema-consistent, relative to schema-irrelevant, information with the passage of time (e.g., Rothbart, Evans, & Fulero, 1979; see Brewer & Nakamura, 1984, for a review). As a result while half the subjects in the 33% and 50% shock base rate groups made estimates immediately after the series of trials (as in Experiments 1 and 2), the other half made contingency estimates one week after exposure to the series of trials. Based on the findings noted above, we expected that delayed recall might also increase illusory biases.

As indicated by Figure 7.3, when subjects received shock 33% of the time, the results were consistent with those of the two previous studies. Once again, High Fear subjects demonstrated a significant bias to associate fear-relevant stimuli with shock, while the Low Fear subjects failed to show any significant bias. However, the results were markedly different in the 50% shock base rate conditions. As evidenced by Figure 7.4, in both the immediate and delayed recall conditions, the probability estimates of High and Low Fear subjects were remarkably similar.

In the Immediate Recall condition, the snake/shock probability estimates of both groups were significantly greater than their flower/shock estimates, and in the Delayed Recall condition, their snake/shock estimates were significantly greater than both their mushroom/shock and flower/shock estimates.

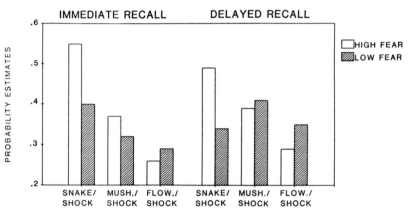

FIG. 7.3. Selected mean probability estimates for High and Low Fear subjects receiving 33% baserate of shock, with Immediate or Delayed recall. (From Tomarken, Mineka & Cook, in preparation).

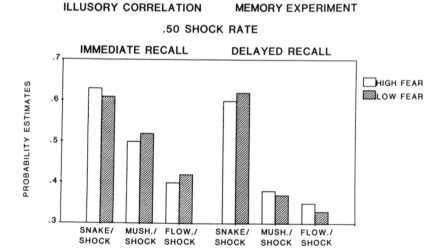

FIG. 7.4. Selected mean probability estimates for High and Low Fear subjects receiving 50% baserate of shock, with Immediate or Delayed recall. (From Tomarken, Mineka & Cook, in preparation).

The findings from the 50% conditions of this experiment are the first in our series indicating that, under certain circumstances, low fear subjects can demonstrate a notable bias to associate fear-relevant stimuli with aversive outcomes. It is significant that an increase in the base rate of shock elicited these illusory correlations. As noted above, in previous experiments, similar manipulations designed to increase the frequency of what could be considered schema-congruent outcomes have also increased the magnitude of covariation bias. This observation suggests that particularly potent situational conditions may be required to elicit covariation bias in low fear subjects. Conversely, high fear subjects demonstrate pronounced biases under even less favorable circumstances. Perhaps, then, high and low fear individuals do not differ so much in the presence or absence of a schema linking fear-relevant stimuli to aversive outcomes but in its relative accessibility under various contextual conditions.

An additional implication of these illusory correlation studies pertains to the marked biases consistently demonstrated by high fear subjects. Simply put, it is tempting to suggest that such pronounced overestimation of the contingency between feared stimuli and aversive outcomes is an important factor acting to promote the maintenance or exacerbation of fears and phobias over time. Admittedly, one potential weakness of this conclusion is the rarity with which animal phobics actually confront feared stimuli. However, just as actual aversive experiences do not appear necessary for the acquisition of phobias (see Vicarious Conditioning section above), actual experience with fear-relevant stimuli may not be necessary for generation of covariation bias. To investigate this possibility in future studies, we will assess the contribution of observational factors and imagery to illusory correlations. In addition, we are currently conducting studies assessing fear-relevant illusory correlations among socially anxious subjects, a group less able than animal phobics to actively avoid threatening stimuli in real life.

Finally, in future experiments, we intend to examine the relationship between biased covariation assessment and enhanced conditioned responding to prepared stimuli. Although the two sets of findings both demonstrate a heightened sensitivity to covariations between fear-relevant stimuli and aversive outcomes, it is possible that the two phenomena may differ in other respects. One issue is the role of individual differences in fear. Most conditioning studies on preparedness have not assessed the effects of this factor, and those that have done so have yielded inconsistent results (McNally, 1987). Similarly, in illusory correlation experiments, the covariation estimates of high and low fear subjects have differed markedly under some conditions and have been highly similar under others. Clearly, further research is necessary to delineate, and to compare, those conditions under which individual differences in fear moderate effects in both paradigms.

A second issue is the relationship between covariation judgments and conditioned responding. Are biased estimates of the covariation between fear-relevant stimuli and aversive outcomes paralleled by enhanced autonomic responding to such stimuli? We intend to address this question by concurrently monitoring subjects' contingency estimates and their autonomic responses over the course of exposure to an illusory correlation sequence (cf. Dawson, Schell, & Banis, 1986).

Selective Processing of Threat Cues

Our illusory correlation studies showed that high fear subjects, and sometimes low fear subjects, selectively process covariations between feared stimuli and aversive outcomes. In recent years, a complementary body of research has shown that phobias, and other anxiety disorders, are associated with selective processing of threat-related stimuli per se, that is, independent of their current association with aversive outcomes. A linkage between anxiety and heightened accessibility of threat- or danger-related cognitions was first proposed by Beck and his colleagues (e.g., Beck, 1967; Beck, Laude, & Bohnert, 1974). Subsequent studies on anxious subjects' naturalistic thoughts (e.g., Hibbert, 1984, cf. Sewitch & Kirsch, 1984) and appraisal strategies (Butler & Mathews, 1983; Goldfried, Padawer, & Robins, 1984; Landau, 1980) have supported Beck's views. Other studies have used the methods and concepts of contemporary information processing theory to assess specific cognitive biases associated with anxiety disorders. These investigations will be the focus of this review.

Anxiety and Attention. One line of research has focused on attentional biases. For example, using a probe-reaction time paradigm (e.g., Navon & Margalit, 1983), MacLeod, Mathews, and Tata (1986) found that patients with generalized anxiety disorder consistently shifted attention to threat words displayed in varying locations on a visual display screen. Conversely, non-anxious controls tended to shift attention away from threat words. Other studies have adopted a different approach by demonstrating that threat-related (but task-irrelevant) content selectively interferes with the processing of other, task-relevant features of stimuli. Using a variation of the familiar Stroop paradigm (Dyer, 1973, Stroop, 1938), Watts, McKenna, Sharrock, & Trezise (1986) found that, relative to non-phobic controls, spider phobics were significantly slower at naming the color of words related to spiders (e.g., 'creepy'). Similarly, Mathews and MacLeod (1985) showed that threat-related words interfered with color-naming for anxious out-patients but not for controls. Of additional interest is the evidence that interference was content-specific in both of these studies. For example, Mathews and MacLeod (1985) found that subjects with predominantly physical fears were more impaired by words denoting physical than social threat, and the converse was true of those with predominantly social fears.

A third paradigm that has been used to assess attentional biases is dichotic listening. In this procedure, subjects are asked to shadow (repeat) a message presented to one ear, while ignoring a message presented to the other ear. Of interest is the frequency with which the content of the rejected channel is semantically processed. Using this paradigm, two studies have shown that phobics (Burgess, Jones, Robertson, & Emerson, 1981) and obsessive-compulsives (Foa & McNally, 1986) demonstrate a heightened sensitivity to fear-relevant words, but not to neutral words, appearing on the unattended channel. Particularly intriguing are the results of a recent dichotic listening study by Mathews and MacLeod (1986). These authors found that patients with generalized anxiety disorder, unlike controls, were slower in performing a simultaneous reaction time (RT) task when threat-related words appeared on the rejected channel. However, subjects were unable to report or recognize the words to which they had been exposed, even when suddenly interrupted in the middle of the procedure. The authors interpret their findings as reflecting the operation of an automatic, preattentive processing of threat-related material that occurs prior to awareness in patients with generalized anxiety. Further, they propose that such preattentive processing results in momentary allocation of resources to either further processing of threat-related material or to the task of preventing such material from reaching consciousness. Either of these effects would account for the slower RTs of the generalized anxiety group.

Öhman (1986; Öhman, Dimberg, & Esteves, this volume) has also recently proposed a similar model for the processing of fear-relevant conditioned stimuli, such as snakes and angry faces. He has argued that conditioned autonomic responses to fear CSs reflect the operation of a preattentive, "unconscious" call for resource-limited controlled processing (see Öhman et al., this volume). To test his model, Öhman has attempted to uncouple pre-attentive and controlled processing through the use of a masking paradigm in which very brief (30 ms) CS presentations are followed by a masking stimulus, thus preventing conscious recognition. Initial experiments have supported this hypothesis by indicating maintenance of differential electrodermal responding to masked fear-relevant, but not fear-irrelevant, CS + s during extinction (see Öhman et al., this volume, for more extensive discussion).

Although evidence of unconscious processing of fear- or threat-related stimuli certainly has important implications, these findings should be viewed with caution at the present time. For example, patients in the Mathews and MacLeod (1986) study may have been more aware of threat-related words than the authors indicate; it has been argued that, in dichotic listening paradigms, retrospective reports of subjects are a less sensitive indicator of awareness than shadowing errors (e.g., Dawson & Schell, 1985; Holender, 1986). In this regard, it is noteworthy that Mathews and MacLeod's patients demonstrated a near-significant trend toward greater shadowing errors after threat-related words. Similarly, although Öhman's findings are intriguing, one of his recent studies has shown that differential conditioning to masked fear-relevant stimuli is abolished when subjects are instructed to attend to the masking stimulus. By indicating that conditioning effects are dependent on the individual's allocation of attention, this result calls into question whether automatic, pre-attentive processes alone can mediate such effects. Interestingly, this evidence is consistent with findings recently obtained in other paradigms that similarly question strong claims for automatic, or unconscious, perceptual processing that is completely independent of resource-limited focal attention (e.g., Kahneman & Triesman, 1984).

Anxiety and Memory. In recent years, several studies have also assessed selective memory biases in anxiety disorders. Two investigations found that socially anxious college students have enhanced memory for self-relevant information, with evidence that this effect is more pronounced for negative traits (O'Banion & Arkowitz, 1977) and under social-evaluative threat (Smith, Ingram, & Brehm, 1983). Similarly, Mueller & Curtois (1980) showed that high test-anxious students recalled more self-descriptive trait terms than low test-anxious students. In this study, however, a recall bias was found for both negative and positive words. Greater inconsistencies are evident in studies of clinical populations. While Nunn, Stevenson, and Whalan (1984) found enhanced memory for fear-relevant material in agoraphobics, Bradley and Mathews (1983) and Mogg, Mathews, and Weinman (1987) found that patients with generalized anxiety had no recall bias for negative self-relevant material. Indeed, in the latter study, anxious patients tended to recall *fewer* threat words than controls.

Further research is clearly necessary to resolve whether these inconsistencies are due to differences in diagnostic groups, experimental procedures, or other factors. In any case, memory studies conducted to date have provided less compelling evidence for selective processing of negative information than studies assessing attentional biases. This disparity between attentional and memory findings appears most notable in the case of generalized anxiety disorder.

In accounting for the stronger evidence for attentional than memory biases, Mogg et. al. (1987) have proposed that anxiety is associated with a vigilant-avoidant pattern of cognitive processing characterized by early detection of threat cues, followed by attempts to cognitively avoid these events. Because of cognitive avoidance, it is argued, heightened recall for negative self-relevant information is unlikely to occur. In addition, citing evidence of a negative self-referent recall bias in depressives, (e.g., Derry & Kuiper, 1981; Kuiper & Derry, 1982), Mogg et. al. propose that depression is associated with absence of avoidance and, thus a prominent memory bias for negative information.

At first glance, it appears that Mogg et. al. may have overstated the difference between anxiety- and depression-related cognitive processes. For example, some studies have failed to find evidence for a depression-induced memory bias for negative information (e.g., Hasher, Rose, Zacks, Sanft, & Doren, 1985; see Isen, 1984, for a review). Conversely, there is evidence that at least some forms of anxiety can be associated with a negative recall bias (e.g., O'Banion & Arkowitz, 1977). Yet, it is important to note that a comparison restricted to *clinically significant* manifestations of both disorders may better corrobate Mogg et. al.'s hypothesis. Among depression studies those using clinically depressed samples have been most likely to find negative recall biases (e.g., compare Hasher et. al., 1985, to Breslow, Kocsis, & Belkin, 1981; see Johnson & Magaro, 1987, for a review). Conversely, anxiety studies using clinical samples, in particular those with generalized anxiety, have been less likely to find such selective recall biases (compare, e.g., O'Banion & Arkowitz, 1977, to Mogg et. al., 1987).

Interestingly, these differences between depression and anxiety in the *stages of processing* that can manifest bias do not necessarily imply differences in the *content* of information that is selectively biased. Indeed, there is evidence that anxiety states are often associated with "depressogenic" cognitions and vice versa (e.g., Clark & Hemsley, 1985; Hollon & Kendall, 1980; Sutherland, Newman, & Rachman, 1982). Clearly, one reason for the substantial cognitive overlap is the overlap in affective states and/or diagnostic status; many clinically depressed patients are significantly anxious and many patients with anxiety disorders are significantly depressed (e.g., Akiskal, 1985; Jablensky, 1985). This symptomatic overlap makes it difficult to ascertain the degree to which depression and anxiety are associated with unique cognitive biases. To resolve this issue, it would be optimal for future studies assessing cognitive biases to classify subjects on the basis of features of both disorders, with an eye toward the possible identification of relatively "pure" subgroups of each and/or a distinct "anxious-depressed" subtype.

It is also necessary that future anxiety studies focus more on delineating those factors responsible for cognitive biases. One question is whether such biases are linked to *state* anxiety or to other, potentially more enduring features of anxiety disorders. In this regard, it is notable that, in college student samples, heightened state anxiety has been associated with selective processing of threat-related cues in both dichotic listening (Nielsen & Sarason, 1981) and Stroop (Ray, 1979) paradigms similar to those that have been used with patient populations. However, because state anxiety is significantly correlated with trait anxiety (e.g., Watson & Clark, 1984), it is possible that more enduring dispositional factors contributed to selective biases in these studies (see also M. Eysenck, this volume). Clearly, future investigations should evaluate the effects of both state and trait factors on selective processing of threat-related cues.

A related issue requiring future research is whether cognitive biases are risk factors predisposing toward anxiety disorders, or are merely consequences of anxiety disorders. Of the studies reviewed above, only Watts et. al. (1986) and Foa and McNally (1986) have begun to address this issue (see also M. Eysenck, this volume). Although methodological problems (e.g., the possible role of practice effects) somewhat limit conclusions, both studies found that attentional biases markedly declined after successful treatment. These results are consistent with what would be expected if biases were consequences of fear. However, they are by no means inconsistent with the possibility that such biases are among those etiological factors causing fear in the first place. This observation highlights the need for longitudinal investigations assessing the developmental interplay between anxiety and cognitive processes in at-risk populations.

One final issue that merits increased attention in future research is the nature of "low anxiety". In particular, do low anxious individuals, like non-depressives (e.g., Alloy & Abramson, 1979), display cognitive biases that act to minimize the impact of stimuli capable of inducing negative affect? The results of several investigations reviewed above are consistent with this hypothesis. In these studies, low anxious groups have tended to selectively *ignore* threat-relevant information (e.g., Mathews, et al., 1986; Nunn et. al., 1984). On the other hand, under certain conditions in illusory correlation experiments, low fear subjects have demonstrated a bias to selectively associate fear-relevant cues with aversive outcomes that is as pronounced as that shown by high fear subjects. Future research, taking into account the heterogeneity of self-reported low anxiety/fear (e.g., Weinberger, Schwartz, & Davidson, 1979), is necessary to delineate those conditions under which it is associated with particular selective biases.

Overgeneralization of fear with the passage of time.

Clinically it has been known for some time that one cardinal characteristic of anxiety disorders is a pronounced tendency to overgeneralize the range of objects or situations that pose a threat (e.g., Beck, 1976; Beck & Emery, 1985). Such clinical observations are now supported by a large amount of research using animals as subjects. In addition, as will be shown below, this research shows that a very important variable moderating the development of overgeneralization is time since the aversive conditioning experience.

Riccio, Richardson, and Ebner (1984) have recently reviewed a number of animal experiments showing that as the retention interval following appetitive or fear conditioning increases, the generalization gradient around the original CS+ flattens. Furthermore, this flattening of the generalization gradient is caused not by lowering of fear to the CS+, but rather by an *increase* in fear to the generalization test stimuli. Riccio et al. argue that this outcome reflects a forgetting with the passage of time of the very specific attributes of a CS; memory for these specific CS attributes is intact right after conditioning, contributing to sharper generalization gradients at that time. Such forgetting of specific CS attributes may well also be involved in the common clinical observation noted above that fears and phobias show increasing generalization over time.

Hendersen, Patterson, and Jackson (1980) have also shown forgetting of specific *UCS* attributes with the passage of time. Further, such forgetting has similar consequences to that noted by Riccio et al. in the form of increasingly conservative behavior in a wider range of situations than occurs immediately following conditioning. These authors showed that a CS that had been paired with an aversive airblast 100 times would not serve to increase the rate of responding on a shock-motivated Sidman avoidance task when animals were tested the day following conditioning. However, after a long interval (45 days) the same CS would serve to increase the rate of the shock-motivated avoidance response. It is as if, after a long interval, the rat remembered that the CS signalled danger, but forgot exactly what the characteristics of that danger were (e.g., shock vs. air blast) and so behaved conservatively by increasing their rate of shock-motivated avoidance when the CS for airblast was presented.

Hendersen (1978) and Thomas (1979) have also shown that conditioned inhibition is forgotten with the passage of time to a much greater extent than is conditioned excitation (although we have seen that using very sensitive procedures for testing conditioned excitation there is some forgetting of specific CS and US attributes). Such forgetting of fear inhibition or safety signals may also facilitate the increasing generalization of objects and situations to which fear is shown with the passage of time. Places or objects that were once safe (actively inhibitory of fear) may lose these properties. This change increases the chance that fear may generalize to these former safety signals.

A complementary set of findings indicate that, although fear CRs are not context specific (i.e., they generalize across situations), extinction of such CRs is context specific (e.g., Bouton & Bolles, 1979, 1985; Bouton & King, 1983). For example, Bouton and Bolles have shown that when fear of a CS is extinguished in context (B) other than the one in which it was conditioned (A), there is no generalization of the extinction of fear of the CS to the original (A) or to new (C) contexts. Just as increasing generalization gradients and forgetting of conditioned inhibition may account for the increasing generalization of fear over time, context-specific extinction may underlie *the maintenance of generalization* once it has occurred. This hypothesis awaits empirical test. Nevertheless, it clearly suggests that important issues can be addressed by exploring the interface between the forgetting and memory issues addressed by Riccio and Hendersen and the context-specific extinction effects addressed by Bouton and colleagues.

In this section we have reviewed evidence that fear generalizes across contexts, and across CSs--especially with the passage of time. In addition to the loss of memory for specific CS attributes with the passage of time, there also appears to be a loss of memory for specific UCS attributes. The consequence of both processes is that the animal shows fear-motivated behaviors in situations that it would not have immediately following conditioning. Furthermore, we have seen that inhibitory CRs are forgotten with time, and that extinguished CSs do not generalize across contexts. The robustness of generalization of excitatory effects, combined with the fragility of inhibitory effects, helps illuminate some of the factors contributing to the maintenance and even enhancement of fears over time. In addition, these findings may have important implications for the treatment of human fears. However, it is important to remember that the research discussed in this section has been done exclusively with rats as subjects. The parallels of these findings with observations of human fears suggest that similar experimental effects would be found in humans, although at present we are unaware of any human investigations that have explicitly examined these issues. We believe that exploring such questions in humans would have important implications for our understanding of the origins and maintenance of fear and anxiety, as well as for understanding some more basic questions about human emotional memory.

CONCLUSIONS

In this chapter we have reviewed experimental approaches to understanding the origins and maintenance of fear and anxiety disorders.

Three major sources of dissatisfaction with traditional conditioning models were discussed, and research pertinent to each of them was reviewed. It is our belief that an adequate understanding of the origins and maintenance of fear and anxiety can only be achieved if a broad, integrative model is developed which incorporates constructs from each of the areas of research we have reviewed. These include (but are not necessarily limited to): Contemporary S-S conditioning theory; vicarious conditioning; interactions of experiential variables occuring prior to, during, and following a traumatic experience; and cognitive biases of several different types (selective associations of certain fear-relevant cues with aversive outcome, biased attention and perhaps memory for threat-related cues, and overgeneralization of fear with the passage of time). In reviewing these areas of inquiry, we have tried to generate bridges among domains of research that often have little contact. For example, we have tried to emphasize the shared concerns and mutual relevance of human and animal research on conditioning and information processing and, in turn, the relevance of each of these areas of basic research to the clinical literature on anxiety and phobic disorders. It is our belief that such bridges are necessary for real progress to be made in understanding the origins and maintenance of fear and anxiety.

ACKNOWLEDGEMENTS

Preparation of this chapter was supported by Grant BNS-8507340 from the National Science Foundation and by a grant from the Hogg Foundation for Mental Health to S. Mineka. The authors' research described in the chapter has been generously supported by the following grants: a Biomed grant from the University of Wisconsin Graduate School, a grant from the Hogg Foundation for Mental Health and Grants BNS-7823612, BNS-8119041, BNS-8216141, BNS-8507340 from the National Science Foundation. The authors would like to especially thank Michael Cook for his help in conducting much of the research described here and for his comments on an earlier version of this chapter.

REFERENCES

Akiskal, H. S. (1985). Anxiety: Definition, relationship to depression, and proposal for an integrative model. In A. H. Tuma & J. D. Maser (Eds.), *Anxiety and the anxiety disorders*, pp. 787-797. Hillsdale, N.J.: Erlbaum.

Alloy, L. B., & Abramson, L. Y. (1979). Judgment of contingency in depressed and nondepressed students: Sadder but wiser?. *Journal of Experimental Psychology: General, 108,* 441-485.

Alloy, L. B., & Abramson, L. Y. (1982). Learned helplessness, depression, and the illusion of control. *Journal of Personality and*

Social Psychology, 42. 1114-1126.

Alloy, L. B., & Tabachnik, N. (1984). Assessment of covariation in humans and animals: The joint influence of prior expectancy and current situational information. *Psychological Review, 91,* 112-149.

Beck, A. T. (1967). *Depression: Clinical, experimental and theoretical aspects.* New York: Harper & Row.

Beck, A. T. (1976). *Cognitive theory and the emotional disorders.* New York: International Universities Press.

Beck, A. T., & Emery, G. (1985). *Anxiety Disorders and Phobias: A Cognitive Perspective.* New York: Basic Books.

Beck, A. T., Laude, R., & Bohnert, M. (1974). Ideational components of anxiety neurosis. *Archives of General Psychiatry, 31,* 319-325.

Bouton, M. (1984). Differential control by context in the inflation and reinstatement paradigms. *Journal of Experimental Psychology: Animal Behavior Processes, 10,* 56-74.

Bouton, M. (1984). Contextual control of the extinction of conditioned fear. *Learning and Motivation, 10,* 445-466.

Bouton, M., & Bolles, R. (1985). Contexts, event-memories, and extinction. In P. D. Balsam & A. Tomie (Eds.), *Context and Learning,* pp. 133-166. Hillsdale, N.J.: Erlbaum.

Bouton, M., & King, D. (1983). Contextual control of the extinction of conditioned fear: Tests for the associative value of the context. *Journal of Experimental Psychology: Animal Behavior Processes, 9,* 248-265.

Bradley, B., & Mathews, A. (1983). Negative self-schemata in clinical depression. *British Journal of Clinical Psychology, 22,* 173-181.

Breslow, R., Kocsis, J., & Belkin, B. (1981). Contribution of the depressive perspective to memory function in depression. *Archives of General Psychiatry, 138,* 227-230.

Brewer, W. F., & Nakamura, G. V. (1984). The nature and function of schemas. In R. S. Wyer & T. K. Srull (Eds.), *Handbook of social cognition,* Vol. 1, pp. 119-160. Hillsdale, N. J.: Erlbaum.

Burgess, I. S., Jones, L. M., Robertson, S. A., Radcliffe, W. N., & Emerson, E. (1981). The degree of control exerted by phobic and non-phobic verbal stimuli over the recognition behaviour of phobic and non-phobic subjects. *Behaviour Research and Therapy, 19,* 233-243.

Butler, G., & Mathews, A. (1983). Cognitive processes in anxiety. *Advances in Behaviour Research and Therapy, 5,* 51-62.

Chapman, L. J., & Chapman, J. P. (1967). Genesis of popular but erroneous psychodiagnostic observations. *Journal of Abnormal Psychology, 72,* 193-204.

Chapman, L. J., & Chapman, J. P. (1969). Illusory correlation as an obstacle to the use of valid diagnostic signs. *Journal of Abnormal Psychology, 74,* 271-280.

Clark, D. A., & Hemsley, D. R. (1985). Individual differences in the experience of depressive and anxious, intrusive thoughts. *Behaviour Research and Therapy, 23,* 625-633.

Cook, M., & Mineka, S. Observational conditioning of fear to fear-relevant versus fear-irrelevant stimuli in rhesus monkeys. In preparation.

Cook, M., Mineka, S., Wolkenstein, B., & Laitsch, K. (1985). Observational conditioning of snake fear in unrelated rhesus monkeys. *Journal of Abnormal Psychology, 93*, 355-372.

Crocker, J. (1981). Judgment of covariation by social perceivers. *Psychological Bulletin, 90*, 272-372.

Dawson, M. E., & Schell, A. M. (1985). Information processing and human autonomic classical conditioning. In P. K. Ackles, J. R. Jennings, & M. G. H. Coles (Eds.), *Advances in psychophysiology,* Vol. 1, pp. 89-165. Greenwich, CT: JAI Press.

Dawson, M. E., Schell, A. M., & Banis, H. T. (1986). Greater resistance to extinction of electrodermal responses conditioned to potentially phobic CSs: A noncognitive process? *Psychophysiology, 23*, 552-561.

Delprato, D. (1980). Hereditary determinants of fears and phobias, *Behavior Therapy, 11*, 79-103.

Derry, P. A., & Kuiper, N. A. (1981). Schematic processing and self-reference in clinical depression. *Journal of Abnormal Psychology, 90*, 286-297.

Desiderato, O., & Newman, A. (1971). Conditioned suppression produced in rats by tones paired with escapable or inescapable shock. *Journal of Comparative and Physiological Psychology, 77*, 427-431.

Dickinson, A., & Shanks, D. (1985). Animal conditioning and human causality judgment. In L. G. Nilsson & T. Archer (Eds.), *Perspectives on learning and memory*, pp. 167-191. London: Erlbaum.

Dollard, J., & Miller, N. (1950). *Personality and Psychotherapy.* New York: McGraw Hill.

Domjan, M. (1983). Biological constraints on instrumental and classical conditioning: Implications for general process theory. In G. Bower (Ed.), *The psychology of learning and motivation*, Vol. 17, pp. 215-277. New York: Academic Press.

Dyer, F. N. (1973). The Stroop phenomenon and its use in the study of perceptual, cognitive and response processes. *Memory and Cognition, 1*, 106-120.

Eysenck, H., & Rachman, S. (1965). *Causes and cures of neurosis.* London: Routledge and Kegan Paul.

Foa, E. B., & McNally, R. J. (1986). Sensitivity to feared stimuli in obsessive-compulsives: A dichotic listening analysis. *Cognitive Therapy and Research, 10*, 477-485.

Goldfried, M. R., Padawer, W., & Robins, C. (1984). Social anxiety and the semantic structure of heterosocial interactions. *Journal of Abnormal Psychology, 93*, 87-97.

Hamilton, D. L., Dugan, P. M., & Trolier, T. K. (1985). The formation of sterotypic beliefs: Further evidence for distinctiveness-based illusory correlations. *Journal of Personality and Social Psychology, 48*, 5-17.

Hamilton, D. L., & Gifford, R. K. (1976). Illusory correlation in interpersonal perception: A cognitive basis of sterotypic judgments. *Journal of Experimental Social Psychology, 12*, 392-407.

Hasher, L., Rose, K. C., Zacks, R. T., Sanft, S., & Doren, B. (1985). Mood, recall, and selectivity effects in normal college students. *Journal of Experimental Psychology: General, 114*, 106-120.

Hastie, R. (1980). Memory for behavioral information that confirms or contradicts a personality impression. In R. Hastie, T. Ostrom, E. Ebbesen, R. Wyer, Jr., D. Hamilton, & D. Carlston (Eds.), *Person memory: The cognitive basis of social perception*, pp. 155-177. Hillsdale, N.J.: Erlbaum.

Hendersen, R. (1978). Forgetting of conditioned fear inhibition. *Learning and Motivation, 8*, 16-30.

Hendersen, R. (1985). Fearful memories: The motivational significance of forgetting. In F. R. Brush & J. B. Overmier (Eds.), *Affect, conditioning and cognition: Essays in the determinants of behavior*, pp. 43-53. Hillsdale, N.J.: Erlbaum.

Hendersen, R., Patterson, J., & Jackson, R. (1980). Acquisition and retention of control of instrumental behavior by a cue-signalling air blast: How specific are conditioned anticipations? *Learning and Motivation, 11*, 407-426.

Hibbert, G. A. (1984). Ideational components of anxiety: Their origin and content. *British Journal of Psychiatry, 144*, 618-624.

Higgins, E. T., & Bargh, J. A. (1987). Social cognition and social perception. In M. R. Rosenzweig & L. Y. Porter (Eds.), *Annual review of psychology*, Vol. 38, pp. 369-425. Palo Alto: Annual Reviews, Inc.

Holender, D. (1986). Semantic activation without conscious identification in dichotic listening, parafoveal vision, and visual masking: A survey and appraisal. *The Behavioral and Brain Sciences, 9*, 1-66.

Hollon, S., & Kendall, P. (1980). Cognitive self-statements in depression: Development of the Automatic Thoughts Questionnaire. *Cognitive Therapy and Research, 4*, 383-395.

Isen, A. M. (1984). Toward understanding the role of affect in cognition. In R. Wyer & T. Srull (Eds.), *Handbook of social cognition*, Vol. 3, pp. 179-226. Hillsdale, N.J.: Erlbaum.

Isen, A. M. (1985). Asymmetry of happiness and sadness in effects on memory in normal college students: Comment on Hasher, Rose, Zacks, Sanft, and Doren. *Journal of Experimental Psychology: General, 114*, 388-391.

Jablensky, A. (1985). Approaches to the definition and classification of anxiety and related disorders in European psychiatry. In A. H. Tuma & J. Maser (Eds.), *Anxiety and the anxiety disorders*, pp. 735-758. Hillsdale, N.J.: Erlbaum.

Johnson, M. H., & Magaro, P. A. (1987). Effects of mood and severity on memory processes in depression and mania. *Psychological Bulletin, 101*, 28-40.

Kahneman, D., & Treisman, A. (1984). Changing views of attention and automaticity. In R. Parasuraman, & D. R. Davies (Eds.),

Varieties of attention, pp. 29-61. Orlando, Fla: Academic Press.

Kuiper, N. A., & Derry, P. A. (1982). Depressed and nondepressed content self-reference in mild depressives. *Journal of Personality, 50,* 67-80.

Landau, R. J. (1980). The role of semantic schemata in phobic word interpretation. *Cognitive Therapy and Research, 4,* 427-434.

Leventhal, H., & Tomarken. A. J. (1986). Emotion: Today's problems. In M. R. Rosenzweig & L. Y. Porter (Eds.), *Annual review of psychology,* Vol. 37. pp. 565-610. Palo Alto: Annual Reviews, Inc.

LoLordo, V. (1978). Selective associations. In A. Dickinson & R. Boakes (Eds.), *Mechanisms of learning and motivation: A memorial to Jerzey Konorski,* pp. 367-398. Hillsdale, N.J.: Lawrence Erlbaum.

MacLeod, C., Mathews, A., & Tata, P. (1986). Attentional bias in emotional disorders. *Journal of Abnormal Psychology, 95,* 15-20.

Marks, I. (1969). *Fears and Phobias.* New York: Academic Press.

Mathews, A., & McLeod, C. (1985). Selective processing of threat cues in anxiety states. *Behaviour Research and Therapy, 23,* 131-138.

McNally, R. (1987). Preparedness and phobias: A review. *Psychological Bulletin, 101,* 283-303.

Mineka, S. (1985a). Animal models of anxiety-based disorders: Their usefulness and limitations. In J. Maser & A. Tuma (Eds.), *Anxiety and the anxiety disorders,* pp. 199-244. Hillsdale, N.J.: Erlbaum.

Mineka, S. (1985b). The frightful complexity of the origins of fears. In F. R. Brush & J. B. Overmier (Eds.), *Affect. conditioning and cognition: Essays in the determinants of behavior,* pp. 55-73. Hillsdale, N.J.: Erlbaum.

Mineka, S. (in press). A primate model of phobic fears. In H. Eysenck & I. Martin (Eds.), *Theoretical Foundations of Behavior Therapy.* New York: Plenum Press.

Mineka, S., & Cook, M. (in press). Social learning and the acquisition of snake fear in monkeys. In T. Zentall and J. Galef (Eds.), *Comparative social learning.* Hillsdale, N.J.: Lawrence Erlbaum.

Mineka, S., & Cook, M. (1986). Immunization against the observational conditioning of snake fear in rhesus monkeys. *Journal of Abnormal Psychology, 95,* 307-318.

Mineka, S., & Cook, M. Mechanisms underlying observational conditioning of fear. Submitted for publication.

Mineka, S., Cook, M., & Miller, S. (1984a). Fear conditioned with escapable and inescapable shock: The effects of a feedback stimulus. *Journal of Experimental Psychology: Animal Behavior Processes, 10,* 307-323.

Mineka, S., Davidson, M., Cook, M., & Keir. R. (1984b). Observational conditioning of snake fear in rhesus monkeys. *Journal of Abnormal Psychology, 93,* 355-372.

Mineka, S., Gunnar, M., & Champoux, M. (1986). Control and socioemotional development: Infant rhesus monkeys reared in controllable versus uncontrollable environments, *Child Development, 57,* 1241-1256.

Mogg, K., Mathews, A., & Weinman, J. (1987). Memory bias in

clinical anxiety. *Journal of Abnormal Psychology, 96,* 94-98.

Mowrer, O. H. (1947). On the dual nature of learning: A reinterpretation of "conditioning" and "problem-solving". *Harvard Educational Review, 179,* 102-148.

Mowrer, O. H., & Viek, P. (1948). An experimental analogue of fear from a sense of helplessness. *Journal of Abnormal and Social Psychology, 43,* 193-200.

Mueller, J. H., & Curtois, M. (1980). Retention of self-descriptive and nondescriptive words as a function of test anxiety level. *Motivation and Emotion, 4,* 229-237.

Navon, D., & Margolit, B. (1983). Allocation of attention according to informativeness in visual recognition. *Quarterly Journal of Experimental Psychology, 35(a),* 497-512.

Nielsen, S., & Sarason, I. (1981). Emotion, personality and selective attention. *Journal of Personality and Social Psychology, 41,* 945-960.

Nisbett. R. E., & Ross, L. (1980). *Human inference: Strategies and shortcomings of social judgment.* Englewood Cliffs, N.J.: Prentice-Hall.

Nunn, J. D., Stevenson, R. J., & Whalan, G. (1984). Selective memory effects in agoraphobic patients. *British Journal of Clinical Psychology, 23,* 195-201.

O'Banion, K., & Arkowitz, H. (1977). Social anxiety and selective memory for affective information about the self. *Social Behavior and Personality, 5,* 321-328.

Öhman, A., Fredrikson, M., & Hugdahl, K. (1978). Toward an experimental model for simple phobic reactions. *Behavioral Analysis and Modification, 2,* 97-114.

Öhman, A., Dimberg, U., & Öst. L.-G. (1985). Animal and social phobias: Biological constraints on learned fear responses. In S. Reiss & R. Bootzin (eds.), *Theoretical issues in behavior therapy,* pp. 123-175. New York: Academic Press.

Öhman, A. (1986). Face the beast and fear the face: Animal and social fears as prototypes for evolutionary analyses of emotion. *Psychophysiology, 23,* 123-145.

Rachman, S. (1978). *Fear and Courage.* San Francisco: Freeman.

Ray, C. (1979). Examination stress and performance on a color--word interference task. *Perceptual and Motor Skills, 49,* 400-402.

Rescorla, R. (1974). Effect of inflation of the unconditioned stimulus value following conditioning. *Journal of Comparative and Physiological Psychology, 86,* 101-106.

Riccio, D., Richardson, R., Ebner, D. (1984). Memory retrieval deficits based upon altered contextual cues: A paradox. *Psychological Bulletin, 96,* 152-165.

Rothbart, M., Evans, M., & Fulero, S. (1979). Recall for confirming events: Memory processes and the maintenance of social stereotypes. *Journal of Experimental Social Psychology, 15,* 343-355.

Seligman, M. (1971). Phobias and preparedness. *Behavior Therapy, 2,* 307-320.

Sewitch, T. S., & Kirsch, I. (1984). The cognitive content of anxiety:

Naturalistic evidence for the predominance of threat-related thoughts. *Cognitive Therapy and Research, 8,* 49-58.

Smith, T. W., Ingram, R. E., & Brehm, S. S. (1983). Social anxiety, anxious self-preoccupation, and recall of self-relevant information. *Journal of Personality and Social Psychology, 44,* 1276-1283.

Solomon, R. L., & Wynne, L. (1954). Traumatic avoidance learning: The principles of anxiety conservation and partial irreversibility. *Psychological Review, 61,* 353-385.

Stroop, J. R. (1938). Factors affecting speed in serial verbal reactions. *Psychological Monographs, 50,* 38-48.

Sutherland, G., Newman, B., & Rachman, S. (1982). Empirical investigations of the relation between mood and intrusive unwanted cognitions. *British Journal of Medical Psychology, 55,* 127-138.

Thomas, D. A., & Riccio, D. (1979). Forgetting of a CS attribute in a conditioned suppression paradigm. *Animal Learning and Behavior, 7,* 191-195.

Tomarken, A. J., Mineka, S., & Cook, M. (in preparation). Prepared fears, selective associations, and covariation bias.

Watson, D., & Clark, L. (1984). Negative affectivity: The disposition to experience aversive emotional states. *Psychological Bulletin, 96,* 465-490.

Watts, F. N., McKenna, F. P., Sharrock, R., & Trezise, L. (1986). Colour naming of phobia-related words. *British Journal of Psychology, 77,* 97-108.

Weinberger, D., Schwartz, G., & Davidson, R. (1979). Low anxious, high-anxious, and repressive coping styles: Psychometric patterns and behavioral and physiological responses to stress. *Journal of Abnormal Psychology, 88,* 369-380. PP

IV Neurobiological Perspectives on Aversively Motivated Behavior

Trevor Archer and Torbjörn U. C. Järbe
University of Umeå and Uppsala

The methods and procedures developed from diverse areas of behavioral research using aversive stimuli such as one-way and two-way active avoidance, passive avoidance, fear retention, electrified maze running, conditioned suppression, etc., have proven to be extremely applicable for the study of the neuropharmacology of psychoactive substances, the brain systems underlying learning and reinforcement processes and neurophysiological or neuroanatomical processes at the cellular level. Thus, avoidance learning procedures have shown great utility for the analyses of the effects of various agents upon different aspects of memory. Generally, these procedures have been used to demonstrate the detrimental effects on memory consolidation and/or retention resulting from manipulations of certain neurotransmitter systems although recent reviews tend to be critical of the unrestricted usage of simple passive or inhibitory avoidance tasks for this purpose (e.g. Bammer, 1982). However, in some cases, as for example in the case of certain neuropeptides acting upon the central nervous system, memory (as measured by avoidance procedures) appears to be enhanced (Ader & de Wied, 1972; Bohus, Ader & de Wied, 1972; de Wied, 1971).

The chapter by James McGaugh describes some of the complex interactions between neuropeptides and neurohormones and their modulatory effects upon the control of memory processes by the central nervous system. McGaugh, who generally applies two basic procedures, inhibitory conditioning and a γ-maze situation, makes an extremely important point in his rejection of the term, passive avoidance, which suggests that the rat or mouse is doing "nothing" while waiting in the test situation to receive or not to receive shock. McGaugh's suggestion (this volume) that the term passive avoidance be done away with and replaced by "Inhibitory conditioning" could well prove to be of enormous service to behavioral pharmacology if it is carefully adhered to by both authors, referees and reviewers of behavioral and neuroscientific journals. In retrospect, it is suggested that continued usage of the term passive avoidance, convenient as it may seem, ought to be regarded as inappropriate and a careless disregard for correct behavioral description. Rick Beninger's chapter describes the general involvement of the classical neurotransmitters in aversive learning and describes a theory for the role of dopaminergic neurotransmission. Dick Thompson describes the neurophysiological circuitry involved in the conditioning and reinforcement of rabbit eyelid conditioning. Lesions confined to discrete regions of the cerebellum abolished conditioned responding from a wide range of procedures and Thompson's application of the blocking phenomenon provides an ingenuous tactic for interpreting cerebellar memory circuitry in the cognitive language currently used to describe Pavlovian conditioning phenomena.

There are other aspects of neuropharmacology that are related to the issues treated in the following chapters but were not quite of central importance to the approaches developed by McGaugh, Beninger and Thompson. A basic orientation to the problem of what is learned in an avoidance situation with regard to the physiological and pharmacological substrates of this type of learning has been unfolded over the last fifteen years by the work of Ivan Izquierdo. Although avoidance and aversion learning is often considered within an associative framework, the influence of non-associative factors is of central importance not only for the procedure used *per se* (Cunningham, Fitzgerald & Francisco, 1977; Mitchell, Kirschbaum & Perry, 1975; Rescorla, 1967; Sjödén & Archer, 1981) but also for a reliable analysis of the neurobiological variables (Anisman, 1975; Bignami, 1976; Izquierdo, 1975). In this regard the relative influence of classical conditioning and instrumental learning is taken into account as Izquierdo and Elisabetsky (1979) indicate "... if these question are left unanswered, it will be impossible to show that the effect of any independent variable (drugs, age, lesions, etc.) on any given behaviour is due to an influence on learning or on other concomitant processes, and it will also be impossible to know if any accompanying physiological activity (unit, firing, slow potentials, biochemical changes) is a correlate of learning or of nonassociative factors" (p. 227).

Izquierdo distinguishes between a *pseudoconditioning* condition, whereby the tone or buzzer signal in a typical shuttlebox procedure is randomly interspersed by the shock presentations, and the typical *two-way avoidance* condition, by which shock presentation is contingent upon the tone or buzzer signal, generally with a trace conditioning procedure (Gattoni & Izquierdo, 1974; Izquierdo, 1974). Izquierdo further distinguishes between classical stimulus pairing (P), an avoidance contingency (C) and the nonassociative effects of footshocks, defined as a "drive" state (D) in the pharmacological dissection of various drugs affecting the central nervous system (e.g. Izquierdo, 1976), and to the analysis of compounds or interventions that affect long-term memory processes (Izquierdo & Elisabetsky, 1979; Lauzi Gozzani & Izquierdo, 1976). The application of the two-way active avoidance procedure represents a most complex strategy to understand the neurobiology of memory but Izquierdo appears, through various combinations of the parameters P, C and D, to have derived an ingenous tactic for harnessing this procedure. This strategy is indeed fortuitous since the two-way active avoidance learning procedure remains a most complex method for studying stimulus associations in aversively motivated behavior.

One aspect of amnesia that has been studied comprehensively and with much success using aversive conditioning techniques, is *retrograde amnesia*, although manipulations of anterograde amnesia have proven interesting both empirically and clinically (Kopp, Bohdanecky & Jarvik, 1968; Springer, Schoel, Klinger & Agranoff, 1975; Milner, Corkin & Teuber, 1968; Zerbolio, 1969).

Retrograde amnesia has been measured consistently using the gradient function whereby the effectiveness of the agent inducing amnesia is greatest when administered soonest after initial training on the inhibitory conditioning or active avoidance task to which it is applied. It is assumed that retrograde amnesia affects processes of memory storage and/or consolidation although not necessarily reinforcement (Landauer, 1969; Lewis, 1969; Wagner, Rudy & Whitlow, 1973). Several techniques for investigating retrograde amnesia may be listed: *Electroconvulsive shock* (ECS) was early used to establish a retrograde amnesia gradient of memory consolidation in a shuttlebox avoidance task (Duncan, 1949). The neurochemical basis of ECS and avoidance learning has since been the object of much research (e.g. Essman, 1972, 1974; Dunn, Giuditta, Wilson & Glassman, 1974; Montanaro, Dall'Olio & Gandolfi, 1979, 1981; Pryor, Peache & Scott, 1972). Gold, Macri and McGaugh (1973) studied the retrograde amnesia resulting from cortical *Direct electrical stimulation of the brain* (DESB) using the inhibitory conditioning technique, whereas Bresnahan and Routtenberg (1972) studied amygdaloid DESB induced amnesia. Other sources of retrograde amnesia in inhibitory conditioning tasks include hypothermia and hyperthermia (e.g. Riccio, Hodges & Randall, 1968), hypoxia (Giurgea, Lefevre, Lescrenier & David-Remacle, 1971; Paolino, Quartermain & Miller, 1966; Sara & Lefevre, 1972) but see also (Vacher, King & Miller, 1968), cortical spreading depression (Bures & Buresova, 1972).

An enormous variety of drugs have been used to induce retrograde amnesia in aversive tasks (for a review of the problems inherent to this enterprise see Jarvik, 1972) but the incidence of posttrial administration of the amnesia inducing drug are relatively limited. Spear (1978) lists four basic accounts of the drug-amnesia effects obtained: "...(1) dampening of electrical activity in certain regions of the brain; (2) decrement in general arousal that might impair neural recruitment or otherwise impede posttraining memory processes or memory retrieval processes; (3) interference with the chemical substances that apparently serve as neurotransmitters in the brain, like acetylcholine, serotonin, dopamine, and norepinephrine; and (4) interference with the syntheses of macromolecules such as proteins, which many scientists suspect serve a vital function in the physiological basis of memory storage." (p. 325).

A different tactic in the investigation of the neurobiological substrates of learning and memory is to seek a "double dissociation" by comparing the effects of two treatments (manipulations of the central nervous system) upon the performance of two avoidance procedures, two-way active avoidance versus fear retention or inhibitory (passive avoidance) conditioning. Noradrenaline depletion following DSP4, a noradrenaline neurotoxin, treatment consistently resulted in a two-way avoidance impairment (e.g. Archer, Jonsson & Ross, 1984a) whereas olfactory bulbectomy generally caused deficits of inhibitory conditioning and for retention of aversive stimuli (e.g. Cairncross, Cox, Forster & Wren, 1978; Garrigou, Broekkamp & Lloyd, 1981).

In a series of experiments, the olfactory bulbectomized rats and DSP4 treated rats were tested for performance of the two-way active avoidance task, a 'step-down' avoidance task and for fear conditioning and retention (Archer, Söderberg, Ross & Jonsson, 1984b). DSP4-treated, but not olfactory bulbectomized, rats were impaired in acquiring two-way avoidance. Bulbectomized, but not DSP4 treated, rats were found to show notable 'step-down' avoidance and fear retention deficits. Surprisingly, the DSP4 treated rats that were later bulbectomized did not show the two-way avoidance deficit of DSP4 treatment alone and bulbectomized rats later treated with DSP4 did not evidence 'step-down' avoidance and fear retention deficits (Archer et al., 1984b). These experiments illustrate an interesting double dissociation especially since DSP4 treatment caused severe but selective noradrenaline depletion while the bulbectomy operation did not result in any neurochemical changes apart from the ablated area. The possible mediation by brain region/neurotransmitter pathway of opponent avoidance processes seems to provide a novel double dissociation which may permit some insight of experimental inverstigations of stress, anxiety and depression.

It is probably safe to suggest that the use of animal models of depression, anxiety, stress, analgesia and perhaps even the active avoidance tests of 'antipsychotic acitivity' have given the neurobiological approach to aversively motivated behavior a wide clinical and applied psychological perspective. Thus, students endeavoring to assessing the efficacy of models, procedures or new therapeutic compounds are recommended to follow closely the concepts derived by Willner (1985), i.e. predictive and constructive validity, as well as the three chapters included under "Clinical Perspectives".

REFERENCES

Ader, R., & de Wied, D. (1972). Effects of vasopressin on active and passive avoidance learning. *Psychonomic Science, 29*, 46-48.

Anisman, H. (1975). Time dependent variations in aversively motivated behaviors: non-associative effects of cholinergic and catecholaminergic drugs. *Psychological Reviews, 82,* 359-385.

Archer, T., Jonsson, G., & Ross, S. B. (1984). A parametric study of the effects of the noradrenaline neurotoxin DSP4 on avoidance acquisition and noradrenaline neurones in the CNS of the rat, *British Journal of Pharmacology, 82,* 249-257. (a)

Archer, T., Söderberg, U., Ross, S. B., & Jonsson, G. (1984). Role of olfactory bulbectomy and DSP4 treatment in avoidance learning in the rat. *Behavioral Neuroscience, 98,* 496-505. (b)

Bammer, G. (1982). Pharmacological investigations of neurotransmitter involvement in passive avoidance responding: A review and some new results. *Neuroscience and Biobehavioral Reviews, 6,* 247-296.

Bignami, G. (1976). Nonassociative explanations of behavioral changes induced by central cholinergic drugs. *Acta Neurobiologica Experientia, 36,* 5-90.

Bohus, B., Ader, R., & de Wied, D. (1972). Effects of vasopressin on active and passive avoidance behavior. *Hormones and Behavior, 3,* 191-197.

Bresnahan, E., & Routtenberg, A. (1972). Memory disruption by unilateral low level, subseizure stimulation of the medial amygdaloid nucleus. *Physiology and Behavior, 9,* 513-525.

Bures, J., & Buresova, O. (1972). Inducing cortical spreading depression. In R. D. Myers (Ed.), *Methods in Psychobiology Vol 2 Specialized laboratory techniques in neuropsychology and neurobiology,* pp. 319-344. New York: Academic Press.

Cairncross, K. D., Cox, B., Forster, C., & Wren, A. F. (1978). A new model for the detection of antidepressant drugs: Olfactory bulbectomy compared with existing models. *Journal of Pharmacological Methods, 1,* 131-143.

Cunningham, C. L., Fitzgerald, R. D., & Francisco, D. L. (1977). Exitatory and inhibitory consequences of explicitly unpaired and truly random conditioning procedures on heart rate in rats. *Animal Learning and Behavior, 5,* 135-142.

Duncan, C. P. (1949). The retroactive effect of electroshock on learning. *Journal of Comparative and Physiological Psychology, 42,* 32-44.

Dunn, A., Giuditta, A., Wilson, J. E., & Glassman, E. (1974). The effect of electroshock on brain RNA and protein synthesis and its possible relationship to behavioral effects. In M. Fink, S. Kety, J. McGaugh and T. Williams (Eds.), *Psychobiology of Convulsive Therapy,* pp. 185-197. Washington: V. H. Winston & Sons.

Essman, W. B. (1972). Neurochemical changes in ECS and ECT. *Seminars in Psychiatry, 4,* 67-77.

Essman, W. B. (1974). Effects of electroconvulsive shock on cerebral protein synthesis. In M. Fink, S. Kety, J. McGaugh and T. A. Williams (Eds.), *Psychobiology of convulsive therapy,* pp. 237-250. New York: Wiley.

Garrigou, D., Broekkamp, C. L., & Lloyd, K. G. (1981).

Involvement of the amygdala in the effects of antidepressants on the passive avoidance deficit in bulbectomized rats. *Psychopharmacology, 74,* 66-70.

Gattoni, R. C., & Izquierdo, I. (1974). The effect of conditioning and pseudoconditioning on hippocampal and neurcortical RNA. *Behavioral Biology, 12,* 67-80.

Giurgea, C., Lefevre, D., Lescrenier, C., & David-Remcle, M. (1971). Pharmacological protection against hypoxia-induced amnesia in rats. *Psychopharmacologia, 20,* 160-168.

Gold, P. E., Macri, J., & McGaugh, J. L. (1973). Retrograde amnesia effects: Effects of direct cortical stimulation. *Science, 179,* 1343-1345.

Izquierdo, I. (1974). Effect on pseudoconditioning of drugs with known central nervous activity. *Psychopharmacologia, 38,* 259-266.

Izquierdo, I (1975). Relations between orienting, conditioned and pseudoconditioned responses in a shuttle-box - a pharmacological analysis by means of LSD and dibenamine. *Behavioral Biology, 15,* 193-205.

Izquierdo, I. (1976). A pharmacological separation of buzzer-shock pairing and of the shuttle-shock contingency as factors in the elicitation of shuttle responses to a buzzer in rats. *Behavioral Biology, 18,* 75-87.

Izquierdo, I., & Elisabetsky, E. (1979). Physiological and pharmacological dissection of the main factors in the acquisition and retention of shuttle behavior. In M. A. B. Brazier (Ed.), *Brain mechanisms in memory and Learning: From the single neuron to man.* New York: Raven Press.

Jarvik, M. E. (1972). Effects of chemical and physical treatments on learning and memory. *Annual Review of Psychology, 23,* 457-486.

Kopp, R., Bohdanecky, Z., & Jarvik, M. E. (1968). Proactive effect of a single electroconvulsive shock (ECS) on one-trial learning in mice. *Journal of Comparative and Physiological Psychology, 65,* 514-517.

Landauer, T. K. (1969). Reionforcement as consolidation. *Psychological Review, 76,* 82-96.

Lauzi Gozzani, J., & Izquierdo, I. (1976). Possible peripheral adrenergic and central dopaminergic influences in memory consolidation. *Psychopharamcology, 49,* 109-112.

Lewis, D. J. (1969). Sources of experimental amnesia. *Psychological Review, 76,* 461-472.

Milner, B., Corkin, S., & Teuber, H. L. (1968). Further analysis of the hippocampal-amnesic syndrome: 14 year follow-up study of H. M. *Neuropsychologia, 6,* 215-234.

Mitchell, D., Kirschbaum, E. H., & Perry, R. L. (1975). Effects of neophobia and habituation on the poison-induce avoidance of exteroceptive stimuli in the rat. *Journal of Experimental Psychology: Animal Behavior Processes, 104,* 47-55.

Montanaro, N., Dall'Olio, R., & Gandolfi, O. (1979). Bromolysergide and methysergide protection against ECS-induced retrograde amnesia. *Neuropsychobiology, 5,* 174-180.

Montanaro, N., Dall'Olio, R., Gandolfi, O. (1981). Reduction of ECS-induced retrograde amnesia of passive avoidance conditioning after 5,7-dihydroxytryptamine median raphe neuleus lesion in the rat. *Neuropsychobiology, 7,* 57-66.

Paolino, R. M., Quartermain, D., & Millser, N. E. (1966). Different temporal gradients of retrograde amnesia produced by carbon dioxide anesthesia and electroconvulsive shock. *Journal of Comparative and Physiological Psychology, 62,* 270-274.

Pryor, G. T., Peache, S., & Scott, M. K. (1972). The effect of repeated electroconvulsive shock on avoidance conditioning and brain monoamine oxidase activity. *Physiology and Behavior, 9,* 623-628.

Rescorla, R. A. (1967). Pavlovian conditioning and its proper control procedures. *Psychological Review, 74,* 71-80.

Riccio, D. C., Hodges, L. A., & Randall, P. K. (1968). Retrograde amnesia produced by hypothermia in rats. *Journal of Comparative and Physiological Psychology, 66,* 618-622.

Sara, S. J., & Lefevre, D. (1972). Re-examination of role of familiarization in retrograde amnesia in the rat. *Journal of Comparative and Physiological Psychology, 84,* 361-364.

Sjödén, P. O., & Archer, T. (1981). Associative and nonassociative effects of exteroceptive context in taste-aversion conditioning with rats. *Behavioral and Neural Biology, 33,* 74-92.

Spear, N. E. (1978). *The processing of memories: Forgetting and retention.* New Jersey: Hillsdale.

Springer, A. D., Schoel, W. M., Klinger, P. D., & Agranoff, B. W. (1975). Anterograde and retrograde effects of electroconvulsive shock and of puromycin on memory formation in the goldfish. *Behavioral Biology, 13,* 467-481.

Vacher, J. M., King, R. A., & Miller, A. T. (1968). Failure of hypoxia to produce retrograde amnesia. *Journal of Comparative Physiological Psychology, 66,* 179-181.

Wagner, A. R., Rudy, J. W., & Whitlow, J. W. (1973). Rehearsal in animal conditioning. *Journal of Experimental Psychology Monograph, 97,* 407-426.

de Wied, D. (1971). Long-term effect of vasopressin on the maintainence of a conditioned avoidance response in rats. *Nature, 232,* 58-60.

Willner, P. (1985). *Depression: A psychobiological synthesis.* New York: John Wiley & Sons.

Zerbolio, D. J. (1969). The proactive effect of electroconvulsive shock on memory storage with and without convulsion. *Communications in Behavioral Biology, 4,* 23-27.

8

Involvement of the Amygdala in Hormonal and Neurotransmitter Interactions in the Modulation of Memory Storage

James L. McGaugh, Ines B. Introini-Collison, Alan H. Nagahara, and Larry Cahill
University of California, Irvine

Hormonal Modulation of Memory Storage

There is extensive evidence indicating that memory storage is modulated by a variety of hormones that are normally released by aversive experiences (de Wied, 1984; McGaugh, 1983; McGaugh & Gold, in press). This chapter summarizes some of our recent studies examining the memory-modulating effects of hormones and drugs affecting adrenergic, noradrenergic and opiate receptor systems. Our findings suggest that the effects of these treatments on memory involve activation of noradrenergic receptors within the amygdaloid complex. And, more generally, the findings support the view that the amygdala is involved in modulating the storage of recent experiences. While our studies have focussed on experiments using aversively-motivated training tasks, our findings indicate that the modulating effects of hormones on memory are not restricted necessarily to tasks using aversive motivation.

Memory-modulating effects of Epinephrine. It is now well documented that, in rats and mice, posttraining administration of the adrenal medullary hormone epinephrine alters subsequent retention (Borell, de Kloet, Versteeg, & Bohus, 1983; Gold & van Buskirk, 1976; McGaugh & Gold, in press). Since epinephrine is known to be released from the adrenal medulla by the kind of aversive stimulation typically used in animal memory experiments (Gold & McCarty, 1981) the findings have been interpreted as supporting the general view that endogenously-released epinephrine modulates the storage of recently acquired information.

To date, most studies of the effects of epinephrine on memory have used one-trial inhibitory (passive) avoidance tasks. If it is assumed that epinephrine effects on memory are due to a general modulating effect on memory storage, then the effects should not be restricted to inhibitory avoidance tasks. There is clear evidence that epinephrine affects learning in a variety of aversively-motivated tasks. We have found, for example, that posttraining administration of epinephrine also affects retention of an active avoidance task (Liang, Bennett & McGaugh, 1985).

The modulating effects of epinephrine on memory are not restricted to tasks, such as active or inhibitory avoidance, in which response latency is used as the measure of retention. Posttraining administration of epinephrine also enhances retention in discrimination tasks where choice rather than response latency is used to assess retention. For example, in a recent study we found that posttraining epinephrine alters subsequent longterm retention of a footshock-motivated visual discrimination task (Introini-Collison & McGaugh, 1986). Mice in this study were trained to escape from a mild footshock by entering the left, lighted arm of a Y-maze

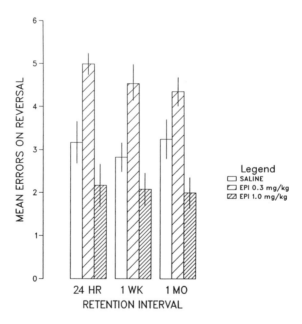

FIG. 8.1. Effects, in mice, of immediate posttraining epinephrine (ip) on discrimination reversal training 1 day, one week, or one month following original training (Mean ± S.E.). Retention of the original discrimination is indexed by errors made on the discrimination reversal. N=18 for 1 day group and N=12 for one week and one month groups. (From Introini-Collison and McGaugh, 1986.)

(criterion of 3 successive correct choices) and were then given posttraining injections of either saline or epinephrine (0.3 or 1.0 mg/kg ip). On retention tested 1 day, 1 week, or 28 days later, the location of the correct alley was reversed and the mice were given 6 trials on which they could escape from the shock only by entering the right, dark alley. As Figure 8.1 shows, at each retention interval the mice given a low dose of epinephrine made more errors than did saline controls on the reversal training, while mice given the high dose made fewer errors.

We interpret these findings as indicating that the low dose of epinephrine enhanced retention of original discrimination while the high dose of epinephrine impaired retention of the original discrimination. These findings are highly comparable to those that we and other investigators have obtained with inhibitory avoidance tasks (Gold & van Buskirk, 1976; Introini-Collison & McGaugh, 1986). It is particularly important to note that the memory-modulating effects of a single posttraining injection of epinephrine are lasting: Effects assessed on the one-month retention test were comparable to those seen one-day following training.

While the effects of epinephrine on memory have been typically studied in experiments using aversive motivation, we have found that epinephrine can also influence the retention of an appetitively-motivated discrimination task (Sternberg, Isaacs, Gold & McGaugh, 1985). In this study, water-deprived mice were placed in a Y-maze and allowed to explore until they found and drank water from a spout located at the end of a lighted alley. They were then given posttraining injections of saline or epinephrine and tested for retention 24 hours later. As Figure 8.2 shows, the animals given immediate posttraining epinephrine entered significantly fewer alleys prior to finding the water spout on the retention test than did controls. Further, the effect of epinephrine was blocked by injections of the β-antagonist dl-propranolol and the α-antagonist phenoxybenzamine administered 30 minutes prior to training. These findings are consistent with other findings from our laboratory indicating that both α- and β-antagonists also block the enhancing effects of epinephrine on retention of an inhibitory avoidance response (Sternberg, Korol, Novack & McGaugh, 1986).

Our findings indicating that epinephrine has highly similar effects in a variety of learning tasks using different motivation and different response measures are consistent with the view that epinephrine has a general role in the modulation of memory storage. This does not mean, of course, that endogenously-released epinephrine normally modulates learning under all training circumstances. For example, Gold, Robertson and Delanoy (1985) have reported that plasma epinephrine is not significantly elevated immediately after thirsty rats find water in a training apparatus. Thus, the learning that occurs under those conditions may not ordinarily be modulated by endogenously-released epinephrine. But, our evidence (Sternberg et al., 1985) argues that learning based on appetitively-motivated training is, none-the-less, subject to the modulating influence of posttraining epinephrine. This argument predicts that the learning of the location of the water should also be enhanced by

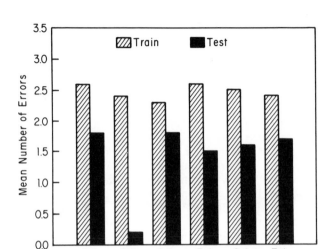

FIG. **8.2.** Effect of posttraining epinephrine on retention in a one trial appetitively-motivated task (Mean ± S.E.). Mice received saline, propranolol or phenoxybenzamine 30 minutes prior to training and saline or epinephrine immediately posttraining. For all conditions errors made on the 24 hr retention test were lower (P < 0.05) than errors on the training. Retention errors of posttraining epinephrine group were lower (P < 0.05) than those of the saline group and all groups given phenoxybenzamine or propranolol. N = 14-19 per group. (From Sternberg et al., 1985.)

posttraining experiences that result in the endogenous release of epinephrine. This possibility has not, as yet, been examined experimentally.

As is discussed below, our current work focusses on the central mechanisms underlying the effects of epinephrine, as well as other treatments affecting adrenergic systems. We have also examined parallel effects obtained with other hormonal and transmitter systems. Our findings strongly suggest that treatments affecting opiate receptor systems as well as adrenergic receptor systems affect memory through influences involving noradrenergic receptors in the amygdala. We will first review some of our findings concerning the involvement of opioid peptide systems and then discuss the interaction of adrenergic and opioid peptide systems in memory modulation.

Involvement of Opiate Receptors. There is extensive evidence that memory, as assessed in a variety of types of training tasks, including aversively-motivated tasks as well as appetitively-motivated tasks, can be modulated by posttraining treatments affecting opiate receptors. Retention is generally impaired by posttraining administration of opiate receptor agonists (e.g. morphine, β-endorphin) and enhanced by opiate receptor antagonists such as naloxone and naltrexone (Castellano, 1975, 1981; Gallagher, 1985; Introini-Collison & Baratti, 1986; Izquierdo, 1979;

Messing, Jensen, Matinez, Spichler, Vasquez, Soumireu-Mourat, Liang & McGaugh, 1979). The memory-enhancing effects of opiate receptor antagonists appear to be based on central effects, since retention is not affected by posttraining i.p. administration of naltrexone methyl bromide (MR2263), an opiate receptor antagonist that does not readily pass the blood-brain barrier. Further, the effects of β-endorphin as well as morphine also appear to be centrally mediated since MR2263 does not antagonize the memory-impairing effects of these treatments (Introini, McGaugh, & Baratti, 1985).

Interaction of Adrenergic and Opiate Systems. Evidence from several studies suggests that epinephrine effects on retention may involve interactions with a brain opioid peptide system. For example, recent findings indicate that the memory-impairing effect of high doses of epinephrine is blocked by naloxone (Introini-Collison & McGaugh, 1987; Izquierdo & Dias, 1985). Such findings are consistent with other evidence indicating that epinephrine releases brain β-endorphin (Carrasco et al., 1982). However, the memory-enhancing effects of low doses of epinephrine clearly do not involve the release of β-endorphin since low doses of epinephrine block the memory-impairment produced by posttraining β-endorphin (Izquierdo & Dias, 1985; Introini-Collison & McGaugh, 1987). Further, as is shown in Figure 8.3, low doses of

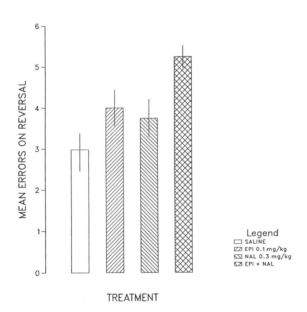

FIG. 8.3. Effect of combined posttraining administration of low doses of epinephrine and naloxone on discrimination reversal training tested 24 hours following original training. Retention of the original discrimination is indexed by errors made on the discrimination reversal (Mean ± S.E.). N=12 per group. (From Introini-Collison and McGaugh, 1987).

naloxone and epinephrine which do not affect memory when administered alone significantly enhance memory when administered together. As is discussed below, such an additive effect is expected in view of evidence suggesting that the effect of both of these treatments involves the release of central norepinephrine (NE).

Izquierdo and his colleagues reported that following a novel training experience hypothalamic β-endorphin immunoreactivity is reduced for several hours (Izquierdo, Souza, Dias, Carrasco, Volkmer, Perry & Netto, 1984). These findings suggest that naloxone may enhance retention by blocking the effects of β-endorphin normally released by a training experience. If this is the case, then naloxone should not be expected to enhance retention in animals given a novel experience prior to training. To examine this implication, mice were given either a ten-minute novel exploratory experience or injections (ip) of β-endorphin or saline one hour prior to training on an inhibitory avoidance task. Immediately following training, the mice were given saline, naloxone or a low dose of epinephrine. As is shown in Table 8.1, neither the novel experience nor β-endorphin given prior to training affected retention (tested 24 hours later) in animals given posttraining saline. Further, posttraining naloxone enhanced retention in mice given either β-endorphin or saline one hour prior to training. However, as was expected on the assumption that

TABLE 8.1

Effect of a Novel Experience (NE) or of an ip Injection of β-endorphin (o.1 μg per Mouse) Given before Training in a Step-through Inhibitory Avoidance Task at 24 h in Mice Receiving a Post-training ip Injection of Saline (0.1 ml per Mouse), Naloxone HCl (0.1 mg per Mouse) or Epinephrine HCl (0.3 μg per Mouse)[a]

Treatments 1 hr before training	Post-training	Median (interquartile range) test minus training latency difference(s)	
Saline	Saline	19.1	(6.8/ 43.8)
Novel Experience	Saline	41.1	(16.0/ 48.2)
β-endorphin	Saline	30.8	(17.4/ 45.1)
Saline	Naloxone	270.9	(115.5/ 300.0)*
Novel Experience	Naloxone	17.4	(7.1/ 32.9)
β-endorphin	Naloxone	133.5	(68.7/ 142.4)*
Saline	Epinephrine	139.2	(47.4/ 167.2)*
Novel Experience	Epinephrine	101.1	(94.2/ 300.0)*
β-endorphin	Epinephrine	117.1	(93.0/ 241.1)*

Note. N = 12 per group.

[a]0.35 mA footshock.

*Significant difference from groups not asterisked at p < .002 level in two-tailed Mann-Whitney U test.

naloxone effects on retention are due to blocking of the effects of β-endorphin released by training, naloxone did not enhance retention in mice given the novel experience prior to training.

In agreement with other evidence discussed above (Introini-Collison & McGaugh, 1987), the enhancing effects of low doses of epinephrine on retention appear to be independent of the effects of β-endorphin: Neither a novel experience nor β-endorphin given prior to training attenuated the enhancing effects of posttraining epinephrine (Izquierdo & McGaugh, 1985).

Interaction of Noradrenergic and Opiate Systems. There is substantial evidence that opiates and opioid peptides exert an inhibitory influence on NE neurons (Walker, Khachaturian & Watson, 1984). Electrophysiological studies have shown that systemically as well as iontophoretically administered opiate receptor agonists induce naloxone-reversible depression of spontaneous as well as stimulation-induced firing rates of locus coeruleus neurons (Bird & Kuhar, 1977; Korf, Bunney & Aghajanian, 1974; Pepper & Henderson, 1980; Young, Bird & Kuhar, 1977; Strahlendorf, Strahlendorf, & Barnes, 1980). Morphine and β-endorphin depress the release of NE from rat cerebral cortex slices (Arbilla & Langer, 1978; Montel, Starke, & Weber, 1974). Further, infusion of morphine into the cortical terminal fields of locus coeruleus neurons depresses excitability to direct stimulation (Nakamura, Tepper, Young, Ling & Grows, 1982). The finding that opiate receptor binding is reduced in NE terminal regions following 6-OHDA destruction of NE cell bodies suggests that opiate receptors may be located presynaptically on NE cells (Llorens, Martres, Baudry & Schwartz, 1978). Tanaka and his colleagues (Tanaka, Kohno, Nakagawa, Ida, Ilimori, Hoaki, Tsuda & Nagasaki, 1982) have reported that stress increases NE turnover in the amygdala and that the turnover is enhanced by naloxone. These findings suggest that endogenous opiod peptides in the amygdala attenuate stress-induced NE turnover.

Evidence from a number of studies strongly suggests that adrenergic as well as opioid peptidergic systems may interact with central NE in their effects on memory. Izquierdo and Graudenz (1980) reported that propranolol (a $\beta_{1,2}$ antagonist) blocked the enhancing effects of naloxone on memory. These findings suggest that opioid antagonists may enhance retention by releasing brain NE neurons from the inhibitory effects of opioid peptides. This interpretation is consistent with the neuropharmacological evidence reviewed above. Other recent evidence has provided additional support for the view that opioid effects on memory involve NE. For example, naloxone potentiates the memory-enhancing effects of the centrally acting β-adrenergic agonist clenbuterol (Introini-Collison & Baratti, 1986). In addition, the findings that the memory-enhancing effects of naloxone are not blocked by a peripherally-acting β-antagonist (sotalol), or by α-antagonists (phenoxybenzamine or phentolamine) argue that naloxone effects on memory may specifically involve central β-adrenergic receptors (Introini-Collison & Baratti, 1986). Gallagher and her colleagues have reported that 6-OHDA lesions of the dorsal noradrenergic bundle block the enhancing effects of naloxone on retention (Fanelli, Rosenberg, & Gallagher, 1985; Gallagher, Rapp, & Fanelli, 1985). Further, Introini-Collison and Baratti (1986) have shown that the enhancing effects of naloxone on memory are also blocked in animals treated with DSP4, a neurotoxin which produces a relatively specific reduction in brain NE.

Involvement of the Amygdala in Noradrenergic and Opioid Modulation of Memory

The evidence discussed above is consistent with the general view that opiate and adrenergic systems modulate memory through interactions involving the release of central NE. While the findings of studies using noradrenergic neurotoxins suggest that naloxone effects on memory require an intact NE system, they do not reveal whether NE in any specific brain region is of particular importance. As we discuss below, other recent findings suggest that effects of naloxone and epinephrine on memory may involve, in particular, the activation of NE receptors within the amygdaloid complex. These recent findings are of interest in view of the evidence suggesting that the amygdaloid complex plays a role in memory storage (Sarter & Markowitsch, 1985a,b).

Involvement of the Amygdaloid Complex. Noradrenergic receptors are found in several amygdala nuclei (U'Prichard, Reisine, Maison, Fibiger & Yamamura, 1980), particularly in the central and basolateral nuclei (Fallon, 1981). Opiate receptors are also found throughout the amygdaloid complex. Enkephalin fibers and cell bodies are located in the central nucleus and β-endorphin is located in the medial and central nuclei (Bloom & McGinty, 1981). Thus, the anatomical evidence suggests that the amygdaloid complex is a likely candidate for a locus of the effects of treatments affecting opiate and noradrenergic receptors.

We have found that, in rats, retention is impaired by bilateral lesions of the amygdala produced shortly after training, but that retention is unaffected if the lesions are made several days after training (Liang, McGaugh, Martinez, Jensen, Vosquez & Messing, 1982). Thus, it seems unlikely that the amygdala is a site of memory storage. It seems more likely that the amygdala is involved in modulating the storage of recently acquired information (e.g. Sarter & Markowitsch, 1985b). Many studies have shown that posttraining low intensity (subseizure) electrical stimulation can modulate retention (Kesner, 1982; McGaugh & Gold, 1976). In view of evidence that the effects of amygdala stimulation on retention are blocked by lesions of the stria terminalis (ST), a major amygdala pathway, (Liang & McGaugh, 1983b) it seems likely that amygdala stimulation affects retention by modulating storage processes at sites in other brain regions. More recently we have found that lesions of the ST also block the memory-enhancing effects of posttraining peripheral injections of both epinephrine and naloxone as well as the memory-impairing effects of β-endorphin (Liang & McGaugh, 1983a; McGaugh, Introini-Collison, Juler, & Izquierdo, 1986). Further, we have found that posttraining naloxone does not affect retention in rats with bilateral lesions (produced by the excitatory neurotoxin NMDA) of the amygdaloid complex (unpublished findings).

Involvement of Intra-amygdala Norepinephrine. While it is generally assumed that epinephrine does not pass the blood-brain barrier it is clear from the studies discussed above that epinephrine has central effects. Moreover, Gold and van Buskirk (1976) have reported that telencephalic NE level is significantly lowered shortly following peripheral injections of epinephrine in doses found to affect retention. The route by which epinephrine affects the brain is not yet known. It is possible that the effects of peripheral epinephrine are mediated by activation of visceral afferents projecting to central noradrenergic systems which are known to project to the amygdala (via the ST and the ventral amygdalo-fugal pathway). If this is the case, interference with the activation of central NE receptors should block the effect of peripheral epinephrine on memory. Evidence summarized below strongly supports this implication.

If modulation of memory storage processes involves noradrenergic activation within the amygdala, then it should be possible to influence retention with posttraining intra-amygdala injections of noradrenergic agonists and antagonists. Extensive recent evidence supports this implication. Gallagher and her colleagues have reported that retention of an inhibitory avoidance response is impaired by posttraining intra-amygdala injections of the β-antagonists, propranolol and alprenolol. The effect is time-dependent, stereo-specific and is attenuated by concurrent intra-amygdala administration of NE (Gallagher, Kapp, Pascoe

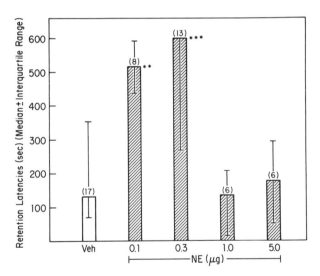

FIG. 8.4. Effects of posttraining intra-amygdala administration of norepinephrine on retention of an inhibitor, avoidance response (Median ± interquartile range). ** P<0.01 *** P<0.002 compared with vehicle controls. N per group is shown in parentheses. (From Liang, Juler and McGaugh, 1986.)

& Rapp, 1981). Kesner and his colleagues found that posttraining intra-amygdala injections of NE can impair retention (Ellis & Kesner, 1981, 1983; Ellis, Berman, & Kesner, 1983).

We have found that posttraining intra-amygdala injections of NE enhance retention in an inhibitory avoidance task (Liang, Juler & McGaugh, 1986). Rats in these studies were implanted bilaterally with amygdala cannulae. They were then trained on an inhibitory avoidance task and given either immediate or delayed intra-amygdala injections. As Figure 8.4 shows, when administered immediately posttraining, low doses of NE enhanced retention on a 24 hr retention test, while higher doses and delayed injections were ineffective.

The effect of NE was blocked by concurrent intra-amygdala injections of propranolol. Further, as is shown in Figure 8.5, we have found that posttraining intra-amygdala injections of propranolol block the retention-enhancing effects of *peripherally* administered epinephrine. This finding provides strong evidence for our view that epinephrine affects memory by influencing the release of NE within the amygdala.

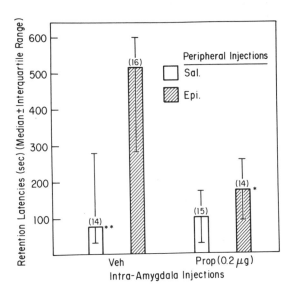

FIG. 8.5. Effects of posttraining intra-amygdala administration of propranolol and ip administration of epinephrine on retention of an inhibitory avoidance response (Median ± interquartile range). N's shown in parentheses. * P<0.05 ** P<0.02 compared with group given vehicle intra-amygdally and epinephrine ip. (From Liang, Juler and McGaugh, 1986.)

Interaction of Noradrenergic and Opiate Systems. Retention can also be modulated by intra-amygdala injections of opioid agonists and antagonists. Gallagher and her colleagues reported that posttraining intra-amygdala injections of the opiate agonist levorphanol produced a naloxone-reversible retention deficit and that posttraining intra-amygdala naloxone administered alone enhanced retention (Gallagher & Kapp, 1978; Gallagher et al., 1981). As discussed above, the findings of studies using peripheral injections of opioid antagonists have suggested that effects of these compounds on memory may be due to blocking of opioid inhibition of NE release. In further support of this interpretation, Gallagher, Rapp and Fanelli (1985) reported that 6-OHDA lesions of the dorsal noradrenergic bundle block the effects of posttraining intra-amygdala injections of naloxone on retention.

Other recent findings provide evidence suggesting that the modulating effects of naloxone on retention may involve activation of noradrenergic receptors within the amygdala (McGaugh, Introini-Collison, & Nagahara, in press). Rats in these experiments received immediate posttraining intra-amygdala injections of α- and β-adrenergic blockers or a buffer control solution, through implanted cannulae, followed by i.p. injections of naloxone. The experiments examined the effects of these treatments on 1-week retention of an inhibitory avoidance task as well as our Y-maze discrimination reversal task discussed above.

The findings obtained in the inhibitory avoidance task are shown in Figures 8.6a, 8.6b and 8.6c. The results obtained in the discrimination reversal task are shown in Figures 8.7a, 8.7b and 8.7c. In both tasks,

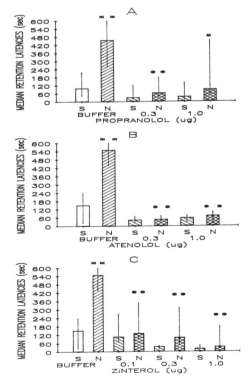

FIG. 8.6. Effect of posttraining ip naloxone on 1-week retention of inhibitory avoidance training in animals given intra-amygdala injections of a) propranolol (0.3 or 1.0 μg), b) atenolol (0.3 or 1.0 μg) or c) zinterol (0.1, 0.3 or 1.0 μg) immediately prior to the naloxone (3 mg/kg). **P < 0.01 vs buffer/saline-injected control group; [O]P < 0.05 and [OO]P < 0.01 vs buffer/naloxone injected group. (From McGaugh, Introini-Collison and Naghara, in press.)

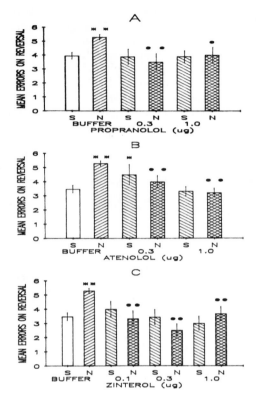

FIG. 8.7. Effect of posttraining ip naloxone on 1-week retention of Y-maze discrimination training in animals given intra-amygdala injections of a) propranolol (0.3 or 1.0 μg), b) atenolol (0.3 or 1.0 μg) or c) zinterol (0.1, 0.3 or 1.0 μg) immediately prior to the nalozone (3 mg/kg). **P<0.01 vs buffer/saline-injected control group; ^{O}P<0.05 and ^{OO}P<0.01 vs buffer/naloxone injected group. (From McGaugh, Introini-Collison and Nagahara, submitted.)

the memory enhancing effect of posttraining naloxone was blocked by propranolol (a $\beta_{1,2}$ antagonist), atenolol (a β_1 antagonist) and zinterol (a β_2 antagonist), in doses that did not affect retention when administered alone. However, the α-antagonists prazosin and yohimbine did not block the effect of naloxone. Moreover, propranolol injected into either the cortex or caudate nucleus immediately above the amygdala injection site did not block the memory-enhancing effects of naloxone.

We have interpreted these findings as indicating that peripherally-administered naloxone influences memory by blocking opioid peptide receptors located within the amygdaloid complex. Thus, on the assumption, as discussed above, that opioid peptides inhibit the release of NE, naloxone would be expected to induce the release of NE within the amygdala. The interpretation that naloxone acts on central receptors seems reasonable since previous studies have shown that retention is enhanced by posttraining intra-amygdala injections of naloxone (Gallagher & Kapp, 1978; Gallagher, et al., 1981) and is not affected by peripheral injections of naltrexone methylbromide (MR2263), a peripherally-acting opiate receptor antagonist (Introini, McGaugh, & Baratti, 1985). Recently we have found that intra-amygdala injections of propranolol also block the memory-enhancing effects of posttraining intra-amygdala injections of naloxone. As shown in Figure 8.8, propranolol injected immediately posttraining blocked the effect of naloxone on retention of the inhibitory avoidance task (8.8a) as well as the Y-maze discrimination task (8.8b). As in the experiments using peripherally-injected naloxone, retention was tested 1-week following training (unpublished findings). Thus, considered together, our findings provide strong support for the view that naloxone affects memory through influences selectively involving β-adrenergic receptors within the amygdaloid complex.

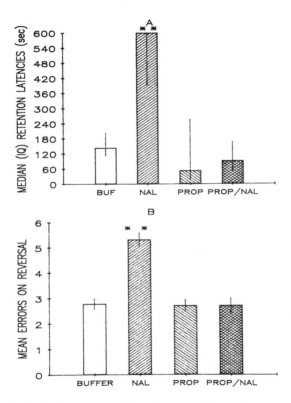

FIG. 8.8. Effect of posttraining intra-amygdala naloxone on 1-week retention of inhibitory avoidance (8a) and Y-maze discrimination (8b) training in animals given intra-amygdala injections of propranolol immediately prior to the naloxone. (Unpublished findings.)

Role of the Amygdala in Memory-Modulation

The findings that retention is influenced by treatments affecting opiate and β-adrenergic receptors within the amygdala provide additional evidence for the view that the amygdaloid complex is part of a brain system involved in processing recently acquired information. It is of interest to note that the amygdala and ST are involved in the memory-modulating effects of a variety of treatments affecting noradrenergic and opiate systems. Preliminary findings of studies in progress indicate that ST lesions block the effect of the cholinergic muscarinic agonist oxotremorine on memory and that memory can be modulated by posttraining intra-amygdala injections of cholinergic agonists and antagonists (unpublished findings). These findings suggest the interesting possibility that nuclei in the amygdaloid complex may be generally involved in neurohormonal modulation of memory. Whether or not this is the case it does appear the amygdala is involved in the memory modulating effects of the three receptor systems that have been examined to date.

As we have noted, it seems unlikely that the amygdala is involved as a locus of changes underlying memory. Our finding that, in rats, bilateral lesions of the amygdala do not impair retention of an inhibitory avoidance task if the lesions are produced several days after training (Liang et al., 1982) indicates that the amygdala is not a site for storage of long-term memory -- at least for this type of learning task. These findings do not rule out the possibility that the amygdaloid complex is involved as a storage site for recent memory. Further, our findings, as well as our interpretation, are not readily reconciled with evidence from other laboratories indicating that nuclei within the amygdala may be involved in circuits mediating rapidly conditioned non-specific autonomic and skeletal responses elicited by aversive stimuli (Cohen, 1975; Kapp, Pascoe & Bixler, 1984; LeDoux, 1986). Additional experiments are needed to determine the involvement of the amygdala in different learning tasks. But, for the types of tasks used in our studies it seems most likely that the amygdala is involved in the modulation and processing of recently acquired information in ways that alter the long-term storage of the information. The modulation might involve attaching affective qualities to sensory information (Mishkin, Malamut & Bachevalier, 1984) or, as we have suggested, by modulating cellular mechanisms at storage sites (McGaugh, Liang, Bennett & Sternberg, 1984).

ACKNOWLEDGEMENT

This research in this chapter was supported by USPHS Research Grant MH12526, and Contract Nooo14-84-K-0391 and N00014-87-K-0518 from the Office of Naval Research.

REFERENCES

Arbilla, S., & Langer, S. Z. (1978). Morphine and beta-endorphin inhibit release of noradrenaline from cerebral cortex but not of dopamine from rat striatum. *Nature, 217,* 559-561.

Bird, S. J., & Kuhar, M. J. (1977). Iontophoretic application of opiates to the locus coeruleus. *Brain Research, 122,* 523-533.

Bloom, F. E., & McGinty, J. F. (1981). Cellular distribution and function of endorphins. In J. L. Martinez Jr., R. A. Jensen, R. B. Messing, H. Rigter, J. L. McGaugh (Eds.): *Endogenous Peptides and Learning and Memory Processes*, pp. 199-230. New York: Academic Press.

Borrell, J., de Kloet, E. R., Versteeg, D. H. G., & Bohus, B. (1983). The role of adrenomedullary catecholamines in the modulation of memory by vasopressin. In E. Endroczi, D. de Wied, L. Angelucci., and V. Scapagnini (Eds.): *Integrative Neurohumoral Mechanisms, Developments in Neuroscience*, pp. 85-90. Amsterdam: Elsevier/North Holland.

Carrasco, M. A., Dias, R. D., Perry, M. L. S., Wofchuk, S. T., Souza, D. O., & Izquierdo, I. (1982). Effect of morphine, ACTH, epinephrine, Met-. Leu-, and des-Tyr-Met-enkephalin on beta-endorphin-like immunoreactivity of rat brain. *Psychoneuroendocrinology, 7*, 229-234.

Castellano, C. (1975). Effects of morphine and heroin on discrimination learning and consolidation in mice. *Psychopharmacology, 42*, 235-242.

Castellano, C. (1981). Strain-dependent effects of naloxone on discrimination learning in mice. *Psychopharmacology, 73*, 291-295.

Cohen, D. H. (1975). Involvement of the avian amygdala-homologue (archistriatum posterior and mediale) in defensively conditioned heart rate change. *Journal of Comparative Neurology, 160*, 13-36.

de Wied, D. (1984). Neurohypophyseal hormone influences on learning and memory processes. In G. Lynch, J. L. McGaugh, and N. M. Weinberger (Eds.): *Neurobiology of Learning and Memory*, pp. 289-312. New York: The Guilford Press.

Ellis, M. E., Berman, R. F., & Kesner, R. P. (1983). Amnesia attenuation specificity: Propranolol reverses norepinephrine but not cycloheximide-induced amnesia. *Pharmacology Biochemistry and Behavior, 19*, 733-736.

Ellis, M. E., & Kesner, R. P. (1981). Physostigmine and norepinephrine: Effects of injection into the amygdala on taste association. *Physiology and Behavior, 27*, 203-209.

Ellis, M. E., & Kesner, R. P. (1983). The noradrenergic system of the amygdala and aversive memory processing. *Behavioral Neuroscience, 97*, 399-415.

Fallon, J. H. (1981). Histochemical characterization of dopaminergic, noradrenergic and serotonergic projections to the amygdala. In Y. Ben-Ari (Ed.): *The Amygdaloid Complex*, pp. 175-184. Amsterdam: Elsevier/North Holland.

Fanelli, R. J., Rosenberg, R. A., & Gallagher, M. (1985). Role of noradrenergic function in the opiate antagonist facilitation of spatial memory. *Behavioral Neuroscience, 99*, 751-755.

Gallagher, M. (1985). Re-viewing modulation of learning and memory. In N. M. Weinberger, J. L. McGaugh and G. Lynch (Eds.): *Memory Systems of the Brain: Animal and Human Cognitive Processes*, pp. 311-334. New York: Guilford Press.

Gallagher, M., & Kapp, B. S. (1978). Manipulation of opiate activity in the amygdala alters memory processes. *Life Sciences, 23,* 1973-1978.

Gallagher, M., Kapp, B. S., Pascoe, J. P., & Rapp, P. R. (1981). A neuropharmacology of amygdaloid systems which contribute to learning and memory. In Y. Ben-Ari (Ed.): *The Amygdaloid Complex,* pp. 343-354. Amsterdam: Elsevier/North Holland.

Gallagher, M., Rapp, P. R., & Fanelli, R. J. (1985). Opiate antagonist facilitation of time-dependent memory processes: Dependence upon intact norepinephrine function. *Brain Research, 347,* 284-290.

Gold, P. E., & McCarty, R. (1981). Plasma catecholamines: Changes after footshock and seizure-producing frontal cortex stimulation. *Behavioral and Neural Biology, 31,* 247-260.

Gold, P. E., Robertson, N. L., & Delanoy, R. L. (1985). Post-training brain catecholamine levels: Lack of response to water-motivated training. *Behavioral and Neural Biology, 44,* 425-433.

Gold, P. E., & van Buskirk, R. (1976). Enhancement and impairment of memory processes with posttrial injections of adrenocorticotrophic hormone. *Behavioral Biology, 16,* 387-400.

Introini-Collison, I. B., & Baratti, C. M. (1986). Opioid peptidergic systems may modulate the activity of b-adrenergic mechanisms during memory consolidation processes. *Behavioral and Neural Biology, 46,* 227-241.

Introini-Collison, I. B., & McGaugh, J. L. (1986). Epinephrine modulates long-term retention of an aversively-motivated discrimination task. *Behavioral and Neural Biology, 45,* 358-365.

Introini-Collison, I. B., & McGaugh, J. L. (1987). Naloxone and beta-endorphin alter the effects of posttraining epinephrine on retention of an inhibitory avoidance response. *Psychopharmacology, 92,* 229-235.

Introini, I. B., McGaugh, J. L., & Baratti, C. M. (1985). Pharmacological evidence of a central effect of naltrexone, morphine and beta-endorphin and a peripheral effect of Met- and Leu-enkephalin on retention of a inhibitory response in mice. *Behavioral and Neural Biology, 44,* 434-446.

Izquierdo, I. (1979). Effect of naloxone and morphine on various forms of memory in the rat: Possible role of endogenous opiate mechanisms in memory consolidation. *Psychopharmacology, 66,* 199-203.

Izquierdo, I., & Dias, R. D. (1985). Influence on memory of posttraining and pre-test injections of ACHT, vasopressin, epinephrine, or B-endorphin, and their interaction with naloxone. *Psychoneuroendocrinology, 10,* 165-172.

Izquierdo, I., & Graudenz, M. (1980). Memory facilitation by naloxone is due to release of dopaminergic and beta-adrenergic systems from tonic inhibition. *Psychopharmacology, 67,* 265-268.

Izquierdo, I., & McGaugh, J. L. (1985). Effect of a novel experience prior to training or testing on retention of an inhibitory avoidance response in mice: Involvement of an opioid system. *Behavioral and Neural Biology,* 44, 228-238.

Izquierdo, I., Souza, D. O., Dias, R. D., Carrasco, M. A., Volkmer, N., Perry, M. L. S., & Netto, C. A. (1984). Effect of various behavioral training and testing procedures on brain B-endorphin-like immunoreactivity, and the possible role of B-endorphin in behavioral regulation. *Psychoneuroendocrinology,* 9, 381-389.

Kapp, B. S., Pascoe, J. P., & Bixler, M. A. (1984). The amygdala: A neuroanatomical systems approach to its contribution to aversive conditioning. In L. Squire & N. Butters (Eds.), *The neuropsychology of memory,* pp. 473-488. New York: The Guilford Press.

Kesner, R. P. (1982). Brain stimulation: Effects on memory. *Behavioral and Neural Biology,* 36, 315-367.

Korf, J., Bunney, B. S., & Aghajanian, G. K. (1974). Noradrenergic neurons: Morphine inhibition of spontaneous activity. *European Journal of Pharmacology,* 25, 165-169.

LeDoux, J. E. (1986). Sensory systems and emotion: A model of affective processing. *Integrative Psychiatry,* 4, 237-248.

Liang, K. C., Bennett, C., & McGaugh, J. L. (1985). Peripheral epinephrine modulates the effects of posttraining amygdala stimulation on memory. *Behavioural Brain Research,* 15, 93-100.

Liang, K. C., Juler, R., & McGaugh, J. L. (1986). Modulating effects of posttraining epinephrine on memory: Involvement of the amygdala noradrenergic system. *Brain Research,* 368, 125-133.

Liang, K. C., & McGaugh, J. L. (1983a). Lesions of the stria terminalis attenuate the enhancing effect of posttraining epinephrine on retention of an inhibitory avoidance response. *Behavioural Brain Research,* 9, 49-58.

Liang, K. C. & McGaugh, J. L. (1983b). Lesions of the stria terminalis attenuate the amnestic effect of amygdaloid stimulation on avoidance responses. *Brain Research,* 274, 309-318.

Liang, K. C., McGaugh, J. L., Martinez Jr., J. L., Jensen, R. A., Vasquez, B. J., & Messing, R. B. (1982). Posttraining amygdaloid lesions impair retention of an inhibitory avoidance response. *Behavioural Brain Research,* 4, 237-249.

Llorens, C., Martres, M. P., Baudry, M., & Schwartz, J. C. (1978). Hypersensitivity to noradrenaline in cortex after chronic morphine: Relevance to tolerance and dependence. *Nature,* 274, 603-605.

McGaugh, J. L. (1983). Hormonal influences on memory. *Annual Review of Psychology,* 34, 297-323.

McGaugh, J. L., & Gold, P. E. (1976). Modulation of memory by electrical stimulation of the brain. In M. R. Rosenzweig and E. L. Bennett (Eds.), *Neural Mechanisms of Learning and Memory,* pp. 549-560. Cambridge: MIT Press.

McGaugh, J. L., & Gold, P. E. (in press). Hormonal modulation of memory. In R. B. Brush and S. Levine (Eds.), *Psychoendocrinology.* New York: Academic Press.

McGaugh, J. L., Introini-Collison, I. B., Juler, R. G., & Izquierdo, I.

248 McGAUGH, INTROINI-COLLISON, NAGAHARA AND CAHILL

(1986). Stria terminalis lesions attenuate the effects of posttraining naloxone and b-endorphin on retention. *Behavioral Neuroscience, 100*, 839-844.

McGaugh, J. L., Introini-Collison. I. B., & Nagahara, A. H. (in press). Memory-enhancing effects of posttraining naloxone: Involvement of β-noradrenergic influences in the amygdaloid complex. *Brain Research.*

McGaugh, J. L., Liang. K. C., Bennett. C., & Sternberg, D. B. (1984). Adrenergic influences on memory storage: Interaction of peripheral and central systems. In G. Lynch, J. L. McGaugh and N. M. Weinberger (Eds.), *Neurobiology of Learning and Memory*, pp. 313-333. New York: The Guilford Press.

Messing, R. B., Jensen, R. A., Martinez Jr., J. L., Spiehler, V. R., Vasquez, B. J., Soumireu-Mourat, B., Liang, K. C., & McGaugh, J. L. (1979). Naloxone enhancement of memory. *Behavioral and Neural Biology, 27*, 266-275.

Mishkin, M., Malamut, B., & Bachevalier, J. (1984). Memories and habits: Two neural systems. In G. Lynch, J. L. McGaugh and N. M. Weinberger (Eds.), *Neurobiology of Learning and Memory*, pp. 65-77. New York: The Guilford Press.

Montel, H., Starke, K., & Weber, F. (1974). Influence of morphine and naloxone on the release of noradrenaline from rat brain cortex slices. *Naunyn-Schmiedeberg's Archives of Pharmacology, 283*, 283-369.

Nakamura, S., Tepper, J. M., Young, S. J., Ling, N., & Groves, P. M. (1982). Noradrenergic terminal excitability: Effects of opioids. *Neuroscience Letters, 30*, 57-62.

Pepper, C. M., & Henderson, G. H. (1980). Opiates and opioid peptides hyperpolarize locus coeruleus neurons in vitro. *Science, 209*, 394-396.

Sarter, M., & Markowitsch, H. J. (1985a). Involvement of the amygdala in learning and memory. A critical review, with emphasis on anatomical relations. *Behavioral Neuroscience, 99*, 342-380.

Sarter, M., & Markowitsch, H. J. (1985b). The amygdala's role in human mnemonic processing. *Cortex, 21*, 7-24.

Sternberg, D. B., Isaacs, K., Gold, P. E., & McGaugh, J. L. (1985). Epinephrine facilitation of appetitive learning: Attenuation with adrenergic receptor antagonists. *Behavioral and Neural Biology, 44*, 447-453.

Sternberg, D. B., Korol, D., Novack, G., & McGaugh, J. L. (1986). Epinephrine-induced memory facilitation: Attenuation by adrenergic receptor antagonists. *European Journal of Pharmacology, 129*, 189-193.

Strahlendorf, H. K., Strahlendorf, J. C., & Barnes, C. D. (1980). Endorphin-mediated inhibition of locus coeruleus neurons. *Brain Research, 191*, 284-288.

Tanaka, M., Kohno, Y., Nakagawa, R., Ida, Y. Ilimori, K., Hoaki, Y., Tsuda, A., & Nagasaki, N. (1982). Naloxone enhances stress-induced increases in noradrenaline turnover in specific brain regions in rats. *Life Sciences, 30*, 1663-1669.

U'Prichard, D. C., Reisine, T. D., Maison, S. F., Fibiger, H. C., & Yamamura, H. I. (1980). Modulation of rat alpha- and beta-adrenergic receptor populations by lesions of the dorsal noradrenergic bundle. *Brain Research, 187*, 143-154.

Walker, J. M., Khachaturian, H., Watson, S. J. (1984). Some anatomical and physiological interactions among noradrenergic systems and opioid peptides. In M. G. Ziegler and C. R. Lake (Eds.), *Norepinephrine*, pp. 74-91. Baltimore: Williams and Wilkins.

Young, W. S., Bird, S. J., & Kuhar, M. J. (1977). Iontophoresis of methionine-enkephalin in the locus coeruleus area. *Brain Research, 129*, 366.370.

9

The Essential Memory Trace Circuit and the Essential Reinforcement System for a Basic Form of Associative Learning

Richard F. Thompson
University of Southern California, Los Angeles

Some years ago we selected classical conditioning of the eyelid closure response as a model system in which to analyze the neuronal substrates of basic associative learning and memory. We adopted this paradigm, and the rabbit as the experimental animal of choice, for two key reasons: 1) There is an extensive literature on the properties and parameters of this basic form of associative learning in both humans and animal (particularly the rabbit) (Black & Prokasy, 1972; Gormezano, 1972), and 2) it obeys the basic "laws" of conditioning and exhibits the basic phenomena of associative learning in a similar manner in humans and in other mammals.

When we began this work about eighteen years ago, we had no idea that we would be led to the cerebellum as the key structure that appears to store the essential memory trace. With the advantage of hindsight, it is perhaps not so surprising. The conditioned eyelid closure response is a very precisely timed movement--over the entire effective CS-US onset interval where learning occurs, from about 100 msec to over 1 sec., the learned response develops such that the eyelid closure is maximal at the time of onset of the US. In this sense it is a maximally adaptive response. It is also a very precisely timed "skilled" movement, perhaps the most elementary form of learned skilled movement. Our results strongly support the general spirit of earlier theories of the role of the cerebellum in motor learning (Albus, 1971; Eccles, 1977; Ito, 1972; Marr, 1969) (see Figure 9.1).

As noted below, this conclusion is not limited to eyelid conditioning in the rabbit but appears to hold for the learning of any discrete behavioral

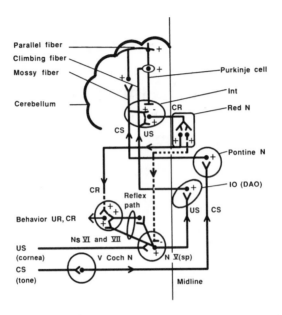

FIG. 9.1. Simplified schematic of hypothetical memory trace circuit for discrete behavioral responses learned as adaptations to aversive events. The US (corneal airpuff) pathway seems to consist of somatosensory projections to the dorsal accessory portion of the inferior olive (DAO) and its climbing fiber projections to the cerebellum. The tone CS pathway seems to consist of auditory projections to pontine nuclei (Pontine N) and their mossy fiber projections to the cerebellum. The efferent (eyelid closure) CR pathway projects from the interpositus nucleus (Int) of the cerebellum to the red nucleus (Red N) and via the descending rubral pathway to act ultimately on motor neurons. The red nucleus may also exert inhibitory control over the transmission of somatic sensory information about the US to the inferior olive (IO), so that when a CR occurs (eyelid closes), the red nucleus dampens US activation of climbing fibers. Evidence to date is most consistent with storage of the memory traces in localized regions of cerebellar cortex and possibly interpositus nucleus as well. Pluses indicate excitatory and minuses inhibitory synaptic action. Additonal abbreviations: N V (sp), spinal fifth cranial nucleus; N VI, sixth cranial nucleus; N VII, seventh cranial nucleus; V Cock N, ventral cochlear nucleus. (From Thompson, 1986; Reprinted by permission of *Science*, 1986.)

response learned to deal with an aversive event by mammals. It is thus a category of associative learning and might be described as "procedural" learning, i.e., learning how. Some years ago we adopted the general strategy of recording neuronal unit activity in the trained animal (rabbit eyelid conditioning) as an initial survey and sampling method to identify putative sites of memory storage. A pattern of neuronal activity that correlates with the behavioral learned response, specifically one that precedes the behavioral response in time within trials, predicts the form of the learned response within trials and predicts the development of learning over trials, is a necessary (but not sufficient) requirement for identification of a storage locus.

We mapped a number of brain regions and systems thought to be involved in learning and memory. Neuronal activity of pyramidal cells in the hippocampus exhibited all the requirements described above (Berger, Rinaldi, Weisz & Thompson, 1983). But the hippocampus itself is not necessary for learning and memory of such discrete behavioral responses (Thompson, Berger & Madden 1983). Recent evidence argues strongly that long-lasting neuronal plasticity is established in the hippocampus in these learning paradigms (Mamounas, Thompson, Lynch & Baudry, 1984; Weisz, Clark & Thompson, 1984). Thus, "memory traces" are formed in the hippocampus during learning but these "higher order" traces are not necessary for learning of the basic association between a neutral tone or light CS and the precisely timed, adaptive behavioral response. However, the hippocampus can become essential when appropriate task demands are placed on the animal, even in eyelid conditioning (Thompson, et al., 1983). But the hippocampus is not a part of the memory trace circuit essential, i.e., necessary and sufficient, for basic associative learning and memory of discrete responses. Indeed, decorticate and even decerebrate mammals can learn the conditioned eyelid response (Norman, Buchwald & Villablanca, 1977; Oakley & Russell, 1972) and animals that are first trained and then acutely decerebrated retain the learned response (Mauk & Thompson, 1986). The essential memory trace circuit is below the level of the thalamus.

In the course of mapping the brain stem and cerebellum we discovered localized regions of cerebellar cortex and a region in the lateral interpositus nucleus where neuronal activity exhibited the requisite memory trace properties--patterned changes in neuronal discharge frequency that preceded the behavioral learned response by as much as 60 msec (minimum behavioral CR onset latency approx. 100 msec), predicted the form of the learned behavioral response (but not the reflex response) and grew over the course of training, i.e., predicted the development of behavioral learning (McCormick, Lavond, Clark, Kettner, Rising & Thompson, 1981; McCormick, Clark, Lavond & Thompson 1982a; McCormick & Thompson, 1984; Thompson, 1986) (Figure 9.2).

We undertook a series of lesion studies -- large lesions of lateral cerebellar cortex and nuclei, electrolytic lesions of the lateral interpositus-medial dentate nuclear region and lesions of the superior cerebellar peduncle ipsilateral to the learned response all abolished the learned response completely and permanently. had no effect on the reflex UR and did not prevent or impair learning on the contralateral side of the body (Clark, McCormick, Lavond & Thompson, 1984; Lavond, McCormick, Clark, Holmes & Thompson. 1981; Lincoln. McCormick & Thompson, 1982; McCormick et al., 1981, 1982a; McCormick, Guyer & Thompson, 1982b; Thompson, Clark, Donegan, Lavond, Madden, Mamounas, Mauk & McCormick 1984). After our initial papers were published, Yeo, Glickstein and associates replicated our basic lesion result for the interpositus nucleus, using light as well as tone CSs and a

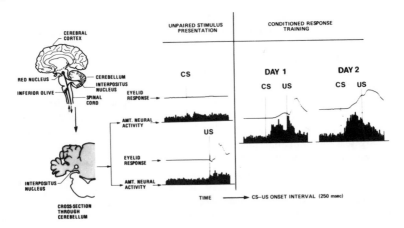

FIG. 9.2. Neuronal unit activity recorded from the lateral interpositus nucleus during unpaired and paired presentations of the training stimuli. The animal was first given pseudorandomly unpaired presentations of the tone and corneal airpuff, in which the neurons responded very little to either stimulus. However, when the stimuli were paired togehter in time, the cells began responding within the CS period as the animal learned the eyeblink response. The onset of this unit activity preceded the behavioral NM response within a trial by 36 to 58 msec. Stimulation through this recording site yielded ipsilateral eyelid closure and NM extension. Each histogram bar is 9 msec in duration. The upper trace of each histogram represents the movement of the NM with up being extension across the eyeball. (From McCormick and Thompson, 1984b.)

periorbital shock US (we had used corneal airpuff US), thus extending the generality of the result (Yeo, Hardiman & Glickstein, 1984).

Electrolytic or aspiration lesions of the cerebellum cause degeneration in the inferior olive--the lesion-abolition of the learned response could be due to olivary degeneration rather than cerebellar damage, per se. We made kainic acid lesions of the interpositus--a lesion as small as a cubic millimeter in the lateral anterior interpositus permanently and selectively ablolished the learned response with no attendant degeneration in the inferior olive (Lavond, Hembree & Thompson, 1985). Additional work suggests that the lesion result holds across CS modalities, skeletal response systems, species, and perhaps with instrumental contingencies as well (Donegan, Lowry & Thompson, 1983; Polenchar, Patterson, Lavond & Thompson, 1985; Yeo et al., 1984). Electrical microstimulation of the interpositus nucleus in untrained animals elicits behavioral responses by way of the superior cerebellar peduncle, e.g., eyeblink, leg-flexion, the nature of the response being determined by the locus of the electrode (McCormick & Thompson, 1984). Collectively, these data build a case that the memory traces are afferent to the efferent fibers of the superior cerebellar peduncle, i.e., in interpositus, cerebellar cortex or systems for which the cerebellum is a mandatory efferent.

The essential efferent CR pathway appears to consist of fibers exiting from the interpositus nucleus ipsilateral to the trained side of the body in the superior cerebellar peduncle, crossing to relay in the contralateral magnocellular division of the red nucleus and crossing back to descend in the rubral pathway to act ultimately on motor neurons (Chapman, Steinmetz & Thompson, 1983; Haley, Lavond & Thompson, 1983; Lavond et al., 1981; Madden, Haley, Barchas & Thompson, 1983; McCormick et al., 1982b; Rosenfield, Devydaitis & Moore, 1985) (see Figure 9.1). Possible involvement of other efferent systems in control of the CR has not yet been determined, but descending systems taking origin rostral to the midbrain are not necessary for learning or retention of the CR, as noted above.

Recent lesion and microstimulation evidence suggests that the esential US reinforcing pathway, the necessary and sufficient pathway conveying information about the US to the cerebellar memory trace circuit, is climbing fibers from the dorsal accessory olive (DAO) projecting via the inferior cerebellar peduncle (see Figure 9.1). Thus, lesions of the appropriate region of the DAO prevent acquisition and produce normal extinction of the behavioral CR with continued paired training in already trained animals (McCormick et al., 1985). Electrical microstimulation of this same region elicits behavioral responses and serves as an effective US for normal learning of behavioral CRs; the exact behavioral response elicited by DAO stimulation is learned as a normal CR to a CS (Mauk, Steinmetz & Thompson, 1986).

Lesion and microstimulation data suggest that the essential CS pathway includes mossy fiber projections to the cerebellum via the pontine nuclei (see Figure 9.1). Thus, sufficiently large lesions of the middle cerebellar peduncle prevent acquisition and immediately abolish retention of the eyelid CR to all modalities of CS (Solomon, Lewis, LoTurco, Steinmetz & Thompson 1986) whereas lesions in the pontine nuclear region can selectively abolish the eyelid CR to an acoustic CS (Steinmetz et al., 1987). Consistent with this result is current anatomical evidence from our laboratory for a direct contralateral projection from the ventral cochlear nucleus to this same region of the pons (Thompson, Lavond, & Thompson, 1986) and electrophysiological evidence of a "primary-like" auditory relay nucleus in this pontine region (Logan, Steinmetz, & Thompson, 1986).

Electrical microstimulation of the mossy fiber system serves as a very effective CS, producing rapid learning, on average more rapid than with peripheral CSs, when paired with, e.g., a corneal airpuff US (Steinmetz et al., 1985a). If animals are trained with a left pontine nuclear stimulation CS and then tested for transfer to right pontine stimulation, transfer is immediate (i.e., 1 trial) if the two electrodes have similar locations in the two sides, suggesting that least under these conditions the traces are not formed in the pontine nuclei but rather in the cerebellum, probably beyond the mossy fiber terminals (Steinmetz et al., 1986b) Finally, appropriate forward pairing of mossy fiber stimulation as a CS and climbing fiber stimulation as a US yields *normal behavioral learning* of the response elicited by climbing fiber stimulation (Steinmetz, Lavond &

Thompson, 1985b). Lesion of the interpositus abolishes both the CR and the UR in this paradigm. All of these results taken together would seem to build an increasingly strong case for localization of the essential memory traces to the cerebellum, particularly in the "reduced" preparation heth stimulation of mossy fibers as the CS and climbing fibers as the US. In the normal animal trained with peripheral stimuli, the possibility of trace formation in brain stem structures has not yet been definitively ruled out.

In current work we have compared electrical stimulation of the dorsolateral pontine nucleus (DLPN) and lateral reticular nucleus (LRN) as CSs. When paired with a peripheral US (corneal airpuff), both yield normal and rapid learning (Knowlton, Beekman. Lavond. Steinmetz & Thompson, 1986; Steinmetz, Rosen. Chapman, Lavond & Thompson, 1986a). DLPN projects almost exclusively to an intermediate region of cerebellar cortex whereas the LRN projects in significant part to the interpositus nucleus (Chan-Palay, 1977, Bloedel & Courville, 1981; Brodal, 1975). Under these conditons, a lesion limited to the general region of cerebellar cortex receiving projections from the DLPN completely and permanently abolishes the CR to the DLPN stimulation CS but not to the LRN stimulton CS (Knowlton et al., 1986). We have thus created a situation where a relatively restricted region of cerebellar cortex is necessary for the CR, which will be most helpful for further analysis of mechanisms of memory trace formation. More generally, these results suggest that the particular region(s) of cerebellar cortex necessary for associative memory formation depend upon the patterns of mossy fiber projections to the cerebellum activated by the CS. We hypothesize that the memory traces are formed in regions of cerebellar cortex (and interpositus nucleus?) where CS activated mossy fiber projections and US activated climbing fiber projections converge.

Recordings from Purkinje cells in the eyelid conditioning paradigm are consistent with the formation of memory traces in cerebellar cortex. Prior to training, a tone CS causes a variable evoked increase in frequency of discharge of simple spikes in many Purkinje cells (Donegan, Foy & Thompson, 1985; Foy & Thompson. 1986). Following training, the majority of Purkinje cells that develop a change in frequency of simple spike discharge that correlates with the behavioral response (as opposed to being stimulus evoked) show decreases in frequency of discharge of simple spikes that precede and "predict" the form of the behavioral learned response, although increases in "predictive" discharge frequency also occur fairly frequently.

Conjoint electrical stimulation of mossy fibers and climbing fibers can yield normal learning of behavioral responses. as noted above (Steinmetz, Rosen, Woodruff-Pak, Lavond & Thompson, 1986b). The properties of these learned responses appear identical to those of the same conditioned responses learned with peripheral stimuli (e.g.. eyelid closure, leg flexion). The temporal requirements for such conjoint stimulation that yields behavioral learning are essentially identical to those required with peripheral stimuli: no learning at all if CS onset does not precede US onset by more than 50 msec, best learning if CS precedes US by 200-400 msec, and progressively poorer learning with increasing CS precedense (Gormezano, 1972). Further, normal learning occurs if the mossy fiber CS consists of only 2 pulses, 5 msec apart, at the beginning of a 250 msec CS-US onset interval (Logan et al, 1985).

Collectively, the evidence reviewed above demonstrates that the cerebellum is essential for the category of procedural memory we have studied. It also builds a very strong case that the essential memory traces are stored in very localized regions of the cerebellum.

THE CEREBELLUM, BLOCKING AND THE NATURE OF REINFORCEMENT

We hasten to add we do not argue that all types of memories are stored in the cerebellum. But the evidence for storage of any kind of memory trace in the cerebellum is very recent, dating from our initial report in 1981 (McCormick, et al.). It is at least possible that the cerebellum is much more generally involved in memory and complex information processing than earlier believed. Indeed, there are tantalizing hints that the cerebellum may play a key role in the sequential aspects of complex cognitive processes (Leiner, Leiner & Dow, 1986).

There is suggestive evidence from our own current work that the essential cerebellar circuit we have defined (Figure 9.1) may in fact be capable of mediating *blocking*, a complex aspect of classical conditioning that is viewed by many as cognitive. The phenomenon of blocking (Kamin, 1968) has become a key issue of modern animal learning theory. In brief, if an animal is first trained on CS_1-US, then given additional training on CS_1 paired simultaneously with CS_2, followed by US, and then tested for response to CS_2, little conditioned responding is seen compared with animals not given the prior CS_1-US training (and other appropriate control conditions). The important message of blocking is that the informational context in which a CS appears determines the degree to which it becomes associated with the US (as opposed to simply the number of times the CS is paired with the US)--contiguity is necessary to produce conditioning, but not sufficient.

Blocking has become the cornerstone of all models of associative learning that address the Pavlovian conditioning literature (e.g., Mackintosh, 1975; Pearce & Hall, 1980; Rescorla & Wagner, 1972; Schull, 1979; Sutton & Barto, 1981; Wagner, 1981). In fact, it seems almost obligatory for a model to predict blocking in order to be taken seriously (see also Gluck & Thompson, 1987). One way blocking could occur is that as the CR becomes established to CS_1 the associative strength added by additional pairings of CS_1 and the US becomes increasingly less, so that after learning to CS_1 is asymptotic, no additional associative strength is added by additional CS_1-US pairings. Hence, if further training is given with CS_1 and a new CS_2, presented simultaneously, and the US, no associative strength will accrue to CS_2-US. This is the essence of the Rescorla-Wagner mathematical formulation of basic associative learning and memory (Rescorla & Wagner, 1972).

The essential learning and memory circuit involving the cerebellum (Figure 9.1) contains within in the hypothetical potential for actualizing the Rescorla-Wagner formulation of associative learning, including blocking. The basic requirement is that as the CR develops to a US, the less effective the US becomes--the less "reinforcing" it is. We make the following assumption: the degree to which the US is reinforcing, i.e., the degree to which it adds associative strength on CS-US trials, is a direct funtion of the occurrence of a climbing fiber volley to the cerebellum evoked by the US onset.

Since the hypothetical memory trace in the cerebellum must involve a population of Purkinje cells and a population of climbing fibers projecting from the dorsal accessory olive portion of the inferior olive, a simple way to conceptualize reinforcement strength is as the proportion of effective climbing fibers activated by the US (by "effective" is meant all those activated by the particular US prior to training).

Before learning, the tone CS does not result in any increase in the activity of interpositus neurons, i.e., the efferent CR pathway from interpositus to red nucleus to motor neurons is not activated (see Figure 9.2). As training proceeds, neurons in the interpositus increase their patterns of discharge in the CS period such that they preceed and predict the occurrence of the behavioral CR, as noted above (see Figure 9.2). In a well-trained animal, activation of neurons in the efferen CR pathway is massive in the CS period (Figure 9.2).

Suppose that in addition to driving the behavioral CR, the efferent CR pathway also exerts an inhibitory influence on the essential US pathway. Then as the CR is increasingly well-learned, activation of the US pathway by the US is increasingly attenuated. In a well-trained animal, the US pathway might be completely shut down. If so, then additional training to the original CS_1 paired with a new CS_2, and the US will result in no association between CS_2 and the US because the US has functionally ceased to occur at the critical regions of memory trace formation in the cerebellum (see Figure 9.1).

Recent evidence suggests that activation of the red nucleus can inhibit somatosensory activation of the inferior olive (IO) (Weiss, et al., 1985). Electrical stimulation of the red nucleus can produce inhibition of activation of IO neurons by tactile stimulation (of the forepaw). Weiss, et al., (1985) suggest that this inhibition acts at the somatosensory relay in the cuneate nucleus (relaying somatosensory information to the IO and to higher brain structures from the forelimbs).

Assume that a comparable descending inhibitory system exists from red nucleus to the spinal trigeminal nucleus regulating projection of somatosensory information from the face to the critical region of the IO, the dorsal accessory olive (dashed line in Figure 9.1). Similar descending inhibitory influences may exist from the interpositus to the trigeminal nucleus and perhaps to the dorsal accessory olive as well.

If this decending system inhibiting somatosensory activation of the IO does in fact exist, then our cerebellar circuit provides the basic architecture for the Rescorla-Wagner formulation and can account fully for blocking. The strong prediction is that as the CR develops to a CS, activation of the essential US pathway in dorsal accessory olive - climbing fibers - cerebellum by the US will decrease, until in a well-trained animal, the US no longer activates the essential US pathway at all. In current work we have two lines of evidence supporting this hypothesis. The first involves recording the activity of single Purkinje neurons. As noted above, there are clear and marked changes in the patterns of simple spike discharges of Purkinje neurons. (Simple spikes are evoked by the mossy fiber-granule cell-parallel fiber system, the essential CS pathway.) But there are also clear and dramatic changes in the patterns of complex spike discharges. (Complex spikes in Purkinje cells are evoked by activation of climbing fibers from the IO--the essential US pathway.) Prior to training, the onset of the US (corneal airpuff) consistently evokes complex spikes in those Purkinje cells receiving climbing fiber projections from the region of the IO that is activated by stimulation of the eye region of the face. In well-trained animals, the US onset typically does not evoke complex spikes in the appropriate Purkinje cells (Foy & Thompson, 1986). It appears that as the CR develops, activation of the Purkinje cells by the US becomes markedly attenuated, as predicted by our blocking hypothesis.

In current and preliminary studies we are obtaining more direct evidence for our blocking hypotheses by recording activity of neurons in the dorsal accessory olive activated by the corneal airpuff US onset (Steinmetz, Donegan & Thompson, in preparation). US alone presentation consistently evoke a phasic increase in responses of these neurons (US onset evoked). As the behavioral CR (eyelid/NM response) begins to develop, this US onset evoked response in dorsal accessory olive neurons becomes markedly attenuated. Indeed, in a well--trained animal, US onset evoked activity may be completely absent in the dorsal accessory olive.

Perhaps the most striking aspect of our blocking hypothesis is that the phenomenon of blocking is a mandatory emergent property of the essential memory trace circuit itself. If the circuit indeed functions as we hypothesize, then the explanation of blocking is purely mechanistic. Terms like "expectation" and "surprise" favored by some cognitive psychologists to "explain" blocking become so much excess baggage. From a different perspective, an identified neuronal memory trace circuit in the mammalian brain can indeed account for the cognitive phenomenon of blocking.

In more general terms, our cerebellar circuit would seem to provide the neuronal substrate for the Rescorla-Wagner formulation of basic associative learning. This emerges from the architecture of the circuit itself rather than from any special synaptic processes. In our circuit, the reason that CS-US pairings add progressively less associative strength as learning develops is because the essential reinforcement provided by the US becomes progressively weaker over the course of training. In a well-trained animal the US provides no reinforcement at all.

If indeed, the "reinforcement" for classical conditioning of discrete behavioral responses with aversive USs consists in climbing fibers to the cerebellum activated by the US, then we have a new and rather interesting view of the nature of reinforcement in classical conditioning, Thus, electrical microstimulation of the dorsal accessory olive that serves as an effective US (see above) is not at all aversive to the animal. It is the essential reinforcing pathway but in and of itself does not convey aversive information. The aversive component of the US. e.g., that activates the spinothalamic (or here, trigeminothalamic) pathway, is not an essential part of the reinforcement system. But, it very likely plays an important modulatory role, perhaps in rates of acquisition and extinction.

ACKNOWLEDGEMENTS

Supported by grants from the National Science Foundation (BNS 8117115), the Office of Naval Research (N00014-83) the McKnight Foundation and the Sloan Foundation.

REFERENCES

Albus, J. B. (1971). A theory of cerebellar function. *Mathematical Bioscience, 10,* 25-61.
Berger, T. W., Rinaldi, P., Weisz D. J., & Thompson. R. F. (1983). Single unit analysis of different hippocampal cell types during classical conditioning of the rabbit nictitating membrane response. *Journal of Neurophysiology, 50,* 1197-1219.
Black, A. H., & Prokasy W. F. (Eds), (1972). *Classical conditioning II: Current research and theory.* New York: Appleton-Century-Crofts.
Bloedel, J. R., & Courville, J. (1981). Cerebellar afferent systems. In J. M. Brookhart, V. B. Mountcastle, V. B. Brooks, & S. R. Geiger, (Eds), *Handbook of Physiology, Vol. 2,* Baltimore: *American Physiological Society,* pp 735-829.
Brodal, P. (1975). Demonstration of a somatotopically organized projection onto the paramedian lobule and the anterior lobe from the lateral reticular nucleus. An experimental study with the horseradish peroxidase method. *Brain Research, 95,* 221-239.
Chan-Palay, V. (1977). *Cerebellar Dentate Nucleus.* New York: Springer.
Chapman, P. F., Steinmetz, J. E., & Thompson, R. F. (1985). Classical conditioning of the rabbit eyeblink does not occur with stimulation of the cerebellar nuclei as the unconditioned stimulus. *Society for Neuroscience Abstracts, 11,* 835.
Clark, G. A., McCormick, D. A., Lavond, D. G., & Thompson R. F. (1984). Effects of lesions of cerebellar nuclei on conditioned behavioral and hippocampal neuronal responses. *Brain Research, 291,* 125-136.
Donegan, N. H., Lowry, R. W., & Thompson, R. F. (1983). Effects of lesioning cerebellar nuclei on conditioned leg-flexion responses. *Neuroscience Abstracts, 9,* 331 (No. 100.7).

Donegan, N. H., Foy, M. R., & Thompson, R. F. (1985). Neuronal responses of the rabbit cerebellar cortex during performance of the classically conditioned eyelid response. *Neuroscience Abstracts, 11*, 835.

Eccles, J. C. (1977). An instruction-selection theory of learning in the cerebellar cortex. *Brain Research, 127*, 327-352.

Foy, M. R., & Thompson, R. F. (1986). Single unit analysis of Purkinje cell discharge in classically conditoned and untrained rabbits. *Society for Neuroscience Abstracts, 12*, 518.

Gluck, M. A., & Thompson, R. F. (1987). Modelling the neural substrates of associative learning and memory: a computational approach. *Psychological Review*, in press.

Gormezano, I. (1972). Investigations of defense and reward conditioning in the rabbit. In Black, A. H. & Prokasy, W. F. (eds): *Classical Conditioning II: Current research and theory*. pp. 151-181. New York: Appleton-Century-Crofts.

Haley, D. A., Lavond, D. G., & Thompson, R. F. (1983). Effects of contralateral red nuclear lesions on retention of the classically conditioned nictitating membrane/eyelid response. *Society for Neuroscience Abstracts, 9*, 643.

Ito, M. (1972). Neural design of the cerebellar motor control system. *Brain Research, 40*, 81-84.

Kamin, L. J. (1968). Attention - like processes in classical conditioning. In M. R. Jones (Ed.), *Miami Symposium on the prediction of Behavior: Aversive Stimulation*. Miami: University of Miami Press.

Knowlton, B., Beekman, G., Lavond, D. G., Steinmetz, J. E., & Thompson, R. F. (1986). Effects of aspiration of cerebellar cortex on retention of eyeblink conditioning using stimulation of different mossy fiber sources as conditioned stimuli. *Society for Neuroscience Abstracts, 12*, 754.

Lavond, D. G., McCormick, D. A., Clark, G. A., Holmes, D. T., & Thompson, R. F. (1981). Effects of ipsilateral rostral pontine reticular lesions on retention of classically conditioned nictitating membrane and eyelid response. *Physiological Psychology, 9*(4), 335-339.

Lavond, D. G. Hembree, T. L., & Thompson, R. F. (1985). Effect of kainic acid lesions of the cerebellar interpositus nucleus on eyelid conditioning in the rabbit. *Brain Research, 326*, 179-182.

Leiner, H. C., Leiner, A. L., & Dow, R. S. (1986). Does the cerebellum contribute to mental skills? *Behavioral Neuroscience, 100*, 443-454.

Lincoln, J. S. McCormick, D. A., & Thompson, R. F. (1982). Ipsilateral cerebellar lesions prevent learning of the classically conditioned nictitating membrane/eyelid response of the rabbit. *Brain Research, 242*, 190-193.

Logan, C. G., Steinmetz, J. E., Woodruff-Pak, D. S., & Thompson, R. F. (1985). Short-duration mossy fiber stimulation is effective as a CS in eyelid classical conditioning. *Society for Neuroscience*

Abstracts, 11, 835.

Logan, C. G., Steinmetz, J. E. & Thompson R. F. (1986). Acoustic related responses recorded from the region of the pontine nuclei. *Society for Neuroscience Abstracts, 12*, 754.

Mackintosh, N. J. (1975). A theory of attention: variations in the associability of stimuli with reinforcement. *Psychological Review, 82*, 276-298.

Madden, J. I., Haley, D. A., Barchas, J. D., & Thompson, R. F. (1983). Microinfusion of picrotoxin into the caudal red nucleus selectively abolishes the classically conditoned nictitating membrane/eyelid response in the rabbit. *Society for Neuroscience Abstracts, 9*, 830.

Mamounas, L. A., Thompson, R. F., Lynch, G., & Baudry, M. (1984). Classical conditioning of the rabbit eyelid respone increases glutamate receptor binding in hippocampal synaptic membranes. *PNAS, 81*, 2548-2552.

Marr, D. (1969). A theory of cerebellar cortex. *Journal of Physiology, 202*, 437-470.

Mauk, M. D. Steinmetz, J. E., & Thompson, R. F. (1984). Classical conditioning using stimulation of the inferior olive as the unconditioned stimulus. *Proceedings of the National Academy of Sciences, USA 83*, 5349-5353.

Mauk. M. D., & Thompson, R. F. (1987). Retention of classically conditoned eyelid responses following acute decerebration. *Brain Research, 403*, 89-95.

McCormick, D. A., Lavond, D. G. Clark, G. A., Kettner, R. E., Rising, C. E., & Thompson, R. F. (1981). The engram found? Role of the cerebellum in classical conditioning of nictitating membrane and eyelid responses. *Bulletin of the Psychonomic Society, 18*(39), 103-105.

McCormick, D. A., Clark, G. A., Lavond, D. G., & Thompson, R. F. (1982a). Initial localization of the memory trace for a basic form of learning. *PNAS, 79*, 2731-2742.

McCormick, D. A., Guyer, P. E., & Thompson R. F. (1982b). Superior cerebellar peduncle lesions selectively abolish the ipsilateral classically conditioned nictitating membrane/eyelid response in the rabbit. *Brain Research, 244*, 347-350.

McCormick, D. A., & Thompson, R. F. (1984). Cerebellum: Essential involvement in the classically conditioned eyelid respone. *Science, 233*, 296-299.

McCormick, D. A., & Thompson, R. F. (1984). Neoronal responses of the rabbit cerebellum during acquisition and performance of a classically conditioned nictitating membrane-eyelid response. *Journal of Neuroscience, 4*, 2811-2822.

McCormick, D. A. Steinmetz, J. E., & Thompson, R. F. (1985). Lesions of the inferior olivary complex cause extinction of the classically conditioned eyeblink response. *Brain Research, 359*, 120-130.

Norman, R. J., Buchwald, J. S., & Villablanca, J. R. (1977).

Classical conditioning with auditory discrimination of the eyeblink decerebrate cats. *Science, 196,* 551-553.
Oakley, D. A., & Russel, I. S. (1972). Neocortical lesions and classical conditioning. *Physiology and Behavior, 8,* 915-926.
Pearce, J. M., & Hall, G. (1980). A model for Paulovian learning: variations in the effectiveness of conditioned but not unconditioned stimuli. *Psychological Review, 87,* 532-552.
Polenchar, B. E., Patterson, M. M., Lavond, D. G., & Thompson, R. F. (1985). Cerebellar lesions abolish an avoidance response in rabbit. *Behavioral and Neural Biology. 44,* 221-227.
Rescorla, R. A., & Wagner, A. R. (1972). A theory of Pavlovian conditioning: Variations in the effectiveness of reinforcement and non-reinforcement. In A. H. Black & W. F. Prokasy (Eds.). *Classical conditioning II: Current research and theory,* pp. 64-99. New York: Appleton-Century-Crofts.
Rosenfield, M. E., Devydaitis, A., & Moore, J. W. (1985). Brachium conjunctivum and rubrobulbar tract: brainstem projections of red nucleus essential for the conditioned nictitating membrane respone. *Physiology and Behavior, 34,* 751-759.
Schull, J. (1979). A conditioned opponent theory of Paulovian conditioning and habituation. In G. H. Bower (Ed.) *The psychology of learning and motivation, 13.* New York: Academic Press.
Seyfarth, R. M., Cheney, D. L., & Marler, P. (1980). Monkey responses to three different alarm calls: evidence of predator classification and semantic communication. *Science, 210,* 801-803.
Solomon, P. R. Lewis, J. L., LoTurco, J. J. Steinmetz, J. E., & Thompson, R. F. (1986). The role of the middle cerebellar peduncle in acquisition and retention of the rabbits classically conditoned nictitating membrane response. *Bulletin of the Psychonomic Society, 24*(1), 75-78.
Steinmetz, J. E., Lavond, D. G., & Thompson, R. F. (1985a). Classical conditioning of the rabbit eyelid response with mossy fiber stimulation as the conditioned stimulus. *Bulletin of the Psychonomic Society, 23*(3), 245-248.
Steinmetz, J. E., Lavond, D. G., & Thompson, R. F. (1985b). Classical conditioning of skeletal muscle responses with mossy fiber stimulation CS and climbing fiber stimulation US. *Society for Neuroscience Abstracts, 11,* 982.
Steinmetz, J. E., Rosen, D. L., Chapman, P. F., Lavond, D. G., & Thompson, R. F. (1986a). Classical conditioning of the rabbit eyelid response with a mossy fiber stimulation CS. I Pontine nuclei and middle cerebellar peduncle stimulation. *Behavioral Neuroscience, 100,* 871-880.
Steinmetz, J. E., Rosen, D. J., Woodruff-Pak., D.S., Lavond, D. G., & Thompson, R. F. (1986b). Rapid transfer of training occurs when direct mossy fiber stimulation is used as a conditioned stimulus for classical eyelid conditioning. *Neuroscience Research, 3,* 606-616.
Steinmetz, J. E., Logan, C. G., Rosen, D. J., Thompson, J. K., Lavond, D. G,. & Thompson, R. F. (1987). Initial localication of

acoustic conditioned stimulus projection system to the cerebellum essential for classical eyelid conditioning. *Proceedings of the National Academy of Sciences, 84,* 3531-3535.

Sutton, R. S., & Barto, A. G. (1981). Toward a modern theory of adaptive networks. *Psychological Review, 88,* 135-170.

Thompson, R. F., Berger, T. W., & Madden, J. IV. (1983). Cellular processes of learning and memory in the mammalian CNS. *Annual Review of Neuroscience, 6,* 447-491.

Thompson, R. F., Clark, G. A., Donegan, N. H., Lavond, D. G., Madden, J. I., Mamounas, L. A., Mauk, M. D., & McCormick. D. A. (1984). Neuronal substrates of basic associative learning. In L. Squire & N. Butters (Eds.), *Neuropsychology of memory,* pp. 424-442. New York: Guilford Press.

Thompson, R. F. (1986). The neurobiology of learning and memory. *Science, 233,* 941-947.

Thompson, J. K., Lavond, D. G., & Thompson, R. F. (1986). Preliminary evidence for a projection from the cochlear nucleus to the pontine nuclear region. *Society for Neuroscience Abstracts, 12,* 754.

Wagner, A. R. (1981). SOP: a model of automatic memory processing in animal behavior. In N. E. Spears and R. R. Miller (Eds.), *Information processing in animals: Memory mechanisms,* pp. 5-48. Hillsdale, NJ: Lawrence Erlbaum Associates.

Weisz, D. J., Clark, G. A., & Thompson, R. F. (1984). Increased activity of dentate granule cells during nictitating membrane response conditioning in rabbits. *Behavioral Brain Research. 12,*145-154.

Yeo, C. H., Hardiman M. J., & Glickstein, M. (1984). Discrete lesions of the cerebel,lar cortex abolish the classically conditioned nictitating membrane response of the rabbit. *Behavioral Brain Research, 13,* 261-266.

10

The Role of Serotonin and Dopamine in Learning to Avoid Aversive Stimuli

Richard J. Beninger
Queen's University

INTRODUCTION

In psychopharmacological research concerned with the possible role played by various neurotransmitter systems in learning, the use of aversive stimuli is extensive. Some researchers may be interested in this class of stimuli per se, they may for example be interested in neurotransmitter systems mediating nociception, but many researchers employ aversive stimuli in learning experiments for convenience. Aversive stimuli such as electrical footshock are easy to deliver in discrete episodes and can easily be quantified. Furthermore, they have unconditioned effects that are less influenced by the animals' state by comparison to many appetitive stimuli such as food, for example, that is most effective in appropriately deprived animals. The effects of aversive stimuli on learning are also relatively free of satiation effects unlike those of food which weaken as the animal eats more.

Operant learning tasks involving the acquisition of responses to escape or avoid electrical footshock are frequently employed. One way to classify these tasks is as passive or active avoidance. Passive avoidance tasks usually involve a learning phase in which particular environmental stimuli are associated with an unconditioned aversive stimulus such as footshock. Testing is done in the absence of shock and the animals' latency to approach the shock-associated stimuli is taken as an index of the strength of original learning. Variations of this task have been employed in an extensive number of studies concerned with the possible role played by neurotransmitter systems in learning and/or memory. A typical approach is to present animals with pairings of environmental stimuli and shock followed by administration of centrally active pharmacological compounds.

The effects of these treatments are assessed in test trials at a later time (cf., McGaugh, Liang, Bennett and Sternberg, 1984). Although studies employing passive avoidance procedures have provided valuable information concerning the involvement of various neurotransmitters in memory (McGaugh, this volume), they will not be discussed here. The present chapter will focus on active avoidance procedures which provide an explicit reward (offset of unconditioned or conditioned aversive stimuli) for an explicit operant response, usually running to a particular place.

Active avoidance tasks can be subdivided into one-way and two-way. Both types of tasks typically involve the use of a long narrow box. In one-way active avoidance, the animal is placed into one side of the box and after a delay (e.g., 10 sec) receives electrical footshock. The shock can be escaped by running to the other (safe) side of the box. The animal is then removed from the safe side and after an intertrial interval, placed again into the side associated with shock and shock again is delivered at the end of the delay period. The latency to make the running response can be taken as an index of learning. Running responses that occur after the delay period when shock has been turned on are termed escape responses; those that eventually occur before shock onset are termed avoidance responses. Running latencies typically show a learning curve, getting shorter from trial to trial as responses shift from escape to avoidance. Theoretically, animals are learning the association between stimuli identifying the shock side of the box and shock itself and the association between stimuli identifying the safe side of the box and safety itself. Reward would be occurring at the time of offset of shock or shock-associated stimuli.

Two-way avoidance training is similar to one-way with one important distinction. After the first trial the animal is not removed from the apparatus. Instead, the animal remains in the original safe side and after a delay a signal (e.g., tone) indicates that shock will occur there. The required response now is to run to the original shock side. This task, although convenient for experimenters because it can be automated and therefore does not require the continuous presence of the experimenter as in one-way avoidance, is difficult for rats to learn because it requires their returning to a place where they previously received shock (cf., Bolles, 1970). In addition, pharmacological treatments that lead to increased locomotor activity (e.g., scopolamine, Bauer, 1982) generally lead to improved performance of two-way avoidance. This may not reflect improved learning, however, as increased activity may simply lead to the occurrence of more shuttle responses. For these reasons, two-way avoidance will not be considered further here.

This chapter will focus on the role of the neurotransmitters serotonin and dopamine in one-way avoidance learning. It will be argued that serotonin may play a role in the modulation of perceptual input and possibly in the modulation of the strength of synapses mediating the learning of associations between stimuli. It will be suggested that the reported effects of dopamine receptor blockers make it possible to identify some of the elements of learning in avoidance tasks and to better understand the effects of reward on learning.

SEROTONIN AND ONE-WAY AVOIDANCE LEARNING

The brain and spinal cord are extensively innervated by serotonergic fibers originating in raphe nuclei of the brainstem (for detailed anatomy see Steinbusch and Nieuwenhuys, 1983). There has been considerable interest in the contribution of these systems to learning (for a review see Ögren, 1982a). Many data suggest that increases in serotonergic neurotransmission lead to impairments in the acquisition and retention of one-way avoidance responding whereas decreases lead to enhanced acquisition.

Perhaps the most thorough psychopharmacological study of the role of serotonin in avoidance behaviour has been carried out by Ögren and his colleagues. Employing acute systemic treatments with p-chloroamphetamine (PCA), a compound that increases the presynaptic release of serotonin, these investigators found that one-way avoidance acquisition and retention was impaired in a dose-dependent manner (Ögren, 1986). This effect was likely due to the effects of PCA on the brain. Thus, animals receiving intrathecal injections of the neurotoxin 5,6-dihydroxytryptamine, that significantly reduced the number of serotonergic synapses in the spinal cord, while showing no change in avoidance acquisition following saline injections, were still seen to be impaired when injected with PCA (Ögren, Berge and Johansson, 1985).

The PCA disruption of avoidance learning seemed to be specific to its action at serotonergic synapses in the brain. Thus, the effect of PCA was blocked by zimeldine or fluoxetine, drugs that prevent serotonin uptake but also inhibit the ability of PCA to stimulate the release of serotonin (Ögren, 1982b; Ögren and Johansson, 1985; Ögren, Johansson, Johansson and Archer, 1982). Furthermore, pretreatment with a large dose of PCA, known to be toxic to serotonergic terminals, blocked the acute effects of PCA on avoidance acquisition (Ögren, 1982b; Ögren and Johansson, 1985; Ögren, et al. 1982). The tryptophan hydroxylase inhibitor parachlorophenylalanine (PCPA) or the serotonin receptor blocker methergoline also blocked the effects of PCA on avoidance learning (Ögren, 1982b, 1985; Ögren and Johansson, 1985). On the other hand, the norepinephrine uptake blocker desipramine failed to mitigate the effects of PCA on avoidance (Ögren, 1982b; Ögren et al. 1982), nor did treatments with the selective norepinephrine neurotoxin DSP4 (Ögren, 1985; Ögren and Johansson, 1985; Ögren et al. 1982). Tyrosine hydroxylase inhibition also failed to influence the effects of PCA on avoidance, nor did the opiate receptor blocker naloxone have any effect (Ögren, 1985; Ögren and Johansson, 1985). Further studies showed that the effect of PCA was related to an increase in serotonin release but not to changes in catecholamine content (Ögren, 1985). Behavioural studies showed that the effect of PCA on avoidance was independent of changes in nociception or locomotor activity (Ögren and Johansson, 1985).

The effect of PCA on avoidance may be due at least in part to its action on serotonergic synapses in the hippocampus and frontal cortex. Intraforebrain injections of 5,7-dihydroxytryptamine produced decreases in prefrontal cortex and hippocampal, but not striatal, serotonin and attenuated the effect of PCA on avoidance learning (Ögren, Johansson and Magnusson, 1985). These excellent and thorough studies of Ögren and his coworkers argue strongly for a role for the brain's serotonergic systems in avoidance learning.

The results of a number of previous studies from other laboratories support those of Ögren and his colleagues. Thus, whereas PCA-induced increases in serotonin release led to deficits in avoidance learning, PCPA-induced decreases in serotonergic neurotransmission led to enhanced acquisition of one-way avoidance responding (Brody, 1970; Schlesinger, Schreiber and Pryor, 1968; Tenen, 1967). Tenen (1967) also found that PCPA-treated rats had increased sensitivity to nociceptive stimuli and hypothesized that this may have led to increased rates of avoidance learning. To examine this possibility, Tenen (1967) conducted further avoidance tests using a higher shock intensity that was highly aversive to both groups. In this study control and PCPA-treated rats did not differ significantly.

Investigators using forebrain serotonin-depleting electrolytic lesions of the dorsal raphe and/or central superior nucleus have found an impairment in one-way avoidance learning (Lorens, Guldberg, Hole, Kohler and Srebro, 1976; Srebro and Lorens, 1975) although one report of increased acquisition has appeared (Plaznik, Kostowski, Bidzinski and Hauptmann, 1980). If these lesions had a selective effect on serotonergic neurons, they would be expected to lead to an enhancement of avoidance learning like that seen following PCPA. Unfortunately, electrolytic lesions are relatively nondiscriminating and would lead to damage to nonserotonergic cells and fibers as well as serotonergic ones. An alternative approach would be to use the selective neurotoxin 5,7-dihydroxytryptamine to place a lesion in the serotonergic cell bodies. When this approach was used, no effect on avoidance learning was seen in spite of substantial depletions of forebrain serotonin (Hole, Fuxe and Jonsson, 1976; Lorens et al. 1976). One possibility suggested by Lorens et al. (1976) is that a compensatory change in brainstem monoamine metabolism may have masked possible effects of the neurotoxic lesion on avoidance learning.

In summary, it appears that increases in forebrain serotonergic neurotransmission lead to deficits in avoidance learning whereas decreases may enhance learning. It may be possible to interpret these results in the context of the hypothesis that serotonin is involved in learning to decrease responding to nonrewarded or irrelevant stimuli. This "tuning-out" hypothesis is supported by the results of a number of studies. Thus, it was found that animals treated with the serotonin synthesis inhibitor PCPA failed to show latent inhibition. This paradigm involves preexposure to a stimulus that subsequently is used as a conditioned stimulus. Animals nondrugged during preexposures in comparison to rats without preexposures showed impaired acquisition during conditioning trials possibly because during preexposure they learned to ignore or tune out the apparently irrelevant stimulus. When serotonergic neurotransmission was blocked during preexposure, this putative tuning out process may have failed to occur and subsequent conditioning was seen to be similar to that without preexposure. One interpretation is that serotonin normally is involved in the tuning out process (Solomon, Kiney and Scott, 1978). Further support for this hypothesis is provided by the observation that animals treated with PCPA during extinction of a food-rewarded operant response or a punished stepdown response showed slower rates of extinction. Possibly, during extinction animals must learn to tune out stimuli that previously signalled reward (Beninger and Phillips, 1978). Also consistent with this hypothesis is the finding that PCPA treatment retarded the rate of habituation (Carlton and Advokat, 1973; Connor, Stolk, Barchas and Levine, 1970) and led to an increased reactivity to novel stimuli (Connor et al. 1970).

The tuning out hypothesis also provides a useful framework for interpreting the results of a series of studies by Archer and his colleagues. These investigators employed a conditioning procedure involving the delivery of inescapable shock in one compartment of a two-compartment chamber. During retention tests the strength of original conditioning was assessed by measuring the activity level of the animal, presumably longer durations of immobility indicating stronger conditioning. Results showed that rats treated with a low dose of PCA during conditioning showed less immobility than untreated controls during retention tests (Archer, 1982; Archer, Ögren and Johansson, 1981; Archer, Ögren and Ross, 1982). The authors argued that their results could not be attributed to state dependent learning. A number of pharmacological manipulations confirmed that the PCA effect was probably a consequence of elevated release of serotonin. Thus, the effects of PCA were blocked by zimeldine and fluoxetine but not desipramine, pretreatment with a large dose of PCA but not DSP4 blocked the PCA effect and methergoline but not the dopamine receptor blocker pimozide blocked the PCA effect (Archer, 1982; Archer et al. 1981, 1982). According to the tuning out hypothesis, during conditioning trials elevated levels of serotonin produced by PCA may have led the rats to ignore or tune out environmental stimuli associated with shock. When subsequently exposed to those stimuli in retention tests, the rats may have failed to remain immobile because they had failed to learn the association of those stimuli with shock.

The effects of manipulations of central serotonergic neurotransmission on one-way avoidance learning may also be interpreted by the tuning out hypothesis. Animals undergoing avoidance training while levels of serotonergic neurotransmission are elevated may show impaired acquisition because excessive tuning out of environmental stimuli leads to poorer learning of the association between stimuli associated with shock and shock itself and between stimuli associated with safety and safety itself. This poorer learning is also reflected in retention tests conducted a day later when the animals are no longer drugged. Conversely, animals undergoing avoidance training while levels of serotonergic neurotransmission are decreased may show enhanced rates of acquisition because of more effective learning of associations. The mechanism by which serotonin influences the formation of associations between stimuli remains to be worked out. These results, however, suggest that serotonin may be involved in the modulation of perceptual input and possibly in the modulation of the strength of synapses mediating the learning of associations between stimuli.

DOPAMINE AND ONE-WAY AVOIDANCE LEARNING

The brain's dopaminergic systems, originating in nuclei of the ventral midbrain have been mapped in detail (see Lindvall and Bjorklund, 1983). There has been much interest in the possible behavioural function of these systems including, for example, their role in the control of locomotor activity (Costall and Naylor, 1979; Ungerstedt, 1979), hedonic processes (Wise, 1982), learning (Beninger. 1983, 1987) and eating and drinking (White, 1986). Many data suggest that manipulations that decrease central dopaminergic neurotransmission impair the acquisition of one-way avoidance learning. Given that dopamine may participate in a number of different behavioural functions, interpretation of the effects of decreased dopaminergic transmission in behavioural situations must be made with caution. It will be argued here that dopamine, unlike serotonin, is not involved in the learning of associations between environmental stimuli in avoidance tasks. Rather, dopamine may be involved in mediating the learning that results from the presentation of reward.

When experimentally naive animals were given treatments that decreased neurotransmission at central dopaminergic synapses and then underwent one-way avoidance training, they were seen to be impaired in acquisition and often never made any avoidance responses. This was observed following treatments with dopamine receptor blockers including chlorpromazine (Posluns, 1962), haloperidol (Fibiger, Zis and Phillips, 1975), pimozide (Anisman, Corradini, Tombaugh and Zacharko, 1982a; Anisman, Irwin, Zacharko and Tombaugh, 1982b; Beninger, Mason, Phillips and Fibiger. 1980a,b; Beninger, Phillips and Fibiger, 1983) and cis-flupenthixol (Koob, Simon, Herman and LeMoal, 1984). Similar results were reported following bilateral destruction of dopaminergic systems with the neurotoxin, 6-hydroxydopamine (6-OHDA). Sites of injection included the substantia nigra or the nigrostriatal bundle (Zis, Fibiger and Phillips, 1974). It is noteworthy that the deficit seen following bilateral destruction of the dopaminergic nigrostriatal bundle was reversed by treatment with the dopamine precursor 3,4-dihydroxy-L-phenylalanine suggesting that the effect was due to destruction of dopaminergic neurons (Zis et al. 1974). Using small injections of 6-OHDA into dopamine terminal regions Koob et al. (1984) found that combined lesions of the caudate nucleus and nucleus accumbens but not lesions of either alone nor lesions of dopaminergic terminals in the frontal cortex impaired acquisition of one-way avoidance.

When animals were pretrained in a one-way avoidance paradigm and then tested while treated with a drug that disrupted dopaminergic neurotransmission, responding was also seen to be impaired. This was reported following treatments with chlorpromazine (Posluns, 1962) and pimozide (Beninger et al. 1983). However, responding did not cease immediately but showed a gradual decline with repeated testing, as illustrated in figure 10.1. Two groups (n = 48) of rats were pretrained for

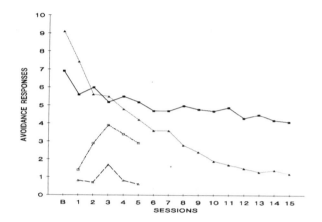

FIG. 10.1. Mean number of avoidance responses per session (10 trials) for groups of rats receiving pretraining or no pretraining prior to testing with pimozide. For the pretrained groups (n = 48) the last training session is shown (B) and 15 sessions where they were treated with doses of 0.5 (■) or 1.0 (▲) mg/kg. The nonpretrained groups (n = 16) received 5 sessions following injections of 0.5 (□) or 1.0 (Δ) mg/kg. (Adapted from Beninger et al., 1983.)

2-10 days on a one-way avoidance task with 10 trials per day. One group then received 0.5 mg/kg and the other 1.0 mg/kg pimozide prior to each of the next 15 sessions. Two additional nonpretrained groups (n = 16) received the same doses of pimozide for 5 sessions. The results showed that the high dose of pimozide blocked the acquisition of avoidance responding in the nonpretrained groups. Pimozide also impaired the avoidance responding of the pretrained animals. gradually reducing performance over 15 sessions to a level near that seen in the nonpretrained group (Beninger et al. 1983). What is particularly noteworthy, however, is the initial large difference in the level of performance of the pretrained and nonpretrained animals when given pimozide. Clearly it is inadequate to argue that the disruptive effects of dopamine receptor blockade on the acquisition of avoidance responding in nonpretrained animals was due to an effect of the drug on the animals' ability to initiate avoidance responses. The initial high level of performance observed in pretrained animals given pimozide argues against this position. These results suggest that intact dopaminergic neurotransmission is required for the acquisition of avoidance responding. Once animals have been trained, they can for some trials perform the avoidance response when dopamine receptors are blocked but with continued testing in the presence of the drug, the ability to avoid gradually is lost.

If the deficits in avoidance responding following treatments that disrupt dopaminergic neurotransmission cannot be attributed to impairments in the animals' ability to initiate responses, to what can they be attributed? One possibility is that the learning of an association between preshock stimuli and shock itself or between safety related stimuli and safety itself requires dopamine for its initial establishment and for its maintenance once that learning is established. However, research has shown this hypothesis to be incorrect. The results of a number of studies showed that animals with impaired dopaminergic neurotransmission were unimpaired in their ability to form associations between stimuli.

Some of the earliest reports were anecdotal. For example, Fibiger et al. (1975) observed that haloperidol disrupted the acquisition of avoidance responding but noted that when in the presence of stimuli that regularly preceded shock (conditioned stimuli; CSs), the drugged animals "...urinated, defecated and showed other signs typically associated with fear in this species, suggesting that these animals were aware of the significance of the CS" (p. 313). In a subsequent study Beninger et al. (1980b) took advantage of the conditioned suppression paradigm to systematically test the hypothesis that animals treated with dopamine receptor blockers, although failing to avoid, learn the association between preshock stimuli and shock. Conditioned suppression was first reported by Estes and Skinner (1941). They trained rats to lever press for food and then presented them with a CS followed by footshock. During subsequent presentation of the CS, responding was observed to be suppressed indicating that the rats had learned the association between the CS and shock. Beninger et al. (1980b) similarly trained rats to lever press for food. They then subjected them to five sessions of one-way avoidance training in which a 10-sec tone was used to signal shock in the shock side of the test chamber. Prior to each of these sessions groups received saline, 0.5 or 1.0 mg/kg pimozide. As already discussed (see figure 10.1), the pimozide-treated animals failed to acquire the avoidance response. All groups were then replaced into the lever press apparatus when drug-free and tested for their response to the tone. Conditioned suppression was observed in the saline and pimozide groups but not in rats never receiving tone-shock pairings. Thus, the animals had learned the association between the preshock stimuli and shock while under the influence of pimozide even though avoidance responding was not observed.

In one of the studies by Archer (1982) discussed in the serotonin section, one of his control groups received the high dose of 2.2 mg/kg of pimozide prior to pairings of environmental stimuli with footshock. When tested for immobility in the presence of the shock-associated stimuli while undrugged on the following day, this group evidenced a level of conditioning comparable to saline-treated controls. This result is in good agreement with the findings of Beninger et al. (1980b). Anisman et al. (1982b) injected animals with vehicle or pimozide and then presented zero or ten pairings of light plus tone with shock. Several days later when tested undrugged for avoidance acquisition with the light plus tone stimulus signalling shock, animals previously receiving vehicle injections and ten pairings acquired the avoidance response significantly faster than those receiving zero pairings. The same effect was observed in animals receiving pairings while under the influence of pimozide. This result, along with those of Beninger et al. (1980b) and Archer (1982) provides strong support for the conclusion that blockade of dopaminergic neurotransmission does not impair an animal's ability to learn the association between environmental cues that signal shock and shock itself.

Data also suggest that animals undergoing avoidance training while under the influence of dopamine receptor blockers learn the association between environmental stimuli signalling safety and safety itself, i.e., they learn the location of safety. This was shown in the study of Beninger et al. (1980b) when mean escape or avoidance latencies of pimozide-treated rats were examined from trial to trial in the first test session. As shown in figure 10.2, mean escape latencies were seen to decline across trials for

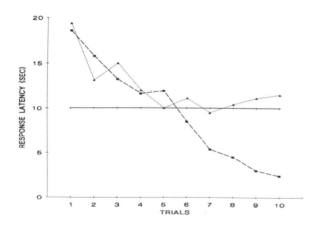

FIG. 10.2. Mean latency (sec) to escape (> 10 sec) or avoid (< 10 sec) for groups of 8 rats receiving 10 trials of one-way avoidance training. Groups were pretreated with vehicle (■) or 1.0 mg/kg (▲) pimozide. (Adapted from Beninger et al., 1980a.)

both the saline-treated group and the drug group. However, whereas the mean latencies of the control group continued to decrease to values of less than 10 sec, indicating avoidance responses, the pimozide group failed to acquire the avoidance response. The declining curve in the pimozide-treated group over the first five trials suggests that they were learning the location of safety from trial to trial in a manner similar to the control group. Anisman et al. (1982a) tested this possibility directly by requiring pimozide-treated mice to perform a discriminated avoidance response. In a Y-maze, shock escape or avoidance could only be made by entering the appropriate arm of the maze as indicated by visual or positional cues. They found that although pimozide impaired acquisition of the avoidance response, it had no significant effect on the animals' ability to select the appropriate arm. Thus, the association of cues signalling safety and safety itself was learned in animals treated with a dopamine receptor blocker.

These results illustrate another interesting aspect of the effects of treatments that reduce dopaminergic neurotransmission on behaviour. Although pimozide-treated animals failed to acquire the avoidance response, they readily escaped when shock was presented. Apparently intense or nociceptive stimulation like that provided by unconditioned aversive stimuli such as electrical shock can induce running responses in pimozide-treated rats even though the presentation of conditioned aversive stimuli such as environmental cues signalling shock cannot. Some researchers have taken advantage of this fact in studying the possible role of dopamine in learning. Price and Fibiger (1975) found that bilateral 6-OHDA lesions of the substantia nigra failed to affect learning of a brightness discrimination in an electrified Y-maze. Corradini, Tombaugh and Anisman (1984) reported that pimozide, although slowing escape times, failed to affect the learning of a place or cue discrimination in a T-maze partially submerged in water requiring the mice to swim to safety. These findings are consistent with the view that disruption of dopaminergic function does not impair the ability of animals to learn associations between stimuli.

Following is a list of points that summarizes the results of studies of the effects of disrupting dopaminergic neurotransmission on avoidance learning:

1) Unconditioned aversive stimuli (e.g., electrical footshock) retain their ability to elicit escape behaviour.

2) The learning of associations between environmental stimuli signalling unconditioned aversive stimuli and those unconditioned aversive stimuli themselves is intact.

3) The learning of associations between environmental stimuli signalling safety and safety itself (i.e., the location of safety) is intact.

4) The ability of pretrained animals to perform the avoidance response is initially intact but becomes lost with repeated testing.

5) The nonpretrained animal has an impaired ability to learn the avoidance response.

The nonpretrained animal with dopaminergic function reduced can learn that shock is imminent and can learn the location of safety in an avoidance task but apparently cannot learn to move to safety prior to shock onset. The use of the term "learn" with respect to the avoidance response is important. It is not simply the case that disrupted dopaminergic function leads to an inability to perform the avoidance response because pretrained animals given dopamine receptor blockers are observed to perform the avoidance response. This learned response is lost, however, with repeated testing while under the influence of dopamine receptor blockade. It can be concluded that dopamine is involved in learning and maintaining the ability to avoid unconditioned aversive stimuli.

DOPAMINE AND INCENTIVE MOTIVATIONAL LEARNING

The type of learning that dopamine appears to mediate in one-way avoidance tasks can be understood in the context of incentive motivational learning theory (Beninger, 1983, 1987; Bindra, 1974). This type of learning is said to take place when reward is presented. In avoidance tasks reward occurs at the time of shock offset. According to incentive motivational learning theory, environmental stimuli that are presented in close temporal contiguity with reward become associated with reward and through this association those stimuli acquire the motivational properties of the reward itself; reward has the unconditioned ability to attract the animal. As a consequence, environmental stimuli associated with reward become conditioned incentive motivational stimuli, having acquired an enhanced ability to attract the animal. In one-way avoidance tasks, the stimuli that are most closely associated with reward (shock offset) are the safety related stimuli, i.e., the side of the chamber where shock never occurs. Thus, the safety related stimuli would be the ones that become conditioned incentive motivational stimuli.

Studies of the effects of disrupted dopaminergic neurotransmission on avoidance learning have revealed important details concerning the components of incentive learning in which dopamine may be involved (figure 10.3). Thus, in the absence of intact dopaminergic function, animals apparently can learn the association between reward (shock offset) and safety related stimuli. However, without intact dopaminergic neurotransmission, the incentive motivational properties of the reward may not be transferred to the safety related stimuli. Ironically, therefore, animals can learn where safety is but cannot learn to go there when dopaminergic neurotransmission is blocked. The studies of the effects of dopamine receptor blockers on avoidance learning further reveal that if animals are pretrained before drug testing, their ability to perform the avoidance response initially is intact and is only seen to diminish with repeated testing. This would suggest that the incentive motivational learning that may be mediated by dopamine involves a change in a nondopaminergic system in the brain. This putative dopamine-mediated change apparently can influence avoidance responding at least transiently even when dopaminergic neurotransmission is blocked. Again it seems ironic that a pretrained animal, when given dopamine receptor blockers initially can avoid but then loses this ability gradually even though the animal retains previous learning concerning the imminence of shock in the shock side of the chamber and the location of safety.

The profile of effects of disrupted dopaminergic neurotransmission on incentive motivational learning in avoidance tasks is in excellent agreement

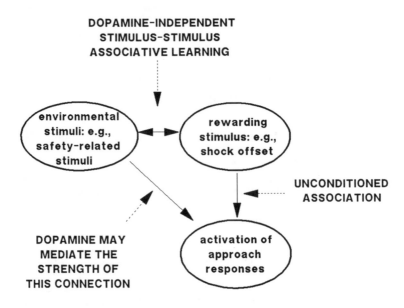

FIG. 10.3. Summary of some of the elements of learning an avoidance response and the possible role of dopamine in each.

with the results of parallel studies of appetitive tasks (cf., Beninger, 1983, 1987). For example, the acquisition of lever pressing for food was impaired by dopamine receptor blockade (Tombaugh, Tombaugh and Anisman, 1979; Wise and Schwartz, 1981) but if animals were trained first and then tested while drugged, responding initially was little affected but was seen to decline gradually within or across sessions (e.g., Wise, Spindler, deWit and Gerber, 1978).

Another form of learning that can be understood within the context of incentive motivational learning theory is stimulant-produced environment-specific conditioned activity. In this paradigm, animals are repeatedly given injections of a drug that enhances dopaminergic neurotransmission in a specific environment and are then tested in the same environment following a vehicle injection. Results showed that the activity level of animals previously receiving the drug in the test environment was significantly higher than that of control animals having a similar drug history and similar number of exposures to the test environment but not having the two associated. As increased dopaminergic neurotransmission is thought to occur when reward is presented, leading to incentive motivational learning, this effect can be understood as an incentive conditioning phenomenon, the stimuli in the test environment acquiring enhanced ability to activate approach responses by association with drug-induced increased dopaminergic neurotransmission. In agreement with the avoidance experiments, studies have shown that pimozide blocked the acquisition of environment-specific conditioned acitivty based on amphetamine or cocaine but once conditioning had occurred, pimozide failed to block the expression of conditioned activity (Beninger and Hahn, 1983; Beninger and Herz, 1986). The results of these and numerous related studies suggest that dopamine may be involved in incentive motivational learning occurring in a wide variety of tasks.

It remains the task of future research to identify the mechanism by which dopamine produces changes in the ability of environmental stimuli to elicit approach responses. The work of Koob et al. (1984) showed that the observation of impaired acquisition of avoidance learning required destruction of the dopaminergic innervation of the caudate nucleus and nucleus accumbens suggesting that dopamine in these regions may mediate incentive learning. These dorsal and ventral striatal regions receive extensive neocortical and allocortical projections and their outputs project to globus pallidus and zona reticulata of the substantia nigra (Nauta and Domesick, 1984), nuclei that project in turn to the mesencephalic locomotor region (Garcia-Rill, 1986). This anatomical organization places the striatal dopaminergic terminals in the right place to modulate the ability of environmental stimuli to influence approach responses via striatal efferents. Environmental stimuli would activate corticostriatal projections. Many authors have emphasized the apparent role of the striatum in gating the influence that sensory input may have on motor output. Evarts and Wise (1984), for example, suggested that the striatum may play a higher order role in motor control than simply controlling movements. They saw the striatum as an interface between motor areas and cortical areas involved in higher brain function. Similarly, Schneider and his colleagues saw the striatum as affecting motor behaviour by gating sensory input to systems controlling movement (Lidsky, Manetto and Schneider, 1985; Schneider, 1984).

Electrophysiological studies have shown that the responses of some cells in the striatum of monkeys were unrelated to movement alone. Instead, these cells were seen to be activated by an auditory stimulus when that stimulus was a cue for food delivery (a conditioned incentive motivational stimulus) but not when that stimulus failed to predict reward (see Evarts and Wise, 1984). Mogenson (1984) and his coworkers showed that the responses of output cells of the nucleus accumbens to stimulation of inputs were modulated by stimulation of dopaminergic afferents to the accumbens. These results provide further support for the suggestion that the striatum may be actively involved in controlling the influence that sensory stimuli have on response systems. The results of Mogenson (1984) further support the suggestion that dopamine in the striatum may subserve this control.

In summary, the effects of reward on behaviour are to mediate a change in environmental stimuli that predict reward leading to an enhanced ability of those stimuli to elicit approach responses, i.e., those stimuli become conditioned incentive motivational stimuli. When reward is removed, conditioned incentive stimuli retain their ability to elicit approach responses transiently but this ability is lost with repeated exposure to those stimuli in the absence of reward. Dopamine in the dorsal and ventral striatum appears to mediate the effects of reward on behaviour. In light of the anatomical organization of the striatum and the apparent function of dopamine in gating the influence of sensory stimuli on motor systems, it might be the case that dopamine modulates the effectiveness of synapses in the striatum where the presynaptic terminals are activated as a result of sensory events and the postsynaptic cells influence response systems.

There is evidence from electrophysiological studies of peripheral nervous system structures that dopamine can modulate synaptic effectiveness leading to an increased influence of presynaptic terminals on postsynaptic cells. The rabbit superior cervical ganglion, which contains cholinergic afferents and dopaminergic interneurons that synapse on the efferent cells, was employed in these studies. Using the sucrose gap method, it was shown that dopamine produced a long-term enhancement of the postsynaptic potential resulting from stimulation of muscarinic cholinergic receptors with exogenous muscarinic agonists (Libet, Kobayashi and Tanaka, 1975; Mochida, Kobayashi and Libet, 1987). It has also been shown that dopamine could similarly modify the response of the postsynaptic cells resulting from orthodromic stimulation of cholinergic afferents to the ganglion (Ashe and Libet, 1981). This modulatory action of dopamine has more recently been shown in the central nervous system. Recording from CA1 pyramidal hippocampal cells in vitro, Gribkoff and Ashe (1984) showed that dopamine produced a long lasting potentiation of the population response resulting from stimulation of the Schaffer-collateral pathway that is afferent to the pyramidal cells. These studies provide strong evidence that dopamine can modulate the effectiveness of nondopaminergic synapses leading to an increased influence of presynaptic terminals on postsynaptic cells.

Although this modulatory action of dopamine has not yet been demonstrated in the striatum, findings in the peripheral nervous system and the hippocampus provide clues to the possible mechanism by which dopamine may produce incentive motivational learning by altering the ability of reward-related stimuli to influence approach responses. It is noteworthy that there are cholinergic interneurons within the dorsal and ventral striatum that have been shown to be influenced by cortical afferents (Simon, 1982). The results of ultrastructural studies suggest that dopaminergic afferents and possibly cholinergic interneurons synapse on medium-size densely spiny neurons that are the major projection neurons of the striatum (Bolam, 1984). Thus, the major elements of the peripheral heterosynaptic mechanism demonstrating a role for dopamine in learning may be found in the central nervous system. These include cells receiving both dopaminergic and cholinergic afferents. Of course, it remains possible that dopamine may influence learning through a different mechanism, involving, for example, the modification of glutaminergic corticostriatal projections. The resolution of the mechanism awaits further study; however, work to date provides intriguing possibilities for the way in which dopamine may mediate the effects of reward on incentive motivational learning.

CONCLUSIONS

This chapter has focused on the possible role of the neurotransmitters serotonin and dopamine in one-way avoidance learning. Results revealed that animals with reduced serotonergic function showed enhanced rates of acquisition whereas animals with elevated levels of synaptic serotonin were impaired in their ability to learn and retain the one-way avoidance task. By integrating these results with others from studies employing various behavioural methodologies it was suggested that serotonin may be involved in tuning out or reducing responsiveness to nonrewarded or irrelevant stimuli. Although the mechanism by which serotonin produces these effects remains unknown, it was concluded that serotonin may be involved in the modulation of perceptual input and possibly in the modulation of the strength of synapses mediating the learning of associations between stimuli.

Research into the possible role of dopamine in avoidance learning has revealed a number of results that lead to a better understanding of the elements of learning in this task. Results showed that decreased dopaminergic function, unlike increased serotonergic function, apparently had little effect on the learning of associations between environmental stimuli signalling shock and shock itself or environmental stimuli signalling safety and safety itself. Instead, blockade of dopaminergic neurotransmission impaired animals' ability to learn to go to safety when presented with conditioned stimuli signalling imminent shock. If a pretrained animal received a dopamine receptor blocker prior to testing, the animal was found to transiently retain avoidance responding but with continued testing while drugged, it gradually lost the avoidance response. It was concluded that dopamine plays a role in reward-related incentive motivation learning involving changes in the ability of reward-related stimuli to elicit approach responses. Possibly this involves a dopamine mediated modification of synapses in the dorsal and ventral striatum where environmental stimuli influence responses systems via corticostriatal projections.

It can be concluded that psychopharmacological studies of aversively motivated behavior have provided valuable insights into the role of the neurotransmitters serotonin and dopamine in learning. The continued integration of the results of these studies with anatomical, physiological and neurochemical results will eventually lead to a more complete knowledge of the mechanisms underlying the manner in which serotonin and dopamine influence learning.

ACKNOWLEDGEMENTS

This chapter is dedicated to John and Lisa Strifler. I would like to thank Diane C. Hoffman and Evalynn J. Mazurski for their helpful comments on the manuscript. The author is supported by a grant from the Ontario Ministry of Health. All correspondence should be sent to the author at the Department of Psychology, Queen's University, Kingston, Ontario, K1L 3N6, Canada.

REFERENCES

Archer, T. (1982). Serotonin and fear retention in the rat. *Journal of Comparative and Physiological Psychology, 96,* 491-516.

Archer, T., Ögren, S.-O., & Johansson, C. (1981). The acute effect of p-chloroamphetamine on the retention of fear conditioning in the rat: Evidence for a role of serotonin in memory consolidation. *Neuroscience Letters, 25,* 75-81.

Archer, T., Ögren, S.-O., & Ross, S. B. (1982). Serotonin involvement in aversive conditioning: Reversal of the fear retention deficit by long-term p-chloroamphetamine but not p-chlorophenylalanine. *Neuroscience Letters, 34,* 75-82.

Anisman, H., Corradini, A., Tombaugh, T. N., & Zacharko, R. M. (1982a). Avoidance performance, cue and response-choice discrimination after neuroleptic treatment. *Pharmacology Biochemistry and Behavior, 17,* 1245-1249.

Anisman, H., Irvin, J., Zacharko, R. M., & Tombaugh, T. N. (1982b). Effects of dopamine receptor blockade on avoidance performance: Assessment of effects on cue-shock and response-outcome associations. *Behavioral and Neural Biology, 36,* 280-290.

Ashe, J. H., & Libet, B. (1981). Modulation of slow postsynaptic potentials by dopamine, in rabbit sympathetic ganglion. *Brain Research, 217,* 93-106.

Bauer, R. H. (1982). Age-dependent effects of scopolamine on avoidance, locomotoractivity, and rearing. *Behavioural Brain Research, 5,* 261-279.

Beninger, R. J. (1983). The role of dopamine in locomotor activity and learning. *Brain Research Reviews, 6,* 173-196.

Beninger, R. J. (1988). Methods for determining the effects of drugs on learning. In A. A. Boulton, G. B. Baker & A. J. Greenshaw (Eds.), *Neuromethods: Psychopharmacology.* Clifton, N.J.: Humana Press.

Beninger, R. J., & Hahn, B. L. (1983). Pimozide blocks establishment but not expression of amphetamine-produced environment-specific conditioning. *Science, 220,* 1304-1306.

Beninger, R. J., & Herz, R. S. (1986). Pimozide blocks establishment but not expression of cocaine-produced environment-specific conditioning. *Life Sciences, 38,* 1425-1431.

Beninger, R. J., Mason, S. T., Phillips, A. G., & Fibiger, H. C. (1980a). The use of extinction to investigate the nature of neuroleptic-induced avoidance deficits. *Psychopharmacology, 69,* 11-18.

Beninger, R. J., Mason, S. T., Phillips, A. G., & Fibiger, H. C.

(1980b). The use of conditioned suppression to evaluate the nature of neuroleptic-induced avoidance deficits. *Journal of Pharmacology and Experimental Therapeutics, 213,* 623-627.

Beninger, R. J., & Phillips, A. G. (1979). Possible involvement of serotonin in extinction. *Pharmacology Biochemistry and Behavior, 10,* 37-41.

Beninger, R. J., Phillips, A. G., & Fibiger, H. C. (1983). Prior training and intermittent retraining attenuate pimozide-induced avoidance deficits. *Pharmacology Biochemistry and Behavior, 18,* 619-624.

Bindra, D. (1974). A motivational view of learning, performance, and behavior modification. *Psychological Review, 81,* 199-213.

Bolam, J. P. (1984). Synapses of identified neurons in the neostriatum. In D. Evered & M. O'Connor (Eds.), *Functions of the basal ganglia,* pp. 30-41. London: Pitman.

Bolles, R. C. (1970). Species-specific defense reactions and avoidance learning. *Psychological Review, 77,* 32-38.

Brody, J. F., Jr. (1970). Behavioral effects of serotonin depletion and of p-chlorophenylalanine (a serotonin depletor) in rats. *Psychopharmacologia.* (Berlin), *17,* 14-33.

Carlton, P. L., & Advokat, C. (1973). Attenuated habituation due to parachlorophenylalnine. *Pharmacology Biochemistry Behavior, 1,* 657-663.

Conner, R. L., Stolk, J. M., Barchas, J. D., & Levine, S. (1970). Parachlorophenylalanine and habituation to repetitive auditory startle stimuli in rats. *Physiology and Behavior,* 1215-1219.

Corradini, A., Tombaugh, T., & Anisman, H. (1984). Effects of pimozide on escape and discrimination performance in a water-escape task. *Behavioral Neuroscience, 1,* 96-106.

Costall, B., & Naylor, R. J. (1979). Behavioural aspects of dopamine agonists and antagonists. In A. S. Horn, J. Korf & B. H. C. Westerink (Eds.), *The neurobiology of dopamine,* pp. 555-576. London: Academic Press.

Estes, W. K., & Skinner, B. F. (1941). Some quantitative properties of anxiety. *Journal of Experimental Psychology, 29,* 390-400.

Evarts, E. V., & Wise, S. P. (1984). Basal ganglia outputs and motor control. In D. Evered & M. O'Connor (Eds.), *Functions of the basal ganglia,* pp. 83-96. London: Pitman.

Fibiger, H. C., Phillips, A. G., & Zis, A. P. (1974). Deficits in instrumental responding after 6-hydroxydopamine lesions of the nigro-neostriatal dopaminergic projection. *Pharmacology Biochemistry and Behavior, 2,* 87-96.

Fibiger, H. C., Zis, A. P., & Phillips, A. G. (1975). Haloperidol-induced disrution of conditioned avoidance responding: Attenuation by prior training or by anticholinergic drugs. *European Journal of Pharmacology, 30,* 309-314.

Garcia-Rill, E. (1986). The basal ganglia and the locomotor regions. *Brain Research Reviews, 11,* 47-63.

Gribkoff, V. K., & Ashe, J. H. (1984). Modulation by dopamine of population responses and cell membrane properties of hippocampal CA1 neurons in vitro. *Brain Research, 292,* 327-338.

Hole, K., Fuxe, K., & Jonsson, G. (1976). Behavioral effects of 5, 7-dihydroxytryptamine lesions of ascending 5-hydroxytryptamine pathways. *Brain Research, 107,* 385-399.

Koob, G. F., Simon, H., Herman, J. P., & Le Moal, M. (1984). Neuroleptic-like disruption of the conditioned avoidance response requires destruction of both the mesolimbic and nigrostriatal dopamine systems. *Brain Research, 303,* 319-329.

Libet, B., Kobayashi, H., & Tanaka, T. (1975). Synaptic coupling into the production and storage of a neuronal memory trace. *Nature, 258,* 155-157.

Lidsky, T. I., Manetto, C., & Schneider, J. S. (1985). A consideration of sensory factors involved in motor functions of the basal ganglia. *Brain Research Reviews, 9,* 133-146.

Lindvall, O., & Björklund, A. (1983). Dopamine- and norepinephrine-containing neuron systems: Their anatomy in the rat brain. In P.C. Emson (Ed.), *Chemical neuroanatomy,* pp. 229-255. New York: Raven Press.

Lorens, S. A., Guldberg, H. C., Hole, K., Kohler, C., & Srebro, B. (1976). Activity, avoidance learning and regional 5-hydroxytryptamine following intrabrain stem 5, 7-dihydroxytryptamine and electrolytic midbrain raphe lesions in the rat. *Brain Research, 108,* 97-113.

McGaugh, J. L., Liang, K. C., Bennett, C., & Sternberg, D. B. (1984). Adrenergic influences on memory storage: Interaction of peripheral and central systems. In G. Lynch, J. L. McGaugh & N. M. Weinberger (Eds.), *Neurobiology of learning and memory,* pp. 229-255. New York: Guilford Press.

Mochida, S., Kobayashi, H., & Libet, B. (1987). Stimulation of adenylate cyclase in relation to dopamine-induced long-term enhancement (LTE) of muscarinic depolarization in the rabbit superior cervical ganglion. *Journal of Neuroscience, 7,* 311-318.

Mogenson, G. J. (1984). Limbic-motor integration - with emphasis on initiation of exploratory and goal-directed locomotion. In R. Bandler (Ed.), *Modulation of sensorimotor activity during alterations in behavioral states,* pp. 121-137. New York: Alan R. Liss.

Nauta, W. J. H., & Domesick, V. B. (1984). Afferent and efferent relationships of the basal ganglia. In D. Evered & M. O'Connor (Eds.), *Functions of the basal ganglia,* pp. 3-23. London: Pitman.

Ögren, S. O. (1982a). Central serotonin neurones and learning in the rat. In N.N. Osborne (Ed.), *Biology of serotonergic transmission,* pp. 317-334. New York: John Wiley & Sons.

Ögren, S. O. (1982b). Forebrain serotonin and avoidance learning: Behavioural and biochemical studies on the acute effect of p-chloroamphetamine on one-way active avoidance learning in the male rat. *Pharmacology Biochemistry and Behavior, 16,* 881-895.

Ögren, S. O. (1985). Central serotonin neurones in avoidance learning: Interactions with noradrenaline and dopamine neurones.

Pharmacology Biochemistry and Behavior, 23, 107-123.

Ögren, S. O. (1986). Analysis of the avoidance learning deficit induced by the serotonin releasing compound p-chloroamphetamine. *Brain Research Bulletin, 16*, 645-660.

Ögren, S. O., Berge, O. G., Johansson, C. (1985). Involvement of spinal serotonergic pathways in nociception but not in avoidance learning. *Psychopharmacology, 87*, 260-265.

Ögren, S. O. & Johansson, C. (1985). Separation of the associative and non-associative effects of brain serotonin released by p-chloroamphetamine: Dissociable serotonergic involvement in avoidance learning, pain and motor function. *Psychopharmacology, 86*, 12-26.

Ögren, S. O., Johansson, C., Johansson, G., & Archer, T. (1982). Serotonin neurons and aversive conditioning in the rat. *Scandinavian Journal of Psychology, Suppl. 1*, 7-15.

Ögren, S. O., Johansson, C., & Magnusson, O. (1985). Forebrain serotonergic involvement in avoidance learning. *Neuroscience Letters, 58*, 305-309.

Plaznik, A., Kostowski, W., Bidzinski, A., & Hauptmann, M. (1980). Effects of lesions of the midbrain raphe nuclei on avoidance learning in rats. *Physiology and Behavior, 24*, 257-262.

Posluns, D. (1962). An analysis of chlorpromazine-induced suppression of the avoidance response. *Psychopharmacologia, 3*, 361-373.

Price, M. T. C., & Fibiger, H. C. (1975). Discriminated escape learning and response to electric shock after 6-hydroxydopamine lesions of the nigro-neostriatal dopaminergic projection. *Pharmacology Biochemistry and Behavior, 3*, 285-290.

Schlesinger, K., Schreiber, R. A., & Pryor, G. T. (1968). Effects of p-chlorophenylalanine on conditioned avoidance learning. *Psychonomic Science. 11*, 225-226.

Schneider, J. S. (1984). Basal ganglia role in behavior: Importance of sensory gating and its relevance to psychiatry. *Biological Psychiatry, 19*, 1693-1710.

Simon, J. R. (1982). Cortical modulation of cholinergic neurons in the striatum. *Life Sciences, 31*, 1501-1508.

Solomon, P. R., Kiney, C. A., & Scott, O. R. (1978). Disruption of latent inhibition following systemic administration of parachlorophenylalanine (PCPA). *Physiology and Behavior, 20*, 265-271.

Srebro, B., & Lorens, S. A. (1975). Behavioral effects of selective midbrain raphe lesions in the rat. *Brain Research. 89*, 303-325.

Steinbusch, H. W. M., & Nieuwenhuys, R. (1983). The raphe nuclei of the rat brainstem: A cytoarchitectonic and immunohistochemical study. In P.C. Emson (Ed.), *Chemical neuroanatomy*, pp. 131-207. New York: Raven Press.

Tenen, S. S. (1967). The effect of p-chlorophenylalanine, a serotonin depletor, on avoidance acquisition, pain sensitivity and related behavior in the rat. *Psychopharmacologia* (Berlin). *10*. 204-219.

Tombaugh, T. N., Tombaugh, J., & Anisman, H. (1979). Effects of dopamine receptor blockade on alimentary behaviors: Home cage food consumption, magazine training, operant acquisition, and performance. *Psychopharmacology, 66.* 219-225.

Ungerstedt, U. (1979). Central dopamine mechanisms and unconditioned behaviour. In A. S. Horn, J. Korf & B. H. C. Westerink (Eds.), *The neurobiology of dopamine,* pp. 577-596. London: Academic Press.

White, N. M. (1986). Control of sensorimotor function by dopaminergic nigrostriatal neurons: Influence on eating and drinking. *Neuroscience and Biobehavioral Reviews, 10,* 15-36.

Wise, R. A. (1982). Neuroleptics and operant behavior: The anhedonia hypothesis. *The Behavioral and Brain Sciences, 5,* 39-88.

Wise, R. A., & Schwartz, H. V. (1981). Pimozide attenuates acquisition of leverpressing for food in rats. *Pharmacology Biochemistry and Behavior, 15,* 655-656.

Wise, R. A., Spindler, J., deWit, H., & Gerber, G. J. (1978). Neuroleptic-induced "anhedonia" in rats: Pimozide blocks reward quality of food. *Science, 201,* 262-264.

Zis, A. P., Fibiger, H. C., & Phillips, A. G. (1974). Reversal by L-dopa of impaired learning due to destruction of the dopaminergic nigro-neostriatal projection. *Science, 185.* 960-962.

V

Cognitive Perspectives

Ingvar Lundberg
University of Umeå

All three papers presented in this section provide nice illustrations of the fact that experimental cognitive psychology has advanced to a level where phenomena can be analyzed and understood. which up till now have been dealt within the domain of more "soft" and so called dynamic psychological inquiry. The gap-bridging efforts that can be witnessed here are indeed welcome signs of the healthy state of cognitive psychology. However, a moment of cautious reflection is needed. We do not know whether results obtained in a laboratory situation will generalize to the very different circumstances that are encountered in actual cases in which. for example. a person claims amnesia in connection with a rape, or detects signs of threat. It is likely that even the most diligent attempts to create a laboratory analogue that faithfully reflects key aspects of the phenomena. will be insufficient in important respects. One cannot. for practical and ethical reasons, induce extreme states of emotions in subjects.

All three papers deal with the most complicated problem of the relationship between emotion and cognition, however without advanced theoretical ambitions to analyse and elaborate the relation like Öhman. Dimberg and Esteves (see Chapter 6) and Mineka and Tomarken (see Chapter 7). We should be concerned with multicomponent mechanisms operating on various levels. like sensory-motor, schematic, and conceptual levels with a sequence of stimulus evaluation checks. which are phylogenetically evolved mechanisms that optimize flexible adaptations to highly complex social and physical environments. We have a long epistemological tradition in which perception has been defined as that which eventuates in *conscious* experience of the world. It was this view that led to the dismissal of *subliminal* perception as inherently paradoxical. This confusion arises out of a failure to distinguish between "perception" as experience and "perception" as the extraction of information from the world. This distinction is certainly implicitly recognized in the papers of the present section where subliminal phenomena play a considerable role.

Although Loftus's red herrings may qualify as aversive stimuli, on the basis of an olfactory variable it is not readily apparent how aversively motivated behaviors are involved unless one assumes that eye-witness accounts may be distorted as a function of the unpleasantness embodied in the to-be-remembered scenes. Red herrings mislead cognitive processes, as for instance memory retrieval, but not always because of their aversive character. In fact, they appear to evoke a Trojan Horse-like effect and alter, disguise or substitute memory images by failing to attract sufficient attention. However, Loftus elegantly succeeds in bringing the reader to the very psychological heart of the book, which is "aversive and to-be-avoided events".

When reading Christiansons and Nilssons paper one is intrigued by the possibility that their close look into a real case of functional retrograde amnesia will ultimately influence theoretical developments within memory research. Take, for instance, the well established and widely recognized distinction between *episodic* and *semantic* memory. Their amnesia case clearly demonstrates a need for finer distinctions. Memories related to the establishment and maintenance of a self concept, a personal identy might be such a separate subcategory of episodic memory. The case of hysterical amnesia presented by Christianson and Nilsson is presumably rather extreme and rare. The rape experience is of course a most traumatic experience. But I doubt that this event by itself has sufficient power to create the extreme state of total identity loss reported here. The pre-morbid personality and relevant prior experiences must certainly also be considered. Moreover, in case studies of the sort discussed by Christianson and Nilsson, there is always a risk that the amnesia seen in the victim is simulated.

Michael Eysenck's paper is a fascinating revival of the "new look" in perception from the fifties (e.g. hungry people are prone to attend to food-related stimuli). We can all recognize occasions when our emotional states, our fears, joys, anger, preceded and biased our interpretations of subsequent situations. And we can all recognize occasions when changes in the way we perceived or interpreted situations served to elicit or alter our emotional states. Thus we have no clear and unidirectional *causal* link between emotional state and cognitive-perceptual bias. Eysenck has selected *anxiety* as his specific field of inquiry. According to Robins et al., (1984), the lifetime prevalence of anxiety neurosis as defined by the DSM III is estimated to 10-12 % of the population. A distinctive feature of this disorder is an unrealistic perception of threat. The probability of a feared event as well as the seriousness of the event is grossly overestimated, while the coping resources and the availability of help from others are underestimated. Is this selective bias and interpretative bias a vulnerability factor, i.e. a cause of anxiety or is it just a reflection of the anxious mood? Those are the extreme alternatives in this chicken- and-egg problem which attract Eysenck's interest. However, an interaction or a reciprocal relationship is more likely.

The research strategy used is not optimal for clarifying the nature of the relationship. Basically, the design is correlational and does not permit causal inferences. Not even the introduction of a group of recovered patients does offer an escape from this correlational trap. I also note the risk of being tempted to propose ad hoc explanations, e.g. by referring to the possibility that certain functions have a slow rate of recovery. There are two kinds of people in this world: those who believe that there are two kinds of people and those who do not. I do not believe there are either anxious people or non-anxious people. In medicine you sometimes find conditions of an all-or-none-type, measles, for example. And you cannot be almost pregnant, or can you? Perhaps the demarcation line between normal persons high in trait anxiety and anxious patients is a very hazy zone, where comparisons easily get obscured. In the exciting series of studies reported here, we can always ask questions about the kinds of stimuli used and the conditions for stimulus presentation. In a majority of cases the stimulus material consists of words, either written or spoken. One of the many problems connected with verbal stimuli is the possibility that other factors than threat are operating and provoke the bias, for instance subjective word frequency which might be only indirectly related to anxiety.

The natural extensions of this theme are of course the use of phobic stimuli, like pictures of spiders or snakes, facial expressions of threat and experimentally induced threat as in the classical subception literature. In a complete design, other emotional dimensions than threat as potential sources of bias should also be included, like e.g. pleasantness, novelty etc.

As far as stimulus presentation is concerned, measures could be taken to keep hemispheric localization under control. In a *dichotic* listening paradigm, threat stimuli could be given either in the left or the right ear. A reasonable prediction would be that anxiety patients will show left ear advantage, since the assumption is that threat or other negative emotional input is evaluated by the right hemisphere. Likewise, a left hemifield advantage is expected in the visual experiments with eye fixation control and rapid exposures.

The papers of the present section demonstrate in different ways how all sorts of methodological and theoretical issues are raised when cognitive psychology is broadened to include emotional aspects. But the papers also provide encouraging examples of the exciting potential of the new look of cognitive psychology.

REFERENCE

Robins, L. N. et al. (1984). Lifetime prevalence of specific psychiatric disorder in three different sites. *Archives of General Psychiatry, 4*, 949-958.

11 Hysterical Amnesia: A Case of Aversively Motivated Isolation of Memory

Sven-Åke Christianson and Lars-Göran Nilsson
University of Umeå

The question of how emotional shock or psychological trauma affect the efficiency of cognitive processing has been of considerable clinical and practical interest for a long time. Early in this century Freud (1915) described how psychiatric patients 'repressed' memories of traumatic events and how these repressions could affect the cognitive functioning of these patients much later in life. Since the time of Freud's pioneering work it has been observed in many clinical settings that a patient who has experienced a psychological trauma sometime fails to remember not only the traumatic event *per se* but also the events that occur prior to and immediately after the psychological trauma. Typically, the memory loss can be quite dramatic when the patient's memory is assessed soon after the traumatic event. In later evaluations of the patient's memory, however, a recovery of memory is usually observed. Excellent reviews of these phenomena of amnesia appear in Abse (1987), Horowitz (1986), Kihlstrom and Evans (1979a), Talland (1969). and Whitty and Zangwill (1977).

The occurrence of amnesia as a function of psychological trauma is by no means limited to clinical situations. As discussed by Schacter (1986) victims of serious crimes and the criminals themselves often display amnesia when questioned about the criminal act in a later court room session. Disregarding for the moment the risk that the witnesses or the criminals may consciously want to simulate amnesia. it is reasonable to assume that amnesia or other memory disorders could occur as a function of the emotional stress involved in witnessing a traumatic event (see Christianson & Loftus, 1987; Christianson & Nilsson, 1984; Christianson. Nilsson. Mjörndal. Perris. & Tjelldén. 1986; Loftus & Burns, 1982).

A general goal of this chapter is to discuss theory and data for the sake of determining possible underlying principles about the relationship between emotional stress and memory disorders. Our general approach in this regard is to consider amnesia or pathological forgetting as an aversively motivated behavior. Our point of departure is a case study which involved a traumatic event and a subsequent hysterical amnesia. Later, we will use this case as a basis for a discussion of how experimental memory research could be used in order to further our understanding of hysterical amnesia.

A Case of Hysterical Amnesia

On a light summer evening of May 29, 1984, a 23 year-old female (to be referred to as C.M.) was raped while she was out jogging close to her home. Lying on a track 10 meters from the regular running route she was found by another runner. Her face showed several bruises, and she was badly shocked. C.M. could not explain what had happened to her and she could not tell the identity of herself. The only person she recognized that night was a policeman, a famous Swedish ice-hockey player[1], who brought her to the hospital. Over the next few days, C.M. had no recollection of her personal identity, relatives , friends, home, or place of work. Recollections of her previous life and the course of the attack by the rapist were totally blocked for her. Her memory of the course of events from the time she was found, onwards, however, was quite normal. That is, she showed a retrograde amnesia, and an amnesia for the specific traumatic event, but no anterograde amnesia.

One and a half weeks after the trauma C.M. was released from the hospital. At that point, her physical injuries were almost healed, and except for that C.M. recognized two close relatives and thought that some friends of her looked familiar, she was still amnesic about events that had occurred up to the moment when she was found. She was also suffering from anxiety attacks and nightmares.

Three weeks after the trauma her retrograde amnesia had receded somewhat: she remembered a repeat TV-program and recognized neutral places she had visited before the trauma. However, only a few very personal memories had returned. At this time she was escorted by two policemen over the area in which the assault had occurred. During the walk with the policemen she appeared continually stressed. C.M. expressed discomfort at different spots in the area, but was totally amnesic for the specific traumatic episode. However, she had no problem pointing out the place where she had been found and she was able to give a detailed description of what happened from the moment she was discovered by the fellow jogger.

---

[1] As will be seen in our discussion of this case, the fact that the person who brought her to the hospital was famous, is relevant to the understanding of the memory dysfunction in this woman.

When C.M. was taken again to the scene of the assault one week later, she felt very uncomfortable at specific places, but had no recollection of the traumatic evening, except that the word "bricks" (Swedish "tegel") crossed her mind. When questioned about what she meant by this word, she answered "bricks and the path" (Swedish "tegel och stigen") without being able to give any further explanation of why these specific words were recalled.

The explanation came later when they passed some crumbled bricks that were found on another small path beside her running route. Being confronted with this track on which pieces of the crumbled bricks were spread out C.M. showed an intense emotional stress, and claimed that she associated the unpleasant feelings with the pieces of bricks on the track she was walking on. She strongly felt that something must have happened at this specific place, although she did not know for certain at this point of time that she had been raped. From the confession by the rapist a few days earlier the policemen knew, however, that this was the place where he had assaulted her and from which she had been forced out onto the small meadow where the actual rape took place.

C.M. was very concerned that she could not remember what had happened to her and she therefore asked (on July 4, five weeks after the assault) to be taken to the place of the crime once again. Visiting the critical area on this third occasion she walked along the crumbled brick path to the small meadow where the actual rape occurred. Standing on the meadow she told the accompanying policemen that there was something specific about this meadow and at the same time she became nauseated and started to cry 'hysterically'.

Her state of amnesia lasted until the 16th of August (i.e., more than 11 weeks after the assault). On that day C.M. was out jogging again, for the first time after the trauma, but in a different surrounding -- at her country-cottage. The cavities in the road where C.M. was running were filled with crushed bricks, which reminded her strongly of those bricks found in the vicinity of her recent experince. After jogging for a while she suddenly became disoriented. The locality became confusing and she became unsure about where she was running; she did not know whether she was back on her usual running track, where the traumatic event occurred, or on the running track at her cottage. C.M. happened to stop at the entrance of another cottage, where a pile of bricks were placed. At that moment, images of the traumatic episode started to return to her. The first memory to return was the smell of beer from the attacker, and she immediately connected this smell with a memory of a sexual assault she was exposed to as a 9-year-old girl. Thereafter, isolated memory-pictures from the traumatic evening started to return in an nonchronological manner, and within a time space of 10-20 minutes she was able to reconstruct the whole traumatic episode.

According to C.M.'s report, the main aspects of the traumatic event were as follows: Along her running route C.M. had been called to sit down by a man sitting on a bench beside the track. After she had turned down his offer, he ran after her, caught her and struck her in the face. In an attempt to escape the attacker she took off along the path with crumbled bricks which led to the meadow where she was raped. On this path she was caught and beaten up and then forced, half-unconscious, out onto the meadow. When C.M. was lying on the ground she was holding her hands in front of her eyes in order to protect herself, and accordingly she did not see the face of the attacker. C.M. remembered that she regained consciousness on the small meadow with her sweatpants and underwear around her ankles and she wondered whether or not she dared to move. When she got up and adjusted her clothes she remembered that one single thought occupied her mind: "Why didn't I tie my pants more tightly at the waist,...if I had tied them more tightly from the beginning, maybe it would not have happened..."[2]. Her state of retrograde amnesia receded almost completely within the time space of 2-3 months after August 16.

When the suspected rapist was cross-examined for the first time, on June 21, he admitted that he had been sitting alone close to the place where C.M was found, but he claimed that he must have had a "black-out" because suddenly he found himself in a shopping center three miles away. During the next few days he suspected that he had done something seriously wrong. And when he read about the assault and suspected rape in the newspaper he felt very anxious since he was afraid that he could have been the perpetrator of the crime. On July 25, he remembered how he had attacked C.M. when she had passed him on her running route, and later the same day he also described that he had tried to rape her, but probably did not succeeded fully[3].

PSYCHOLOGICAL TRAUMA AND AMNESIA

What are the mechansisms of C.M.'s cognitive and emotional systems that could account for this pattern of memory disturbance? The problem as such is of a long standing nature in the clinical literature, and in recent years it has also been tackled in some laboratory analogues of amnesia within the realm of experimental cognitive psychology. The purpose of this chapter is to extract information from these studies with the intention of arriving at a comprehensive interpretation of the phenomenon of hysterical amnesia like that described in this case study. First, we will briefly review some of the clinical and experimental literature in this area.

Second, a theoretical view concerning attentional narrowing and the isolation of memory information is put forward as one possible way of explaining the process of hysterical amnesia. Finally, we will discuss the phenomenon of hysterical amnesia on the basis of recent general knowledge within human memory research.

---

[2] C.M.'s description of the traumatic event was more detailed than described here; the details given here were the most salient ones found in interviews with the victim and in protocols from the police department and the court session.

[3] The man was recommended by the courts to a closed psychiatric ward.

Clinical and Experimental Descriptions of Traumatic Amnesia

According to the clinical literature, the case presented here demonstrates the typical post-traumatic symptoms that occur in relation to hysterical neurosis (see Nemiah, 1969, 1979). Such hysterical neuroses could be expressed either in terms of dissociative reactions or conversion reactions (Buss, 1966). Dissociative reactions comprise cognitive symptoms such as a limited and transient inability to recall past events and events associated with an emotional trauma. The onset is usually acute and the patient is typically disoriented to time, place, and his or her own person. In the neurological literature, this state is assumed to develop as a means of escaping intolerable stress and it is interpreted as a process of psychological "inability to reopen voluntarily the pathways where memories are retained" (Walton, 1971, p. 106). Conversion reactions refer to states in which the patient exhibits physiological/sensorimotor symptoms (e.g., paralysis, numbness) without any organic basis for the symptoms (see Abse, 1987). Generally, these conversion symptoms have been interpreted as a kind of unconscious indirect recall of aspects that are central to the repressed emotional trauma (see e.g., Breuer & Freud, 1895; Erdelyi & Goldsberg, 1979).

An early theoretical interpretation of the phenomena of hysterical amnesia and conversion hysteria was offered through the repression hypothesis (see Breuer & Freud, 1895; Freud, 1915; MacKinnon & Dukes, 1962). The essence of this view is that an emotional trauma is repressed from a conscious state by the individual in order to avoid, and to cope with, an overwhelming psychological 'pain'. Excessive stimulation is seen as the inciting cause of the repressive state. Freud described this type of amnesia in terms of "motivated forgetting", referring to an unconscious effort to master an extremely powerful evocative event. This view suggests that the repressed events are registered and retained, but cannot be recalled until the associations or ideas make contact with the emotional response appropriate to the repressed material.

Remarkable for both the hysterical amnesia and the hysterical conversion symptoms is that the patient either spontaneously in the course of time or by means of various therapeutic techniques manages to remember the previously inaccessible traumatic episode (see Erdelyi & Goldberg, 1979). A similar recovery has also been observed in (a) experimental studies of the repression hypothesis, (b) in laboratory analogues of amnesia, and (c) in studies of arousal and memory. Under the next rubric we will consider each of these three settings which have all demonstrated amnesia and recovery phenomenons.

Experimental Studies of Memory and Emotion

Studies of the Repression Hypothesis. A few experimental studies of the repression hypothesis have produced results that seem to be in line with the ideas suggested by Freud (see e.g., Erdelyi, 1970; Flavell, 1955;

Glucksberg & King, 1967; Holmes, 1972; Jung, 1906; Levinger & Clark, 1961; Zeller, 1950a, b, 1951). The essence of these results is that events associated with certain feelings of unpleasantness are remembered worse than neutral events and that memory performance for emotional events is better at a delayed as compared to an immediate test. According to Freud's theory, these results indicate that there is a desire to exclude the emotional events from consciousness; that is, the emotional content is subjected to repressive mechanisms. Following a delayed test interval these events are less threatening and thus more accessible to consciousness. Although the repression interpretation by all means is reasonable, it should be noted that there are at least two other theoretical interpretations that can account for the same data. One of these is the consolidation notion proposed by Walker (1958, 1967) and Kleinsmith and Kaplan (1963, 1964), and the other is our own theoretical contribution to be discussed shortly.

Laboratory Analogues of Amnesia. Although not usually treated as studies on hysterical amnesia, some experiments have been conducted which may be conceived of as simulations of retrograde and anterograde amnesia (Bond & Kirkpatrick, 1982; Brenner, 1973; Detterman, 1975, 1976; Detterman & Ellis, 1972; Ellis, Detterman, Runcie, McCarved & Craig, 1971; Fisk & Wickens, 1979; Loftus & Burns, 1982; Runcie & O'Bannon, 1977; Saufley & Winograd, 1970; Schultz, 1970; Tulving, 1969). The amnesic agents used in these studies have usually been a critical event with high novelty or an item differing in nature from an otherwise homogeneous set of items (e.g., the name of a famous person in a list of common nouns, a word presented at the intensity of a loud shout in a list of words presented in a conversational level, or a photograph of a nude in a list of common neutral objects). In line with clinical cases of amnesia these laboratory analogues have been successful in demonstrating retrograde and/or anterograde amnesia. Furthermore, similar to the clinical observations that exist, recovery has been demonstrated for induced retrograde amnesia (Detterman, 1975, 1976; Detterman & Ellis, 1972).

However, whereas the traumatic critical event in clinical cases is normally less well remembered, the critical event (amnesic agent) in these laboratory studies is very well remembered. Although no amnesia has been obtained with respect to the amnesic agent (cf. the psychological trauma), these studies constitute an interesting simulation of the retrograde and anterograde aspects of clinical amnesia.

Studies of Arousal and Memory. Experimental studies of arousal and memory (see Eysenck, 1982 for review), have also shown findings that are characteristic of traumatic amnesia. First, it has been found that high arousal events -- often emotional loaded stimuli -- are initially less well remembered than low arousal, or 'neutral', events (see e.g. Kleinsmith & Kaplan, 1963, 1964). In contrast to the results of the experimental simulations mentioned above the results from these arousal studies are, thus, comparable to the clinically observed amnesia of the traumatic event proper. Second, a recovery effect has been demonstrated for those events associated with high arousal (Kleinsmith & Kaplan, 1963, 1964), which is similar to the observation of recovery of retrograde amnesia in clinical cases.

The Relationship Between Emotional Arousal and Induced Amnesia

In experimental studies of the repression hypothesis, in laboratory analogues of amnesia, and in studies on arousal and memory, the most stable findings of memory impairments have been demonstrated by manipulations of emotional arousing agents. In view of this, we are probably safe to generalize that there is both experimental and clinical evidence supporting the notion that emotional arousing events and the information associated with these events are initially more difficult to remember than neutral events. An important issue is therefore to what extent a state of high emotional arousal *per se* mediate the clinical and experimental findings on traumatic amnesia. This issue was brought to a closer investigation in a series of studies by Christianson and his colleagues (Christianson, 1984a, 1986; 1987; Christianson & Loftus, 1987; Christianson & Mjörndahl, 1985; Christianson & Nilsson, 1984; Christianson, Nilsson, Mjörndahl, Perris, & Tjelldén, 1986).

In a study by Christianson and Nilsson (1984), subjects were presented with a series of slides, consisting of photographs of faces, and with each face accompanied by four verbal descriptors. For subjects in the 'emotional' condition, faces in the middle of the slide sequence were horrible disfigured, showing grotesque forensic patology photographs of facial injuries, and were thus considered as 'traumatic' events. In the control condition, all faces were of a neutral character. Memory performance was measured by means of recall and recognition of four verbal descriptors presented along with each face. In the recall test an amnesia was found for the to-be-remembered (TBR) verbal items presented along with the traumatic pictures, as well as for the TBR items succeeding these 'horror'pictures (i.e., an anterograde amnesia). In the subsequent recognition test the amnesia for the events associated with the traumatic pictures was slightly reduced; and the anterograde amnesia receded completely. These results indicate that the differences between recall and recognition data are most probably due to an interaction between altered encoding operations and the amount of retrieval information aiding reconstructive processes.

Christianson and Mjörndal (1985) and Christianson, Nilsson, Mjörndal, Perris, and Tjelldén (1986) designed a series of experiments in which the explicit aim was to investigate to what extent the laboratory amnesia shown by Christianson and Nilsson is mediated by a heightened level of emotional arousal *per se*. In the study by Christianson and Mjörndal (1985) subjects in one condition were injected with adrenalin and presented with a series of neutral pictures. Subjects in an other condition were injected with saline and presented with the same neutral pictures. (The stimulus material used was the same as presented to the control groups in the Christianson and Nilsson, 1984 study.)

Despite the fact that subjects were brought to a state of high emotional arousal due to the adrenalin and the enhanced emotional reactions by the experimental situation (a paradigm adopted from Schachter, 1971), no amnesia effects were obtained. This pattern of results was confirmed in a follow-up study by Christianson, et al. (1986), and the interpretation offered was that a general increase in emotional arousal as induced by an 'external' source[4] like adrenaline, does not affect memory processes in the same way as a source of emotional arousal directly associated with the TBR events.

Thus, a state of emotional arousal is significant as an intervening variable in explaining traumatic amnesia only when the emotional reaction is an inherent property of the TBR events. Under such conditions it can be assumed that the cognitive activity of the individual is focussed upon the most critical and arousing aspects of the emotional event. That is, coping activities and perseverative tendencies in thinking about the critical aspects expend so much conscious attentional resources that further processing of other, more peripheral information may be severely restricted. This restriction upon the elaboration of encoding of the event might be critical to an explanation of traumatic amnesia.

This line of reasoning was also put forward in a study by Christianson (1984a). In that study it was shown that subjects who watched an emotional version of a thematic sequence of pictures, remembered the story equally well as compared to subjects presented with a neutral version of the slide sequence when asked to recall the story short after presentation. At a delayed recall test, however, the emotionally aroused subjects were superior in remembering the critical main information of the emotional slides, for example "a boy being hit by a car and bleeding heavily from the eye". When tested by means of recognition, no difference was found between the 'emotional' and the 'neutral' group, irrespective of the time of test. In this recognition test the main features of each stimulus slide were held constant and only the peripheral information was manipulated. Furthermore, a retrograde amnesia effect was obtained, such that subjects presented with the emotional version of the story remembered the pictures preceding the emotional loaded pictures in the series at a lower level at a short test interval compared with the control subjects, but were superior at the delayed test.

Two observations of potential importance for the issues discussed here should be noted and related to the case study described at the outset of the chapter. First, Christianson (1984a) found a retrograde amnesia when the TBR information consisted of a thematic story. Using a similar design but a non-thematic TBR information Christianson and Nilsson (1984) found no retrograde amnesia. The events preceding and including the rape in the case study were supposedly of a thematic nature and it is therefore important to notice that a retrograde amnesia was found in the case study as well. In the same way as for the experimentally induced retrograde

---

[4] By external we mean affecting the sympathetic nervous system and only indirectly affecting cognitive centers in the central nervous system.

amnesia (Christianson, 1984a) the retrograde amnesia in the case study receded some time after the traumatic event. Secondly, an interpretation of amnesia and recovery of memory after elapsed time can better be accounted for by encoding and retrieval processes than by storage or consolidation processes (e.g., Kleinsmith & Kaplan, 1963, 1964; Walker, 1958, 1967). The main reason for this view is that the amount of information recalled or recognized seems to be directly related to manipulations made at study and test (see e.g., Christianson, 1984a; Christianson & Loftus, 1987; Christianson & Nilsson, 1984; Christianson et al., 1986).

Taken into consideration the close relationship between the data patterns found in the Christianson (1984a) study on laboratory induced amnesia and the case study reported here, we claim that the retrograde amnesia found in the case study is due to the influence of traumatic factors on encoding rather than on consolidation. Likewise the recovery of the traumatic memories 11 weeks later is due to the fact that retrieval cues made the stored information accessible. The fact that these cues were effective in this respect at this particular moment in time is due to an interaction between encoding and retrieval processes. This aspect of the case study will be discussed in the light of general memory research, to which we now turn.

HYSTERICAL AMNESIA IN THE LIGHT OF GENERAL MEMORY RESEARCH

Attentional Narrowing and Isolation of Memory

It has long been assumed that arousal and cognitive efficiency are strongly interrelated. Yerkes and Dodson (1908) attempted to generalize this relationship by proposing an inverted U-form relation between tension or arousal and performance. Easterbrook's (1959) cue-utilization theory, which describes this U-formed relationship, suggests that there is a progressive restriction of the range of cues utilized or attended to as a function of an increase in emotional arousal. At states of high emotional arousal this restriction in cue-utilization is benificial to performance, because relevant central information is supposed to be attended to at the expence of peripheral cues. An increase in emotional arousal, as in states of high stress or anxiety, implies a reduction of relevant and critical cues attended to and would therefore be deleterious to cognitive efficiency (see also Bacon, 1974; Baddeley, 1972; Korchin, 1964; Mueller, 1979; Wachtel, 1967, 1968).

Easterbrook's view (1959) was extended by Mandler (1975) who suggested that physiological aspects of the autonomic nervous system arousal require attention. This attention to physiological responding is the critical component that relate emotional arousal to restricted cue-utilization. "Given the limited capacity of attention-consciousness and the presence of additional events that make demands on the limited capacity, it is not surprising that with increasing arousal the number of other events (cues) that can share conscious attention will be decreased" (p. 124). In situations where the sympathetic nervous system arousal, or emotions become very intense, Mandler states that "It floods attentional mechanisms and decreases the amount of information that the organism can recruit effectively either from environment or from its own memory store" (Mandler, 1975, p. 123). This theoretical point of view was further developed by Eysenck (1982) who suggested that high arousal leads to a reduced ability to engage in parallel processing due to that a "smaller proportion of attentional capacity is available for task processing" (Eysenck, 1982, p. 176). Thus, the narrowing of the attention span at states of high emotional arousal should be benificial to memory of central aspects of an event, but detrimental to recall of a wide range of aspects or cues including peripheral information.

The results of the studies by Christianson (1984a) and Christianson and Nilsson (1984) support the notion that amnesic effects obtained for information related to strong emotional events are caused by a restriction in attention and depth of encoding, and by a failure at retrieval to gain access to the peripherally encoded information. In line with the theoretical analyses by Easterbrook (1959), Eysenck (1982), and Mandler (1975), we argue that events of traumatic nature reduces available attentional capacity, which in turn will lead to a restriction in elaboration of encoding of the total event. We assume that the traumatic pictures presented in the studies by Christianson (1984a) and Christianson and Nilsson (1984) directed the attentional resources of the subjects to the most central and critical aspects of the traumatic episode. This in turn means that fewer aspects of the traumatic event and associated information were attended to.

As an analogue to pathological forgetting observed in clinical settings, we conceive of narrowed attention as a potential underlying mechanism for the phenomena of hysterical amnesia. It is commonly observed in clinical cases, that subjects who have undergone a psychological trauma, exhibit a memory loss of the traumatic episod, but preserve some features or cues associated to the trauma. In some cases this cue information is expressed as physical symptoms such as paralysis of an arm (a conversion reaction), or, a compulsive repetition in thought, and may serve as a type of non-conscious recall of some central information from the traumatic experience (see Breuer & Freud, 1895; Erdely & Goldberg, 1979; Janet, 1965). This preservation of single aspects without a conscious relation to a relevant context was also demonstrated in our case study. The victim in the present casy study, C.M., showed a recollection of an isolated memory of "bricks" or "bricks and the path", without being able to explain why these words came to mind. C.M. also showed an intense stress when she was confronted with a path with pieces of bricks.

It is conceivable, that this type of traumatic amnesia with preserved isolated memories, results from an extreme variant of attentional selectivity associated with extreme states of emotion, and that it constitutes an extension of the process of narrowed attention that has been observed in laboratory studies with traumatic pictures (see Christianson, 1984a;

Christianson & Loftus, 1987; Christianson & Nilsson, 1984). Thus, in order to avoid extreme psychological 'pain' the individual may isolate, at a conscious level, some critical details of the traumatic event from its original context. This process of isolation may hence be one critical cognitive mechanism underlying the traumatic amnesia symptoms found in our case study.

A related failure to recall a complete episode has been demonstrated by means of posthypnotic suggestion (see Kihlstrom & Evans, 1979b). Following a hypnotic state, susceptible subjects show an initial difficulty in remembering events that occurred while being deeply hypnotized. However, if the subjects are provided with copy cues as in a recognition test or with other cues as in a cued recall test the amnesia recedes.

Kihlstrom and Evans (1979b) have also demonstrated that hypnotized subjects fail to recall the TBR information in the same logic order as under normal non-hypnotized conditions. This finding is interesting in the present context for at least two reasons. First, the finding suggests that order information, not only item information (cf. Murdock, 1974), is affected in amnesia. Since Kihlstrom and Evans have demonstrated this phenomenon for posthypnotic amnesia we got for a strategy effect at encoding or retrieval to be more likely than an effect of consolidation. Second, the ideas proposed here about isolation of memories would seem to be congenial with this finding of post-hypnotic amnesia in retaining order information. Under normal condition it is assumed that encoding and retrieval occur according to a coherent synthesis of a sequence of events that have a causal relationship. In a traumatic situation, however, the same type of coherent structuring of information appears not to occur. Thus, the fragmented encoding and the isolation of the traumatic event appear to obscure the act of reconstruction of the original traumatic event.

Attentional Narrowing and Coping

So far we have stressed attentional narrowing as a process associated with limited cognitive processing capacity in states of intense emotional stress. However, narrowing of attention can also be seen as a mechanism involved in *coping* with the traumatic experience. This latter aspect has been discussed by Horowitz (1979) in terms of selection of information and self-images as coping responses in post-traumatic disorders.

Horowitz (1979) discussed signs and symptoms of stress after serious life events like loss of a loved one by death, or personal loss caused by accident or violence. According to Horowitz, memory failure of stressful life events is one way to control and cope with a traumatic experience (usually without conscious awareness). This and other types of control operations are similar to the Freudian defensive-mechanisms concept. In Freud's terminology defence mechanisms (i.e., ego controls) are activated to regulate levels of tension evoked by intense emotional stimulation. When the repression mechanisms fail to master a powerful emotional event, the victim may exhibit symptoms such as hysterical amnesia or symptoms of conversion hysteria. Thus, "hysteria is essentially the result of a disturbance in the process of repression" (Abse, 1987, p. 259). The Freudian ideas have been translated by Horowitz (1979) into an information processing theoretical tradition, in which the traumatic intrapsychic conflict postulated by Freud is interpreted in terms of an interaction between new stressful information, pre-existent cognitive schemata, and control operations.

Horowitz would probably argue that the victim in our case study cannot alter the traumatic rape situation. This in turn means that C.M.'s inner models (cognitive schemata) have to be revised so that they conform to the new reality. Processes interact through shifts in these schemata to meet the new reality. In this situation of incongruence between the new experience of having been raped and inner schemata, strong emotions will be evoked, and control operations will be activated.

There are two types of control operations stated by Horowitz (1979) that are of special interest to the hysterical amnesia shown by C.M. in our case story. First, there are control operations that select information during emotional states, and second, there are control operations that select self-images during such states. If the victim's initial interpretation of the rape and its consequences produce a defensive shift in her inner models, this could result in partial or total inhibition of the traumatic event. This type of active inhibition of information is an example of a control operation in which the victim by selecting certain train of thoughts can restrain threatening ideas and feelings. "After being raped, for instance, a woman might find herself thinking only of what to do next, whom to call, what to say, and would rigourly avoid re-experiencing and remembering the terrifying event or any similar past experience." (Horowitz, 1979,p 259).

Horowitz argued that in order to cope with the trauma some people remember a traumatic event such as a rape only as a fragment (i.e., in isolation), obscuring images and details to avoid emotional stress. This control process of selection of information flow is exemplified in our case study by C.M.'s fragmented memory of some isolated details; "bricks and the path", and by her strong concern for fastening her sweatpants, which immediately occupied her mind when she was left by the attacker.

These control operations also work through selecting possible self-images, resulting in various progressions or regressions of identity that commonly occur after a traumatic experience. A control failure in choice of available self-images, or the stabilizing of a self-image, can lead to a chaotic lapse of identity. This loss of identity was also seen in our case study in which C.M. initially showed a dissociation between common general knowledge (e.g. her identification of a famous Swedish hockey player) and her personal past (her loss of identity and autobiographical memories).

The Distinction Between Episodic and Semantic Memory

In addition to the accurate recollection of the name of the famous hockey player, C.M. was also capable of recalling several other facts of a general-knowledge nature. When specifically asked, C.M. could tell the names of capitals of countries and the names of several other notable cities. She could also tell the names of persons in the royal family of Sweden, and she had no difficulties in recalling the names of common places in her neighbourhood. Thus, it seems fair to conclude that her memory for general knowledge was intact.

This accuracy in memory for general facts should be contrasted to C.M.'s apparent difficulties in remembering more personally related information, even if this information was not related to the traumatic episode she had experienced. For example, C.M. failed to recognize her boyfriend and a close girlfriend, and she was unable to recall their names. These obervations, thus, give further support to the notion of a dissociation between memory for general knowledge and memory for more private and personally related information.

The distinction between memory for general facts and memory for personal events is commonly conceptualized in human memory research as a distinction between semantic and episodic memory (Tulving, 1972, 1983). Whereas semantic memory is conceived of as memory for general knowledge not related to a specific individual, episodic memories are defined as carrying information about personally related episodes. Moreover, the acquisition of information in semantic memory is not defined in terms of time and place, whereas information in episodic memory is (Tulving, 1972, 1983).

Taken together, these observations which demonstrate a dissociation between episodic and semantic memory, may be regarded as a support for the notion of separate memory systems for episodic and semantic information (Tulving, 1972, 1983, 1985). However, a few curious observations found in the interviews with C.M. complicate matters and make a firm conclusion on separate memory systems somewhat premature. A couple of weeks after the trauma, C.M. showed recollection of memories that would seem to be of an episodic rather than a semantic nature. One such example is that she happened to watch a repeat program on TV. C.M. reported that she did not remember that she had seen the program before, but the cues provided by the play in the beginning of the program made her recollect the rest of the plot in that program. Another example is that C.M. failed to recognize her own apartment, but managed to recall that one of her neighbours always used to have their curtains lowered. Moreover, she discovered changes in the looks and the apparance of a close friend without being able to say anything about how she knew this person. She also "felt" that some persons were familiar to her, but she was unable to describe in what way she knew them. These observations suggest that C.M. failed to remember information that was closely related to her personally, but was succesful in recollection of non-personal episodic information. Similar observations regarding episodic/semantic and personal/non-personal memories have also been reported by Schacter, Wang, Tulving, and Freedman (1982).

It could be argued that these memories were of an episodic rather than a semantic nature in the sense that they were related to her personally rather than to general knowledge. Memory for those episodic aspects actually recalled at this period in time might be examples of a gradual recovery, although we have argued that it was not until much later, on August 16, when she rememberd the specific traumatic episode, that she gradually started to gain access to her personal episodic memories. Alternatively, it could be the case that the episodic information actually recalled only two or so weeks after the trauma, indicates a qualitatively different, yet undefined, type of information, and possibly also another memory system in addition to the episodic and semantic memory systems proposed by Tulving (1972, 1983). In fact, Tulving (1985) has posed the question of how many memory systems there are and has recently argued for a trichotomy (procedural, semantic, and episodic memory) rather than the dictotomy between semantic and episodic memory. Whether the examples given of recollective memories are instances of procedural memory or of an unknown memory system that Tulving (1985) has dubbed QM (for question mark) remains an open question.

Functional or Organic amnesia?

In the previous section we discussed the distinction between episodic and semantic memory. Such a dissociation has also been observed in cases of organic amnesia, that is, pathological forgetting due to damage to the brain caused by e.g., chronic abuse of alcohol, anesthetics, electroconvulsive shock, epilepsy, closed-head injury, tumors, encephalitis (see Christianson, 1984b, for a review). Patients with organic amnesia typically show a dissociation, such that memory disturbances are more likely to occur for episodic tasks than for semantic tasks (see e.g., Christianson, Nilsson, & Silfvenius, in press; Jacoby, 1982; Kinsbourne & Wood, 1982; Warrington & Weiskrantz, 1974,1982). Since C.M. was hit in the forehead and the neck it is of importance to know whether her pathological forgetting was caused by any neurological damage to her brain. According to the medical examination C.M. underwent when she was brought to the Karolinska Hospital in Stockholm, approximately one and a half hours after the attack, she was not oriented in time, place, or to her own person, but she was fully conscious, and participated in the examination without problems. X-ray examinations of the brain, and the facial and neck skeleton were negative. Thus, there were no oral and radiographic symptoms to her amnesia found in the neurological examination. C.M. was, accordingly, sent to a psychiatrist who diagnosed her state as hysterical amnesia.

Furthermore, C.M. did not show an anterograde amnesia. When questioned at the hospital and later during the police investigation, C.M. could readily describe, detail by detail, the course of events from the point of time she was spoken to by the fellow jogger who first found her on the track. The only sign of anterograde amnesia concerns a very short moment after she awoke and adjusted her clothes until she was found about 30 meters down on the path[5]. The fact that C.M. did not show an

---

[5] Three years after the trauma this immediate post-traumatic period is still blurred to her.

extended anterograde amnesia, suggests that her amnesia had exclusively functional origins.

Internal and External Cues

The amnesic state reported in the present case study might be regarded in part as a phenomenon of state-dependent memory (Bower, 1981: Eich, 1980). The traumatic events encountered at the time of the crime were difficult to remember because C.M. was in a different state of mind, when questioned about the assault afterwards than she was at the time of the assault. Strictly speaking, in order to test this hypothesis one would have to create the same state at the later "test" occasion as was present in the original event. For obvious reasons this would be extremely unethical and such a test of the hypothesis simply cannot be done.

However, on the basis of post-hoc inference we would like to argue for an interpretation of C.M.'s memory recovery in terms of state-dependent memory. As previously mentioned it was not until August 16 that C.M. was able to recollect what had happened that day, 11 weeks earlier, when the rape took place. Our basic claim is that recollection of the traumatic event that day was possible because several cues brought back the same physiological and cognitive state of C.M. as that prevailing during the assault.

On August 11, C.M. was out jogging for the first time since the rape. Thus, the muscle movements were, supposedly, the same as those involved in the jogging just before the rape took place. Moreover, the heightened body temperature, hyperventilation, and cardiac activity from jogging were probably also more or less the same at the two occasions. In addition, there were also a number of external cues in the environment (the environmental scene, the pieces of bricks and the pile of bricks etc) that gave rise to a cognitive state of the same kind at the two occasions. Taken together, the internal and the external cues probably provided a reasonably coherent picture that aided C.M. to recollect aspects of the situation just preceding the actual rape. Bits and pieces of the original situation did then successively build up to a reconstructed memory trace of the traumatic event *per se*.

The main feature of this interpretation is that the complete recollection of the traumatic experience would be arrived at successively by means of approaching the aversive experience not directly, but rather from the relatively 'safe' and controlled state of mind C.M. would have experienced minutes before she was assaulted, even before she had seen the attacker. Another aspect of this interpretation is that the internal and external contexts combine to form a relatively complete code of the experience. This combination of contexts also facilitates the reconstruction of the memory trace of the specific traumatic episode.

A related but different interpretation of the memorial consequences of this traumatic experience can also be made in the realm of the encoding specificity principle (Tulving & Thomson, 1973). In its most general form this principle states that "What is stored is determined by what is perceived and how it is encoded, and what is stored determines what retrieval cues are effective in providing access to what is stored" (Tulving & Thomson, 1973, p. 353). In other words, recall is the consequence of a complex interaction between encoding and retrieval processes. Thus, for this particular case one may assume that a large number of aspects of the original event are encoded. When recall of this event is tested soon after the event, C.M. cannot utilize the retrieval information provided to such an extent that the information extracted makes contact with the original memory trace.

There might be several different reasons for this; one reason might be that C.M. experiences difficulties in focussing her attention towards the most crucial aspects of the retrieval information provided. The reason for this inability to focus attention on relevant aspects or components of the context might be, as suggested by Horowitz (1979), that the individual, after a traumatic experience, is occupied by intrusive thoughts about the threatening event (see also Christianson & Nilsson, 1984; Horowitz, 1975; Zachary, 1982).

Thus, Horowitz' notion of control operations may be suitable here. Control operations change the state of the individual and prevent a continuous processing of the threatening event; this change helps C.M. to work through the disturbing experience and to conform to the new reality. In instances in which individuals have difficulties in mastering the emotionally provoking experiences, the meaning of the events will be avoided, or altered by control operations. This altered state will continue until a situation of personal safety and tolerable levels of emotions can be reinstated and allow the traumatic content to enter awareness. The specific stress response will of course differ among individuals due to differences in developmental history, earlier experiences of similar character, and the current life situation. The fact that C.M. had been sexually assaulted as a child, makes it most probable that her emotional experience became even more threatening by the actualization of this earlier trauma. In order to handle this intense emotional burden an altered state of consciousness seems necessary.

At the time when C.M. is assured personal safety and tolerable levels of emotions, she is prepared to retrieve the details of the traumatic experience. When she is mastering these strong emotions the recollection of the event should be as accurate as remembering any other experience provided that the conditions needed for the encoding specificity are at hand.

In terms of the encoding specificity principle and the notion of state dependent memory, the encoding, storage, and retrieval processes as such should function just about the same as in the normal case. The problem is that strong emotions by means of intrusive thinking about what had happened to her prevents these processes to come into play. Once the negative effects of these strong emotions have been reduced or eliminated, regular principles for how the cognitive system functions are as valid as in the normal case.

SUMMARY OF THE THEORETICAL INTERPRETATION OF THE CASE C.M.

The issue for this chapter was to extract basic knowledge within recent cognitive psychology in order to explain a rather unusual but most interesting phenomenon of pathological forgetting, referred to as hysterical amnesia in the clinical literature. In summing up our theoretical interpretation of the present case of hysterical amnesia, we propose the following circumstances, which taken together, contribute to the development of amnesia and the process of recovery.

1) High emotional arousal will lead to a re-distribution of attentional resources such that only a limited amount of central information will be processed and that peripheral information will be excluded.

When C.M. attempted to escape the attacker, her emotional state limited her available attentional resources from elaborating the information in the external environment. Most of her conscious mind was presumably occupied with possible concerns about finding a way to escape the attacker, with thoughts like "I'm going to be killed", and with feelings of physical and emotional stress and fear.

2) The fact that C.M.'s attention was restricted with respect to the external information made her attention focus upon details in the environmental context that were most central[6] and critical to her in that specific situation. In our case this information was the pieces of bricks which were spread out along the track C.M. chosed as an escaping route. The path with crumbled bricks was the information focused upon and hence will have the strongest cue validity to the traumatic event.

3) The excessive emotional strain evoked during the act of rape, including the actualization of an earlier sexual assault that C.M. had been exposed to at an early age, produced a defensive shift in C.M.'s inner models of reality. In terms of the Horowitz (1979) theory, C.M. limited, by means of control operations, her thoughts to rather illogical aspects of the traumatic situation immediately after the rape. Her concern about fastening her sweatpants "which might had prevented her from being raped" is an example of this. Moreover, the rape implied such an unbearable insult to her identity and assault upon her self-image, that a temporal loss of identity perhaps became necessary in order to handle the immediate post-traumatic stress.

4) Due to her heightened level of emotion and intrusive thoughts concerning her apparent lack of any real knowledge about what had happened to her, C.M. was not able to focus her attention towards the most crucial aspects of the retrieval information provided. Thus, C.M. could not utilize critical retrieval information to such an extent that the information extracted would make contact with the specific traumatic experience until she was assured a situation of personal safety.

---

[6] We realize that it is difficult to determine what the central information is in advance outside the laboratory, and we are aware of the risk of circularity when we say that the detail information that was remembered probably was the most central information.

5) At the situation in which C.M. was successful in remembering the traumatic event, a tolerable level of stress and personal safety was at hand. Now when C.M. was running for the first time after the trauma, the same internal context was reinstated as was experienced the moment just preceding the attack. At this time, C.M. was also exposed to external cues that strongly reminded her of the place for the attack: a country environment with brushwood, a gravelled track with pieces of bricks, and a pile of bricks. Her earlier memory of "bricks and path" -- isolated from the initial context -- suggests that this detailed information was focused upon during the attack and hence high in cuing validity to the specific traumatic event.

As far as we know, interpretations of hysterical amnesia in terms of experimental memory data and cognitive psychological theory have been sparse so far in the literature. The present chapter attempts to remedy this state of affairs, and hopefully to instigate additional studies in which clinical and experimental knowledge will be used jointly to further our understanding of pathological forgetting.

ACKNOWLEDGEMENT

Preparation of this chapter was supported in part by Grant F 158/87 from the Swedish Council for Research in the Humanities and Social Sciences and Grant 84/253:1 from the Bank of Sweden Tercentenary Foundation. We are grateful to Ingvar Lundberg for helpful comments on an earlier draft of this chapter. Address all correspondance concerning this case study to Sven-Åke Christianson, Department of Psychology, University of Umeå, S-901 87 Umeå, Sweden.

REFERENCES

Abse, D. W. (1987). *Hysteria and related mental disorders.* (2nd ed). Bristol: Wright.

Bacon, S. J. (1974). Arousal and the range of cue utilization. *Journal of Experimental Psychology, 102,* 81-87.

Baddeley, A. D. (1972). Selective attention and performance in dangerous environments. *British Journal of Psychology, 63,* 537-546.

Bond, C. F. Jr., & Kirkpatrick, K. C. (1982). Distraction, amnesia, and the next-in-line effect. *Journal of Experimental Social Psychology, 18,* 307-323.

Bower, G. H. (1981). Mood and memory. *American Psychologist, 36,* 129-148.

Brenner, M. (1973). The next-in-line effect. *Journal of Verbal Learning and Verbal Behavior, 12,* 320-323.

Breuer, J., & Freud, S. (1895). Studies on hysteria. In J. Strachey (Ed.), *The standard edition of the complete psychological works of*

Sigmund Freud. (Vol. 2). London: Hogarth Press, 1955.
Buss, A. R. (1966). *Psychopathology.* New York: Wiley & Sons, Inc.
Christianson, S.-Å. (1984a). The relationship between induced emotional arousal and amnesia. *Scandinavian Journal of Psychology, 25,* 147-160.
Christianson, S.-Å. (1984b). *Amnesia and emotional arousal.* Doctoral Dissertation, University of Umeå, Sweden.
Christianson, S.-Å. (1986). Effects of positive emotional events on memory. *Scandinavian Journal of Psychology, 27,* 287-299.
Christianson, S.-Å. (1987). Emotional and autonomic responses to visual traumatic stimuli. *Scandinavian Journal of Psychology, 28,* 83-87.
Christianson, S.-Å., & Loftus, E. F. (1987). Memory for traumatic events. *Applied Cognitive Psychology, 1,* 225-239.
Christianson, S.-Å., & Mjörndal, T. (1985). Adrenalin, emotional arousal, and memory. *Scandinavian Journal of Psychology, 26,* 237-248.
Christianson, S.-Å., & Nilsson, L.-G. (1984). Functional amnesia as induced by a psychological trauma. *Memory and Cognition, 12,* 142-155.
Christianson, S.-Å., Nilsson, L.-G., Mjörndal, T., Perris, C., & Tjellden, G. (1986). Psychological versus physiological determinants of emotional arousal and its relationship to laboratory amnesia. *Scandinavian Journal of Psychology, 27,* 302-312.
Christianson, S.-Å., Nilsson, L.-G., & Silfvenius, H. (1987). Initial memory deficits and subsequent recovery in two cases of head trauma. *Scandinavian Journal of Psychology. 28,* 267-280.
Detterman, D. K. (1975). The von Restorff effect and induced amnesia: Production by manipulation of sound intensity. *Journal of Experimental Psychology: Human Learning and Memory, 1,* 614-628.
Detterman, D. K. (1976). The retrieval hypothesis as an explanation of induced retrograde amnesia. *Quarterly Journal of Experimental Psychology, 28,* 623-632.
Detterman, D. K., & Ellis, N. R. (1972). Determinants of induced amnesia in short-term memory. *Journal of Experimental Psychology, 95,* 308-316.
Easterbrook, J. A. (1959). The effect of emotion on cue utilization and the organization of behavior. *Psychological Review, 66,* 183-201.
Eich, J. E. (1980). The cue-dependent nature of state-dependent retrieval. *Memory & Cognition, 8,* 157-173.
Ellis, N. R., Detterman, D. K., Runcie, D., McCarver, R. B., & Craig, E. M. (1971). Amnesic effects in short-term memory. *Journal of Experimental Memory, 89,* 357-361.
Erdelyi, M. H. (1970). Recovery of unavailable perceptual input. *Cognitive Psychology, 1,* 99-113..
Erdelyi, M. H., & Goldberg, B. (1979). Let's not sweep repression under the rug: Toward a cognitive psychology of repression. In J. F. Kihlstrom, & F. J. Evans (Eds.), *Functional disorders of memory,* pp. 355-402. Hillsdale, N.J.: Lawrence Erlbaum Associates, Publishers.

Eysenck, M. W. (1982). *Attention and arousal: Cognition and performance.* Berlin: Springer-Verlag.

Fisk, A. D., & Wickens, D. D. (1979). On the locus of the Tulving retrograde amnesia effect. *Bulletin of the Psychonomic Society, 14,* 3-6.

Flavell, J. H. (1955). Repression and the "Return of the Repressed". *Journal of Consulting Psychology, 19,* 441-443.

Freud, S. (1915). Repression. In J. Strachey (Ed.), *The standard edition of the complete psychological works of Sigmund Freud,* Vol. 14, pp. 146-158. London: Hogarth Press, 1957.

Glucksberg, S., & King, L. J. (1967). Motivated forgetting mediated by implicit verbal chaining: A laboratory analogue of repression. *Science, 158,* 517-519.

Holmes, D. S. (1972). Repression or interference? A further investigation. *Journal of Personality and Social Psychology, 22,* 163-170.

Horowitz, M. J. (1975). Intrusive and repetitive thoughts after experimental stress: a summary. *Archives of General Psychiatry, 32,* 1457-1463.

Horowitz, M. J. (1979). Psychological response to serious life events. In V. Hamilton and D. M. Warburton (Eds.), *Human stress and cognition.* New York: Wiley & Sons.

Horowitz, M. J. (1986). *Stress Response Syndromes* (2nd edition). New Jersey: Aronson.

Jacoby, L. L. (1982). Knowing and remembering: Some parallels in the behavior of Korsakoff patients and normals. In L. S. Cermak (Ed.). *Human memory and amnesia,* pp. 97-122. Hillsdale, N.J.: Lawrence Erlbaum Associates.

Janet, P. (1965). *The major symptoms of hysteria* (2nd edition). New York: Hafner Publishing Company.

Jung, C. G. (1906). Experimental researches. In *Collected Works.* London: Routledge and Keagan Paul, 1972.

Kihlstrom, J. F., & Evans, F. J. (Eds.). (1979a). *Functional disorders of memory.* Hillsdale, N.J.: Lawrence Erlbaum Associates, Publishers.

Kihlstrom, J. F., & Evans, F. J. (1979b). Memory retrieval processes during posthypnotic amnesia. In J. F. Kihlstrom & F. J. Evans (Eds.), *Functional disorders of memory,* pp. 179-218. Hillsdale, N.J.: Lawrence Erlbaum Associates, Publishers.

Kinsbourne, M., & Wood, F. (1982). Theoretical considerations regarding the episodic - semantic memory distinction. In L. S. Cermak (Ed.), *Human memory and amnesia,* pp. 195-217. Hillsdale, N.J.: Lawrence Erlbaum Associates.

Kleinsmith, L. J., & Kaplan, S. (1963). Paired-associate learning as a function of arousal and interpolated interval. *Journal of Experimental Psychology, 65,* 190-193.

Kleinsmith, L. J., & Kaplan, S. (1964). The interaction of arousal and recall interval in nonsense syllable paired-associate learning. *Journal of Experimental Psychology, 67,* 124-126.

Korchin, S. J. 1964). Anxiety and cognition. In C. Scheerer (Ed.), *Cognition: Theory, research, promise,* pp. 58-78. New York: Harper & Row.

Levinger, G., & Clark, J. (1961). Emotional factors in the forgetting of word associations. *Journal of Abnormal and Social Psychology, 62,* 99-105.

Loftus, E. F., & Burns, T. (1982). Mental shock can produce retrograde amnesia. *Memory & Cognition, 10,* 318-323.

MacKinnon, D. W., & Dukes, W. F. (1962). Repression. In L. Postman (Ed.). *Psychology in the making.* New York: Knopf.

Mandler, G. (1975). *Mind and emotion.* New York: Wiley.

Mueller, J. H. (1979). Anxiety and encoding processes in memory. *Personality and Social Psychology Bulletin, 5,* 288-294.

Nemiah, J. C. (1969). Hysterical amnesia. In G. A. Talland & N. C. Waugh (Eds.), *The pathology of memory,* pp. 107-113. New York: Academic Press.

Nemiah. J. C. (1979). Dissociative amnesia: A clinical and theoretical reconsideration. In J. F. Kihlstrom & F. J. Evans (Eds.), *Functional disorders of memory,* pp. 303-323. Hillsdale, N.J.: Lawrence Erlbaum Associates, Publishers.

Runcie, D., & O'Bannon, R. M. (1977). An independence of induced amnesia and emotional response. *America Journal of Psychology, 90,* 55-61.

Russel, W. R. (1971). *The traumatic amnesias.* London: Oxford University Press.

Saufley, W. H. Jr., & Winograd, E. (1970). Retrograde amnesia and priority instructions in free recall. *Journal of Experimental Psychology, 85,* 150-152.

Schachter, S. (1971). *Emotion, obesity, and crime.* New York: Academic Press.

Schacter, D. L., Wang, P. L., Tulving, E., & Freedman, M. (1982). Functional retrograde amnesia: A quantitative case study. *Neuropsychologia, 20,* 523-532.

Schacter, D. L. (1986). Amnesia and Crime. How Much Do We Really Know? *American Psychologist, 41,* 286-295.

Schulz, L. S. (1971). Effects of high-priority events on recall and recognition of other events. *Journal of Verbal Learning and Verbal Behavior, 10,* 322-330.

Talland, G. A., & Waugh, N. C. (1969). (Eds.). *The Pathology of memory.* New York: Academic Press.

Tulving, E. (1969). Retrograde amnesia in free recall. *Science, 164.* 88-90.

Tulving, E. (1972). Episodic and semantic memory. In E. Tulving & W. Donaldson (Eds.), *Organization of memory,* pp. 381-403. New York: Academic Press.

Tulving, E. (1983). *Elements of episodic memory.* Oxford: Clarendon Press.

Tulving, E. (1985). How many memory systems are there? *American Psychologist, 40,* 385-398.

Tulving, E., & Thomson, D. M. (1973). Encoding specificity and retrieval processes in episodic memory. *Psychological Review, 80,* 352-373.

Wachtel, P. L. (1967). Conceptions of broad and narrow attention. *Psychological Bulletin, 68,* 417-429.

Wachtel, P. L. (1968). Anxiety, attention, and coping with threat. *Journal of Abnormal Psychology, 73,* 137-143.

Walker, E. L. (1958). Action decrement and its relation to learning. *Psychological Review, 65,* 129-142.

Walker, E. L. (1967). Arousal and the memory trace. In D. P. Kimble (Ed.), *The organization of recall,* Vol. 2, pp. 186-233. New York: The New York Academy of Sciences.

Walton, J. N. (1971). *Essentials of neurologi,* (3rd edition), London: Pitman Medical & Scientific Publishing Company Ltd.

Warrington, E. K., & Weiskrantz, L. (1974). The effect of prior learning on subsequent retention in amnesic patients. *Neuropsychologia, 12,* 419-428.

Warrington, E. K., & Weiskrantz, L. (1982). Amnesia: A disconnection syndrome? *Neuropsychologia, 20,* 233-247.

Whitty, C. W. M., & Zangwill, O. L. (1977). (Eds.), *Amnesia.* (2nd edition). London: Butterworth.

Zachary, R. A. (1982). Imagery, ambiguity, emotional arousal, and ongoing thought. *Journal of Mental Imagery, 6,* 93-108.

Zeller, A. F. (1950a). An experimental analogue of repression. I. Historical summary. *Psychological Bulletin, 47,* 39-51.

Zeller, A. F. (1950b). An experimental analogue of repression. II. The effect of individual failure and success on memory measured by learning. *Journal of Experimental Psychology, 40,* 411-422.

Zeller, A. F. (1951). An experimental analogue of repression. III. The effect of induced failure and success on memory measured by recall. *Journal of Experimental Psychology, 42,* 32-38.

12 Malleability of Memory for Emotional Events

Elizabeth F. Loftus and Sven-Åke Christianson
University of Washington and University of Umeå

How well do people remember emotional experiences from the past? When something traumatic happens, like an accident, it may seem at the time as if it will never be forgotten. The issue that we concern ourselves with in this chapter is the fate of these memories over the course of life.

A body of research has examined the fate of memory. Once information is stored in memory, it does not necessarily wait there in a pristine form for attempts to recover it. Rather new inputs appear to alter, transform, or change the earlier memories. Thus, we talk about the malleability of memory. A question that has received relatively little attention is whether highly emotional events differ from their less emotional counterparts in terms of the extent to which they are malleable.

In this chapter, we first review some studies on the malleability of memories that result from simulated events presented in the laboratory. This work shows the relative ease with which people's memories can be changed by post-event inputs. We then ask this question: Are memories of highly emotional events more or less malleable? We present some preliminary data suggesting that the details of highly emotional events are less well remembered in general and more susceptible to post-event inputs. Even if some details of an emotional event would ordinarily be well retained in memory, these details are still vulnerable to interfering influences.

What do these results tell us about real life traumatic experiences, and the extent to which they are retained in memory? Applying experimental findings to real life events is always a risky business; we discuss the extent to which it is legitimate to do that in this domain.

Post-Event Information and Memory Distortion

Over the past decade, one of the present authors has been studying distortions in memory from post-event information. The basic procedure used in this research is quite simple. Subjects witness a complex event, like a film of a crime or accident. Subsequently some subjects receive new misleading information about the event. Control subjects do not. Finally, all subjects attempt to recall details from the original event.

When exposed to misleading post-event information, subjects have misrecalled the color of a car that was green as being blue, a yield sign as a stop sign, broken glass or tape recorders that never existed, and even recalled something as large and conspicuous as a barn when no barn was ever seen (See Loftus, 1979; Loftus, 1983; and Hall, Loftus, & Tousignant, 1984, for reviews of this work.)

To give a more specific example, in one study subjects first watched a film of a car accident. Misled subjects were asked "How fast was the white sports car going when it passed the barn while travelling along the country road?" There was no barn in the film. Control subjects answered a question that did not mention a barn. A week later, all subjects were asked whether they had seen a barn in the film.

Misled subjects were more likely to later "recall" having seen the non-existent barn than were subjects who had not been asked the misleading question. Why does this occur? One hypothesis is that the questions are effective because they contain information -- in this case false information -- that becomes integrated into the person's recollection of the event, thereby supplementing that memory.

In other studies, it has been shown that new information can do more than simply supplement a recollection: it can occasionally alter, or transform, a recollection. For example, in several studies, subjects have received misleading information about the color of certain key objects. In one study (Loftus, 1977), subjects saw a series of slides depicting successive stages in an accident involving a car and a pedestrian. In the series, a green car drives past the accident but does not stop. After viewing the slides of the accident, some subjects were exposed to the information that the car that had passed the accident was blue. Finally subjects looked at a color wheel containing color stripes and were given a list of objects that had appeared in the slides. Among other colors, the wheel contained some green strips, some blue ones, and some that were intermediate bluish-green. The task was to pick out the color that best represented the subjects' recollection of each of the objects.

This study showed that subjects given the "blue" information tended to pick a blue or bluish-green as the color that represented their recollection of the car that passed the accident. Some of these subjects picked a solid blue while others picked a bluish-green, indicating greater or lesser influence of the misleading information. The choice of bluish-green and simultaneous rejection of the true green indicates that subjects have some elements of the original information in memory but have been shifted toward a bluer color by the post-event suggestion. This research suggests that new information can not only supplement memory, it can sometimes alter it.

The Fate of Memory

Although research on the misinformation effect is clear in showing that post-event information can influence a person's reported recollection, many questions remain about the misinformation effect. One question concerns the fate of the underlying memory traces. When a person sees an accident involving a car racing through an intersection with a red traffic light, and later "learns" that the light was green and now remembers seeing green, what happened to the original memory for a red light? Has the memory truly been updated or altered by the post-event information so that the original traces could not be recovered in the future? This has been referred to as the "alteration" hypothesis, and it suggests that the original memory representations are altered when post-event information is encoded that differs from what was originally experienced. Another position is the "coexistence" hypothesis, which assumes that the original and the post-event information coexist in memory. The introduction of post-event information, under this position, is thought to make the original memories simply less accessible, but still potentially recoverable at some future time.

The coexistence-alteration dichotomy bears on one of the most fundamental questions about memory: the permanence of memory traces. The coexistence view is consistent with the idea that all information, once stored in memory remains there more or less permanently. The alteration view implies a true loss of information from memory due to the updating, substitution, or blending in of new inputs.

Coexistence theories derive their support from studies that show successful recovery of original memories. For example, by reinstating the context of the original event more fully, or by warning people that they may have been exposed to misleading information. Despite these successful recoveries of the allegedly altered memories, this still does not mean that all memories are similarly recoverable.

Alteration theories derive their support by numerous empirical failed attempts to recover original memory. Even the mysterious technique of hypnosis has failed to lead to the original memories once they have been altered. Of course such failures do not prove that the original memories do not exist, because it can always be argued that the original memory does exist but that the appropriate retrieval method was not used, or that the method used was not sufficiently powerful.

Recently a third position on the misinformation effect appeared. McCloskey and Zaragoza (1985) maintain that both the alteration and the coexistence views are wrong. Their claim is that misleading post-event information neither alters the original memory nor makes it less accessible. Concider the empirical work that led them to this assertion. McCloskey and Zaragoza used the standard three-phase paradigm, with one modification. Subjects saw a simulated office burglary. The simulation contained a number of critical items, one of which shows a man holding a hammer. Then subjects read a narrative describing the events shown in the slides. In the Control condition, the narrative gave no specific information about the critical item -- it was reffered to simply as a tool. In the Misled condition, the narrative referred to the critical item as a screwdriver. After reading the narrative, the subjects were tested on what they saw. The original test procedure required subjects to choose between hammer -- the originally-seen item, and screwdriver -- the item presented to the Misled subjects as misleading information.

McCloskey and Zaragoza felt that the traditional test procedure was not adequate for telling whether the original memory has been modified since the post-event information could simply bias some subjects towards choosing the other object. So they created a modified procedure in which the bias could not operate. In the modified procedure, the misleading information -- screwdriver -- was not included as an option on the test. Instead subjects were asked to choose between the original item -- hammer -- and a new item: wrench. If misleading information impairs subjects' memory (by erasing the original or by making it less accessible) then Misled subjects should show poorer test performance than Control subjects, even in the Modified procedure. However, if misleading information does not influence memory for the original information, then Control and Misled conditions should not differ.

Six replications of this test, using nearly 800 college students, were conducted. Misled and Control subjects performed about equally on recognition tests. They averaged 72% and 75% correct, respectively. (With the traditional procedure -- a test between hammer and screwdriver, for example -- the researchers obtained the usual effect of misleading information, 37% correct for Misled subjects and 72% correct for Control subjects.). It was these data that led McCloskey and Zaragoza to conclude that misleading information has no effect on a person's ability to remember the original event.

At the heart of the McCloskey and Zaragoza's work is the complaint that the usual testing procedure, where the suggested item is included on the test, is inappropriate for assessing the effects of misleading information on memory. Yet the usual testing procedure is quite appropriate for answering certain kinds of questions about the misinformation effect. Consider a case in which subjects see a man with a hammer. Later some subjects receive misleading information about a screwdriver. How shall we now test these subjects to assess the impact of post-event information? If we wanted to know whether misled subjects would adopt the suggestion and choose it on a recognition test, it would be perfectly appropriate to give subjects a choice between the original and the suggested item.

But suppose that we were interested in whether the misleading information impaired memory. In this case. McCloskey and Zaragoza may be right that the presence of the suggested item on the test and the choice by subjects of that item cannot be easily interpreted. Subjects could be choosing the item not because their memory is impaired but because they feel that the experimenter must know more than they do. Or, they could choose the item because they failed to encode the original information and the misleading information supplemented their memory. Or, finally they could be choosing the item because their memory was altered by the misleading information. Past researchers have recognized these possibilities before, and have used a variety of techniques to attempt to disentangle the various interpretations. In one study designed explicitly to identify those who were simply succumbing to the experimenter's wishes or apparent knowledge, it was concluded that only a small percentage of misled subjects could be characterized this way.

If the presence of the suggested item as a response possibility leads to problems in interpreting performance, does the absence of the suggested item solve those problems? Certainly if subjects cannot chose the suggested item, then they cannot respond to that particular demand characteristic. This is one apparent benefit of the modified test. However there are other problems with the modified test that must be recognized. One problem is that it may not be sufficiently sensitive to detect small impairments in memory. Put another way, the test between hammer and wrench (when the suggested item was screwdriver) may not have been sensitive enough to capture a loss in accessibility of hammer. This arises in part because many subjects will simply guess when they do not know the right answer. With the two-item test (hammer versus wrench), subjects can quess the correct answer half the time. The particular items used by McCloskey and Zaragoza were difficult items (as evidenced by the fact that the nonmisled subjects were correct only 72% of the time). Thus they were not particularly accessible even for subjects who were not misled. If items are not particularly accessible to begin with, it is hard to make them less accessible. This reasoning motivated some new research by Chandler (1987). When Chandler utilized critical items that were indeed accessible to begin with, misleading post-event information impaired memory performance even in a test that did not permit the choice of the misleading item, (see also Ceci, Ross & Toglia, 1987).

Untimately, the current debate regarding the most appropriate way to conceptualize the fate of post-event information requires addressing some critical questions about the nature of memory representation. Since we cannot get inside subjects heads to see how their memories are represented, we must rely on indirect inferences based on reports of what is recalled. Unfortunately what subjects claim to experience may not actually represent the true nature of their memories. Even if we demonstrate that subjects truly believe that their memories represent what they originally saw, we can never know whether somewhere in the recesses of mind lies an inaccessible but pristine memory trace. Thus rather than trying to make inferences about representation issues that may be unanswerable, researchers may more profitably shift the focus of research to new questions. Under what conditions will we observe a change in memory performance after exposure to new information?

When Does Memory Performance Change?

The alteration of recollection appears to be a fact of life. It is of theoretical and practical interest to know something about the conditions under which people accept suggestive information and the conditions under which they resist such information. One type of situation that promotes the acceptance of post-event information is a situation in which the new information is presented in a fairly subtle way, so as to minimize the likelihood that a subject will detect a discrepancy between the new information and what is already stored in memory. Subtly presented post-event information is more powerful in its ability to misguide our cognitive processes. It invades us like Trojan horses because it does not attract our attention (Ingvar Lundberg, this volume. p. 286).

Other variables are also important. One variable concerns the time interval between the viewing of an initial event, the encountering of misinformation, and the engaging in a final test of recollection. Studies have shown that if time passes after an event occurs, a person's recollection for details becomes increasingly susceptible to misinformation. Put another way, recollection change is enhanced by the fading of original memory with the passage of time. Again the principle of discrepancy detection can be used to account for this result. With the passage of time, it becomes increasingly likely that an individual will fail to detect a discrepancy between the misinformation and what is already stored in memory. For a more detailed discussion of discrepancy detection, see Tousignant, Hall, and Loftus (1986).

In addition to the nature of the misinformation itself, and when that information is introduced, another important factor that potentially can influence the misinformation effect is the nature of the event itself. Unfortunately relatively little is known about which types of events are more prone to distorting influences and which types of events are more resistant to such influences. It seems reasonable to posit that any variable that causes event details to be poorly stored would create a situation that is ripe for the acceptance of post-event information. So, for example, events that are witnessed under conditions of high emotional stress might be expected to be more vulnerable to subsequent post-event misinformation, if the emotionality caused a poorer memory to be formed in the first place. To explore this issue, we must first ask what is known about memory for emotional events.

Eyewitness Memory of Emotional Events

Eyewitness research generally shows that information acquired in the course of viewing a life-stressing event is more difficult to recollect as compared with a neutral event. On the basis of a number of laboratory studies investigating the role of arousal on accuracy in recollection of a natural event (see Deffenbacher, 1983, for a review). we conclude that a high level of emotional arousal reduces the accuracy of eyewitness memory (see e.g., Clifford & Scott, 1978; Clifford & Hollin, 1981; Loftus & Burns, 1982). Moreover, it is memory for peripheral detail information that is especially susceptible to forgetting, compared to memory for the central details of the original event (Hall, Loftus, & Tousignant, 1984).

One explanation offered to account for these findings, in accordance with Easterbrook (1959), is that states of increased emotional arousal are associated with narrowing of attention. and thus, a reduction in the range of task-relevant cues attended to (e.g., Christianson, 1984; Siegel & Loftus, 1978). Thus, peripheral details should be more vulnerable to forgetting because people fail to attend to this information appropriately.

While most empirical work on eyewitness memory has shown a relatively poor recollection of violent events, there are some observations which indicate that certain aversive events seem subjectively to be well remembered. For example, images of public events such as the assassination of President Kennedy (Brown & Kulik, 1977; Winograd & Killinger, 1983), and more private events such as witnessing an auto accident (Rubin & Kozin, 1984), seem to persist with little subjectively experienced loss of memory. In line with these findings, Christianson (1984) reported resonably good performance for some aspects of emotional events. Christianson showed that subjects who watched an emotional version of slide sequence remembered the slides at a short test interval as well as subjects presented with a neutral version of the sequence. At a delayed test interval, however, subjects presented with the emotional version were superior in recall of certain central details of the emotional slides. Christianson discussed these data in terms of attention-demanding characteristics of the emotional event.

In considering the empirical discrepancy observed in studies on memory of emotional events, it is important to elucidate what it means to say that a person remember an emotional event. To what extent is thematic information remembered? What about central detail information, and what about peripheral detail information? The matter of reliability of testimony for emotionally arousing events depends heavily on which type of information we ask about. Someone who has witnessed a traffic accident might be quite good at remembering that the event occurred and even remembering detail information concerning a car involved in the accident but quite poor at remembering detail information about a car parked in the background.

In a study by Christianson and Loftus (1987), memory for a traumatic event was compared with memory for a nontraumatic version of the same event. The purpose of this study was to try to distinguish between people's memory of the occurrence of an emotional event and the degree to which they accurately remember the details of the emotional event.

Subjects watched a short pictorial story consisting of an emotionally arousing sequence placed between preceding and succeeding neutral sequences. Control subjects watched a sequence that contained the same neutral events in the beginning and the end, but also neutral events in the middle. In both conditions subjects were instructed to pay close attention to the slides, and to choose and write down the most distingishing feature from each of the slides. Memory was assessed by asking the subjects to freely recall as many as possible of those features previously selected for each slide. Subjects were also given a recognition test on the specific pictures they had seen. This recognition test was primarily designed to measure the ability to remember peripheral details.

We expected to find that the central information (i.e., the selected items) of emotional events would be more likely to be attended to and rehearsed. We also expected (in line with Easterbrook, 1959 and

Eysenck, 1982) that the range of cues attented to would be more restricted because of a reduced proportion of attentional capacity available for processing of peripheral information (i.e., an inferior recognition of the specific pictures).

In accordance with the predictions, we found that subjects who saw the emotional version were better able to recall the essential features (or theme) of the event, however they were less able to recognize the specific pictures they had seen.

In a second experiment subjects watched either an emotional or a nonemotional version of a filmed event and about six months later were asked to remember the essence of the film. We found that subjects who watched the emotional version were better able to recall the essence of the film.

These findings suggest that the essence (the theme) and some central details of an emotionally arousing event might be relatively well retained, while memory seems to be impaired for many specific, and especially peripheral, details.

Emotional Events and Acceptance of Post-Event Information

We now turn to the issue of whether information acquired in the course of viewing an emotional event is more or less susceptible to misinformation. Relevant to this issue is the work of Loftus and Burns (1982), who presented subjects with one of two versions of an event -- a violent version or a nonviolent one. All subjects saw a film lasting for 2 minutes and 15 seconds. The violent version presented a bank robbery in the first two minutes and ended with a young boy being shot in the face. The nonviolent version also began with the bank robbery but ended in a neutral way. The results showed that compared with subjects who saw the neutral version of the film, those who saw the violent version showed poorer retention of the details of the bank robbery itself (the first two minutes) of the film. For example, in the neutral version, almost 28% of the subjects recalled a detail about the boy's shirt, whereas less than 5% could recall it from the violent version of the film. One explanation for this result is that violent events disrupt full storage of information in memory. In a follow-up study using these stimuli it was shown that the details of the violent event were more vulnerable to misinformation. Put another way, it was easier to mislead a subject about the details of the boy's shirt when that subject had seen the violent rather than the neutral version of the film (Loftus, 1983).

The study just described provides a single demonstration that it is easier to manipulate some details when a violent event is witnessed, compared to a neutral event. But the detail about the boy's shirt was a rather minor detail. Would more salient details behave in the same way? If the critical event were an accident, would it be possible to change memory both for something peripheral like a car that passed without stopping, as well as something central like the car involved in the accident? We might predict that central details associated with emotional events would be hard to influence, and peripheral details easy to influence. Some preliminary work bears on this issue (Christianson & Loftus, unpublished data). Subjects were presented with a slide sequence depicting an accident in which a car hit a young boy. After this emotional event, subjects were presented with two pieces of misinformation. One piece was about the car that hit the boy (a central detail), and the other piece was about a car that passed in the distance (a peripheral detail). Performance on these two items was compared to that of subjects who received no misinformation.

The results showed that the misleading information had a significant effect on memory for the peripheral detail. However, it also negatively influenced memory for the central detail albeit to a lesser degree. All control subjects accurately remembered the central information that the car that hit the boy was white. However, about half of the subjects who received misinformation were wrong about the color of the car. This study suggests that even central information from an emotionally shocking event is susceptible to post-event influences. (See Dritsas & Hamilton, 1977, for a further demonstration that peripheral details are easier than central details to manipulate in memory.)

Taken together, the experimental work on memory for emotional events has shown the following. By and large, details of emotional events seem to be by and large less well retained than the details of more neutral events. This is particularly true of the more peripheral details. While occasionally some central details are well retained from an emotional event, memory for those details is still susceptible to interferring inputs.

Experimental Research Versus Real-Life Trauma

What do these findings tell us about real-life emotional events? Even if one has to be cautious in applying laboratory data to real-life events, recent knowledge within human memory research has been found to be most useful and relevant in interpreting different real-life situations. One example of this is the phenomenon of hysterical amnesia discussed by Christianson and Nilsson (this volume). However, more confident statements on the basis of experimental research can of course be made to less unusual events, such as the witnessing of an car accident. The laboratory results suggest to us that, contrary to the belief that there can be an indelible fixation in the mind when traumatic events occur, such traumata are in fact often associated with impairments of memory (see e.g., Christianson, 1984; Christianson & Nilsson, 1984; Loftus & Burns, 1982).

The belief that emotional events lead to the formation of indelible memories was held by many observers of a trial that occurred in Israel in 1987. The man on trial, John Demjanjuk, was accused of being Ivan the Terrible -- the operator of the gas chambers that killed perhaps as many as a million people at the Treblinka concentration camp in Poland during World War II. Ivan the Terrible acquired his name and notorious reputation from the sadistic pleasure he took in splitting the skulls of his prisoners with an iron pipe and otherwise mutilating them. The critical issue in the Ivan case is whether the face identified at trial by the survivors out of that sea of sadism is the right face. Do we know anything scientifically about memories of atrocities that are 40 years old? The facts of the Ivan case are so distinctly different from the experimental simulations that our discomfort at generalizing from these results is especially great. For example, in the Ivan case, the surviving eyewitnesses were exposed to critical individuals perhaps hundreds of times. In the experimental simulations the subject witnesses are exposed to a critical event but once. In the Ivan case 40 years elapsed between the events and court testimony. In the experimental simulations, elapsed time is on the order of minutes or weeks. While the basic perceptual and memorial processes come into play in both the real-life and the experimental events, it is very difficult to know what degree of confidence one should have in analogizing from one situation to the other.

Consider, however, a real-life situation that on the surface more closely matches the experimental simulations. Suppose the real-life event is an armed robbery that lasts for three minutes. Several weeks later a witness is interviewed. Do the experimental results apply here? One immediate problem that arises when we try to apply the experimental findings to real-life events is to determine which type of details would be expected to be better or worse retained, as well as their vulnerability to interfering influences. Even if we believe, on the basis of laboratory results, that some central details from emotional events are relatively well retained and less susceptible to interference, we still have the problem of classifying central and peripheral details from a particular event outside the laboratory setting. Is the face of the robber a central or peripheral detail? Is the weapon used a central or peripheral detail? What about the gloves worn by the robber? Commonsense thinking would suggest that the source of emotional arousal or fright (or strongly connected pieces of information) would comprise of the most central details. However, it is easy to say when someone remembers something that it must have been a central detail. It is much harder to specify in advance outside the laboratory whether some detail is likely to be central or not. Who would have predicted in advance that the rape victim described by Christianson and Nilsson (this volume) would preserve some isolated memories of crumbling bricks along a path when the victim was questioned shortly after the incident?

Final Remarks

The research described constitutes one step towards the understanding of memory for emotional events. We are beginning to learn some things about the ability of people to retrieve the details of emotional events, and the extent to which memory for emotional events is malleable. We know that many details of emotional events suffer in memory, and this is especially true of the more peripheral events. Peripheral events are less well retained, and are more susceptible to interfering inputs. More work is needed before we can fully apply these findings to real-life emotional experiences. It seems likely that some of the same perceptual and memorial processes that are involved in laboratory simulations of emotional experiences will also be involved in the real world.

REFERENCES

Brown, R., & Kulik, J. (1977). Flashbulb memories. *Cognition, 5,* 73-99.

Ceci, S. J., Ross, D. F., & Toglia, M. P. (1987). Age differences in suggestibility: Narrowing the uncertainties. In S. J. Ceci, M. P. Toglia & D. F. Ross (Eds.), *Children's Eyewitness Memory,* pp. 178-208. New York: Springer-Verlag.

Chandler, C. (1987). *Does interpolated learning make original learning inaccessible?* Unpublished manuscript, University of Toronto, Canada.

Christianson, S.-Å. (1984). The relationship between induced emotional arousal and amnesia. *Scandinavian Journal of Psychology, 25,* 147-160.

Christianson, S.-Å. & Loftus, E. F. (1987) Memory for traumatic events. *Applied Cognitive Psychology, 1,* 225-239.

Christianson, S.-Å., Nilsson, L.-G. (1984). Functional amnesia as induced by a psychological trauma. *Memory and Cognition, 12,* 142-155.

Clifford, B. R., & Hollin, C. (1981). Effects of the type of incident and the number of perpetrators on eyewitness memory. *Journal of Applied Psychology, 66,* 364-370.

Clifford, B. R., & Scott, J. (1978). Individual and situational factors in eyewitness testimony. *Journal of Applied Psychology, 63,* 352-359.

Deffenbacher, K. (1983). The influence of arousal on reliability of testimony. In B. R. Clifford and S. Lloyd-Bostock (Eds.), *Evaluating witness evidence,* pp. 235-251. Chichester: Wiley.

Dritsas, W. J. & Hamilton, V. L. (1977) *Evidence about evidence: Effects of presuppositions, item salience, stress and perceiver set on accident recall.* Unpublished manuscript, University of Michigan.

Easterbrook, J. A. (1959). The effect of emotion on cue utilization and the organization of behavior. *Psychological Review, 66,* 183-201.

Eysenck, M. W. (1982). *Attention and arousal: Cognition and performance.* Berlin: Springer-Verlag.

Hall, D. H., Loftus, E. F., & Tousignant, J. P. (1984). Postevent information and changes in recollection for a natural event. In G. L. Wells & E. F. Loftus (Eds.), *Eyewitness testimony: Psychological perspectives,* pp. 124-141. Cambridge: Cambridge University Press.

Loftus, E. F. (1977). Shifting human color memory. *Memory & Cognition, 6,* 696-699.

Loftus, E. F. (1979). *Eyewitness testimony.* Cambridge, Mass: Harvard University Press.

Loftus, E. F. (1983). Misfortunes of memory. *Philosophical*

Transactions of the Royal Society, 302, 413-421. London.

Loftus, E.F. & Burns, T. E. (1982) Mental shock can produce retrograde amnesia. *Memory and Cognition, 10,* 318-323.

McCloskey, M., & Zaragoza, M. (1985). Misleading post-event information and memory for events: Arguments and evidence against memory impairment hypothesis. *Journal of Experimental Psychology: General, 114,* 3-18.

Rubin, D. C., & Kozin, M. (1984). Vivid memories. *Cognition, 16,* 81-95.

Siegel, J. M., & Loftus, E. F. (1978). Impact of anxiety and life stress upon eyewitness testimony. *Bulletin of the Psychonomic Society, 12,* 479-480.

Tousignant, J. P., Hall, D., & Loftus. E. F. (1986). Discrepancy detection and vulnerability to misleading post-event information. *Memory and Cognition, 14,* 329-338.

Winograd, E., & Killinger, W. A., Jr (1983). Relating age at encoding in early childhood to adult recall: Development of flashbulb memories. *Journal of Experimental Psychology: General, 112,* 413-422.

13 Anxiety and Cognition: Theory and Research

Michael W. Eysenck
University of London, England

INTRODUCTION

This chapter is concerned with the general issue of individual differences in anxiety as viewed from the cognitive perspective. It would, of course, be possible to address this issue in a number of different ways. For example, patients suffering from clinical anxiety could be compared with normal controls, or normals high in the personality dimension of trait anxiety could be compared with normals low in trait anxiety. While it might be supposed that these two approaches have little in common, this is not necessarily so. There are reasonable theoretical grounds for assuming that normals high in trait anxiety are more vulnerable to clinical anxiety than those low in trait anxiety. There is less empirical evidence relevant to this assumption than one might imagine, but such evidence as does exist tends to support it (e.g., Ingham, 1966; McKeon, Roa, & Mann, 1984).

So far as cognitive functioning is concerned, there are various approaches which could be adopted. Eysenck (1986) identified four different strands of research, but for present purposes it is of particular importance to distinguish between two major approaches. One approach is based on performance level, whereas the other approach considers differences in processing between threatening and non-threatening stimuli.

The most extensively used approach (especially in the United States) essentially addresses the question of whether high levels of anxiety lead to improved or to impaired performance on cognitive tasks. This approach perhaps owes its origins to the famous 'Yerkes-Dodson law' (Yerkes & Dodson, 1908), according to which increasing levels of arousal, motivation, or anxiety lead to improved performance up to a certain level, after which further increases impair performance. Various explanations of this putative inverted-U shaped curve have been offered, of which the best known is Easterbrook's hypothesis. According to Easterbrook (1959),

323

there is a progressive narrowing of cue utilization as arousal or anxiety increases. Initially this prevents processing of irrelevant stimuli and so improves performance, but with greater narrowing some of the task stimuli can no longer be processed, and so performance suffers.

The second approach is based on the assumption that differences in information processing between those high and low in anxiety will often depend on the content of the stimuli which are presented. More specifically, it seems reasonable to assume that differences are more likely to occur in the presence of threatening or anxiety-inducing stimuli than non-threatening or neutral stimuli. In other words, the emphasis is not on whether anxiety makes performance better or worse but on differential patterns of response as a function of stimulus content.

Which of these approaches is preferable depends, of course, on the specific questions one is interested in. From the perspective of clinical psychology, the latter approach is likely to prove more fruitful than the former. A crucial characteristic of clinically anxious patients is that they engage in excessive processing of threat-related information (e.g. worry), and one of the aims of therapy is to reduce or eliminate the tendency of anxious patients to exaggerate the threat posed by environmental events. If it were possible to specify more precisely the different ways in which individuals high and low in anxiety process threatening stimuli, then this might increase our understanding of some of the processes involved in clinical anxiety. It is to such matters that we now turn.

ANXIETY AND THREAT: NORMALS

Byrne's hypothesis

Byrne (1964) was interested in the notion that there are important individual differences in the response to threat in normal populations. In his theoretical formulation, he distinguished between repressors (who avoid threatening stimuli) and sensitizers (who approach threatening stimuli), and he devised the Repression-Sensitization Scale to permit individuals to be classfied as repressors or sensitizers. Byrne (1964) was adamant that his scale was not simply measuring trait anxiety. However, the fact that the Repression-Sensitization Scale correlates approximately +.85 with standard questionnaires of trait anxiety (Watson & Clark, 1984) indicates that his scale can appropriately be regarded as a measure of trait anxiety. In other words, sensitizers are high in trait anxiety and allegedly approach threatening stimuli, whereas repressors are low in trait anxiety and avoid threatening stimuli.

The relevant experimental evidence has been considered in detail elsewhere (e.g., Eysenck, MacLeod, & Mathews, 1987; Eysenck & Mathews, 1987). In essence, it has proved rather difficult to demonstrate the predicted differences in processing of threatening stimuli. The most used paradigm is that of perceptual defence, in which the exposure duration needed to recognize threatening or emotionally-loaded stimuli is often greater than that required to recognize neutral stimuli. If repressors or those low in trait anxiety avoid processing threatening stimuli, then one might anticipate that they would manifest a greater perceptual defence effect than sensitizers or those high in trait anxiety. However, this predicted difference in perceptual defence has usually not been obtained. As Watson and Clark (1984) concluded in their review of the literature, the results have been "overwhelmingly negative" (p. 481).

According to Byrne's (1964) conceptualization, it is as if there are individual differences in a volume control: those high in trait anxiety (sensitizers) turn up this control when confronted by threat, whereas those low in trait anxiety (repressors) do the opposite. It may well be more realistic to assume that there are individual differences in a selective mechanism which determines how processing resources are allocated among stimuli differing in their threat value. For example, if one threatening and one neutral stimulus were presented concurrently, then one might predict that individuals high in trait anxiety would tend to allocate more processing resources to the threatening than to the neutral stimulus, whereas those low in trait anxiety would do the opposite.

One of the advantages of thinking in terms of a selective mechanism is that it helps to explain why most of the experimental tests of Byrne's (1964) hypothesis have failed to support it. In nearly all of those experiments only one stimulus was presented at a time, and under such circumstances the selective mechanism would not operate. More convincing evidence of the existence of a selective mechanism has recently been obtained, and is discussed below.

Selective mechanism

The basic paradigm for investigating the selective mechanism was first used by Halkiopoulos, a student of mine, in a study reported briefly in Eysenck et al. (1987). Pairs of words were presented concurrently to the two ears, with all of the words presented to one ear needing to be shadowed (i.e., repeated back). Some of the shadowed words were threatening (e.g., grave, fail), whereas others were neutral (e.g., chairs, sale); all of the words on the unattended ear were neutral. In order to assess the allocation of processing resources, subjects were asked to respond as rapidly as possible to occasional tones which were presented to either ear very shortly after a pair of words had been presented.

Subjects were classified as high or low in trait anxiety on the basis of their scores on the Facilitation-Inhibition Scale (Ullmann, 1962), which correlates very highly with measures of trait anxiety. In essence, speed of responding to the tones indicated that those high in trait anxiety (i.e., facilitators) preferentially allocated processing to the ear on which a threatening word had just been presented, whereas those low in trait anxiety (i.e., inhibitors) actively avoided attending to the ear on which a threatening word had been presented. These basic findings have been replicated by Broadbent (pers. comm.) using a visual analog of this auditory task.

These findings indicate that a modified version of Byrne's (1964) hypothesis may be tenable. It is not true, as he argued, that there are always consistent individual differences in the extent to which threatening stimuli are processed. However, consistent differences in the processing of threatening stimuli of the kinds predicted by Byrne (1964) can be obtained provided that the situation permits selection between concurrent threatening and neutral stimuli.

Selection in a different sense has also been demonstrated by Eysenck et al. (1987). They used auditory presentation of homophones having a threatening and a neutral interpretation (e.g., die, dye; guilt, gilt), with the subjects' task simply being to write down the spelling of each word. Normals high in trait anxiety wrote down many more threatening interpretations of the homophones than did those low in trait anxiety.

In sum, those high in trait anxiety tend to allocate more processing resources to mildly threatening stimuli than do those low in trait anxiety, and they are also more likely to interpret ambiguous stimuli in a threatening fashion. These findings make intuitive sense. An individual who engages in excessive processing of threatening stimuli and who regards ambiguous situations as threatening will clearly experience the environment as more subjectively threatening than others, and will as a consequence more frequently be in a state of high anxiety (cf., Watson & Clark, 1984). However, it is not clear whether these differences in cognitive functioning between those high and low in trait anxiety are a cause or a consequence of trait-anxiety level. The causality issue has not been resolved here. As we will see later, there has been some progress so far as cognitive functioning in clinically anxious patients is concerned.

ANXIETY AND THREAT: PATIENTS

Basic findings

It is assumed that normal individuals high in trait anxiety are more likely than those low in trait anxiety to become clinically anxious. As a consequence, one might predict that those aspects of cognitive functioning which are found in normals high in trait anxiety would also tend to be found in anxious patients. The evidence broadly supports this prediction, at least so far as generalized anxiety disorder is concerned.

MacLeod, Mathews, and Tata (1986) utilized a visual version of the auditory selective processing task first used by Halkiopoulos and reported in Eysenck et al. (1987). They were interested in the allocation of processing resources between concurrent threat-related and neutral stimuli in generalized anxiety disorder patients and in normal controls. They discovered that the anxious patients tended to allocate more processing resources to threatening than to neutral stimuli, whereas the normal controls did the opposite. This is, of course, the same pattern of results reported by Eysenck et al. (1987) with normals high and low in trait anxiety.

An issue of obvious importance concerns the kinds of threatening stimuli which are effective in producing selective biases in the allocation of processing resources. In the study by MacLeod et al. (1986), they divided the threatening words they presented into those referring to physical health concerns (e.g., injury, agony) and those referring to social threats (e.g., criticized, ashamed). They also divided the patients with generalized anxiety disorder into two groups on the basis of whether they indicated that physical health or social concerns formed the major source of their worries. The allocation of processing resources between the threatening and neutral stimuli was unaffected by whether or not the nature of the threatening stimulus matched the primary area of concern of the patients.

Various other experimental paradigms have been used to compare patients with generalized anxiety disorder and normal controls. It has usually been found that the nature of the threat does not interact with the reported domain of concern in determining performance. It may well be that the early stages of processing involve only the simple categorization of stimulus material as potentially threatening or not, with a more precise analysis of the type of threat occurring only later. According to this view, allocation of processing resources in the selective processing task presumably occurs at a relatively early stage of processing.

Some relevant information concerning the processing stage at which the selective bias operates has recently been obtained in research involving Andrew Mathews, Anne Richards, and myself. Subjects were asked to name strips of colour while at the same time threatening or neutral words were presented subliminally. Despite the fact that the words could not be perceived at the conscious level, it was discovered that patients with generalized anxiety disorder took longer to name the colours when threatening rather than neutral words were presented concurrently. In contrast, speed of colour naming in normal controls was faster when neutral words were presented concurrently. These findings indicate rather clearly that the selective bias in anxious patients can operate at a pre-attentive level. The same conclusion was reached on the basis of a study using the dichotic listening paradigm (Mathews & MacLeod, 1986).

A number of additional aspects of cognitive functioning have been considered. For example, two different paradigms have been used in order to investigate the notion that anxious patients differ from normal controls in their interpretation of ambiguous stimuli having possible threatening and neutral meanings. In unpublished research, homophones having threat-related and neutral spellings (e.g., die, dye) were presented auditorily, with the subjects being instructed to write down the spelling of each word as it was presented. Patients with generalized anxiety disorder wrote down on average approximately 15% more threat-related spellings than normal controls, presumably reflecting a difference in terms of the interpretation of ambiguity.

Similar findings with a somewhat different paradigm were obtained by Eysenck, Mathews, and Richards (in preparation). Ambiguous sentences (e.g., "The chest was opened") were presented along with unambiguous sentences at presentation. On a subsequent recognition test, sentences consistent with either the threat-related or the neutral interpretation of the ambiguous sentences were presented, and the subjects' task was to decide whether each sentence meant the same as one of the sentences presented initially. Patients with generalized anxiety disorder were relatively more likely than normal controls to select the threat-related rather than the neutral interpretation sentences.

Consistently negative findings have been obtained when long-term memory for unambiguously threatening or non-threatening stimulus material in anxious patients and normal controls has been considered (see Mathews and Eysenck, 1987). This is surprising, both because of the evidence that anxious patients selectively process information related to threat, and also because of a phenomenon known as mood-congruent learning (e.g., Bower, Gilligan, & Monteiro, 1981). In this phenomenon, emotionally-loaded stimulus material is learned best when its affective value is congruent or consistent with the learner's current mood. It would thus be anticipated that anxious patients would have a bias in learning (and therefore memory also) favouring material related to threat.

It is still not entirely clear why anxious patients fail to show the predicted memory-bias effect. However, one possibility is that anxious patients have developed cognitive avoidance strategies (e.g., failure to rehearse) which they make use of after a stimulus has been identified as threatening. Such strategies would have obvious utility, in that in their absence clinically anxious patients would be almost constantly processing threatening material stemming from the pre-attentive selective bias.

Problems of interpretation

There are obvious similarities betweeen the findings obtained when comparing anxious patients with normal controls and when comparing normals high and low in trait anxiety. In both cases, there is evidence for a pre-attentive selective bias and for an interpretative bias favouring threat-related interpretations of ambiguous stimuli. However, the memory findings are less similar across the two comparisons. There is evidence that high trait anxiety (or neuroticism) is associated with a bias favouring recall of negative information about oneself (e.g., Martin, Ward, & Clark, 1983), but this finding has not been replicated with generalized anxiety disorder patients (e.g., Mogg, Mathews, & Weinman, 1987).

The fundamental limitation of all of these findings relating to non-normal cognitive functioning in anxious patients is that it is not possible to interpret them in an unequivocal fashion. In essence, we do not know whether non-normal cognitive functioning is one of the factors involved in the aetiology of clinical anxiety, or whether it is merely a reflection and secondary consequence of anxious mood state. The theoretical significance of the findings would, of course, be much greater in the former than in the latter case.

In order to elucidate the issue of causality, it is necessary to investigate cognitive functioning in other groups of individuals. The most revelant group would consist of normal individuals who subsequently develop anxiety neurosis. If the non-normal cognitive functioning exhibited by currently anxious patients were also found in pre-morbid individuals, then the implication would be that those aspects of cognition are associated with vulnerability to anxiety. On the other hand, if pre-morbid individuals did not exhibit non-normal cognitive functioning, then it could be assumed that non-normal cognitive functioning among the currently anxious is merely a reflection of current mood state.

There are very real practical problems associated with investigating cognitive functioning in a pre-morbid group. In order to obtain a satisfactory group size, it would obviously be necessary to conduct a long-lasting longitudinal study on an extremely large sample. As a consequence, no such study has been carried out. However, it could be argued (albeit with a number of qualifications) that the cognitive functioning of normals high in trait anxiety may resemble that of a pre-morbid group. If one were willing to make such an assumption, then the research discussed above suggests that the pre-attentive selective bias and the biased interpretation of ambiguous stimuli are both reflections of a vulnerability factor rather than of anxious mood state.

While the findings from normals high in trait anxiety are probably of some relevance, it remains a fact that high trait anxiety has not definitely been established as a factor associated with vulnerability to clinical anxiety. Accordingly, it is necessary to consider other ways in which the issue of causality might be approached experimentally. The current research programme of Andrew Mathews and myself, discussed below, does precisely that.

Research strategy: recovered patients

We have adopted the research strategy of comparing the cognitive task performance of currently anxious patients with a diagnosis of generalized anxiety disorder, individuals who have recovered from clinical anxiety at least six months prior to taking part in our research, and normal controls. It is assumed that those cognitive measures reflecting stable characteristics associated with vulnerability to anxiety should distinguish the matched controls from the other two groups. On the other hand, those cognitive measures reflecting anxious mood state should distinguish the currently anxious group from both the recovered anxious and control groups.

It should be noted that there are some potential problems of interpretation with this research strategy. If the cognitive performance of the recovered anxious group resembles that of the currently anxious group but differs from that of the normal controls, it does not necessarily follow that a stable characteristic associated with vulnerability to anxiety is being assessed. An alternative possibility is simply that different functions and processes recover at different rates, with cognitive functioning taking somewhat longer than other indices of recovery.

If the cognitive performance of the recovered anxious group is comparable to that of the control group but different from that of the currently anxious group, then the likelihood is that the performance reflects currrent anxious mood state. However, it is also possible for comparable performance to camouflage important differences. For example, recovered anxious subjects and normal controls might indicate equal optimism about the future on a questionnaire designed to assess attitudes, but this comparability in expressed attitudes would not necessarily also be found in internal cognitive processes.

Despite these possible interpretative problems, the proposed research strategy discussed above can provide valuable evidence. In the study by Eysenck, Mathews, and Richards (in preparation) which was discussed above, currently anxious patients were relatively more likely than normal controls to select the threatening interpretations of ambiguous sentences on a test of recognition memory. A group of recovered anxious patients was also run in this experiment. Their performance approximated closely to that of the normal controls, but was quite different from that of the currently anxious patients. According to the logic of the experimental design, this pattern of results indicates that the relative bias in favour of threatening interpretations shown by currently anxious patients is a function of their current mood state rather than a reflection of a vulnerability factor.

The same basic research strategy has been applied to a study of a priming paradigm designed to investigate the negative priming effect (Tipper, 1985). In some of Tipper's research, the subject was initially presented with two drawings. One of these drawings was to be attended to and the other was to be ignored, and the instructions made it clear which was which. Shortly after this initial presentation, a further drawing was presented. The subject's task was to name the drawing as rapidly as possible. There were three different conditions of present relevance: (1) when the drawing was the same as the previously attended drawing; (2) when it was the same as the previously ignored drawing; and (3) when it differed from both the attended and ignored drawings (baseline or control condition).

Tipper (1985) obtained a negative priming effect when the final drawing was the same as the previously ignored drawing. In other words, subjects take longer to name a previously ignored drawing than to name a previously unpresented drawing. While the correct interpretation of these data remains unclear, Tipper (1985) favoured the notion that ignoring a drawing involves inhibitory processes which delay subsequent naming of that drawing.

Tipper (1985) also obtained evidence for a positive priming effect. In this effect, naming of the drawing was faster when it was identical with the previously attended drawing than when it was a previously unpresented drawing.

We made use of a modified version of Tipper's (1985) paradigm. Words were used instead of drawings, and the subject's task was to decide whether or not a string of letters formed a word (i.e., a lexical decision task). When the letter string formed a word, there were three conditions of interest: (1) when the letter string was the same as the attended word; (2) when the letter string was the same as the ignored word; (3) when the letter string was a previously unpresented word. In view of our interest in individual differences in the processing of threatening and neutral material, some of the words were threat-related (social and physical health threat) and the remainder were neutral.

On positive trials (i.e., where the letter string was a word), there was a significant interaction between groups (current anxious, recovered anxious, and control) and conditions (attended, ignored, and baseline or control). This interaction was unaffected by the threat value of the words presented. Control subjects showed evidence of a positive priming effect in the attended condition and of a negative priming effect in the ignored condition, whereas currently anxious patients showed a positive priming effect but no negative priming effect. The findings for the recovered anxious subjects approximated much more closely to those of the currently anxious patients than to those of the normal controls.

There is increasing evidence that the negative priming effect is affected by a number of individual differences in addition to anxiety level. For example, Tipper (unpublished data) has discovered that those who report a high incidence of cognitive failures show less of a negative priming effect than those who do not. Claridge (pers. comm.) has discovered that individuals high in schizotypy differ systematically from those low in schizotypy in the Tipper paradigm. Thus, the effects we have obtained may reflect something rather broader than simply anxiety level per se.

It is difficult to provide a full interpretation of these data. However, it is probably correct to argue that the normal pattern of a positive priming effect in the attended condition and a negative priming effect in the ignored condition reflects a relatively precise focussing of attention. The fact that the currently anxious patients and the recovered anxious subjects fail to exhibit this pattern suggests that both groups have difficulty in focussing attention in a precise fashion.

These findings resemble those obtained in studies of distraction. For example, Dornic (1977) discovered that neurotic introverts (who are high in trait anxiety) were more distractible than stable extraverts (who are low in trait anxiety). Distractibility obviously has much in common with an inability to focus attention in the desired way.

The finding of greatest theoretical importance, however, is that the recovered anxious group resemble the current anxious group much more than the normal control group. In terms of the rationale being adopted, the implication is that the imprecision of attentional focus demonstrated by the current anxious group is a reflection of a vulnerability factor rather than a consequence of anxious mood state. If, for example, an individual is unable to focus attention precisely, he or she is more at risk of having his or her thought processes being interrupted by unwanted intrusive thoughts (e.g., worries, personal concerns).

A third paradigm in which currently anxious patients, recovered anxious subjects, and normal controls have been compared is a modified version of the Stroop task. As was mentioned earlier, Andrew Mathews, Anne Richards, and myself have investigated the speed with which colours can be named when threatening and neutral words are presented concurrently at a subliminal level. Currently anxious patients with generalized anxiety disorder named the colours slower in the presence of subliminal threat-related rather than neutral words, but normal controls were faster in the presence of threat. Recovered anxious subjects were slightly faster in the presence of threat, but basically showed very little effect of the type of concurrent subliminal word. In other words, the performance of the recovered anxious subjects was intermediate between that of the other two groups.

These findings suggest that the tendency for currently anxious patients to allocate more processing resources to subliminal threat stimuli than to subliminal neutral stimuli cannot be regarded as reflecting a vulnerability factor. The reason for arguing this is the failure of the recovered anxious subjects to exhibit the same performance pattern. On the other hand, the fact that the recovered anxious subjects also appeared to differ from the normal controls suggests that we are not dealing entirely with a mood-based effect. Presumably the tendency to allocate extra processing resources to threat-related stimuli at a pre-attentive level changes only slowly during the process of recovery, since even those individuals who have been recovered from generalized anxiety disorder for six months or more still fail to exhibit an entirely normal pattern of performance.

Theoretical interpretation

The first important point to make is that the research strategy which we have been using makes it clear that the various differences in cognitive functioning between currently anxious patients and normal controls which have been discovered differ in their theoretical status. So far, we have data on three aspects of cognitive functioning in recovered anxious subjects, and the relationship of their performance to that of currently anxious and normal control subjects differs in each case.

On present evidence, it appears that imprecision of attentional focus in the modified Tipper paradigm reflects a vulnerability factor, whereas the relative favouring of threatening interpretations of ambiguous stimuli reflects anxious mood state. Allocation of extra processing resources to subliminal threat-related stimuli appears to constitute an intermediate case which does directly exemplifies neither a vulnerability factor nor anxious mood state. At the simplest level, the findings from the modified subliminal Stroop suggest that we should contemplate replacing the dichotomy between vulnerability and mood state effects with a continuum. In other words, in should be recognized that non-normal cognitive functioning in currently anxious patients can vary in its temporal stability from great stability at one extreme (i.e., vulnerability factor) to relative transience at the other extreme (i.e., anxious mood state factor).

It is obvious that more data are required before any proper interpretation of the various aspects of non-normal cognitive functioning in generalized anxiety disorder is possible. However, one or two speculations can be offered even at this early stage. A reasonable starting point is to assume that there is a valid distinction between cognitive processes which are relatively automatic and over-learned and processes which are more flexible and under greater control (cf. Shiffrin &

Schneider, 1977). Theoretically, it would be expected that automatic processes would be much more resistant to change than controlled processes, and the experimental evidence marshalled by Shiffrin and Schneider (1977) supports this expectation. It would thus follow that those aspects of non-normal cognitive functioning in anxious patients involving relatively automatic processes would tend to reflect a vulnerability factor, whereas those aspects involving more controlled processes would be more likely to reflect anxious mood state.

The above hypothesis will be tested directly in future research. However, some of the presently available evidence is relevant to it. While the interpretation of ambiguous stimuli undoubtedly involves some relatively automatic processes, it almost certainly also makes use of controlled processes as well. It could be the involvement of these controlled processes which makes non-normal interpretation of ambiguity a reflection of anxious mood state. The tendency of currently anxious patients to allocate extra processing resources to subliminal threat-related words is much less a reflection of anxious mood state, presumably because automatic, pre-attentive processes are involved to a greater extent.

The imprecision of attentional focussing shown by currently anxious patients appeared to reflect a vulnerability factor. In terms of the theoretical analysis presented above, this should occur because the precision of attentional focussing depends on relatively automatic processes. Unfortunately, insufficient is known of the processes involved to be able to draw any firm conclusions as to whether or not the findings with the modified Tipper paradigm are consistent with our theoretical analysis.

In sum, a start has been made on the difficult issue of why it is that patients with generalized anxiety disorder differ from normals in their cognitive functioning. It seems almost certain that the reasons vary depending on which aspect of cognitive functioning one is considering. However, an adequate theoretical formulation which can predict which aspects of non-normal cognitive functioning in anxious patients reflect vulnerability and which reflect anxious mood state must await further research.

REFERENCES

Bower, G. H., Gilligan, S. G., & Monteiro, K. P. (1981). Selectivity of learning caused by affective states. *Journal of Experimental Psychology: General, 110*, 451-473.

Byrne, D. (1964). Repression-sensitization as a dimension of personality. In B. A. Maher (Ed.), *Progress in Experimental Personality Research*, pp. 169-220. New York: Academic Press.

Dornic, S. (1977). Mental load, effort, and individual differences. *Reports of the Department of Psychology, University of Stockholm*, No. 509.

Easterbrook, J. A. (1959). The effect of emotion on cue utilization and the organization of behaviour. *Psychological Review, 66,* 183-201.

Eysenck, M. W. (1986). Individual differences in anxiety, cognition and coping. In G. R. J. Hockey, A. W. K. Gaillard, and M. G. H. Coles (Eds.), *Energetics and Human Information Processing,* pp. 255-269. Dordrecht: Martinus Nijhoff.

Eysenck, M. W., MacLeod, C., & Mathews, A. (1987). Cognitive functioning and anxiety. *Psychological Research, 49,* 189-195.

Eysenck, M. W., & Mathews, A. (1987). Trait anxiety and cognition. In H. J. Eysenck and I. Martin (Eds.), *Theoretical Foundations of Behaviour Therapy,* pp. 197-216. New York: Plenum.

Ingham, J. G. (1966). Changes in M.P.I. scores in neurotic patients: A three year follow-up. *British Journal of Psychiatry, 112,* 931-939.

MacLeod, C., Mathews, A., & Tata, P. (1986). Attentional bias in emotional disorders. *Journal of Abnormal Psychology, 95,* 15-20.

Mathews, A., & Eysenck, M. W. (1987). Clinical anxiety and cognition. In H. J. Eysenck and I. Martin (Eds.), *Theoretical Foundations of Behaviour Therapy,* pp. 217-234. New York: Plenum.

Mathews, A., & MacLeod, C. (1986). Discrimination of threat cues without awareness in anxiety state. *Journal of Abnormal Psychology, 95,* 131- 138.

McKeon, J., Roa, B., & Mann, A. (1984). Life events and personality trait in obsessive-compulsive neurosis. *British Journal of Psychiatry, 144,* 185-189.

Mogg, K, Mathews, A., & Weinman, J. (1987). Memory bias in clinical anxiety. *Journal of Abnormal Psychology, 96,* 94-98.

Shiffrin, R. M., & Schneider, W. (1977). Controlled and automatic human information processing: II. Perceptual learning, automatic attending, and a general theory. *Psychological Review, 84,* 127-190.

Tipper, S. P. (1985). The negative priming effect: Inhibitory priming by ignored objects. *Quarterly Journal of Experimental Psychology, 37A,* 571-590.

Ullmann, L. P. (1962). An empirically derived MMPI scale which measures facilitation-inhibition of recognition of threatening stimuli. *Journal of Clinical Psychology, 18,* 127-132.

Watson, D., & Clark, L. A. (1984). Negative affectivity: The disposition to experience aversive emotional states. *Psychological Bulletin, 96,* 465-490.

Yerkes, R. M., & Dodson, J. D. (1908). The relation of strength of stimulus to rapidity of habit-formation. *Journal of Comparative and Neurological Psychology, 18,* 459-482.

VI Neuroethological Perspectives on Aversively Motivated Behavior

Richard J. Beninger and Trevor Archer
Queen's University and University of Umeå

From an ethological perspective, the behavioral effects of independent variables and the selection of dependent variables are viewed with regard to the natural habit and to the specific responses or response patterns used in that habitat by the species under study. Neuroscience is the study of the nervous system and behavioral neuroscience is concerned with the function of the central nervous system in the control of behavior. Therefore, a neuroethological perspective would involve the study of central nervous system function within the context of ethological considerations. In the previous topic sections, the usefulness of the neuroethological perspective has already been emphasized. For example, the importance of gustatory cues in the learning of food aversions by rats and the relative unimportance of auditory or visual cues (see Garcia, this volume) can be understood from a consideration of the natural habitat of the rodent. Thus, whereas visual and auditory cues in the environment may be associated with a particular food source, they may be less likely to be associated consistently with a particular food type; taste cues, on the other hand, would be highly predictive of a particular type of food and could, therefore, be the better predictor of toxic substances.

Furthermore, odor cues associated with taste cues followed by nausea might be expected to lead to powerful aversions for the same reason. Odor cues on their own might be expected to be poor cues for aversion learning because they, like visual and auditory cues, may be encountered in the absence of ingestion of the toxic substance. This is exactly what has been found in laboratory studies (Garcia, this volume). Further analyses of the taste, odor and exteroceptive cues in aversion learning indicated that Garcia's double dissociation was even more complicated than was originally thought and place a greater descriptive burden upon the configurations of the compound stimuli presented in the typical taste-aversion experiment (Archer, Sjödén & Nilsson, 1985; Archer, Sjödén, Nilsson & Carter, 1980). Notwithstanding these complications, the excellent work of Bermudez-Rattoni and Prado-Alcala (this volume), has of late demonstrated different neuroanatomical substrates for gustatory-illness versus olfactory-illness conditioning and provides a good example of a neuroethological perspective on aversively motivated behavior.

Apart from its neuroethological perspectives, the long-delay learning effect of taste-aversion conditioning, by which taste aversions are learned even over long taste-poison intervals has important consequences for the general processes of the laws of learning (e.g. Garcia, McGowan & Green, 1972, but see also Overmier & Archer, this volume). On both counts Revusky's interference theory (1971) bears some consideration. This account suggests that long-delay conditioning depends on two general factors: retention of the conditioned stimulus (CS) at the time the unconditioned stimulus (US) is presented and mutual "relevance" in the relationships of the CS, US and the contextual events. In accordance with the principle of *stimulus relevance*, introduced by Capretta (1961), associations are learned more readily between two events of the same class than if one belongs to a different class. Thus, the associative strength of a cue with some consequence depends, in part, on the nature of the consequence (Dietz & Capretta, 1967). Associations between taste and illness are more powerful than any other "interfering" associations, since the stimulus events which predominate at the time of conditioning and in any CS-US interval (i.e., exteroceptive stimuli) belong to a different class. The principle of *situational relevance* implies that associations are more likely to occur between two events (e.g., taste and illness) that occur in the same environment than between events occurring in different environments. These two principles have been incorporated by Revusky (1977) in a rule of concurrent interference by which "... the strength of an association between any cue and an aftereffect changes as an inverse function of the number and strengths of the competing associations of other cues with the same aftereffects". (p. 42).

The neuroethological section was represented by two presentations (one by Stephen Suomi, the other by Giorgio Bignami) that differed widely with respect to the species being studied (rhesus monkeys versus rats and mice), the types of aversive independent variables being manipulated (separation from the social group versus electrical footshock) and the behavioral dependent variables recorded (social behavior upon reintroduction to the group versus escape and avoidance running responses). (Stephen Suomi's chapter never materialized. He made an excellent presentation at the conference and we shall try to outline a few salient aspects.) Suomi discussed the effects of genetic pedigree as an independent variable and measured catecholamines and metabolites as additional dependent variables that may provide indications regarding the possible contribution of these neurotransmitter systems to the observed behaviors. Bignami compared rats to mice, using ethological information regarding their behavior in a naturalistic environment to better understand the differential responses of these two species to a variety of independent variables in avoidance learning including prehandling, time of shock offset/onset, size of door (hurdle) between compartments, length of intertrial interval, modality of conditioned stimulus, shock intensity and a variety of pharmacological compounds. In spite of the differences in the approaches taken by Suomi and Bignami to their study of aversively motivated behavior, the work of both of these scientists can be related from the neuroethological perspective. Thus, both were concerned with the ways that a consideration of the behaviors of the species under study in its natural environment can contribute to a better understanding of the behaviors observed in their experiments and the possible neural and/or neuropharmacology mechanisms involved.

Suomi's presentation described a long series of longitudinal studies of the social behavior of rhesus monkeys, both in captive colonies and in natural environments. He found large inter-monkey variability in responses to isolation from the social group and sought to identify the contribution of genetic and neurochemical variables to this phenomenon. His results revealed that individual responses to aversive events such as separation from the social group were highly heritable. Moreover, physiological changes including levels of catecholamine metabolites or adenocorticotrophic hormone varied among individuals and seemed to be correlated with the perception of or ability to cope with the aversive stimulus. In recent exciting work Suomi has found that the behaviors of freeranging monkeys of a different species showed similar inter-individual variability in response to aversive events and is seeking to identify genetic and biochemical components in the response. These studies, by virtue of a unique width (species), duration (time span) and depth (numbers of individuals), provide an excellent neuroethological perspective on the aversively motivated behavior of monkeys.

The studies of Bignami, reported in this section, with their focus upon a very standard behavior (i.e. two-way active avoidance) and the species most commonly used for animal experiments, rats and mice, complement those of Suomi. Bignami demonstrates that the acquisition of active avoidance responses of rats and mice is affected by a wide range of methodological and neuropharmacological variables. Furthermore, he has found that the effects of some of these variables on rats and mice differ. For example, when required to approach a lighted area to escape and learn to avoid electrical footshock, rats were found to be more impaired than mice. From an ethological perspective this might be understood with reference to the behavior of the two species within a naturalistic setting. Thus, the rat is usually almost totally inactive during the day but the mouse, with a higher metabolic rate, is seen to be active both during the night and day. Perhaps rats are less inclined than mice to approach a lighted area to avoid shock because of this stronger natural tendency to remain inactive in the light. Of course this hypothesis should be tested in other paradigms to establish its generality, but it provides a useful neuroethological perspective that aids in unravelling the meaning of striking species differences in the effects of relatively minor procedural variations in avoidance methodologies.

There are many other aversively motivated behaviors that could also have been included in this section covering neuroethological perspectives. Indeed, it should eventually be possible to relate all aversively motivated behaviors to the behavior of the species under study in its natural habit and to identify the neural basis of these behaviors (à la Bolles, 1985). Some of the other behaviors include taste aversion learning, defensive burying, swimming to safety and predator escape and avoidance. Defensive burying is a phenomenon that involves returning to the source of an aversive stimulus and burying the source (Pinel & Treit, 1978). The act of approaching environmental stimuli that signal an aversive event seemed contrary to the widely held belief that animals avoid such stimuli.

However, burying will only be seen if appropriate burying material is available and if the source of the unconditioned aversive stimulus can be identified; neither condition is normally met in a shock avoidance paradigm. Here again, a consideration of the behavior of rats and other species in their natural habitat provides some clues to understanding this behaviour. Thus, a number of species, including rats, are seen to bury potentially harmful stimuli. Rats' species-specific predisposition to bury objects potentially associable with or associated with aversive stimuli is now well documented (Terlecki, Pinel & Treit, 1979; Wilkie, MacLennan & Pinel, 1979) and is certainly important from a neuroethological viewpoint in conforming to the species-specific-defence-repertoire (SSDR) formulation by Bolles (e.g., 1970, 1975). The possible involvement of neurotransmitter systems in this phenomenon has also been studied (Beninger, MacLennan & Pinel, 1981; Treit, 1985a). From a neuropharmacological perspective it is of interest to note the mitigating effects of anxiolytic agents, e.g., the benzodiazepines, upon defensive burying (e.g., Treit, Pinel & Fibiger, 1981, 1982). This action has been shown also to be independent of any possible analgesic effects of these compounds (Treit, 1985b).

A related phenomenon to conditioned defensive burying in rats is marble burying generally shown by single mice placed alone in a cage in which a large number (generally 20 to 25) of brightly coloured glass marbles are placed upon the sawdust bedding material. Glass marbles appear to (collectively) provide an effective unconditioned aversive stimulus which "provokes" burying behavior in both rats and mice (Broekkamp, Rijk, Jol-Gelouin & Lloyd, 1986; Poling, Cleary & Monaghan, 1981). One important condition seems to be the removal of socially housed mice to a test cage where they are isolated and confronted by the novel marbles. It is possible that this isolation experience is the aversive stimulus "triggering" defensive burying in a similar manner to that of shock presentation in conditioned defensive burying (Treit, Pinel & Terlecki,

1980). Recently, Archer, Fredriksson, Lewander and Söderberg (1987) developed a technique for measuring marble burying concomitantly with spontaneous motor activity in mice by utilising automated activity cages; an interesting interaction between burying behavior and locomotor activity was revealed. The mice were assigned to either a "marbles" or a "no marbles" group and measures were taken during 60 min sessions over sessions on each of three consecutive days. The "marbles" groups performed significantly less locomotor behavior than the "no marbles" group on the first day of testing but showed significantly more locomotion by the third and final day of testing (see Fig. VI.1). However, the "marbles" group mice buried all their marbles on all three occasions.

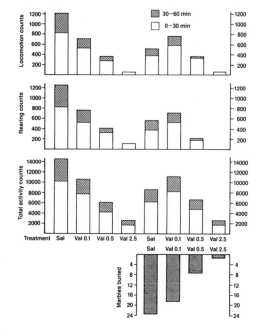

FIG. VI.1. Mean locomotion, rearing and total activity counts over 30 (unshaded) and 60 (shaded) min periods following acute treatment with diazepam (0.1, 0.5 and 2.5 mg/kg, "val") or saline. Half the mice were not exposed to marbles (left-hand side) the other half were (right-hand side). The mean number of marbles buried by each group is indicated on the bottom figure.

Two points can be made from the neuroethological perspective: (1) Burying initially interfered with locomotor activity, and (2) the mice learned to bury their marbles more quickly by Day 3 and then indulged in their locomotor activity, implying a need for locomotor activity suppressed initially by the presence of the aversive marbles. The concurrent behavior analysis has been applied to assess the efficacy of anxiolytic compounds but swim-induced grooming activity has been used as the "activity" variable (Broekkamp et al., 1986). There are both procedural and conceptual (i.e., physiological changes following submergence in a water bath) grounds for suggesting that the concomitant burying-locomotor activity technique is preferable to the concurrent burying-grooming technique but it is clear that reliability and robustness of the burying phenomenon in general offers much scope for further investigation of animal models of drug action in a neuroethological perspective.

For the purpose of a neuroethological *awareness* certain points may be considered: (1) macromolecular as opposed to specific characteristics of behavior must be weighed in the neuroethological analysis of any given situation. (2) In the application of neuroethological principles the selection of species for the study of animal models of behavioral disturbances may prove to be essential, e.g., primates for affective disorders and rats for stereotypy models of schizophrenia. (3) The utilization and exploitation of individual differences in the behavior of a given population may lead to inferences necessary to the neuroethological analysis. Thus, Suomi has found that individual monkeys sitting on a stretch of road may vary considerably in their response to the approach of an automobile or truck. A few individual disappear immediately, the majority move off to a position of observation out of immediate danger but a few individuals remain unconcerned and expectant. Given a vehicle of evil intent (hunters and/or dangerous drivers) the disappearing individuals ought to be selected for survival whereas in conditions of chronic food shortage the approach of a possible food source provides advantages for the unconcerned individual. In a controlled laboratory analysis (Archer, unpublished data) it was found that the degree of taste-aversion conditioning to saccharin was positively correlated with the degree of taste neophobia shown at the initial presentation of the novel taste saccharin (see Fig. VI.2). Given the aversive circumstances of taste-aversion

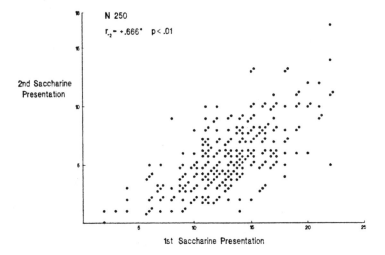

FIG. VI.2. Saccharin intake of 250 rats on two successive presentations. Rats in different conditions (see Table 2) received both saccharin presentations in identical contexts on both presentations. An i.p. LiCl injection followed the 1st presentation. The correlation between saccharin intake values on the 1st and 2nd presentation was positive and significant ($r_{12} = +.666$, $p < .01$).

learning the survival benefits of a high degree of taste neophobia (assuming that the novel taste contained poison) are determined by a low intake of toxin and developed by a stronger avoidance of the taste. However, in conditions of limited access to nutritients the individuals consuming the large amounts of saccharin might be at an advantage. This positive correlation confirmed that of earlier studies (Archer & Sjödén, 1979a, b). Thus, it is to be hoped that analyses of aversively motivated behavior in terms of a neuroethological perspective may prove to be of long term benefit.

REFERENCES

Archer. T., Fredriksson, A., Lewander, T., & Söderberg. U. (1987). Marble burying and spontaneous motor activity in mice: Interactions over days and the effect of diazepam. *Scandinavian Journal of Psychology, 28,* 242-249.

Archer, T., & Sjödén, P. O. (1979). Positive correlation between pre- and postconditioning saccharin intake in taste-aversion learning. *Animal learning and Behaviour, 7,* 144-148(a).

Archer. T., & Sjödén, P. O. (1979). Neophobia in taste-aversion conditioning: Individual differences and effects of contextual changes. *Physiological Psychology, 7,* 364-369(b).

Archer, T., Sjödén, P. O., Nilsson, L.-G. (1985). Contextual control of taste-aversion conditioning and extinction. In P. D. Balsam & A. Tomie (Eds.), *Context and Learning,* pp. 225-271. Hillsdale, N. J.: Lawrence Erlbaum Associates.

Archer, T., Sjödén, P. O., Nilsson, L.-G., & Carter, N. (1980). Exteroceptive context in taste-aversion conditioning and extinction: Odour, cage, and bottle stimuli. *Quarterly Journal of Experimental Psychology, 32,* 197-214.

Beninger, R. J., MacLennan, A. J., & Pinel, J. P. J. (1980). The use of conditioned defensive burying to test the effects of pimozide on associative learning. *Pharmacology Biochemistry and Behavior, 12,* 445-448.

Bolles, R. C. (1970). Species-specific defence reactions and avoidance learning. *Psychological Reviews, 77,* 32-48.

Bolles, R. C. (1975). *Learning Theory.* New York: Holt, Rinehart & Winston.

Bolles, R. C. (1985). Associative processes in the formation of conditioned food aversions: an emerging functionalism. *Annals of the New York Academy of Sciences, 443,* 1-7.

Broekkamp, C. L., Rijk, H. W., Jol-Gelouin, J., & Lloyd, K. L. (1986). Major tranquillizers can be distinguished from minor tranquillizers on the basis of effects on marble burying and swim-induced grooming in mice. *European Journal of Pharmacology, 126,* 223-229.

Capretta, P. J. (1961). An experimental modification of food preference in chickens. *Journal of Comparative and Physiological Psychology, 54,* 238-242.

Dietz, M. N., & Capretta, P. J. (1967). Modification of sugar and sugar-saccarin preference in rats as a function of electric shock to the mouth. *Proceedings of the 75th Annual Convention of the American Psychological Association*, 161-162.

Garcia, J., McGowan, B. K., & Green, K. F. (1972). Biological contraints on conditioning. In M. E. P. Seligman and J. L. Hager (Eds.), *Biological boundaries of learning*, pp. 21-43. New York: Appleton-Century-Crofts.

Pinel, J. P. J., & Treit, D. (1978). Burying as a defensive response in rats. *Journal of Comparative and Physiological Psychology, 92,* 208-212.

Poling, A., Cleary, J., & Monaghan, M. (1981). Burying by rats in response to aversive and nonaversive stimuli. *Journal of Experimental Analysis of Behaviour, 35,* 31-36.

Revusky, S. (1971). The role of interference in association over a delay. In W. K. Honig and P. H. R. James (Eds.), *Animal memory*, pp. 155-213. New York: Academic Press.

Revusky, S. (1977). Learning as a general process with an emphasis on data from feeding experiments. In N. W. Milgram, L. Krames and T. M. Alloway (Eds.), *Food Aversion Learning*, pp. 3-15. New York: Plenum Press.

Terlecki, L. J., Pinel, J. P. J., & Treit, D. (1979). Conditioned and unconditioned defensive burying in the rat. *Learning and Motivation, 10,* 337-350.

Treit, D. (1985). Animal models for the study of anti-anxiety agents: A review. *Neuroscience and Behavioral Reviews, 9,* 203-222(a).

Treit, D. (1985). The inhibitory effect of diazepam on defensive burying: Anxiolytic vs analgesic effects. *Pharmacology, Biochemistry and Behavior, 22,* 47-52(b).

Treit, D., Pinel, J. P. J., & Fibiger, H. C. (1981). Conditioned defensive burying: A new paradigm for the study of anxiolytic agents. *Pharmacology, Biochemistry and Behavior, 15,* 619-626.

Treit, D., Pinel, J. P. J., & Fibiger, H. C. (1982). The inhibitor effect of diazepan on defensive burying is reversed by picrotoxin. *Pharmacology, Biochemistry and Behavior, 17,* 359-361.

Treit, D., Pinel, J. P. J., & Terlecki, L. J. (1980). Shock intensity and conditioned defensive burying in rats. *Bulletin of the Psychonomic Society, 16,* 5-7.

Wilkie, D. M., MacLennan, A. J., & Pinel, J. P. J. (1979). Rat defensive behavior: Burying noxious food. *Journal of Experimental Analysis of Behavior, 31,* 229-306.

14 To Go or Not to Go in Aversive Paradigms: Preparedness and Other Questions

Giorgio Bignami
Istituto Superiore Di Sanità, Roma

Over the past years, the methods and contructs of experimental and physiological psychology have been seriously questioned by comparative psychologists, ethologists, and neuroethologists. Essentially, these criticisms have emphasized the subordination of many analyses of animal behaviour to models of human function and dysfunction, ranging from learning and motivation processes to the interpretation of CNS damage and drug treatment effects. More specifically, the charge is that of using highly "artificial" testing situations, a limited range of domesticated species (mainly rats), and inappropriate problem definitions, with little relevance for the understanding of "real world" phenomena, processes and mechanisms. This campaign often makes a liberal use of aggressive tones. It is claimed that the sacred precincts of the behavioural sciences should be promptly cleared from all sorts of obsolete paraphernalia -- mazes, shuttle-boxes, Skinner-boxes, and of course the innumerable conflicting models evolved by the various psychological and neuropsychological schools.

More interesting, however, is the confrontation with those analysts who continue the tradition of criticizing any illegitimate use of behavioural responses as convenient (and interchangeable) dependent variables (McCleary, 1961). In this context, Dantzer (1986) has used the example of the mechanisms by which an animal forms and utilizes internal representations of the surrounding environment, be they spatial maps, organoleptic properties of foods in conditioned aversion phenomena, or olfactory features of offspring at the time when mother-young relationships are established. One cannot disagree with his statement that new approaches to the problem just mentioned have "considerable chances of being more fruitful than an academic debate on the respective roles of associative and nonassociative factors in conditioned avoidance responding ..." (Dantzer, 1986; author's dots, translation mine).

However, one could also cite numerous cases in which updated versions of the "traditional" approaches have been quite successful in dealing with important aspects of behaviour modulation, as is shown by the considerable heuristic impact of models such as those proposed by Konorski (1948, 1967) and by Rescorla and Wagner (1972. Incidentally, any causal peruser of media like Journal of Experimental Psychology-Animal Behavior Processes, Learning and Motivation, The Quarterly Journal of Experimental Psychology, Animal Learning and Behavior, and Acta Neurobiologiae Experimentalis will have difficulties reconciling the liveliness of the "traditional" fields with the repetitive issuance of death certificates bearing their names).

Quite interestingly, the rumor that tests and theoretical approaches borrowed from experimental and physiological psychology may not be any more fashionable has spread to related areas, such as neuropsychopharmacology. The paradoxical consequence is that substantial information on the intimate nature of the behavioural changes produced by treatments is available only for ancient drugs like amphetamine, LSD-25, scopolamine, chlorpromazine, and chlordiazepoxide (see e.g. Anisman & Bignami, 1978). By contrast, the information on clinically important agents developed in more recent times, such as "atypical" neuroleptics and new (non-benzodiazepine) anxiolytics, is mostly limited to the results obtained by operationally convenient assays. In other words, behavioural test strategies tend to be increasingly subordinate to the biochemical and clinical models; embarrassing questions about the meaning of important drug-behaviour interactions are often avoided.

The present paper, however, cannot deal further with the contribution given by drug and lesion studies to the analysis of behaviour processes and regulatory mechanisms; nor can it extend the historical analysis of the conflicts between approaches and models, considering also that history (Samuel Taylor Coleridge speaking) "gives us a lantern on the stern, which shines only on the waves behind us". The more modest aim is rather that of examining some aspects of the variability of rat and mouse behaviour in the face of different contingencies in avoidance tasks. In spite of the highly "artificial" features of these tasks, the available data appear to be able to contribute to our understanding of the mechanisms by which different components of the defensive repertoire -- particularly locomotor activation versus staying in the same place, "to go or not to go" -- are modulated as a joint function of stimulus and other factors.

At this point, it is only fair to warn the reader that a large portion of the observed variance in avoidance learning and performance still remains unexplained. In a sense, the well-known statement made by Bolles (1978) several years ago maintains its validity: "I suspect that if all the avoidance-learning data ever reported could be combined and subjected to a gigantic analysis of variance, we would find that about 80% of the total variance would be attributable to situational factors, and only about 10 %

could be attributed to all the other parameters that are usually considered to be of theoretical interest. (The remaining 10% would be error variance.) The existence of these great situational differences is, I repeat, the most salient fact about avoidance learning" (Bolles, 1978, p. 90).

But, this position avoids a confrontation with two important problems. Firstly, the variation within a given situation requiring a given response to a given cue, due to higher-order interactions between several factors (see later), can be as large as the variation between situations, responses, and cues. Secondly, explanations based on "preparedness", besides having a tautological flavour, can be self-limiting from the heuristic viewpoint. In fact, these models can discourage the search for processes and mechanisms which have so far escaped an adequate definition (for further discussion on this and related points see Crawford & Masterson, 1982). One of the aims of the present paper is to assess whether it is possible to combine an anlysis of preparedness phenomena from a neuroethological perspective with that of associative and reinforcement processes as viewed from the perspective of classical learning models.

AVOIDANCE INTERACTIONS BETWEEN STIMULI AND OTHER VARIABLES IN ACTIVE AVOIDANCE

Great emphasis is placed in the literature on the role of stimulus factors either *per se* or in relation to the category of the reinforcer. As already mentioned, however, higher-order interactions between stimuli, responses, response-reinforcement contingencies within a given reinforcer category, and several other variables account for a much larger portion of the overall variance than the main effects of individual factors or lower-order interactions. A formal statement on this problem from the viewpoint of the physiologist can be found in one of the latest writings by Konorksi (1972). Summarizing an extensive experience with several discrimination and differentiation tasks using directional and nondirectional cues and response requirements, Kornoski wrote "[W]e cannot be sure which factor is responsible for the localization of the motor-act differentiation control, whether only the category of the cue [...], or the category of the response [...], or else, both the category of the cue and that of the response. *So far the last supposition seems to be the most probable*" (Konorski, 1972, p. 605-606; emphasis mine. See also the avoidance discrimination data and models in Dabrowska, 1975).

Posing the Right Question on Cue Factors

As concerns active avoidance learning by small rodents, it has long been known (i) that acoustic CS are generally more effective than visual CS, which applies almost uniformly to noise stimuli, but often not to pure tones, and (ii) that learning is impeded by the use of "stimulus off" instead of "stimulus on" as CS, and by the requirement to move towards, rather than away from, the warning signal (for references see Bignami, Alleva, Amorico, De Acetis, & Giardini, 1985).

The former effect, which includes ample evidence on the overshadowing of visual stimuli by acoustic stimuli, has been the object of considerable controversies about whether or not visual simuli are *per se* ineffective as active avoidance signals (see e.g. Bignami et al., 1985; Cicala & Azorlosa, 1985; Jacobs & LoLordo, 1977, 1980). In these terms, however, the question is ill posed. What needs to be explained is why noise stimuli tend to be uniformly effective, while light-cued avoidance learning varies tremendously as a function of several other factors, particularly when the task cannot be learned on the basis of the location of safe and unsafe places. As is well known, this is the critical difference between two-way and one-way locomotor avoidance. The former is not only more difficult than the latter, but also much more sensitive to the adverse influence of high shock intensities and high initial shock densities (short intertrial intervals, ITI's).

As concerns the processes and mechanisms involved in these differences, the reader must be referred to studies such as those by Freedman, Hennessy, and Groner (1974) and by Modaresi (1978, and previous experiments quoted therein). The former provided direct evidence on the role of passive avoidance in two-way tasks, by manipulating separately shock levels in the two compartments of the shuttle-box. The latter succeeded in eliminating the differences between two-way and one-way avoidance (including the adverse influence of a high shock level in the bidirectional task), by making response end-points more discriminable. Except for the digression on some apparatus variables in the next section, this line of analysis, which includes highly significant lesion and drug data, cannot be developed here. The emphasis will rather be on the conditions with determine a high, or vice versa, a low rate of two-way avoidance acquisition with a discrete visual cue.

In mice, for example, two-way avoidance with a light-on CS is made quite difficult by the use of a short (30 sec) ITI in a wide range of different conditions -- with or without intertrial response (ITR) punishment, with both high and low shock intensities, and with or without a midline partition with an opening at floor level. By contrast, the learning of noise-cued avoidance is uniformly rapid. Slow learning can eventually result in a fairly high asymptotic performance with a light CS, but only if ITR's are not punished and the partition is absent (Bignami et al., 1985). In rats (Fig. 14.1), the interaction just mentioned is even more evident.

Light-cued avoidance learning with a short ITI and a high shock level is similarly impaired by either partition, ITR punishment, or both, but takes place fairly rapidly in the absence of both ITR punishment and partition (Bignami, Amorico, Frontali, & Rosic, 1971; remark that the term ITI is used throughout to avoid confounding the reader. In the experiments performed in the author's laboratory, what was set was the duration of CS-CS intervals; the real ITI's were somewhat shorter and varied slightly depending on response latencies, which were measured only in a few selected instances). An analysis of the relations between CS

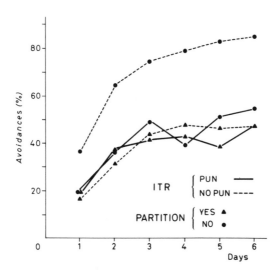

FIG. 14.1. Shuttle-box avoidance learning by male albino Wistar-derived rats (N = 12 per group) with a non-directional light-on CS (bright illumination provided by two 10-W bulbs on either side of the centre of the ceiling), a CS-US interval of 5 sec, a 1.5 mA shock, CS termination by escape and avoidance responses, and a CS-CS interval of 30 seconds. The animals were given six daily sessions of 50 trials each, without or with punishment of intertrial responses (ITR) until recrossing occurred, and without or with a midline partition that had a 7 x 7 cm doorway at floor level. The maximal shock duration in the ITR NO PUN condition was 15 seconds. In the shuttle-box used for the ITR PUN groups (49 x 21 x 22.5 cm), the two halves of the tilting grid floor were electrified separately on alternate trials; therefore, escape from shock was completed so soon as the rat crossed the midline. In the shuttle-box used for the ITR NO PUN groups (same size), the whole floor was electrified and de-electrified at the appropriate moments; therefore, shock was terminated when the floor tilted. Considering the facilitation produced by the former condition in the presence of ITR punishment (Fig. 14.2), the difference just mentioned does not bias the inference that fast learning with a light cue, a high shock intensity and a high initial shock density can occur only in the absence of both ITR punishment and partition.

responding and ITR rates can be found in the original papers and is not necessary in the present context. Suffice it to say that the two measures are often correlated; but, most of the times the differences in ITR's cannot account for the large differences in responding to the discrete cue. For example, the superiority of noise avoidance over light avoidance in mice which has just been mentioned was not accompanied by substantial differences in ITR's (Bignami et al., 1985).

A Digression on Apparatus Variables Affecting Response "Tendencies"

The data so far discussed impose a digression on the effects of some apparatus variables, considering in particular that escape latencies are initially longer with than without a partition. In fact, the adverse influence of an increase in shock exposure at the start of light-cued avoidance training appears to weigh more than any beneficial effect of apparatus cues which may help the animal in fulfilling the response criterion and/or in coping with the repeated switching of safe and unsafe places (for further data and discussion on the role of place learning in two-way avoidance see Moot, Nelson, & Bolles, 1974; Weisman, Denny, & Zerbolio, 1967).

This tentative inference is strengthened by the results of a recent experiment concerning the effects of response criterion and prehandling on light-cued two-way avoidance learning by rats with a short (30 sec) ITI and with ITR punishment. Half of the animals were trained in an apparatus in which only one half of the floor was electrified on the appropriate side at the end of the CS-US interval; that is, shock reception was terminated so soon as the rats crossed the midline. The other animals were trained in a box of the same size in which the whole floor was electrified, and the shock was stopped when the completion of the crossing response produced floor tilting; this inevitably produced a slight delay in shock termination after midline crossing. (Remark that both types of shuttle-box had tilting floors). As expected, avoidance learning was faster in the former, than in the latter condition (Fig. 14.2).

The other variable was presence or absence of an extended period of daily handling and mild painful stimulation prior to the beginning of training (see legend of Fig. 14.2). As expected on the basis of previous results on avoidance (Joffe & Levine, 1973) and on several other tasks (for data and references see West & Michael, 1987), previously stimulated rats learned faster than the others. The effects of the stimulation and the apparatus variables were purely additive. This suggests that quite different factors which can reduce the initial stressfulness of exposure to the escape-avoidance paradigm can contribute to the attenuation of the response impairment resulting from unfavourable test conditions.

Several literature data confirm the importance of apparatus features in relation to the extent of initial shock exposure and to response topographies. For example, rats required to jump over a hurdle learn shuttle-box avoidance faster than rats required to use a narrow doorway at floor level (Dalby & Shuttlesworth, 1978. Quite interestingly, the use of a wide doorway -- 12.5 x 15 cm instead of 7 x 7 cm in our experiment and 10 x 10 cm in that of Dalby and Shuttlesworth -- produced similar rates of learning of running and hurdle-jumping avoidance at most shock intensities, and better running than hurdle-jumping avoidance at the lowest and at the highest intensities: Henderson, 1970. Of shock intensity effects, more later). Together with the other data mentioned above, this shows how carefully one must take into account those apparatus features which can influence the availability of different responses, such as running

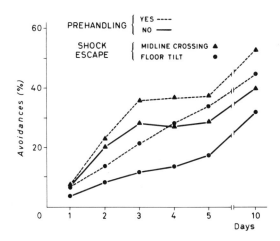

FIG. 14.2. Shuttle-box avoidance learning by rats (N = 28-44 per group) in conditions like those of the ITR PUN group without partition in Fig. 14.1, but with half of the animals trained in an apparatus like that used for the ITR NO PUN group in the said figure ("floor tilt"). Prior to the start of training, half of the animals were briefly handled and given an injection of water five days a week for six weeks. The data show additive facilitative effects of the "midline crossing" condition and prehandling. Bignami, De Acetis, Amorico, and Valanzano, unpublished data.

and jumping. When the former, which seems to have the highest priority in escape from painful paw stimulation, is made ineffective and must be substituted by the latter, the chances of a subsequent response impairment are increased. This, incidentally, appears to be just one more nail in the coffin of those models which emphasize the similarity of UR's and CR's, at least as far as instrumental tasks are concerned. When avoidance becomes established in a shuttle-box without a hurdle, jumping gives place to leisurely locomotion, independently of presence or absence of a partition with a narrow doorway at floor level.

With more space available, this analysis could be extended to several other results which point in the same direction. Before concluding this extensive digression, brief mention must be made of some data showing that an increase in the size of the apparatus can reduce mouse activity and impair shuttle-box avoidance learning (Kuribara & Tadokoro, 1986). Admittedly, these data do not allow one to separate the influence of an increase in the amount of shock received initially in the larger box from other influences; e.g., the role of thigmotaxis (wall hugging) in aversive situations (Kelley, 1985), which may have different consequences as a function of apparatus size and/or presence or absence of a partition. But, they add to the considerable variation in two-way avoidance learning due to the factors which have been analyzed in the present section; and therefore, to the *caveats* to be kept in mind when confronting results from diffferent sources and when interpreting the interactions between stimulus and other variables.

Further Analysis of the Variability in Light-Cue Effectiveness

As already mentioned, two-way avoidance can be quite sensitive to the adverse influence of high shock densities (short ITI's) and of high shock intensities. Several data, however, are not entirely compatible with the models which propose similar explanations for the effects of both variables. According to our experience, for example, the facilitation of light-cued two-way avoidance obtained in rats by lowering the shock intensity (from 1.5 mA to 0.85 mA) in the presence of a short ITI (30 sec) is much less marked than the facilitation obtained by prolonging the ITI (70 sec instead of 30 sec) in the presence of a high shock intensity (1.5 mA) (Bignami et al., 1971). More importantly, data from different laboratories indicate that bidirectional avoidance learning by mice varies little over a fairly wide range of shock intensities above the escape threshold, while mice are at least as sensitive as rats to ITI differences (for data and additional references see Bignami et al., 1985).

In the experiments performed in the author's laboratory, highly traumatic shock intensities (above 1.5 mA) were not used. But, a 1.5 mA shock produces both in rats and in mice substantial signs of distress which are absent at levels closer to the escape threshold. Therefore, the tentative hypothesis that shock intensity and shock density effects may be produced by different mechanisms might have a least some heuristic value when attempting to understand the differences in light-cue effectiveness in various conditions. It is only fair to add that an experiment on rats by Kurtz and Shafer (1967) showed differential effects of shock intensity as a function of ITI duration; that is, fast two-way avoidance learning occurred with a low shock level and either short or long ITI's, but only with a long ITI in the case of strong shock. This, however, does not suffice to conclude that the intensity and the density variables act by the same mechanism (see also a later section).

Additional data can be presented to show some of the consequences of using different variants of a light cue. As already mentioned, rats do consistently better with an "away-from-light", than with a "toward-light", contingency. By contrast, mouse avoidance is apparently unaffected by such a difference in stimulus arrangement (Bignami et al., 1985). This is in agreement with literature data showing no effects, or only slight effects, of the said variable in this species (Anisman, 1976; Oliverio, 1968). This difference between rats and mice may be important for understanding the constraints which contribute to the variability in light-cue effectiveness. As discussed elsewhere (Bignami et al., 1985) several data suggest that rats, but not mice, may be "prepared" to use light and darkness as danger and safety signals, respectively. Both species are more active in the dark periods; but, mice have a much smaller body mass, and presumably for metabolic reasons they engage in repeated bouts of activity, feeding, and drinking during light periods. This contrasts with the near-complete diurnal inactivity of rats.

In one of the mouse experiments with different ITI's which have already been mentioned, the CS was light turned on either in both compartments of the shuttle-box or only in the start compartment (directional signal identical to that offered to the "away-from-light" groups in the previous experiment). The directional cue resulted in further improvement in the animals trained with a 60 sec ITI, but was unable to modify the very low performance of those trained with a 30-sec ITI (Fig. 14.3).

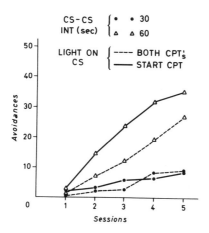

FIG. 14.3. Shuttle-box avoidance learning by Swiss-derived male albino mice (N=12 per group) with either a non-directional or a directional light-on CS (bright illumination provided by two 3-W bulbs on either side of the centre of the ceiling), a CS-US interval of 5 sec, a 1.5 mA shock (maximal duration 10 sec), CS termination by escape and avoidance responses, no punishment of intertrial responses, and different durations of the CS-CS interval (30 vs 60 sec). The animals were given five daily sessions of 50 trials each in a 39 x 9 x 17 cm shuttle-box with a central partition that had a 4.5 cm-diameter circular opening (maximal width 1.25 cm above floor level). The use of a directional CS facilitated avoidance at the long, but not at the short intertrial interval.

Another experiment in the same series provided additional evidence on the joint role of stimulus, reinforcer, apparatus, and temporal variables. This experiment exploited both the facilitation produced by a 60-sec ITI, relative to a 30-sec ITI, and the increased effectiveness of a non-directional light cue when a short ITI is combined with absence of both ITR punishment and partition. The main result (Fig. 14.4) was an enhancement of the latter effect by a reduction of the maximal shock duration in the case of escape failure (5 sec instead of 10 sec). This strengthened the notion that the amount of punishment received at the start

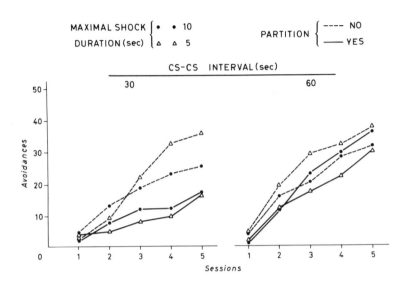

MAXIMAL SHOCK { • • 10   PARTITION { ---- NO
DURATION (sec) { ∆ ∆ 5   { —— YES

CS-CS   INTERVAL (sec)

FIG. 14.4. Shuttle-box avoidance acquisition by mice (N=10 per group) trained in conditions like those of the non-directional CS groups of Fig. 14.3, but either without or with a midline partition and with different maximal shock durations (5 vs 10 sec). The data show better avoidance with the lower shock duration in the absence of the partition, particularly in animals trained with the shorter intertrial interval. Animals trained with a partition performed slightly better with the longer, than with the shorter shock duration.

of training is a critical factor in determining the greater or lesser effectiveness of a light cue. The fact that a facilitation did not occur in the presence of a partition was not surprising. Actually, the mice that were required to find their way through an opening of limited size were not only not helped, but were even further impaired, by a reduction of maximal shock duration.

Since comparisons between experiments must always be made with caution, these particular experiments are perhaps those that best illustrate the very large differences in avoidance learning which can occur with the same CS modality, the same apparatus and response requirement, and the same shock intensity, depending on variables such as stimulus directionality, maximal shock duration, and ITI duration. In each experiment, avoidance responding covered the whole range between little or no learning at one extreme and efficient learning by most animals at the opposite extreme. There remains, however, an important difference with respect to noise-cued tasks, since in the latter a substantial number of avoidances appears already in the first session under most training conditions. A similar difference at the start of training was found by Cicala and Azorlosa (1985) when comparing two-way avoidance learning by rats with acoustic and visual cues which otherwise yielded similar rates of acquisition and similar asymptotic performances.

Preliminary Inferences on the Nature of Differences in Avoidance Ability

The data so far discussed and several others, which cannot be analysed here, suggest some preliminary inferences on the relative roles of preparedness and other phenomena in two-way avoidance learning with CS's of different modalities. Apparently, only an organismic process such as that proposed by Bolles (1970) can account for the readiness to acquire noise-cued avoidance under a wide range of different conditions; however, this process still awaits to be defined more accurately than it has been possible up to now. Noise can be intrinsically aversive and is more effective than light in activating pseudoconditioned and classically conditioned motor responses in a punishment context. But, the hypothesis that noise *per se* favours active components of the defensive repertoire at the expense of others contrasts with the fact that noise is uniformly effective in producing freezing, and more generally, response suppression, in a variety of classical and punishment paradigms. Therefore, Crawford and Masterson (1982) are likely to be right when they emphasize that flight responses appear to be established and maintained by their consequences, although considerable differences in rate of acquisition and in asymptotic levels depend on organismic processes such as that involved in the uniform effectiveness of noise cues.

By contrast, it appears more difficult to define the nature of the constraints which make that rats and mice show such large differences in light-cued avoidance learning in different variants of the same task. Numerous data indicate that it would be naive to support an exclusive role of reinforcement and other processes not amenable to preparedness, as usually defined, in producing this situation. For example, genetic selection has yielded rats which learn two-way avoidance very quickly under conditions that determine mediocre performances in unselected rats, with little or no learning in a fairly high proportion of the animals; that is, a light cue, a short ITI, and ITR punishment (Bignami, 1965. With more space available, one should also analyze the extensive literature concerning avoidance differences between mouse and rat strains, showing that these differences can vary considerably from one to the other version of the same task).

When an organismic process creates a constraint which acts in some conditions, but not in others, one must attempt to understand the nature of other ("non-preparedness") processes which may account for response acquisition and maintenance when learning occurs. It is perhaps easier, however, to ask the alternative question first -- what may be the nature of the deficit when animals fail to meet reinforcement requirements in avoidance tasks like those which have been discussed here and in several others, particularly those with manipulatory response requirements. Many data suggest that this deficit is unlikely to be of an associative or a motivational nature, since several types of manipulations can allow rats and mice to achieve high avoidance levels under otherwise very unfavourable conditions.

For example, massed training (e.g., Bignami et al., 1971) and several different drug treatments can abolish the learning impairment in a wide range of avoidance tasks, although fine-grain analyses have often shown differential effects of the same drug on apparently similar deficits created by different contingencies in the same task. In addition, animals which continue to show little or no avoidance responding after innumerable sessions can start responding, and often achieve a 100% avoidance level, in the later phases of more extended sessions or under drug treatments (see data and references in Anisman & Bignami, 1978). In other words, it may be misleading to label the animal as a "non-learner" *tout court* when the use of unfavourable combinations of stimulus and other varibles prevents active unfavourable combinations of stimulus and other variables prevents active responding. The problem seems rather to be that of the conflict which occurs between opposite response tendencies, creating ample room for quite different outcomes in apparently similar tasks, and for dramatic shifts in either direction in animals faced with a given task.

FURTHER ANALYSIS OF THE PROCESSES INVOLVED IN THE DIFFERENCES IN CUE EFFECTIVENESS

The tentative definition given above of the nature of differences in avoidance ability is of course not an explanation; except for the fact that it tends to rule out some explanations and to favour others. In addition, this or other related accounts are doomed to maintain a strong tautological flavour until the underlying processes and mechanisms are unvealed. What cues do we have at present to help us in this search?

CS, Contextual Cues, Response Topographies, and Initial Response Tendencies

An important starting point in any further analysis is the apparently greater ability of noise than of light cues to take on a wide range of different, or even opposite, functions in aversive contexts. In classical conditioning paradigms, the freezing produced by noise CS's is proportional to shock intensity and inversely proportional to cue intensity (Sigmundi, Bouton, & Bolles, 1980; Sigmundi & Bolles, 1983). When a flight response has functional value, the former effect appears to be overshadowed by the latter. For example, a high noise intensity can counteract the adverse effect of a high shock intensity on two-way avoidance learning (Bauer, 1972).

Freezing produced by a classically conditioned light signal also decreases as a function of CS intensity, but does not seem to vary with shock intensity (Sigmundi, Bouton, & Bolles, 1980; Sigmundi & Bolles,

1983). In two-way avoidance paradigms, the greater or lesser effectiveness of a light CS appears to be strongly related to the relative amounts of fear conditioning to the discrete and to the contextual cues. In fact, a high shock intensity simultaneously impairs light-cued avoidance and enhances responses which allow the rat to escape from the apparatus (McAllister, McAllister, & Douglass, 1971). Pre-exposure to the apparatus yields a direct, instead of an inverse, relationship between shock intensity and light-cued avoidance learning (McAllister, McAllister, Dieter, & James, 1979). This effect can be explained by a reduced salience of contextual cues (latent inhibition), whether or not one is willing to accept the reinforcement model favoured by the authors of these studies. Conversely, dim illumination during the ITI's prevents most of the facilitation obtained by lowering shock intensity in two-way avoidance with a compound cue, consisting of an increase in both noise level and illumination level (McAllister, McAllister, & Dieter, 1976). Another relevant finding is that after classical fear conditioning with a light CS and different ITI's, learning of responses which allow the animal to escape from the CS shows a direct relation with ITI duration, while escape from contextual stimuli is reduced at longer ITI's (McAllister, McAllister, Weldin, & Cohen, 1974).

Additional evidence on the nature of the interactions between cue modality, cue intensity, and shock intensity has been provided by the recent results of Callen (1986). In these experiments, each rat was exposed to both noise-cued and light-cued trials. When intensity varied between subjects, the expected differences were observed: that is, avoidance learning was faster with a low, than with a high shock intensity, and responses to the noise CS were initially more frequent than responses to the light CS. In a within-subject design, avoidance developed faster in noise-high shock trials than in light-low shock trials, while acquisition rates were practically identical with the opposite arrangement. This asymmetry was largely eliminated by reducing noise intensity and increasing light intensity in the within-subject design, which resulted in a positive correlation between shock intensity and avoidance responding, independently of cue modality. In the present context, however, a residual asymmetry in stimulus utilization appears to be far from negligible. Specifically, more avoidances were given in the first training session to the noise signalling strong shock that to the light signalling weak shock, but rats trained in the light-strong shock, noise-weak shock condition responded similarly in the two types of trials.

The data so far mentioned and many of those discussed in previous sections allow one at this point to refine the account on the differences between noise-cued and light-cued two-way avoidance. In the former, the flight response to CS onset is quickly selected at the expense of others, which is just opposite to what happens in classical and in punishment paradigms, where noise quickly becomes an effective response suppressor. Simultaneous shock and noise termination by the initial escapes plays a critical role in the prompt establishment of the functional value of the flight response. This is shown by the adverse effects of CS non-termination in escape trials in the presence of CS termination in avoidance trials (Bolles, Hargrave, & Grossen, 1970). In addition, there is one point of unanimous agreement in the controversy on stimulus nonequivalences, concerning the fact that noise is ineffective in signalling safety in situations where painful stimulation is received.

One could argue at this point about the relative roles of different mechanisms -- aversiveness of noise, pseudoconditioning, and classical conditioning of motor components of the repertoire -- which may contribute to the early appearance of crossing responses preceding shock onset. But, all data point to the fact that a favourable chain of events is started quite early in active avoidance training with a noise cue. These events include at least (i) a minimization of the fear elicited by apparatus cues, relative to fear elicited by CS plus apparatus cues, and (ii) an early exploitation of the information provided jointly by exteroceptive and interoceptive feedbacks in signalling safety when place learning is ineffective (but, see later for the differences in the functional value of CS termination and other feedback signals).

By contrast, the game appears to be initially much more problematic when a light cue is offered in the absence of topographical cues for danger and safety, resulting in a wide range of different outcomes in subsequent stages of training. (Remark that even more striking than the differences in rate of two-way avoidance learning occurring with different combinations of test variables can be the wide range of performances of individual rats and mice in a particular task of intermediate average difficulty -- from no learning in an extended series of sessions to rapid learning and high asymptotic performance). Light onset is an effective CS in fear conditioning, and light offset is also quite effective as a safety signal. But, light is *per se* much less aversive than noise. Moreover, simultaneous shock and light offset by the initial escapes is likely not to be a combination of events as salient as simultaneous noise and shock offset, for the purpose of establishing quickly the functional value of the flight response at the expense of other components of the repertoire. (As will be discussed later, this suspicion is strengthened by the findings which suggest that CS termination determines a slow dissipation of the fear elicited by the CS itself, rather than producing prompt fear inhibition as appears to be the case with other exteroceptive feedback signals). In finer detail, which processes and mechanisms are more likely to determine whether or not light-cued two-way avoidance is eventually learned after such an unfavourable start of the game?

As is well known, the fear elicited by the CS presented without the contextual cues increases in successive avoidance trials up to a maximum, and then starts to decrease (Kamin, Brimer, & Black, 1953; for data illustrating the nature of this phenomenon and for additional references see Neuenschwander, Fabrigoule, & Mackintosh, 1987; Starr & Mineka, 1977). More importantly for the purposes of the present analysis, as avoidance learning progresses a discrimination is formed, resulting in a substantial amount of fear elicited by the CS plus situational cues and in an extinction of fear to the situational cues alone (McAllister, McAllister, & Benton, 1983; for the role of within-compound associations between the context and the CS in fear conditioning see e.g. Marlin, 1982).

A delay in the appearance of responses to a light cue in the initial stage of avoidance training may therefore facilitate the establishment and maintenance of a high level of fear elicited by contextual cues alone, relative to the fear elicited by the CS plus situational cues. This unfavourable trend could easily lead to a point of no return when shock density and shock intensity are high, ITR's are punished, and initial escapes are somewhat impeded by a narrow doorway. Incidentally, this line of reasoning points to a major flaw in the work so far conducted in the author's laboratory. In fact, appropriate independent tests of the functional value of discrete and contextual cues as a joint function of cue modality, other test variables, and different stages of training have not yet been performed.

Response topographies and their modifications after exposure to noxious stimuli also have special relevance in the present context. Jumping of rats to shock, particularly when expressed as percent of total possible responses, is maximal at low and intermediate intensities (0.4-1 mA) and is drastically reduced at higher intensities (1.6 mA or more; Goodman, Dyal, Zinser, & Golub, 1966). Illumination has been shown to increase jumping latency and to decrease jumping frequency upon exposure to shock (Nishikawa, Tsuda, Toshima, Tanaka, & Nagasaki, 1981). In addition, running elicited by shock is proportional to shock level, but the reduction of running produced by escape delays is more marked at high that at low intensities (Bell, Noah, & Davis, 1965). These data are quite helpful in accounting for the initial handicap of animals trained with a light cue, a high shock intensity, and a narrow doorway.

Equally important is the information provided by fine-grain analyses of response distribution in various conditions. In an experiment by McAllister and McAllister (1979), the number of pseudoavoidances -- that is, of responses occurring during the CS-US interval prior to the initial receipt of shock -- was reduced when a neutral rather an intense auditory stimulus was used, and when the shuttle-box compartments were separated by a small rather than a large guillotine door. The number of pseudoavoidances is correlated to that of subsequent avoidances; moreover, as already mentioned, the effects on two-way avoidance of differences in cue modality can be attenuated by reducing noise intensity and increasing light intensity (Callen, 1986). Therefore, the effects of cue intensity and doorway size on operant response level are of great potential relevance for understanding the course of events in the early training stage.

Other analyses of response tendencies in the early stages of shock exposure (Cicala, Masterson, & Kubitsky, 1971; Cicala, Ulm, & Drews, 1971), although conducted with a single intensity of a noise CS, suggest that one could further exploit the interactions between type of cue, shock intensity, and shock density. The first of these studies showed that in the absence of response-reinforcement contingencies, shuttle responding is directly related to shock intensity early in the ITI and inversely related to shock intensity during the CS. More importantly, the second study showed that responding during CS presentation, but not responding in the pre-CS period, is proportional to ITI duration, while both CS and pre-CS responding are inversely proportional to shock intensity. This confirms that ITI manipulations affect mainly the relative proportion of fear elicited by situational cues alone and by CS plus situational cues, respectively. By contrast, intensity effects appear to be mediated by differences in overall fear level, resulting in changes of the relative prepotency of locomotor responses in an aversive situation where safe and unsafe areas are not clearly defined.

Overall, the impression is that we are inching our way towards the understanding of the mechanisms which determine whether or not light-cued avoidance is eventually learned in the absence of a clear definition of safe and unsafe places. However, there remain considerable uncertainties about the relative roles of the various phenomena so far discussed. This is even more evident when one turns to other types of data which also need to be considered for both explanatory and heuristic purposes.

CAVEATS ON SOME ADDITIONAL TOPICS

The possibilities offered by still other lines of analysis should be discussed at this point, but this cannot be done here in adequate detail. In fact, the empirical analysis presented in previous sections could not be extended to include experiments dealing with the effects of prior shock exposure, with the functions of CS termination and of other feedback signals, and with stimulus nonequivalences in go-no go avoidance discriminations. One can only warn the reader that there are substantial gaps in our knowledge of several important phenomena when these are considered from the viewpoint of cue effects and interactions.

Prior Exposure to Shock or CS plus Shock

An extensive literature deals with the variable effects of prior exposure to shock alone or to CS-shock pairings on subsequent avoidance learning (for discussion and references see Alleva, De Acetis, Amorico, & Bignami, 1983) and more generally, with the proactive effects of shock received in different conditions upon subsequent response topographies (e.g., Anisman, Kokkinidis, & Sklar, 1981; Fanselow, 1986; Maier & Jackson, 1979). However, there is little information on possible higher-order interactions between cue modality, amount and distribution of pre-exposure, and conditions of subsequent avoidance training. This is a serious gap, considering the confounding that inevitably occurs in the initial stages of avoidance learning, between real and perceived contingencies. As any inveterate rat and mouse runner knows, the time of the shift from random responding during shock periods to effective escape can vary considerably between situations and between animals in the same situation. But, to what extent is this shift affected by the type of cue preceding and accompanying shock administration? Thanks to the widespread use of automated apparatus, we still do not have substantial information on this important point.

CS Termination Versus Other Feedback Signals

Several data strongly suggest that the marked differences in the functions of CS and contextual cues which depend on test conditions need to be viewed in the context of the variable effects of CS termination (usually called warning stimulus termination, WST) and of exteroceptive feedback stimuli other than WST occurring upon completion of the response criterion (FS). With noise as CS and light off as FS, for example, both WST and FS are needed for the acquisition of two-way avoidance in unfavourable conditions as defined in earlier sections. This has been shown (i) in a discrete-trial task with a short ITI of fixed duration and a high shock intensity (Cicala, Owen, & Hill, 1976), and (ii) in a discriminated continuous (operant) task with a short response-shock interval (Bolles & Grossen, 1970). By contrast, either WST alone or FS alone can suffice for avoidance learning with a low shock intensity in the former task. WST alone, but not FS alone, is effective with a long response-shock interval in the latter task. Moreover, data from animals exposed to a random shock schedule with or without an escape contingency show an FS effect on fear of shock context with a long, but not with a short ITI (Rosellini, DeCola, & Warren, 1986).

Additional data (e.g., Cicala & Owen, 1976, Owen, Cicala, & Herdegen, 1978) suggest that a major difference between WST and FS in the avoidance paradigms considered here is that the former acts by a slow process of fear dissipation -- hence, probably, its effectiveness when the overall level of fear is low (low shock intensity) and when there is sufficient extinction of fear elicited by contextual cues (long ITI) -- while FS acts promptly by conditioned fear inhibition. Further strong evidence on the latter point has been provided by Morris (1974), confirming and extending earlier evidence by Soltysik and Kowalska (1960; see also Konorski, 1967). Overall, the impression is that further studies of the effects of CS, contextual cues, WST, and FS as a joint function of stimulus modality and other variables could help explaining different profiles of noise-cued and light-cued avoidance in various conditions.

Unexplained Stimulus Nonequivalences in Go-No Go Avoidance Discriminations

The present analysis has already emphasized the importance of the discrimination between contextual cues alone and CS plus contextual cues, as well as the differential effects of ITR punishment on noise-cued and light-cued avoidance. (Remark that discrete-trial avoidance without ITR punishment is a go-no go discrimination with asymmetrical reinforcement. In fact, CS plus contextual cues signal shock and an avoidance contingency, while contextual cues alone signal nonreinforcement. By contrast, discrete-trial avoidance with ITR punishment is a go-no go discrimination with symmetrical reinforcement. Both CS and no-CS signal shock, but with active and passive avoidance contingencies, respectively). At this point, one should also consider the stimulus nonequivalences which are found in go-no go discriminations with discrete cues both in active avoidance trials and in passive avoidance or extinction trials (for data on rats, see Rosic, Frontali & Bignami, 1969; Frontali, & Bignami, 1973, 1974; data on mice and more recent data on rats have not yet been published).

Among these nonequivalences, it is easy to account for the fact that feature-positive discriminations (XA^+, A^-) are generally easier than the corresponding feature-negative discriminations (A^+, XA^-). But, there also are important stimulus nonequivalences revealed by comparisons within each pair of discriminations with opposite stimulus arrangements (A = noise, N; X = light, L; or viceversa). Again, one can easily explain the greater tendency to respond to an acoustic, than to a visual signal in the extinction trials of feature-positive discriminations with asymmetrical reinforcement (Fig. 14.5, left portion of upper graph). The same applies to the fact that in mice the difference between L^+, NL^- discriminations and those with the opposite stimulus arrangement is due mainly to the expected difference in effectiveness of active avoidance cues from different modalities (Fig. 14.5, right portion of upper graph). In rats, however, the greater difficulty of the former tasks consists also of substantial differences in commission (no-go trial) errors, which are not easy to explain.

These differences occur both in active-passive avoidance tasks and in active avoidance-extinction tasks (for the former see Fig. 14.6 and Rosic et al., 1969; for the latter see Frontali & Bignami, 1974). Moreover, the stimulus nonequivalence is not substantially modified by variations of test conditions which can determine considerable changes in absolute response levels. These include omission of active avoidance pretraining and different noise intensities in the symmetrical tasks different noise intensities in the symmetrical tasks (Frontali & Bignami, 1973) and several variants of the asymmetrical tasks, with (i) either simultaneous or successive onset of the two stimuli in compound no go signals, (iI) different durations of the no go signals, and (iii) different durations of the intertrial interval producing different initial shock densities (Frontali & Bignami, unpublished data). These profiles exclude any explanation of the nonequivalence involving either the different mechanisms brought into play by the two types of reinforcement contingencies in asymmetrical and symmetrical tasks (e.g., Konorski, 1967; Dabrowska, 1975) or the mechanisms which may account for the well-known differences between serial and simultaneous feature-negative discriminations (e.g., Holland & Gory, 1986).

Even more surprisingly, in one of the asymmetrical tasks (N^+, LN^-), but not in the other (L^+, NL^-), mice show more suppression of responses to the compound signal in the presence than in the absence of a partition (Fig. 14.5, right portion of the lower graph). This difference does not occur in rats, most of which maintain responding to no-go signals for several months of daily training in all four versions of the feature-negative task with asymmetrical reinforcement (different stimulus arrangements x presence vs. absence of partition; Bignami, Alleva, Amorico, De Acetis, & Valanzano, unpublished data).

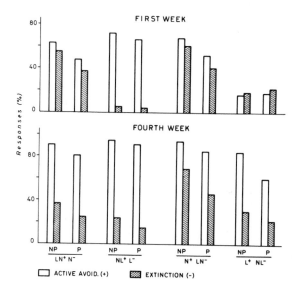

FIG. 14.5. Go-no go avoidance discrimination learning by mice in a shuttle-box (active avoidance-extinction task; same apparatus as in Fig. 14.3 and 14.4; N = 12 per group). The animals were given five daily sessions in each of four consecutive weeks. Each session consisted of 25 active avoidance trials (+) and 25 extinction trials (-), according to the sequence +-+ +-+--; +..., and with an interval of 30 sec between any two successive trials. Two symmetrically opposite stimulus arrangements were used in each of the feature-positive and feature-negative discriminations (90 dB buzzer noise, N; non-directional light, L, see Fig. 14.3).

When a simple signal was appropriate, the CS-US interval was 5 sec in + trials, while the duration was fixed (6 sec) in - trials. When a compound signal was presented, the first stimulus preceded by 1 sec the second one, which started a CS-US interval of 5 sec in + trials and a fixed period of presentation of both stimuli (5 sec) in - trials. In addition, half of the animals in each stimulus condition were trained with a partition (P, see Fig. 14.3) and the other half without partition (NP). Intertrial responses were not punished. As expected, in the initial phase the animals responded more to the extinction signal in the LN^+, N^- than in the NL^+, L^- condition. The feature-negative discrimination was more difficult in the L^+, NL^- than in the N^+, LN^- condition, due mostly to the expected difference in effectiveness between L and N as active avoidance signals. The partition facilitated the suppression of extinction responding in the latter, but not in the former condition; this unexpected interaction was even more evident in two partial replications of the present experiment. Bignami, Alleva, Amorico, De Acetis, and Valanzano, unpublished data.

Our ignorance of the mechanisms that might be responsible for unexplained stimulus nonequivalences is revealed by the comments elicited by the data which were published many years ago. These comments include formally correct, although limited, statements concerning the role

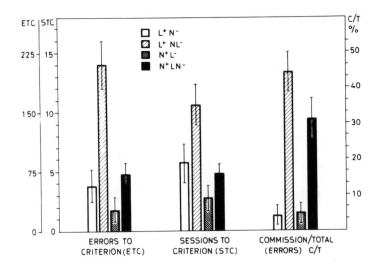

FIG. 14.6. Go-no avoidance discrimination learning by rats in a shuttle-box (active-passive avoidance task; N = 11-26 per group) after active avoidance pretraining to an 80% or more criterion with either an acoustic or a visual CS (90 dB buzzer noise, N; non-directional light, L, see Fig. 14.1). Simple and compound signal presentations and contingencies in active avoidance trials (+) were as indicated in the legend of Fig. 14.5. In passive avoidance trials (-), responses were punished until recrossing occurred. Intertrial responses were also punished. The difference between the easier N^+, LN^- task and the more difficult L^+, NL^- task was even larger than is indicated in the figure, particularly with respect to the frequency of passive avoidance failures (commission errors). In fact, in the former task all rats (24) reached criterion (no more than six omission errors and two commission errors in each of two consecutive sessions), while in the latter task 8 rats out of 26 stabilized below criterion level in spite of extended training. For the consistency of this stimulus nonequivalence in a wide variety of different test conditions, including active avoidance-extinction tasks, see text.

of relative cue salience (Kowalska & Zielinski, 1980), but also statements such as "However, the complicated design of their [Frontali & Bignami's, 1973, 1974] experiments made it difficult to identify the source of group differences" (Domjan, 1983, p. 233). Remark also that in the discussion that follows Domjan defines as "a more definitive study" that of Jacobs & LoLordo, 1977. On the basis of data obtained in particular conditions the latter authors had concluded that light onset is, in general, a poor warning signal in avoidance tasks, rather than emphasizing our insufficient knowledge of the mechanisms that produce a marked variation in the effectiveness of this cue).

In most discrimination experiments using classical aversive paradigms, the trend is to pool data from animals trained with opposite stimulus arrangements within a given feature-negative or feature-positive discrimination, with or without the explicit statement that there were no (or at least, no significant) differences due to stimulus arrangement. However, there is at least one study which shows a marked stimulus nonequivalence similar to one of those found by us, except for the use of a tone (T), instead of a noise signal. Specifically, Reberg and Leclerc (1977) found that rats discriminate much better in the T^+, TL^-, than in the L^+, LT^- task. As expected, both feature-positive discriminations developed rapidly, without differences due to stimulus arrangement. The authors point out that these data could be reconciled with the Rescorla-Wagner theory by adding a "preparedness" element to it; that is, by postulating that visual and acoustic signals are about equally salient as stimuli for distinguishing shock trials in feature-positive discriminations, while a visual signal is more salient than an acoustic signal for distinguishing no-shock trials in feature-negative discriminations.

But, what about the fact that in instrumental paradigms similar stimulus nonequivalences are found both when comparing active avoidance-extinction tasks and when comparing active-passive avoidance tasks? The latter type of discrimination is not between shock and no shock, but between different response requirements in order to avoid shock. Moreover, the suppression of responses to extinction signals in instrumental tasks with asymmetrical reinforcement may be due at least in part to the punishing properties of signal non-termination (Dabrowska, 1975). This makes it even more unlikely that the tentative explanation proposed by Reberg and Leclerc (1977) can account for the stimulus nonequivalences found in instrumental paradigms. Overall, this and several other unsolved problems show how far we still are from an adequate understanding of cue utilization in different situations.

SUMMARY AND CONCLUDING COMMENTS

The present paper was written with several aims. The first was to document the fact that stimulus factors considered either *per se*, or in relation to the category of the reinforcer, can account only for a tiny portion of the variability in active avoidance acquisition and performance in two-way tasks; that is, in situations where the animal cannot meet reinforcement requirements on the basis of the location of safe and unsafe places. Higher-order interactions between stimulus and other variables -- particularly shock density, shock intensity and duration, intertrial interval duration, presence or absence of intertrial response punishment, number of trials per session, and apparatus features which influence the initial availability of escape responses -- account for a much larger portion of the observed variance. The main difference between noise and light cues is that the former show relatively minor changes in effectiveness across a wide variety of different conditions, while the latter can produce a very wide range of learning abilities, depending on the joint influence of the factors just mentioned. This difference in the profiles of cue effectiveness, and not the difference in cue effectiveness *per se*, is the phenomenon which awaits to be explained.

The second aim was to provide a tentative account of the nature of the difference just mentioned, starting with a definition of the learning deficit when avoidance does not develop with a light cue. This deficit is unlikely to be of a general associative and/or motivational kind, since it can be reversed by a variety of manipulations ranging from exposure to a large number of trials within the same session to treatment by several drugs with quite different mechanisms of action. A more likely account is that organismic processes, that is, preparedness-like phenomena, indeed exert an important influence in determining different response "tendencies" at the start of training; for example, by allowing the flight response to a noise signal to acquire quickly a functional value, and viceversa, by postponing until later the outcome of the game when the animal is offered a light cue.

The third aim was to provide a highly tentative analysis of the processes and mechanisms which eventually determine whether or not light-cued avoidance develops. Variation in the relative amount of fear conditioning to the CS plus contextual cues and to contextual cues alone, respectively, and different response topographies determined jointly by the cue and the reinforcer in the early stages of training, appear to be vigorous competitors in this explanatory and heuristic contest. Considering also the variable effects of warning signal termination and feedback stimuli in different situations, one could attempt at this point to reformulate an integrated model; that is, to redefine the relative roles of preparedness phenomena and of reinforcement and other mechanisms, along the lines of the analysis by Crawford and Masterson (1982) which examines the pro's and contra's of the successive versions of Bolles' model.

However, additional problems arise when the analysis is extended to include some unexplained stimulus nonequivalences in feature-negative avoidance discriminations with either asymmetrical or symmetrical reinforcement; that is, to active avoidance-extinction and active-passive avoidance tasks with opposite arrangements of noise and light cues in the A^+, XA^- paradigm. At this point, an explanatory truce becomes imperative, and much additional speculation for heuristic purposes (and of course, much additional research) appears to be necessary. At present, it is still difficult to foresee which kind of changes to current models may eventually be necessary in order to cope with a series of embarrassing facts. Here one is reminded of some recent remarks made by Bolles (1985), challenging the claim of the associationists that the differences between various conditioning and learning phenomena are just a matter of degree. With more space available, Bolles' analogy comparing the 1-2 mm bumps on the vertebrae of some snakes with the legs of race horses (but while we are up, why not with those of giraffes?) should be quoted fully. In fact, at what point does a large quantitative difference become a qualitative difference?

Here we complete a full circle back to the problems and controversies mentioned in the Introduction. Specifically, can one justify the heroic efforts required to understand the interactions which occur in highly "artificial" testing situations? These may be entirely irrelevant when attempting to define the processes and mechanisms which serve behavioural functions in more "natural" environments. At the present state of the behavioural arts -- be they experimental and physiological psychology, comparative psychology and behavioural ecology, or ethology and neuroethology -- any clear-cut positive or negative answer to such a question can be dictated only by pride, prejudice, or anxiety about the outcome of the race for research funds. We really do not have right now any answer better than that given by the famous climber when asked why he tried so hard to conquer Mount Everest ("because it is there"), or that given by the equally famous astronomer when asked about the possible benefits of his studies on stars ("we may end up with a lower price of potatoes").

A vast literature suggests that one needs not to be discouraged by these uncertainties. Speaking from the perspective of a much harder discipline, and with the freedom granted by the Swedish laurels, Sir Peter Medawar has repeatedly reminded us that "The purely logical element in scientific discovery is a comparatively small one". More specifically, even the most objective scientific truths can be shown to rest on a puzzling background of social construction of the basic facts -- striving and fighting to modify the inscriptions, according to the detailed account by Latour and Woolgar (1986) of the long and memorable duel between Guillemin and Schally.

Dealing with a much tinier problem, the present paper has tried hard to show the inadequacy of some of the inscriptions in the records of the go-no go dilemma in aversive paradigms. It was clear from the start that it might be difficult, at the present state of the art, to propose modified working models endowed with at least some heuristic value. But in spite of the many unsolved problems, it appears that further analyses of the interactions between preparedness phenomena and associative and reinforcement processes may eventually benefit both neuroethology and the disciplines which have been traditionally involved in the study of aversively motivated learning.

ACKNOWLEDGEMENTS

The preparation of this paper was supported as part of the Sub-project on Neural and Behavioural Pathophysiology (Project on Non-infectious Pathology) of the Istituto Superiore di Sanità. The reader must be referred to the quotations of published and unpublished data from the authors's laboratory for an acknowledgement of the essential role played by several coworkers in this and in related research. However, special mention must be made of the expert collaboration and unremitting encouragement given by Luigi Amorico and Luigi De Acetis over a period of more than 25 years. This long-term association has been the single most important factor in the achievement of data reliability and of continuity in research which often requires boring and exhausting replications of complex and lengthy experiments before accepting unconventional results.

REFERENCES

Alleva, E., De Acetis, L., Amorico, L., & Bignami, G. (1983). Amphetamine, conditioned stimulus, and nondebilitating preshock effects on activity and avoidance: Further evidence for interactions between associative and nonassociative changes. *Behavioral and Neural Biology, 39*, 78-104.

Anisman, H. (1976). Role of stimulus locale on strain differences in active avoidance after scopolamine or d-amphetamine treatment. *Pharmacology Biochemistry and Behavior, 4,* 103-106.

Anisman, H., & Bignami, G. (1978). *Psychopharmacology of aversively motivated behavior.* New York: Plenum.

Anisman, H., Kokkinidis, L., & Sklar, L. S. (1981). Contribution of neurochemical change to stress-induced behavioral deficits. In S. J. Cooper (Ed.), *Theory in psychopharmacology: Volume 1*, pp. 65-102. London: Academic Press.

Bauer, R. H. (1972). The effects of CS and US intensity on shuttlebox avoidance. *Psychonomic Science, 27*, 266-268.

Bell, R. W., Nohan, J. C., & Davis, J. R., Jr. (1965). Interactive effects of shock intensity and delay of reinforcement on escape conditioning. *Psychonomic Science. 3*, 505-506.

Bignami, G. (1965). Selection for high rates and low rates of avoidance conditioning in the rat. *Animal Behaviour, 13,* 221-227.

Bignami, G., Alleva, E., Amorico, L., De Acetis, L., & Giardini, V. (1985). Bidirectional avoidance by mice as a function of CS, US, and apparatus variables. *Animal Learning and Behavior, 13,* 439-450.

Bignami, G., Amorico, L., Frontali, M., & Rosic, N. (1971). Central cholinergic blockade and two-way avoidance acquisition: The role of response disinhibition. *Physiology and Behavior, 7*, 461-470.

Bolles, R. C. (1970). Species-specific defense reactions and avoidance learning. *Psychological Review, 77*, 32-48.

Bolles, R. C. (1978). The role of stimulus learning in defensive behavior. In S. H. Hulse, H. Fowler, & W. K. Honig (Eds.), *Cognitive processes in animal behavior*, pp. 89-107. Hillsdale: Erlbaum.

Bolles, R. C. Short-term memory and attention. In L.-G. Nilsson, & T. Archer (Eds.), *Perspectives on learning and memory*, pp. 137-146. Hillsdale: Erlbaum.

Bolles, R. C., & Grossen, N. E. (1970). Function of the CS in shuttle-box avoidance learning by rats. *Journal of Comparative and Physiological Psychology, 70,* 165-169.

Bolles, R. C., Hargrave, G. E., & Grossen, N. E. (1970). Avoidance learning as a function of CS quality and CS termination on escape trials. *Psychological Reports. 26.* 27-32.

Callen, E. J. (1986). Fear of the CS and of the context in two-way avoidance learning: Between- and within-subjects manipulations. *Animal Learning and Behavior, 14,* 80-89.

Cicala, G. A., & Azorlosa, J. L. (1985). Stimulus specificity in avoidance learning. *Learning and Motivation. 16.* 83-94.

Cicala, G. A., Masterson, F. A., & Kubitsky, G. (1971). Role of initial response rate in avoidance learning by rats. *Journal of Comparative and Physiological Psychology, 75.* 226-230.

Cicala, G. A., & Owen, J. W. (1976). Warning signal termination and feedback signal may not serve the same function. *Learning and Motivation, 7,* 356-367.

Cicala, G. A., Owen, J. W., & Hill, D. (1976). Successful shuttle avoidance learning with high-intensity USs is sustained if a feedback signal accompanies warning-signal termination. *Bulletin of the Psychonomic Society, 7,* 533-535.

Cicala, G. A., Ulm, R. R., & Drews, D. R. (1971). The effects of shock intensity and intertrial interval duration on the operant level of a shuttle-avoidance response. *Psychonomic Science, 22,* 7-8.

Crawford, M., & Masterson, F. A. (1982). Species-specific defense reactions and avoidance learning. *The Pavlovian Journal of Biological Science, 17,* 204-214.

Dabrowska, J. (1975). Prefrontal lesions and avoidance reflex differentiation in dogs. *Acta Neurobiologiae Experimentalis, 35,* 1-15.

Dalby, D. A., & Shuttlesworth, D. E. (1978). Effect of septal lesions, required response, and shock on the acquisition of a two-way conditioned avoidance response in rats. *Physiological Psychology, 6,* 11-14.

Dantzer, R. (1986). La neurobiologie des comportements peut-elle se passer du comportement? *Comportements, No. 5,* 15-23.

Domjan, M. (1983). Biological constraints on instrumental and classical conditioning: Implications for general process theory. *The Psychology of Learning and Motivation, 17,* 215-277.

Fanselow, M. (1986). Associative vs topographical accounts of the immediate shock-freezing deficit in rats: Implications for the response selection rules governing species-specific defensive reactions. *Learning and Motivation, 17,* 16-39.

Freedman, P. E., Hennessy, J. W., & Groner, D. (1974). Effects of varying active/passive avoidance shock levels in shuttle box avoidance in rats. *Journal of Comparative and Physiological Psychology, 86,* 79-84.

Frontali, M., & Bignami, G. (1973). Go-no go avoidance discriminations in rats with simple "go" and compound "no go" signals: Stimulus modality and stimulus intensity. *Animal Learning and Behavior, 1,* 21-24.

Frontali, M., & Bignami, G. (1974). Stimulus nonequivalences in go/no-go avoidance discriminations: Sensory. drive, and response factors. *Animal Learning and Behavior, 2,* 153-160.

Goodman, E. D., Dyal, J. A., Zinser, O., & Golub, A. (1966). UCR morphology and shock intensity. *Psychonomic Science, 5,* 431-432.

Henderson, N. D. (1970). Motivation-performance relationships using different shock-avoidance shuttlebox techniques. *Psychonomic Science, 21,* 314-315.

Holland, P. C., & Gory, J. (1986). Extinction of inhibition after serial and simultaneous feature negative discrimination training. *The Quarterly Journal of Experimental Psychology, 38B,* 245-265.

Jacobs, W. J., & LoLordo, V. M. (1977). The sensory basis of avoidance responding in the rat. Relative dominance of auditory or visual warning signals and safety signals. *Learning and Motivation, 8,* 448-466.

Jacobs, W. J., & LoLordo, V. M. (1980). Constraints on Pavlovian aversive conditioning: Implications for avoidance learning in the rat. *Learning and Motivation, 11,* 427-455.

Joffe, J. M., & Levine, S. (1973). Effects of weaning age and adult handling on avoidance conditioning, open-field behavior, and plasma corticosterone of adult rats. *Behavioral Biology, 9,* 235-244.

Kamin, L. J., Brimer, C. J., & Black, A. H. (1963). Conditioned suppression as a monitor of fear of the CS in the course of avoidance training. *Journal of Comparative and Physiological Psychology, 56,* 497-501.

Kelley, M. J. (1985). Species-typical taxic behavior and event-reinforcer interactions in conditioning. *Learning and Motivation, 16,* 301-314.

Konorski, J. (1948). *Conditioned reflexes and neuron organization.* Cambridge: Cambridge University Press.

Konorski, J. (1967). *Integrative activity of the brain.* Chicago: University of Chicago Press.

Konorski, J. (1972). Some hypotheses concerning the functional organization of prefrontal cortex. *Acta Neurobiologiae Experimentalis, 32,* 595-613.

Kowalska, D. M., & Zielinski, K. (1980). Avoidance responding in dogs trained in symmetrical or asymmetrical go, no-go differentiation. *Acta Neurobiologiae Experimentalis, 40,* 403-432.

Kuribara, H., & Tadokoro, S. (1986). Differences in acquisition of discrete lever-press and shuttle avoidance responses in 6 strains of mice. *Japanese Journal of Pharmacology, 40,* 303-310.

Kurtz, P. S., & Shafer, J. N. (1967). The interaction of UCS intensity and intertrial interval in avoidance learning. *Psychonomic Science, 8,* 465-466.

Latour, B., & Woolgar, S. (1986). *Laboratory life. The construction of scientific facts.* 2nd ed. Princeton: Princeton University Press.

Maier, S. F., & Jackson, R. L. (1979). Learned helplessness: All of us were right (and wrong): Inescapable shock has multiple effects. *The Psychology of Learning and Motivation, 13,* 155-218.

Marlin, N. A. (1982). Within-compound associations between the context and the conditioned stimulus. *Learning and Motivation, 13,* 526-541.

McAllister, D. E., & McAllister, W. R. (1979). Pseudoavoidance responses in two-way avoidance learning. *Bulletin of the Psychonomic Society, 13*, 317-319.

McAllister, D. E., McAllister, W. R., & Dieter, S. E. (1976). Reward magnitude and shock variables (continuity and intensity) in shuttle-box-avoidance learning. *Animal Learning and Behavior, 4*, 204-209.

McAllister, W. R., McAllister, D. E., & Benton, M. M. (1983). Measurement of fear of the conditioned stimulus and of situational cues at several stages of two-way avoidance learning. *Learning and Motivation, 14*, 92-106.

McAllister, W. R., McAllister, D. E., Dieter, S. E., & James, J. H. (1979). Preexposure to situational cues produces a direct relationship between two-way avoidance learning and shock intensity. *Animal Learning and Behavior, 7*, 165-173.

McAllister, W. R., McAllister, D. E., & Douglass, W. K. (1971). The inverse relationship between shock intensity and shuttle-box avoidance learning in rats: A reinforcement explanation. *Journal of Comparative and Physiological Psychology, 74*, 426-433.

McAllister, W. R., McAllister, D. E., Weldin, G. H., & Cohen, J. M. (1974). Intertrial interval effects in classically conditioning fear to a discrete conditioned stimulus and to situational cues. *Journal of Comparative and Physiological Psychology, 87*, 582-590.

McCleary, R. A. (1961). Response specificity in the behavioral effects of limbic system lesions in the cat. *Journal of Comparative and Physiological Psychology, 54*, 605-613.

Modaresi, H. A. (1978). Facilitating effects of a safe platform on two-way avoidance learning. *Journal of Experimental Psychology: Animal Behavior Processes, 4*, 83-94.

Moot, S. A., Nelson, K., & Bolles, R. C. (1974). Avoidance learning in a black and white shuttlebox. *Bulletin of the Psychonomic Society, 4*, 501-502.

Morris, R. G. M. (1974). Pavlovian conditioned inhibition of fear during shuttlebox avoidance behavior. *Learning and Motivation, 5*, 424-447.

Neuenschwander, N., Fabrigoule, C., & Mackintosh, N. J. (1987). Fear of the warning signal during overtraining of avoidance. *The Quarterly Journal of Experimental Psychology, 39B*, 23-33.

Nishikawa, T., Tsuda, A., Toshima, N., Tanaka, M., & Nagasaki, N. (1981). Interaction of developmental and environmental variables on shock-induced jumping behavior in rats. *Physiology and Behavior, 27*, 539-541.

Oliverio, A. (1968). Effects of scopolamine on avoidance conditioning and habituation of mice. *Psychopharmacologia, 12*, 214-226.

Owen, J. W., Cicala, G. A., & Herdegen, R. T. (1978). Fear inhibition and species specific defense reaction termination may contribute independently to avoidance learning. *Learning and Motivation, 9*, 297-313.

Reberg, D., & Leclerc, R. (1977). A feature positive effect in conditioned suppression. *Animal Learning and Behavior, 5*, 143-147.

Rescorla, R. A., & Wagner, A. R. (1972). A theory of Pavlovian conditioning: Variations in the effectiveness of reinforcement and nonreinforcement. In A. H. Black, & W. F. Prokasy (Eds.), *Classical conditioning II*, pp. 64-99. New York: Appleton-Century-Crofts.

Rosellini, R. A., DeCola, J. P., & Warren, D. A. (1986). The effect of feedback stimuli on contextual fear depends upon the length of the minimum intertrial interval. *Learning and Motivation. 17*, 229-242.

Rosic, N., Frontali, M., & Bignami, G. (1969). Stimulus factors affecting go-no go avoidance discrimination learning by rats. *Communications in Behavioral Biology. 4*, 151-156.

Sigmundi, R. A., & Bolles, R. C. (1983). CS modality, context conditioning, and conditioned freezing. *Animal Learning and Behavior, 11*, 205-212.

Sigmundi, R. A., Bouton, M. E., & Bolles, R. C. (1980). Conditioned freezing in the rat as a function of shock intensity and CS modality. *Bulletin of the Psychonomic Society. 15*, 254-256.

Soltysik, S., & Kowalska, M. (1960). Studies on the avoidance conditioning. I. Relations between cardiac (type I) and motor (type II) effects in the avoidance reflex. *Acta Biologiae Experimentalis, 20*, 157-170.

Starr, M. D., & Mineka, S. (1977). Determinants of fear over the course of avoidance learning. *Learning and Motivation, 8*, 332-350.

Weisman, R. G., Denny, M. R., & Zerbolio, D. J., Jr. (1967). Discrimination based on differential non-shock confinement in a shuttle box. *Journal of Comparative and Physiological Psychology, 63*, 34-38.

West, C. H. K., & Michael, R. P. (1987). Handling facilitates the acquisition of lever-pressing for brain self-stimulation in the posterior hypothalamus of rats. *Physiology and Behavior, 39*, 77-81.

VII

Methodological and Conceptual Perspectives on Aversive Conditioning

Tommy Gärling and Trevor Archer
University of Umeå

Several methodological and conceptual issues stand out as important and in need of resolution through future research endeavors on aversively motivated behavior. These issues range from conceptual ones, such as how the role of higher-order mental processes in human instrumental and classical conditioning should be conceptualized and assessed, through questions about what kinds of experimental designs are most efficient and strategical in studies of various problems within the field, to ethical issues which are raised by both human and animal studies using aversive stimuli. Thus, in the application of experimental procedures in animal studies more care could be taken to design experiments that may not only be less distressful to the animal under study but also may prove to be more effective scientifically (e.g. Archer, Fredriksson, Lewander, & Söderberg, 1987).

Conditioning is assumed to be the simplest form or unit of the learning process, presumably with strong similarities in humans and in animal species. This assumption would be questionable if it is shown that conditioning is controlled by higher-order mental processes. In humans, awareness (defined as a conscious experience that may be recalled) of the relationship to be learned has been taken as an indication of the role of higher-order mental processes in conditioning. If awareness of contingencies is a necessary condition for their acquisition, then one may doubt whether the considerable recent advances in the study of animal learning (see, e.g., Chapters 1-4, 7, 8-10, 14-17 of this volume) is important for the resolution of fundamental issues in human psychology as well as whether the results of animal studies are informative for the practical issues of psychological application by, for instance, those clinicians who have recently found a coherent framework for their practice in learning theory (cf. Chapters 5, 6, 11-13). The relative gains and losses in seeking a close application of contemporary animal learning theory to, for example, the field of human memory and decision have been discussed at length in a previous volume (Nilsson & Archer, 1985) but the problem is closely analysed by Rönnberg and Ohlsson (1985).

The chapter by Robert Boakes (this volume) sets its sights beyond the general issues dealing solely with the conceptual bases of aversively motivated behavior. Boakes does much to clarify the present empirical status of the notion that human adults learn, in classical conditioning, the relationship between stimulus and reinforcer, or, in instrumental conditioning, the relationship between response and reinforcer, without being aware of the learned relationship. It appears as true as it was in 1974 when Brewer wrote his review (Brewer, 1974), that there exist no convincing supporting evidence. In this regard, the problem of *pseudoconditioning* might be considered. As a result of a particular experimental arrangement, pseudoconditioning, the unconditioned response (UR) to a given aversive stimulus (US) may become elicited by any other discrete stimulus in the absence of any explicit correlation between that stimulus and the US (Grether, 1938). Thus, without any conditioning process actually 'in effect' or any awareness of a contingency arrangement a pseudoconditioning process could provide a necessary and adaptive form of behavior (Evans, 1966; Wells, 1968).

Related to the general issue of pseudoconditioning in aversion paradigms is the problem of selecting appropriate controls in conditioning, e.g. in contextual conditioning experiments the TRC stimulus (i.e. a randomly presented discrete keylight stimulus intermittently presented during the administration of a positive reinforcer, e.g. food) although unpredictive of the US may become excitatory (e.g. Tomie, 1985), to which the problem of individual differences can be considered a related issue. Further, in a conditioned emotional response (CER) paradigm, Ayres, Benedict and Witcher (1975) found that the training stimulus suppressed barpressing if the CS-US pairing occurred early during training but if the early US presentations were isolated from the presentations of the CS, later CS-US pairings were not effective in conditioning the random CS (but see also Keller, Ayres & Mahoney, 1977). Thus, several investigations using aversive Pavlovian-conditioning procedures have demonstrated that the conditioning of a randomly presented discrete CS is blocked by the concurrent conditioning accrueing to the presentaiton of contextual cues (e.g. Kremer, 1974; Odling-Smee, 1975; Witcher & Ayres, 1975).

The acquisition of shuttlebox or barpress responses by rats of different genetic strains is quite variable; even different batches of rats or mice within a given strain show surprising and often frustrating variation (e.g.

Anisman & Waller, 1972; Broadhurst & Levine, 1963; Gray & Lalljee, 1974; Joffe, 1964; Katzer & Mills, 1974; Levine & Broadhurst, 1963; Wilcock & Fulker, 1973). In addition, a significant variation has been found between animals of the same strain but obtained from different commercial breeders (Nakamura & Anderson, 1962; Ray & Barrett, 1975). The presence of greater between-litter than within-litter variance within a given rat or mouse strain appears to be a microenvironmental effect which may reflect genetic differences whereas the possibility of an influence of environmental variation upon avoidance learning may be both the result of an interaction with or even independent of the genetic differences (cf. Brush, 1985). Bearing these evidence in mind, it is necessary ot be aware of the extra-experimental conditions that have been shown to affect performance in avoidance paradigms (Bignami, 1965; Brush, 1966; Herrnstein, 1969; Holland & Gupta, 1966).

In attempting a resolution, Boakes makes two arguments which are somewhat difficult to reconcile. First, awareness in human conditioning may not have a causal role, and could therefore be considered to be epiphenomenal. Thus higher-order mental processes are after all not important in human conditioning. Secondly, in addition to the lack of empirical evidence for so called primitive conditioning (Razran, 1971) in humans, conditioning in animals is very often not an automatic development of a reflex-like reaction which do not involve expectancies. Therefore, it might have been a mistake from the outset to expect to obtain primitive conditioning in humans. The implication is now that the issue of cognitive factors in human conditioning is not crucial for cross-species generalizations. However, tactics may differ with regard to how the human - animal similarities and/or dissimilarities may be resolved and even exploited to achieve these generalizations. Dickinson and Shanks (1985) suggest that the conditional response (for example, in an animal conditioning experiment) could be regarded the response measure analogous to mental processes or a state of "awareness". In this context, they suggest"..... if the strength of the response is taken as reflecting the animal's judgement of the event relationships involved in the conditioning procedure, a direct parallel can be drawn with the processes involved in human judgements of causal effectiveness" (p. 169). To support this approach one may evoke studies on the possible relationship between animal conditioning and human judgements of control in learned helplessness studies (Alloy & Abramson, 1979; Alloy & Tabachnik, 1984). Thus, we seek to pursue the issues raised and developed by the discussions involving information processing and cognition in human and animal studies.

Another approach to the resolution of the problems inherent to human-animal cognition may be to try to delineate and define the *role* of higher-order mental processes in human conditioning paradigms, and to compare this *role* to the influences of higher-order mental processes in animal conditioning paradigms, rather than to investigate whether awareness is a necessary condition for human conditioning. Whether or not the existence of awareness is important for the more general issue of cognition is questionable. As already noted, Boakes addresses this issue

374 GÄRLING AND ARCHER

when questioning whether awareness has a causal role. In related
research on expectancy-value models in cognitive motivational psychology
(Feather, 1982) or in decision making (Payne, 1982), higher-order mental
processes are considered to be causally related to behavior or actions (see
also a current position in philosophical action theory, Brand, 1984). Such
mental processes may nevertheless be only partially conscious, that is,
open to introspection (Erikson & Simon, 1984; Nisbett & Wilson, 1977).

What then are the possibilities to derive the role of higher-order
mental processes in conditioning in general and in human conditioning in
particular, or, more specifically, what paradigms should be used for
infering the causal role of awareness (e.g., conscious plans and
intentions)? Complementary to a number of suggestions given by Boakes,
close on-line monitoring of mental processes, rather than of autonomous
responses, in conjunction with computer modeling of these processes may
be suggested as one possibility. In humans the data could be secured
from introspective reports whereas animal data are confined to
observations of overt behavior. If the findings from human studies, where
more detailed and conclusive data can be obtained, generalize to animal
studies would be an interesting question to ask, in addition to the question
of whether animal data generalize to humans (e.g. Dickinson & Shanks,
1985).

The following two chapters are both concerned with the need for other
types of experimental designs. Russell Church (Chapter 16) notes that
even though his three published articles (Church, 1964; Church & Getty,
1972; Church & Lerner, 1976), in which the yoked control design is
critized for leading to biased estimates of treatment effects, have not gone
completely unnoticed, they seem to have had little effect on actual practice.
According to a recent literature search by Church, the yoked control
design has been used with about the same frequency since 1967. In this
design the control subjects or yoked controls receive a reinforcer (or
punishment) exactly at the same time, irrespective of the response, as the
experimental subject receives it, contingent on the response to be
reinforced. The problem is that it cannot be validly inferred that the
response is controlled by the reinforcer if there is random variability in
effectiveness of the reinforcer. The apparent control features of the design
may conceal this bias. Other factors may however more readily explain
why the practice is not changed. The yoked control problem may be of
substanial consequence in view of widespread use of this procedure in
studies investigating the behavioral and neurochemical consequences of
uncontrollable shock (e.g. Overmier & Seligman, 1967; Weiss,
Goodman, Losito, Corrigan, Charry & Bailey, 1981) and is therefore a
methodological consideration of some consequence.

One argument for using the yoked control design, discussed by
Church, is the (untestable) assumption that the bias is small and
unimportant. Against this point, Church argues that if an experimental
design does not permit unbiased estimates of treatment effects, it should be
abandoned in favour of another design. However, the zeitgeist, contrary
to this argument, seems to favour a pragmatic rather than a puristic view
on these matters. The recent popularity of quasiexperimental designs

(Cook & Campbell, 1979), in which biases are in principle accepted, witness to this. Confounding has furthermore been a principle of incomplete experimental designs for a long time, as exemplified by, for instance, confounding of error variance and interaction effects in a latin square design (Kirk, 1982). The fact is that no simpler alternative than the yoked control design probably exists. If the degree of bias was known, then it would perhaps be possible to "correct" the bias in a way similar to how analysis of covariance is used in connection with quasiexperimental designs. An unfortunate feature of the yoked control design is nevertheless that the bias is never conservative. Using this design may thus be immediately rewarding. This is hopefully not important: Whether or not cognitive factors are involved in human conditioning, we certainly expect such factors to be operative in the design of experiments.

In the third chapter of this topic (Chapter 17), Terje Sagvolden discusses a series of studies of instrumental conditioning and avoidance learning which illustrate the point that parametric experimental designs should be used more often in the future than they have been in the past. Preferably one independent variable should be varied in many steps whilst all other variables are kept constant. Blocking may perhaps also be used more often by means of more complex factorial designs. These sound recommendations, although not completely novel ones, do appear to have only one serious drawback: They are seldom practically feasible. If psychologists learned more about so called incomplete experimental designs (Kirk, 1982), this would be one possibility to overcome the difficulties. In such designs one takes the risk of confounding various effects but achieves about the same efficiency for less investment of work. This raises however other problems such as what to do with missing data in such designs.

Sometimes statistical control, requiring that more measurements are taken on the same number of sample units, is perhaps a viable alternative to experimental control. Because one concern of Sagvolden is that interaction effects are the rule rather than the exception, it should be noted that such interactions are not reflections of nature. They may very much vary with which dependent measures are chosen (Loftus, 1978). Thus, reconsidering one's choice of dependent variable is another possibility. In this connection it may furthermore be noted that the value of parametric designs increases if the independent variable(s) can be measured quantitatively without errors.

Sagvolden benefits greatly from hindsight when drawing conclusions from his research examples, therefore he might have missed that these examples also demonstrate nicely the decisive role of hypotheses in research. If one had no hypothesis, how would it then be possible to know what factors to vary systematically and what factors to control for? Perhaps Sagvolden's claim for more complex experimental designs in future research should be extended to or replaced by the claim that more complex questions be asked. Then complex designs will be needed for answering these questions, and hopefully, if the field has reached the required degree of maturation, the answers will be more general and reliable.

Starting with a discussion of a conceptual issue, this introduction to methodological and conceptual perspectives has complete a full circle by noting the importance of such issues for the practice of experimental designs. This is as it should be because a clear dividing line can obviously not be drawn between methodological and conceptual issues. However, another issue, defined here as a methodological one, is definitely less related to the logic of research. This is the issue of whether and under what circumstances it is ethical to conduct experiments with aversive stimuli.

We maintain that it is beyond the scope and purpose of this volume to pursue arguments centred upon the ethical issue even though careful consideration must be given to the design of experiments involving aversive conditioning; this consideration being of paramount importance to the acquisition of methodological stringence. It should also considered that action groups and/or committees applying unrestricted and superficial recommendations could, on a long term basis, punish the very individuals that ought to be of central importance, i.e. the experimental animals, by unwitting interference with experimental design such that larger numbers of subjects be the results of increases in within-subject error or in cases where numbers of animals are severely reduced the same individual may become subjected a painfully excessive repetition of tests. Thus, the ethical issue in methodology requires much more careful and sober analysis by qualified members of both the scientific community and those groups representing animal rights. For a cold, direct and explicit treatise of unrestricted or amateurish attempts to control ethical issues the reader is referred to the recent paper by Revusky (1987).

We would also maintain that the relevance of animal aversive conditioning to human psychology is not limited to solely behavioral criteria, for instance the illumination of phobic anxiety as similar behavioral reactions are involved, although it may not be useful to seek a close parallel between say a cognitive causality judgement and conditional emotional reponse in the rat. The usefulness of, say avoidance learning, for the human conditions becomes more apparent if the conditioning procedures are treated as various measures of knowledge acquisition (mental processes) and the individual is then considered to be learning about negative event correlations (Dickinson, 1980). Thus, a necessary requirement must be to pursue a reappraisal of conditioning procedures and concepts in cognitive terms which means that we may have to abandon some of the conditioning and reinforcement terminology and acquire a language to suit such a knowledge-based orientation.

REFERENCES

Alloy, L. B., & Abramson, L. Y. (1979). Judgment of contingency in depressed and nondepressed students: Sadder but wiser? *Journal of Experimental Psychology: General, 108*, 441-485.

Alloy, L. B., & Tabachnik, N. (1984). Assessment of covariation by humans and animals: The joint influence of prior expectations and current situational information. *Psychological Review, 91*, 112-149.

Anisman, H., & Waller, T. G. (1972). Facilitative and disruptive effects of prior exposure to shock on subsequent avoidance performance. *Journal of Comparative and Physiological Psychology, 78*, 113-122.

Archer, T., Fredriksson, A., Lewander, T., & Söderberg, U. (1987). Marble burying and spontaneous motor activity in mice: Interactions over days and the effect of diazepam. *Scandinavian Journal of Psychology, 28*, 242-249.

Ayres, J. J. B., Benedict, J. O., & Witcher, E. S. (1975). Systematic manipulation of individual events in a truly random control in rats. *Journal of Comparative and Physiological Psychology, 88*, 97-103.

Bignami, G. (1965). Selection for high rates and low rates of avoidance conditioning in the rat. *Animal Behavior, 13*, 221-227.

Brand, M. (1984). *Intending and acting: Towards a naturalized action theory.* Cambridge, MA: MIT Press.

Brewer, W. F. (1974). There is no convincing evidence for operant or classical conditioning in adult humans. In W. B. Weimar & D. S. Palermo (Eds.), *Cognition and the symbolic processes*, pp. 1-42. Hillsdale, NJ: Erlbaum.

Broadhurst, P. L., & Levine, S. (1963). Behavioral consistency in strains of rats selectively bred for emotional elimination. *British Journal of Psychology, 54*, 121-125.

Brush, F. R. (1966). On the differences between animals that learn and do not learn to avoid electric shock. *Psychonomic Science, 5*, 123-124.

Brush, F. R. (1985). Genetic determinants of avoidance learning: Mediation by emotionality. In F. R. Brush and J. B. Overmier (Eds.), *Affect, conditioning and cognition: Essays on the determinants of behavior*, pp. 27-42. Hillsdale, NJ: Erlbaum.

Church, R. M. (1964). Systematic effect of random error in the yoked control design. *Psychological Bulletin. 62*, 122-131.

Church, R. M., & Getty, D. J. (1972). Some consequences of the reaction to an aversive event. *Psychological Bulletin, 78*, 21-27.

Church, R. M., & Lerner, N. D. (1976). Does the headless roach learn to avoid? *Physiological Psychology, 4*, 439-442.

Cook, T. D., & Campbell, D. T. (1979). *Quasi-experimentation: Design & analysis issues for field settings.* Chicago: Rand McNally.

Dickinson, A. (1980). Contemporary animal learning theory. Cambridge: Cambridge University Press.

Dickinson, A., & Shanks, D. (1985). Animal conditioning and human causality judgment. In L.-G. Nilsson & T. Archer (Eds.), *Perspectives on learning and memory*, pp. 167-191. Hillsdale, NJ: Erlbaum.

Ericsson, K. A., & Simon, H. A. (1984). *Protocol analysis: Verbal reports as data.* Cambridge, MA: MIT Press.

Evans, S. M. (1966). Non-associative avoidance learning in Nereid polychaetes. *Animal Behaviour, 14,* 102-106.

Feather, N. T. (Ed.) (1982). *Expectations and actions: Expectancy-value models in psychology.* Hillsdale, NJ: Erlbaum.

Gray, J. A., & Lalljee, B. (1974). Sex differences in emotional behavior in the rat: Correlation between open-field defecation and active avoidance. *Animal Behavior, 22,* 856-861.

Grether, W. F. (1938). Pseudo-conditioning without paired stimulation encountered in attempted backward conditioning. *Journal of Comparative Psychology, 25,* 91-96.

Herrnstein. R. J. (1969). Method and theory in the study of avoidance. *Psychological Review, 76,* 49-69.

Holland, H. C., & Gupta, B. D. (1966). Some correlated measures of activity and reactivity in two strains of rats selectively bred for differences in the acquision of a conditioned avoidance response. *Animal Behavior, 14,* 574-580.

Joffe, J. (1964). Avoidance learning and failure to learn in two strains of rats selectively bred for emotionality. *Psychonomic Science, 1,* 185-186.

Kirk, R. E. (1982). *Experimental design: Procedures for the behavioral sciences (2nd ed.).* Belmont, CA: Brooks/Cole.

Keller, R. J., Ayres, J. J. B., & Mahoney, W. J. (1977). Brief vs extended exposure to truly random control procedures. *Journal of Experimental Psychology: Animal Behavior Processes, 3,* 53-65.

Kremer, E. F. (1974). The truly random control procedure: Conditioning to the static cues. *Journal of Comparative and Physiological Psychology, 86,* 700-707.

Levine, S., & Broadhurst, P. L. (1963). Genetic and ontogenetic determinants of adult behavior in the rat. *Journal of Comparative and Physiological Psychology, 56,* 423-428.

Loftus, G. R. (1978). On interpretation of interactions. *Memory & Cognition, 6,* 312-319.

Nakamura, C. Y., & Anderson, N. H. (1962). Avoidance behavior differences within and between strains of rats. *Journal of Comparative and Physiological Psychology, 55,* 740-747.

Nilsson, L.-G., & Archer, T. (Eds.). (1985). *Perspectives on learning and memory.* Hillsdale. N.J: Erlbaum.

Nisbett, R. E., & Wilson, T. D. (1977). Telling more than we can know: Verbal reports on mental processes. *Psychological Review, 84,* 231-259.

Overmier, J. B., & Seligman, M. E. P. (1967). Effects of inescapable shock upon subsequent escape and avoidance learning. *Journal of Comparative Physiological Psychology, 78,* 340-343.

Payne, J. W. (1982). Contingent decision behavior. *Psychological Bulletin, 92,* 382-402.

Ray, O. S., & Barrett, R. J. (1975). Behavioral, pharamcological and biochemical analysis of genetic differences in rats. *Behavioral Biology, 15,* 391-418.

Razran, G. (1971). *Mind in Evolution: An East-West Synthesis of Learned*

Behavior and Cognition. Boston: Houghton Mifflin.

Revusky, S. (1987). About the Canadian council on animal care. *The Newfoundland Psychologist, 9,* 33-44.

Rönnberg, J., & Ohlsson, K. (1985). The challenge of integrating animal learning and human memory research. In L.-G. Nilsson & T. Archer (Eds.), *Perspectives on learning and memory,* pp. 293-324. Hillsdale, N. J.: Lawrence Erlbaum Associates.

Weiss, J. M., Goodman, P. A., Losito, B. G., Corrigan, S., Charry, J. M., & Bailey, W. H. (1981). Behavioral depression produced by an uncontrollable stressor: Relationship to norepinephrine, dopamine, and serotonin levels in various regions of rat brain. *Brain Research Reviews, 3,* 167-205.

Wells, M. (1968). *Lower Animals.* London: Weidenfeld and Nicolson.

Wilcock, J., & Fulker, D. W. (1973). Avoidance learning in rats: Genetic evidence for two distinct behavioral processes in the shuttlebox. *Journal of Comparative and Physiological Psychology, 82,* 247-253.

Witcher, E. S., & Ayres, J. J. B. (1975). Effect of removing background white noise during CS presentation on conditioning in the truly random control procedure. *Bulletin of the Psychonomic Society, 6,* 25-27.

15

How One Might Find Evidence for Conditioning in Adult Humans

Robert A. Boakes
University of Sussex, England

1. Conditioning and Awareness

This chapter is concerned with a paradoxical state of affairs which needs to be resolved. The paradox can be stated quite simply. On the one hand the term 'conditioning' has become a term in our everyday language reflecting widespread belief that people's actions, attitudes, beliefs and feelings can be profoundly influenced by processes of learning over which they have little voluntary control and of which normally they are largely unaware. On the other hand the research tradition in psychology which, since the early days of Behaviorism, has done most to strengthen this popular belief and which has provided the label 'conditioning', has failed to provide good evidence to support it. There are two obvious ways of resolving this paradox: either popular belief is mistaken or psychologists studying human conditioning have failed to use appropriate methods.

Before examining relevant research it will be useful to clarify the nature of lay belief on the matter using the distinction between instrumental and classical conditioning which, although taught to beginning students of psychology for many decades now, strangely does not appear yet to have entered everyday language. 'Awareness' here will be used in the sense of conscious experience which could potentially be reported at the time to someone else.

Thus, 'instrumental conditioning without awareness' might mean making some response that was acquired and is maintained as a result of some consistent temporal relationship with a reinforcing event either 1) without present awareness of the response; 2) without present awareness of the nature of the reinforcing event; or 3) without any awareness *during the period when the response is acquired* of the relationship between response and reinforcer.

Neither 1) nor 2) is particularly contentious: general psychological theorists going back at least a century, current information processing theory, contemporary learning theory and everyday belief all agree that many responses which are frequently repeated under similar conditions become automatic in the sense of occurring without awareness of either the involvement of any decision process or the occurrence of the response. This is a separate issue from that of whether a response can become *autonomous* in the sense of independence from the response-reinforcer contingency which first established the response; this issue *is* contentious at present (Dickinson, 1985; Colwill & Rescorla, 1985).

The question at issue here is whether a response can be acquired by a normal, adult human being without that person perceiving the relationship between the response and its consequences. Most of us would probably agree that at least some aspects of the way we interact with others and some of our idiosyncratic mannerisms are acquired in this way.

Similar distinctions may be made with regard to classical conditioning, which will be taken here in the broad sense to denote any learning that arises from a temporal relationship between two external events. In this case 'conditioning without awareness' might mean either: 1) that a stimulus of whose presence we are not currently conscious can affect our present feelings or actions due to its past relationship with some reinforcing event; 2) that a stimulus can acquire such properties even though we have *never* been aware of its presence; that is, the question of subliminal perception; or 3) that a stimulus which we consciously perceived can acquire some influence over us even though we were at no time aware of its essential relationship with some other important event.

Again, the first interpretation is relatively uncontentious: many areas of research in psychology, such as those examining nonverbal aspects of communication or the perception of emotion, have demonstrated the powerful influence of perceptual events of which people are unaware, when it seems likely that some stimuli of this kind acquired their properties as a result of a temporal relationship with some other event in the past.

What is in dispute is whether a stimulus can acquire such properties without its essential relationship to some other event being perceived. If the answer is no, then the question of subliminal perception of the stimulus during acquisition (2 above) does not arise.

Three other issues need some discussion before concluding these introductory remarks.

First, a major achievement of current theories of conditioning in animals is to have demonstrated the need for a careful distinction between learning and performance. Thus, with respect to human conditioning awareness of the relationship between two events may be necessary for conditioning to occur, but nevertheless the person may be quite unaware of the consequences of such conditioning. Thus, to take as examples two of the most popular procedures for experiments on human conditioning, subjects may know that a click regularly precedes a puff of air to their eye, but not know whether they blinked to the click; or they may know that a pattern appearing on a screen means that shock is coming, but not know whether their skin conductance has changed accordingly. The degree to which people perceive their own behaviour is a different question from that of whether they perceive the relationships which may affect that behaviour.

Second, the traditional prototype of classical conditioning has been Pavlovian salivary conditioning with its emphasis on the measurement in animals of the kind of response over which human beings have very limited voluntary control. Consequently, past discussion of the present issue has often been intermingled with concern over the question of involuntary behaviour. Animal research of the past two decades indicates that, although conditioned changes in involuntary responses are indeed likely to reflect processes of classical conditioning (Dworkin & Miller, 1986), various kinds of behaviour in animals corresponding to what would normally be classed as voluntary behaviour in people can be affected by classical conditioning; a notable example is autoshaped keypecking by pigeons (Hearst & Jenkins, 1974).

This simply shows that the prototype most readily used for thinking about human conditioning may be misleading. The main point is again the need to distinguish between learning and performance. The question of learning without awareness is independent of that of voluntary control. I may, for example, discover that I display a conditioned asthmatic reaction to some situation or a hostile reaction to some person for reasons that completely elude me, yet this need not stop me from taking an effective decision to change such reactions. Alternatively, the view that conditioning cannot take place without the perception of the crucial contingency is entirely compatible with the idea that this might produce a response beyond voluntary control. A teenager may well know that her anxiety at the prospect of joining a group of people reflects the acute self-consciousness she suffered on the last occasion she was with them, but this may not make it any easier to stop blushing when she does so.

Finally, there is the developmental issue. Often the term 'condition' is used loosely to refer to the effects of early learning on later development. An example would be to claim that an adult's role in a relationship is 'conditioned' by some relationship in childhood. Since both classical and instrumental conditioning have been demonstrated very early in life at a time when the baby's perception of relationships must be much more limited than those of an adult, it is arguable that human conditioning without awareness might at least occur very early in life. However, this is not an issue that will receive much discussion here.

Such speculation may prompt the kind of unease that psychology tried to escape from seventy years ago by accepting Watson's Behaviorism and his promise that conditioning would provide a method to substitute for reliance on subjective reports (Boakes, 1984). Why bother with the question of awareness in conditioning? The question would perhaps not arise if Watson's promise had been realized. Instead, it is argued here that the question needs to be resolved if we are to understand how the considerable recent advances in the study of animal learning relate to fundamental issues in human psychology; and also if such studies are to inform the practice of psychology by those, such as clinicians, who previously found a coherent framework for their work in learning theory.

One way of summarizing the problem introduced in this section is to use the terms employed by Razran (1971). He distinguished various levels of human learning of which the two most pertinent here were 'primitive conditioning', the form of learning commonly studied in animals, and 'perception of relations', abrupt changes in behaviour resulting from the sudden awareness of a temporal relationship between two events. His view that both kinds of learning can occur has been very pervasive. The problem is that good evidence for 'primitive conditioning' has proved so hard to find.

2. Cognitive Factors in Human Conditioning

The issues introduced here provided the background to a large amount of experimental work during the late 1950s and 1960s. Reflecting the rapidly changing theoretical context to the study of learning during that era, these studies were at first largely concerned to test the direct applicability of S-R theory (e.g., Spence, 1966) or of the principles of operant conditioning to human behaviour (e.g., Hefferline, Keenan, & Harford, 1959), but then became more and more concerned with the influence of cognitive factors.

This research was comprehensively reviewed in a key paper by Brewer (1974) whose provocative title, 'There is no convincing evidence for operant or classical conditioning in adult humans', expressed the conclusion he reached. What he termed his radical position in contrast to the previously dominant Behaviorist approach to human conditioning was that 'the college sophomore does not leave his higher mental processes outside the door when he walks into the experimental room, but he uses them to try to understand what is going on and what he should do about it'. Brewer's argument was that the data from human conditioning experiments can be entirely understood in terms of such conscious and active processes. He looked at two main types of experiment related to this issue and subsequent research has continued to employ both of them. The primary aim of one design, called here the 'information design', is to compare the effects of giving subjects information likely to affect their expectations of what is going to happen with the effects of their direct experience of events; the latter usually consist of some contingency between a response or stimulus and a reinforcer (Grings, 1973). The second, 'masking', design makes it difficult for subjects to become aware of the contingencies between events intended to promote conditioning and usually has the aim of discovering whether conditioning can take place in the absence of such awareness.

The most common forms of experiment using the information design are ones that either tell the subject beforehand that, for example, a picture of a snake will be followed by a shock - this is sometimes called a 'threat' condition - or that some contingency no longer holds; for example, that there will be no more shock. The latter procedure is usually termed 'instructed extinction'. Readers unfamiliar with this literature will probably not be surprised to learn that both kinds of information can be highly effective. If skin conductance measures are taken, the threat procedure can result in a large response to the snake before the subject has ever directly experienced the snake-shock contingency, while learning that there will be no more shock usually results in immediate decrease of a previously established response to some stimulus.

What is more surprising is the magnitude of such effects. As we have found in our experiments, simply telling a subject that a snake will be followed by a shock, but that a spider will not - while, in fact, not delivering shock at all - may produce a much clearer differentiation of responding to the two stimuli than in subjects who actually experience the event contingencies. Brewer (1974) notes that this outcome has been obtained from three out of the four studies that have directly made this comparison. Similarly, even when quite intense shocks, at a level one suspects that few of today's ethical committees would allow, are used in an instructed extinction design (e.g., Bridger & Mandel, 1964), telling the subject that there will be no more shock results in near immediate abolition of the response.

A particularly satisfactory procedure for examining the degree to which instructions can override possible effects of past experience is the 'reversed cue' design first introduced by Wilson (1968). Telling a subject that a blue light would no longer be followed by shock, but that a previously nonreinforced yellow light now would be, led to the effective disappearance of a skin conductance response to the blue light on the very first trial on which it was presented. The superiority of this procedure lies in the fact that the instructions are not intended to change the subject's beliefs about what events are to occur, but about the contingency between them. Simple threat and instructed extinction procedures confound these two kinds of expectation. In any experiment using autonomic measures overall expectancies about the likelihood of shock may well have a large effect on baseline arousal levels against which a stimulus effect is assessed.

Wilson's (1968) findings were extended by Grings, Schell and Carey (1973) by using both long and short duration stimuli to test the possibility that 'verbal control' might be less complete with brief stimuli and, more importantly, to include a control group given non-contingent conditions during the first phase of the experiment. Some of the data from this study are shown in Figure 15.1. The crucial result to note is that on the first trial of the reversal phase subjects in the experimental group responded at the same low level to the light, which on all previous occasions had been followed by shock, as the control subjects, for whom the light had never been paired with shock. Thus, in the experimental group the information that the previous cue-shock contingency would be reversed had completely eliminated any effect of prior light-shock pairings.

Such studies indicate that, if primitive conditioning does affect human autonomic responding, then it is relatively fragile in the face of a change in conscious expectations brought about by instructions from the experimenter. However, these studies do not directly bear on the question of awareness. This has been the focus of experiments using a masking design in which subjects are usually deliberately misled as to the purpose

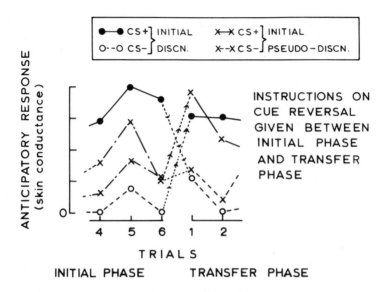

FIG. 15.1. Instructed reversal of a discrimination compared with a group given a 'pseudo discrimination' (random control condition) during the initial phase. Redrawn from Grings, Schell and Carey (1973; Fig. 3).

of the experiment. As summarized by Brewer (1974), early studies that reported successful conditioning without awareness of the contingencies were marred by the lack of sensitive assessment of awareness and, as more refined efforts to make such assessment were developed, evidence for conditioning without awareness became progressively harder to find. A pervasive problem was that in many studies subjects would develop beliefs about the nature of the experiment which, although incorrect, could be sufficient to generate a pattern of responding identical to that expected on the basis of a simple conditioning model. Some notable examples of this occurred in the context of the disputes over verbal conditioning (Greenspoon, 1955). Thus, in Dulany (1961) a subgroup of subjects, who showed an increased frequency of plural nouns when these were reinforced and yet could not report this contingency, had developed 'correlated hypotheses' about what the experimenter was after which appeared to be responsible for their data.

The most persistent group to use the masking design has been that of Dawson and his colleagues. At the time of Brewer's review they had started to use a differential conditioning paradigm which they have continued to exploit ever since. Thus, in Dawson (1970) subjects were told that they were taking part in a study designed to determine whether 'physiological activation' produced by a periodic brief electric shock would facilitate auditory perception. A series of trials each contained five tones and subjects were instructed to identify verbally which of the last four tones sounded similar to the first one. Half of the subjects were given the additional information that the last tone of a trial would always be either the lowest or highest, and the shock would occasionally occur after one of these (the highest, say), but not the other. This additional information was not given to the subjects in the 'masked' condition. Using skin conductance as the measure of learning, differential responding was found in the informed group, but there was no sign of conditioning in the masked group, even though scores on the auditory task confirmed that they had been attending to the tones throughout the experiment.

Dawson and his colleagues have subsequently employed this procedure to explore the relationship between awareness of contingencies and conditioning in a variety of ways. For example, in the experiment illustrated in Figure 15.2 Dawson and Biferno (1973) asked subjects to indicate their expectancy of a shock during each tone; they found that the trial on which subjects began to make accurate predictions coincided with that on which differential skin conductance responses began to appear. Most importantly their work has indicated the importance of employing an immediate recognition questionnaire to assess awareness, rather than asking a subject to recall the conditions of the experiment after some delay (Dawson & Reardon, 1973). This work has consistently shown that conditioning measured by skin conductance does not occur without awareness of the contingencies, provided that a sufficiently sensitive measure is used to assess the latter (Dawson & Schell, 1987).

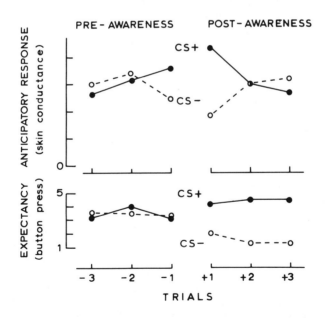

FIG. 15.2. Concurrent measurement of 'anticipatory response' (skin conductance) and 'expectancy' (selection of response buttons 1-5) on trials immediately preceding and immediately following the 'moment of awareness' as indicated by the button measure. Redrawn from Dawson and Biferno (1973; Fig. 2).

Confirmation of Brewer's (1974) conclusions has also come from work on instrumental conditioning. He suggested that extant data on the performance of human subjects exposed to various schedules of reinforcement were entirely consistent with the idea that their response patterns depend on the verbalizable hypotheses they reach about the contingency, whether or not this corresponds to the actual schedule. Lowe and his colleagues have subsequently confirmed this claim (Lowe, 1979) and find that only when human subjects at an age of limited language abilities i.e. 2 years or under, are tested on reinforcement schedules are the patterns of responding typical of non-human animals found (Bentall, Lowe, & Beasty, 1985).

One of the most interesting attempts to find a limit to Brewer's claim has been the work of Öhman, Hugdahl and others cited elsewhere in this volume (see Chapter by Öhman et al.). Briefly, this accepts that most of the data from human conditioning studies reflect the influence of cognitive variables, but suggests that primitive conditioning may be found when human subjects are exposed to certain 'prepared' pairings of stimuli and reinforcers, notably when pictures of phobia-related stimuli such as snakes precede the arrival of shock. The main support proposed for this claim has been the finding that the effects of such exposure decline less rapidly than those of equivalent neutral stimuli e.g. flowers and mushrooms, when shock is withdrawn (e.g., Öhman, Eriksson & Olofsson, 1975) and are less affected by instructions that extinction is about to begin (e.g., Hugdahl & Öhman, 1977).

There has been some scepticism over these claims, partly because of problems of replicability (e.g., McNally, 1987), partly because of methodological problems (e.g., Gray, 1982) and partly because of conceptual difficulties. An example of the latter is provided by the parallel Öhman draws between such 'phobic' conditioning and the best documented example of prepared animal learning, conditioned taste aversion. Despite early belief to the contrary, there is in fact no good evidence that the latter is slow to extinguish. There do not seem to have been any attempts to compare rates of extinction of conditioned taste aversions, but nonetheless there are several examples indicating that such conditioning is both rapidly acquired and rapidly lost (e.g., Sjödén & Archer, this volume; Westbrook, Smith & Charnock, 1985).

For present purposes the most important point to make about conditioning involving phobia-related stimuli is that it turns out not to be an exception after all to the general pattern of results from human conditioning studies already described. Just because a group of subjects is told that there will be no more shock or notice that shocks have been omitted, it does not mean that all of them wholeheartedly believe that there is zero probability of any more shocks. Dawson, Schell and Tweddle-Banis (1986) used the kind of stimuli and procedures employed by Öhman and his colleagues, but embedded them within a 'visual memory' variant of the masking procedure described above. They found no evidence of conditioning among unaware subjects, but did replicate the finding of slower extinction of skin conductance responses to phobic stimuli. However, their procedure also incorporated trial-by-trial reports on subjects' confidence that no shock would occur. This turned out to develop more slowly in subjects presented with phobic stimuli and when degree of 'cognitive extinction' was equated differences in skin conductance responding between phobic and neutral groups could no longer be found.

It is now thirteen years since Brewer's review was published. 'Convincing evidence' can be taken to mean appropriately analysed and statistically significant data which have been obtained from a theoretically coherent experimental procedure employing suitable control conditions and which have not proved difficult to replicate, preferably by researchers holding different presuppositions. By such criteria his conclusion still stands that there is no convincing evidence for conditioning in human subjects without awareness of the contingencies.

The surprising thing is that this research has had so little impact on belief about human conditioning. Both the beginning student and the informed cognitive scientist seem to find the idea of primitive conditioning quite acceptable. Introductory textbooks to psychology may be partly responsible. Thus, to take two examples of highly popular American textbooks which, as tradition demands, carefully describe the concepts of conditioning, Gleitman (1980; 1986) simply does not mention human conditioning and Atkinson, Atkinson and Hilgard (8th edition; 1983) imply that research has confirmed the direct application of conditioning principles to human behaviour, explaining that learning can still occur when 'subjects are not consciously aware of what the experimenter is doing' (p. 206). In England an increasing number of 18- and 19-year olds study psychology and many use a textbook by Radford and Govier (1980). This confidently states that conditioning without awareness is a well-established phenomenon (p. 230) and many students, intrigued by this idea, routinely run small experiments on the topic which inevitably fail. This is, of course, attributed by them and by their teachers to their lack of experimental skill.

3. Human Conditioning and Contemporary Animal Learning Theory

When in 1974 Brewer decided that there was no evidence for conditioning in adult humans, he meant by conditioning the development of a reflex-like reaction in an automatic fashion which did not involve expectancies. As most recently Davey (1987) has pointed out, it has proved hard to find evidence for such 'primitive' conditioning even in the laboratory rat or pigeon. The steady trend in animal learning theory over the past fifteen years or more has been towards associationist theories which stress that changes in responding are the outward sign of internal relationships between the animal's representation of events (e.g.. Mackintosh, 1983). Despite Pavlov's early rejection of such an approach (Boakes, 1984), it seems quite clear now that the increase of salivation by a dog to a bell which precedes the arrival of food can only be satisfactorily explained by appealing to associations between bell and food which correspond to the dog's expectation, when the bell sounds, that food will shortly follow. Similarly, Thorndike's (1898) rejection of the idea that animals learn to associate actions with their consequences, which for so long dominated the analysis of instrumental conditioning, has been abandoned in the face of evidence that the maintained associations between a response and a reinforcing event are critical for the acquisition and maintenance of instrumentally conditioned behaviour (Adams & Dickinson, 1981; Colwill & Rescorla, 1985).

At one time it seemed that conditioned taste aversion might provide a notable exception to the cognitive trend in learning theory (Rozin & Kalat, 1971; Seligman, 1970). With some objections (see Garcia, this volume,) it is now widely accepted that taste aversion shares the same properties as other kinds of associative learning and is remarkable only because of its high degree of selectivity, that is, the relative difficulty that many mammals and birds show in associating sickness with stimuli other than tastes (Domjan, 1983; Revusky, 1977). The associations that are acquired as a result of some classical conditioning procedure may be highly specific, reflecting 'consummatory conditioning' according to Konorski's (1967) terminology, or non-specifically evaluative, Konorski's (1967) preparatory conditioning. In people the latter might correspond to a feeling of dread or anxiety when an event occurs, without being able to anticipate exactly what is likely to happen. Taste aversion learning clearly comes at this end of the consummatory-preparatory continuum.

The implication of such contemporary views of animal learning for the study of human conditioning are quite straightforward: there is no such process as 'primitive conditioning' and therefore it was a mistake to expect to detect its presence in experiments using human subjects. Non-human animals can develop expectancies on the basis of past experience of event contingencies and, perhaps to a much more limited extent, on the basis of observing the behaviour of other individuals (e.g., Mineka & Cook, in press; Mineka & Tomarken, this volume). People can also form such expectancies on the basis of what they are told. Whether I actually experience a sequence in which a picture of a mushroom is followed by shock; see someone else, who is also wearing shock electrodes, look at a mushroom and subsequently flinch and say 'Ouch'; or am told by an experimenter that a mushroom always precedes shock delivery, the result is the same: I form an association between mushrooms and shock such that when the next mushroom appears on the screen I expect a shock to follow. Thus, to return to the paradox with which this chapter started, the only remaining puzzle is why in general people appear so ready to believe that there is something more to conditioning.

Such a conclusion also raises the serious question of whether there is any point to human conditioning studies. In animal research conditioning procedures may be thought of as a set of methods for determining what an animal knows about its world (Dickinson, 1980). Since most other adults are very skilled at telling us what they know and expect, either in ordinary language or, for example, as in the experiment by Dawson and Biferno (1973) mentioned earlier, by following instructions to select a button to indicate their present level of confidence, why use conventional conditioning procedures at all with human subjects? The decrease in research on human conditioning since the early 1970s may partly reflect implicit acceptance of this point. Furthermore, if Brewer (1974) is correct in claiming that even in conditioning experiments what people do is the result of complex mental processes of the kind underlying, say, problem solving, episodic memory and language, does the study of animal learning have anything to say about human behaviour?

In a previous volume in this series Dickinson and Shanks (1985) argued that models gained from the study of animal learning can provide insight into the way people make attributions about the causes of events. In particular, their research has shown that in a computer game where there are two possible causes of an event - a tank can blow up either because the subject hit it with a shell or because the tank ran into a mine - contingencies between events can affect human judgements in much the same way as they affect an animal's responses. In such experiments the subject is very much in a reflective, problem-solving mode, concentrating on the crucial events and on the decision that is required. What such research indicates in elegant fashion is how ideas derived from the study of associative learning in animals can be applied to certain aspects of human behaviour. What they fail to illuminate are the question of how such contingency effects interact with the various kinds of human cognitive process which do not have much counterpart in the animal mind - the students in Dickinson and Shanks study clearly had a number of beliefs about the actions of tanks, shells and mines and some understanding of probability theory which almost certainly affected their judgements - and the question of why awareness of a contingency appears to be such a prominent factor in more conventional human conditioning research.

4. Awareness is an Effect not a Cause

On reflection the opposition between contingencies and awareness or hypotheses set up by Brewer (1974), Dawson and Schell (1987) and many others before them is seen to be a very odd one. Why should observation of a correlation between changes in a skin response and in awareness be explained in terms of awareness of the contingency, rather than the contingency itself *causing* the response? The question as to how such awareness occurs does not seem to get asked. The change in viewpoint I am proposing here is to treat 'awareness' as an effect which is caused by the contingency.

A visual analogy may clarify this point. When someone is shown a picture such as that in Figure 15.3 for the first time, they may take some time to see what it represents. Some verbal hints as to what it is can reduce this time considerably. At a certain point they might say: 'Oh, I see, it's a dog!' We would not say that this perception is *caused* by 'sudden awareness'. Rather we would assume that in the preceding period various perceptual processes have been operating that are mainly inaccessible to consciousness. When a subject in one of Dawson's experiments, who has been diligently making matching judgements on a

FIG. 15.3. Degraded photograph (by R. C. James). Reproduced from Lindsay and Norman (1972).

series of tones against a background of occasional shocks, suddenly realizes that the high tone is always followed by the shock, then we might assume that this occurs as a result of automatic processes concerned with detecting temporal relationships and contingencies which are largely inaccessible to consciousness. We might *not* make this assumption if there were reasons to believe that the subject was actively searching for a way to predict the arrival of shock.

One important reason for the apparent lack of relationship between the processes described by learning theories and the subjective experience of perceiving a contingency may be that the latter is typically abrupt. We suddenly become aware of a relationship in apparent all-or-none fashion - just as we suddenly become aware that Figure 15.3 contains a dog. In contrast all theories of conditioning, whether of the old Behaviorist variety or of the modern associationist kind, appeal to incremental processes whereby some link or excitatory connection changes in progressive fashion, albeit in large steps under certain conditions. However, if awareness is regarded as an *effect* of some contingency - in other words some kind of response - then this contrast becomes less problematic. As illustrated in the diagram from Dickinson (1980) shown in Figure 15.4, it follows from the distinction made by associative theories between learning, as represented by associative strength, and performance that incremental changes in associative strength may be reflected by an all-or-none change in some response. Thus, for the subject in Dawson's experiment there

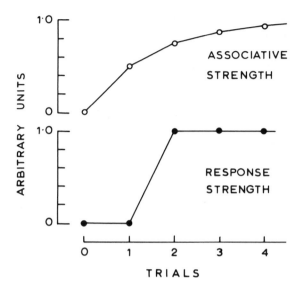

FIG. 15.4. Illustration of how grade changes in associative strength from trial to trial may be expressed as all-or-none traditions in response strength due to threshold and ceiling factors. Redrawn from Dickinson (1980; Fig. 29).

may have been a steady increase in associative strength between the high tone and the shock, but only when this reached some threshold value did it trigger the response we call 'awareness of the relationship'.

I would like to suggest that the human brain contains a preattentive system which is dedicated to detecting temporal relationships and which can operate in parallel with a variety of other mental processes. When this system registers relationships between two events of a strength in excess of some threshold, then it interrupts whatever else the central, serial processer is doing and this corresponds to the 'awareness response'. At this point the relationship becomes verbalizable, the information is evaluated and then either ignored or other cognitive processes brought to bear upon it. For example, if it suddenly occurs to me that, quite often when I have seen Joan enter the park, I am somewhat more likely than on other occasions to see Brian enter by another gate some time later, my curiosity might prompt me to search very actively my knowledge about Joan and Brian in order to make sense of a relationship I had hitherto not suspected. Alternatively, I might think no more about it, in which case some time later I might well have forgotten noticing anything at all about these two people. 'Forgetting' here is intended to refer to loss of the ability to consciously recall the idea of a possible connection between Joan and Brian (i.e. loss of episodic or explicit memory), but allows the possibility that some associative link between Joan and Brian might remain in my mind (i.e. some form of implicit or semantic memory).

Within this kind of framework the way to make sense of the long history of studies of conditioning and awareness using skin conductance or other autonomic measures is to conclude that a potential physiological reaction is triggered at the same threshold value as the awareness response. For decades psychologists have been wanting to believe that peripheral autonomic measures provide privileged access to central cognitive processes which are not accessible to consciousness. Research in various domains - selective attention (e.g., Dawson & Schell, 1982), lie detection (British Psychological Society, 1986), hemispheric differences (e.g., Hugdahl, 1987; this volume), as well as human classical conditioning - suggests that, with a few possible exceptions, this is a mistaken belief.

In animal learning research it has become accepted that the principles governing the formation of associations between two relatively neutral events, as in the phenomenon misleadingly called 'sensory preconditioning', are the same as those governing associations between a neutral and a biologically significant event of the kind referred to as a reinforcer (Mackintosh, 1983); the point of using reinforcement in animal learning experiments is that this usually ensures that any learning by the subject will result in detectable changes in its behavior (Dickinson, 1980).

In human conditioning research it is common to use as powerful a reinforcing event - almost always an aversive one - as ethical and practical considerations will allow (but see, for example, Maltzman, Gould, Bartnett, Raskin, & Wolff, 1977; Pendery & Maltzman, 1977). When the above arguments concerning the use of reinforcers in animal research are applied to human experiments, it is no longer clear that studies designed to find out how people form associations as a result of experiencing certain event contingencies need to employ reinforcers. One advantage of presenting a subject with, say, light-shock pairings instead of light-tone pairings might be simply to ensure that a convenient index of when the association reaches a certain strength is provided by some measure of an involuntary autonomic reaction. In fact, Maltzman et al., (1977) found little difference when they compared skin conductance measures to a word which subjects knew to predict a shock and to one which warned them of the arrival of tone demanding a rapid foot response.

There are other ways of assessing associative strengths than measuring the current ability of a stimulus to evoke some kind of autonomic or other physiological response. It is striking that human conditioning research has relied almost entirely on concurrent measures of learning, in contrast to animal research where it is commonplace to use various forms of post-conditioning tests to reveal what or how much an animal has learned from some particular event contingency.

Many of the points made so far have been made by others, using somewhat different terms and providing a far more extensive review of the relevant literature than that attempted here (e.g., Dawson & Schell, 1985, 1987; Maltzman, 1977; Öhman, 1983). Such authors agree that to a large extent the autonomic measures used in human conditioning studies assess the degree to which a stimulus elicits an orienting reflex or is attended to (see also Siddle & Remington, 1987; Siddle, Booth, & Packer,

1987). In Maltzman's (1977) terms, the skin conductance response to a stimulus indicates how 'noteworthy' it is, whether this is because of its inherent physical properties, its novelty, the imminent need to do something, or even just to think about it, and not just its possible affective value. These arguments are clearly valid ones. However, the main point of this section does not appear to have been made before, namely, the need to view awareness of a relationship as a response which occurs when associative strength exceeds some threshold. This viewpoint suggests a new way of examining the question of whether the theories of associative learning developed from animal research bear directly on the way people learn about event contingencies.

5. What Kind of Experimental Procedures are Required?

When a human subject comes to take part in an experiment, the experimenter is faced with the choice of telling him what the experiment is about, leaving him in the dark or giving information intended to give him a false belief about its aims and procedures. If some classical conditioning procedure is used and the experimenter tells the subject exactly what is to happen, then in most senses of the word the learning process is complete before the first trial begins. At most, any doubt the subject might have felt over the experimenter's instruction that, say, the circle would always be followed by an unpleasantly loud noise and the triangle would be safe, will be transformed into complete acceptance within a few trials. A curious feature of graphs showing the 'course of conditioning' in studies using autonomic measures is that with repeated trials the 'conditioned' response becomes weaker. As Öhman (1983) and others have suggested, such functions are often better regarded as showing habituation of an orienting response than as representing the acquisition of associative strength.

However, if the experimenter fails to explain anything about the experiment to her subject, then, unless the latter is completely bored or pathologically uninterested in his surroundings, he is going to try quite hard to work out what is going on. If successful - and this is not very difficult with the simple contingencies employed in most conditioning studies - he is going to arrive at the same state as the subject who was fully informed from the beginning. If unsuccessful, so that he comes to some wrong conclusions about the experiment, then, as we have seen earlier, his reactions are likely to reflect these false beliefs and expectations and remain insensitive to the contingencies that are of concern to the experimenter. Whatever the outcome then, the subject's behaviour will reflect the 'higher mental processes' brought in through the cubicle door, as in the quotation by Brewer (1974) early in this chapter, rather than any kind of associative learning process conceivably similar to those displayed by animals.

Regrettably then we are forced to mislead our subjects. We do not wish to ask whether, or how, they might *discover* some contingency, but rather how awareness of the contingency might *occur*. Take, for example, the reaction time task used by Maltzman and his colleagues (1977), where subjects are asked to release a foot pedal as soon as they hear a tone and such tones are embedded in a series of spoken words; uninformed subjects are not told that, for example, the word 'plant' always precedes the tone by 10 sec. It would be possible to vary such a plant-tone contingency in different groups to determine whether such variations determine the time taken for a subject to notice the contingency in a way that is predicted by current associative theories. How would one detect the point at which such awareness occurs? Asking for some kind of continuous self-report is liable to alert the subject to the fact that there is more to the experiment than the masking task described in the instructions. It is here that a skin conductance measure becomes invaluable, since all the evidence described above shows that the point at which a large response to 'plant' suddenly occurs corresponds exactly to the time at which the subject perceives the relationship between 'plant' and tone.

It was proposed earlier that such a perception marks the point at which the associative strength reaches some threshold. Is there any way of detecting such an association before it reaches threshold? Perhaps techniques developed by cognitive psychologists might succeed where those of psychophysiology have failed. The various kinds of priming recently employed to investigate the distinction between implicit and explicit memory might prove valuable (e.g., Mandler, Graf, & Kraft, 1986; Schacter & Graf, 1986). One example is associative priming: if the word 'butter' is briefly flashed onto a screen, I am more likely to recognize it if a few seconds beforehand I have read the word 'bread'. It is feasible that, if a subject has served in a reaction time experiment requiring a response to the word 'butter' and has failed to realize that during the task 'butter' was regularly preceded by 'hen', nonetheless 'hen' might serve to prime 'butter' in a subsequent recognition test.

If such approaches succeed in detecting sub-threshold associative learning - or 'learning without awareness' - then they may provide tools for the subtle investigation of such learning. If they fail, it does not mean that such learning does not take place, but simply that it may be impossible to detect it in any direct fashion.

6. Resolving the Paradox

This chapter began by suggesting a large discrepancy between what is commonly believed about human conditioning and the outcome of laboratory research on this topic. Two reasons for this discrepancy are suggested here. One of them has been discussed at length, namely, that to a large extent conditioning experiments using human subjects have been mistakenly conceived: first, they have often viewed awareness of contingencies and the contingencies themselves as alternative causes; second, they have often not taken into account the problem-solving mode which subjects are liable to adopt in order to make sense of what is happening; and, third, they have put misplaced faith in psychophysiological measures. The view proposed here is that lay belief must be correct. Logically there *must* be associative processes preceding awareness of a contingent relationship between two events. The important empirical questions are: Can they be detected in any direct fashion? And do they correspond to the processes studied in conditioning experiments using animals as subjects?

The role of forgetting as the other possible reason for the discrepancy has been hinted at above, but space does not allow full discussion. It may be that many associations develop to a state of full awareness or are based on an immediate 'first-trial' perception of some temporal relationship, but later become inaccessible to conscious recall. Various independent lines of research point to the importance of this factor. We have already noted that in human conditioning experiments a delay between exposure to the contingencies and some subsequent questionnaire will reduce the number of subjects correctly reporting the contingency (Dawson & Reardon, 1973). From the neuropsychological literature the fact that amnesics condition as rapidly as normal subjects suggests that the difference between the two groups does not lie in the process of learning, but in the degree of conscious recall (Shimamura, 1986; Weiskrantz & Warrington, 1979).

Studies of animal memory have found that after long retention intervals between the original conditioning procedure and some test session, although the effects of the conditioned stimulus on the animal's behavior are still very well preserved, it is as if the animal has forgotten various details of the original experience (Riccio, Richardson, & Ebner, 1984). Thus, a pigeon trained to peck at a blue light will show little generalization to other colours if tested immediately, but broad generalization in a delayed test (Thomas, 1981). A particularly pertinent example is provided by Hendersen (1985): rats which were trained to respond to a warning signal to avoid exposure to a heat lamp, when tested a day later responded to the signal in a warm environment, but not in a cold one; those tested ninety days later responded in the same way in both environments, thus suggesting that they had remembered what to do, but had forgotten the specific events involved in the original training. In the everyday life of normal people what passes for the effects of unconscious conditioning may be simply a matter of forgetting; it may no longer be possible to recall the crucial events and their relationship, all of which were consciously perceived at the time.

The discussion in this chapter has concentrated on classical conditioning because there has been little systematic research on these issues in the context of human instrumental conditioning. However, the proposals made here are intended to apply equally to this second type of conditioning. Consequently it may be appropriate to end by making this explicit. When someone makes some very gross response or action and this is followed by some salient and unexpected event, then especially under conditions of strong temporal and spatial contiguity, the person is likely to become aware immediately of the response-outcome relationship and all sorts of 'higher mental' processes will become engaged, including decisions as to whether to repeat the response or try to refrain from doing so. Where the response is more subtle, perhaps because of less feedback, where the consequence is less salient and the contingency weaker, then conscious perception of a response-outcome relationship may not occur until several 'pairings' have occurred.

The example of non-verbal aspects of communication used earlier may be appropriate here: our tone of voice, gestures and facial expressions as we speak are not usually responses that we pay much attention to, while the effects they produce on our listener may be scarcely detectable. My proposal is that associations between such responses and their consequences may increase in strength according to the kind of principles indicated by research on animal learning to the point at which they reach a threshold and trigger some possibly momentary awareness of the relationship, as well as decision processes that can affect the future frequency of the response. From then on performance may become completely automatic and recall of the relationship increasingly difficult to retrieve. So that when it is pointed out to the person that he tends to frown or sound tense whenever talking with some particular person, he will find this surprising and, if trying to explain it, may well reply: 'I suppose it's just a conditioned response'.

ACKNOWLEDGEMENTS

This chapter was very much influenced by the experimence of running human conditioning experiments in collaboration with Bob Stainer, during the time in which he was supported by a UK MRC Research Studentship. I am grateful for all that he has contributed toward this research and for his comments on an earlier version of the chapter. I would also like to acknowledge my appreciation of a brief remark made by John Pearce which, after a very long delay, turned out to serve as the seed for the central idea of this chapter.

The copyright for the data on which Figures 15.1 and 15.2 are based is held by the American Psychological Association, which gave permission for their use in this chapter, as did the main authors of the papers in which they first appeared. I am grateful to Dr. W. W. Grings (Figure 15.1) and Dr. M. E. Dawson (Figure 15.2) for agreeing to this. I would also like to acknowledge Dr. A. Dickinson's kind permission to base Figure 15.4 on a diagram which was first published in Dickinson (1980) and the agreement of the publishers of his book, Cambridge University Press.

REFERENCES

Adams, C. D. & Dickinson, A. (1981). Actions and habits: variations in associative representation during instrumental learning. In N. E. Spear & R. R. Miller (Eds.), *Information processing in animals: Memory mechanisms*, pp. 143-165. Hillsdale, NJ: Lawrence Erlbaum

Associates.

Atkinson, R. L., Atkinson, R. C., & Hilgard, E. R. (1983). *Introduction to psychology.* 8th Edition. New York: Harcourt Brace Jovanovich, Inc.

Bentall, R. P., Lowe, C. F., & Beasty, A. (1985). The role of verbal behavior in human learning: II. Developmental differences. *Journal of the Experimental Analysis of Behavior, 43,* 165-181.

Boakes, R. A. (1984). *From Darwin to Behaviourism.* Cambridge: Cambridge University Press.

Brewer, W. F. (1974). There is no convincing evidence for operant and classical conditioning in human beings. In W. B. Weimer & D. J. Palermo (Eds.), *Cognition and the symbolic processes,* pp. 1-42. Hillsdale, NJ: Lawrence Erlbaum Associates.

Bridger, W. & Mandel, I. J. (1965). Abolition of the PRE by instructions in GSR conditioning. *Journal of Experimental Psychology, 69,* 476-482.

British Psychological Association (1986). Report of the working party on the use of the polygraph in criminal investigation and personnel screening. *Bulletin of the British Psychological Society, 39,* 81-94.

Colwill, R. W. & Rescorla, R. A. (1985). Instrumental responding remains sensitive to reinforcer devaluation after extensive training. *Journal of Experimental Psychology: Animal Behavior Processes, 11,* 520-536.

Davey, G. C. L. (1987). An integration of human and animal models of Pavlovian conditioning: Associations, cognitions and attributions. In G. C. L. Davey (Ed.), *Cognitive processes and Pavlovian conditioning in humans,* pp. 83-144. Chichester: John Wiley.

Dawson, M. E. (1970). Cognition and conditioning: Effects of masking the CS-UCS contingency on human GSR classical conditioning. *Journal of Experimental Psychology, 85,* 389-396.

Dawson, M. E. & Biferno, M. A. (1973). Concurrent measurement of awareness and electrodermal classical conditioning. *Journal of Experimental Psychology, 101,* 82-86.

Dawson, M. E. & Reardon, D. P. (1973). Construct validity of recall and recognition postconditioning measures of awareness. *Journal of Experimental Psychology, 98,* 308-315.

Dawson, M. E. & Schell, A. M. (1982). Electrodermal responses to attended and nonattended significant stimuli during dichotic listening. *Journal of Experimental Psychology: Human Perception and Performance, 8,* 315-324.

Dawson, M. E. & Schell, A. M. (1985). Information processing and human autonomic classical conditioning. In P. K. Ackles, J. R. Jennings & M. G. H. Coles (Eds.), *Advamcres in Psychophysiology,* Vol. I, pp. 89-165. Greenwich, Conn: JAI Press.

Dawson, M. E. & Schell, A. M. (1987). Human autonomic and skeletal conditioning: The role of conscious cognitive factors. In G. C. L. Davey (Ed.), *Cognitive processes and Pavlovian conditioning in humans,* pp. 27-56. Chichester: John Wiley.

Dawson, M. E., Schell, A. M., & Tweddle-Banis, H. T. (1986).

Greater resistance to extinction of electrodermal responses conditioned to potentially phobic CSs: A noncognitive process? *Psychophysiology*, *23*, 552-561.

Dickinson, A. (1980). *Contemporary animal learning theory*. Cambridge: Cambridge University Press.

Dickinson, A. (1985). Actions and habits: the development of behavioral autonomy. In L. Weiskrantz (Ed.), *Animal intelligence*, pp. 67-78. Oxford: Clarendon Press.

Dickinson, A. & Shanks, D. R. (1985). Animal conditioning and human causality judgement. In L. G. Nilsson & T. Archer (Eds.), *Perspectives on learning and memory*, pp. 167-191. Hillsdale, NJ: Lawrence Erlbaum Associates.

Domjan, M. (1983). Biological constraints on instrumental and classical conditioning: Implications for general process theory. In G. H. Bower (Ed.), *The psychology of learning and motivation*, *17*, pp. 215-277. New York: Academic Press.

Dulany, D. E. Jnr (1961). Hypotheses and habits in verbal 'operant conditioning'. *Journal of Abnormal and Social Psychology*, *63*, 251-263.

Dworkin, B. R. & Miller, N. E. (1986). Failure to replicate visceral learning in the acute curarized rat preparation. *Behavioral Neuroscience*, *100*, 299-314.

Gleitman, H. (1981; 2nd edtn. 1986). *Psychology*. New York: Norton.

Gray, J. A. (1982). *The neuropsychology of anxiety*. Oxford: Clarendon.

Greenspoon, J. (1955). The reinforcing effect to two spoken sounds on the frequency of two responses. *American Journal of Psychology*, *68*, 409-416.

Grings, W. W. (1973). Cognitive factors in electrodermal conditioning. *Psychological Bulletin*, *79*, 200-210.

Grings, W. W., Schell, A. M., & Carey, C. A. (1973). Verbal conditioning of an autonomic response in a cue reversal situation. *Journal of Experimental Psychology*, *99*, 215-221.

Hearst, E & Jenkins, H. M. (1974). *Sign tracking: the stimulus reinforcer relation and directed action*. Monograph of the Psychonomic Society. Austin, Texas.

Hefferline, R. F., Keenan, B., & Harford, R. (1959). Escape and avoidance conditioning in human subjects without their observation of the response. *Science*, *130*, 1338-1339.

Hendersen, R. W. (1985). Fearful memories: the motivational significance of forgetting. In F. R. Brush and J. B. Overmier (Eds.), *Affect, conditioning and cognition: essays on the determinants of behavior*, pp. 43-54. Hillsdale, NJ: Lawrence Erlbaum Associates.

Hugdahl, K. (1987). Pavlovian conditioning and hemispheric asymmetry: A perspective. In G. C. L. Davey (Ed.), *Cognitive processes and Pavlovian conditioning in humans*, pp. 147-182. Chichester: John Wiley.

Hugdahl, K. & Öhman, A. (1977). Effects of instruction on acquisition and extinction of electrodermal responses to fear relevant stimuli.

Journal of Experimental Psychology: Human Learning and Memory, 3, 608-618.

Konorski, J. (1967). *Integrative activity of the brain: An interdisciplinary approach.* Chicago: University of Chicago Press.

Lowe, C. F. (1979). Determinants of human operant behavior. In M. D. Zeiler & P. Harzem (Eds.), *Advances in the analysis of behavior, 1,* pp. 159-192. New York: Wiley.

Mackintosh, N. J. (1983). *Conditioning and associative learning.* Oxford: Clarendon Press.

Maltzman, I. (1977). Orienting in classical conditioning and generalization of the galvanic skin response to words: an overview. *Journal of Experimental Psychology: General, 106,* 111-119.

Maltzman, I., Gould, J., Barnett, O. J., Raskin, D. C., & Wolff, C. (1977). Classical conditioning components of the orienting reflex to words using innocuous and noxious unconditioned stimuli under different conditioned stimulus-unconditioned stimulus intervals. *Journal of Experimental Psychology: General, 106,* 185-212.

Mandel, I. J. & Bridger, W. H. (1967). Interaction between instructions and ISI in conditioning and extinction of the GSR. *Journal of Experimental Psychology, 74,* 36-43.

Mandler, G., Graf, P., & Kraft, D. (1986). Activation and elaboration effects in recognition and word priming. *Quarterly Journal of Experimental Psychology, 38A,* 645-662.

McNally, R. J. (1987). Preparedness and phobias. *Psychological Bulletin, 101,* 283-303.

Mineka, S & Cook, M. (in press). Social learning and the acquisition of snake fear in monkeys. In T. Zentall & J. Galef (Eds.), *Comparative social learning.* Hillsdale, NJ: Lawrence Erlbaum Associates.

Öhman, A. (1983). The orienting response during Pavlovian conditioning. In D. Siddle (Ed.), *Orienting and habituation: Perspectives in human research,* pp. 315-369. Chichester: John Wiley.

Öhman, A., Ericsson, A., & Olofsson, C. (1975). One-trial learning and superior resistance to extinction of autonomic responses conditioned to potentially phobic stimuli. *Journal of Comparative and Psyciological Psychology, 88,* 619-627.

Pendery, M. & Maltzman, I. (1977). Instructions and the orienting reflex in 'semantic conditioning' of the galvanic skin response in an innocuous situation. *Journal of Experimental Psychology: General, 106,* 120-140.

Radford, J & Govier, E. (1980). *A textbook of psychology.* London: Sheldon Press.

Razran, G. (1971). *Mind in evolution: an East-West synthesis of learned behavior and cognition.* Boston: Houghton Mifflin.

Revusky, S. (1977). Learning as a general process with an emphasis on data from feeding experiments. In N. W. Milgram, L. Krames & T. M. Alloway (Eds.), *Food aversion learning,* pp. 1-51. New York: Plenum Press,

Riccio, D. D., Richardson, R., & Ebner, D. L. (1984). Memory retrieval deficits based upon altered contextual cues: a paradox. *Psychological Bulletin, 96,* 152-165.

Rozin, P. & Kalat, J. W. (1971). Specific hungers and poisoning as adaptive specializations of learning. *Psychological Review, 78,* 459-486.

Schachter, D. L. & Graf, P. (1986). Effects of elaborative processing on implicit and explicit memory for new associations. *Journal of Experimental Psychology: Learning, Memory and Cognition, 12,* 432-444.

Seligman, A. P. (1970). On the generality of the laws of learning. *Psychological Review, 77,* 406-418.

Shimamura, A. P. (1986). Priming effects in amnesia: evidence for a dissociable memory function. *Quartely Journal of Experimental Psychology, 38A,* 619-644.

Siddell, D. A. T. & Remington, B. (1987). Latent inhibition and human Pavlovian conditioning: research and relevance. In G. C. L. Davey (Ed.), *Cognitive processes and Pavlovian conditioning in humans,* pp. 115-146. Chichester: John Wiley.

Siddle, D. A. T., Booth, M. L., & Packer, J. S. (1987). Effects of stimulus pre-exposure on omission responding and omission produced dishabituation of the human electrodermal response. *Quarterly Journal of Experimental Psychology, 39B,* in press.

Spence, K. W. (1966). Cognitive and drive factors in the extinction of the conditioned eye-blink in human subjects. *Psychological Review, 13,* 445-458.

Thomas, D. R. (1981). Studies of long-term memory in the pigeon. In N. E. Spear & R. R. Miller (Eds.), *Information processing in animals: Memory mechanisms,* pp. 257-290. Hillsdale, NJ: Lawrence Erlbaum Associates.

Thorndike, E. L. (1898). *Animal intelligence: an experimental study of the associative processes in animals.* Monograph Supplement No. 8, *Psychological Review,* 68-72.

Weiskrantz, L. & Warrington, E. K. (1979). Conditioning in amnesic patients. *Neuropsychologia, 17,* 187-194.

Westbrook, R. F., Smith, F. J., & Charnock, D. J. (1985). The extinction of an aversion: role of the interval between nonreinforced presentations of the averted stimulus. *Quarterly Journal of Experimental Psychology, 37B,* 255-273.

Wilson, G. D. (1968). Reversal of differential GSR conditioning by instructions. *Journal of Experimental Psychology, 76,* 491-493.

16 The Yoked Control Design

Russell M. Church
Brown University

ABSTRACT

The yoked control design involves pairs of subjects randomly assigned to experimental and control conditions. An experimental subject and its yoked control subject receive consequences as a function of the responding of the experimental subject. This chapter summarizes three articles that claim that, with this design, sources of random error (between-subject variability, within-subject variability, or variable effects of a consequence) can produce systematic differences between an experimental group and its yoked control. Such effects can appear in studies of punishment, avoidance, and positive reinforcement. Reactions to these claims are then reviewed. Despite some opinion to the contrary, the conclusion is that the design is flawed for making inferences about the influence of the contingency of the response and consequence, that the flaws are serious, and that they cannot be corrected by modifications of the yoked control design.

DESCRIPTION OF THE YOKED CONTROL DESIGN

Responses have consequences, and one of the major problems of psychology is to determine how these consequences affect behavior. A rat presses a lever and receives food; a mouse steps off a platform and is shocked; a cockroach flexes its leg and avoids shock. Subsequently, the rat presses the lever at a higher rate, the mouse remains on the platform longer, and the cockroach flexes its leg more quickly. We suspect that this was due to the fact that the consequence was contingent upon the response, but how do we prove it was not due to the mere occurrence of the consequence? A control condition is needed--one in which the subject receives the consequence not contingent upon the response. The problem is to determine when the consequence should occur. One popular solution has been the yoked control design.

For a yoked control design individuals are paired and one member of each pair is assigned at random to the two groups: experimental and control. A subject in the experimental group receives a consequence (C) contingent upon some response (R); its paired subject in the control group receives the same consequence at the same time, independently of its response. (See Table 16.1.) The same measure of performance is taken for subjects in the two groups.

TABLE 16.1

	Yoked Control Design	
	Response	Consequence
Experimental	R	C
Control	--	C

This yoked control appears to be an ideal control group. The yoked control subject receives the same consequence at the same time as its paired experimental subject. The only difference between them is that the consequence to the experimental subject is contingent upon its own response, but the consequence to the control subject is contingent upon the response of another subject. Therefore, any difference between the experimental subject and its yoked control appears to be due to either (a) the effect of contingency of the consequence on the response, or (b) random error. Random error can be reduced as much as desired by an increase in sample size, and it can be estimated by standard methods of statistical analysis.

CRITICISM OF THE YOKED CONTROL DESIGN

In the early 1960's I was impressed by this argument, and I used the yoked control design in studies of differential reinforcement of response latency (Carnathan & Church, 1964; Church, 1961; Church & Carnathan, 1963). I first expressed my concern about the yoked control design in a review of studies of punishment (Church, 1963), and in the following year, I published an article devoted to this concern (Church, 1964). The title of the article was "Systematic effect of random error in the yoked control design." The abstract was as follows:

"The yoked control design has been employed to determine whether the effect of an event on a response is related to the temporal relationship between the event and that response. A number of specific examples of this design are discussed, and the conclusion is reached that the results are necessarily ambiguous. If the event does have an effect on behavior, systematic differences between the experimental group and its matched control group will emerge: (a) if the temporal relationship between response and event is relevant or (b) if various sources of random error are present, such as individual differences in the effectiveness of the event."

The claim was that random error could produce a systematic difference between an experimental group and its yoked control group. The main example was based upon random variability in the effectiveness of an event. The first table in that article dealt with a dichotomy of effectiveness with the following cases shown in Table 16.2.

TABLE 16.2

Case	Experimental	Control
1	Effective	Effective
2	Effective	Ineffective
3	Ineffective	Effective
4	Ineffective	Ineffective

An example from a study of punishment (passive avoidance) would be as follows. Pairs of rats are trained to press a lever for food reinforcement, and then one of the rats from each pair is randomly assigned to the experimental treatment and the other rat is assigned to the control treatment. Each response of the rat in the experimental treatment is followed by a brief shock; its yoked control subject receives a brief shock whenever the experimental subject receives the shock. As a result of this treatment, rats in the experimental group may press the lever less often than rats in the control group. This may be due to the fact that the shock immediately followed the response in the experimental group but not in the control group, but there are other possibilities.

Suppose that shock affected some rats more rapidly than others, and that the effect was a suppression of responding. If an experimental subject required a few more shocks than its yoked control before it became suppressed, the experimental subject would make only a few more responses than its yoked control (Case 3); if a control subject required a few more shocks than its yoked experimental before it became suppressed, the control subject would continue to respond indefinitely (Case 2). This asymmetry would lead to a substantially greater number of responses in the control group than its yoked experimental group, even though the temporal relationship between response and shock was irrelevant.

The article generalized the argument in several ways: It applied it to positive reinforcement, helplessness, and avoidance as as well as to punishment; it applied it to a continuum of effectiveness as well as discrete categories; it applied it to differences in initial probability of a response and asymptotic level of response, as well as to differences in the effectiveness of an event; and, most importantly, it applied it to within-subject variability as well as between-subject variability.

Eight years later I was coauthor of another criticism of the yoked control design (Church & Getty, 1972). In a review of the difficulty of distinguishing between anticipation of an aversive event and reaction to an aversive event, a section was included entitled "Failure of the yoked control design." The example was the same one described above. The major function of this article was to apply the general argument to the case in which the subjects are perfectly matched and have a constant value of all parameters throughout the experiment. Even under these conditions, the yoked control design can produce spurious results. The other function of this article was to present the argument formally and quantitatively. Estimates of the probability of suppression after the kth shock, with $p = 1-q$ as the probability of suppression after any given shock, were given for an experimental subject, q^k/q^{zk}, and for a control subject, $(q^k/q^{zk}+q)/(1+q)$. Thus, with a sufficiently large number of shocks, the probability that an experimental subject will not be suppressed approaches zero, while the probability that a yoked control subject will not be suppressed approaches $q/(1+q)$.

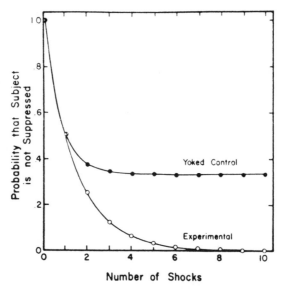

FIG. 16.1. Probability that a subject in the experimental group and its yoked control subject are not suppressed as a function of successive shocks. (The probability that any given shock will produce permanent suppression was set at .5 for both groups.)

My last public comment on the yoked control design was published over ten years ago (Church & Lerner, 1976), and it was in response to an invitation to participate in a workshop sponsored by the Social Science

Research Council (Teyler, Baum, & Patterson, 1975). The example was from avoidance, rather than punishment. Like the previous article, it used subjects that were perfectly matched and had a constant value of all parameters throughout the experiment. Results were obtained from both simulation and explicit solution. The abstract was as follows:

> "The headless roach has been identified as a relatively simple model system for the physiological analysis of instrumental learning. The basic observation is that an experimental roach that receives shock contingent upon leg extension raises its leg more often and keeps it raised for a longer time than its yoked control roach. This evidence is inadequate to demonstrate learning, since these results are also consistent with a purely reactive model. The asymptotic results based on one such reactive model were similar to previously reported data."

The assumptions were that (a) when stimulated by electric shock, the leg withdraws, and (b) when not stimulated, the leg extends in a probabilistic manner. On the basis of these purely reactive assumptions, the proportion of the time that the leg of an experimental roach was up was greater than the proportion of the time that the leg of its yoked control was up, and the number of withdrawals per minute was greater. The most important difference between this application and the previous ones was that, because of the use of a nonabsorbing state (up) rather than an absorbing one (suppression), differences emerged between all pairs in one direction, even though the assumptions involved only reaction and no anticipation.

The basic idea in all three manuscripts was the same--that systematic differences between an experimental and a yoked control design could emerge even if the temporal interval between a response and a consequence was irrelevant. In the initial article, systematic differences between the groups were found to occur when there were random differences in the effectiveness of a consequence; in the latter two articles, systematic differences between groups were found to occur when there were random differences in the reaction of the animal to an event. Several examples in the initial manuscript assumed some drift in the state of an animal, and this was not required in the applications of the argument in latter manuscripts. The initial manuscript described the ideas verbally and applied them to many different examples; the latter manuscripts described the ideas quantitatively and applied them to single examples. Thus, during this ten-year period the argument became simpler and more quantitative, but it was not changed fundamentally.

EXPERIMENTS USING THE YOKED CONTROL DESIGN

In the Spring of 1987 I did a computer search of the Psychological Abstract data base (since 1967) for the word "yoked" either in the title or abstract of articles. The number obtained is a reasonable minimum estimate since an inspection of the abstracts indicated that nearly all of them used the yoked control design. The number obtained may be a considerable underestimate of the number published, however, since some studies using the yoked control design may have been published in journals not be in this data base, some titles and abstracts may refer to the yoked control design under some other name, such as "the matched control design," or the "triadic design," and some titles and abstracts may not refer to the design. The cumulative number is shown as a function of year in Figure 16.2.

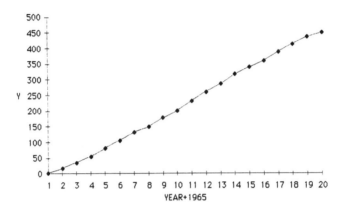

FIG. **16.2.** The cumulative number of articles (Y) as a function of year (1967-1985).

The number of articles using the yoked control design has been relatively constant in the 20-year period since 1967, at about 24 per year. There was no noticeable increase or decrease at about the time of my articles.

Most of the studies have used human subjects (40%) or rats (36%); fewer have used pigeons (6%), mice (4%), monkeys (3%) or fish (2%). Other species used each represent 1% of the total or less (dogs, cats, rabbits, chipmonks, hamsters, chickens, frogs, lobsters, honeybees, cockroaches, and aplysia).

One purpose of the yoked control design has been to determine whether the probability of a response that was followed by a consequence was changed because it was followed by the consequence. The results have almost always been positive. Reliable differences between an experimental group and its yoked control group have been reported for the following responses: Leg flexion of headless cockroach (Horridge, 1962); Leg flexion of the spinal rat (Sherman, Hoehler, & Buerger, 1982); Heart rate changes of the curarized rat (Trowell, 1967); Movement of planaria (Crawford & Skeen, 1967); Variability of response sequence of pigeons (Page & Neuringer, 1985); Salivation of dogs (Shapiro & Herendeen, 1975); and electric organ response of mormyrid fish (Mandriota, Thompson & Bennett, 1968). One exception was that rats that received a food pellet following each intromission did not exhibit more sexual behavior than their yoked controls following castration or testosterone replacement therapy (Broere, van derSchoot, & Slob, 1985).

Some psychologists use the yoked control design not to make inferences about the role of contingency between response and event, but simply as a way to creative group differences to explain. Normally they will observe a dependent variable different from the one upon which the consequence is contingent. This is typically the case in studies of helplessness. One subject is given escapable shock; its yoked control subject is given shock of the same intensity and duration whenever its yoked experimental subject is shocked. The control subjects tend to move less, to be more emotional and to learn new responses less readily (Maier & Jackson, 1979). This may be due to their lack of control of the shock (the original purpose of using the yoked control) or because inescapable shock may be more stressful (Desiderato & Newman, 1971; Brennan & Riccio, 1975) or for other reasons. Of course, it is appropriate to use the yoked control design to obtain data that needs to be explained.

Although the total number of articles using the yoked control design has been relatively constant, the proportion of the articles with the dependent variable the same as the one upon which the consequence is contingent has been decreasing and the proportion of the articles with the dependent variable different from the one upon which the consequence is contingent has been increasing. In the 10-year period beginning in 1967 about a third of the studies used a different dependent variable; in the 10-year period beginning in 1977 over half of the studies used a different dependent variable ($\lambda^2 = 15.7$, df = 1, p < .001).

REACTIONS TO THE CRITICISM OF THE YOKED CONTROL DESIGN

The continued use of the yoked control design was not because my criticism was unknown. According to Science Citations over 80 articles have referenced my 1964 article. In the 10-year period beginning in 1967 the citation rate was about 6 per year, and in the 10-year period beginning in 1977 it was about 2 per year. In 1978 I declined an invitation to contribute a methodological article on the status of the yoked control design. I wrote to the editor, "I considered repeating the same arguments against the yoked control design (with new examples). That would not be beating a dead horse, since the horse is still very much alive. But if I failed to kill it after 15 years of trying, I think I should leave the job to someone else."

The design is not flawed

The vast majority of articles that use the yoked control design make no reference to any systematic difference between groups that may emerge if only random variability is present. Probably most of the investigators believe the design is not flawed, although the reasons for this belief is not stated. The author of one manuscript wrote me as Editor of Animal Learning & Behavior, "...despite your 1964 article the triadic design has been the basis of the learned helplessness literature and has been used in literally thousands of published experiments (including many in Animal Learning & Behavior). Therefore, I believe that the manuscript cannot be rejected on this ground." The fact that the design is used frequently by thoughtful and able psychologists conveys a degree of legitimacy to the design, and studies using the yoked control design have continued to appear in Animal Learning & Behavior and elsewhere. But common practice is not a strong defense.

The design is flawed

Some psychologists believed that the yoked control design is only biased in some instrumental training procedures and not others. For example, in a reply to Katkin and Murray (1968), who I believe correctly identified the problem of using the yoked control design to demonstrate instrumental autonomic conditioning, Crider, Schwartz, and Shnidman (1969) claimed that the criticism applied to positive reinforcement, but not to punishment or avoidance. They wrote, "If the nonspecific effect of punishment is to suppress responding, a poorer experimental subject will not suppress and will produce many stimuli for his better control, who will then suppress. In the case of avoidance, if a poorer experimental subject is not activated to avoid, the better control will receive many negative reinforcers and will respond more." They claim that this results in "equalizing bias effects." I do not believe this is correct, but verbal arguments are often difficult to follow because all assumptions are not explicitly stated. Quantitative examples of bias in punishment (Church & Getty, 1972) and avoidance (Church & Lerner, 1976) are now available.

The identification of errors in my criticism is another defense of the design. Many psychologists must have read the 1964 article carefully because at least four of them (A. Black, J. Moore, I. Pollock, H. Fishbein, and C. Peterson & L. Jaffe) independently wrote me about an unfortunate misstatement I made on page 124, and many others talked to me about it. In an application of the argument to avoidance conditioning of the eyelid response (Moore & Gormezano, 1961), I wrote as if the procedure were punishment, rather than avoidance. Although I recognized that this error confused some readers, I decided that it was not worthy of a published correction since the purpose of the specific examples was only to illustrate the general argument. The misstatement of the eyelid conditioning experiment as passive rather than active avoidance was finally corrected in print by Crider, Schwartz, & Shnidman (1969), Katkin, Murray, & Lachman, (1969), Grings & Carlin (1966), and by Gormezano (Teyler, Baum, & Patterson, 1975), but some readers undoubtedly thought that there was no systematic error of the yoked control design when it was applied to avoidance learning.

The following might be a reasonable application of this argument for the yoked eyelid experiment and it was the one I used in personal communication to various interested individuals in 1964: "An experimental subject that learns quickly (that is strongly affected by the event) receives relatively few unconditioned stimuli but, by assumption, enough to reach its asymptotic level of performance. When such an experimental subject is matched with a control subject that learns slowly, however, (i.e., one that is relatively unaffected by the event) the latter will not receive an adequate number of events to reach its asymptotic level of performance. An experimental subject that learns slowly (that is relatively unaffected by the event) receives a great many unconditioned stimuli but in time it will reach its asymptotic level of performance. When such an experimental subject is matched with a control subject that learns quickly (i.e., one that is strongly affected by the event) both subjects will reach their asymptotic levels of performance. Thus in the yoked eyelid experiment, under the null hypothesis, individual differences in the degree to which subjects are affected by an event can result in a reliable difference between the experimental and control group."

Although the necessary assumptions to produce systematic effects based on random error are very weak (some reaction to the event or some variability in the effect of the event), the assumptions I made to obtain quantitative results in specific in simple examples were more restrictive. For example, in the reactive model of headless roach avoidance (Church & Lerner, 1976) some states not theoretically possibly, occasionally may occur (Buerger, Eisenstein & Reep, 1981). Of course, a model with some random variability allows for the occurrence of these otherwise impossible states.

The flaws in the design can be corrected

If stable individual differences were the only source of random variation, the flaws in the design could be corrected. As noted in the 1964 article, in a between-subjects yoked design, the bias would not lead to significantly more than half the subjects being affected.

In addition, a within-subject yoked control procedure can be used (Lattal & Ziegler, 1980) or a reciprocal yoked control design (Kimmel & Terrant, 1968). In a reciprocal yoked control design, two stimuli are used; subjects are paired and each subject receives the experimental treatment in one stimulus and the yoked control treatment in the other. This effectively eliminates individual differences in the effectiveness of the consequence as a basis for systematic differences between groups. Another extension of the yoked control design is to pair each experimental subject with two yoked control subjects (Job, in press). The differences between the two yoked control subjects provide an estimate of the magnitude of individual differences. No proposals have been made to deal with random variation within-subjects in the effectiveness of a consequence, or with models without any between-subject or within-subject variability.

The flaws in the design are not serious

Probably the dominent current view of systematic effects of random error in the yoked control design is that the problem is present, but it probably does not interfere with conclusions. For example, Lattal and Ziegler (1980) wrote that although moment-to-moment variability in the effectiveness of the independent variable can lead to systematic bias, "the demonstrated utility, power, and generality of within-subject comparisons in the experimental analysis of behavior lend credence to their value in the context of yoked-control designs." A more common opinion is the following, "Although the yoking technique has received some criticism (Church, 1964), it is difficult to believe that what one is seeing here is nothing but the differential influence of the aversive stimulation itself" (Abramson & Bitterman, 1986). I agree a flawed design can lead to a correct conclusion; it can also lead to an incorrect conclusion, and there is no formal way to decide whether or not the conclusion is correct.

The flaws in the design are serious

Some psychologists have accepted the arguments of the 1964 article and use them as basis for criticism of research that uses the yoked control design. For example, Katkin and Murray (1968) criticize some evidence for instrumental conditioning of autonomic responses on the basis of systematic effects of random error. Farley and Alkon (1985) criticizes some evidence for chemosensory aversion learning in lobster on the basis of possible individual differences in shock threshold for a withdrawal response. Some psychologists may not use the yoked control design because of its serious flaws. For the last 25 years I have been among them.

CONCLUSION

The primary use of the yoked control design has been to determine whether the tendency to make a response is affected by the temporal relationship of the response and a consequence. All of my criticisms of the design have been concerned with its use for this purpose. For this purpose, I continue to believe that the design is flawed; the flaws cannot be corrected by extensions to the design; and that the flaws are serious.

The design is flawed

In an attempt to be general in the 1964 article, some of my remarks were vague. An effective event was one that promoted rapid learning, that was particularly intense, or that elicited a particularly great reaction, which could either be an increase or a decrease in something that was measured.

The examples were designed to convince the readers that variability in such effectiveness did not balance out in the yoked control design, as it would in any proper experimental design. The yoked control design appears to be a proper experimental design--there is random assignment of subjects to treatments, and one group receives response-consequence pairings while the other one receives only consequences. The problem is that the response-consequence pairings are controlled by a subject, not the experimenter.

In some examples the responses produced consequences that increased the probability of the response (positive feedback). Examples were positive reinforcement, and bursts of response elicited by shock. In these cases the typical mechanism to produce familiar results was variation in elicitation. In other examples the responses produced consequences that decreased the probability of the response (negative feedback). Examples were suppression by punishment and avoidance learning. In these cases, the typical mechanism to produce familiar results was variation in the speed of learning. My major point was not that the systematic effects had to be in the observed direction, but that systematic effects occurred on the basis of reasonable assumptions.

The flaws in the design cannot be corrected

Extensions of the yoked control design to handle these problems are not promising. If stable individual differences were the only problem, a simple sign test would be a solution, but the problem is much more pervasive. Nobody knows how to deal with within-subject differences. Even if one could find a solution for random variation within-subject in the effectiveness of an event, the systematic effects remain. A probabilistic model with no between-subject or within-subject differences in the parameters will produce systematic differences between an experimental group and a random control group in punishment (Church & Getty, 1972) and avoidance (Church & Lerner, 1976), and many other procedures.

The flaws in the design are serious

Bias in an experimental design is serious when its magnitude is unknown. I believe that an experimental design should be absolutely free of bias--it should not contain a small and unknown amount of bias. Therefore, the yoked control design should not be used to infer the role of response-consequence continency. Other methods to rule out one variable at a time may be the best available. To know whether or not a single control group will ever be sufficient to demonstrate that contingency is the responsible variable, we need a deeper understanding of the term "contingency."

REFERENCES

Abramson, C. I., & Bitterman, M. E. (1986). The US-preexposure effect in honeybees. *Animal Learning & Behavior, 14,* 374-379.

Brennan, J. F., & Riccio, D. C. (1975). Stimulus generalization of suppression in rats following aversively motivated instrumental or Pavlovian training. *Journal of Comparative and Physiological Psychology, 88,* 540-579.

Broere, F., van der Schoot, P., Slob, K. A. (1985). Food conditioning, castration, testosterone administration and sexual behavior in the male rat. *Physiology & Behavior, 35,* 627-629.

Buerger, A. A., Eisenstein, E. M., & Reep, R. L. (1981). The yoked control in instrumental avoidance conditioning: an empirical and methodological analysis. *Physiological Psychology, 9,* 351-353.

Carnathan, J., & Church, R. M. (1964). The effect of competitive allocation of reinforcements to rats in a straight alley. *Journal of General Psychology, 71,* 137-144.

Church, R. M. (1961). Effect of a competititive situation on the speed of response. *Journal of Comparative and Physiological Psychology, 54,* 162-166.

Church, R. M. (1963). The varied effects of punishment on behavior. *Psychological Review, 70,* 369-402.

Church, R. M. (1964). Systematic effect of random error in the yoked control design. *Psychological Bulletin, 62,* 122-131.

Church, R. M. & Carnathan, J. (1963). Differential reinforcement of short latency responses in the white rat. *Journal of Comparative and Physiological Psychology, 56,* 120-123.

Church, R. M., & Getty, D. J. (1972). Some consequences of the reaction to an aversive event. *Psychological Bulletin, 78,* 21-27.

Church, R. M., & Lerner, N. D. (1976). Does the headless roach learn to avoid? *Physiological Psychology, 4,* 439-442.

Crawford, F. T., & Skeen, L. C. (1967). Operant responding in the planarian: A replication study. *Psychological Reports, 20,* 1023-1027.

Crider, A., Schwartz, G. E., & Shnidman, S. (1969). On the criteria for instrumental autonomic conditioning: A reply to Katkin and Murray. *Psychological Bulletin, 71,* 455-461.

Desiderato, O., & Newman, A. (1971). Conditioned suppression produced in rats by tones paired with escapable or inescapable shock. *Journal of Comparative and Physiological Psychology, 77,* 427-431.

Farley, J., & Alkon, D. L. (1985). Cellular mechanisms of learning, memory, and information storage. In *Annual Review of Psychology, 36,* 419-494.

Grings, W. W., & Carlin, S. (1966). Instrumental modification of autonomic behavior. *Psychological Record, 16,* 153-159.

Horridge, G. A. (1962). Learning of leg position by headless insects. *Nature, 193,* 697-698.

Job, R. F. S., (1987). Learned helplessness in chickens. *Animal Learning & Behavior, 15,* 347-350.

Katkin, E. S., & Murray, E. N. (1968). Instrumental conditioning of autonomically mediated behavior: Theoretical and methodological issues. *Psychological Bulletin, 70,* 52-68.

Katkin, E. S., Murray, E. N., & Lachman, R. (1969). Concerning instrumental autonomic conditioning: A rejoinder. *Psychological Bulletin, 71,* 462-466.

Kimmel, H. D., & Terrant, F. R. (1968). Bias due to individual differences in youked control designs. *Behavior Research Methods in Instrumentation, 1,* 11-14.

Lattal, K. A., & Ziegler, D. R. (1980). Recording and storing data for yoked-control comparisons. *Journal of Experimental Analysis of Behavior, 34,* 131-132.

Maier, S. & Jackson, R. (1979). Learning helplessness: All of us were right (and wrong): Inescapable shock has multiple effects. In G. Bower (ed). *Advances in learning and motivation,* Vol 13, pp 155-218. New York: Academic Press.

Mandriota, F. J., Thompson, R. L., & Bennett, M. V. (1968). Avoidance conditioning of the rate of electric organ discharge of the mormyrid fish. *Animal Behaviour, 16,* 448-455.

Moore, J. W., & Gormezano, I. (1961). Yoked comparisons of instrumental and classical eyelid conditioning. *Journal of Experimental Psychology, 62,* 552-559.

Page, S. & Neuringer, A. (1985). Variability is an operant. *Journal of Experimental Psychology: Animal Behavior Processes, 11,* 429-452.

Shapiro, M. M. & Herendeen, D. L. (1975). Food-reinforced inhibition of conditioned salivation in dogs. *Journal of Comparative & Physiological Psychology, 88,* 628-632.

Sherman, B. S., Hoehler, F. K., & Buerger, A. A. (1982). Instrumental avoidance of increased leg lowering in the spinal rat. *Physiology & Behavior, 29,* 123-128.

Teyler, T. T., Baum, W. M., & Patterson, M. M. (1975). Behavioral and biological issues in the learning paradigm. *Physiological Psychology, 3,* 65-72.

Trowill, J. A. (1967). Instrumental conditioning of the heart rate in the curarized rat. *Journal of Comparative and Physiological Psychology, 63,* 7-11.

17 Experimental Designs in Behavioral Studies

Terje Sagvolden
University of Oslo

ABSTRACT

Choice of experimental design is very important in every study because the choice affects what conclusions one is able to draw. The present article argues in favour of parametric designs where the most important situation variable, or variables, is changed systematically in order to observe how different levels of this variable affects the behavior under study. A non-parametric design is one where for example a brain-lesioned group and a control group are tested with a single value on all variables. Data from studies of behavioral effects of septal lesions are used for illustrating these points. Two-dimensional parametric designs showed that the behavioral changes in the brain-lesioned group compared to a control group depend upon level of water deprivation in appetitively motivated tasks and shock intensity in aversively motivated tasks. The implications of these results were analyzed in a more detailed three-dimensional parametric design. This study showed that the behavioral changes following septal lesions are response-rate dependent in the sense that the septal animals showed increased response rates only when the baseline rates were above a certain level. In parametric studies of avoidance behavior, the control of the shock parameters is very important. The present article discusses the use of continuous versus the use of brief electric shocks with a fixed duration. It is shown that the traditionally-used continuous shocks, where the animal's escape latency controls the duration of each shock, causes several problems that very well could jeopardize the conclusions one is able to draw. In addition, brief shocks have other advantages: the acquisition of the avoidance task is much faster, the stressfulness of the task is probably less than what is the case with continuous shocks, and the experiments may even be cheaper to conduct.

Researchers are not always aware of how the choice of experimental design affects the conclusions one is able to draw. The reason for this is that one does not always realize assumptions implicit in the design chosen. Most behavioral experiments are conducted according to non-parametric designs where for example a brain-lesioned group and a control group are tested with a single value on all environmental variables that may be involved in the control of the behavior.

A NOT SO HYPOTHETICAL EXPERIMENT

Assume that we are interested in investigating the behavioral effects of septal lesions on responding for water in a standard one-lever operant chamber.

Figure 17.1 shows a typical septal lesion. Figure 17.2A shows the behavioral results of our hypothetical experiment. The rats with septal lesions had a 15-per cent response-rate increase which in the present case was statistically significant. A typical conclusion would be something like: "Following septal lesions in rats there is increased lever pressing for water on an operant schedule of continuous reinforcement". In support of this conclusion we typically cite other experiments with similar results.

What may our hypothetical researcher do next? The most common strategy is then to proceed to another experimental paradigm and look for more behavioral changes following septal lesions. This new paradigm may be a two-way active avoidance, or "shuttle-box" avoidance, test.

In a typical procedure, each trial starts with the presentation of the CS, the conditioned stimulus. If the rat moves into the other compartment within 5 s, the CS presentation is terminated, the floor is not electrified

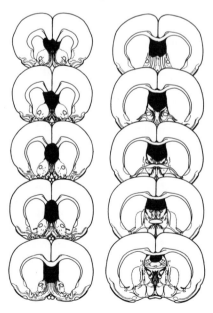

FIG. 17.1. Typical septal lesion not interfering with the hippocampal acetylcholinesterase level.

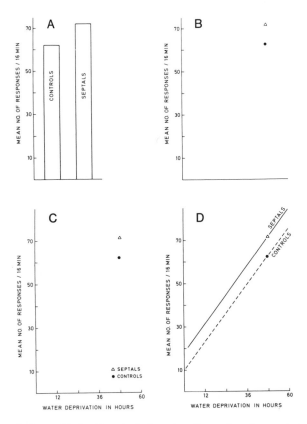

FIG. 17.2A-D. Hypothetical results. For explanation see text.

and the response is recorded as an avoidance response. However, if the rat does not cross fast enough, the grid floor is electrified by a scrambled shock until the rat escapes into the other compartment and the rat's response is recorded as an escape response. Following a pause lasting 25 s, a new trial is started. The experiment is usually run a fixed number of trials every day.

It has been reported repeatedly that rats with septal lesions acquire this task faster than controls (for references see Sagvolden, 1975a). The results of these experiments are very typical and shown repeatedly. Having completed this second experiment, our researcher may proceed to a third and a fourth experiment and try to find a unitary explanation of the increased lever pressing for water following septal lesions, the faster acquisition of shuttle-box avoidance and the results from the other experiments. In doing this, it is very easy, and very typical, to draw erroneous conclusions like: "The increased lever pressing for water following septal lesions" and "the faster acquisition of shuttle-box avoidance following septal lesions". Such statements assume implicitly that increased lever-pressing for water will occur for all values of the important variables controlling lever-pressing for water in the operant chamber. In order to see this more clearly, the results of the initial experiment are presented in Figure 17.2B which in terms of information is identical to Figure 17.2A. However, it is obvious that Figure 17.2B is not quite standard. Among other things, the x-axis of the graph is not specified. Firstly, this independent variable ought to have been kept constant; it ought to be a variable likely to affect rats' lever pressing for water. The most obvious variable to select is probably how thirsty the rat is. Thus, "Water deprivation in hours" could be the independent variable (Figure 17.2C).

The next obvious step in a research process is to ask what the behavioral results would be if the water deprivation had been varied systematically. The argument is that by concluding: "Following septal lesions in rats there is increased lever pressing for water on an operant schedule of continuous reinforcement", one implicitly, and probably without being aware of it, assumes curves or functions similar to the ones shown on Figure 17.2D. These functions may not necessarily be straight lines, but may be curved, inverted U-shaped and so on. The point is that implicit in the conclusion above is the assumption that for all values of the water-deprivation variable, rats with septal lesions will press more than control rats, that is, there should not be any statistical interaction.

OPERATIONALIZING CHANGED AROUSAL

I accepted such generalizations or more correctly, I was not aware of this implicit generalization before I had been struggling for some time with an overarousal hypothesis for changes following septal lesions (Sagvolden, 1979a). "Arousal" is a tremendously difficult concept that is very hard to measure. In operationalizing the overarousal hypothesis (Fig. 17.3A), the first assumption may be that the relationship between arousal and performance would still exist because this is probably a very fundamental relationship (Hebb, 1955). The second assumption would be that "overarousal" means that the overaroused organism responds with more arousal than the normally-aroused organism to the same intensity of the arousing stimulus (Fig. 17.3B). The arousal variable may be eliminated by combining these assumptions mathematically. The result is shown on Figure 17.3C. Now both the dependent and the independent variables may be measured. It is obvious that the behavioral implications would most easily be detected in tasks where there were inverted U-shaped relations between the intensity of the arousing stimulus and performance. For the case of the overaroused organism, this inverted U-shaped relation should be shifted to the left.

This interpretation of the overarousal hypothesis predicts quite dramatic performance changes by increasing stimulus intensity. The behavioral effect of septal lesions, compared to normal control rats' behavior, is predicted to be in one direction, namely improved performance, when the intensity of the arousing stimulus is weak.

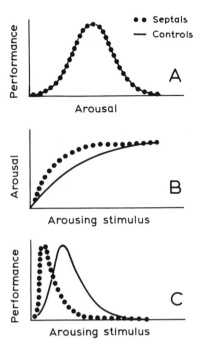

FIG. 17.3. A: The hypothetical arousal-performance curve of rats with septal lesions and control rats. B: Functions relating level of arousal to arousing stimulus. C: Functions based on A and B relating performance to the value of the arousing stimulus in septal and control rats. For details see text. (Based on Sagvolden, 1979a.)

But, the opposite behavioral effect of the lesions, namely poor performance, should be the result when the arousing stimulus is intense. Finally, this hypothesis could even predict no behavioral change. These predictions were startling: The overarousal hypothesis could evidently explain all kinds of behavioral changes as long as the studies used non-parametric designs!

PARAMETRIC STUDIES OF THE BEHAVIOR OF ANIMALS WITH SEPTAL LESIONS

There are few studies in the experimental literature systematically investigating behavioral effects of septal lesions as functions of variables that may effect the behavior, i.e., with a parametric design. A parametric design is one where the most important situation variable, or variables, is changed systematically in order to observe how different levels of this variable affects the behavior under study. It turned out that there were few experiments with more than two values on any independent variable (Doty & Forkner, 1971; Harvey & Hunt, 1965; Johnson & Thatcher, 1972). But, two values are hardly enough for establishing curves for relations between an independent and a dependent variable with a high degree of precision. Evidently, parametric experiments were needed.

EFFECTS OF THE LEVEL OF WATER DEPRIVATION ON WATER-REINFORCED LEVER PRESSING -- FR-1 SCHEDULE

Doing parametric experiments with lever pressing for water using an operant paradigm was a logical start for several reasons. There is an inverted U-shaped relation between the rate of water pressing and the duration of water deprivation (Belanger & Feldman, 1962). With operant methods most other variables affecting the behavior could easily be controlled. A continuous reinforcement schedule of water delivery was used in one study (Sagvolden, 1975b). Following shaping and stabilization of the rats' behavior, the duration of water deprivation was varied systematically.

The behavioral results were quite unexpected: rats with septal lesions show increased lever-press response rates only when the water deprivation had lasted for a long time (Figure 17.4). When the water deprivation had lasted only 12 hr, they pressed less for water than control rats. Note that this parametric design required deprivations starting during the night. One has to be devoted to parametric studies in order to do something like that! The behavioral results show at least three ways of reaching wrong conclusions: (i) If only 12-hr deprivations had been used, we might have concluded erroneously that rats with septal lesions press less for water than control rats. (ii) By using only 24- or 36-hr deprivations, we might have concluded that septal lesions do not affect lever pressing for water. (iii) By using only long-lasting deprivations, we might have concluded that rats with septal lesions press more for water than control rats. Only the entire parametric functions gave a correct picture of the effect of septal lesions under the present experimental conditions. Further, when the results show functions that are not parallel, the most interesting question to ask a statistical test is whether the lack of parallelism is significant. Both main effects and tests of paired values are trivial when interactions are statistically and behaviorally significant.

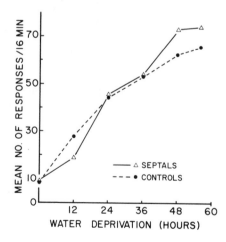

FIG. 17.4. Mean number of responses as a function of level of water deprivation and lesion. (Based on Sagvolden, 1975b).

EFFECTS OF THE LEVEL OF WATER DEPRIVATION ON WATER REINFORCED LEVER PRESSING -- VI 60-s SCHEDULE

In order to replicate the results of Sagvolden (1975b), a variable interval (VI) 60-s schedule of water reinforcement was used as the behavioral baseline for systematic variations of the level of deprivation (Sagvolden, 1979b). In this study, the rats were used as their own controls in order to be sure that the results were seen in all rats and not due to averaging or other statistical phenomena. The results showed interactions between the level of water deprivation and the septal lesions in all rats (Figure 17.5). Rats with septal lesions pressed less for water when the level of water deprivation was 0, 6, or 12 hr, but showed a non-statistically significant increase following the longest-lasting deprivation. These results were neither consistent with the overarousal hypothesis, nor any other existing

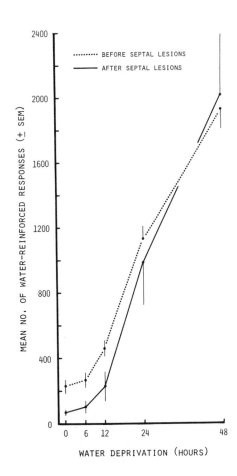

FIG. 17.5. Mean number of water-reinforced lever presses (+SEM) as a function of level of water deprivation before and after septal lesions. (From Sagvolden, 1979).

hypothesis. The septal area is not unitary. It consists of several distinct nuclei with their characteristic input-output relations to the hippocampus neurotransmitters and morphology (see, e.g., Storm-Mathisen, 1978; Swanson & Cowan, 1979). A later study (Sagvolden, 1982) showed that the interaction effects between level of deprivation and lesion would be produced   by   dorsolateral   septal   lesions   not   affecting   the acetylcholinesterase activity in the hippocampus.

There are some problems with these studies (Sagvolden, 1975b; 1979b; 1982): Firstly, there are group differences in the density of reinforcement in all three studies. During VI responding the number of reinforcements was reduced by almost 50 per cent by the septal lesions when the deprivation was short-lasting (Figure 17.6). Secondly, although

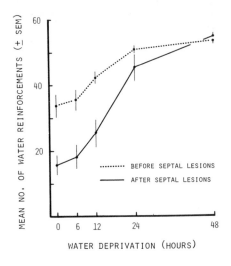

FIG. 17.6. Mean number of water reinforcements (+SEM) as a function of level of water deprivation before and after septal lesions.

the systematically-investigated independent variable in all three studies had been water deprivation and the statistical conclusion has been that there is a significant interaction between septal lesions and the level of water deprivation, it might be that it is the baseline response rate, not water deprivation, that is the crucial variable. The reason for this is that these two were variables confounded: The response rates increased by increasing level of water deprivation. Were we led astray by these relatively simple two-dimensional parametric studies? Maybe we need more sophisticated three-dimensional parametric designs to be able to tease apart the water-deprivation and the response-rate effects?

DISSECTING CONFOUNDED VARIABLES -- A THREE-DIMENSIONAL PARAMETRIC DESIGN

In contrast to the studies above (Sagvolden, 1975b; 1979b; 1982), this study varied the response rate independent of the level of deprivation. If the deprivation variable is the critical one for the behavioral effects of the septal lesion, then the interaction between lesion and level of water deprivation should be present both when the response rates are low and when they are high. If however, the response rate is the crucial variable, then there should be a critical response rate, above which rats with septal lesions should show elevated response rates. At the same time, the behavioral paradigm should allow all other variables, especially the reinforcement density, to be kept as constant as possible.

The septal lesions were closely similar to the dorsolateral lesion of Sagvolden (1982). Following habituation to the operant chamber, magazine training and shaping of responses, lever pressing was reinforced according to a conjoint variable interval 25-s differential reinforcement of low rate X-s (conjoint VI 25-s drl X-s) schedule of water reinforcement. A conjoint schedule specifies that responding is only on one lever and that the requirements of both schedule components have to be fulfilled before a reinforcer is delivered. The VI 25-s component schedules reinforcers at variable intervals with a mean of 25 s. This component ensures that the reinforcement density is relatively constant and reasonably independent of the rate of responding because as long as the response rate is above a certain minimum, further increases do not increase the density of reinforcement. The drl component, the first independent variable, was used for programming a minimum time (X) between two responses. This schedule component was used for reinforcing low-rate and high-rate behavior. Four values of X were used: 0 s (which means that the schedule operated like a simple VI 25 s), 2 s, 4 s and 8 s. When, e.g., the drl 8 s was used, the rat had to space responses at least 8 s; but at the same time it had to press with a steady rate, because the VI component had to be fulfilled too and there was no external stimulus signalling when the reinforcer was set up. Each rat was trained on only one drl-value. The sessions lasted 1 hr. Each animal was run for at least 6 weeks to stabilize the behavior.

When stable-state behavior was obtained, systematically-varied water deprivations were introduced. This was the second independent variable. The following water deprivations were used: 0, 12, 22, and 48 hr. After deprivations, the animals were given ample time for recovering from the effects of the deprivation (see, e.g. Sagvolden, 1975b). The results showed that the densities of reinforcement were closely similar under all four drl-values (Figure 17.7). There are no obvious differences between the groups and drl values. Figure 17.8 shows response rates as functions of drl- value, deprivation level and lesion. The results show that the level of water deprivation is not the critical variable because there is no interaction between deprivation and lesion when the baseline response rates were low (drl values of 4 and 8 s). But there was a small effect when the drl value was 2 s and a large when the drl 0-s schedule was used. In sum, these results show that when the rates were above 10 responses per min, rats with septal lesions pressed more than controls. Thus, the response rate, not level of water deprivation was the important variable. Changing from non-parametric, through two-dimensional to

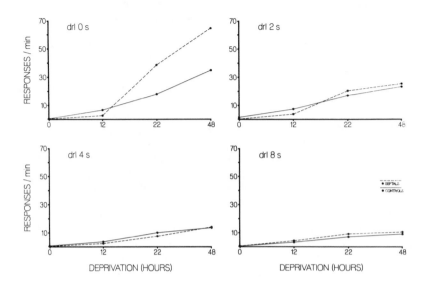

FIG. 17.7A-D. Mean number of water reinforcements as functions of value of the drl component (X) in a conjoint variable interval 25-s differential reinforcement of low rate X-s schedule, level of water deprivation and lesion.

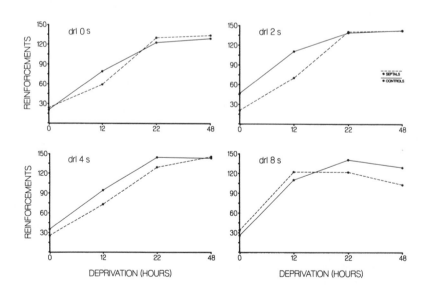

FIG. 17.8A-D. Mean number of responses as functions of value of the drl component (x) in a conjoint variable interval 25-s differential reinforcement of low rate X-s schedule, level of water deprivation and lesion.

three-dimensional parametric designs gave some quite startling insights we probably could not have got elsewhere.

One implication of these results is an hypothesis that any experimental manipulation increasing the response rates, whether it be the reinforcement schedule used, the level of deprivation or something else, may produce elevated response rates in rats with septal lesions when the rate induced is above a certain critical value. Future studies will have to determine whether this critical value depends upon the task. Effects of septal lesions have been interpreted in many ways (for reviews see Caplan, 1973; Gray,1982; Lubar & Numan, 1973; O'Keefe & Nadel, 1978). This might mean that septal lesions have several behavioral effects. The results of the three-dimensional parametric study show that the behavioral effects of septal lesions depend upon the response rate. This implies that an updated version of the Kaada-McCleary response disinhibition hypothesis, originally suggesting that responses high in the response hierarchy of the particular situation are released from inhibitory control after septal lesions (Kaada, Rasmussen & Kveim, 1962; McCleary, 1961), would be the best description of the present results.

PARAMETRIC STUDIES OF AVERSIVELY-MOTIVATED BEHAVIOR

It might be that there are some serious problems with the design and conclusions of avoidance studies similar to the ones in experiments studying water-reinforced behavior of septal animals. Rats with septal lesions show a faster acquisition of two-way avoidance, or shuttle-box avoidance, than control animals (for references, see Sagvolden, 1975a). This task is very different from the previous task: it is aversively motivated rather than appetitively, the topography of the response required is quite different from lever presses and it is an acquisition task, not a task requiring stable-state performance. The most obvious variable to select for systematic study in avoidance tasks is shock intensity. However, control of the shock is difficult because the aversive effect of electric shocks is determined by the logarithm of the product shock intensity in mA times shock duration in seconds. This has been shown in several different behavioral tasks and by several researchers: Church, Raymond and Beauchamp (1967) studying degree of suppression of responding on a VI schedule, by Seligman and Campbell (1965) studying punished extinction of one-way avoidance responding, and by Leander (1973) using a Sidman avoidance paradigm.

Thus, studies of two-way active- avoidance behavior as a function of shock have to control both shock intensity and shock duration. This is best done by using brief, discontinuous shocks which are extremely uncommon in shuttle-box avoidance experiments. but standard in Sidman avoidance. The brief shocks have another advantage too: the rat learns this avoidance task much faster than the traditional one (see Sagvolden, 1975a). Using brief shocks Sagvolden (1975a) showed that when the intensity of these brief shocks was weak, the rats with septal lesions received many more shocks and had a longer latency to the first escape response, but when shock intensity was higher, there was no difference between the control animals and the animals with septal lesions (Figure 17.9). Further, the animals with septal lesions used many trials to obtain a learning criterion of 10 consecutive avoidances both when the shocks were weak and when they were intense (Figure 17.10). At a medium

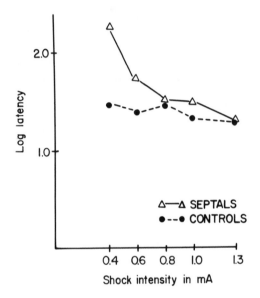

FIG. 17.9. Mean log latency of the first escape response as a function of shock intensity and lesion. (From Sagvolden, 1975a).

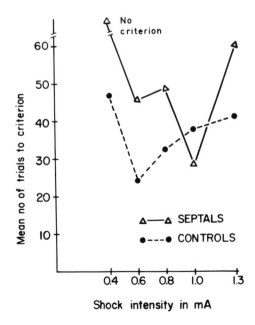

FIG. 17.10. Mean number of trials required to obtain the 10 consecutive avoidance responses in 10 trials learning criterion as a function of shock intensity and lesion. (From Sagvolden, 1975a).

intensity, the rats with septal lesions learned the task faster than the control animals receiving the same shock. Thus, the avoidance behavior of septal rats depend upon the intensity of brief shocks.

In another study (Sagvolden & Johnsrud, 1982) three different types of septal lesions were used. Some rats received lesions in the medial septal area, some in the lateral septal area and some received total septal lesions. The purpose of this study was: what are the behavioral effects of these different lesions and are these effects dependent upon the intensity of brief shocks? The results showed that the number of shocks received on the first trial depended both on the shock intensity and the lesion. Rats with total septal lesion and rats with dorsolateral septal lesions showed profoundly increased escape latencies when the shock was relatively weak. The behavior of the rats with medial septal lesions was quite similar to that of the control rats.

In terms of per cent avoidance responses as a function of shock intensity, the control animals' behavior was not very much affected by the shock intensity (Figure 17.11). However, rats with total septal lesions, showed a lower percentage avoidance responses than control animals when the shock intensity was 1.0 mA or less. This behavior is quite different from the one of animals with dorsolateral septal lesions. Their behavior did not deviate from the control animals' when the shocks were either 0.4 or 0.7 mA, but above these intensities they had a higher percentage avoidance. Finally, the rats with medial septal lesions had a lower percentage avoidance responses than the control animals, when the shocks

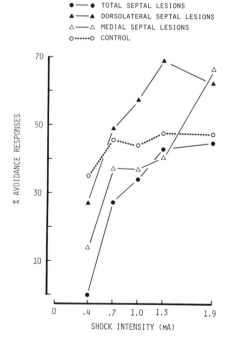

FIG. 17.11. Per cent avoidance responses as a function of shock intensity and lesion (From Sagvolden & Johnsrud, 1982).

were 1.3 mA or weaker, but had a much higher percentage when the shocks were above this level.

The data from these parametric avoidance studies all point in one direction: namely, the behavioral effects of septal lesions strongly depend upon the shock intensity: (i) Small medial septal lesions, interfering with hippocampal acetylcholinesterase activity, produce a learning deficit when the shocks are weak. (ii) Small dorsolateral lesions, not interfering with hippocampal acetylcholineasterase activity, produce faster learning probably related to increased ambulation plus reduced shock reactivity. (iii) Total septal lesions produce reduced shock reactivity. It is hard to see how conclusions like these could be reached without having the entire parametric curves available. The next step should now have been to investigate to what degree these results are response-rate dependent.

OTHER PROBLEMS DUE TO THE USAGE OF CONTINUOUS SHOCKS

As shown above, the escape latencies differ between animals and between groups of animals depending upon treatment. If the traditional continuous shock is used, then the shock effect (log mAs) will differ not only between groups, but also between animals within the same trial and within animals from trial to trial. Figure 17.12 shows what could happen if the experimental group has longer escape latencies than the control group. The control group makes one scatter plot and the experimental group another. The startling conclusion is that our control group in such an experiment actually is no control group for experimental group. Consequently, it is hard to believe that results obtained with continuous shocks could give rise to correct conclusions! In addition, it is reasonable to believe that the fewer trials and sessions needed to obtain the learning criterion when brief shocks are used cause less stress to the animals than procedures using continuous shocks.

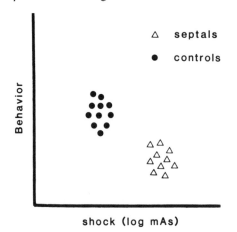

FIG. 17.12. Hypothetical scatter plots relating behavior to the product shock intensity (in mA) times shock duration (in s) in a group with increased escape latencies (septals) and controls.

CONCLUSION

It is easy to see that in the future, researchers ought to perform parametric experiments keeping everything constant except for the variable, or variables, systematically studied. The conclusions one may reach following parametric experiments would in many cases be quite different from what one can reach with non-parametric ones. Figure 17.13 shows some hypothetical results. There are three graphs, all with ambulation as the dependent variable and shock as the independent variable. In Figure 17.13A, the curve describing the behavior of the experimental group is displaced upwards for all levels of the shock intensity. Changes like this indicate increased activity in the experimental group. In Figure 17.13B, the curve describing the behavior of the experimental group is displaced towards higher shock intensities. In that case the behavioral changes indicate reduced shock sensitivity or reduced fear in the experimental group. In Figure 17.13C, the experimental group shows a combination of the changes observed in A and B, namely both an increased activity and a reduced shock sensitivity. Studies conducted according to non-parametric designs do not have the power to reveal the nature of the changes seen in 17.13B and C. Quite on the contrary, non-parametric designs might in such cases give rise to results that are not reproducible causing a wastage of animals and research funds.

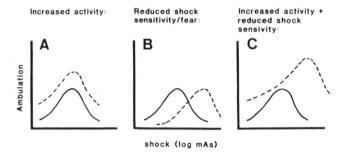

FIG. 17.13A-C. Hypothetical results relating behavior to the product shock intensity (in mA) times shock duration (in s) in an experimental (- - -) and a control group (----). A. Shows the predicted results when the experimental group has increased activity; B, when the experimental group shows reduced shock sensitivity; and C, when the experimental group shows both increased activity and reduced shock sensitivity.

One might argue that it could be difficult to select which of potentially important independent variables to study systematically. However, the available theories and hypotheses will guide the researcher in this selection process. Finally, when some of the basic parametric functions have been established, it ought to be possible to avoid the most time-consuming, expensive designs.

REFERENCES

Belanger, D., & Feldman, S. M. (1962). Effects of water deprivation upon heart rate and instrumental activity in the rat. *Journal of Comparative and Physiological Psychology, 55,* 220-225.

Caplan, M. (1973). An analysis of the effects of septal lesions on negatively reinforced behavior. *Behavioral Biology, 9,* 129-167.

Church, R. M., Raymond, G. A., & Beauchamp, R. D. (1967). Response suppression as a function of intensity and duration of punishment. *Journal of Comparative and Physiological Psychology, 63,* 39-44.

Doty, B.A., & Forkner, M.R. (1971). Alterations in pain thresholds and avoidance conditioning in rats with septal lesions. *Neuropsychologia, 9,* 325-330.

Gray, J.A. (1982). *The neuropsychology of anxiety: an enquiry into the functions of the septo-hippocampal system.* Oxford: Clarendon Press.

Harvey, J.A. & Hunt, H.F. (1965). Effect of septal lesions on thirst in the rat as indicated by water consumption and operant responding for water reward. *Journal of Comparative and Physiological Psychology, 59,* 49-56.

Hebb, D.O. (1955). Drives and the C. N. S. (conceptual nervous system). *Psychological Review, 62,* 243-354.

Johnson, D.A. & Thatcher, K. (1972). Differential effects of food deprivation on the fixed ratio behavior of normal rats and rats with septal lesions. *Psychonomic Science, 26,* 45-46.

Kaada B.R., Rasmussen E.W., & Kveim, O. (1962). Impaired acquisition of passive avoidance behavior by subcallosal, septal, hypothalamic, and insular lesions in rats. *Journal of Comparative and Physiological Psychology, 55,* 661-670.

Leander, J.D. (1973). Shock intensity and duration interactions on free-operant avoidance behavior. *Journal of the Experimental Analysis of Behavior, 19,* 481-490.

Lubar, J.F. & Numan R. (1973). Behavioral and physiological studies of septal function and related medial cortical structures. *Behavioral Biology, 8,* 1-25.

McCleary, R.A. (1961). Response specificity in the behavioral effects of limbic system lesions in the cat. *Journal of Comparative and Physiological Psychology, 54,* 605-613.

O'Keefe, J. & Nadel, L. (1978). *The hippocampus as a cognitive map.* Oxford: Clarendon Press.

Sagvolden, T. (1975). Acquisition of two-way active avoidance following septal lesions in the rat: effect of intensity of discontinuous shock. *Behavioral Biology, 14,* 59-74. (a)

Sagvolden, T. (1975). Operant responding for water in rats with septal lesions: effect of deprivation level. *Behavioral Biology, 13,* 323-330. (b)

Sagvolden, T. (1979). Behavioral Changes in Rats with Septal Lesions: Effects of Water-Deprivation Level and Intensity of Electric Shocks. Doctoral dissertation, University of Oslo, Norway. (a)

Sagvolden, T. (1979). Behavior of rats with septal lesions during low levels of water deprivation. *Behavioral and Neural Biology, 26,* 431-441. (b)

Sagvolden, T. (1982). Continuous reinforcement of responding for water in rats with medial or dorsolateral septal lesions: effect of deprivation level. *Behavioral and Neural Biology, 34,* 372-383.

Sagvolden, T. & Johnsrud, G. (1982) Two-way active avoidance learning following medial, dorsolateral, or total septal lesions in rats: effect of intensity of discontinuous shock. *Behavioral and Neural Biology, 35,* 17-32.

Seligman, M.E.P., & Campbell, B.A. (1965). Effect of intensity and duration of punishment on one-way and shuttle avoidance conditioning. *Journal of Experimental Psychology, 59,* 295-297.

Storm-Mathisen, J. (1978). *Location of putative transmitters in the hippocampal formation. With a note on the connections to septum and hypothalamus.* In K. Elliot & J. Whelan (Eds.), Functions of the Septo-Hippocampal System, Ciba Foundation Symposium 58 (new series). pp. 49-79. Amsterdam: Elsevier.

Swanson, L.W., & Cowan, W.M. (1979). The connections of the septal region in the rat. *Journal of Comparative Neurology, 186,* 621-656.

VIII

SUMMARY AND INTEGRATION

18 Aversively Motivated Behavior: Which Are the Perspectives?

Lars-Göran Nilsson and Trevor Archer
University of Umeå

At the very beginning of Chapter 1 it was stated that two aspects of aversively motivated behavior were to be examined: The historical background to current research in this area and the six perspectives upon which this volume was based. It was established also that the contingencies of aversively motivated behavior controlled an extraordinarily large portion of our everyday behavior (e.g. Archer, 1979), but apart from this practical perspective lasting and fundamental theoretical developments have been obtained from the study of aversively based behaviors. One purpose of this final chapter will be to try to identify some "trends" within and across the various perspectives reviewed here. It is hoped that these trends will facilitate the identification of some key concepts to allow the derivation of animal models of human "dysfunctions", surely the most worthy of perspective enterprises.

Perspectives on aversion, avoidance and anxiety

There is much general consensus that the *Perspectives on the determinants of hedonic value* (or perspectives on taste-aversion learning) give us a global conceptualization of the learning process and the particular organism doing the learning. The present perspectives were centred upon the neurobiological correlates of this taste-aversion/shock-avoidance learning paradigm and permit a unique analysis of the neuroanatomical substrates of the feeding approach-avoidance behavior. Animals, humans included, do require the means to select nutrients and avoid poisonous agents which, probably as a result of evolutionary pressures, they have developed (e.g. Chapman & Blaney, 1979; Garcia, Rusiniak & Brett, 1977; Rhoades, 1979). These principles, as described by the learning of external and visceral consequences of cues and the different neurobiological systems subserving them, are developed to full extent in the chapters by Bermúdez-Rattoni, Sandez and Prado-Alcalá (Chapter 4) and Garcia (Chapter 2), but see also Garcia, Rusiniak, Kiefer & Bermúdez-Rattoni (1982). The influences of contextual variables upon these principles is developed in the chapter by Sjödén and Archer (Chapter 3). However, as Garcia develops in his treatise, the issue of taste-aversion learning and general process theory is not completely resolved as "Taste aversions do not fit comfortably within the present framework of classical or instrumental conditioning ..." (p. 46); and, from these beginnings John Garcia develops the theme concerning the determinants of hedonic value to a level of outstanding generality, with an historic perspective bearing fruit from the seeds of Tolman's functionalism (but see also Bolles, 1985).

The chapters by Hugdahl (Chapter 5), Öhman, Dimberg and Esteves (Chapter 6), and Mineka and Tomarken (Chapter 7) discuss various methodological and theoretical considerations of aversively motivated behavior from a clinical perspective. In line with the tradition from previous research on aversively motivated behavior in the domain of animal learning and conditioning, the focus of attention in the present three chapters is that of the study of fear through classical conditioning. That is, we conceive of this research of the acquisition, maintenance, and extinction of fear and anxiety as somewhat of a prolongation of the research on escape and avoidance conditioning in the animal learning domain. Whereas the general topic of research appears to be in line with previous studies, the theoretical orentation of the present three chapters differ quite markedly from that of previous theoretical enterprises in this field. The prime difference in this regard is that cognitive factors now seem to be a rule rather than an exception in this type of learning and there is, of course, a strong relationship between the main thrust of these three chapters and that of the three chapters by Christianson and Nilsson (Chapter 11), Loftus and Christianson (Chapter 12), and Eysenck (Chapter 13) explicitly directed towards the study of aversively motivated behavior from a cognitive perspective.

The cognitive orientation, as such, of the research reported by Hugdahl (Chapter 5) pertains to the notion of brain asymmetry and lateralization in cognitive function. Hugdahl builds his arguments on previous research (e.g., Bradshaw & Nettleton, 1981; Kimura, 1961; Sperry, Stamm & Miner, 1956; Wada & Rasmussen, 1960) generally postulating that the two cerebral hemispheres are functionally different for the processing of various types of sensory information. In general, the left hemisphere has been said to be specialized for the processing of verbal-linguistic information, whereas the right hemisphere has been said to be specialized for the processing of visuo-spatial information and especially so if this information has an emotional tone.

The particular task that Hugdahl tackles in his investigation is the extent to which human Pavlovian conditioning is related to the notion of lateralization of cognitive functions. Hugdahl admits that the ideas he proposes about this relationship are somewhat speculative, but argues convincingly that they should be explored. Based on the general contention that aversively motivated behavior most commonly is a result of non-verbal stimuli, Hugdahl argues that the question of the relationship between human Pavlovian conditioning and lateralization of cognitive functions is particularily appropriate to discuss and explore in a context like the present one. In a straightforward manner Hugdahl predicts that conditioning to fear-relevant CSs like pictures of snakes and spiders (e.g., Bernstein & Allen, 1969; Braun & Reynolds, 1969; Landy & Gaupp, 1971; Marks, 1969; Öhman, Erixon & Löfberg, 1975) should be more easily acquired and more resistent to extinction when the fear-relevant CSs are initially processed by the right cerebral hemisphere.

Hugdahl presents interesting data in support of this prediction at the same time as he points out several methodological difficulties as potential sources of misinterpretation. Although the dichotic extinction paradigm proposed by Hugdahl seems to be a promising technique to overcome these difficulties, a more general word of caution should be mentioned.

Whereas much research has been conducted on the issue of lateralization of cognitive functions, as of yet very few studies have been undertaken with respect to the role of lateralization in conditioning. This means that the data base is relatively limited and all the potential pitfalls may not yet have been discovered. One source of possible misinterpretation may lie in the task of unconfounding the cognitive effects that are known to exist from the effects of 'pure' conditioning. The results demonstrated in the dichotic extinction paradigm may certainly reflect differential conditioning, but could equally well reflect differences in these more known cognitive functions. For example, it might be the case that the effects Hugdahl attributes to pure conditioning are effects of differences in the way information is accessed and subsequently retrieved from memory after having been initially processed in a unilateral way.

Cognitive factors are also paramount in the conditioning model proposed by Öhman, Dimberg and Esteves (Chapter 6). The model provides a possible desynchrony among verbal, motor, and physiological responses similarily to that proposed by Lang (1968) in his conceptualization of three systems of fear. Of primary concern here is that the model by Öhman et al. allows such a desynchrony because the physiological responses are assumed to reflect the automatic affective reaction more directly; these responses are not assumed to be influenced by controlled processes in this direct fashion.

The idea of disconnecting controlled processes by means of the method of backward masking is indeed interesting. The technique may mean a substantial contribution of the understanding not only of aversively motivated behavior but also of the role of automatic versus controlled processes in emotions in general. However, in the same way as for the dichotic extinction paradigm proposed by Hugdahl in Chapter 5, there are some methodological considerations that need to be made in relation to the backward masking paradigm proposed by Öhman et al. as well. First, the evidence Öhman et al. use for the disconnection of controlled processes via backward masking is solely the failure by the subject to verbally report the masked stimulus. In drawing the attention to the

analysis of the perceptual defence phenomenon more than 30 years ago
(e.g., McGinnies, 1949; Postman, Bronson & Gropper, 1953; Zajonc,
1962), we conceive of this verbal report test as a somewhat bleak means of
control. Moreover, in the last experiment reported by Öhman et al., it
could be argued that the sensitization condition may be somewhat
problematic. One alternative may be to use a pseudoconditioning control
that would not involve the novelty stimulus effects at testing. Such effects
may invalidate the sensitization control.

The role of cognitive factors in understanding the origins and
maintenance of fear and anxiety is thoroughly discussed by Mineka and
Tomarken (Chapter 7) as well. Students of aversively motivated behavior
nowadays incorporate concepts that traditionally have been confined only to
the cognitive theories themselves. This development calls to our attention
the apparent need in contemporary conditioning theory to broaden the
conceptual machinery for the sake of accomodating fine grain analyses of
new data from conditioning research. Mineka and Tomarken explicitly
state in their chapter that an adequate understanding of the origins and
maintenance of fear and anxiety can be achieved only if a broad integrative
model is developed which incorporate theoretical constructs from several
sources. Some of these sources, according to Mineka and Tomarken, are
contemporary S-S conditioning theory and models of vicarious
conditioning, but also various theoretical accounts pertaining to
interactions of experiential variables occurring prior to, during, and after a
traumatic experience (cf. Christianson & Nilsson, Chapter 11).
Moreover, according to Mineka and Tomarken, various cognitive biases of
several different types should be included; among these are selective
associations of certain fear-relevant cues with aversive outcome, biased
attention and memory for threat-related cues, and overgeneralization of
fear with the passage of time. Note that only few exposures of the
primates to fearful snake/reptile stimuli was necessary for the learning of
strong fears (Mineka, Davidson, Keir & Cook. 1984), and these fear
responses were very resistant to extinction (Mineka & Keir, 1983;
Mineka, Keir & Prince, 1980). Monkeys will even show an aversion to a
particular food a long time after having been presented a toy snake in the
feeding place (Solomon, 1977).

As already mentioned cognitive factors also play a crucial role in the
chapters by Christianson and Nilsson (Chapter 11), Loftus and
Christianson (Chapter 12), and Eysenck (Chapter 13). These chapters
were explicitly aimed at covering the cognitive perspectives of aversively
motivated behavior. The research reported in these chapters was directed
exclusively towards theoretical accounts in terms of cognitive psychology;
no attempts were made to try to include any of the concepts used in
traditional conditioning theory. It should be noted, however, that some of
the results discussed might be possible to interpret within the boundaries
of conditioning theory.

The cognitive concepts at these chapters all focus on memory and
attention. Christianson and Nilsson (Chapter 11) place an emphasis on
encoding and retrieval factors (rather than storage or consolidation) as
being the sources for the aversively motivated behavior, i.e. the amnesia

for the traumatic event and the retrograde and anterograde amnesia for events preceding and succeeding the traumatic event per se. By means of the model of narrowed attention, Christianson and Nilsson manage to account for (a) the amnesia of the traumatic event, (b) the retrograde amnesia, (c) the anterograde amnesia, and (d) the recovery of memories of the traumatic event, and the events preceding and succeding the traumatic event. Moreover, the experimental paradigm described (cf. Christianson, 1984; Christianson & Nilsson, 1984) makes it possible to bridge the gap between clinical and experimental findings. Finally, the reinstatement of internal physiological states in the context of the case study reported by Christianson and Nilsson constitutes a potentially important bridge to laboratory studies on state dependency. The rape victim in that case study could gain access to apparently available but previously inaccessible information in memory (cf. Tulving & Pearlstone, 1966) by means of the internal physiological states that were reinstated when the woman was out jogging for the first time since the assault took place several weeks earlier. This observation would seem to suggest a useful therapeutic technique at least for some cases of aversively motivated behavior.

Loftus and Christianson (Chapter 12) present a clear account of the notion of "blending" of memories. This notion has had a controversial but clear impact on the theoretical debate in memory research (see Loftus & Burns, 1982; McClosky & Zaragoza, 1985). It is also interesting to note that the 'memory blending' notion provides a clear analogue to the 'revaluation, studies of Rescorla (1984, 1985) for changing memories.

The chapter by Eysenck (Chapter 13) is certainly based on a modern cognitive ground although it also gives connotations to the perceptual defence propositions of the 1950s. More explicitly, the emphasis on cognitive factors is on automatic and controlled processes in a similar way as that discussed by Öhman et al. in Chapter 6. This similarity between Eysenck's approach and the approach taken by Öhman et al. is interesting in its own right since it suggest a convergence of ideas from quite different backgrounds and perspectives that should not pass without notice. However, it should also be noted that some of the difficulties that Öhman at al. are facing with respect to the desynchronizing of automatic and controlled processes apply to the approach taken by Eysenck as well. More explicitly, until it can be determined in a non-circulatory way whether or not the putative preprocessing is automatic or controlled it is difficult to generate a prediction in experiments.

Implicit or explicit emphasis on the role of cognitive factors in aversively motivated behavior can also be found in the chapters by McGaugh (Chapter 8) and Boakes (Chapter 15). McGaugh's main contribution is that of showing how the study of brain mechanisms can serve as a key to understanding global psychological functions. The search for neural mechanisms of learning and memory should reasonably engage cognitive psychologists and the approach McGaugh has proposed is inspiring in this regard. However, it should be noticed that there are some problems within McGaugh's framework that are still waiting for a solution. For example, the trials by dose metric is interesting but would seem to deserve much further pursuit and development. Are the obtained effects really due to enhancement or are they due to state dependency arising from placing the animal in the fear eliciting test context? Moreover, why is it the case that peripheral adrenaline requires activation of both α and β adrenergic pathways to produce the effects on memory mediated in the amygdala? Bearing these questions in mind, it is interesting to note recent attempts to assess the interactive influences of conditioning and anxiety with the effects of the neurohormones (Eysenck & Kelley, 1987).

The chapter by Boakes (Chapter 15) on methodological problems in human conditioning also expresses a cognitive tone. Boakes is basically doubtful towards research on human conditioning. His main thrust is that there is really no point in doing conditioning experiments in humans since there are better and more straightforward cognitive methods of finding out what humans think is frightening and which the stimuli are that provoke anxiety. Boakes' argument is that such methods should be limited to animal studies. Since animals cannot be asked in any other way what they know about the world, conditioning techniques are appropriate (cf. Dickinson & Shanks, 1985).

This critique of human conditioning and the increasing use of cognitive concepts in much research on aversively motivated invited us to propose an underlying dimension on which aversively motivated behavior might be based. This dimension ranges from automatic processing requiring no conscious involvement. These two end points on the continuum are similar to the two types of processes intended by the distinction proposed by Hasher and Zachs (1979) in terms of automatic and effortful processes. Hasher and Zachs (1979) proposed this distinction to account for the memory impairments demonstrated in elderly as compared to young adults with the notion being that such deficits are found in tasks requiring effortful processes, but not in tasks that are tapping automatic processes. Furthermore, Mogg, Mathews and Weinman (1987) suggest that depression may be associated with an absence of avoidance relating to a memory bias for negative information from evidence of a negative self-referent recall bias in depressives (e.g. Derry & Kuiper, 1981; Kuiper & Derry, 1982) although some results are non supportive (Hasher, Rose, Zacks, Sanft & Doren, 1985; Isen, 1984; Johnson & Magaro, 1987). Note that anxiety problems too may be associated with negative recall bias (Nunn, Stevenson & Whalan, 1984; O'Banion & Arkowitz, 1977). Yet another dichotomy of memory processes should also be mentioned as a source of inspiration for the continuum of processes proposed here. This is the distinction between implicit and explicit memory proposed by Graf and Schacter (1985) to account for differences in memory performance demonstrated for amnesic patients and normal control subjects.

Thus, our claim is that aversively motivated behavior is not based on a single process but rather on a several different processes that can be allocated to various portions of the continuum between automatic processing and deliberate processing. Supposedly, the intention in using Pavlovian conditioning is to deal with automatic processes only. However, as pointed out by Öhman et al. (Chapter 6) several processes are combined in the conditioning paradigm and in line with Öhman et al. we think that it is essential that these processes are desyncronized. As mentioned the backward masking technique proposed by Öhman et al. is an important means to accomplish this. And indeed those processes that Öhman et al. are primarily interested in are similar to the processes involved in implicit memory (cf. Graf & Schacter, 1985). In addition to the possibility that the theoretical development that has taken place in memory research might influence further development of theories in the domain of aversively motivated behavior, it might be the case that a technique like the one proposed by Öhman et al. (Chapter 6) could be used to fertilize further studies of implicit memory.

Perspectives on animal models

Several aspects of aversively motivated behavior relating to the clinical, neurobiological and neuroethological perspectives are important from the therapeutical neuroscientific perspective. These topics each involve current and wide areas of neuropharmacological research and some brief mention can be made: (1) Anxiety and the status of animal models, (2) Depressive illness and problems involving derivation and application of animal models, and (3) Stress induced analgesia of various types. These first two points, in a very general sense, include both neurotic pathology, e.g. phobias and compulsions, depression and helplessness, and problems involving guilt, psychosomatic pathology and stress disorders. As will be developed in our consideration of some aspects of unpleasant stimuli, these problems do bear some relation to a discussion of stress induced analgesia. In this respect, neuroimmunemodulation should be considered also. The present discussion pretends only to provide a very rudimentary perusal of features of the three topics. These features have no immediate bearing upon either the theoretical or empirical status of the topics but are meant to allow the interested reader to obtain new channels of investigation amongst the wider horizons of behaviors that are related to aversive events whether real or perceived only (but see also Bignami, Chapter 14; and Sagvolden, Chapter 17 this volume).

The increasing interest for anxiety related conditions in the last decade may be indexed by the proliferation of potential therapeutic psychoactive agents currently under investigation. The preclinical study of possible, clinically effective antianxiety agents centers, traditionally, around a plethora of animal models that may be divided broadly into three main types: (1) models based on conflict or conditioned fear procedures, (2) novelty induced anxiety or fear procedures, neophobia, (3) models in which the behavioral responses (whether anxiety or aversion) are chemically induced, (File, 1985). A perennial question arising out of the search for anxiolytic agents is the question: How predictive are the current models of anxiety? There is a prevailing attitude that the animal models of anxiety have been 'tailored' to fit the anxiolytic properties of the benzodiazepine class of compounds. This proposal (whether or not unfair) is of some pertinence since the benzodiazepines are also muscle relaxants and anticonvulsant as well as causing sedation, amnesia, and ataxia. Therefore, does the detection of a behavioral change following benzodiazepine treatment constitute a propensity for anxiolytic action? One essential quest therefore is to demonstrate that the particular behavioral change resulting from the drug treatment does reflect a reduction (alteration) of the anxiety level.

Does experimental induced anxiety provide a valid and reliable model of anxiety in the clinic? Given the complexity of anxiety conditions (Klein, 1981) it is not surprising that the status of current animal models is questionable (Abbott, 1987; File, 1985, but see also Estes & Skinner, 1941). Are there satisfactory treatments for anxiety? Traditional benzodiazepine treatment has the above-mentioned drawbacks and although antidepressant compounds have been used their efficacy is not clear (Telch, Agras, Taylor, Roth & Gallen, 1985; Zitrin, Klein & Woerner, 1980). It may be of interest to note then the notably higher success rate obtained from behavior therapeutic procedures (Jansson & Ost, 1982).

Although the chapters by Öhman, Hugdahl, Mineka, Eysenck, Loftus and Christianson, and Christianson and Nilsson provide much illustration of anxiety states in animals and humans the only potential animal model or illustration of a depressed state appears to be provided by Suomi (for discussion see Beninger & Archer, this volume). But, animal models of depression proliferate and new claims for potential models appear almost on a monthly basis. The fact is that at present there are no animal models of depression worthy of that status (Nagayama, Hingten & Aprison, 1981; Willner, 1984, 1985) although there do exist a very large number of drug screens and bioassays (about thirty at the last count) of varying reliability for predicting antidepressant efficacy. Bearing this in mind, it is necessary to describe two animal models that may eventually lay claim to validity: (1) The procedure by which rats are subjected to the unpredictable and chronic administration of various different mild stressors over periods of one to two weeks (e.g. Katz, 1984; Katz & Sibel, 1982; Soblosky & Thurmond, 1986; but see also Willner, Towell, Sampson, Sophokleous & Muscat, 1987). (2) Berger and co-workers (e.g. Berger, Mesch & Schuster, 1980; Berger & Schuster, 1982; Schuster, Rachlin, Rom & Berger, 1982) have developed an animal model of social interaction in which pairs of rats learn to coordinate their movements in space by attending to each others behavior to optimise the acquisition of a reinforcer. It may be that the social interaction measures following treatment with mild stressor and/or social isolation will produce a valid model. Nevertheless, the status of any animal model bears careful consideration, as Keehn (1986) argues the behavior of one organism may be a model of that of another not only when the behaviors look alike but also when the conditons giving rise to and maintaining them share common processes.

The 'behavioral despair' model, also referred to as forced swim or Porsolt test, provides a case example of a rhetorically and anthropomorphically attractive test that does not quite attain the required status of an animal model. Developed by Porsolt and co-workers (e.g. Porsolt, Anton, Blanet & Jalfre, 1978; Porsolt, Le Pichon & Jalfre, 1977) the procedure requires the placement of a rat in a confined water bath (generally a 18 cm cylinder containing 15-20 cm water. The animals, forced to remain in the bath for upto 10 min, generally shows on initial period of vigorous activity and then remains immobile. On subsequent occasions of immersion the onset of immobility is much more rapid and has been suggested to constitute a state of 'despair'. Whether this is because the animal has learned that escape is impossible or for someother reason is not clear. For example, O'Neill and Valentino (1982) have questioned the relationship between inescapable shock and immobility and Borsini, Volterra and Meli (1986) have attempted to ascertain whether the 'behavioral despair' was the cause of immobility. Borsini et al. (1986) varied the depth of water in which the rats were places (4, 15 and 30 cm) and observed that the immobility duration following exposure to 4 cm of water was not modified by the prior conditions (previous immersion in the water bath), an indication that "despair" had not been produced. Furthermore, the total duration of immobility was significantly shorter when the rats were placed in 30 cm of water as compared to 4 or 15 cm water, independent of the pretest condition (No immersion, 0, 4, 15 or 30 cm; see Fig. 18.1).

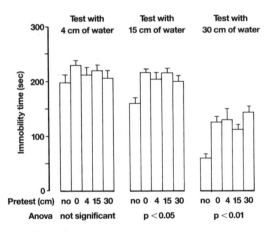

FIG. 18.1. Effect of various levels of water on immobility time. Each column represents mean +S.E. of 6-10 rats. (Redrawn from Borsini et al. 1986)

Borsini et al. (1986) suggest that familiarity with the environment rather than "despair" was responsible for the prolongation of immobility. We have a simpler explanation: it is possible at the shallower depths (4 or 15 cm) that the most 'convenient' position for the rat was one of immobile 'floating' in contact with the bottom. This is essentially what would be suggested by Hawkins, Hicks, Phillips and More (1978) who showed behavioral immobility to be a consequence of adaptive responding to a stressful situation. Finally, the stress-inducing properties and the physiological inbalance resulting from a forced immersion in a water bath have been discussed also with regard to the 'behavioral despair' test (Thierry, Stern, Simon & Porsolt, 1986). At present, it may be stating the obvious to say that no predictive *and valid* animal model exists when each potential model is subjected to the type of dissection with which the 'despair' test has been investigated.

The stress induced adaptive properties of the 'despair' test could also be a means to illustrate that effects of stress on pain perception, i.e. in the study of stress induced analgesia. Exposure to stressful stimuli has been shown to elicit a reliable analgesic effect in rats (Akil, Madden, Patrick & Barchas, 1976; Hayes, Bennet, Newlon & Mayer, 1976; Rosecrans & Chance, 1976). Thus, elevated pain thresholds in response to, for example, heat stimuli have been obtained consistently following inescapable footshock or tail-shock (e.g. Buckett, 1981; Madden, Akil, Patrick & Barchas, 1977). As with water bath immersion induced immobility, one fundamental question is whether the analgesic effects of stress (whether cold water, shock or immobility) represents an adaptive or a 'dispairing' type of response. Certainly, one property of certain stressors is the release of endogenous opioids (Chihara, Arimura, Coy & Schally, 1978; Rossier, French, River, Ling, Guillemin & Bloom, 1977; Siegel, Chowers, Conforti, Feldman & Weidenfeld, 1982) and opioid mechanisms of stress induced analgesia are well documented (Chance, 1980; Hayes, Bennett, Newlon & Mayer, 1978).

Generally, inescapable shock has been used to induce analgesia (e.g. Chance, Krynock & Rosecrans, 1978; Chance, White, Krynock & Rosecrans, 1977; Chester & Chan, 1977; Madden et al., 1977) but other treatments have been applied including, cold water immersion (Bodnar, Kelly & Glusman, 1978; Bodnar, Glusman, Brutus, Spiaggia & Kelly, 1979), immobilization restraint (Amir & Amit, 1976; Blair, Galina, Holmes & Amit, 1982), food deprivation (Bodnar, Kelly, Spiaggia, Glusman, 1978; Dinsmoor, 1958; Franchina, 1966), aggression induced defeat (Miczek, Thompson & Shuster, 1982), heat exposure (Kulkarni, 1980) and body pinch (Ornstein & Amir, 1981). As a general rule it has been found that those environmental manipulations which are regarded as stressors have increased nociceptive thresholds although some exceptions exist, e.g. tailpinch had an analgesic effect using certain nociception tests (Levine, Wilcox, Grace & Morley, 1982) but produced an hyperalgesia in other tests (Simone & Bodnar, 1982).

Several aspects of stress, pain and stress-induced analgesia may be pivotal to our considerations of the perspectives within aversively motivated behavior. *First*, as a result of selective processes, pain mechanisms and the responses to painful stimuli are controlled by the central nervous system and accordingly it is understandable that survival contingencies may result in the analgesia following from stress or extreme fear. In this context it is timely to consider the "working memory hypothesis" proposed by James Grau (1987b), by which the central representation of an aversive event in working memory activates the analgesic systems. Grau's procedure involves the removal of the subjects from the shock apparatus in order to test pain reactivity which exposes the animal to a variety of distracting stimuli. These stimuli act to desplace the representation of shock from working memory thereby undermining the degree to which analgesic systems are activated by memorial processes (Grau, 1986, 1987a). Also, removal of the animals from the shock chamber removes them from cues associated with shock, which minimizes the degree to which memory processes activates the analgesic systems (Fanselow, 1984). Grau's hypothesis is interesting not least of all because it captures certain aspects of the formalized *Standard Operating Procedures of Memory Systems* (SOP) model as proposed by Wagner (see Donegan & Wagner, in press; Mazur & Wagner, 1982; Wagner, 1981). *Second,* responses to aversive stimuli represent a basic adaptive mechanism of animals and humans mediated by an integrated neuroendocrine response, involving pituitary-adrenal-cortical and sympathomedullary activation (Selye, 1952).

Third, the adaptive behavior ensuing will often take the form of species-specific defensive behaviors, e.g. freezing, fleeing or fighting (Bolles, 1970), but will also be dependent upon the state of the organism following the aversive event (stressor), i.e. whether defense, flight or recovery from injury are most essential, the perceptual-defensive-recuperative (PDR) theory (cf. Bolles & Fanselow, 1980). PDR theory rejects the assumption that nociceptive stimuli derectly activate the analgesic systems and assumes that conditioned fear mediates the activation. Thus, animals associate the aversive event to the context in which it occurred, and, the association elicits a state of fear leading, in turn, to hypoalgesia. This account differs from the "coulometric hypothesis" which suggests that the degree to which analgesic systems are activated depends upon the severity of the aversive event (cf. Terman, Shavit, Lewis, Cannon & Liebeskind, 1984), but for relevant discussion see also (Maier & Keith, 1987; Mineka, Cook & Miller, 1984; Rosellini, DeCola & Warren, 1986).

Fourth, we have noted that the consequences of stress involve both disturbances of instrumental avoidance and appetitive behaviours (Anisman, 1977; Maier & Seligman, 1976; Rosellini, 1978; Zacharko & Anisman, 1978) as well as analgesia. Thus, under certain conditions stress is believed to be the main predisposing and precipitating factor in depression (Anisman & Zacharko, 1982; Breslau & Davis, 1986). Clinical observations indicate some relationship between previous stressful (traumatic) events like the loss of parents or loved-one (predisposing factor), subsequent other stressors (precipitating factor) and the occurrence of a state of depression (Cornell, Milden & Shimp, 1985). Depressed patients, at the time, report themselves to be deeply upset by recent stressful events in their lives (Hammen & Cochran, 1981). Also, the frequency of the unpleasant stimuli occurrence (preceived) has been found to correlate with the severity of depressed mood (see also Willner, 1985). In some respects, then, it appears as if the stress induced analgesia may be similar to the depressed state observed in animals and humans.

On the other hand, there is some historical support for the possibility that stressful events may produce certain 'antidepressant-like' effects. REM (rapid eye movement) sleep deprivation and physical exercise (jogging) have been pronounced effective for the treatment of melancholia and depression (Greist, Klein, Eishens, Fairs. Gurman & Morgan, 1979;

Vogel, 1983), but it was shown also that aerobic exercise which resulted in a significant improvement in cardiovascular functioning had no more effect on psychological mood states than did the placebo control of participation in nonaerobic recreational games or no exercise and sport at all. Beta-endorphin levels with the 41 depressed subjects were not a link that might explain the possible influence of physical activity on depression (Williams & Getty, 1986).

Bearing this in mind, it is interesting to note in this respect the effects of exercise and jogging on the release of endogenous opiates (e.g. Farrell, Gates, Maksud & Morgan, 1982; Harber & Sutton, 1984). For example, Goldfarb, Hatfield, Sfarzo and Flynn (1987) found that following exercise, β-endorphin levels were significantly increased compared to resting values and, additionally, the psychological state of the subjects (untrained male college students) was unaffected by exercise. Other investigations (Farrell, Gustafsson, Garthwaite, Kalkhoff, Cowley & Morgan, 1986; Grossman, Bouloux, Price, Drury, Lam, Turner, Thomas, Besser & Sutton, 1984; de Meirleir, Naaktgeboren, Van Steirteghem, Gorus, Olbrecht & Block, 1986) demonstrate a complex interaction between endogenous opiate release and the pituitary-adrenal axis (relating to the role of stress-hormones) during and after strenuous exercise. All of which suggests a highly intricate concatenation of empirical and conceptual factors, behavioral and neurobiological, that ought to bear some mention in association with aversive situations, though obviously not constituting examples of such (e.g. Morgan, 1985; Steinberg & Sykes, 1985).

In situations of continuous stress exposure, as for example under front-line or behind-enemy-line battle conditions or in prisoner-of-war camps, depressive symptoms and attempts at suicide are believed to be a rarity. Here, it has been reported that behavior patterns that put a premium on survival are the most dominant (Haslam, 1984; Solomon & Benbenishty, 1986). Frontline and battle exposure treatment was found to correlate well with lowered rates of posttraumatic stress disorder and elevations of performance, fitness and mood (but see also Bäckman & Molander, 1986a, b). Thus, Bäckman and Molander (1986a) found that the performance of older golfers (miniature golf competitions) deteriorated in conditions of high arousal (and presumably stress resulting from the greater importance of certain championships) the younger golfers performed at the same level, throughout. Furthermore, the performance decline of the older golfers was correlated with a related deterioration in the performance of a test of cognitive ability which was to remember details of previous shots played (Bäckman & Molander, 1986b). These studies offer an ingenuous application of a "real-life", yet controlled, situation to investigate aspects of anxiety associated behavior in the context of both sensory-motor performance and cognitive skills (but see also Welford, 1977).

In several instances the similarities and parallels between chronic stress exposure and antidepressant treatment have been found in experimental studies (cf. Danysz, Kostowski & Archer, 1988). On the other hand, chronic stress models of depression are relevant to an understanding of biological mechanisms of depression (Katz, 1981) as stress (and distressful) events in everyday life are frequently associated with depressive disorders (Bidzinska, 1984). Thus, for example, Garcia Marguez and Armario (1987) applied the chronic stress (various stressor like food and water deprivation, lighting changes etc) animal model of Katz and co-workers (e.g. Katz, Roth & Carroll, 1981) to compare the effects of chronic and acute stress on certain behaviors and levels of adrenocorticotropic (ACTH) hormone (e.g. Armario, Restrepo, Castellanos & Balasch, 1985). Utilising these procedures, Garcia-Marguez and Armario (1987) found that chronic and not acute stress decreased hole-board exploration and increased immobility in the Porsolt (forced swim) test, but neither treatment altered ACTH levels (see Fig. 18.2). This study is of some special interest with regard to the earlier discussions regarding problems of validity with the Porsolt test since Garcia-Marguez and Armario have applied the Porsolt test as a dependent variable for the animal model, chronic stress (but see also Danysz, Plaznik, Kostowski, Malatynska, Järbe, Hiltunen & Archer, 1987).

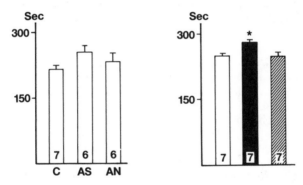

FIG. 18.2. The effect of a single session of stress (left) and the effect of cronic resistant vs. cronic shock (right) on the period of immobility in the Porsolt's test. Mean and SEM are represented. Number of animals per groups inside bars. Left: C = control, AS = shock, AN = noise. The ANOVA revealed no significant effect of the treatment. Right: Open bars indicate control, closed bars indicate chronically shocked and shaded bars indicate chronically restrained rats. $P < 0.05$ vs the other two groups with Duncan's test. (Redrawn from Garcia-Marquez and Armario, 1987)

Fifth, the purported 'antidepressant-like' property of stress, which seems to be a paradox to the stress (distress)-depression connection, serves to remind us of the hyperalgesic properties of certain stressors (e.g. Simone & Bodnar, 1982; Vidal & Jacob, 1982). If we accept the definition of a stressor as a stimulus that activates the adrenocortical system, then it should be noted that stress may not necessarily increase pain thresholds (cf. Bodnar, 1984). Unfortunately, only a portion of the investigations utilising stress in antinociception or depression paradigms actually measure corticosterone or adrenocorticotropic hormone levels so that the endocrinal monitoring of stress as a correlate to the behavioral analyses is rudimentary.

Sixth, it has been shown that controllable and uncontrollable shock treatments differentially influence nociceptive response thresholds whereby uncontrollable, but not controllable shock increased response latencies (Jackson, Maier & Coon, 1979; Mair, Drugan & Grau, 1982), just as it is well established that uncontrollable, and not controllable, shock causes severe deficits of later escape performance (Maier & Seligman, 1976; Overmier & Seligman, 1976).

Indeed, it has suggested that variables influencing escape performance after inescapable/uncontrollable shock also modify the analgesic effects. However, some evidence indicate that uncontrollable shock *per se* is not the essential requirement for either the escape deficit or the analgesic effect (e.g. Mah, Suissa & Anisman, 1980).

Finally, the work of several investigors suggest hat both opioid and non-opioid mechanisms of stress shock induced analgesia are involved (Chance, 1980; Hayes et al., 1978; Lewis, Cannon & Liebeskind, 1980; Lewis, Sherman & Liebeskind, 1981). Brief electric footshock has been reported to produce a non-opioid (naloxone-insensitive) antinociceptive effect in rats (Lewis, Cannon & Liebeskind, 1983) whereas chronic shock was reversible by naloxone and cross-tolerant with morphine-induced analgesia (e.g. Maier, Davis, Grau, Jackson, Morrison, Moye, Madden & Barchas, 1980) which suggests an opioid mediation. These various aspects of stress induced analgesia suggest a behavioral, neurochemical and neuroendocrinal complexity that may be central to our considerations of anxiety, aversion and avoidance behavior.

Aggressive behavior has close in-roads with aversively motivated behavior (Bandura 1973; Berkowitz, 1974): the *aggressor* being affected by some unpleasant stimulus or stimuli (e.g. frustration) and is at the same time an aversive stimulus for the *victim.* Thus, the term aggression, through purely functional consequences, subsumes both aggressive (attacking or threatening) behavior as well as fear-related behaviors (often resulting in phobic anxiety). The chapter by Christianson and Nilsson (this volume) offers a lucid description of both attack (rape) and its traumatic consequences. In the laboratory, frustration induced aggression has been commonly studied in birds (Azrin, Hutchinson & Hake, 1966; Duncan & Wood-Gush, 1971; Looney, Cohen & Yoburn, 1976; Yoburn & Cohen, 1979) and in rodents (Blanchard, Blanchard, Takahashi & Kelley, 1977; Gallup, 1965; Miczek, 1974, 1977). Comparative analyses using cats (Leyhausen, 1979), bears (Blanchard, Blanchard, Takahasi & Suzuki, 1978), undulates (Geist, 1971), primates (Adams & Shoel, 1981) and rodents (Adams, 1980) suggest important phylogenetic continuity between aggression and fear relations. The characteristics of frustration aggression and its relation to other types of aggression have been reviewed by Dantzer (1987) especially with regard to instances of human aggression seen in juveniles (Haner & Brown, 1955; Kelly & Hake, 1970; but see Miller, 1973, for discussions on the frustration-aggression hypothesis).

In the laboratory certain aspects of the victim's behavior have been studied under the general classification of "flight behavior" which pertains to all activity intended to remove the victim from the vicinity of the threatening stimulus (aggressive individual or others). Flight is used in a broad sense generally which does not exclude retaliatory behavior (Adams, 1980). Note that flight followed by successful escape is a consummatory behavior and thus has clear reinforcing properties (see Dixon & Kaesermann, 1987). However, flight and active escape may be blocked (as in the case described above). Animals that cannot perform to flight and escape resort to "cut-off" behavioral acts and postures (Chance, 1962). The "cut-off" behaviors have also been found to occur in humans and are especially apparent in psychotic patients (Dixon, 1986; Grant, 1968). Submissive or "crouching" posture may also be observed on occasions of blocked escape (Grant, 1963) and this behavior, too, has been observed in psychotic patients (Grant, 1972).

Although most laboratory studies investigate male aggression (Moyer, 1968), there are numerous examples of aggression by female rats (e.g. Blanchard & Blanchard, 1984; DeBold & Miczek, 1984). Comprehensive reviews of the various factors influencing aggresive behavior are provided by Olivier, Mos and their co-workers (Mos, Witte, Olivier, Van der Poel & Kruk, 1984; Olivier, 1981; Olivier & Mos, 1986), who have set out several experimental models of the ethopsychopharmacological basis of aggression, e.g. maternal aggression, male pairs with access to one female, colonies, swimming in a runway to attain limited amounts of food, mouse killing, shock induced or hypothalamus stimulation induced aggression (for further reading, see Olivier, Mos & Brain, 1987). In all these cases careful monitoring and scoring of a multitude of different behavioral parameters was shown to be essential (see Olivier & Mos, 1986; Olivier et al., 1985). Figure 18.3 presents different components of aggression and socially interaction behaviors in the agonistic repertoire of rats described by Timmermans (1978). Olivier and Mos (1986) have developed a unique specificity to encompass both aggressive behavior and the pharmacological profile of drugs that put a premium upon serenic action (i.e. antiaggression) rather than sedation. Indeed, the collective battery of these authors would appear to provide an animal model with predictiveness, reliability and validity that is hardly matched by any current animal model of anxiety or depression.

The various areas of research or approaches to aversion, avoidance and anxiety divulge the enormous conceptual and mechanistic support that is provided by the biological considerations within behavior. This does not necessarily suggest that other aspects of neurobiology are overlooked. The chapters by Beninger (Chapter 10) and Thompson (Chapter 9) describe the role of dopamine and serotonin in avoidance, as well as the essential neural circuitry involved in basic conditioning phenomena. Beninger has managed to describe quite adequately the dopaminergic and serotonergic involvement in active and passive avoidance and space could not allow the separate treatment of the other classical neurotransmitters, acetyl choline and noradrenaline, in his chapter. Both the cholinergic and noradrenergic involvement in avoidance deserve separate treatises but for present purposes a few sentences may suffice.

FIG. 18.3. Timmerman's unique sketches of aggressive and defensive behaviors in pairs/groups of rats.

Generally, treatments that destroy or reduce cholinergic neurotransmission also impair active and passive avoidance whereas elevations of cholinergic neurotransmission may improve performance (cf. Bammer, 1982). The position with noradrenaline is probably more complicated since some investigations have reported consistent impairments of two-way active avoidance (Archer, 1982; Archer, Ögren, Ross & Johansson, 1982; Crow, Longden, Smith & Wendlandt, 1977) but others have not (Mason & Fibiger, 1979). One-way active avoidance and passive avoidance do not appear, in general, to be affected by lesions to central noradrenergic systems (Archer, Söderberg, Ross & Jonsson, 1984; Fibiger, Roberts & Price, 1975; Mason & Fibiger, 1978; Roberts & Fibiger, 1977). Drugs and treatments elevating noradrenergic neurotransmission may under some circumstances improve avoidance performance (e.g. Haycock, van Buskirk & McGaugh, 1977; Haycock, van Buskirk, Ryan & McGaugh, 1977; but see also McGaugh, this volume). Thus, the sophistication and diversity of the extent to which the biological approach to avoidance and aversion has developed does require some comments. It appears that the observation made by Bob Bolles (1985) is not only true in the present day but is as implacable in its curse. Technology and methodology are continuing to outstrip the theoretical formulations even though some fundamental aspects of methodology are persistently neglected (Church, this volume). Nothwithstanding this bleak reality, the spirit imbued in this volume should serve to inspire our further endeavors. We may well be on the threshold of deriving mechanisms; certainly the requirement for persistence of effort is there.

At this point in the volume we stand in somewhat a position of hindsight and are able, at least to some extent, to pronounce certain perspectives that have been instrumental to a better understanding of aversively motivated behavior. What of the consolidation of these perspectives? Some indication of their content was perused over at the beginning of this final chapter and a little glimpse was taken of the animal model perspective. But, consolidation requires a different dimension; this dimension should include an analysis of the previously undiscovered aspects of the topics discussed, the distinctions as well as the interactions between them, their constraints and constraining influences, and finally the ecological validity and representativity of the behavior under analysis, i.e. aversively motivated behavior.

REFERENCES

Abbott, A. (1987). Can animal models really predict anxiety? *Trends in Pharmacological Sciences, 8,* 157-158.

Adams, D. B. (1980). Motivational systems of agonistic behavior in myroid rodents. A comparative review and neural model. *Aggressive Behavior, 6,* 295-346.

Adams, D. B., & Shoel, W. M. (1981). Motor patterns and motivational systems of social behavior in male rats and stumptail macaques - are they homologous? *Aggressive Behavior, 7,* 267-280.

Amir, S., & Amit, Z. (1978). Endogenous opioid ligands may mediate stress-induced changes in the affective properties of pain related behavior in rats. *Life Sciences, 23,* 1143-1152.

Akil, H., Madden, J., Patrick, R. L., & Barchas, J. D. (1976). Stress-induced increase in endogenous opiate peptides: Concurrent analgesia and its partial reversal by naloxone. In H. W. Kosterlitz (Ed.), *Opiates and endogenous opiate peptides,* pp. 63-70. Amsterdam: Elsevier.

Anisman, H. (1977). Time-dependent changes in activity, reactivity and responsivity during shock: effects of cholinergic and catecholaminergic manipulations. *Behavioral Biology, 21,* 1-31.

Anisman, H., & Zacharko, R. M. (1982). Depression: the predisposing influence of stress. *Behavior and Brain Sciences, 5,* 89-137.

Archer, J. (1979). Behavioural aspects of fear. In W. Sluckin (Ed.), *Fear in animals and man*, pp. 56-85. New York: Van Nostrand.

Archer, T. (1982). DSP4-(N-2-chloroethyl-N-ethyl-2-bromoben-zylamine), a new noradrenaline neurotoxin, and the stimulus conditions affecting acquisition of two-way active avoidance. *Journal of Comparative and Physiological Psychology, 96*, 476-490.

Archer, T., Ögren, S. O., Johansson, G., & Ross, S. B. (1982). DSP4-induced two-way active avoidance impairment in rats: Involvement of central and not peripheral noradrenaline depletion. *Psychopharmacology, 76*, 303-309.

Archer, T., Söderberg, U., Ross, S. B., & Jonsson, G. (1984). Role of olfactory bulbectomy and DSP4 treatment in avoidance learning in the rat. *Behavioral Neuroscience, 98*, 496-505.

Armario, A., Restrepo, C., Castellanos, J. M., & Balasch, J. (1985). Dissociation between adrenocorticotropin and corticosterone responses to restraint after previous chronic exposure to stress. *Life Sciences, 36*, 2085-2099.

Azrin, N. H., Hutchinson, R. R., & Hake, D. F. (1966). Extinction induced aggression. *Journal of Experimental Analysis of Behavior, 9*, 191-204.

Bäckman, L., & Molander, B. (1986). Adult age differences in the ability to cope with situations of high arousal in a precision sport. *Psychology and Aging, 1*, 133-139. (a)

Bäckman, L., & Molander, B. (1986). Effects of adult age and level of skill on the ability to cope with high stress conditions in a precision sport. *Psychology and Aging, 1*, 334-336. (b)

Bammer, G. (1982). Pharmacological investigations of neurotransmitter involvement in passive avoidance responding: A review and some new results. *Neuroscience and Biobehavioral Reviews, 6*, 247-296.

Bandura, A. (1973). *Aggression: A social learning analysis*. New Jersey: Prentice Hall, Englewood Cliffs.

Berger, B. D., Mesch, D., & Schuster, R. (1980). an animal model of "Cooperation" learning. In R. F. Thompson., L. H. Hicks and V. B. Shvyrkov (Eds.), *Neural mechanisms of goal-directed behavior*, pp. 481-492. New York: Academic Press.

Berger, B. D., & Schuster, R. (1982). An animal model of social interaction: Implications for the analysis of drug action. In M. Y. Spiegelstein and A. Levy (Eds.), *Behavioral models and the analysis of drug action*, pp. 415-428. Amsterdam: Elsevier.

Berkowitz, L. (1974). Some determinants of impulsive aggression: role of mediated associations with reinforcement. *Psychological Review, 81*, 165-176.

Bernstein, D. A., & Allen, G. J. (1969). Fear survey schedule (II): Normative data and factor analyses based upon a large college sample. *Behaviour Research and Therapy, 7*, 403-407.

Bidzinska, E. J. (1984). Stress factors in affective diseases. *British Journal of Psychiatry, 144*, 161-166.

Blair, R., Galine, Z. H., Holmes, L. J., & Amit, Z. (1982). Stress-induced analgesia: a performance deficit or a change in pain

responsiveness. *Behavioral and Neural Biology, 34,* 152-158.
Blanchard, D. C., & Blanchard, R. J. (1984). Affect and aggression: An animal model applied to human behavior. In R. J. Blanchard & D. C. Blanchard (Eds.), *Advances in the study of aggression,* pp. 1-62. New York: Academic Press.
Blanchard, R. J., Blanchard, D. C., Takahashi, T., & Kelley, M. J. (1977). Attack and defensive behavior in the albino rat. *Animal Behavior, 25,* 622-634.
Blanchard, D. C., Blanchard, R. J., Takahashi, T., & Suzuki, N. (1978). Aggressive behaviors of the Japanese Brown Bear. *Aggressive Behavior, 4,* 31-41.
Bodnar, R. J. (1984). Types of stress which induce analgesia. In M. D. Tricklebank and G. Curzon (Eds.), *Stress-induced analgesia,* pp. 19-32. Chicester: John Wiley & Sons.
Bodnar, R. J., Glusman, M., Brutus, M., Spiaggia, A., & Kelly, D. D. (1979). Analgesia induced by cold-water stress: attennation following hypophysectomy. *Physiology and Behavior, 23,* 53-62.
Bodnar, R. J., Kelly, D. D., & Glusman, M. (1978). Stress-induced analgesia: time course of pain reflex alterations following cold-water swims. *Bulletin of the Psychonomic Society, 11,* 333-336.
Bodnar, R. J., Kelly, D. D., Spiaggia, A., & Glusman, M. (1978). Biphasic alteration of niciceptive thresholds induced by food deprivation. *Physiological Psychology, 6,* 391-395.
Bolles, R. C. (1970). Species-specific defense reactions and avoidance learning. *Psychological Review, 77,* 32-48.
Bolles, R. C. (1985). Associative processes in the formation of conditioned food aversions: An emerging functionalism. *Annals of the New York Academi of Scinces, 443,* 1-7. (a)
Bolles, R. C. (1985). Short-term memory and attention. In L.-G. Nilsson & T. Archer (Eds.), *Perspectives on Learning and Memory,* pp. 137-146. Hillsdale, N. J.: Lawrence Erlbaum Associates. (b)
Bolles, R. C., & Fanselow, M. S. (1980). A perceptual-defensive recuperative model of fear and pain. *Behavior and Brain Sciences, 3,* 291-323.
Borsini, F., Volterra, G., & Meli, A. (1986). Does the behavioral "despair" test measure "despair"? *Physiology and Behavior, 38,* 385-386.
Bradshaw, J., & Nettleton, N. C. (1981). The nature of hemispheric specialization in man. *The Behavioral and Brain Sciences, 4,* 51-91.
Braun, P. R., & Reynolds, P. J. (1969). A factor analysis of a 100-item fear survey inventory. *Behaviour Research and Therapy, 7,* 399-409.
Breslau, N., & Davis, G. C. (1986). Chronic stress and major depression. *Archives of General Psychiatry, 43,* 309-314.
Buckett, W. R. (1981). Pharmacological studies on stimulation-produced analgesia in mice. *European Journal of Pharmacology, 69,* 281-290.
Chance, M. R. A. (1962). An interpretation of some agonistic postures: the role of "cut-off" acts and postures. *Proceedings of the*

Zoological Society of London, 8, 71-89.

Chance, W. T. (1980). Autoanalgesia: Opiate and non-opiate menchnisms. *Neuroscience and Biobehavioral Reviews, 4*, 55-68.

Chance, W. T., Krynock, G. M., & Rosecrans, J. A. (1978). Antinociception following lesion-induced hyperemotionality and conditioned fear. *Pain, 4*, 243-252.

Chance, W. T., White, A. C., Krynock, G. M., & Rosecrans, J. A. (1977). Autoanalgesia: behaviorally activated antinociception. *European Journal of Pharmacology, 44*, 283-284.

Chapman, R. F., & Blaney, W. M. (1979). How animals perceive secondary compounds. In G. A. Rosenthal & D. H. Jenzen (Eds.), *Herbivores: their interaction with secondary plant metabolities*, pp. 4-54. New York: Academic Press.

Chester, G. B., & Chan, B. (1977). Footshock induced analgesia in mice: its reversal by naloxone and cross tolerance with morphine. *Life Sciences, 21*, 1569-1574.

Chihara, K., Arimura, A., Coy, D. H., & Schally, A. V. (1978). Studies on the interactions of endorphins, Substance P, and endogenous somatostatin in Growth Hormone and Prolactin release in rats. *Endocrinology, 102*, 281-290.

Christianson, S.-Å. (1984). The relationship between induced emotional arousal and amnesia. *Scandinavian Journal of Psychology, 25*, 147-160.

Christianson, S.-Å., & Nilsson, L.-G. (1984). Functional amnesia as induced by a psychological trauma. *Memory & Cognition, 12*, 142-155.

Cornell, D. G., Milden, R. S., & Shimp, A. (1985). Stressful life events associated with endogenous depression. *Journal of Nervous and Mental Disorders, 173*, 470-476.

Crow, T. J., Longden, A., Smith, A., & Wendlandt, S. (1977). Pontine tegmental lesions, monoamines neurones, and varieties of learning. *Behavioral Biology, 20*, 184-196.

Dantzer, R. (1987). Frustration, aggression and drugs. In B. Olivier, J. Mos & P. F. Brain (Eds.), *Ethopharmacology of agonistic behavior in animals and humans*, pp. 1-13. Dordrecht, Holland: Martinus-Nijhoff.

Danysz, W., Kostowski, W., & Archer, T. (1988). Some aspects of stress and depression. *Progress in Neuro-Psychopharmacology & Biological Psychiatry*, in press.

Danysz, W., Plaznik, A., Kostowski, W., Malatynska, E., Järbe, T. U. C., Hiltunen, A. J., & Archer, T. (1987). Comparison of desipramine, amitryptiline, zimeldine and alaproclate in six animal models used to investigate antidepressant drugs. *Pharmacology & Toxicology, 62*, 42-50.

De Bold, J. F., & Miczek, K. A. (1984). Aggression persists after ovariectomy in female rats. *Hormones and Behavior, 18*, 177-190.

Derry, P. A., & Kuiper, N. A. (1981). Schematic processing and self-reference in clinical depression. *Journal of Abnormal Psychology, 90*, 286-297.

Dickinson, A., & Shanks, D. (1985). Animal conditioning and human causality judgements. In .-G. Nilsson & T. Archer (Eds.), *Perspectives on learning and memory*, pp. 167-191. Hillsdale, N. J.: Lawrence Erlbaum Associates.

Dinsmoor, J. A. (1958). Pulse duration and food deprivation in escape-from-shock training. *Psychological Reports, 4,* 531-534.

Dixon, A. K. (1986). Ethological aspects of psychiatry. *Swiss Archives of Neurology and Psychiatry, 137,* 151-163.

Dixon, A. K., & Kaesermann, H. P. (1987). Ethopharmacology of flight behaviour. In B. Olivier, J. Mos, & P. F. Brain (Eds.), *Ethoparmacology of agonistic behaviour in animals and humans*, pp. 46-79. Dordrecht: Nijhoff.

Donegan, N. H., & Wagner, A. R. (1987). Conditioned diminution and facilitation of the UR: A sometimes opponent-process interpretation. In I. Gormezano, W. F. Prokasy, & R. F. Thompson (Eds.), *Classical conditioning III: Behavioral, neurophysiological, and neurochemical studies in the rabbit.* Hillsdale, N. J.: Lawrence Erlbaum Associates.

Duncan, I. J. H., & Wood-Gush, D. G. M. (1971). Frustration and aggression in the domestic fowl. *Animal Behavior, 19,* 500-504.

Estes, W. K., & Skinner, B. F. (1941). Some quantitative properties of anxiety. *Journal of Experimental Psychology, 29,* 390-400.

Eysenck, H. J., & Kelley, M. J. (1987). The interaction of neurohormones with Pavlovian A and Pavlovian B conditioning in the causation of neurosis, extinction, and incubation of anxiety. In G. Davey (Ed.), *Cognitive processes and Pavlovian conditioning in humans*, pp. 251-286. New York: John Wiley & Sons.

Fanselow, M. S. (1984). Shock-induced analgesia on the formalia test: Effects of shock severity, naloxone, hypophysectomy, and associative variables. *Behavioral Neuroscience, 98,* 79-95.

Farrell, P. A., Gates, W. K., Maksud, M. G., & Morgan, W. P. (1982). Increases in plasma beta-endorphin/beta-lipotropin immunoreactivity after treadmill running in humans. *Journal of Applied Physiology, 52,* 1245-1249.

Farrell, P. A., Gustafson, A. B., Garthwaite, T. L., Kalkhoff, R. K., Cowley, A. W., & Morgan, W. P. (1986). Influence of endogenous opioids on the response of selected hormones to exercise in humans. *Journal of Applied Physiology, 61,* 1051-1057.

Fibiger, H. C., Roberts, D. C. S., & Price, M. T. C. (1975). On the role of telencephalic noradrenaline in learning and memory. In G. Jonsson, T. Malmfors & C. Sachs (Eds.), *Chemical tools in catecholamine research*, pp. 349-356. Amsterdam: North-Holland Publishing.

File, S. E. (1985). Models of anxiety. *British Journal of Clinical Practice, 39,* 15-19.

Franchina, J. J. (1966). Combined sources of motivation and escape responding. *Psychonomic Science, 6,* 221-222.

Gallup, G. G. (1965). Aggression in rats as a function of frustrative nonreward in a straight alley. *Psychonomic Science, 11,* 99-100.

Garcia, J., Rusiniak, K. W., & Brett, L. P. (1977). Conditioning food-illness aversions in wild animal: caveant canonici. In H. David & H. M. B. Hurwitz (Eds.), *Operant Pavlovian interactions*, pp. 273-316. Hillsdale, N. J.: Lawrence Erlbaum Associates.

Garcia, J., Rusiniak, K. W., Kiefer, S. W., & Bermúdez-Rattoni, F. (1982). The neural integration of feeding and drinking habits. In C. D. Woody (Ed.), *Conditioning: representation of involved neural functions*, pp. 567-579. New York: Plenum Press.

Garcia-Marguez, C., & Armario, A. (1987). Cronic stress depresses exploratory activity and behavioral performance in the forced swimming test without altering ACTH response to a novel acute stressor. *Physiology & Behavior, 40,* 33-38.

Geist, V. (1971). *Mountain sheep: A study in behavior and evolution.* Chicago: University of Chicago Press.

Goldfarb, A. H., Hatfield, B. D., Sforzo, G. A., & Flynn, M. G. (1987). Serum beta-endorphin levels during a graded exercise test to exhaustion. *Medical Science and Sports Exercise, 19,* 78-82.

Graf, P., & Schacter, D. L. (1985). Implicit and explicit memory for new associations in normal and amnesic subjects. *Journal of Experimental Psychology: Learning, Memory and Cognition, 11,* 501-518.

Grant, E. C. (1963). An analysis of the social behaviour of the male laboratory rat. *Behaviour, 21,* 260-281.

Grant, E. C. (1968). An ethological description of non-verbal behaviour during interviews. *British Journal of Medical Psychology, 41,* 172-184.

Grant, E. C. (1972). Non-verbal communication in the mentally ill. In R. A. Hinde (Ed.), *Non-verbal communication,* pp. 349-358. Cambridge: Cambridge University Press.

Grau, J. W. (1986). The central representation of an aversive event maintains the opioid and nonopioid forms of analgesia (Doctoral Dissertation, University of Pennsylvania, 1985). *Dissertation Abstracts International, 46,* 4434B.

Grau, J. W. (1987). The central representation of an aversive event maintains the opiod and nonopiod forms of analgesia. *Behavioral Neuroscience, 101,* 272-288. (a)

Grau, J. W. (1987). Activation of the opioid and nonopioid analgesic systems: Evidence for a memory hypothesis and against the coulometric hypothesis. *Journal of Experimental Psychology: Animal Behavior Processes, 13,* 215-225. (b)

Grau, J. E., & Wagner, A. R. (1982). An episodic model of associative memory. In M. Commons, R. Herrnstein, & A. R. Wagner (Eds.), *Quantitative analyses of behavior: Acquisition,* Vol. 3. pp. 3-39. Cambridge: MA.: Ballinger.

Greist, J. H., Klein, M. H., Eishens, R. R., Fairs, J., Gurman, A. S., & Morgan, W. P. (1979). Running as treatment for depression. *Comparative Psychiatry, 20,* 41-54.

Grossman, A., Bouloux, P., Price, P., Drury, P. L., Lam, K. S., Turner, T., Thomas, J., Besser, G. M., & Sutton, J. (1984). The role of opioid peptides in the hormonal responses to acute exercise in man. *Clinical Science, 67,* 483-491.

Hammen, C. L., & Cochran, S. D. (1981). Cognitive correlates of life stress and depression in college students. *Journal of Abnormal Psychology, 90,* 23-27.

Haner, C. F., & Brown, P. A. (1955). Clarification of the instigation to action concept in the frustration-aggression hypothesis. *Journal of Abnormal and Social Psychology, 51,* 204-206.

Harber, V. J., & Sutton, J. R. (1984). Endorphins and exercise. *Sports Medicine, 1,* 154-171.

Hasher, L., & Zachs, R. T. (1979). Automatic and effortful processes in memory. *Journal of Experimental Psychology: General, 108,*

Haslam, D. R. (1984). The military performance of soldiers in sistained operations. *Aviation, Space and Environmental Medicine, 55,* 216-221.

Hawkins, J., Hicks, R. A., Phillips, N., & Moore, J. D. (1978). Swimming rats and human depression. *Nature, 274,* 512.

Haycock, J. W., van Buskirk, R., & McGaugh, J. L. (1977). Effects of catecholaminergic drugs upon memory storage processes in mice. *Behavioral Biology, 20,* 281-310.

Haycock, J. W., van Buskirk, R., Ryan, J. R., & McGaugh, J. L. (1977). Enhancement of retention with centrally administered catecholamines. *Experimental Neurology, 54,* 199-208.

Hayes, R. L., Bennet, G. J., Newlon, P. G., & Mayer, D. J. (1976). Analgesic effects of certain noxious and stressful manipulations in the rat. *Society of Neuroscience Abstracts, 2,* 939.

Hayes, R. L., Bennett, G. J., Newlon, P. G., & Mayer, D. J. (1978). Behavioral and physiological studies of non-narcotic analgesia in the rat elicited by certain environmental stimuli. *Brain Research, 155,* 69-90.

Isen, A. M. (1984). Toward understanding the role of affect in cognition. In R. Wayer & T. Srull (Eds.), *Handbook of social cognition, Vol. 3.* pp. 176-226. Hillsdale, N. J.: Erlbaum.

Jackson, R. L., Maier, S. F., & Coon, D. J. (1979). Long-term analgesic effects of inescapable shock and learned helplessness. *Science, 206,* 91-93.

Johnson, M. H., & Magaro, P. A. (1987). Effects of mood and severity on memory processes in depression and mania. *Psychological Bulletin, 101,* 28-40.

Katz, R. (1981). Animal models and human depressive disorders. *Neuroscience and Biobehavioral Reviews, 5,* 231-246.

Katz, R. (1984). Effects of zometapine, a structural antidepressant, in an animal model of depression. *Pharmacology, Biochemistry & Behavior, 21,* 487-490.

Katz, R. J., Roth, K. A., & Carroll, B. J. (1981). Acute and chronic stress effects on open field activity in the rat. Implications for a model of depression. *Neuroscience and Behavioral Reviews, 5,* 247-251.

Katz, R., & Sibel, M. (1982). Animal model of depression: Tests of three structurally and pharmacologically novel antidepressant compounds. *Pharmacology, Biochemistry & Behavior, 16,* 973-977.

Keehn, J. D. (1986). *Animal models for psychiatry.* London: Routledge & Kegan Paul.

Kelly, J. F., & Hake, D. F. (1970). An extinction-induced increase in an aggressive response with humans. *Journal of Experimental Analysis of Behavior, 14,* 153-164.

Kimura, D. (1961). Some effects of temporal-lobe damage on auditory perception. *Canadian Journal of Psychology, 15,* 156-165.

Klein, D. F. (1981). Anxiety reconceptualized. In D. F. Klein and J. Rabkin (Eds.), *Anxiety: New research and changing concepts,* pp. 1-13. New York: Raven Press.

Kuiper, N. A., & Derry, P. A. (1982). Depressed and nondepressed content of self-reference in mild depressives. *Journal of Personality, 50,* 67-80.

Kulkarni, S. K. (1980). Heat and other physiological stress-induced analgesia: catecholamine mediated and naloxone reversible respons. *Life Sciences, 27,* 185-188.

Landy, F. J., & Gaupp, L. A. (1971). A factor analysis of the fear suvey schedule - III. *Behaviour Research and Therapy, 9,* 89-93.

Lang, P. J. (1968). Fear reduction and fear behavior: Problems in treating a construct. In J. M. Shlein (Ed.), *Research in Psychotherapy, Vol. III,* pp. 90-103. Washington, D. C.: American Psychological Association.

Levine, A. S., Wilcox, G. L., Grace, M., & Morley, J. E. (1982). Tail pinch induced consummatory behaviors are associated with analgesia. *Physiology and Behavior, 28,* 959-962.

Lewis, J. W., Cannon, J., & Liebeskind, J. C. (1980). Opioid and non-opioid mechanisms of stress analgesia. *Science, 208,* 623-625.

Lewis, J. W., Cannon, J., & Liebeskind, J. C. (1983). Involvement of central muscarinic cholinergic mechanisms in opioid stress analgesia. *Brain Research, 270,* 289-293.

Lewis, J. W., Sherman, J. E., & Liebeskind, J. C. (1982). Opioid and non-opioid stress analgesia: Assessment of tolerance and cross-tolerance with morphine. *Journal of neuroscience, 1,* 358-363.

Layhausen, P. (1979). *Cat behavior: The predatory and social behavior of domestic and wild cats.* New York: Garland STPM Press.

Loftus, E. F., & Burns, T. E. (1982). Mental shock can produce retrograde amnesia. *Memory and Cognition, 10,* 318-323.

Looney, T. A., Cohen, P. S., & Yoburn, B. C. (1976). Variables affecting the establisment of schedule-induced attack on pictorial targets in White King pigeons. *Journal of Experimental Analysis of Behavior, 26,* 349-360.

Madden, J., Akil, H., Patrick, R. L., & Barchas, J. D. (1977). Stress-induced parallel changes in central opioid levels and pain responsiveness in rat. *Nature, 265,* 358-360.

Mah, C., Suissa, A., & Anisman, H. (1980). Dissociation of antinociception and escape deficits induced by stress in mice. *Journal of Comparative and Physiological Psychology, 94,* 1160-1171.

Maier, S. F., Davies, S., Grau, J. W., Jackson. R. L., Morrison, D. H., Moye, T., Madden, J., & Barchas, J. D. (1980). Opiate antagonists and the long-term analgesia reaction induced by inescapable shock in rats. *Journal of Comparative and Physiological Psychology, 94,* 1172-1183.

Maier, S. F., Drugan, R. C., & Grau, J. W. (1982). Controllability, coping behavior, and stress-induced analgesia in the rat. *Pain, 12,* 47-56.

Maier, S. F., & Keith, J. R. (1987). Shock signals and the development of stress-induced analgesia. *Journal of Experimental Psychology: Animal Behavior Processes, 13,* 226-238.

Maier, S. F., & Seligman, M. E. P. (1976). Learned helplessness: theory and evidence. *Journal of Experimental Psychology: General, 105,* 3-46.

Marks, I. (1969). *Fears and phobias.* London: Heineman Medical Books.

Mason, S. T., & Fibiger, H. C. (1978). 6-OHDA leison to the dorsal noradrenergic bundle alters extinction of passive avoidance. *Brain Research, 152,* 209-216.

Mason, S. T., & Fibiger, H. C. (1979). Noradrenaline and avoidance learning in the rat. *Brain Research, 161,* 321-334.

Mazur, J. E., & Wagner, A. R. (1982). An episodic model of associative memory. In M. Commons, R. Herrnstein, & A. R. Wagner (Eds.), *Quantitative analyses of behavior: Acquisition,* Vol. 3, pp. 3-39. Cambridge, MA.: Ballinger.

McCloskey, M., & Zaragoza, M. (1985). Misleading post-event information and memory for events: Arguments and evidence against memory impairment hypothesis. *Journal of Experimental Psychology: General, 114,* 3-18.

McGinnies, E. (1949). Emotionality and perceptual defense. *Psychological Review, 56,* 244-251.

de Meirleir, K., Naaktgeboren, N., Van Steirteghem, A., Gorus, F., Olbrecht, J., & Block, P. (1986). Beta-endorphin and ACTH levels in peripheral blood during and after aerobic and anaerobic exercise. *European Journal of Applied Physiology, 55,* 5-8.

Miczek, K. A. (1974). Intraspecies aggression in rats: effects of D-amphetamine and chlordiazepoxide. *Psychopharmacologia, 39,* 275-301.

Miczek, K. A. (1977). Effects of alcohol on attack and defensive-submissive reactions in rats. *Psychopharmacology, 52,* 231-237.

Miczek, K. A., Thompson, M. L., & Shuster, L. (1982). Opioid-like analgesia in defeated mice. *Science, 215,* 1518-1520.

Miller, N. E. (1973). The frustration-agression hypothesis. In T. Marple & D. W. Matheson (Eds.), *Aggression, hostility and violence, nature or nurture,* pp. 103-115. New York: Holt Rinehart and Winston.

Mineka, S., Cook, M., & Miller, S. (1984). Fear conditioned with escapable and inescapable shock: Effects of a feedback stimulus.

Journal of Experimental Psychology: Animal Behavior Processes, **10**, 307-324.

Mineka, S., Davidson, M., Keir, R., & Cook, M. (1984). Observational conditioning of snake fear in Rhesus monkeys. *Journal of Abnormal Psychology, 93*, 355-372.

Mineka, S., & Keir, R. (1983). The effects of flooding on reducing snake fear in Rhesus monkeys. Six-month follow-up and further flooding. *Behaviour Research and Therapy, 21*, 527-536.

Mineka, S., Keir, R. & Price, V. (1980). Fear of snakes in wild- and laboratory-reared rhesus monkeys (macaca mulatta). *Animal Learning and Behavior, 8*, 653-66.

Mogg, K., Mathews, A., & Weinman, J. (1987). Memory bias in clinical anxiety. *Journal of Abnormal Psychology, 96*, 94-98.

Morgan, W. P. (1985). Affective beneficence of vigorous physical activity. *Medical Science and Sports Exercise, 17*, 94-100.

Mos, J., Witte, M. M., Olivier, B., Van der Poel, A. M., & Kruk, M. R. (1984). Behavioural voltammetry: its application in aggression research. In K. A. Miczek, M. R. Kruk & B. Olivier (Eds.), *Ethopharmacological Aggression Research*, pp. 179-189. New York: Alan R. Liss.

Moyer, K. E. (1968). Kinds of aggression and their physiological basis. *Communications in Behavioral Biology, 2*, 65-87.

Nagayama, H., Hintgen, J. N., & Aprison, M. H. (1981). Postsynaptic action by four antidepressant drugs in an animal model of depression. *Pharmacology, Biochemistry and Behvior, 15*, 125-130.

Nunn, J. D., Stevenson, R. J., & Whalan, G. (1984). Selective memory effects in agoraphobic patients. *British Journal of Clinical Psychology, 23*, 195-201.

O'Banion, K., & Arkowitz, H. (1977). Social anxiety and selective memory for affective information about the self. *Social Behavior and Personality, 5*, 321-328.

Öhman, A., Erixon, G., & Löfberg, I. (1975). Phobias and preparedness: Phobic versus neutral pictures as conditioned stimuli for human autonomic responses. *Journal of Abnormal Psychology, 84*, 41-45.

Olivier, B. (1981). Selective anti-aggressive properties of DU 27725: ethological analysis of intermale and terriforial aggression in effect on "behavioral despair". *European Journal of Pharmacology, 78*, 379-380.

Ornstein, K., & Amir, S. (1981). Pinch induced catalepsy in mice. *Journal of Comparative and Physiological Psychology, 95*, 827-835.

Overmier, J. B., & Seligman, M. E. P. (1976). Effects of inescapable shock upon subsequent escape and avoidance responding. *Journal of Comparative and Physiological Psychology, 63*, 28-33.

Porsolt, R. D., Anton, G., Blavet, N., & Jalfre, M. (1978). Behavioural despair in rats: A new model sensitive to antidepressant treatments. *European Journal of Pharmacology, 47*, 379-391.

Porsolt, R. D., Le Pichon, M., & Jalfre, M. (1977). Depression: A new animal model sensitive to antidepressant treatment. *Nature, 266*,

730-732.

Postman, L., Bronson, W. C., & Gropper, G. L. (1953). Is there a mechanism of perceptual defence? *Journal of Abnormal Social Psychology, 48*, 215-224.

Rescorla, R. A. (1984). Associations between Pavlovian CS_s and context. *Journal of Experimental Psychology: Animal Behavior Processes, 10*, 195-205.

Rescorla, R. A. (1985). Conditioned inhibition and facilitation. In R. R. Miller & N. S. Spear (Eds.), *Information processing in animals: Conditioned inhibition*, pp. 64-99. Hillsdale, N. J.: Lawrence Erlbaum Associates.

Rhoades, D. F. (1979). Evolution of plant chemical defense against herbivoures. In G. A. Rosenthal & D. H. Jensen (Eds.), *Herbivores: Their interaction with secondary plant metabolites*, pp. 138-149. New York: Academic Press.

Roberts, D. C. S., & Fibiger, H. C. (1977). Evidence for interactions between central noradrenergic neurons and adrenal hormones in learning and memory. *Pharmacology, Biochemistry & Behavior, 7*, 191-194.

Rosellini, R. A. (1978). Inescapable shock interferes with the acquisition of a free appetitive operant. *Animal Learning and Behavior, 6*, 515-519.

Rosellini, R. A., DeCola, J. P., & Warren, D. A. (1986). The effect of feedback stimuli on contextual fear depends upon the length of the minimum [T]. *Learning and Motivation, 17*, 229-242.

Rosecrans, J. A., & Chance, W. T. (1976). Emotionality-induced antinociception. *Society for Neuroscience Abstracts, 2*, 919.

Rossier, J., French, E. D., Rivier, C., Ling, N., Guillemin, R., & Bloom, F. E. (1977). Foot-schock induced stress increases β-endorphin levels in blood but not brain. *Nature, 270*, 618-620.

Selye, H. (1956). *The stress of life*. New York: McGraw-Hill Book Company, Inc.

Schuster, R. H., Rachlin, H., Rom, M., & Berger, B. D. (1982). An animal model of dyadic social interaction: Influence of isolation, competition and shock-induced aggression. *Aggressive Behavior, 8*, 116-121.

Siegel, R. A., Chowers, I., Conforti, N., Feldman, S., & Weidenfeld, J. (1982). Effects of naloxone on basal and stress-induced ACTH and corticosterone secretion in the male rat-site and mechanism of action. *Brain Research, 249*, 103-109.

Simone, D. A., & Bodnar, R. J. (1982). Modulation of antinociceptive responses following tail pinch stress. *Life Sciences, 30*, 719-729.

Soblosky, J. S., & Thurmond, J. B. (1986). Biochemical and behavioural correlates of chronic stress: effects of tricyclic antidepressants. *Pharmacology, Biochemistry & Behavior, 24*, 1361-1368.

Solomon, R. L. (1977). An opponent-process theory of motivation. V. Affective dynamics of eating. In L. M. Barker, M. R. Best & M. Domjan (Eds.), *Learning mechanisms in food selection*, pp. 255-269.

Waco, Tx: Baylor University Press.

Solomon, Z., & Benbenishty, R. (1986). The role of proximity, immediacy, and expectancy in frontline treatment of combat stress reaction among Israelis in the Lebanon war. *American Journal of Psychiatry, 143*, 613-617.

Sperry, R. W., Stamm, J. S., & Miner, N. (1956). Relearning tests for interocular transer following division of optic chiosma and corpus callosum in cats. *Journal of Comparative and Physiological Psychology, 49*, 529-533.

Steinberg, H., & Sykes, E. A. (1985). Introduction to symposium on endorphins and behavioural processes; review of literature on endorphins and exercise. *Pharmacology, Biochemistry and Behavior, 23*, 857-862.

Telch, M. J., Agras, W. S., Taylor, C. B., Roth, W. T., Gallen, C. C. (1985). Combined pharmacological and behavioral treatment for agoraphobia. *Psychopharmacology, 90*, 284-285.

Terman, G. W., Shavit, Y., Lewis, J. L., Cannon, T. J., & Liebeskind, J. C. (1984). Intrinsic mechanisms of pain inhibition: Activation by stress. *Science, 221*, 1270-1277.

Thierry, B., Stérn, L., Simon, P., & Porsolt, R. D. (1986). The tail-suspension test: Ethical considerations. *Psychopharmacology, 90*, 284-285.

Timmermans, P. J. A. (1978). Social behaviour in the rat. Ph. D. Thesis, Nijmegen. Pp. 1-260.

Tulving, E., & Pearlstone, Z. (1966). Availability versus accessibility of information in memory for words. *Journal of Verbal Learning and Verbal Behavior, 5*, 381-391.

Wagner, A. R. (1981). SOP: A model of automatic memory processes in animal behavior. In N. E. Spear & R. R. Miller (Eds.), *Information processing in animals: Memory mechanisms*, pp. 5-47. Hillsdale, N. J.: Lawrence Erlbaum Associates.

Wada, J., & Rasmussen, T. (1960). Intracarotid injection of Sodium Amytal for lateralization of cerebral speech dominance: Experimental and clinical observations. *Journal of Neurosurgery, 17*, 266-282.

Vidal, C., & Jacob, J. J. C. (1982). Stress hyperalgesia in rats: an experimental animal model of anxiogenic hyperalgesia in human. *Life Sciences, 31*, 1241-1244.

Vogel, G. W. (1983). Evidence for REM sleep deprivation as the mechanism of action of antidepressant drugs. *Progress in Neuropsychopharmacology, 7*, 343-349.

Welford, A. T. (1977). Motor performance. In J. E. Birren & K. W. Schaie (Eds.), *Handbook of the psychology of aging*, pp. 450-496. New York: Van Nostrand.

Willner, P. (1984). The validity of animal models of depression. *Psychopharmacology, 83*, 1-16.

Willner, P. (1985). *Depression: a psychobiological synthesis.* New York: John Wiley & Sons.

Willner, P., Towell, A., Sampson, D., Sophokleous, S., & Muscat, R. (1987). Reduction of sucrose preference by chronic unpredictable mild stress, and its restoration by a tricyclic antidepressant. *Psychopharmacology*, *93*, 358-364.

Yoburn, B. C., & Cohen, P. S. (1979). Assessment of attack and drinking in White King pigeons on response-independent food schedules. *Journal of Experimental Analysis of Behavior, 36,* 101-117.

Zacharko, R. M., & Anisman, H. (1984). Motor motivational and anti-nociceptive consequences of stress: contribution of neurochemical changes. In M. D. Tricklebank and G. Curzon (Eds.), *Stress-induced Analgesia,* pp. 33-65. New York: John Wiley & Sons.

Zajonc, R. (1962). Response suppresion in perceptual defence. *Journal of Experimental Psychology, 64,* 206-215.

Zitrin, C. M., Klein, D. F., & Woerner, M. G. (1980). Treatment of agoraphobia with group exposure in vivo and imipramine. *Archives of General Psychiatry, 37,* 63-72.

Author Index

Bold face denotes pages with bibliographic information

A

Subject Index